Investing for Canadians

ALL-IN-ONE

D1128338

A Wiley Brand

Investing for Canadians

ALL-IN-ONE

PAPL
DISCARDED

by Andrew Bell; Bryan Borzykowski; Andrew Dagys, CPA, CMA; Kiana Danial; Matthew Elder; Douglas Gray, LLB; Ann C. Logue, MBA; Tony Martin, B.Comm; Peter Mitham; Paul Mladjenovic, CFP; and Eric Tyson, MBA

A Wiley Brand

Investing for Canadians All-in-One For Dummies®

Published by: **John Wiley & Sons, Inc.,** 111 River Street, Hoboken, NJ 07030-5774, www.wiley.com

Copyright © 2021 by John Wiley & Sons, Inc., Hoboken, New Jersey

No part of this publication may be reproduced, stored in a retrieval system or transmitted in any form or by any means, electronic, mechanical, photocopying, recording, scanning or otherwise, except as permitted under Sections 107 or 108 of the 1976 United States Copyright Act, without the prior written permission of the Publisher. Requests to the Publisher for permission should be addressed to the Permissions Department, John Wiley & Sons, Inc., 111 River Street, Hoboken, NJ 07030, (201) 748-6011, fax (201) 748-6008, or online at http://www.wiley.com/go/permissions.

Trademarks: Wiley, For Dummies, the Dummies Man logo, Dummies.com, Making Everything Easier, and related trade dress are trademarks or registered trademarks of John Wiley & Sons, Inc., and may not be used without written permission. All other trademarks are the property of their respective owners. John Wiley & Sons, Inc., is not associated with any product or vendor mentioned in this book.

LIMIT OF LIABILITY/DISCLAIMER OF WARRANTY: WHILE THE PUBLISHER AND AUTHOR HAVE USED THEIR BEST EFFORTS IN PREPARING THIS BOOK, THEY MAKE NO REPRESENTATIONS OR WARRANTIES WITH RESPECT TO THE ACCURACY OR COMPLETENESS OF THE CONTENTS OF THIS BOOK AND SPECIFICALLY DISCLAIM ANY IMPLIED WARRANTIES OF MERCHANTABILITY OR FITNESS FOR A PARTICULAR PURPOSE. NO WARRANTY MAY BE CREATED OR EXTENDED BY SALES REPRESENTATIVES OR WRITTEN SALES MATERIALS. THE ADVICE AND STRATEGIES CONTAINED HEREIN MAY NOT BE SUITABLE FOR YOUR SITUATION. YOU SHOULD CONSULT WITH A PROFESSIONAL WHERE APPROPRIATE. NEITHER THE PUBLISHER NOR THE AUTHOR SHALL BE LIABLE FOR DAMAGES ARISING HEREFROM.

For general information on our other products and services, please contact our Customer Care Department within the U.S. at 877-762-2974, outside the U.S. at 317-572-3993, or fax 317-572-4002. For technical support, please visit https://hub.wiley.com/community/support/dummies.

Wiley publishes in a variety of print and electronic formats and by print-on-demand. Some material included with standard print versions of this book may not be included in e-books or in print-on-demand. If this book refers to media such as a CD or DVD that is not included in the version you purchased, you may download this material at http://booksupport.wiley.com. For more information about Wiley products, visit www.wiley.com.

Library of Congress Control Number: 2020947484

ISBN 978-1-119-73665-3 (pbk); ISBN 978-1-119-73667-7 (ebk); ISBN 978-1-119-73668-4 (ebk)

Manufactured in the United States of America

SKY10026249_041521

Contents at a Glance

Table of Contents

Introduction

Making investment decisions can be intimidating and overwhelming. Investors have a ton of options available to them, and sorting through the get-rich-quick hype can be exhausting. *Investing for Canadians All-in-One For Dummies* is here to help you with an overview of the investing landscape unique to Canada.

About This Book

Investing for Canadians All-in-One For Dummies provides guidance, tools, and resources for determining and making the right investments for your needs. Here, you get tips on investment choices, risks, and returns as well as the basics on stocks, mutual funds, precious metals, day trading, cryptocurrencies, and real estate.

A quick note: Sidebars (shaded boxes of text) dig into the details of a given topic, but they aren't crucial to understanding it. Feel free to read them or skip them. You can pass over the text accompanied by the Technical Stuff icon, too. The text marked with this icon gives some interesting but nonessential information about investing.

One last thing: Within this book, you may note that some web addresses break across two lines of text. If you're reading this book in print and want to visit one of these web pages, simply key in the web address exactly as it's noted in the text, pretending as though the line break doesn't exist. If you're reading this as an e-book, you've got it easy — just click the web address to be taken directly to the web page.

Foolish Assumptions

Here are some assumptions about why you're picking up this book:

>> You're a millennial or novice investor and eager to find out more about saving, investing, and taking care of long-term needs.

>> You're an experienced investor who wants even more sound guidance and trusted investment strategies.

>> You want to improve your financial situation and build your wealth.

>> You're interested in methods beyond stocks, such as mutual funds, day trading, gold and silver, and cryptocurrencies.

>> You're intrigued by real estate investing and want to know more about available opportunities.

Icons Used in This Book

Like all *For Dummies* books, this book features icons to help you navigate the information. Here's what they mean.

REMEMBER

If you take away anything from this book, it should be the information marked with this icon.

TECHNICAL STUFF

This icon flags information that digs a little deeper than usual into a particular topic.

TIP

This icon highlights especially helpful advice about investing.

WARNING

This icon points out situations and actions to avoid as you enter and move through the world of investing.

Beyond the Book

In addition to the material in the print or e-book you're reading right now, this product comes with some access-anywhere goodies on the web. Check out the free Cheat Sheet for information on Canadian ownership investments, Canadian stock exchanges, and the risks of real estate investing in Canada. To get this Cheat Sheet, simply go to www.dummies.com and search for "*Investing for Canadians All-in-One For Dummies* Cheat Sheet" in the Search box.

Where to Go from Here

You don't have to read this book from cover to cover, but you can if you like! If you just want to find specific information on a type of investment strategy, take a look at the table of contents or the index, and then dive into the chapter or section that interests you.

For example, if you want the basics of investing, flip to Book 1. If you want to explore stock and mutual fund investing, check out Books 2 and 3. If you prefer to find out more about investing in gold and silver, day trading, and cryptocurrencies, flip to Books 4, 5, and 6. Or if you're considering real estate, Book 7 is the place to be.

No matter where you start, you'll find the information you need to enter the world of investing and make the right decisions for your needs. Good luck!

1
Entering the World of Investing

Contents at a Glance

Chapter **1**

Exploring Your Investment Choices

I n many parts of the world, life's basic necessities — food, clothing, shelter, and taxes — consume the entirety of people's meager earnings. Although some Canadians do truly struggle for basic necessities, the bigger problem for other Canadians is that they consider just about *everything* — eating out, driving new cars, hopping on airplanes for vacation — to be a necessity. However, you should recognize that investing — that is, putting your money to work for you — is a necessity. If you want to accomplish important personal and financial goals, such as owning a home, starting your own business, helping your kids through university or college (and spending more time with them when they're young), retiring comfortably, and so on, you must know how to invest well.

It's been said, and too often quoted, that the only certainties in life are death and taxes. To these two certainties you can add one more: being confused by and ignorant about investing. Because investing is a confounding activity, you may be tempted to look with envious eyes at those people in the world who appear to be savvy with money and investing. Note that everyone starts with the same level of financial knowledge: none! *No one* was born knowing this stuff! The only difference between those who know and those who don't is that those who know have devoted their time and energy to acquiring useful knowledge about the investment world.

Getting Started with Investing

Before this chapter discusses the major investing alternatives, consider a question that's quite basic yet important. What exactly does "investing" mean? Simply stated, *investing* means you have money put away for future use.

You can choose from tens of thousands of stocks, bonds, mutual funds, exchange-traded funds, and other investments. Unfortunately for the novice, and even for the experts who are honest with you, knowing the name of the investment is just the tip of the iceberg. Underneath each of these investments lurks a veritable mountain of details.

REMEMBER

If you wanted to and had the ability to quit your day job, you could make a full-time endeavour out of analyzing economic trends and financial statements and talking to business employees, customers, suppliers, and so on. However, you shouldn't be scared away from investing just because some people do it on a full-time basis. Making wise investments need not take a lot of your time. If you know where to get high-quality information and you purchase well-managed investments, you can leave the investment management to the best experts. Then you can do the work that you're best at and have more free time for the things you really enjoy doing.

An important part of making wise investments is knowing when you have enough information to do things well on your own versus when you should hire others. For example, foreign stock markets are generally more difficult to research and understand than domestic markets. Thus, when investing overseas, investing in a mutual fund where a good money manager decides what stocks to hold is often a wise move.

In most cases, you can reap competitive returns while only paying minimal fees by investing in *exchange-traded funds*, or *ETFs*. ETFs are what's known as *index funds*. They are designed to give investors the same return as a particular stock market index, such as the Toronto Stock Exchange. (A stock market index is a measurement of the overall performance of a basket of stocks. The S&P/TSE Composite Index, for example, measures the overall performance of about 250 large companies in a variety of different industries.) If an index rises by 8.5 per cent in 12 months, investors in an ETF that tracks that particular index will see their investment gain by a similar amount, minus a fraction of a percent for the fees paid to the fund's managers.

This book gives you the information you need to make your way through the complex investment world. The rest of this chapter helps you identify the major investments and understand the strengths and weaknesses of each.

Building Wealth with Ownership Investments

REMEMBER

If you want your money to grow faster than the rate of inflation over the long term and you don't mind a bit of a roller-coaster ride from time to time in the value of your investments, ownership investments are for you. *Ownership investments* are those investments where you own an interest in some company or other types of assets (such as stocks, real estate, or a small business) that have the ability to generate revenue and profits.

Observing how the world's richest people have built their wealth is enlightening. Not surprisingly, many of the champions of wealth around the globe gained their fortunes largely through owning a piece (or all) of a successful company that they (or others) built.

In addition to owning their own businesses, many well-to-do people have built their nest eggs by investing in real estate and the stock market. With softening housing prices in many regions in the late 2000s, some folks newer to the real estate world incorrectly believed that real estate is a loser, not a long-term winner. Likewise, the stock market goes through down periods but does well over the long term. (See Chapter 2 in Book 1 for the scoop on investment risks and returns.)

And of course, some people come into wealth through an inheritance. Even if your parents are among the rare wealthy ones and you expect them to pass on big bucks to you, you need to know how to invest that money intelligently.

REMEMBER

If you understand and are comfortable with the risks, and take sensible steps to *diversify* (you don't put all your investment eggs in the same basket), ownership investments are the key to building wealth. For most folks to accomplish typical longer-term financial goals, such as retiring, the money that they save and invest needs to grow at a healthy clip. If you dump all your money in bank accounts that pay little if any interest, you're likely to fall short of your goals (and inflation).

Not everyone needs to make his or her money grow, of course. Suppose you inherit a significant sum and/or maintain a restrained standard of living and work well into your old age simply because you enjoy doing so. In this situation, you may not need to take the risks involved with a potentially faster-growth investment. You may be more comfortable with *safer* investments, such as paying off your mortgage faster than necessary. Chapter 3 in Book 1 helps you think through such issues.

Entering the stock market

Stocks, which are shares of ownership in a company, are an example of an ownership investment. If you want to share in the growth and profits of companies like Skechers (footwear), you can! You simply buy shares of its stock through a brokerage firm. However, even if Skechers makes money in the future, you can't guarantee that the value of its stock will increase.

Some companies today sell their stock directly to investors, allowing you to bypass brokers. You can also invest in stocks via a stock mutual fund where a fund manager decides which individual stocks to include in the fund.

REMEMBER

You don't need an MBA or a PhD to make money in the stock market. If you can practise some simple lessons, such as making regular and systematic investments, and investing in proven companies and funds while minimizing your investment expenses and taxes, you should make decent returns in the long term.

However, you shouldn't expect that you can "beat the markets," and you certainly can't beat the best professional money managers at their own full-time game. This book shows you time-proven, non-gimmicky methods to make your money grow in the stock market as well as in other financial markets. Book 2 explains more about stocks, and mutual funds are covered in Book 3.

Owning real estate

People of varying economic means build wealth by investing in real estate. Owning and managing real estate is like running a small business. You need to satisfy customers (tenants), manage your costs, keep an eye on the competition, and so on. Some methods of real estate investing require more time than others, but many are proven ways to build wealth.

John, who works for a city government, and his wife, Linda, a computer analyst, have built several million dollars in investment real estate *equity* (the difference between the property's market value and debts secured by that property) over the past three decades. "Our parents owned rental property, and we could see what it could do for you by providing income and building wealth," says John. Investing in real estate also appealed to John and Linda because they didn't know anything about the stock market, so they wanted to stay away from it. The idea of *leverage* — making money with borrowed money — on real estate also appealed to them.

John and Linda bought their first property, a duplex, when their combined income was just $35,000 per year. Every time they moved to a new home, they kept the prior one and converted it to a rental. Now in their 50s, John and Linda own seven pieces of investment real estate and are multimillionaires. "It's like a second retirement, having thousands in monthly income from the real estate," says John.

John readily admits that rental real estate has its hassles. "We haven't enjoyed getting calls in the middle of the night, but now we have a property manager who can help with this when we're not available. It's also sometimes a pain finding new tenants," he says.

Overall, John and Linda figure that they've been well rewarded for the time they spent and the money they invested. The income from John and Linda's rental properties also allows them to live in a nicer home.

REMEMBER

Ultimately, to make your money grow much faster than inflation and taxes, you must take some risk. Any investment that has real growth potential also has shrinkage potential! You may not want to take the risk or may not have the stomach for it. In that case, don't despair: This book discusses lower-risk investments as well. You can find out about risks and returns in Chapter 2 of Book 1. Book 7 gives you more details on real estate investing.

Running a small business

Some people have hit investing home runs by owning or buying businesses. Unlike the part-time nature of investing in the stock market, most people work full time at running their businesses, increasing their chances of doing something big financially with them.

WARNING

If you try to invest in individual stocks, by contrast, you're likely to work at it part time, competing against professionals who invest practically around the clock. Even if you devote almost all your time to managing your stock portfolio, you're still a passive bystander in businesses run by others. When you invest in your own small business, you're the boss, for better or worse.

WHO WANTS TO INVEST LIKE A MILLIONAIRE?

Having a million dollars isn't nearly as rare as it used to be. In fact, according to a Boston Consulting Group report, more than 485,000 Canadian households now have at least $1 million in wealth (excluding the value of real estate). Interestingly, wealthy households rarely let financial advisors direct their investments. According to the Spectrum Group, a firm that conducts research on wealth, only 10 per cent of households in the United States or Canada with wealth of at least $1 million allow advisors to call the shots and make the moves, whereas 30 per cent don't use any advisors at all. The remaining 60 per cent may or may not consult an advisor on an as-needed basis and then make their own moves.

As in past surveys, recent wealth surveys show that affluent investors achieved and built on their wealth with ownership investments, such as their own small businesses, real estate, and stocks.

For example, a decade ago, Calvin set out to develop a corporate publishing firm. Because he took the risk of starting his business and has been successful in slowly building it, today, in his 50s, he enjoys a net worth of more than $10 million and can retire if he wants. Even more important to many business owners — and the reason that financially successful entrepreneurs such as Calvin don't call it quits after they've amassed a lot of cash — are the non-financial rewards of investing, including the challenge and fulfilment of operating a successful business.

Similarly, Sandra has worked on her own as an interior designer for more than two decades. She previously worked in fashion as a model, and then she worked as a retail store manager. Her first taste of interior design was redesigning rooms at a condominium project. "I knew when I did that first building and turned it into something wonderful and profitable that I loved doing this kind of work," says Sandra. Today, Sandra's firm specializes in the restoration of landmark hotels, and her work has been written up in numerous magazines. "The money is not of primary importance to me," she says. "My work is driven by a passion but obviously it has to be profitable." Sandra has also experienced the fun and enjoyment of designing hotels in many parts of Canada and overseas.

Most small-business owners know that the entrepreneurial life isn't a smooth walk through the rose garden — it has its share of thorns. Emotionally and financially, entrepreneurship is sometimes a roller coaster. In addition to receiving financial rewards, however, small-business owners can enjoy seeing the impact of their work and knowing that it makes a difference. Combined, Calvin's and Sandra's firms created dozens of new jobs.

TIP

Not everyone needs to be sparked by the desire to start his or her own company to profit from small business. You can share in the economic rewards of the entrepreneurial world through buying an existing business or investing in someone else's budding enterprise.

Generating Income from Lending Investments

Besides ownership investments (which are discussed in the earlier section "Building Wealth with Ownership Investments"), the other major types of investments include those in which you lend your money. Suppose that, like most people, you keep some money in your local bank — most likely in a chequing account but perhaps also in a savings account or guaranteed investment certificate (GIC). No matter what type of bank account you place your money in, you're lending your money to the bank.

THE DOUBLE WHAMMY OF INFLATION AND TAXES

Bank accounts and bonds that pay a decent return are reassuring to many investors. Earning a small amount of interest sure beats losing some or all of your money in a risky investment.

The problem is that money in a savings account that pays 3 per cent, for example, isn't actually yielding you 3 per cent. It's not that the bank is lying; it's just that your investment bucket contains some not-so-obvious holes.

The first hole is taxes. When you earn interest, you have to pay tax on it. If you're a moderate-income earner, you end up losing about a third of your interest to taxes. Your 3 per cent return is now down to 2 per cent. (Interest earned inside a Tax-Free Savings Account [TSFA], however, is not taxed, while interest earned inside an RRSP is only taxed when you withdraw money from your plan.) But the second hole in your investment bucket can be even bigger than taxes: inflation. Although a few products become cheaper over time (computers, for example), most goods and services increase in price. Inflation in Canada has been running about 3 per cent per year over the long term. Inflation depresses the purchasing power of your investments' returns. If you subtract the 3 per cent "cost" of inflation from the remaining 2 per cent after payment of taxes, you've lost 1 per cent on your investment.

To recap: For every dollar you invested in the bank a year ago, despite the fact that the bank paid you your 3 pennies of interest, you're left with only 99 cents in real purchasing power for every dollar you had a year ago. In other words, thanks to the inflation and tax holes in your investment bucket, you can buy less with your money now than you could have a year ago, even though you've invested your money for a year.

TECHNICAL STUFF

How long and under what conditions you lend money to your bank depends on the specific bank and the account you use. With a GIC, you commit to lend your money for a specific length of time — perhaps six months, a year, or more. In return, the bank probably pays you a higher rate of interest than if you put your money in a bank account offering you immediate access to the money. (You may demand termination of the GIC early; however, you'll be penalized.) You can also invest your money in *bonds*, another type of lending investment. When you purchase a bond that's been issued by the government or a company, you agree to lend your money for a predetermined period of time and receive a particular rate of interest. (If you sell a bond before it matures, the difference between what you paid and what you get back may also give you a capital gain or capital loss.) But if you lend your money to Skechers through one of its bonds that matures in, say, ten years, for example, even if Skechers triples in size over the next decade, you won't share in that growth. Skechers' stockholders and employees reap the rewards of the company's success, but as a bondholder, you don't.

WARNING

Many people keep too much of their money in lending investments, thus allowing others to reap the rewards of economic growth. Although lending investments appear safer because typically you know in advance what (nominal) return you'll receive, they aren't that safe. The long-term risk of these seemingly safe money investments is that your money will grow too slowly to enable you to accomplish your personal financial goals. In the worst cases, the company or other institution to which you're lending money can go under and stiff you for your loan.

Considering Cash Equivalents

Cash equivalents are any investments that you can quickly convert to cash without cost to you. With most chequing accounts, for example, you can write a cheque or withdraw cash by visiting a teller — either the live or the automated type.

Money market mutual funds are another type of cash equivalent. Investors, both large and small, invest hundreds of billions of dollars in money market mutual funds because the best money market funds historically have produced higher yields than bank savings accounts. (Some online banks offer higher yields, but you must be careful to understand ancillary service fees that can wipe away any yield advantage.) The yield advantage of a money market fund over a savings account almost always widens when interest rates increase because banks move to raise savings account rates about as fast as molasses on a cold winter day.

Why shouldn't you take advantage of a higher yield? Many bank savers sacrifice this yield because they think that money market funds are risky — but they're not. Money market mutual funds generally invest in safe things such as GICs, short-term bank certificates of deposit, Canadian and provincial government-issued Treasury bills, and commercial paper (short-term bonds) that the most creditworthy corporations issue.

Another reason people keep too much money in traditional bank accounts is that the local bank branch office makes the cash seem more accessible. Money market mutual funds, however, offer many quick ways to get your cash. Sometimes you can write a cheque (most funds stipulate the cheque must be for at least a few hundred dollars), or you can call the fund and request that it mail or electronically transfer your money.

TIP

Move extra money that's dozing away in your bank savings account into a higher-yielding money market mutual fund. Even if you have just a few thousand dollars, the extra yield more than pays for the cost of this book.

Steering Clear of Futures and Options

Suppose you think that IBM's stock is a good investment. The direction that the management team is taking impresses you, and you like the products and services that the company offers. Profits seem to be on a positive trend. Things are looking up.

You can go out and buy the stock. Suppose it's currently trading at around $100 per share. If the price rises to $150 in the next six months, you've made yourself a 50 per cent profit ($150 − $100 = $50) on your original $100 investment. (Of course, you have to pay some brokerage fees to buy and then sell the stock.)

But instead of buying the stock outright, you can buy what are known as *call options* on IBM. A call option gives you the right but not the obligation to buy shares of IBM under specified terms from the person who sells you the call option. You may be able to purchase a call option that allows you to exercise your right to buy IBM stock at, say, $120 per share in the next six months. For this privilege, you may pay $6 per share to the seller of that option (and you'll also pay trading commissions).

If IBM's stock price skyrockets to, say, $150 in the next few months, the value of your options that allow you to buy the stock at $120 will be worth a lot — at least $30. You can then simply sell your options, which you bought for $6 in the example, at a huge profit — you've multiplied your money five-fold!

WARNING

Although this talk of fat profits sounds much more exciting than simply buying the stock directly and making far less money from a stock price increase, call options have two big problems:

>> **You could easily lose your entire investment.** If a company's stock price goes nowhere or rises only a little during the six-month period when you hold the call option, the option expires as worthless, and you lose all — that is, 100 per cent — of your investment. In fact, in the example, if IBM's stock trades at $120 or less at the time the option expires, the option is worthless.

>> **A call option represents a short-term gamble on a company's stock price, not an investment in the company itself.** In the example, IBM could expand its business and profits greatly in the years and decades ahead, but the value of the call option hinges on the ups and downs of IBM's stock price over a relatively short period of time (the next six months). If the stock market happens to dip in the next six months, IBM may get pulled down as well, despite the company's improving financial health.

Futures are similar to options in that both can be used as gambling instruments. The main difference is that futures contracts represent an obligation to buy or sell, unlike an option contract which gives you, well, the option to exercise or not. Futures, for example, can deal with the value of commodities such as oil, corn, wheat, gold, silver, and pork bellies. (There are also option markets for most commodities.) Futures have a delivery date that's in the not-too-distant future. (Do you really want bushels of wheat delivered to your home? Or worse yet, pork bellies?) You can place a small down payment — around 10 per cent — toward the purchase of futures, thereby greatly leveraging your "investment." If prices fall, you need to put up more money (called "posting margin") to keep from having your position sold. (*Note:* Futures on financial instruments like stock market indices and interest rates are generally cash settlements rather than physical delivery, and they're an increasingly large part of the market.) All in all: Don't gamble with futures and options.

TECHNICAL STUFF

The only real use that you may (if ever) have for these *derivatives* (so called because their value is "derived" from the price of other securities) is to *hedge*. Suppose you hold a lot of a stock that has greatly appreciated, and you don't want to sell now because of the taxes you would owe on the profit. Perhaps you want to postpone selling the stock until next year because you plan on not working or because you can then benefit from a lower tax rate. You can buy what's called a *put option*, which increases in value when a stock's price falls (because the put option grants its seller the right to sell his stock to the purchaser of the put option at a preset stock price). Thus, if the stock price does fall, the rising put option value offsets some of your losses on the stock you still hold less the cost of what you paid for your put option. Using put options allows you to postpone selling your stock without exposing yourself to the risk of a falling stock price.

Counting Out Collectibles

The term *collectibles* is a catch-all category for antiques, art, autographs, hockey and baseball cards, clocks, coins, comic books, dolls, gems, photographs, rare books, rugs, stamps, vintage wine, fine musical instruments, writing utensils, and a whole host of other items.

Although connoisseurs of fine art, antiques, and vintage wine wouldn't like to compare their pastime with buying old playing cards or chamber pots, the bottom line is that collectibles are all objects with little intrinsic value. Wine is just a bunch of old mushed-up grapes. A painting is simply a canvas and some paint that at retail would set you back a few bucks. Stamps are small pieces of paper, usually less than an inch square. What about hockey and baseball cards? Heck, kids used to stick these between their bike spokes! You shouldn't diminish contributions that artists and others make to the world's culture. And some people place a high value on some of these collectibles. But true investments that can make your money grow, such as stocks, real estate, or a small business, are assets that can produce income and profits. Collectibles have little intrinsic value and are thus fully exposed to the whims and speculations of buyers and sellers. (Of course, as history has shown, and as discussed elsewhere in this book, the prices of particular stocks, real estate, and businesses can be subject to the whims and speculations of buyers and sellers, especially in the short term. Over the longer term, however, market prices return to reality and sensible valuations.)

WARNING

Here are some other major problems with collectibles:

- **>> Markups are huge.** The spread between the price that a dealer pays for an object and the price he then sells the same object for is often around 100 per cent. Sometimes the difference is even greater, particularly if a dealer is the second or third middleman in the chain of purchase. So, at a minimum, your purchase must typically double in value just to get you back to even. And a value may not double for 10 to 20 years or more!

- **>> Lots of other costs add up.** If the markups aren't bad enough, some collectibles incur all sorts of other costs. If you buy more-expensive pieces, for example, you may need to have them appraised. You may have to pay storage and insurance costs as well. And unlike the markup, you pay some of these fees year after year of ownership.

- **>> You can get stuck with a pig in a poke.** Sometimes you may overpay even more for a collectible because you don't realize some imperfection or inferiority of an item. Worse, you may buy a forgery. Even reputable dealers have been duped by forgeries.

- **>> Your pride and joy can deteriorate over time.** Damage from sunlight, humidity, temperatures that are too high or too low, and a whole host of vagaries can ruin the quality of your collectible. Insurance doesn't cover this type of damage or negligence on your part.

- **>> The returns stink.** Even if you ignore the substantial costs of buying, holding, and selling, the average returns that investors earn from collectibles rarely keep ahead of inflation, and they're generally inferior to stock market, real estate, and small-business investing. Objective collectible return data are hard to come by. Never, ever trust "data" that dealers or the many collectible trade publications provide.

The best returns that collectible investors reap come from the ability to identify, years in advance, items that will *become* popular. Do you think you can do that? You may be the smartest person in the world, but you should know that most dealers can't tell what's going to rocket to popularity in the coming decades. Dealers make their profits the same way other retailers do: from the spread or markup on the merchandise that they sell. The public and collectors have fickle, quirky tastes that no one can predict. Did you know that Beanie Babies, Furbies, Pet Rocks, or Cabbage Patch Kids were going to be such hits (for however long they lasted)?

You can find out enough about a specific type of collectible to become a better investor than the average person, but you're going to have to be among the best — perhaps among the top 10 per cent of such collectors — to have a shot at earning decent returns. To get to this level of expertise, you need to invest hundreds if not thousands of hours reading, researching, and educating yourself about your specific type of collectible.

REMEMBER

Nothing is wrong with spending money on collectibles. Just don't fool yourself into thinking that they're investments. You can sink lots of your money into these non-income-producing, poor-return "investments." At their best as investments, collectibles give the wealthy a way to buy quality stuff that doesn't depreciate.

TIP

If you buy collectibles, here are some tips to keep in mind:

» **Collect for your love of the collectible, your desire to enjoy it, or your interest in finding out about or mastering a subject.** In other words, don't collect these items because you expect high investment returns, because you probably won't get them.

» **Keep quality items that you and your family have purchased and hope will be worth something someday.** Keeping these quality items is the simplest way to break into the collectible business. The complete sets of baseball cards that one collector gathered as a youngster are now (30-plus years later) worth hundreds of dollars to, in one case, $1,000!

» **Buy from the source and cut out the middlemen whenever possible.** In some cases, you may be able to buy directly from the artist. Some folks, for example, purchase pottery and art directly from the artists.

» **Check collectibles that are comparable to the one you have your eye on, shop around, and don't be afraid to negotiate.** An effective way to negotiate, after you decide what you like, is to make your offer to the dealer or artist by phone. Because the seller isn't standing right next to you, you don't feel pressure to decide immediately.

» **Get a buyback guarantee.** Ask the dealer (who thinks that the item is such a great investment) for a written guarantee to buy back the item from you, if you opt to sell, for at least the same price you paid or higher within five years.

» **Do your homework.** Use a comprehensive resource, such as the books by Ralph and Terry Kovel or their website at www.kovels.com, to research, buy, sell, maintain, and improve your collectible.

Chapter **2**

Weighing Risks and Returns

A woman passes up eating a hamburger at a picnic because she heard that she could contract a deadly *E. coli* infection from eating improperly cooked meat. The next week, that same woman hops in the passenger seat of her friend's old-model car that lacks airbags. This example isn't meant to depress or frighten anyone. However, it's trying to make an important point about risk — something everyone deals with on a daily basis. Risk is in the eye of the beholder. Many people base their perception of risk, in large part, on their experiences and what they've been exposed to. In doing so, they often fret about relatively small risks while overlooking much larger risks.

Sure, a risk of an *E. coli* infection from eating poorly cooked meat exists, so the woman who was leery of eating the hamburger at the picnic had a legitimate concern. However, that same woman got into the friend's car without an airbag and placed herself at far greater risk of dying in that situation than if she had eaten the hamburger. In North America, some 37,000 people die in automobile accidents each year.

In the world of investing, most folks worry about certain risks — some of which may make sense and some of which may not — but at the same time they completely overlook or disregard other, more significant risks. This chapter discusses a range of investments and their risks and expected returns.

Evaluating Risks

Everywhere you turn, risks exist; some are just more apparent than others. Many people misunderstand risks. With increased knowledge, you may be able to reduce or conquer some of your fears and make more sensible decisions about reducing risks. For example, some people who fear flying don't understand that statistically, flying is much safer than driving a car. You're approximately 110 times more likely to die in a motor vehicle than in an airplane. But when a plane goes down, it's big news because dozens and sometimes hundreds of people, who weren't engaging in reckless behaviour, perish. Meanwhile, the national media seem to pay less attention to the 100 people, on average, who die on the road every day.

Then there's the issue of control. Flying seems more dangerous to some folks because the pilots are in control of the plane, whereas in your car, you can at least be at the steering wheel. Of course, you can't control what happens around you or mechanical problems with the mode of transportation you're using.

This doesn't mean that you shouldn't drive or fly or that you shouldn't drive to the airport. However, you may consider steps you can take to reduce the significant risks you expose yourself to in a car. For example, you can get a car with more safety features, or you can bypass riding with reckless taxi drivers.

Although some people like to live life to its fullest and take "fun" risks (how else can you explain mountain climbers, parachutists, and bungee jumpers?), most people seek to minimize risk and maximize enjoyment in their lives. The vast majority of people also understand that they'd be a lot less happy living a life in which they sought to eliminate all risks, and they likely wouldn't be able to do so anyway.

REMEMBER

Likewise, if you attempt to avoid all the risks involved in investing, you likely won't succeed, and you likely won't be happy with your investment results and lifestyle. In the investment world, some people don't go near stocks or any investment that they perceive to be volatile. As a result, such investors often end up with lousy long-term returns and expose themselves to some high risks that they overlooked, such as the risk of having inflation and taxes erode the purchasing power of their money.

You can't live without taking risks. Risk-free activities or ways of living don't exist. You can minimize but never eliminate risks. Some methods of risk reduction aren't palatable because they reduce your quality of life. Risks are also composed of several factors. The following sections discuss the various types of investment risks and go over proven methods you can use to sensibly reduce these risks while not missing out on the upside that growth investments offer.

Market-value risk

Although the stock market can help you build wealth, most people recognize that it can also drop substantially — by 10, 20, or 30 per cent (or more) in a relatively short period of time. After peaking in 2000, Canadian and U.S. stocks, as measured by the major indexes representing the value of large companies (for Canada, the S&P/TSX Composite Index, and for the United States, the S&P 500 index), dropped about 50 per cent by 2002. Stocks on the NASDAQ, which is heavily weighted toward technology stocks, plunged more than 76 per cent from 2000 through 2002!

After a multi-year rebound, stocks peaked in 2007 and then dropped sharply during the "financial crisis" of 2008. From peak to bottom, Canadian, U.S., and global stocks dropped by some 50 — or more — per cent.

In a mere six weeks (from mid-July 1998 to early September 1998), large-company Canadian and U.S. stocks fell about 20 per cent. An index of smaller-company U.S. stocks dropped 33 per cent over a slightly longer period of two and a half months.

If you think that the stock market crash that occurred in the fall of 1987 was a big one (the market plunged by about a third in a matter of weeks), take a look at Tables 2-1 and 2-2, which list major declines over the past 100-plus years that were all *worse* than the 1987 crash. Note that two of these major declines happened in the 2000s: 2000 to 2002 and 2007 to 2009.

TABLE 2-1

Most Depressing Canadian Stock Market Declines*

Period	Size of Fall
1929–1932	80% (ouch!)
1937–1942	56%
2000–2002	50%
2007–2009	48%
1980–1982	44%
1973–1974	38%
2020	37%
1987–1987	31%
1956–1957	30%

As measured by changes in the TSE/TSX Composite Index

TABLE 2-2

Largest U.S. Stock Market Declines*

Period	Size of Fall
1929–1932	89% (ouch!)
2007–2009	55%
1937–1942	52%
1906–1907	49%
1890–1896	47%
1919–1921	47%
1901–1903	46%
1973–1974	45%
1916–1917	40%
2000–2002	39%
2020	37%

As measured by changes in the Dow Jones Industrial Average

Real estate exhibits similar unruly, annoying tendencies. Although real estate (like stocks) has been a terrific long-term investment, various real estate markets get clobbered from time to time.

When the oil industry collapsed in Alberta in the early 1980s, real estate prices in the province dropped by 25 per cent. And after a massive run-up in prices in the mid-1980s, house prices in the Toronto area plummeted by nearly 28 per cent over the next few years. Across Canada, after a whopping 50 per cent rise from 1978 to 1981, house prices dropped by 35 per cent in just over a year. Then, after hitting a new high in 1990, the market fell by 15 per cent in just 12 months, and by 1996 was down 22 per cent.

In the United States, housing prices took a 25 per cent tumble from the late 1920s to the mid-1930s. Later, in the 1980s and early 1990s, the northeastern United States became mired in a severe recession, and real estate prices fell by 20-plus per cent in many areas. After peaking near 1990, many of the West Coast housing markets, especially those in California, experienced falling prices — dropping 20 per cent or more in most areas by the mid-1990s.

Declining U.S. housing prices in the mid- to late 2000s garnered unprecedented attention. Some folks and pundits acted like it was the worst housing market ever. Foreclosures increased in part because of buyers who financed their home purchases with risky mortgages. But note that housing market conditions also vary tremendously by area. For example, housing prices in Toronto and Vancouver have often shown double-digit increases while smaller cities and towns were experiencing down-markets. In the United States, some portions of the Pacific Northwest and South actually appreciated during the mid- to late 2000s, while other U.S. markets experienced substantial declines.

After reading this section, you may want to keep all your money in the bank — after all, you know you won't likely lose your money, and you won't have to be a nonstop worrier. Since the Canada Deposit Insurance Corporation (CDIC) came into existence, which protects deposits at banks and trust companies up to $100,000, people don't lose 20, 40, 60, or 80 per cent of their bank-held savings vehicles within a few years, but major losses prior to then did happen. Just keep in mind, though, that just letting your money sit around would be a mistake.

REMEMBER

If you pass up the stock and real estate markets simply because of the potential market-value risk, you miss out on a historic, time-tested method of building substantial wealth. Instead of seeing declines and market corrections as horrible things, view them as potential opportunities or "sales." Try not to give in to the human emotions that often scare people away from buying something that others seem to be shunning.

Later in this chapter, you'll discover the generous returns that stocks and real estate as well as other investments have historically provided. The following sections suggest some simple things you can do to lower your investing risk and help prevent your portfolio from suffering a huge fall (or "drawdown").

Diversify for a gentler ride

If you worry about the health of the economy, the government, and the dollar, you can reduce your investment risk by investing outside of Canada. Most large Canadian companies do business in the United States and overseas, so when you invest in larger Canadian company stocks, you get some international investment exposure. You can also invest in international company stocks, ideally via mutual funds and exchange-traded funds (see Book 3).

Of course, investing overseas can't totally protect you in the event of a global economic catastrophe. If you worry about the risk of such a calamity, you should probably also worry about a huge meteor crashing into Earth. Maybe there's a way to colonize outer space.

TIP

Diversifying your investments can involve more than just your stock portfolio. You can also hold some real estate investments to diversify your investment portfolio. Many real estate markets appreciated in the early 2000s while North American stock markets were in the doghouse. Conversely, when real estate in many regions entered a multi-year slump in the mid-2000s, stocks performed well during that period. In the late 2000s, stock prices fell sharply while real estate prices in many major centres rose, but then stocks came roaring back. See Book 7 for details on real estate investing.

Consider your time horizon

Investors who worry that the stock market may take a dive and take their money down with it need to consider the length of time that they plan to invest. In a one-year period in the stock and bond markets, a wide range of outcomes can occur (as shown in Figure 2-1). History shows that you lose money about once in every three years that you invest in the stock and bond markets. However, stock market investors have made money (sometimes substantial amounts) approximately two-thirds of the time over a one-year period. (Bond investors made money about two-thirds of the time, too, although they made a good deal less on average.)

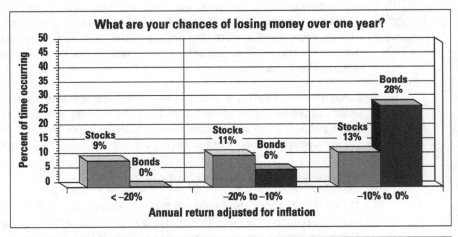

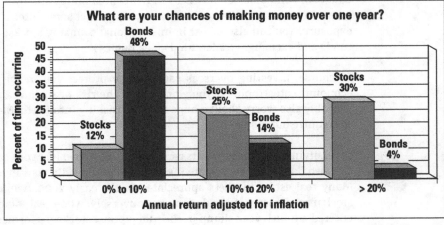

© John Wiley & Sons, Inc.

FIGURE 2-1: What are the odds of making or losing money in the Canadian markets? In a single year, you win far more often (and bigger) with stocks than with bonds.

Although the stock market is more volatile than the bond market in the short term, stock market investors have earned far better long-term returns than bond investors have. (See the later section "Stock returns" for details.) Why? Because stock investors bear risks that bond investors don't bear, and they can reasonably expect to be compensated for those risks. Keep in mind, however, that bonds generally outperform a boring old bank account.

History has shown that the risk of a stock or bond market fall becomes less of a concern the longer that you plan to invest. Figure 2-2 shows that as the holding period for owning stocks increases from 1 year to 3 years to 5 years to 10 years and then to 20 years, there's a greater likelihood of seeing stocks increase in value. In fact, over any 20-year time span, the U.S. stock market, as measured by the S&P 500 index of larger company stocks, has *never* lost money, even after you subtract the effects of inflation.

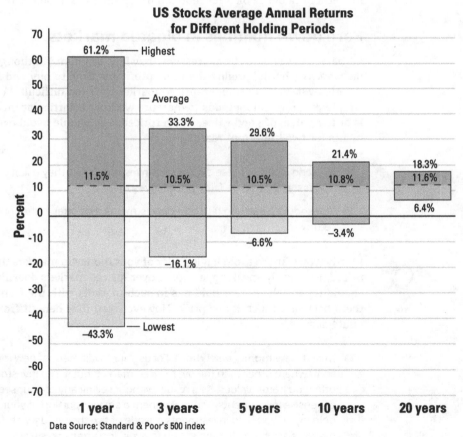

US Stocks Average Annual Returns for Different Holding Periods

Data Source: Standard & Poor's 500 index

© John Wiley & Sons, Inc.

FIGURE 2-2: The longer you hold stocks, the more likely you are to make money.

Figure 2-2 uses U.S. data simply because several more decades of market data are available, giving a better sense of the long-term behaviour of the stock market. However, the same basic point is true for Canada. Since 1957, only one five-year period has had a negative return. In other words, if you had invested in the broad market (meaning your returns were similar to the composite index) and held on for five years, in only one period would you have had less after five years than you started with. If you had invested and *stayed* invested for ten years, you would always have come out ahead. To put it another way, starting in 1957, if you had invested in any year and held those investments for a minimum of ten years, you would always have ended up with a profit, assuming your returns matched those of the index.

REMEMBER

Most stock market investors are concerned about the risk of losing money. Figure 2-2 clearly shows that the key to minimizing the probability that you'll lose money in stocks is to hold them for the longer term. Don't invest in stocks unless you plan to hold them for at least five years — and preferably a decade or longer. Check out Book 2 for more on using stocks as a long-term investment.

Pare down holdings in bloated markets

Perhaps you've heard the expression "buy low, sell high." Although you can't *time the markets* (that is, predict the most profitable time to buy and sell), spotting a greatly over-priced or under-priced market isn't too difficult. You can use some simple yet powerful methods to measure whether a particular investment market is of fair value, of good value, or overpriced. You should avoid overpriced investments for two important reasons:

>> If — and when — these over-priced investments fall, they usually fall farther and faster than more fairly priced investments.

>> You should be able to find other investments that offer higher potential returns.

TIP

Ideally, you want to avoid having a lot of your money in markets that appear over-priced. Practically speaking, avoiding over-priced markets doesn't mean that you should try to sell all your holdings in such markets with the vain hope of buying them back at a much lower price. However, you may benefit from the following strategies:

>> **Invest new money elsewhere.** Focus your investment of new money somewhere other than the over-priced market; put it into investments that offer you better values. As a result, without selling any of your seemingly expensive investments, you make them a smaller portion of your total holdings. If you hold investments outside of tax-sheltered plans, focusing your money elsewhere also allows you to avoid incurring taxes from selling appreciated investments.

>> **If you have to sell, sell the expensive stuff.** If you need to raise money to live on, such as for retirement or for a major purchase, sell the pricier holdings. As long as the taxes aren't too troublesome, it's better to sell high and lock in your profits.

Individual-investment risk

A down-draft can put an entire investment market on a roller-coaster ride, but healthy markets also have their share of individual losers. For example, from the early 1980s through the late 1990s, Canadian and U.S. stock markets had one of the greatest appreciating markets in history. You'd never know it, though, if you held one of the great losers of that period.

Consider a company now called Navistar, which has undergone enormous transformations in recent decades. This company used to be called International Harvester and manufactured farm equipment, trucks, and construction and other industrial equipment. Today, Navistar makes mostly trucks.

In late 1983, this company's stock traded at more than US$140 per share. It then plunged more than 90 per cent over the ensuing decade (as shown in Figure 2-3). Even with a rally in recent years, Navistar stock still trades at less than US$20 per share (after dipping below US$10 per share). Lest you think that's a big drop, this company's stock traded as high as US$455 per share in the late 1970s! If a worker retired from this company in the late 1970s with $200,000 invested in the company stock, the retiree's investment would be worth about $6,000 today! On the other hand, if the retiree had simply swapped his stock at retirement for a diversified portfolio of stocks, which you find out how to build in Book 2, his $200,000 nest egg would've instead grown to more than $5 million!

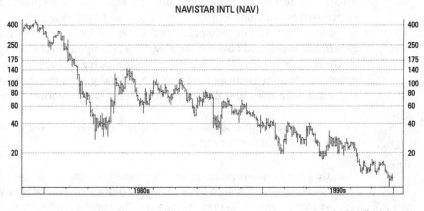

FIGURE 2-3: Even the bull market of the 1990s wasn't kind to every company.

© John Wiley & Sons, Inc.

Like most other markets, the Canadian stock market paled by comparison with the US juggernaut in the 1990s, but this country has had its share of stocks that have plummeted in value. How about Dylex, which through its many brand-name outlets, such as Suzy Shier, at one time took in one out of every ten dollars consumers spent in retail clothing outlets? The stock, which began the 1990s at $24, ended the decade languishing beneath the $10 mark, dwindling lower and lower until the company eventually went under in 2001.

And then, of course, there's Nortel. In the late 1990s, many investors happily recounted how well they'd done by buying Nortel. They often had made two, three, even ten times or more on their original investment. Nortel, or so people were told, just couldn't keep up with the Internet-driven demand for its products. At its peak, Nortel employed 90,000 workers worldwide and was worth nearly $300 billion.

And the press was cheering them on. Nortel even got feature stories written about it when, due to a chronic shortage of workers, it sent a bus to travel around the United States, trying to hire folks. That turned out to be not a sign of great things to come, but a last great gasp. The stock soon peaked at over $120 in August 2000. After that?

Well, in a matter of months, the company's cheerleaders were proven to be completely, hopelessly wrong. Nortel crumbled, and by October 2002 it had literally turned into a penny stock, trading at under a buck. Many investors were now calling Nortel one of their "worst moves." By the end of 2008, the stock was taken off the New York Stock Exchange because it had had an average closing price below US$1 for more than 30 days. By the end of the decade, Nortel had been also delisted by the Toronto Stock Exchange, and went bankrupt.

Just as individual stock prices can plummet, so can individual real estate property prices. In California during the 1990s, for example, earthquakes rocked the prices of properties built on landfills. These quakes highlighted the dangers of building on poor soil. In the decade prior, real estate values in the communities of Times Beach, Missouri, and Love Canal, New York, plunged because of carcinogenic toxic waste contamination. (Ultimately, many property owners in these areas received compensation for their losses from the federal government as well as from some real estate agencies that didn't disclose these known contaminants.)

TIP

Here are some simple steps you can take to lower the risk of individual investments that can upset your goals:

>> **Do your homework.** When you purchase real estate, a whole host of inspections can save you from buying a money pit. With stocks, you can examine some measures of value and the company's financial condition and

business strategy to reduce your chances of buying into an overpriced company or one on the verge of major problems. Book 2 gives you information on researching your stock investment.

>> **Diversify.** Investors who seek growth invest in securities such as stocks. Placing significant amounts of your capital in one or a handful of securities is risky, particularly if the stocks are in the same industry or closely related industries. To reduce this risk, purchase stocks in a variety of industries and companies within each industry. (See Book 2 for details.)

>> **Hire someone to invest for you.** The best funds offer low-cost, professional management and oversight as well as diversification. Stock funds typically own 25 or more securities in a variety of companies in different industries.

THE LOWDOWN ON LIQUIDITY

The term *liquidity* refers to how long and at what cost it takes to convert an investment into cash. The money in your wallet is considered perfectly liquid — it's already cash.

Suppose that you invested money in a handful of stocks. Although you can't easily sell these stocks on a Saturday night, you can sell most stocks quickly through a broker for a nominal fee any day that the financial markets are open (normal working days). You pay a higher percentage to sell your stocks if you use a high-cost broker or if you have a small amount of stock to sell.

Real estate is generally much less liquid than stock. Preparing your property for sale takes time, and if you want to get fair market value for your property, finding a buyer may take weeks or months. Selling costs (agent commissions, fix-up expenses, and closing costs) can approach 8 to 10 per cent of the home's value.

A privately-run small business is among the least liquid of the better growth investments that you can make. Selling such a business typically takes longer than selling most real estate.

To protect yourself from being forced to sell one of your investments that you intend to hold for long-term purposes, keep an emergency reserve of three to six months' worth of living expenses in a money market account or high-interest savings account. Also consider investing some money in highly rated bonds (see Chapter 5 in Book 3), which pay higher than money market yields without the high risk or volatility that comes with the stock market.

Purchasing-power risk (aka inflation risk)

Increases in the cost of living (that is, inflation) can erode the value of your retirement resources and what you can buy with that money — also known as its *purchasing power*. When Teri retired at the age of 60, she was pleased with her retirement income. She was receiving an $800-per-month pension and $1,200 per month from money that she had invested in long-term bonds. Her monthly expenditures amounted to about $1,500, so she was able to save a little money for an occasional trip.

Fast-forward 15 years. Teri still receives $800 per month from her pension, but now she gets only $900 per month of investment income, which comes from some certificates of deposit. Teri bailed out of bonds after she lost sleep over the sometimes roller-coaster-like price movements in the bond market. Her monthly expenditures now amount to approximately $2,400, and she uses some of her investment principal (original investment). She's terrified of outliving her money.

Teri has reason to worry. She has 100 per cent of her money invested without protection against increases in the cost of living. Although her income felt comfortable in the beginning of her retirement, it doesn't at age 75, and Teri may easily live another 15 or more years.

The erosion of the purchasing power of your investment dollar can, over longer time periods, be as bad as or worse than the effect of a major market crash. Table 2-3 shows the effective loss in purchasing power of your money at various rates of inflation and over differing time periods.

TABLE 2-3 Inflation's Corrosive Effect on Your Money's Purchasing Power

Inflation Rate	10 Years	15 Years	25 Years	40 Years
2%	−18%	−26%	−39%	−55%
4%	−32%	−44%	−62%	−81%
6%	−44%	−58%	−77%	−90%
8%	−54%	−68%	−85%	−95%
10%	−61%	−76%	−91%	−98%

REMEMBER

Skittish investors have tried to keep their money in bonds and money market accounts, thinking they were playing it safe. The risk in this strategy is that your money won't grow enough over the years for you to accomplish your financial goals. In other words, the lower the return you earn, the more you need to save to reach a particular financial goal.

A 40-year-old wanting to accumulate $500,000 by age 65 would need to save $722 per month if she earns a 6 per cent average annual return, but she needs to save only $377 per month if she earns a 10 per cent average return per year. Younger investors need to pay the most attention to the risk of generating low returns, but so should younger senior citizens. Even by the age of 65, seniors need to recognize that a portion of their assets may not be used for a decade or more from the present.

INFLATION RAGIN' OUTTA CONTROL

You think 6, 8, or 10 per cent annual inflation rates are bad? How would you like to live in a country that experienced that rate of inflation *in a day*? Too much money in circulation chasing after too few goods causes high rates of inflation.

A government that runs amok with the nation's currency and money supply usually causes excessive rates of inflation — dubbed *hyperinflation*. Over the decades and centuries, hyperinflation has wreaked havoc in more than a few countries.

What happened in Germany in the late 1910s and early 1920s demonstrates how bad hyperinflation can get. Consider that during this time period, prices increased nearly one-billionfold! What cost 1 reichsmark (the German currency in those days) at the beginning of this mess eventually cost nearly 1,000,000,000 reichsmarks. People had to cart around so much currency that at times they needed wheelbarrows to haul it! Ultimately, this inflationary burden was too much for the German society, creating a social climate that fueled the rise of the Nazi party and Adolf Hitler.

During the 1990s, a number of countries, especially many that made up the former USSR and others such as Brazil and Lithuania, got themselves into a hyperinflationary mess with inflation rates of several hundred per cent per year. In the mid-1980s, Bolivia's yearly inflation rate exceeded 10,000 per cent. In Zimbabwe today, beggars on the street refuse to accept Zimbabwe dollars!

Governments often try to slap on price controls to prevent runaway inflation (Pierre Trudeau did this in Canada in the 1970s, as did Richard Nixon in the United States), but the underground economy, known as the *black market,* usually prevails.

Career risk

REMEMBER

Your ability to earn money (also called "human capital" by economists) is most likely your single biggest asset or at least one of your biggest assets. Most people achieve what they do in the working world through education and hard work. By education, we're not simply talking about what one learns in formal schooling. Education is a lifelong process. We've learned far more about business from our own front-line experiences and those of others, as well as training others, than we've learned in educational settings. We also read a lot.

If you don't continually invest in your education, you risk losing your competitive edge. Your skills and perspectives can become dated and obsolete. Although that doesn't mean you should work 80 hours a week and never do anything fun, it does mean that part of your "work" time should involve upgrading your skills.

The best organizations are those that recognize the need for continual knowledge and invest in their workforce through training and career development. Just be sure to look at your own career objectives, which may not be the same as your company's.

Analysing Returns

When you make investments, you have the potential to make money in a variety of ways. Each type of investment has its own mix of associated risks that you take when you part with your investment dollar and, likewise, offers a different potential rate of return. The following sections cover the returns you can expect with each of the common investing avenues. But first, you go through the components of calculating the total return on an investment.

The components of total return

To figure out exactly how much money you've made (or lost) on your investment, you need to calculate the *total return*. To come up with this figure, you need to determine how much money you originally invested and then factor in the other components, such as interest, dividends, and capital appreciation (or depreciation), also known as capital gains.

If you've ever had money in a bank account that pays *interest*, you know that the bank pays you a small amount of interest when you allow it to keep your money. The bank then turns around and lends your money to some other person or organization at a much higher rate of interest. The rate of interest is also known as the *yield*. So, if a bank tells you that its savings account pays 2 per cent interest, the bank may also say that the account yields 2 per cent. Banks usually quote interest rates or yields on an annual basis. Interest that you receive is one component of the return you receive on your investment.

If a bank pays monthly interest, the bank also likely quotes a *compounded effective annual yield*. After the first month's interest is credited to your account, that interest starts earning interest as well. So, the bank may say that the account pays 2 per cent, which then compounds to an effective annual yield of 2.04 per cent.

When you lend your money directly to a company — which is what you do when you invest in a bond that a corporation or a government issues — you also receive interest. Bonds, as well as stocks (which are shares of ownership in a company), fluctuate in value after they're issued.

When you invest in a company's stock, you hope that the stock increases *(appreciates)* in value. Of course, a stock can also decline, or *depreciate,* in value. This change in market value is part of your return from a stock or bond investment: (Current investment value – Original investment) ÷ Original investment = Appreciation or depreciation.

For example, if one year ago you invested $10,000 in a stock (you bought 1,000 shares at $10 per share) and the investment is now worth $11,000 (each share is worth $11), your investment's appreciation looks like this: ($11,000 – $10,000) ÷ $10,000 = 10%.

Stocks can also pay *dividends,* which are the company's sharing of some of its profits with you as a shareholder. Some companies, particularly those that are small or growing rapidly, choose to reinvest all their profits back into the company. (Of course, some companies don't turn a profit, so they don't have anything to pay out!) You need to factor any dividends into your return as well.

Suppose that in the previous example, in addition to your stock investment appreciating from $10,000 to $11,000, it paid you a dividend of $100 ($1 per share). Here's how you calculate your total return: ([Current investment value – Original investment] + Dividends) ÷ Original investment = Total return.

You can apply this formula to the example like so: (([$11,000 – $10,000] + $100) ÷ $10,000 = 11%.

After-tax returns

Although you may be happy that your stock has given you an 11 per cent return on your invested dollars, note that unless you held your investment in a tax-deferred Registered Retirement Savings Plan (RRSP), registered retirement plan, Registered Education Savings Plan, or Tax-Free Savings Account (TFSA), you owe taxes on your return. Specifically, the dividends and investment appreciation that you realize upon selling are taxed, although often at relatively low rates. The tax rates on so-called long-term capital gains and stock dividends are lower than the tax rates on other income. Chapter 3 discusses the different tax rates that affect your investments and explains how to make tax-wise investment decisions that fit with your overall personal financial situation and goals.

If you've invested in savings accounts, money market accounts, or bonds outside of a tax-deferred registered retirement plan or a TFSA, you owe the Canada Revenue Agency taxes on the interest income.

Often, people make investing decisions without considering the tax consequences of their moves. This is a big mistake. What good is making money if the government takes away a substantial portion of it?

If you're in a moderate tax bracket, taxes on your investment probably run in the neighborhood of 30 per cent (federal and provincial). So, if your investment returned 6 per cent before taxes, you're left with a net return of about 4.2 per cent after taxes.

Psychological returns

Profits and tax avoidance can powerfully motivate your investment selections. However, as with other life decisions, you need to consider more than the bottom line. Some people want to have fun with their investments. Of course, they don't want to lose money or sacrifice a lot of potential returns. Fortunately, less expensive ways to have fun do exist!

Psychological rewards compel some investors to choose particular investment vehicles such as individual stocks, real estate, or a small business. Why? Because compared with other investments, such as managed mutual and exchange-traded funds, they see these investments as more tangible and, well, more fun.

TIP

Be honest with yourself about why you choose the investments that you do. Allowing your ego to get in the way can be dangerous. Do you want to invest in individual stocks because you really believe that you can do better than the best full-time professional money managers? Chances are high that you won't. Such questions are worth considering as you contemplate which investments you want to make.

Savings, high-interest, and money market account returns

You need to keep your extra cash that awaits investment (or an emergency) in a safe place, preferably one that doesn't get hammered by the sea of changes in the financial markets. By default and for convenience, many people keep their extra cash in a bank savings account. Although the bank offers the backing of the Canada Deposit Insurance Corporation (CDIC), it comes at a price. Most banks pay a relatively low interest rate on their savings accounts.

TIP

A far better place to keep your liquid savings are the growing number of high-interest savings accounts (HISAs) offered by companies such as Alterna Bank, DUCA Credit Union, or Tangerine, and now most mutual fund companies and big banks as well. These accounts typically offer rates anywhere from 4 to 40 — yes, 40 — times the rate on savings accounts.

Another good place to keep your liquid savings is in a money market mutual fund. These are the safest types of mutual funds around and, for all intents and purposes, equal a bank savings account's safety. The best money market funds generally pay higher yields than most bank savings accounts. Unlike a bank, money market mutual funds tell you how much they deduct for the service of managing your money.

TIP

If you don't need immediate access to your money, consider using Treasury bills (T-bills) or guaranteed investment certificates (GICs; see Chapter 5 in Book 3), which are usually issued for terms of anywhere from three months to five years. Your money will generally earn more in one of these vehicles than in a bank savings account. (In recent years, the yields on T-bills have been so low that the best CDIC-insured bank savings accounts have higher yields.) Rates vary by institution, so it's essential to shop around. The drawback to T-bills and guaranteed investment certificates is that you incur a penalty (with GICs) or a transaction fee (with T-bills) if you withdraw your investment before the term expires.

Bond returns

When you buy a bond, you lend your money to the issuer of that bond (borrower), which is generally the federal government, a provincial government, or a corporation, for a specific period of time. When you buy a bond, you expect to earn a higher yield than you can with a money market or savings account. You're taking more risk, after all. Companies can and do go bankrupt, in which case you may lose some or all of your investment.

Generally, you can expect to earn a higher yield when you buy bonds that

>> **Are issued for a longer term:** The bond issuer is tying up your money at a fixed rate for a longer period of time.

>> **Have lower credit quality:** The bond issuer may not be able to repay the principal.

Wharton School of Business professor Jeremy Siegel has tracked the performance of bonds and stocks back to 1802. Although you may say that what happened in the 19th century has little relevance to the financial markets and economy of today, the decades since the Great Depression of the 1930s, which most other return data track, are a relatively small slice of time. Figure 2-4 presents the data, so if you'd like to give more emphasis to the recent numbers, you may.

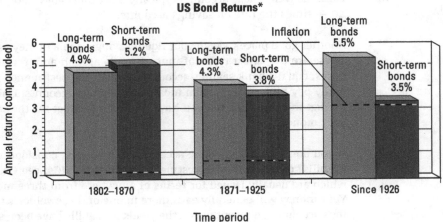

© John Wiley & Sons, Inc.

FIGURE 2-4: A historical view of U.S. bond performance: Inflation has eroded bond returns more in recent decades.

Note that although the rate of inflation has increased since the Great Depression, bond returns haven't increased over the decades. Long-term bonds maintained slightly higher returns in recent years than short-term bonds. The bottom line: Bond investors typically earn about 4 to 5 per cent per year. See Chapter 5 in Book 3 for more about bonds.

Stock returns

Investors expect a fair return on their investments. If one investment doesn't offer a seemingly high enough potential rate of return, investors can choose to move their money into other investments that they believe will perform better. Instead of buying a diversified basket of stocks and holding, some investors frequently buy and sell, hoping to cash in on the latest hot investment. This tactic seldom works in the long run.

WARNING

Unfortunately, some of these investors use a rear-view mirror when they purchase their stocks, chasing after investments that have recently performed strongly on the assumption (and the hope) that those investments will continue to earn good returns. But chasing after the strongest performing investments can be dangerous if you catch the stock at its peak, ready to begin a downward spiral. You may have heard that the goal of investing is to buy low and sell high. Chasing high-flying investments can lead you to buy high, with the prospect of having to sell low if the stock runs out of steam. Even though stocks as a whole have proved to be a good long-term investment, picking individual stocks is a risky endeavour. See Book 2 for advice on making sound stock investment decisions.

A tremendous amount of data exists regarding stock market returns. In fact, in the U.S. markets, data going back more than two *centuries* document the fact that stocks have been a terrific long-term investment. The long-term returns from stocks that investors have enjoyed, and continue to enjoy, have been remarkably constant from one generation to the next.

Going all the way back to 1802, the U.S. stock market has produced an annual return of 8.3 per cent, while inflation has grown at 1.4 per cent per year. Thus, after subtracting for inflation, stocks have appreciated about 6.9 per cent faster annually than the rate of inflation. The U.S. stock market returns have consistently and substantially beaten the rate of inflation over the years (see Figure 2-5).

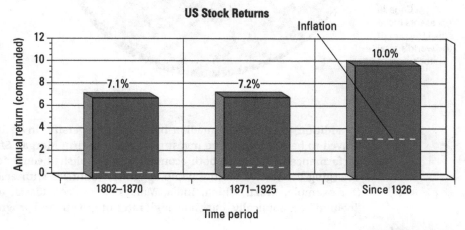

FIGURE 2-5: History shows that stocks have been a consistent long-term winner.

© John Wiley & Sons, Inc.

Stocks don't exist only in Canada and the United States, of course (see Figure 2-6). More than a few investors seem to forget this fact, as they did during the sizzling performance of the Canadian and U.S. stock markets during the late 1990s. As discussed in the earlier section "Diversify for a gentler ride," one advantage of buying and holding overseas stocks is that they don't always move in tandem with North American stocks. As a result, overseas stocks help diversify your portfolio.

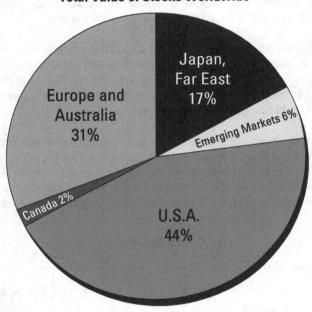

Total Value of Stocks Worldwide

© John Wiley & Sons, Inc.

FIGURE 2-6: Canada represents just a small fraction of the world's total stock market value.

In addition to enabling Canadian investors to diversify, investing overseas has proved to be profitable. The investment banking firm Morgan Stanley tracks the performance of stocks in both economically established countries and so-called emerging economies. As the name suggests, countries with *emerging economies* (for example, Brazil, China, India, Malaysia, Mexico, Russia, and Taiwan) are "behind" economically, but show high rates of growth and progress.

REMEMBER

Stocks are the best long-term performers, but they have more volatility than bonds and Treasury bills. A balanced portfolio gets you most of the long-term returns of stocks without much of the volatility.

ARE SMALLER-COMPANY STOCK RETURNS HIGHER?

Stocks are generally classified by the size of the company. Small-company stocks aren't stocks that physically small companies issue; they're simply stocks issued by companies that haven't reached the size of corporate behemoths like the big banks, Bombardier, and Barrick, or U.S. giants like IBM, Walmart, and Coca-Cola. The S&P/TSX SmallCap Index tracks the smallest companies that qualify for the S&P/TSX compound index, while the S&P/TSX Venture Composite Index measures the performance of the larger and more actively traded companies listed on the TSX Venture Exchange, where smaller or more speculative companies are listed. In the United States, the Standard & Poor's 500 index tracks the performance of 500 large-company stocks in the United States. The Russell 2000 index tracks the performance of 2,000 smaller-company U.S. stocks.

Small-company stocks have outperformed larger-company stocks during the past seven decades. Historically, small-company stocks have produced slightly higher compounded annual returns than large-company stocks. However, nearly all this extra performance is due to just one high-performance time period, from the mid-1970s to the early 1980s. If you eliminate this time period from the data, small stocks have had virtually identical returns to those of larger-company stocks.

Also, be aware that small-company stocks can get hammered in down markets. For example, during the Great Depression, small-company stocks plunged more than 85 per cent between 1929 and 1932, while the S&P 500 fell 64 per cent. In 1937, small-company stocks plummeted 58 per cent, while the S&P 500 fell 35 per cent. And in 1969 to 1970, small-company stocks fell 38 per cent, while the S&P 500 fell just 5 per cent.

Real estate returns

REMEMBER

Over the years, real estate has proved to be about as lucrative as investing in the stock market. Whenever there's a real estate downturn, folks question this historic fact. However, just as stock prices have down periods, so, too, do real estate markets.

The fact that real estate offers solid long-term returns makes sense because growth in the economy, in jobs, and in population ultimately fuels the demand for real estate.

Consider what has happened to the Canadian population over the past two centuries. In 1867 a mere 3.5 million people lived within Canada's borders. In 1900 that figure grew to over 5 million, and by 1929 it had doubled to over 10 million. Today it's about 37 million. All these people need places to live, and as long as jobs exist, the income from jobs largely fuels the demand for housing.

Businesses and people have an understandable tendency to cluster in major cities and suburban towns. Although some people commute, most people and businesses locate near major highways, airports, and so on. Thus, real estate prices in and near major metropolises and suburbs generally appreciate the most. Consider the areas of the world that have the most expensive real estate prices: Hong Kong, Singapore, London, San Francisco, New York, and Boston. Here at home, the most expensive cities are Vancouver and Toronto. What these areas have in common are lots of businesses and people and limited land.

Contrast these areas with the many rural parts of Canada where the price of real estate is relatively low because of the abundant supply of buildable land and the relatively lower demand for housing.

See Book 7 for an introduction to real estate investing.

Small-business returns

You have several choices for tapping into the exciting potential of the small-business world. If you have the drive and determination, you can start your own small business. Or perhaps you have what it takes to buy an existing small business. If you obtain the necessary capital and skills to assess opportunities and risk, you can invest in someone else's small business.

What potential returns can you get from small business? Small-business owners who do something they really enjoy will tell you that the non-financial returns can be major! But the financial rewards can be attractive as well.

Every year, *Forbes* magazine publishes a list of the world's wealthiest individuals. Perusing this list shows that most of these people built their wealth by taking a significant ownership stake and starting a small business that became large. These individuals achieved extraordinarily high returns (often in excess of hundreds of per cent per year) on the amounts they invested to get their companies off the ground.

You may also achieve potentially high returns from buying and improving an existing small business. Such small-business investment returns may be a good deal lower than the returns you may gain from starting a business from scratch.

Unlike the stock market, where plenty of historic rate-of-return data exists, data on the success — or lack thereof! — that investors have had with investing in small private companies is harder to come by. Smart venture capitalist firms operate a fun and lucrative business: They identify and invest money in smaller start-up companies that they hope will grow rapidly and eventually go public. Venture capitalists allow outsiders to invest with them via limited partnerships.

To gain entry, you generally need $1 million to invest, although there are some exceptions from time to time. (This isn't an equal-opportunity investment club!)

Venture capitalists, also known as *general partners*, typically skim off 20 per cent of the profits and also charge limited partnership investors a hefty 2 to 3 per cent annual fee on the amount that they've invested. The return that's left over for the limited partnership investors isn't always stupendous. According to Venture Economics, a U.S. firm that tracks limited partners' returns, venture funds have averaged comparable annual returns to what stock market investors have earned on average over this same period. The general partners that run venture capital funds make more than the limited partners do.

You can attempt to do what the general partners do in venture capital firms and invest directly in small private companies. But you're likely to be investing in much smaller and simpler companies. Earning venture capitalist returns isn't easy to do.

Considering Your Goals

REMEMBER

How much do you need or want to earn? That may seem like an extraordinarily silly question to ask you. Who doesn't want to earn a high return? However, although investing in stocks, real estate, or a small business can produce high long-term returns, investing in these vehicles comes with greater risk, especially over the short term.

Some people can't stomach the risk. Others are at a time in their lives when they can't afford to take great risk. If you're near or in retirement, your portfolio and nerves may not be able to wait a decade for your riskier investments to recover after a major stumble. Perhaps you have sufficient assets to accomplish your financial goals and are concerned with preserving what you do have rather than risking it to grow more wealth.

If you work for a living, odds are that you need and want to make your investments grow at a healthy clip plus lower your income taxes. If your investments grow slowly, you may fall short of your goal of owning a home or retiring or changing careers.

IN THIS CHAPTER

» **Saving money for emergencies**

» **Managing your debt and setting financial goals**

» **Funding retirement and university savings plans**

» **Understanding tax issues**

» **Exploring diversification strategies**

Chapter **3**

Getting Your Financial House in Order

Before you make any great, wealth-building investments, you should get your financial house in order. Understanding and implementing some simple personal financial management concepts can pay-off big for you in the decades ahead.

You want to know how to earn healthy returns on your investments without getting clobbered, right? Who doesn't? Although you generally must accept greater risk to have the potential for earning higher returns (see Chapter 2 in Book 1), this chapter tells you about some high-return, low-risk investments. You have a right to be skeptical about such investments, but don't stop reading this chapter yet. Here, you find some easy-to-tap opportunities for managing your money that you may have overlooked.

Establishing an Emergency Reserve

You never know what life will bring, so having a readily accessible reserve of cash to meet unexpected expenses makes good financial sense. If you have a sister who works on Bay Street as an investment banker or a wealthy and understanding parent, you can use one of them as your emergency reserve. (Although you should ask them how they feel about that before you count on receiving funding from them!) If you don't have a wealthy family member, the ball's in your court to establish a reserve.

REMEMBER

Make sure you have quick access to at least three months' to as much as six months' worth of living expenses. Keep this emergency money in a high-interest savings account or a Tax-Free Savings Account (TFSA). You may also be able to borrow against your home equity should you find yourself in a bind, but these options are much less desirable.

SHOULD YOU INVEST EMERGENCY MONEY IN STOCKS?

As interest rates drifted lower during the 1990s, keeping emergency money in money market accounts became less and less rewarding. When interest rates were 8 or 10 per cent, fewer people questioned the wisdom of an emergency reserve. However, in the late 1990s, which had low money market interest rates and stock market returns of 20 per cent per year, more investors balked at the idea of keeping a low-interest stash of cash. Some articles suggested you simply keep your emergency reserve in stocks. After all, the thinking went, you can easily sell stocks (especially those of larger companies) any day the financial markets are open. Why not treat yourself to the 20 per cent annual returns that stock market investors enjoyed during the 1990s rather than earning a paltry few per cent?

At first, that logic sounds great. But, as discussed in Chapter 2 of Book 1, stocks historically have returned about 9 to 10 per cent per year. In some years — in fact, about one-third of the time — stocks decline in value, sometimes substantially.

Stocks can drop and have dropped 20, 30, or 50 per cent or more over relatively short periods of time. Consider what happened to stock prices in the early 2000s and then again in the late 2000s. Suppose that such a drop coincides with an emergency — such as the loss of your job, major medical bills, and so on. Your situation may force you to sell at a loss, perhaps a substantial one.

Here's another reason not to keep emergency money in stocks: If your stocks appreciate and you need to sell some of them for emergency cash, you get stuck paying taxes on your gains. You should invest your emergency money in stocks (ideally through well-diversified mutual funds) only if you have a relative or some other resource to tap for money in an emergency. Having a backup resource for money minimizes your need to sell your stock holdings on short notice. As discussed in Book 2, stocks are intended to be a longer-term investment, not an investment that you expect (or need) to sell in the near future.

WARNING

If you don't have a financial safety net, you may be forced into selling an investment that you've worked hard for. And selling some investments, such as real estate, costs big money (because of transaction costs, taxes, and so on).

Consider the case of Warren, who owned his home and rented an investment property on the west coast. He felt, and appeared to be, financially successful. But then Warren lost his job, accumulated sizable medical expenses, and had to sell his investment property to come up with cash for living expenses. Warren didn't have enough equity in his home to borrow. He didn't have other sources — a wealthy relative, for example — to borrow from either, so he was stuck selling his investment property. Warren wasn't able to purchase another investment property and missed out on the large appreciation the property earned over the subsequent two decades. Between the costs of selling and taxes, getting rid of the investment property cost Warren about 15 per cent of its sales price. Ouch!

Evaluating Your Debts

Yes, paying down debts is boring, but it makes your investment decisions less difficult. Rather than spending so much of your time investigating specific investments, paying off your debts (if you have them and your cash coming in exceeds the cash going out) may be your best high-return, low-risk investment. Consider the interest rate you pay and your investing alternatives to determine which debts you should pay off.

Conquering consumer debt

Borrowing via credit cards, auto loans, and the like is an expensive way to borrow. Banks and other lenders charge higher interest rates for consumer debt than for debt for investments, such as real estate and business. The reason: Consumer loans are the riskiest type of loan for a lender.

Many folks have credit card or other consumer debt, such as an auto loan, that costs 8, 10, 12, or perhaps as much as 18-plus per cent per year in interest (some credit cards whack you with interest rates exceeding 20 per cent if you make a late payment). Reducing and eventually eliminating this debt with your savings is like putting your money in an investment with a guaranteed *tax-free* return equal to the rate that you pay on your debt.

For example, if you have outstanding credit card debt at 15 per cent interest, paying off that debt is the same as putting your money to work in an investment with a guaranteed 15 per cent tax-free annual return. Because the interest on consumer debt isn't tax-deductible, you need to earn more than 15 per cent by investing your money elsewhere in order to net 15 per cent after paying taxes. Earning such high investing returns is highly unlikely, and in order to earn those returns, you'd be forced to take great risk.

Consumer debt is hazardous to your long-term financial health (not to mention damaging to your credit score and future ability to borrow for a home or other wise investments) because it encourages you to borrow against your future earnings. People often say such things as "I can't afford to buy most new cars for cash — look at how expensive they are!" That's true, new cars *are* expensive, so you need to set your sights lower and buy a good used car that you *can* afford. You can then invest the money you'd otherwise spend on your auto loan.

However, using consumer debt may make sense if you're financing a business. If you don't have home equity, personal loans (through a credit card or auto loan) may actually be your lowest-cost source of small-business financing.

Mitigating your mortgage

Paying off your mortgage more quickly is an "investment" for your spare cash that may make sense for your financial situation. However, the wisdom of making this financial move isn't as clear as paying off high-interest consumer debt because mortgage interest rates are generally lower. When used properly, debt can help you accomplish your goals — such as buying a home or starting a business — and make you money in the long run. Borrowing to buy a home generally makes sense. Over the long term, homes generally appreciate in value.

If your financial situation has changed or improved since you first needed to borrow mortgage money, you need to reconsider how much mortgage debt you need or want. Even if your income hasn't escalated or you haven't inherited vast wealth, your frugality may allow you to pay down some of your debt sooner than the lender requires. Whether paying down your debt sooner makes sense for you depends on a number of factors, including your other investment options and goals (in other words, your "opportunity cost").

When evaluating whether to pay down your mortgage faster, you need to compare your mortgage interest rate with your investments' rates of return (which is defined in Chapter 2 of Book 1). Suppose you have a fixed-rate mortgage with an interest rate of 6 per cent. If you decide to make investments instead of paying down your mortgage more quickly, your investments need to produce an average annual rate of return, of about 6 per cent to come out ahead financially. If this money is being invested outside of a tax-deferred Registered Retirement Savings Plan (RRSP) or Tax-Free Savings Account (TFSA), you'll need to earn anywhere from 8 to 12 per cent — depending on the type of investment — so that *after* taxes, you have earned 6 per cent.

Besides the most common reason of lacking the money to do so, other good reasons *not* to pay off your mortgage any quicker than necessary include the following:

» **You contribute instead to your RRSP or other retirement plan, especially if your employer matches your contribution.** Paying off your mortgage faster has no tax benefit. By contrast, putting additional money into a retirement plan can immediately reduce your income tax burden. The more years you have until retirement, the greater the benefit you receive if you invest in your retirement plans. Thanks to the compounding of your retirement plan investments without the drain of taxes, you can actually earn a lower rate of return on your investments than you pay on your mortgage and still come out ahead. (The various retirement plans are discussed in detail in the later section "Funding Your Registered Retirement Savings Plan.")

» **You're willing to invest in growth-oriented, volatile investments, such as stocks and real estate.** In order to have a reasonable chance of earning more on your investments than it costs you to borrow on your mortgage, you must be aggressive with your investments. As discussed in Chapter 2 of Book 1, stocks and real estate have produced annual average rates of return of about 8 to 10 per cent. You can earn even more by creating your own small business or by investing in others' businesses. Paying down a mortgage ties up more of your capital, and thus reduces your ability to make other attractive investments. To more aggressive investors, paying off the house seems downright boring — the financial equivalent of watching paint dry.

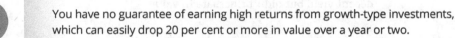

You have no guarantee of earning high returns from growth-type investments, which can easily drop 20 per cent or more in value over a year or two.

WARNING

» **Paying down the mortgage depletes your emergency reserves.** Psychologically, some people feel uncomfortable paying off debt more quickly if it diminishes their savings and investments. You probably don't want to pay down your debt if doing so depletes your financial safety cushion. Make sure that you have access — through a high-interest savings account, money market fund, or other sources (a family member, for example) — to at least three months' worth of living expenses (as explained in the earlier section "Establishing an Emergency Reserve").

REMEMBER

Don't be tripped up by the misconception that somehow a real estate market downturn, such as the one that most areas experienced in the mid- to late 2000s, will harm you more if you pay down your mortgage. Your home is worth what it's worth — its value has *nothing* to do with your debt load. Unless you're willing to walk away from your home and send the keys to the bank (also known as *default*), you suffer the full effect of a price decline, regardless of your mortgage size, if real estate prices drop.

Establishing Your Financial Goals

You may have just one purpose for investing money, or you may desire to invest money for several different purposes simultaneously. Either way, you should establish your financial goals before you begin investing. Otherwise, you won't know how much to save.

For example, when Eric was in his twenties, he put away some money for retirement, but also saved a stash so he could hit the eject button from his job in management consulting. Eric knew that he wanted to pursue an entrepreneurial path and that in the early years of starting his own business, he couldn't count on an income as stable or as large as the one he made from consulting.

Eric invested his two "pots" of money — one for retirement and the other for his small-business cushion — quite differently. As discussed in the later section "Choosing the Right Investment Mix," you can afford to take more risk with the money you plan on using longer term. So, he invested the bulk of his retirement nest egg in stock mutual funds.

With the money he saved for the start-up of his small business, he took an entirely different track. He had no desire to put this money in risky stocks — what if the market plummeted just as he was ready to leave the security of his full-time job? Thus, he kept this money safely invested in a money market fund that had a decent yield but didn't fluctuate in value.

Tracking your savings rate

To accomplish your financial goals (and some personal goals), you need to save money, and you also need to know your savings rate. Your *savings rate* is the percentage of your past year's income that you saved and didn't spend. Without even doing the calculations, you may already know that your rate of savings is low, non-existent, or negative and that you need to save more.

REMEMBER

Part of being a smart investor involves figuring out how much you need to save to reach your goals. Not knowing what you want to do a decade or more from now is perfectly normal — after all, your goals and needs evolve over the years. But that doesn't mean you should just throw your hands in the air and not make an effort to see where you stand today and think about where you want to be in the future.

An important benefit of knowing your savings rate is that you can better assess how much risk you need to take to accomplish your goals. Seeing the amount that you need to save to achieve your dreams may encourage you to take more risk with your investments or find other sources of income if you are not willing to take on more risk.

During your working years, if you consistently save about 10 per cent of your annual income, you're probably saving enough to meet your goals (unless you want to retire at a relatively young age). On average, most people need about 75 per cent of their pre-retirement income throughout retirement to maintain their standards of living.

If you're one of the many people who don't save enough, you need to do some homework. To save more, you need to reduce your spending, increase your income, or both. For most people, reducing spending is the more feasible way to save.

TIP

To reduce your spending, first figure out where your money goes. You may have some general idea, but you need to have facts. Get out your chequebook register, examine your online bill-paying records, and review your credit card bills and any other documentation that shows your spending history. Tally up how much you spend on dining out, operating your car(s), paying your taxes, and on everything else. After you have this information, you can begin to prioritize and make the necessary trade-offs to reduce your spending and increase your savings rate. Earning more income may help boost your savings rate as well. Perhaps you can get a higher-paying job or increase the number of hours that you work. But if you already work a lot, reining in your spending is usually better for your emotional and economic well-being.

If you don't know how to evaluate and reduce your spending or haven't thought about your retirement goals, looked into what you can expect from the Canada Pension Plan (or Quebec Pension Plan) and social security, or calculated how much you should save for retirement, now's the time to do so. Pick up the latest edition of *Personal Finance For Canadians For Dummies* (written by Eric Tyson and Tony Martin, and published by Wiley) to find out all the necessary details for retirement planning and much more.

Determining your investment tastes

Many good investing choices exist: You can invest in real estate, the stock market, mutual funds, exchange-traded funds, or your own or some else's small business. Or you can pay down mortgage debt more quickly. What makes sense for you depends on your goals as well as your personal preferences. If you detest risk-taking and volatile investments, paying down your mortgage, as recommended earlier in this chapter, may make better sense than investing in the stock market.

To determine your general investment tastes, think about how you would deal with an investment that plunges 20 per cent, 40 per cent, or more in a few years or less. Some aggressive investments can fall fast. (See Chapter 2 in Book 1 for examples.) You shouldn't go into the stock market, real estate, or small-business investment arena if such a drop is likely to cause you to sell low or make you a miserable, anxious wreck. If you haven't tried riskier investments yet, you may want to experiment a bit to see how you feel with your money invested in them.

INVESTING AS COUPLES

You've probably learned over the years how challenging it is just for you to navigate the investment maze and make sound investing decisions. When you have to consider someone else, dealing with these issues becomes doubly hard given the typically different money personalities and emotions that come into play.

In many couples, usually one person takes primary responsibility for managing the household finances, including investments. As with most marital issues, the couples that do the best job with their investments are those who communicate well, plan ahead, and compromise.

Here are a couple of examples to illustrate this point. Martha and Alex scheduled meetings with each other every three to six months to discuss financial issues. With investments, Martha came prepared with a list of ideas, and Alex would listen and explain what he liked or disliked about each option. Alex would lean toward more aggressive, growth-oriented investments, whereas Martha preferred conservative, less volatile investments. Inevitably, they would compromise and develop a diversified portfolio that was moderately aggressive. Martha and Alex worked as a team, discussed options, compromised, and made decisions they were both comfortable with. Ideas that made one of them very uncomfortable were nixed.

Henry and Melissa didn't do so well. The only times they managed to discuss investments were in heated arguments. Melissa often criticized what Henry was doing with their money. Henry got defensive and counter-criticized Melissa for other issues. Much of their money lay dormant in a low-interest bank account, and they did little long-term planning and decision making. Melissa and Henry saw each other as adversaries, argued and criticized rather than discussed, and were plagued with inaction because they couldn't agree and compromise. They needed a motivation to change their behaviour toward each other and some counselling (or a few advice guides for couples) to make progress with investing their money.

Aren't your long-term financial health and marital harmony important? Don't allow your problems to fester! One of the most valuable — and difficult — things for couples stuck in unproductive patterns of behaviour to do is to get the issue out on the table. For these couples, the biggest step is making a commitment to discuss their financial management. Once they do, it's a lot easier for them — or their financial advisor — to explain their different points of view and then offer compromises.

TIP

A simple way to "mask" the risk of volatile investments is to *diversify* your portfolio — that is, to put your money into different investments. Not watching prices too closely helps, too — that's one of the reasons real estate investors are less likely to bail out when the market declines. Stock market investors, on the other hand, can get daily and even minute-by-minute price updates. Add that fact to the quick phone call or click of your computer mouse that it takes to dump a stock in a flash, and you have all the ingredients for short-sighted investing — and potential financial disaster.

Funding Your Registered Retirement Savings Plan

Saving money is difficult for most people. Don't make a tough job impossible by forsaking the tax benefits that come from contributing money to — and investing inside — a Registered Retirement Savings Plan (RRSP).

Understanding RRSPs

The only condition you have to meet to be able to contribute to an RRSP is you have to have what the government calls *earned income.* You work hard for any kind of dollars that flow into your household, but it doesn't all qualify. For most people, their *earned income* is their salary, along with any bonuses or commissions. If you're self-employed or an active partner in a business, it includes any net income from your business. Earned income also includes any taxable alimony and maintenance payments as well as any research grants, royalties, and net rental income.

If you have any earned income in a year, you can contribute up to 18 per cent of that total to your RRSP in the following year. That is only one of three limitations that put a ceiling on how much you can contribute. There is a straight dollar ceiling set, plus your maximum may be further reduced if you belong to a company pension plan. Here are the specific rules:

>> Regardless of how much earned income you have, there is an absolute maximum dollar amount you can contribute for any one year. For 2020 the maximum RRSP contribution limit was $27,230.

>> The maximum amount you are allowed to contribute may be further reduced if you belong to a company pension plan. The government calculates the value of contributions made to your employer-sponsored pension plan, called a pension adjustment (PA), and deducts this from whichever is less — the absolute dollar maximum allowed for the year or 18 per cent of your earned income — to arrive at your allowable contribution.

Your pension adjustment for a given year should appear in that year's T4 slip you receive from your employer. (It should also be stated on the Notice of Assessment you receive in the spring after you file your tax return for the previous year.)

Gaining tax benefits

RRSPs should be called "tax-reduction accounts" — if they were, people may be more motivated to contribute to them. Contributions to these plans are tax deductible. Suppose you pay about 36 per cent between federal and provincial income taxes on your last dollars of income. (See the later section "Figuring your tax bracket.") With an RRSP, you can save yourself about $360 in taxes for every $1,000 you contribute in the year that you make your contribution.

After your money is in a retirement plan, any interest, dividends, and appreciation grow inside the account without current taxation. You defer taxes on all the accumulating gains and profits until you withdraw your money down the road. In the meantime, more of your money works for you over a long period of time.

Understanding deductions and contributions

It pays to understand the language around RRSPs, which can be confusing. Not understanding the basics can leave you missing out on some of their benefits.

The key danger comes from the use of two phrases. The first is "contribution limit." One might assume this refers to just how much money you can put into your RRSP in any one year. Not so. The second phrase is similar: "deduction limit." Again, you might understandably think this refers to how much of your RRSP deduction you can claim in any one year. Wrong again.

In both cases, what is actually being addressed is how much your earned income in any one year gives you in terms of a dollar amount you can contribute to your RRSP. But you aren't required to contribute that money in that same year. Further, in prior years, you may not have put in the maximum for each individual year. These unused sums — often called "contribution room" — are carried forward, and can be both contributed to your RRSP and deducted from your income in future years. As a result, the amount you contribute to your RRSP, and subsequently claim as a deduction on your tax return, can be far in excess of your "contribution limit" or "allowable deduction" for that same year.

Say that based on your last year's salary, your new allowable contribution is $5,000, but you only contribute $2,000. Next year, your new allowable contribution is another $5,000, based on your income this year. This means the amount you can put into your RRSP will then be the sum of $5,000 and the $3,000 of allowable contribution you didn't use this year, for a total of $8,000.

REMEMBER

When it comes to your RRSP contribution, it's not a case of "use it or lose it." If you don't put in the full amount you're allowed to in any given year, you can carry forward that amount — your *RRSP deduction limit* — and use it in the future. Think of it as having an ongoing allowable contribution account. Any time you have earned income, the next year you can add to your allowable contribution account the difference between the amount that year's earned income gave you the right to contribute and what you actually put into your RRSP.

Starting early for maximum profits

WARNING

Failing to take full advantage of registered retirement plans early in their working lives is one of the single most common mistakes investors make when it comes to RRSPs and RPPs (Registered Pension Plans). Often this is because of their enthusiasm to spend or invest outside of registered retirement plans. Not investing inside tax-sheltered retirement plans can cost you hundreds, perhaps thousands, of dollars per year in lost tax savings. Add that loss up over the many years that you work and save, and not taking advantage of an RRSP or RPP can easily cost you tens of thousands to hundreds of thousands of dollars in the long term. Ouch!

To take advantage of registered retirement plans and the tax savings that accompany them, you must first spend less than you earn. Only after you spend less than you earn can you afford to contribute to a registered retirement plans (unless you already happen to have a stash of cash from previous savings or inheritance).

REMEMBER

If you enjoy spending money and living for today, you should be more motivated to start saving sooner. The longer you wait to save, the more you ultimately need to save and, therefore, the less you can spend today!

The sooner you start to save, the easier it will be to save enough to reach your goals because your contributions have more years to compound. Each decade you delay saving approximately doubles the percentage of your earnings that you need to save to meet your goals. For example, if saving 5 per cent per year in your early 20s gets you to your retirement goal, waiting until your 30s to start may mean socking away 10 per cent to reach that same goal; waiting until your 40s, 20 per cent. Beyond that, the numbers get truly daunting.

CHOOSING AN RRSP AND OTHER TAX-DEFERRED INVESTMENTS

When you establish a registered plan or account such as an RRSP, RESP (Registered Education Savings Plan), or TFSA, you may not realize that you're simply putting your money into a shell or shield that keeps the government from taxing your investment earnings each year. You still must choose what investments you want to hold inside your registered retirement plan shell. (RESPs are a great way to save for the costs of helping your children pay for a post-secondary education. In addition to tax-deferred growth on your investments, when you put money into a RESP, the government will also contribute on your behalf! Find out more about RESPs later in this chapter.)

Money inside your tax-deferred plans can be invested in a wide range of stocks, bonds, and mutual funds. Mutual funds (offered in most employer-based plans), which are covered in detail in Book 3, are an ideal choice because they offer diversification and professional management. After you decide which financial institution you want to invest through, simply obtain and complete the appropriate paperwork for establishing the specific type of account you want.

Taming Your Taxes in Non-Retirement Accounts

When you invest outside of tax-deferred retirement plans, the profits and distributions on your money are subject to taxation. So, the non-retirement investments that make sense for you depend (at least partly) on your tax situation.

REMEMBER

If you have money to invest, or if you're considering selling current investments that you hold, taxes should factor into your decision. But tax considerations alone shouldn't dictate how and where you invest your money. You should also weigh investment choices, your desire and the necessity to take risk, personal likes and dislikes, and the number of years you plan to hold the investment (see the later section "Choosing the Right Investment Mix" for more information on these other factors).

Figuring your tax bracket

You may not realize it, but even though you only see one income tax deduction on your pay statement, you pay both federal and provincial income tax. And in any year, you pay less tax on the *first* dollars of your earnings and more tax on the *last* dollars of your earnings. To make things even more complicated, each province uses different tax rates and applies them at different income levels.

For example, consider someone who is single and had a taxable income totaling $60,000 during 2020. They would pay 15 per cent federal tax on their first $48,535 of income. On the remaining $11,465 ($48,535 up to $60,000) they would pay 20.50 per cent federal tax.

In addition, the province in which they live would also charge taxes in a similar tiered or laddered fashion, but using different rates and tax brackets. To make matters even more complicated, no two provinces use the same brackets or rates. For example, if our $60,000 earner lived in B.C., they would pay 5.06 per cent provincial tax on the first $41,725 of income, and 7.70 per cent on the remainder. If they called Nova Scotia home, their provincial taxes would be 8.79 per cent on the first $29,590, 14.95 per cent on the next $29,589 (the income from $29,591 up to $59,180), and 16.67 per cent on the last $819 (the income from $59,181 to $60,000).

One further wrinkle is that, thanks to a tax credit called the *basic personal amount*, Canadians effectively do not pay any federal tax on the first $12,296 of income they earn in a year. Each province also has its own basic personal amount, meaning there is no provincial tax on anywhere from your first $9,498 to $19,369, depending on where you live.

TIP

Your *marginal tax rate* is the rate of tax you pay on your *last*, or so-called *highest*, dollars of income. Knowing your marginal tax rate allows you to quickly calculate the following:

>> Any additional taxes that you would pay on additional income, like interest income from investments

>> The amount of taxes that you save if you contribute more money into retirement plans or reduce your taxable income (for example, if you choose investments that produce tax-free income)

Table 3-1 shows the federal marginal brackets and tax rates for 2020.

Table 3-2 shows the approximate combined federal and provincial marginal tax brackets for B.C. residents. Your actual rates will vary, depending on the province you live in. Note that not only does each province have its own, different rates for different income ranges for calculating your taxes, they have many more marginal tax rates and different levels of tax credits.

TABLE 3-1

2020 Federal Income Tax Rates

Taxable Income	Tax Rate
Up to $48,535	15%
48,536 to $97,069	20.5%
$97,070 to $150,473	26%
$150,474 to $214,368	29%
$214,369 and higher	33%

TABLE 3-2

Example of Approximate 2020 Combined Federal and Provincial Income Tax Rates for B.C. Residents

Approximate Taxable Income	Approximate Marginal Tax Rate
$0 to $41,725	21%
$41,725 to $48,535	23%
$48,535 to $83,451	28%
$83,451 to $95,812	31%
$95,812 to $97,069	33%
$97,069 to $116,344	38%
$116,344 to $150,473	41%
$150,473 to $157,748	44%
$157,748 to $214,368	46%
$214,368 and higher	50%

Knowing what's taxed and when to worry

Interest you receive from bank accounts, guaranteed investment certificates (GICs), and bonds is generally taxable. It's treated just like your regular income, and taxed at the same marginal rate. (We discuss bonds in Chapter 5 of Book 3.)

If you sell stocks, bonds, rental property, or a position in a small business for more than what you paid, the profit is called a *capital gain*. Taxation on your *capital gains*, which is the *profit* (sales minus associated costs) on an investment, works under a unique system. You have to include half (50 per cent) of your net gain in your income, which is then taxed at your marginal tax rate. The result is that the tax rate you effectively pay on capital gains — your *effective* tax rate — will be half of your marginal tax rate.

Suppose that you're in a marginal tax bracket of approximately 24 per cent (note that exact tax rates and marginal tax brackets vary from province to province). Your effective tax rate on capital gains will be 12 per cent. If you are in the next tax bracket, where your salary is taxed at 36 per cent, your effective tax rate on capital gains is 18 per cent, while those in the 42 per cent marginal tax bracket will have an effective capital gains tax rate of 21 per cent. Finally, those in the top 46 per cent marginal tax bracket will have capital gains taxed at 23 per cent.

Any *eligible dividends* you receive from Canadian corporations are taxed at the lowest effective rate. (Dividends from foreign corporations are treated and taxed just like your regular income.) A rather strange formula is used to determine the tax rate on Canadian dividends. This is because dividends are the distribution of a company's after-tax profits, so you receive a special tax credit (the dividend tax credit) to prevent the same profits being taxed twice.

First, the amount of the dividend actually received is increased — *grossed up* — to reflect what the corporation is assumed to have made pre-tax. The gross-up percentage, which is regularly adjusted, was 38 per cent in 2020. This inflated number is what you show on your tax return as the amount of your dividend income. To offset this, you then get a federal dividend tax credit, which in 2020 was 15.0198 per cent. Combined with a provincial tax credit, this means the top tax rate on dividends from public Canadian companies, depending on the province, will be approximately 30 to 40 per cent.

The levels of the provincial tax credits for dividends range widely, as do the levels of income at which they apply. That said, in most provinces you can receive just shy of $40,000 in income from eligible dividends before you have to pay any tax on that income. Table 3-3 shows the approximate tax rates for dividends.

TABLE 3-3   **2020 Approximate Eligible Dividend Income Tax Rates**

Approximate Taxable Income	Approximate Effective Tax Rate on Eligible Dividends
$16,000 to $20,000	−14% to 6%
$20,000 to 47,000	10% to 15%
$47,000 to $93,000	6% to 20%
$93,000 to $144,000	15% to 30%
$144,000 to $206,000	22% to 36%
$206,000 and higher	30% to 40%

TIP

The lower your overall income level, the lower the tax rate for any dividends you receive. But there's more. In most provinces, if your income is below certain levels, not only is your dividend income not taxed, the tax you owe on income from other sources, including your regular job, is reduced. How? For lower-income earners, the marginal tax rate for eligible dividends is actually negative. When there is a negative marginal tax rate for dividends, the dividend tax credit you earn not only offsets any tax due on the dividend income, but also reduces tax payable on other income.

TIP

Use these strategies to reduce the taxes you pay on investments that are exposed to taxation:

>> **Invest in tax-friendly stock funds.** Mutual funds that tend to trade less tend to produce lower capital gains distributions. For mutual funds held outside tax-sheltered registered retirement plans, this reduced trading effectively increases an investor's total rate of return. *Index funds* are mutual funds that invest in a relatively static portfolio of securities, such as stocks and bonds (this is also true of most exchange-traded funds). They don't attempt to beat the market. Rather, they invest in the securities to mirror or match the performance of an underlying index, such as the S&P/TSX Composite Index or the Standard & Poor's 500. Although index funds can't beat the market, the typical actively managed fund doesn't either, and index funds have several advantages over actively managed funds, such as lower fees.

>> **Invest in tax-friendly stocks.** Companies that pay little in the way of dividends reinvest more of their profits back into the company. If you invest outside of a retirement plan, unless you need income to live on, minimize your exposure to stocks with dividends. Be aware that low-dividend stocks tend to be more volatile.

>> **Invest in small business and real estate.** The growth in value of business and real estate assets isn't taxed until you sell the asset. However, the current income that small business and real estate assets produce is taxed as ordinary income.

Choosing the Right Investment Mix

Diversifying your investments helps buffer your portfolio from being sunk by one or two poor performers. This section explains how to mix up a great recipe of investments.

Considering your age

When you're younger and have more years until you plan to use your money, you should keep larger amounts of your long-term investment money in *growth* (ownership) vehicles, such as stocks, real estate, and small business. As discussed in Chapter 2 of Book 1, the attraction of these types of investments is the potential to really grow your money. The risk: The value of your portfolio can fall from time to time.

The younger you are, the more time your investments have to recover from a bad fall. In this respect, investments are a bit like people. If a 30-year-old and an 80-year-old both fall on a concrete sidewalk, odds are higher that the younger person will fully recover and the older person may not. Such falls sometimes disable older people.

TIP

A long-held guiding principle says to subtract your age from 110 and invest the resulting number as a percentage of money to place in growth (ownership) investments. So, if you're 35 years old:

> 110 − 35 = 75 per cent of your investment money can be in growth investments.

If you want to be more aggressive, subtract your age from 120:

> 120 − 35 = 85 per cent of your investment money can be in growth investments.

Note that even retired people should still have a healthy chunk of their investment dollars in growth vehicles like stocks. A 70-year-old person may want to totally avoid risk, but doing so is generally a mistake. Such a person can live another two or three decades. If you live longer than anticipated, you can run out of money if it doesn't continue to grow.

REMEMBER

These tips are only general guidelines and apply to money that you invest for the long term (ideally for ten years or more). For money that you need to use in the shorter term, such as within the next several years, more-aggressive growth investments aren't appropriate.

Making the most of your investment options

No hard-and-fast rules dictate how to allocate the percentage that you've earmarked for growth among specific investments like stocks and real estate. Part of how you decide to allocate your investments depends on the types of investments that you want to focus on. As discussed in Book 2, diversifying in stocks worldwide can be prudent as well as profitable.

REMEMBER

Here are some general guidelines to keep in mind:

>> **Take advantage of your registered retirement plans.** Unless you need accessible money for shorter-term non-retirement goals, why pass up the free extra returns from the tax benefits of an RRSP or Registered Pension Plan (a company or corporate plan)? Find out more about RRSPs earlier in this chapter.

>> **Take advantage of a Tax-Free Savings Account (TFSA).** The capital gains, dividends, and interest you earn on money inside these accounts are tax-free, as are any withdrawals. Put short-term money such as your emergency funds into a TFSA. Also consider sheltering savings in a TFSA if you're already contributing the maximum to your RRSP.

>> **Don't pile your money into investments that gain lots of attention.** Many investors make this mistake, especially those who lack a thought-out plan to buy stocks.

>> **Have the courage to be a contrarian.** No one likes to feel that he is jumping on board a sinking ship or supporting a losing cause. However, just like shopping for something at retail stores, the best time to buy something of quality is when its price is reduced.

>> **Diversify.** As discussed in Chapter 2 of Book 1, the values of different investments don't move in tandem. So, when you invest in growth investments, such as stocks or real estate, your portfolio's value will have a smoother ride if you diversify properly.

>> **Invest more in what you know.** Over the years, many successful investors have built substantial wealth without spending gobs of their free time researching, selecting, and monitoring investments. Some investors, for example, concentrate more on real estate because that's what they best understand and feel comfortable with. Others put more money in stocks for the same reason. No one-size-fits-all code exists for successful investors. Just be careful that you don't put all your investing eggs in the same basket (for example, don't load up on stocks in the same industry that you believe you know a lot about).

>> **Don't invest in too many different things.** Diversification is good to a point. If you purchase so many investments that you can't perform a basic annual review of all of them (for example, reading the annual report from your mutual fund), you have too many investments.

>> **Be more aggressive with investments inside retirement plans.** When you hit your retirement years, you'll probably begin to live off your non-retirement plan investments first. Allowing your retirement accounts to continue growing can generally defer your tax dollars. Therefore, you should be relatively less aggressive with investments outside of retirement plans because that money may be invested for a shorter time period.

Easing into risk: Dollar cost averaging

Dollar cost averaging (DCA) is the practice of investing a regular amount of money at set time intervals, such as monthly or quarterly, into volatile investments, such as stocks and stock mutual funds. If you've ever deducted money from a paycheque and pumped it into a retirement savings plan that holds stocks and bonds, you've done DCA.

Most people invest a portion of their employment compensation as they earn it, but if you have extra cash sitting around, you can choose to invest that money in one fell swoop or to invest it gradually via DCA. The biggest appeal of gradually feeding money into the market via DCA is that you don't dump all your money into a potentially overheated investment just before a major drop. Thus, DCA helps shy investors psychologically ease into riskier investments.

DCA is made to order for skittish investors with large lump sums of money sitting in safe investments like guaranteed investment certificates (GICs) or savings accounts. For example, using DCA, an investor with $100,000 to invest in stock funds can feed her money into investments gradually — say, at the rate of $12,500 or so quarterly over two years — instead of investing her entire $100,000 in stocks at once and possibly buying all of her shares at a market peak. Most large investment companies, especially mutual funds, allow investors to establish automatic investment plans so the DCA occurs without an investor's ongoing involvement.

WARNING

Of course, like any risk-reducing investment strategy, DCA has drawbacks. If growth investments appreciate (as they're supposed to), a DCA investor misses out on earning higher returns on his money awaiting investment. Finance professors Richard E. Williams and Peter W. Bacon found that approximately two-thirds of the time, a lump-sum stock market investor earned higher first-year returns than an investor who fed the money in monthly over the first year. (They studied data from the U.S. market over the past seven decades.)

York University business professor Moshe Arye Milevsky came to the same conclusion in his book *Money Logic*. According to Milevsky's research, if you invested a $10,000 lump sum in a Canadian equity mutual fund, you would likely have $11,000 after a year had passed. In short, his research showed that two-thirds of the time, your initial investment would be worth between $9,500 and $12,500. In contrast, if you invested the money in equal amounts over 12 months, by the end of that year your initial investment would likely be worth $10,748. More specifically, two-thirds of the time you could anticipate having somewhere between $9,898 and $11,598. However, knowing that you'll probably be ahead most of the time if you dump a lump sum into the stock market is little solace if you happen to invest just before a major plunge in the stock market. In the fall of 2008, the Canadian stock market, as measured by the S&P/TSX composite index, plummeted

30 per cent in just over four weeks. From late 2007 to the fall of 2008, the market shed 42 per cent of its value.

Investors who fear that stocks are due for such a major correction should practise DCA, right? Well, not so fast. Apprehensive investors who shun lump-sum investments and use DCA are more likely to stop the DCA investment process if prices plunge, thereby defeating the benefit of doing DCA during a declining market.

What's an investor with a lump sum of money to do?

>> **First, weigh the significance of the lump sum to you.** Although $100,000 is a big chunk of most people's net worth, it's only 10 per cent if your net worth is $1,000,000. It's not worth a millionaire's time to use DCA for $100,000. If the cash that you have to invest is less than a quarter of your net worth, you may not want to bother with DCA.

>> **Second, consider how aggressively you invest (or invested) your money.** For example, if you aggressively invested your money through an employer's retirement plan that you roll over, don't waste your time on DCA.

DCA makes sense for investors with a large chunk of their net worth in cash who want to minimize the risk of transferring that cash to riskier investments, such as stocks. If you fancy yourself a market prognosticator, you can also assess the current valuation of stocks. Thinking that stocks are pricey (and thus riper for a fall) increases the appeal of DCA.

TIP

If you use DCA too quickly, you may not give the market sufficient time for a correction to unfold, during and after which some of the DCA purchases may take place. If you practise DCA over too long of a period of time, you may miss a major upswing in stock prices. Consider using DCA over one to two years to strike a balance.

As for the times of the year that you should use DCA, mutual fund investors should use DCA early in each calendar quarter because mutual funds that make taxable distributions tend to do so late in the quarter.

Your money that awaits investment in DCA should have a suitable parking place. Select a high-interest savings account or a high-yielding money market fund that's appropriate for your tax situation.

REMEMBER

One last critical point: When you use DCA, establish an automatic investment plan so you're less likely to chicken out. And for the more courageous, you may want to try an alternative strategy to DCA — *value averaging*, which allows you to invest more if prices are falling and invest less if prices are rising.

Suppose, for example, that you want to value average $500 per quarter into an aggressive stock mutual fund. After your first quarterly $500 investment, the fund drops 10 per cent, reducing your account balance to $450. Value averaging suggests that you invest $500 the next quarter plus another $50 to make up the shortfall. (Conversely, if the fund value had increased to $550 after your first investment, you would invest only $450 in the second round.) Increasing the amount that you invest requires confidence when prices fall, but doing so magnifies your returns when (if) prices ultimately turn around.

Treading Carefully When Investing for University or College

There's no doubt that having kids is one of — if not *the* — most expensive decisions you'll ever make. From paying for diapers to having to buy a heck of a lot more groceries when your kids become teenagers, having children is a costly affair. But it can feel downright punitive when you start thinking about what it will cost to get them a post-secondary education.

That's not exactly welcome news for those already trying to pay off their mortgage and save for retirement. What can you do? Surprisingly, one of the best tactics is often to only focus on your first two goals and ignore the third. If you work hard and knock down your mortgage, you'll have a good chance of being able to reduce or even eliminate your mortgage payments by the time the little ones are ready to go to university. If you've knocked a good deal off of your mortgage, you'll also be in the position to borrow against the equity you've built up in your home to pay for educational expenses.

REMEMBER

By working hard to grow your RRSP, hopefully you'll accumulate a good-sized sum that has built up some compounding steam. If you're accustomed to "paying yourself first" — regularly diverting a portion of your income to your RRSP — you can turn your financial sights away from your old age and toward your children's educational bills while they're at school, and resume your RRSP contributions after they graduate. Some people feel that education is so important that they don't feel comfortable unless they're putting away some dollars specifically earmarked for that purpose. Others may be in the enviable position of being able to set aside savings for future educational costs while also taking care of their mortgage and building up their RRSP. If you want to start an education savings program, you have two basic ways to do it, each with some distinct benefits and drawbacks you need to consider. The approach that works best for you will be determined by your family circumstances, your outlook, and your sense of where your children are heading.

Making the most out of a Registered Education Savings Plan

If you've already got a basic understanding of how RRSPs work, then you're already halfway to making sense of *Registered Education Savings Plans* (RESPs). However, there are also some key differences to be aware of. Much like an RRSP, a RESP lets you set money aside and defer tax on the gains you make on that money while it's inside the plan. When you put money into an RRSP, you also get a tax deduction for your contribution. In contrast, you don't get to deduct money you put into a RESP from your income when figuring out your tax bill for the year.

And, as with your RRSP, when you withdraw money from a RESP it is treated as income and taxed accordingly. But the big difference is it's treated as income for your child. Given that their other income — if they have any — will be low, the amount of tax they'll have to pay will be negligible or non-existent.

You can set up a RESP for each of your children, with a lifetime maximum contribution ceiling of $50,000. When RESPs were first introduced, there was also an annual limit on how much you could contribute, but that has been eliminated.

What makes RESPs financially friendly is that the government tops up your contributions. Under the Canada Education Savings Grant (CESG), the federal government will put in another 20 per cent of any contribution you make, to a maximum of $500 a year. The grant is available every year the beneficiary of the RESP is under the age of 18, up to a maximum of $7,200. (The grant amounts aren't included when calculating your contribution limits.) In addition, children from middle- and low-income families may be eligible for an extra 10 per cent or 20 per cent grant on the first $500 contributed to an RESP each year.

If you don't make the most use of the CESG in any one year by contributing $2,500 and receiving the maximum annual grant of $500, don't worry. If you put in less in any one year, you can earn the untapped grant in future years. However, in any one single year, the CESG grant per beneficiary is limited to the lesser of $1,000 or 20 per cent of the unused CESG room.

TIP

Like RRSPs, you can invest money inside a RESP in a wide choice of investments, including the many types of mutual funds and even individual stocks. (Be sure to opt for a self-directed RESP, not one of the group plans that have higher fees and more restrictions.) If you have more than one child, you can set up a family plan that makes it simpler and easier as you can use a single RESP for all of your children.

TIP

If your child does not pursue a further education that allows him or her to use the money inside the plan, you can take out the original contributions without any penalty. However, you'll have to return any grants you've received under the CESG. In addition, the money you've made on any grants as well as on your own contributions may be taxable.

HOW TO PAY FOR UNIVERSITY OR COLLEGE

If you keep stashing away money in an RRSP, it's reasonable for you to wonder how you'll actually pay for education expenses when the momentous occasion arises. Even if you have some liquid assets that can be directed to your child's college bill, you will, in all likelihood, need to borrow some money. Only the affluent can truly afford to pay for university or college with cash.

One good source of money is your home's equity. You can borrow against your home at a relatively low interest rate. The Canada Student Loans Program, run by the federal governments in consultation with the provinces, is another place to look for funds. To apply, contact your provincial ministry of education. Interest while your child is attending school is paid by the federal government. Repaying the loan has to begin six months after your child graduates. In addition to loans, a number of grant programs are available through schools and the government, as well as through independent sources. Begin by speaking with your child's guidance counselling office. Most schools have lists of local government and private bursaries, grants and awards, and scholarships. You should also consider your family's various employers. A surprising number of companies have student grants available for their employees or children of employees. Contact the university or college your child is considering to see what other sources of funding are available. You can find easy links to their financial resources page by visiting www.canadian-universities.net/index.html and clicking on Financial Aid. You can then choose a province, and you'll get a page listing links to the financial aid page of each school.

Other lists of funding sources are available online. Visit the sites of the universities or colleges your child is considering attending. You can find descriptions of a number of grant and loan programs along with application forms, as well as links to all the provincial and territorial student assistance offices, at the federal government's website at www.canada.ca/en/services/benefits/education/student-aid.html www.canada.ca. Another good source for information on grants and scholarships is www.scholarshipscanada.com. Your child can also work and save money for university during high school. Besides giving your gangly teen a stake in his or her own future, this training encourages sound personal financial management down the road.

If the beneficiary is not a post-secondary student by age 21 and the plan has been running for at least ten years, you can transfer up to $50,000 of the plan's profits to your own or your spouse's RRSP. However, you must have sufficient unused RRSP contribution room available. (The result is that the RRSP deduction you receive will offset any taxes including the RESP's earnings in your income). Any of the plan's profits that don't get sheltered in this way are taxed at your full marginal tax rate. In addition, you pay an extra 20 per cent penalty. On top of your tax bill, that could mean giving up as much as 65 per cent of the profits. Ouch!

Allocating university investments

If you keep up to 80 per cent of your university investment money in stocks (diversified worldwide) with the remainder in bonds when your child is young, you can maximize the money's growth potential without taking extraordinary risk. As your child makes his way through the later years of elementary school, you need to begin to make the mix more conservative — scale back the stock percentage to 50 or 60 per cent. Finally, in the years just before he enters college, whittle the stock portion down to no more than 20 per cent or so.

TIP

Diversified mutual funds (which invest in stocks in Canada and internationally) and bonds are ideal vehicles to use when you invest for college. Be sure to choose funds that fit your tax situation if you invest your funds in non-retirement plans.

Protecting Your Assets

You may be at risk of making a catastrophic investing mistake: not protecting your assets properly due to a lack of various insurance coverages. Manny, a successful entrepreneur, made this exact error. Starting from scratch, he built up a successful million-dollar business. He invested a lot of his own personal money and sweat into building the business over 15 years.

One day, catastrophe struck: An explosion ripped through his building, and the ensuing fire destroyed virtually all the firm's equipment and inventory, none of which was insured. The explosion also seriously injured several workers, including Manny, who didn't carry disability insurance. Ultimately, Manny had to file for bankruptcy.

WARNING

Decisions regarding what amount of insurance you need to carry are, to some extent, a matter of your desire and ability to accept financial risk. But some risks aren't worth taking. Don't overestimate your ability to predict what accidents and other bad luck may befall you.

Here's what you need to protect yourself and your assets:

>> **Adequate liability insurance on your home and car to guard your assets against lawsuits:** You should have at least enough liability insurance to protect your *net worth* (assets minus your liabilities/debts) or, ideally, twice your net worth. If you run your own business, get insurance for your business assets if they're substantial, such as in Manny's case. Also consider professional liability insurance to protect against a lawsuit. You may also want to consider incorporating your business.

>> **Long-term disability insurance:** What would you (and your family) do to replace your income if a major disability prevents you from working? Even if you don't have dependents, odds are that *you* are dependent on you. Most larger employers offer group plans that have good benefits and are much less expensive than coverage you'd buy on your own. Also, check with your professional association for a competitive group plan.

>> **Life insurance, if others are dependent on your income:** If you're single or your loved ones can live without your income, skip life insurance. If you need coverage, buy term insurance that, like your auto and home insurance, is pure insurance protection. The amount of term insurance you need to buy largely depends on how much of your income you want to replace.

>> **Estate planning:** At a minimum, most people need a simple will to delineate to whom they would like to leave all their worldly possessions. If you hold significant assets outside retirement plans, you may also benefit from establishing a living trust, which keeps your money from filtering through the hands of probate lawyers. Living wills and medical powers of attorney are useful to have in case you're ever in a medically incapacitated situation. If you have substantial assets, doing more involved estate planning is wise to minimize taxes and ensure the orderly passing of your assets to your heirs.

In our work, we've seen that although many people lack particular types of insurance, others possess unnecessary policies. Many people also keep very low deductibles. Be sure to insure against potential losses that would be financially catastrophic for you — don't waste your money to protect against smaller losses. (See the latest edition of our book *Personal Finance For Canadians For Dummies*, published by Wiley, to discover the right and wrong ways to buy insurance, what to look for in policies, and where to get good policies.)

2

Investing in Stocks

Contents at a Glance

IN THIS CHAPTER

» **Using Canadian and other stock exchanges to get investment information**

» **Applying accounting and economic know-how to your investments**

» **Keeping up with financial news**

» **Deciphering stock tables and interpreting dividend news**

» **Recognizing good (and bad) investing advice**

Chapter **1**

Gathering Information

K nowledge and information are two critical success factors in stock investing. (Isn't that true about most things in life?) Canadians who plunge headlong into stocks without sufficient knowledge of the stock market in general, and current information in particular, quickly learn the lesson of the eager diver who didn't find out ahead of time that the pool was only an inch deep (ouch!). In their haste not to miss so-called golden investment opportunities, investors too often end up losing money.

REMEMBER

Opportunities to *make* money in the stock market will always be there, no matter how well or how poorly the Canadian and world economies are performing in general. There's no such thing as a single (and fleeting) magical moment, so don't feel that if you let an opportunity pass you by, you'll always regret that you missed your one big chance.

For the best approach to stock investing, build your knowledge and find quality information first so you can make your fortune more assuredly. For example,

Before you buy an individual stock, you need to know that the company you're investing in is

>> Financially sound and growing

>> Offering products and services that are in demand by consumers

>> In a strong and growing industry (and general economy)

Where do you start, and what kind of information do you want to acquire? Keep reading.

Looking to Stock Exchanges for Answers

Before you invest in stocks, you need to be completely familiar with the basics of stock investing. At its most fundamental, stock investing is about using your money to buy a piece of a company that will give you value in the form of appreciation or income (or both). Fortunately, many resources are available to help you find out about stock investing. Some great places are the websites of stock exchanges themselves.

Stock exchanges are organized marketplaces for the buying and selling of stocks (and other securities). The New York Stock Exchange (NYSE), Nasdaq, and the Toronto Stock Exchange (TSX) are the premier North American stock exchanges. They provide a framework for stock buyers and sellers to make their transactions. The Toronto and New York exchanges, like all others, make money not only from a cut of every transaction but also from fees (such as listing fees) charged to companies and brokers that are members of their exchanges.

REMEMBER

The Toronto Stock Exchange, often referred to as the TSX, is one of the world's larger stock exchanges by market capitalization. It offers a range of businesses from Canada and abroad. The TSX, like the NYSE and Nasdaq, offers a wealth of free (or low-cost) resources and information on its websites for all stock investors.

There are peripheral exchanges to be mindful of as well. Formerly known as the American Stock Exchange, NYSE American is an exchange designed for growing companies. In Canada, other exchanges you may see in some newspaper business sections or online include the following:

>> **TSX Venture Exchange:** This is a public stock market for emerging innovative companies that are not yet big enough to be listed on larger exchanges like the TSX.

>> **Canadian Securities Exchange (CSE):** Considered to be an alternative stock exchange for entrepreneurs, it is an option for companies looking to access Canadian capital markets. The CSE lists hundreds of micro-cap equities, government bonds, and other financial instruments.

>> **Montreal Exchange (MX):** The MX is low profile in that it's a derivatives exchange — a place to trade futures contracts and options.

>> **Nasdaq Canada:** This is a subsidiary of the Nasdaq Stock Market in the U.S. Its purpose is to ensure Canadian investors quick availability of all key information of all Nasdaq securities and the ability for companies to raise capital more efficiently.

>> **Aequitas NEO Exchange:** The NEO Exchange, or NEO, aims to help companies and investors by creating a better trading and listing experience (for example, with free stock quotes and faster listing times).

REMEMBER

On the U.S. side, the Dow Jones Industrial Average (DJIA) is the most widely watched index worldwide (although technically it's not an index, it's still used as one). It tracks 30 widely owned, large cap stocks, and it's occasionally rebalanced to drop (and replace) a stock that's not keeping up. The Nasdaq Composite Index covers a cross-section of stocks from Nasdaq. It's generally considered a mix of stocks that are high-growth (riskier) companies with an over-representation of technology stocks. The S&P 500 Index tracks 500 leading, publicly traded companies considered to be widely held.

Go to the NYSE, Nasdaq, and TSX websites to find useful resources such as these:

>> Tutorials on how to invest in stocks, common investment strategies, and so on

>> Glossaries and free information to help you understand the language, practice, and purpose of stock investing

>> A wealth of news, press releases, financial data, and other information about companies listed on the exchange or market, usually accessed through an on-site search engine

>> Industry analysis and Canadian and foreign news

>> Stock quotes and other market information related to the daily market movements of Canadian and other stocks, including data such as volume, new highs, new lows, and so on

>> Free tracking of your stock selections (you can input a sample portfolio or the stocks you're following to see how well you're doing)

TIP

What each exchange/market offers keeps changing and is often updated, so explore them periodically at their respective websites:

>> **Nasdaq:** www.nasdaq.com

>> **New York Stock Exchange:** www.nyse.com

>> **Toronto Stock Exchange:** www.tmx.com

TIP

The federal and provincial governments have been planning to create a national securities regulator, like the Securities and Exchange Commission in the United States, for some time now. The objective is to create a single Canadian securities watchdog, rather than have a dozen or so separate securities regulators in the provinces and territories. Unfortunately, while the federal government and some provincial regulators continue to exchange a lot of hot air on this very important topic, concrete results have yet to emerge. Stay tuned to the resources we mention in this chapter to watch for any developments.

Grasping the Basics of Accounting and Economics

Stocks represent ownership in companies. Before you buy individual stocks, you want to understand the companies whose stock you're considering and find out about their operations. It may sound like a daunting task, but you'll digest the point more easily when you realize that companies work very similarly to the way you work. They make decisions on a daily basis just like you.

Think about how you grow and prosper as an individual or family, and you see the same issues with businesses and how they grow and prosper. Low earnings and high debt are examples of financial difficulties that can affect both people and companies. You can better understand companies' finances by taking the time to pick up some information in two basic disciplines: accounting and economics. These two disciplines, discussed in the following sections, play a significant role in understanding the performance of a firm's stock.

Accounting for taste and a whole lot more

REMEMBER

Accounting. Ugh! But face it: Accounting is the language of business, and believe it or not, you're already familiar with the most important accounting concepts! Just look at the following three essential principles:

» **Assets minus liabilities equals net worth.** In other words, take what you own (your *assets*), subtract what you owe (your *liabilities*), and the rest is yours (your *net worth*)! Your own personal finances work the same way as Microsoft's (except yours have fewer zeros at the end).

A company's balance sheet shows you its net worth at a specific point in time (such as December 31). The net worth of a company is the bottom line of its asset and liability picture, and it tells you whether the company is *solvent* (has the ability to pay its debts without going out of business). The net worth of a successful company grows regularly. To see whether your company is successful, compare its net worth with the net worth from the same point a year earlier. A firm that had a $4 million net worth last year and has a $5 million net worth this year is doing well; its net worth has gone up 25 percent ($1 million) in one year.

» **Income minus expenses equals net income.** In other words, take what you make (your income), subtract what you spend (your expenses), and the remainder is your *net income* (or *net profit* or *net earnings* — your gain).

A company's profitability is the whole point of investing in its stock. As it profits, the business becomes more valuable, and in turn, its stock price becomes more valuable. To discover a firm's net income, look at its income statement. Try to determine whether the company uses its gains wisely, either by reinvesting them for continued growth or by paying down debt.

» **Do a comparative financial analysis.** That's a mouthful, but it's just a fancy way of saying how a company is doing now compared with something else (like a prior period or a similar company).

If you know that the company you're looking at had a net income of $50,000 for the year, you may ask, "Is that good or bad?" Obviously, making a net profit is good, but you also need to know whether it's good compared to something else. If the company had a net profit of $40,000 the year before, you know that the company's profitability is improving. But if a similar company had a net profit of $100,000 the year before and in the current year is making $50,000, then you may want to either avoid the company making the lesser profit or see what (if anything) went wrong with the company making less.

Accounting can be this simple. If you understand these three basic points, you're ahead of the curve (in stock investing as well as in your personal finances). For more information on how to use a company's financial statements and reports to pick good stocks, see Chapter 5 in Book 2.

Understanding how economics affects stocks

Economics. Double ugh! No, you aren't required to understand "the inelasticity of demand aggregates" (thank heavens!) or "marginal utility" (say what?). But having a working knowledge of basic economics is crucial (and we mean crucial) to your success and proficiency as a stock investor. The stock market and the economy are joined at the hip. The good (or bad) things that happen to one have a direct effect on the other. The following sections give you the lowdown.

Getting the hang of the basic concepts

REMEMBER

Alas, many Canadian investors get lost on basic economic concepts (as do some so-called experts that you see on TV). Understanding basic economics will help you filter the financial news to separate relevant information from the irrelevant in order to make better investment decisions. Be aware of these important economic concepts:

>> **Supply and demand:** How can anyone possibly think about economics without thinking of the ageless concept of supply and demand? *Supply and demand* can be simply stated as the relationship between what's available (the supply) and what people want and are willing to pay for (the demand). This equation is the main engine of economic activity and is extremely important for your stock investing analysis and decision-making process. Do you really want to buy stock in a company that makes elephant-foot umbrella stands if you find out that the company has an oversupply and nobody wants to buy them anyway?

>> **Cause and effect:** If you pick up a prominent news report and read, "Companies in the table industry are expecting plummeting sales," do you rush out and invest in companies that sell chairs or manufacture tablecloths? Considering cause and effect is an exercise in logical thinking, and believe us, logic is a major component of sound economic thought.

When you read Canadian and U.S. business news, play it out in your mind. What good (or bad) can logically be expected given a certain event or situation? If you're looking for an effect ("I want a stock price that keeps increasing"), you also want to understand the cause. Here are some typical events that can cause a stock's price to rise:

- **Positive news reports about a company:** The news may report that the company is enjoying success with increased sales or a new product. BlackBerry's introduction of new security software services to underserved or new markets like autonomous cars is a perfect example of how news can move the price of a stock one way or another.

- **Positive news reports about a company's industry:** The media may be highlighting that the industry is poised to do well.

- **Positive news reports about a company's customers:** Maybe your company is in industry A, but its customers are in industry B. If you see good news about industry B, that may be good news for your stock.

- **Negative news reports about a company's competitors:** If the competitors are in trouble — say, due to their deficient customer service and poor overall reputation — their customers may seek alternatives to buy from, including your company.

>> **Economic effects from government actions:** Political and governmental actions have economic consequences. As a matter of fact, nothing (seriously, nothing!) has a greater effect on investing and economics than government. Government actions usually manifest themselves as taxes, laws, or regulations. They also can take on a more ominous appearance, such as war or the threat of war. Government can willfully (or even accidentally) cause a company to go bankrupt, disrupt an entire industry, or even cause a depression. Government has a very strong influence on the money supply, credit, and public securities markets.

Gaining insight from past mistakes

Because most investors ignored some basic observations about economics during the Great Recession, they subsequently lost trillions in their stock portfolios during 2008–2009. Even today, the U.S. and Canada are experiencing the greatest expansion of total debt in history, coupled with a record expansion of their respective money supplies. To be sure, part of this government behavior fueled a bull market. But when will this "fun" stop?

Of course, you should always be happy to earn double-digit annual returns with your investments, but such a return can't be sustained and encourages speculation. Financial market stimulation by the central banks which includes monetary policy actions like increased money supply and lowered interest rates, tends to result in the following:

>> More and more people depleted their savings. After all, why settle for 1–3 percent in a Canadian chartered bank when you can get 20 percent in the stock market? This phenomenon is called the "search for yield."

>> More and more Canadians bought real estate on credit, as they were driven by rates below historic norms. This in turn caused home prices to rise, resulting in even more debt needing to be incurred by households as time progressed. This interaction between home prices and rates quickly became a vicious circle. If the economy is booming, why not buy now and pay later? Canadian consumer credit recently and not surprisingly hit record per capita highs.

>> More and more Canadians borrowed against their homes. Why not borrow and get rich now? "I can pay off my debt later" was at the forefront of these folks' minds at the time.

>> More and more companies sold more goods as consumers took more vacations and bought SUVs, electronics, and so on. Companies then borrowed to finance expansion, open new stores, and so on.

>> More and more Canadians made lower and lower down payments, simply because they could. "Why shouldn't I own a house too?" they asked. That is a reasonable question. However, the risk profile of many Canadian homeowners got so bad that the Canada Mortgage and Housing Corporation eventually imposed a minimum percentage down payment limit before it would write any new mortgages.

>> More and more companies went public and offered stock to take advantage of the increase in money that was flowing to the markets from banks and other financial institutions.

In summary, the economic cycle as it relates to stocks goes something like this: North American spending starts to slow down because consumers and businesses become too indebted. This slowdown in turn causes the sales of goods and services to taper off. Companies are left with too much overhead, capacity, and debt because they expanded too quickly. At this point, businesses get caught in a financial bind. Too much debt and too many expenses in a slowing economy mean one thing: Profits shrink or disappear. To stay in business, companies have to do the logical thing — cut expenses. What's usually the biggest expense for companies? People! Many companies start laying off employees. As a result, consumer spending drops further because more people were either laid off or had second thoughts about their own job security.

Because people had little in the way of savings and too much in the way of debt, they had to sell their stock to pay their bills. Stocks drop. This rinse and repeat trend is one major reason that stocks can fall for an extended period.

REMEMBER

The lessons from years past are important ones for investors today:

>> Stocks aren't a replacement for savings accounts or guaranteed investment certificates (GICs). Always have some money in the bank.

>> Stocks should never occupy 100 percent of your investment funds.

>> When anyone (including an expert) tells you that the economy will keep growing indefinitely, be skeptical and read diverse sources of information.

>> If stocks do well in your portfolio, consider protecting your stocks (both your original investment and any gains) with stop-loss orders.

» Keep debt and expenses to a minimum.

» If the U.S. and Canadian economy is booming, a decline is sure to follow as the ebb and flow of the economy's business cycle continues.

Staying on Top of Financial News

Reading the financial news can help you decide where or where not to invest. Many newspapers, magazines, and websites offer great coverage of the financial world. Obviously, the more informed you are, the better, but you don't have to read everything that's written. The information explosion in recent years has gone beyond overload, and you can easily spend so much time reading that you have little time left for investing. The following sections describe the types of information you need to get from the financial news.

TIP

The most obvious publications of interest to stock investors are the two Canadian national dailies — the *National Post* (www.nationalpost.com) and *The Globe and Mail* (www.theglobeandmail.com). Other useful publications include *The Wall Street Journal* and *Investor's Business Daily*, U.S. newspapers that also cover world financial news. These leading publications report the news and stock data on a regular basis. Some other leading websites are MarketWatch (www.marketwatch.com) and Bloomberg (www.bloomberg.com), which include Canadian company news and information. The websites of all of these information providers can also give you news and stock data within minutes of a transaction.

KNOW THYSELF BEFORE YOU INVEST IN STOCKS

If you're reading this book, you're probably doing so because you want to become a successful investor. Granted, to be a successful investor, you have to select great stocks, but having a realistic understanding of your own financial situation and goals is equally important. One investor lost $10,000 in a speculative Canadian resource stock. The loss wasn't that bad because he had most of his money safely tucked away elsewhere. He also understood that his overall financial situation was secure and that the money he lost was "play" money — the loss wouldn't have a drastic effect on his life. But many investors often lose even more money, and the loss does have a major, negative effect on their lives. You may not be like the investor who can afford to lose $10,000. Take time to understand yourself, your own financial picture, and your personal investment goals before you decide to buy stocks. Refer to Chapter 3 in Book 1 for guidance.

Figuring out what a company's up to

REMEMBER

Before you invest, you need to know what's going on with the company. When you read about a company, either in the firm's literature (its annual report, for example) or in media sources, be sure to get answers to some pertinent questions:

>> **Is the company making more net income than it did last year?** You want to invest in a company that's growing, with sustainable cash flows.

>> **Are the company's sales greater than they were the year before?** Keep in mind that you won't make money if the company isn't making money.

>> **Is the company issuing press releases on new products, services, inventions, or business deals?** All these achievements indicate a strong, vital company.

Knowing how the company is doing, no matter what's happening with the Canadian, U.S., or world economy, is obviously important. To better understand how companies tick, and to identify their strengths and weaknesses, see Chapter 5 in Book 2.

Discovering what's new with an industry

As you consider investing in a stock, make a point of knowing what's going on in that company's industry. If the industry is doing well, your stock is likely to do well, too. But then again, the reverse is also true.

Yes, some investors have picked successful stocks in a failing industry, but those cases are exceptional. By and large, succeeding with a stock is easier when the entire industry is doing well. As you're watching the news, reading the financial pages, or viewing financial websites, check out the industry to ensure that it's strong and dynamic.

Knowing what's happening with the economy

No matter how well or how poorly the overall economy is performing, you want to stay informed about its general progress. It's easier for the value of stock to keep going up when the economy is stable or growing. The reverse is also true: If the economy is contracting or declining, the stock has a tougher time keeping its value. Here are some basic items to keep tabs on:

>> **Gross domestic product (GDP):** The GDP is roughly the total value of output for a particular nation, measured in the dollar amount of goods and services. It's reported quarterly, and a rising GDP bodes well for your stock. When the GDP is rising 3 percent or more on an annual basis, that's solid growth. If it rises but is less than 3 percent, that's generally considered less than stellar (or mediocre). A GDP under zero (a negative number) means that the economy is shrinking (heading into recession).

>> **The index of leading economic indicators (LEI):** The LEI is a snapshot of a set of economic statistics covering activity that precedes what's happening in the economy. Each statistic helps you understand the economy in much the same way that barometers (and windows!) help you understand what's happening with the weather. Economists don't just look at an individual statistic; they look at a set of statistics to get a more complete picture of what's happening with the economy.

Seeing what politicians and government bureaucrats are doing

Being informed about what public officials are doing is vital to your success as a stock investor. Because federal, provincial, and local governments pass literally thousands of laws, rules, and regulations every year, monitoring the political landscape is critical to your success. The news media report what the prime minister and Parliament are doing, so always ask yourself, "How does a new law, tax, trade treaty, or regulation affect my stock investment?"

TIP

Some great organizations inform the Canadian public about tax laws and their impact, such as the Canadian Taxpayers Federation (www.taxpayer.com). Laws being proposed or enacted by the U.S. federal government can be found through the Thomas legislative search engine, which is run by the Library of Congress (www.loc.gov).

Checking for trends in society, culture, and entertainment

As odd as it sounds, trends in society, popular culture, and entertainment affect your investments, directly or indirectly. For example, a CTV or *Maclean's* headline such as "The Greying of Canada — More People Than Ever Before Will Be Senior Citizens" gives you some important information that can make or break your stock portfolio. With that particular headline, you know that as more and more people age, companies that are well positioned to cater to that growing market's wants and needs will do well — meaning a successful stock for you.

Keep your eyes open for emerging trends in society at large by reading and viewing the media that cover such matters (*Time* magazine, CNN, BNN Bloomberg, and so on). What trends are evident now? Can you anticipate the wants and needs of tomorrow's society? Being alert, staying a step ahead of the public, and choosing stocks appropriately gives you a profitable edge over other investors. If you own stock in a solid company with growing sales and earnings, other investors eventually notice. As more investors buy up your company's stocks, you're rewarded as the stock price increases.

Reading and Understanding Stock Tables

The stock tables in major business publications such as *The Wall Street Journal* and *Investor's Business Daily* are loaded with information that can help you become a savvy investor — *if* you know how to interpret them. You need the information in the stock tables for more than selecting promising investment opportunities. You also need to consult the tables after you invest to monitor how your stocks are doing. The *National Post* (www.nationalpost.com) and *The Globe and Mail* (www.theglobeandmail.com) also produce stock tables for a selection of mostly Canadian equities in their print editions. As well, they let you check just about any stock (U.S. or Canadian) in their online editions.

Looking at the stock tables without knowing what you're looking for or why you're looking is the equivalent of reading *War and Peace* backwards through a kaleidoscope — nothing makes sense. But this section can help you make sense of it all (well, at least the stock tables). Table 1-1 shows a sample stock table. Each item gives you some clues about the current state of affairs for that particular company. The sections that follow describe each column to help you understand what you're looking at.

TABLE 1-1   A Sample Stock Table

52-Wk High	52-Wk Low	Name (Symbol)	Div	Vol	Yld	P/E	Day Last	Net Chg
21.50	8.00	SkyHighCorp (SHC)		3,143		76	21.25	+0.25
47.00	31.75	LowDownInc (LDI)	2.35	2,735	5.9	18	41.00	−0.50
25.00	21.00	ValueNowInc (VNI)	1.00	1,894	4.5	12	22.00	+0.10
83.00	33.00	DoinBadly Corp (DBC)		7,601			33.50	−0.75

REMEMBER

Every newspaper's financial tables are a little different, but they give you basically the same information. Updated daily, these tables aren't the place to start your search for a good stock; they're usually where your search ends. The stock tables are the place to look when you own, or are about to own, a stock or know what you want to buy, or possibly sell, and you're just checking to see the most recent price.

52-week high

The column in Table 1-1 labelled "52-Wk High" gives you the highest price that particular stock has reached in the most recent 52-week period. Knowing this price lets you gauge where the stock is now versus where it has been recently. SkyHighCorp's (SHC) stock has been as high as $21.50, whereas its last (most recent) price is $21.25, the number listed in the "Day Last" column. (Flip to the later section "Day last" for more on understanding this information.) SkyHigh-Corp's stock is trading very high right now because it's hovering near its overall 52-week high figure.

Now, take a look at DoinBadlyCorp's (DBC) stock price. It seems to have tumbled big time. Its stock price has had a high in the past 52 weeks of $83, but it's currently trading at $33.50. Something just doesn't seem right here. During the past 52 weeks, DBC's stock price has fallen dramatically. If you're thinking about investing in DBC, find out why the stock price has fallen. If the company is strong, it may be a good opportunity to buy stock at a lower price. If the company is having tough times, avoid it. In any case, research the firm and find out why its stock has declined. (Chapter 5 in Book 2 provides the basics of researching companies.)

52-week low

The column labelled "52-Wk Low" gives you the lowest price that particular stock reached in the most recent 52-week period. Again, this information is crucial to your ability to analyse stock over a period of time. Look at DBC in Table 1-1, and you can see that its current trading price of $33.50 in the Day Last column is close to its 52-week low of $33.

REMEMBER

Keep in mind that the high and low prices just give you a range of how far that particular stock's price has moved within the past 52 weeks. They can alert you that a stock has problems, or they can tell you that a stock's price has fallen enough to make it a bargain. Simply reading the 52-Wk High and 52-Wk Low columns isn't enough to determine which of those two scenarios is happening. They basically tell you to get more information before you commit your money.

Gathering Information

Name and symbol

The "Name (Symbol)" column is the simplest in Table 1-1. It tells you the company name (usually abbreviated) and the stock symbol (also known as the "ticker") assigned to the company.

TIP

When you have your eye on a Canadian or other stock for potential purchase, get familiar with its symbol. Knowing the symbol makes it easier for you to find your stock in the financial tables, which list stocks in alphabetical order by the company's name (or symbol, depending on the source). Stock symbols are part of the language of stock investing, and you need to use them in all stock communications, from getting a stock quote at your broker's office to buying stock over the Internet.

Dividend

Dividends (shown under the "Div" column in Table 1-1) are basically payments to owners (stockholders). If a company pays a dividend, it's shown in the dividend column. The amount you see is the annual dividend quoted for one share of that stock. If you look at LowDownInc (LDI) in Table 1-1, you can see that you get $2.35 as an annual dividend for each share of stock that you own. Companies usually pay the dividend in quarterly amounts. If you own 100 shares of LDI, the company pays you a quarterly dividend of $58.75 ($235 total per year). A healthy company strives to maintain or upgrade the dividend for stockholders from year to year. (Find additional dividend details later in this chapter.)

The dividend is very important to investors seeking income from their stock investments. For more about investing for income, see Chapter 4 in Book 2. Investors buy stocks in companies that don't pay dividends primarily for growth. For more information on growth stocks, see Chapter 3 in Book 2.

Volume

Normally, when you hear the word "volume" on the news, it refers to how much stock is bought and sold for the entire market: "Well, stocks were very active today. Trading volume at the New York Stock Exchange hit 2 billion shares." Volume is certainly important to watch because the stocks that you're investing in are somewhere in that activity. For the "Vol" column in Table 1-1, though, the volume refers to the individual stock.

Volume tells you how many shares of that particular stock were traded that day. If only 100 shares are traded in a day, then the trading volume is 100. SHC had 3,143 shares change hands on the trading day represented in Table 1-1. Is that good or bad? Neither, really. Usually the business news media mention volume for a particular stock only when it's unusually large. If a stock normally has volume in the 5,000 to 10,000 range and all of a sudden has a trading volume of 87,000, then it's time to sit up and take notice.

REMEMBER

Keep in mind that a low trading volume for one stock may be a high trading volume for another stock. You can't necessarily compare one stock's volume against that of any other company. The large cap stocks like IBM or Microsoft typically have trading volumes in the millions of shares almost every day, whereas less active, smaller stocks may have average trading volumes in far, far smaller numbers.

The main point to remember is that trading volume that is far in excess of that stock's normal range is a sign that something is going on with that stock. It may be negative or positive, but something newsworthy is happening with that company. If the news is positive, the increased volume is a result of more people buying the stock. If the news is negative, the increased volume is probably a result of more people selling the stock. What are typical events that cause increased trading volume? Some positive reasons include the following:

» **Good earnings reports:** The company announces good (or better-than-expected) earnings.

» **A new business deal:** The firm announces a favourable business deal, such as a joint venture, or lands a big client.

» **A new product, service, or discovery:** The company's research and development department creates a potentially profitable new product, or the company finds something new and of value, such as oil reserves in a northern territory.

» **Indirect benefits:** The business may benefit from a new development in the economy, or from a new law passed by Parliament.

Some negative reasons for an unusually large fluctuation in trading volume for a particular stock include the following:

» **Bad earnings reports:** Profit is the lifeblood of a company. When its profits fall or disappear, you see more volume.

» **Governmental problems:** The stock is being targeted by government action, such as a lawsuit or an Ontario Securities Commission (OSC) probe.

» **Liability issues:** The media report that the company has a defective product or similar problem.

» **Financial problems:** Independent analysts report that the company's financial health or cash flow is deteriorating.

Gathering Information

REMEMBER

Check out what's happening when you hear about heavier-than-usual volume (especially if you already own the stock).

Yield

In general, yield is a return on the money you invest. However, in the stock tables, *yield* ("Yld" in Table 1-1) is a reference to what percentage that particular dividend is of the stock price. Yield is most important to income investors. It's calculated by dividing the annual dividend by the current stock price. In Table 1-1, you can see that the yield of ValueNowInc (VNI) is 4.5 percent (a dividend of $1 divided by the company's stock price of $22). Notice that many companies report no yield; because they have no dividends, their yield is zero.

REMEMBER

Keep in mind that the yield reported in the financial pages changes daily as the stock price changes. Yield is always reported as if you're buying the stock that day. If you buy VNI on the day represented in Table 1-1, your yield is 4.5 percent. But what if VNI's stock price rises to $30 the following day? Investors who buy stock at $30 per share obtain a yield of just 3.3 percent (the dividend of $1 divided by the new stock price, $30). Of course, because you bought the stock at $22, you essentially locked in the prior yield of 4.5 percent. Lucky you. Pat yourself on the back.

P/E

REMEMBER

The *P/E ratio* is the ratio between the price of the stock and the company's earnings. P/E ratios are widely followed and are important barometers of value in the world of stock investing. The P/E ratio (also called the *earnings multiple* or just *multiple*) is frequently used to determine whether a stock is expensive (a good value). Value investors find P/E ratios to be essential to analyzing a stock as a potential investment. As a general rule, the P/E should be 10 to 20 for large cap or income stocks. For growth stocks, a greater P/E is generally preferable. (See Chapter 5 in Book 2 for full details on P/E ratios.)

In the P/E ratios reported in stock tables, *price* refers to the cost of a single share of stock. *Earnings* refers to the company's reported earnings per share as of the most recent four quarters. The P/E ratio is the price divided by the earnings. In Table 1-1, VNI has a reported P/E of 12, which is considered a low P/E. Notice how SHC has a relatively high P/E (76). This stock is considered too pricey because you're paying a price equivalent to 76 times earnings. Also notice that DBC has no available P/E ratio. Usually this lack of a P/E ratio indicates that the company reported a loss (i.e., negative earnings) in the most recent four quarters.

Day last

The "Day Last" column tells you how trading ended for a particular stock on the day represented by the table. In Table 1-1, LDI ended the most recent day of trading at $41. Some Canadian newspapers report the high and low for that day in addition to the stock's ending price for the day.

Net change

The information in the "Net Chg" column answers the question, "How did the stock price end today compared with its price at the end of the prior trading day?" Table 1-1 shows that SHC stock ended the trading day up 25 cents (at $21.25). This column tells you that SHC ended the prior day at $21. VNI ended the day at $22 (up 10 cents), so you can tell that the prior trading day it ended at $21.90.

Using News about Dividends

Reading and understanding the news about dividends is essential if you're an *income investor* (someone who invests in stocks as a means of generating regular income; see Chapter 4 in Book 2 for details). The following sections explain some basics you should know about dividends.

TIP

You can find news and information on dividends in newspapers such as *The Wall Street Journal* (www.wsj.com/), *Investor's Business Daily* (www.investors.com/), and *Barron's* (www.barrons.com/).

Looking at important dates

REMEMBER

In order to understand how buying stocks that pay dividends can benefit you as an investor, you need to know how companies report and pay dividends. Some important dates in the life of a dividend are as follows:

>> **Date of declaration:** This is the date when a company reports a quarterly dividend and the subsequent payment dates. On January 15, for example, a company may report that it "is pleased to announce a quarterly dividend of 50 cents per share to shareholders of record as of February 10." That was easy. The date of declaration is really just the announcement date. Whether you buy the stock before, on, or after the date of declaration doesn't matter in regard to receiving the stock's quarterly dividend (but it will affect your purchase price). The date that matters is the date of record (see that bullet later in this list).

>> **Date of execution:** This is the day you actually initiate the stock transaction (buying or selling). If you call a broker (or contact her online) today to buy a particular stock, then today is the date of execution, or the date on which you execute the trade. You don't own the stock on the date of execution; it's just the day you put in the order. For an example, skip to the following section.

>> **Closing date (settlement date):** This is the date on which the trade is finalized, which usually happens three business days after the date of execution. The closing date for stock is similar in concept to a real estate closing. On the closing date, you're officially the proud new owner (or happy seller) of the stock.

>> **Ex-dividend date:** *Ex-dividend* means *without dividend.* Because it takes three days to process a stock purchase before you become an official owner of the stock, you have to qualify (that is, you have to own or buy the stock) *before* the three-day period. That three-day period is referred to as the "ex-dividend period." When you buy stock during this short time frame, you aren't on the books of record, because the closing (or settlement) date falls after the date of record. See the next section to see the effect that the ex-dividend date can have on an investor.

>> **Date of record:** This is used to identify which stockholders qualify to receive the declared dividend. Because stock is bought and sold every day, how does the company know which investors to pay? The company establishes a cutoff date by declaring a date of record. All investors who are official stockholders as of the date of record receive the dividend on the payment date.

>> **Payment date:** The date on which a company issues and mails its dividend cheques to shareholders. Finally!

For typical dividends, the events in Table 1-2 happen four times per year.

TABLE 1-2   **The Life of the Quarterly Dividend**

Event	Sample Date	Comments
Date of declaration	January 15	The date that the company declares the quarterly dividend
Ex-dividend date	February 7	Starts the three-day period during which, if you buy the stock, you don't qualify for the dividend
Date of record	February 10	The date by which you must be on the books of record to qualify for the dividend
Payment date	February 27	The date that payment is made (a dividend cheque is issued and mailed to stockholders who were on the books of record as of February 10)

Understanding why certain dates matter

Three business days pass between the date of execution and the closing date. Three business days also pass between the ex-dividend date and the date of record. This information is important to know if you want to qualify to receive an upcoming dividend. Timing is important, and if you understand these dates, you know when to purchase stock and whether you qualify for a dividend.

As an example, say that you want to buy ValueNowInc (VNI) in time to qualify for the quarterly dividend of 25 cents per share. Assume that the date of record (the date by which you have to be an official owner of the stock) is February 10. You have to execute the trade (buy the stock) no later than February 7 to be assured of the dividend. If you execute the trade right on February 7, the closing date occurs three days later, on February 10 — just in time for the date of record.

But what if you execute the trade on February 8, a day later? Well, the trade's closing date is February 11, which occurs *after* the date of record. Because you aren't on the books as an official stockholder on the date of record, you aren't getting that quarterly dividend. In this example, the February 7–10 period is called the *ex-dividend period.*

TIP

Fortunately, for Canadians who buy the stock during this brief ex-dividend period, the stock actually trades at a slightly lower price to reflect the amount of the dividend. If you can't get the dividend, you may as well save on the stock purchase. How's that for a silver lining?

Evaluating or Ignoring Investment Tips

Psssst. Have we got a stock tip for you! Come closer. You know what it is? Research! Don't automatically invest just because you get a hot tip from someone. Good investment selection means looking at several sources before you decide on a stock. No shortcut exists. That said, getting opinions from others never hurts — just be sure to carefully analyze the information you get. Here are some important points to bear in mind as you evaluate tips and advice from others:

>> **Consider the source.** Frequently, people buy stock based on the views of some market strategist or analyst. People may see an analyst being interviewed on a television financial show and take that person's opinions and advice as valid and good. The danger here is that the analyst may be biased because of some relationship that isn't disclosed on the show.

WARNING

It happens on TV all too often. The show's host interviews analyst U.R. Kiddingme from the investment firm Foollum&Sellum. The analyst says, "Implosion Corp. is a good buy with solid, long-term upside potential." You later find out that the analyst's employer gets investment banking fees from Implosion Corp. Do you really think that analyst would ever issue a negative report on a company that's helping to pay the bills? It's not likely. Don't trust analyst recommendations. Just use them as one of several data points that inform your investment decisions.

>> **Get multiple views.** Don't base your investment decisions on just one source unless you have the best reasons in the world for thinking that a particular, single source is outstanding and reliable. A better approach is to scour current issues of independent financial publications, such as *Barron's* (www.barrons.com/), *Canadian Business* (www.canadianbusiness.com/), *MoneySense* (www.moneysense.ca/), and other publications (and websites).

Chapter **2**

Going for Brokers

W hen you're ready to dive in and start investing in stocks, you first have to choose a broker. It's kind of like buying a car: You can do all the research in the world and know exactly what kind of car you want, but you still need a venue to conduct the actual transaction. Similarly, when you want to buy stock, your task is to do all the research you can to select the company you want to invest in. Still, you need a Canadian — yes, it has to be a Canadian — broker to actually buy the stock, whether over the phone or online. This chapter introduces you to the intricacies of the investor/broker relationship.

Defining the Broker's Role

The broker's primary role is to serve as the vehicle through which you either buy or sell stock. When people talk about brokers, they're referring to companies such as TD Waterhouse, BMO InvestorLine, and many other Canadian organizations that can buy stock on your behalf. Brokers can also be individuals who work for such firms. Although you can buy some stocks directly from the companies that issue them, to purchase most stocks, you still need a broker.

The distinction between institutional stockbrokers and personal stockbrokers is important:

>> **Institutional stockbrokers** make money from institutions and companies through investment banking and securities placement fees (such as initial public offerings and secondary offerings), advisory services, and other broker services.

>> **Personal stockbrokers** generally offer the same services to individuals and small businesses.

Although the primary task of brokers is the buying and selling of securities around the world (the word *securities* refers to the world of financial or paper investments, and stocks are only a small part of that world), they can perform other tasks for you, including the following:

>> **Providing advisory services:** Investors pay brokers a fee for investment advice. Customers also get access to the firm's research.

>> **Offering limited banking services:** Brokers can offer features such as interest-bearing Canadian and U.S. dollar trading accounts, cheque writing, electronic deposits and withdrawals, and credit/debit cards.

>> **Brokering other securities:** In addition to stocks, brokers can buy bonds, options, exchange-traded funds (ETFs), mutual funds, and other investments on your behalf.

Personal stockbrokers make their money from individual investors like you through various fees, including the following:

>> **Brokerage commissions:** This fee is for buying or selling stocks and other securities.

>> **Margin interest charges:** This interest is charged to investors for borrowing against their brokerage account for investment purposes. (Margin accounts are discussed in more detail later in this chapter.)

>> **Service charges:** These charges are for performing administrative tasks and other functions. Brokers charge account opening, maintenance, and other fees to investors for Registered Retirement Savings Plans (RRSPs), Registered Education Savings Plans (RESPs), and Tax-Free Savings Accounts (TFSAs). See Chapter 3 in Book 1 for more about these plans.

REMEMBER

Any smaller broker (some individual brokers are now called financial or investment advisors) that you deal with should be a member in good standing of IIROC — the Investment Industry Regulatory Organization of Canada. IIROC is a self-regulatory organization that oversees all member investment dealers. It also watches out for suspicious and questionable trading activity on debt and equity markets in Canada. It sets regulatory and investment industry standards, tries to protect investors' interests, and attempts to strengthen market integrity while maintaining smoothly operating capital markets.

REMEMBER

To further protect your money after you deposit it into a brokerage account, that broker should be a member of the Canadian Investor Protection Fund (CIPF). CIPF doesn't protect you from losses from market fluctuations; it protects your money, within limits, in case the brokerage firm goes out of business or if your losses are due to brokerage fraud. CIPF's coverage limit is $1 million for any combination of cash and securities. If you have both a general and a retirement account, each account qualifies for $1 million coverage.

To find out whether a broker is registered with these organizations, contact IIROC (www.iiroc.ca) and CIPF (www.cipf.ca).

Distinguishing between Full-Service and Discount Brokers

Stockbrokers fall into two basic categories, which are discussed in the following sections: full-service and discount. The type you choose really depends on what type of investor you are. Here are the differences in a nutshell:

>> **Full-service brokers** are suitable for investors who need some guidance, advice, and personal attention.

>> **Discount brokers** are better for those investors who are sufficiently confident and knowledgeable about stock investing to manage with minimal help (usually through the broker's website).

At your disposal: Full-service brokers

Full-service brokers provide two things: brokerage and advisory services. They try to provide as many services as possible for Canadians who open accounts with them. When you open an account at a brokerage firm, a representative is assigned to your account. This representative is usually called an account executive, a registered rep, or a financial advisor by the brokerage firm. This person usually has a securities licence (meaning that she's registered with IIROC and at a minimum has passed the Canadian Securities Course or an equivalent).

Examples of full-service brokers are HSBC InvestDirect (http://invest.hsbc.ca), RBC Dominion Securities (www.rbcds.com), and TD Waterhouse's (www.td.com) Private Investment Advice service. All brokers now have full-featured websites to give you information about their services. Get as informed as possible before you open your account. A full-service broker is there to help you build wealth, not make you uh broker.

What they can do for you

Your account executive is responsible for assisting you, answering questions about your account and the securities in your portfolio, and transacting your buy and sell orders. Here are some things full-service brokers can do for you:

>> **Offer guidance and advice:** The greatest distinction between full-service brokers and discount brokers is the personal attention you receive from your account rep. You get to be on a first-name basis with a full-service broker, and you disclose a lot of information about your finances and financial goals. The rep is there to make recommendations about stocks and funds that are hopefully suitable for you.

>> **Provide access to research:** Full-service brokers can give you access to their investment research department, which can give you in-depth information and analysis on a particular company. This information can be very valuable, but be aware of the pitfalls. (See the later section "Judging Brokers' Recommendations.")

>> **Help you achieve your investment objectives:** A good rep gets to know you and your investment goals and *then* offers advice and answers your questions about how specific investments and strategies can help you accomplish your wealth-building goals.

>> **Make investment decisions on your behalf:** Many investors don't want to be bothered when it comes to investment decisions. Full-service brokers can actually make decisions for your account with your authorization (this is also referred to as a *discretionary* account). This service is fine, but be sure to require brokers to explain their choices to you.

What to watch out for

Although full-service brokers, with their seemingly limitless assistance, can make life easy for an investor, you need to remember some important points to avoid problems:

>> Brokers and account reps are salespeople. No matter how well they treat you, they're still compensated based on their ability to produce revenue for the brokerage firm. They generate commissions and fees from you on behalf of the company. (In other words, they're paid to sell you things.)

REMEMBER

>> Whenever your rep makes a suggestion or recommendation, be sure to ask why and request a complete answer that includes the reasoning behind the recommendation. A good advisor is able to clearly explain the reasoning behind every suggestion. If you don't fully understand and agree with the advice, don't take it. This is an important discipline to hone.

>> Working with a full-service broker costs more than working with a discount broker. They always charge extra for the advice. Discount brokers, on the other hand, are paid for simply buying or selling stocks for you and therefore cost less. Also, most full-service brokers expect you to invest at least $5,000 to $10,000 just to open an account, although many require higher minimums.

>> Handing over decision-making authority to your rep can be a possible negative because letting others make financial decisions for you is always dicey — especially when they're using *your* money. If they make poor investment choices that lose you money, you may not have any recourse because you authorized them to act on your behalf.

WARNING

>> Some brokers engage in an activity called churning. Churning is basically buying and selling stocks for the sole purpose of generating commissions. Churning is great for brokers but really bad for customers. If your account shows a lot of activity, ask for justification. Commissions, especially by full-service brokers, can take a big bite out of your wealth, so don't tolerate churning or other suspicious activity.

Just the basics: Discount brokers

Perhaps you don't need any hand-holding from a broker (that'd be kinda weird anyway). You know what you want, and you can make your own investment decisions. All you need is a convenient way to transact your buy/sell orders. In that case, go with a discount broker. These brokers let you buy or sell stocks two ways: through the Internet or by phone (touch tone, automated voice prompt, or via a live representative). They don't offer advice or premium services — just the basics required to perform your stock transactions.

Canadian discount brokers, as the name implies, are cheaper to engage than full-service brokers. Because you're advising yourself (or getting advice and information from third parties such as newsletters, hotlines, or independent advisors), you can save on costs you'd incur if you used a full-service broker.

REMEMBER

If you choose to work with a discount broker, you must know as much as possible about your personal goals and needs. You have a greater responsibility for conducting adequate research to make good stock selections, and you must be prepared to accept the outcome, whatever that may be. (See Chapter 5 in Book 2 for details on researching stock selections.)

For a while, the regular Canadian investor had two types of discount brokers to choose from: conventional discount brokers and Internet discount brokers. But the two are basically synonymous now, so the differences are hardly worth mentioning. Through industry consolidation in Canada, most of the conventional discount brokers today have fully featured websites, while Internet discount brokers have adapted by adding more telephone and face-to-face services. There really are no more pure discount brokers left.

What they can do for you

Discount brokers offer some significant advantages over full-service brokers:

>> **Lower cost:** This lower cost is usually the result of lower commissions, and it's the primary benefit of using discount brokers.

>> **Unbiased service:** Because they don't offer advice, discount brokers have no vested interest in trying to sell you any particular stock.

>> **Access to information:** Established discount brokers offer extensive educational materials at their offices or on their websites. In this regard, they can provide you with valuable passive advice.

What to watch out for

Of course, doing business with discount brokers also has its downsides, including the following:

>> **No guidance:** Because you've chosen a discount broker, you *know* not to expect guidance, but the broker should make this fact clear to you anyway. If you're a knowledgeable investor, the lack of advice is considered a positive thing — no interference.

WARNING

>> **Hidden fees:** Discount brokers may shout about their lower commissions, but commissions aren't their only way of making money. Many discount brokers charge extra for services that you may think are included, such as issuing a stock certificate or mailing a statement. Ask whether they assess fees for maintaining tax-deferred savings accounts like RRSPs or for transferring stocks and other securities (like bonds) in or out of your account, and find out what interest rates they charge for borrowing through brokerage accounts.

>> **Minimal customer service:** If you deal with an Internet brokerage firm, find out about its customer service. If you can't transact business on its website, find out where you can call for assistance with your order.

Choosing a Broker

Before you choose a broker, you need to analyze your personal investing style (as explained in Chapter 3 of Book 1), and then you can proceed to finding the kind of broker that fits your needs. It's almost like choosing shoes; if you don't know your size, you can't get a proper fit (and you can be in for a really uncomfortable future).

REMEMBER

When it's time to choose a broker, keep the following points in mind:

>> Match your investment style with a brokerage firm that charges the least amount of money for the services you're likely to use most frequently.

>> Compare all the costs of buying, selling, and holding stocks and other securities through a broker. Don't compare only commissions; compare other costs, too, like margin interest and other service charges (see the earlier section "Defining the Broker's Role" for more about these costs).

>> Use broker comparison services available in financial publications such as *Report on Business* and *Maclean's* (and, of course, their websites) and online sources such as Canoe Money (https://canoe.com/category/business).

TIP

Finding brokers is easy. Just search for "Canadian online discount brokers" in your favorite search engine. The search results will also pull up many online articles rating each broker and itemizing their services and fees. (A general review site to use is www.stockbrokers.com.) Start your search by using the following sources:

>> **BMO InvestorLine** (www.bmoinvestorline.com)

>> **CIBC Investor's Edge** (www.investorsedge.cibc.com)

>> **Disnat Direct** (www.disnat.com)

>> **HSBC InvestDirect** (http://invest.hsbc.ca)

>> **National Bank Direct Brokerage** (http://w3.nbdb.ca)

>> **QTrade Investor** (www.qtrade.ca/investor)

>> **Questrade** (http://questrade.com)

>> **RBC Direct Investing** (www.rbcdirectinvesting.com)

>> **Scotiabank iTrade Canada** (www.scotiabank.com/itrade)

>> **TD Waterhouse Canada** (www.tdwaterhouse.ca)

Discovering Various Types of Brokerage Accounts

When you start investing in the stock market, you have to somehow actually pay for the stocks you buy. Most brokerage firms offer investors several types of accounts, each serving a different purpose. The following sections present three of the most common types. The basic difference boils down to how particular brokers view your creditworthiness when it comes to buying and selling securities. If your credit isn't great, your only choice is a cash account. If your credit is good, you can open either a cash account or a margin account. After you qualify for a margin account, you can (with additional approval) upgrade it to do options trades.

REMEMBER

To open an account, you have to fill out an application and submit a cheque or money order, or execute an online bank transfer for at least the minimum amount required to establish an account.

Cash accounts

A cash account (also referred to as a Type 1 account) means just what you'd think. You must deposit a sum of money along with the new account application to begin trading. The amount of your initial deposit varies from broker to broker. Some brokers have a minimum of $10,000; others let you open an account for as little as $500. Once in a while you may see a broker offering cash accounts with no minimum deposit, usually as part of a promotion. Qualifying for a cash account is usually easy, as long as you have cash and a pulse.

With a cash account, your money has to be deposited in the account before the closing (or settlement) date for any trade you make. The closing occurs three business days after the date you make the trade (the date of execution). You may be required to have the money in the account even before the date of execution. See Chapter 1 in Book 2 for details on these and other important dates.

In other words, if you call your broker on Monday, October 10, and order 50 shares of CashLess Corp. at $20 per share, then on Thursday, October 13, you better have $1,000 in cash sitting in your account (plus commission). Otherwise, the purchase doesn't go through.

WARNING

In addition, ask the broker how long it takes deposited cash (such as a cheque) to be available for investing. Some brokers put a hold on cheques for up to ten business days (or longer), regardless of how soon that cheque clears your account.

TIP

See whether your broker will pay you interest on the uninvested cash in your brokerage account. Some Canadian brokers offer a service in which uninvested money earns money market rates, and you can even choose between a regular money market account and a more exotic municipal bond money market account.

Margin accounts

A margin account (also called a Type 2 account) allows you to borrow money against the securities in the account to buy more stock. Because you can borrow in a margin account, you have to be qualified and approved by the broker. After you're approved, this newfound credit gives you more leverage so you can buy more stock or do short-selling.

For stock trading, the margin limit is 50 per cent. For example, if you plan to buy $10,000 worth of stock on margin, you need at least $5,000 in cash (or securities owned) sitting in your account. The interest rate you pay varies depending on the broker, but most brokers generally charge a rate that's considerably higher than their own borrowing rate.

Why use margin? Margin is to stocks what mortgage is to buying real estate. You can buy real estate with all cash, but using borrowed funds often makes sense because you may not have enough money to make a 100 per cent cash purchase, or you may just prefer not to pay all cash. With margin, you can, for example, buy $10,000 worth of stock with as little as $5,000. The balance of the stock purchase is acquired using a loan (margin) from the brokerage firm.

WARNING

Margin is a form of leverage that can work out fine if you're correct but can be very dangerous if the market moves against you. It's best applied with stocks that are generally stable and dividend-paying. That way, the dividends help pay off the margin interest.

Option accounts

An option account (also referred to as a Type 3 account) gives you all the capabilities of a margin account (which in turn also gives you the capabilities of a cash account) plus the ability to trade options on stocks and stock indexes. To upgrade your margin account to an option account, the broker usually asks you to sign a statement that you're knowledgeable about options and familiar with the risks associated with them.

TIP

Options can be a very effective addition to a stock investor's array of wealth-building investment tools. A more comprehensive review of options is available in *Trading Options For Dummies*, 3rd Edition, by Joe Duarte (Wiley). Options can be a great tool in your wealth-building arsenal. But use them very carefully.

Judging Brokers' Recommendations

Canadians and Americans have become enamoured with a new sport: the rating of stocks by brokers on financial TV channels like BNN Bloomberg and MSNBC. Frequently, these channels feature shows with a dapper market strategist talking up a particular stock. Some stocks have been known to jump significantly right after an influential analyst issues a buy recommendation. Analysts' speculation and opinions make for great fun, and many people take their views very seriously. However, most investors should be wary when analysts, especially the glib ones on TV, make a recommendation. It's often just showbiz. The following sections define basic broker recommendations and list a few important considerations for evaluating them.

Understanding basic recommendations

Brokers issue their recommendations (advice) as a general idea of how much regard they have for a particular stock. The following list presents the basic recommendations (or ratings) and what they mean to you:

>> ***Strong buy*** **and** ***buy:*** Hot diggity dog! These ratings are the ones to get. The analyst loves this pick, and you would be very wise to get a bunch of shares. The thing to keep in mind, however, is that *buy* recommendations are probably the most common because (let's face it) brokers sell stocks.

>> ***Accumulate*** **and** ***market perform:*** An analyst who issues these types of recommendations is positive, yet unexcited, about the pick. This rating is akin to asking a friend whether he likes your new suit and getting the response "It's nice" in a monotone voice. It's a polite reply, but you wish his opinion had been more definitive.

>> ***Hold*** **or** ***neutral:*** Analysts use this language when their backs are to the wall, but they still don't want to say, "Sell that loser!" This recommendation is like a mother telling her children to be nice and to either say something positive or keep their mouths shut. In this case, the rating is the analyst's way of keeping his mouth shut.

>> ***Sell:*** Many analysts should have issued this recommendation before and even during the early part of the bear markets of 2000–2002 and 2008–2009 but didn't. What a shame. So many investors lost money because some analysts

were too nice (or biased?) or just afraid to be honest, sound the alarm, and urge people to sell.

>> *Avoid like the plague:* If only this recommendation was available! Plenty of stocks have been dreadful investments — stocks of companies that made no money, were in terrible financial condition, and should never have been considered at all. Yet investors gobble up billions of dollars' worth of stocks that eventually become worthless.

Asking a few important questions

An analyst's recommendation is certainly a better tip than what you'd get from your barber or your sister-in-law's neighbour, but you want to view recommendations from analysts with a healthy dose of reality. Analysts have biases because their employment depends on the very companies that are being presented. What investors need to listen to when a broker talks up a stock is the reasoning behind the recommendation. In other words, why is the broker making this recommendation?

Keep in mind that analysts' recommendations can play a useful role in your personal stock investing research. If you find a great stock and then you hear analysts give glowing reports on the same stock, you're on the right track! Here are some questions and points to keep in mind:

>> **How does the analyst arrive at a rating?** The analyst's approach to evaluating a stock can help you round out your research as you consult other sources such as newsletters and independent advisory services.

>> **What analytical approach is the analyst using?** Some analysts use fundamental analysis — looking at the company's financial condition, key financial ratios, and factors related to its success, such as its standing within the industry and the overall market. Other analysts use technical analysis — looking at the company's stock price history and judging past stock price movements to derive some insight regarding the stock's future price movement. Many analysts use a combination of the two. Is this analyst's approach similar to your approach, or to those of sources that you respect or admire?

>> **What is the analyst's track record?** Has the analyst had a consistently good record through both bull and bear markets? Major financial publications and websites, such as Barron's (www.barrons.com), MarketWatch (www.marketwatch.com), Canoe Money (https://canoe.com/category/business), and the National Post (www.nationalpost.com), regularly track recommendations from well-known analysts and stock pickers. Also check out www.adviceforinvestors.com, which as a subscriber gives you free online access to *Investor's Digest of Canada*, *The TaxLetter*, and *The MoneyLetter*.

>> **How does the analyst treat important aspects of the company's performance, such as sales and earnings?** How about the company's balance sheet? The essence of a healthy company is growing sales and earnings coupled with strong assets, low debt, and good cashflows. (See Chapter 5 in Book 2 for more details on these topics.)

>> **Is the industry that the company's in doing well?** Does the analyst give you insight on this important information? A strong company in a weak industry can't stay strong for long. The right industry and sector is a critical part of the stock selection process.

>> **What research sources does the analyst cite?** Does the analyst quote the federal or provincial government or industry trade groups to support her thesis? These sources are important because they help give a more complete picture regarding the company's prospects for success. Imagine that you decide on the stock of a strong company. What if the provincial government (through agencies like the Ontario Securities Commission) is penalizing the company for fraudulent activity? Or what if the company's industry is shrinking or has ceased to grow (making it tougher for the company to continue growing)? The astute investor looks at a variety of sources before buying stock.

>> **Is the analyst rational when citing a target price for a stock?** When he says, "We think the stock will hit $100 per share within 12 months," is he presenting a rational model, such as basing the share price on a projected price/earnings ratio (see Chapter 5 in Book 2)? The analyst must be able to provide a logical scenario explaining why the stock has a good chance of achieving the cited target price within the time frame mentioned. You may not necessarily agree with the analyst's conclusion, but the explanation can help you decide whether the stock choice is well thought out.

WARNING

>> **Does the company that's being recommended have any ties to the analyst or the analyst's firm?** To this day, the financial industry gets occasional bad publicity because some analysts continue to give shining recommendations on stocks of companies that are doing business with the very firms that employ those analysts. This conflict of interest is probably the biggest reason why analysts can be so wrong in their recommendations. Ask your broker to disclose any conflict of interest.

REMEMBER

The bottom line with brokerage recommendations is that you shouldn't use them to buy or sell a stock. Instead, use them as a back-end check to confirm your own up-front research. If you buy a stock based on your own research and later discover the same stock being talked up on the financial shows, that's just the icing on the cake. The experts may be great to listen to, and their recommendations can augment your own opinions, but they're no substitute for your own careful research. Flip to Chapter 5 in Book 2 for more on researching and picking winning stocks.

Robo-advisors and Fintech

Financial technology, or *fintech,* is a term you'll be hearing about more and more. Fintech represents digital technology and those electronic processes that directly compete with traditional financial services. This is not the only distinction. Your access to fintech is empowered by multiple channels you can use — such as your home computer, smartphone, or tablet — all to give you convenient, fast, and flexible access to mobile banking and stock trading, services that are now entrenched in the Canadian financial industry.

One of the more recent, cooler applications of fintech is the provision of something you've likely heard of already — robo-advisors — also known as *online wealth managers* or *virtual advisers. Robo-advisors* represent great ways for younger Canadians and those new to stock investing to pick stocks and easily sock away some money in a Registered Retirement Savings Plan (RRSP), Tax Free Savings Account (TFSA), or other tax-smart financial vehicle or plan.

Robo-advisors help you do the following:

>> Obtain almost all the preliminary information you need to invest in equities.

>> Devise a basic equity ETF (exchange-traded fund) investment plan based on questionnaire results you provide.

>> Select appropriate investment portfolios by recommending an optimal portfolio.

>> Access a human advisor or representative to help you iron out any kinks and answer administrative and other questions.

Currently, robo-advisors are managing hundreds of million dollars in Canada and billions of dollars worldwide. This segment of the financial services industry is growing incredibly fast. One fascinating factoid is that in Canada, robo-advisors are better regulated than many traditional financial advisors! (Find out more on that later in this chapter.)

High tech meets equity investing

The term *robo-advisor* can be a bit of a misnomer. That's because there is no robot involved. Instead, it's really a paperless electronic platform powered by brainy artificial intelligence and wild but complex algorithms (formulae). These electronic advisors are not just advisors, but actual businesses. So when you think of a robo-advisor, think of an "advice business" with electronic advisors, in much the same way banks are businesses that employ bankers.

Although the robo-advisor platform is indeed operated by humans behind the scenes, there is no actual carbon-based life form that will select an investment portfolio for you. That's where the *robo* part comes in. Robo-advisors will provide you with a selection of tailored investment portfolios (made up of stocks, but more on that later) that are electronically aligned with your financial needs. Robo-advisors use the results of an online questionnaire you fill out. This in turn allows the robo-advisor to generate and determine your risk tolerance and investment objectives. Once your portfolio is selected, it is periodically and automatically rebalanced should the composition of your portfolio deviate significantly from plan.

Terminating bad investment decisions with artificial intelligence

Robo-advisors are a natural evolution of fintech. The online brokerage revolution allowed you to economically take control of your stock trades with powerful tools and resources. Robo-advice is an extension of fintech into the more non-mechanical and judgmental aspect of investing — the provision of actual advice based on the artificial intelligence of robots programmed with algorithms.

The advantage here is that the algorithms, though of course not guarantees of success, are proven best-case scenarios of stock investing that have been tested over the years. These models are being continuously improved and tweaked. In this way, you get a measure of consistency, expertise, and immediacy in your investment decision making.

Advantages of an inhuman touch

Canadians have no doubt seen a few robo-advisor commercials where the client sits across the desk of a smug stockbroker or investment advisor and asks why results are so poor. The broker or advisor smiles and glibly answers, "Just wait, it's a long-term game." The client replies, "It's not a game. That's my kids' education we're talking about," and is far from smiling. The advisor is still smug.

Robo-advisors have no attitude. They generally don't get tempted by selling higher-commission financial products that don't suit your needs but pay them great commissions. They're not tempted by selling you more than you need or selling you with high frequency to rack up fees and commissions. The reputation of the entire industry has been harmed by an array of bad apples and unqualified pretenders who work as "advisors."

It's important to point out, however, that the robo-advisor ecosystem is not all about programming stuff and artificial intelligence. It's not all bits and bytes. Invariably, you will communicate and interact with humans through different channels, including email, phone or video conversations, and computer chat windows.

REMEMBER

Robo-advisors are businesses owned and run by people.

Research has shown that many Canadians actually prefer the robo-advisor option to the traditional approach, especially millennials. Although the inhuman touch has clear advantages, it's incredibly important to be able to access real people to make sure you understand how the robo-advisor process works. This is, after all, your money at stake.

REMEMBER

Although robo-advisors won't be able to match everything that a full-service financial planner or broker could do for you, they will do the lion's share of it — and for much cheaper. The good news is that if, after all this, you still need more advice, you can still use a professionally certified and qualified planner, accountant, or tax expert to help you with estate planning, insurance, and complex tax planning. It's ultimately a question of knowing *when* to use robo-advisors, and this chapter is here to help you.

Exceeding standards

Whenever people deal with artificial intelligence, including robo-advisors, it's a natural instinct to worry a bit. You've seen the headlines of self-driving cars crashing into other vehicles or, worse, people. Yet all great ideas have challenges to learn from and overcome.

From a business governance and practice perspective, you may be surprised to learn that robo-advisors in North America must also follow fiduciary duty standards. Fiduciary standards exist to protect *your* best interests, not the advisor's interests. This reduces conflicts of interest that are rampant in the softly regulated Canadian investment advice industry. (The preceding section discusses some of these problems.) But fiduciary duty itself is not the greatest surprise. The real surprise is that robo-advisor fiduciary standards actually exceed the standards governing most investment advisors and financial planners. In a way, this is sad, but it makes the case for considering robo-advisors even more compelling for newbies to stock investing.

WARNING

In Canada, human advisors generally do not have a strict fiduciary duty. In Canada's wishy-washy regulatory landscape, that's too bad. A *fiduciary* (a person) is supposed to, by definition, "prudently and with due care take great care of your investments and represent the highest standard of care in equity or law." Human investment advisors just have to follow a weaker "suitability standard." As Canada's Justin Bieber would say, "What do you mean?" The suitability obligation means making recommendations that are consistent with the best interests of you, the client. Though Canadian advisors are self-regulated, under the softer suitability standard human advisors just have to "reasonably believe" that any recommendations made are "suitable" for clients. There is no specific requirement not to place the advisor's interests below that of the client, as a fiduciary standard requires.

Unlike *The Terminator* series of movies, where the machines run amok, robo-advisors are restricted in the choices they can make. They can't "short-circuit." Their strength lies in the fact they are really good at wielding algorithms to match a predetermined set of standard portfolios, covering all the key equity asset categories, to your specified needs and risk profile. Robo-advisors follow sound investment practices and are not distracted by higher fees they can get if they sell you substandard investment products.

Robo-advisors are as secure as any credit union, investment broker, or even to an extent a Canadian chartered bank. The term *secure* means two things:

>> **Financially secure:** Like other investment accounts under the custodianship of a member of the Investment Industry Regulatory Organization of Canada (IIROC), your robo-advisor account is eligible for protection of up to $1,000,000 by the Canadian Investor Protection Fund (CIPF). This protection is invoked should the custodian become insolvent. That shouldn't be a problem, as your investment funds are typically held separately in an account in your name at a chartered bank-owned custodian.

>> **Cyber threat secure:** Most robo-advisors use the cyber security standards and measures of Canada's OSFI (Office of the Superintendent of Financial Institutions) and NIST (National Institute of Standards and Technology) to ensure that your sensitive financial and other information is held and processed securely.

Robo-advisors are also transparent and instantly let you see where your money is held. The robo-advisor model has been used around the world for several years now, and at the time of writing robo-advisors manage about $4 billion in assets. They are a growing and trusted investment advice alternative.

Checking Out Canadian Robo-advisors

There are about 15 robo-advisors operating in Canada today. This number is expected to grow as the popularity of the platform continues to grow. Some of the names, which you may recognize through Canadian TV and radio commercials, are listed here. Almost all of these have been established since 2015, and most but not all operate across Canada.

>> BMO SmartFolio

>> Idema Investments

>> Invisor

>> Justwealth

>> ModernAdvisor

>> Nest Wealth

>> Questwealth Portfolios

>> RoboAdvisors+

>> Smart Money Capital Management

>> Virtual Brokers

>> VirtualWealth

>> WealthBar

>> Wealthsimple

Not just for millennials

You may be thinking that fintech is the plaything of millennials and robo-advisors are just for the young. Well, it turns out that both millennials as well as older Canadians are very much at ease within an online investment advice platform. Both age cohorts interact well with robo-advisor interfaces. Research indicates that the average age of Canadian robo-advisor customers is about 45 years old. In fact, the average age of robo-advisor customers, depending on the robo-advisor, ranges from as low as 34 to as high as 50 years old. In the United States, about half of robo-advisor clients are over 35 years old.

Asset allocation: What is the robo-advisor investing your money in?

Age, risk appetite, personal goals, return objectives, and other factors are important in stock investment allocation decisions. With robo-advisors, it's no different. (Again, there is no "robot" — just a simple but very smart computer managed and supported by a person who will execute your portfolio.) The process starts with *you*. Your robo-advisor journey begins with you telling the robo-advisor (a company) a bit about yourself. Based on that little human-to-robot chat, the robo-advisor will recommend a certain exchange traded fund (ETF) or array of ETFs that will suit your needs. The number of portfolio choices ranges from 5 (which appears to be the current norm) up to 10 or more funds.

Most if not virtually all of Canadian robo-advisors invest your funds in ETFs. Those that don't invest exclusively in ETFs, such as RoboAdvisors+ and WealthBar, also invest in mutual funds (see Book 3), pooled funds, and private funds. Typical and main ETF providers across all of Canada's robo-advisors include BMO, Vanguard, Horizons, iShares, Purpose, and many more ETF providers.

REMEMBER

Each recommended ETF portfolio is usually top-heavy with *stock* equities and bolstered with some non-equities. Stocks within the ETF will come in different flavours. They may be Canadian, U.S., global (outside of Canada and the U.S.), or any combination of stocks. ETFs may also include real estate investment trusts — discussed in Chapter 4 of Book 2 — and other equity asset categories like emerging market equities or sectors like commodities.

Some of the sexier ETFs will delve into concepts like futures, sectors like commodities and cannabis, and themes like growth. The ETFs recommended by your robo-advisor may be capped off with fixed-income (non-equity) components and financial instruments such as high-quality investment-grade bonds, lower-quality but higher-return corporate bonds, and money market funds.

The allocation possibilities are many and go even further than this section has indicated. Your portfolios can be embedded within RRSPs, TFSAs, and (if you're older) RRIFs.

After that comes another key feature: You can, should you choose, turn over the day-to-day management of your portfolio to the robo-advisor. You can even choose between robo-advisor offerings that come with passive asset allocation approaches (where the ETF portfolio mirrors a market index) or active asset management (which focuses on outperforming the stock benchmark indexes by buying and selling securities and not sitting still).

Finally, most robo-advisors can execute free or low-fee automatic portfolio rebalances and tax-loss harvesting — which is a big deal, because these duties can be time consuming, tedious, and costly under the traditional investment advisor model.

What to watch for

The first thing to watch for with robo-advisors is the very thing that is obvious from the previous section: Your investment vehicle choice is essentially limited to ETFs. This is neither a good or bad thing. It simply restricts your potential for outsized returns, unless of course the ETF your robo-advisor recommends is of a higher growth but higher risk variety (for example, emerging market or high technology stock) or some sort of active management is being done.

The second risk area is that robo-advisors vary in the extent and nature of the "personal touch" advice they provide and the time of day when such advice can be accessed. Some robo-advisors pitch the word *advice* in every second sentence, yet offer very little of it. Again, note that the robos are there to give you the solution to an algorithmic equation. They give you options and a recommendation. You still have to make a few decisions after that.

WARNING

Finally, even though robo-advisors are regulated more stringently than human advisors, that regulation deals with governance and business processes. What may *not* be governed, and where your exposure lies, is in the fact that the algorithms may be flawed or even hacked and destroyed at your expense. Speaking of hacking, your personal data may even be stolen. There is no such thing as 100 per cent data security.

Fees

Fees are low with robo-advisors, and that is a key appeal. Low fees are possible because robo-advisors don't have to incur the type of office space overhead that financial advisors of similar profile require. Robo-advisors save the most, however, by the fact that they automate so much of their key administrative and operational business processes like registration, monitoring, and reporting to you. The key operational saving stems from the fact that a computer does the thinking and solving for you, not a higher-priced human advisor. If that human advisor is not even qualified or properly trained — and many are not — then you are really getting fleeced.

Every robo-advisor has a distinct fee structure. Some levy a flat rate. Most charge a certain percentage fee. Others utilize a hybrid of flat and percentage fees. Still others charge more (up to 7 per cent with Nest Wealth) with lower balances but drastically reduce the fee once you reach higher minimum balances. Some, like WealthBar and Wealthsimple, charge fees that are well below 1 per cent across a wide range of portfolio balances.

In general, though, robo-advisor clients often pay fees under 1 per cent even if they have a limited amount to invest. Investors who are just beginning their stock-investing journey can open accounts with minimums of $5,000 — and in other cases a lot less. In many cases, robo-advisors that invest in Canada's less-expensive ETFs can charge about one half of a percentage point. One thing that's certain is that they compete as lower-cost alternatives to traditional advisors.

Make no mistake, though: The quality of advice you can get from traditional fee for service advisors, assuming they are experienced and certified, is going to be deeper and broader in scope. It's just that they typically charge at least 2 per cent of your portfolio size in total fees. If you have a very large portfolio, that can build to thousands and tens of thousands of dollars in total annual fees.

REMEMBER

Do the fee math before selecting a robo-advisor.

Putting it all together

This book is all about investing and is written to enable you to do it yourself. It empowers you with the fundamental knowledge and resources to make you a do-it-yourself investor. But there are situations where you may want to have advisors, be they human or robotic, to help you out. It may be when you are starting out. It may be when you are older and have emerging retirement-planning considerations. It may be after you claim an inheritance and suddenly have complex investing decisions to make.

You may want to choose a robo-advisor if

>> You hesitate to invest hours of research learning about the intricacies of index investing.

>> You don't want to rebalance your investment portfolio multiple times annually.

>> You appreciate an easy-to-use and intuitive online platform.

>> You value the 24/7 accessibility and automated nature of robo-advisors to do things like register, deposit funds, verify your balance, and withdraw money.

>> You rightly get exasperated by crazy terms like *efficient market hypothesis* and *smart beta.*

If you don't need or want to use a robo advisor, you don't have to. This book teaches you how to be a do-it-yourself stock investor anyway, or to fill in loose ends. If you are just starting out, it's not too difficult to do for yourself what robo-advisors do — build a basic portfolio of index exchange traded funds for essentially no fee.

Chapter **3**

Investing for Long-Term Growth

What's the number-one reason people invest in stocks? To grow their wealth (also referred to as capital appreciation). Yes, some Canadians invest for income (in the form of dividends), but that's a different matter (see Chapter 4 in Book 2). Investors seeking growth would rather see the money that could have been distributed as dividends be reinvested in the company so that (hopefully) a greater gain is achieved when the stock's price rises or appreciates. People interested in growing their wealth see stocks as one of the convenient ways to do it. Growth stocks tend to be riskier than other categories of stocks, but they offer excellent long-term prospects for making the big bucks. Just ask Warren Buffett, Peter Lynch, and other successful, long-term investors.

Although someone like Buffett is not considered a growth investor, his long-term, value-oriented approach has been a successful growth strategy. If you're the type of investor who has *enough time* to let somewhat risky stocks trend upward or who has enough money so that *a loss won't devastate you* financially, then growth stocks are definitely for you. As they say, no guts, no glory. The challenge is to figure out which stocks make you wealthier quicker; you get tips on how to do so in this chapter.

REMEMBER

Short of starting your own business, stock investing is the best way to profit from a business venture. To make money in stocks consistently over the long haul, you must remember that you're investing in a company; buying the stock is just a means for you to participate in the company's success (or failure). Why does it matter that you think of stock investing as buying a company versus buying a stock? Invest in a stock only if you're just as excited about it as you would be if you were the CEO in charge of running the company. If you're the sole owner of the company, do you act differently than one of a legion of obscure stockholders? Of course you do. As the firm's owner, you have a greater interest in the company. You have a strong desire to know how the enterprise is doing. As you invest in stocks, make believe that you're the owner, and take an active interest in the company's products, services, sales, earnings, and so on. This attitude and discipline can enhance your goals as a stock investor. This approach is especially important if your investment goal is growth.

Becoming a Value-Oriented Growth Investor

REMEMBER

A stock is considered a growth stock when it's growing faster and higher than the overall stock market. Basically, a growth stock performs better than its peers in categories such as sales and earnings. Value stocks are stocks that are priced lower than the value of the company and its assets — you can identify a value stock by analyzing the company's fundamentals and looking at key financial ratios, such as the price-to-earnings (P/E) and price-to-sales (P/S) ratios. (Company finances and ratios are covered in Chapter 5 in Book 2.) Growth stocks tend to have better prospects for growth in the immediate future (from one to four years), but value stocks tend to have less risk and steadier growth over a longer term.

Over the years, a debate has quietly raged in the financial community about growth versus value investing. Some people believe that growth and value are mutually exclusive. They maintain that large numbers of people buying stock with growth as the expectation tend to drive up the stock price relative to the company's current value. Growth investors, for example, aren't put off by P/E ratios of 30, 40, or higher. Value investors, meanwhile, are too nervous to buy stocks at those P/E ratio levels.

However, you can have both. A value-oriented approach to growth investing serves you best. Long-term growth stock investors spend time analyzing the company's fundamentals to make sure that the company's growth prospects lie on a solid foundation. But what if you have to choose between a growth stock and a value stock? Which do you choose? Seek value when you're buying the stock and analyze the company's prospects for growth. Growth includes but is not limited to the health and growth of the company's specific industry, the economy at large, and the general political climate.

REMEMBER

The bottom line is that growth is much easier to achieve when you seek a one-two punch of solid, value-oriented companies in growing industries. It's also worth emphasizing that time, patience, and discipline are key factors in your success — especially in the tumultuous and uncertain stock investing environment of the current world.

TECHNICAL STUFF

Value-oriented growth investing probably has the longest history of success compared to most stock investing philosophies. The track record for those people who use value-oriented growth investing is enviable. Warren Buffett, Benjamin Graham, John Templeton, and Peter Lynch are a few of the more well-known practitioners. Each may have his own spin on the concepts, but all have successfully applied the basic principles of value-oriented growth investing over many years.

Surveying Handy Growth Stock Tips

Although the information in the previous section can help you shrink your stock choices from thousands of stocks to maybe a few dozen or a few hundred (depending on how well the general stock market is doing), the purpose of this section is to help you cull the so-so growth stocks to unearth the go-go ones. It's time to dig deeper for the biggest potential winners. Keep in mind that you probably won't find a stock to satisfy all the criteria presented here. Just make sure that your selection meets as many criteria as realistically possible. But hey, if you do find a stock that meets all the criteria cited, buy as much as you can!

Verifiably, 80 to 90 percent of our stock picks are profitable. People ask us how we pick a winning stock. We tell them that we don't just pick a stock and hope that it does well. In fact, our respective stock-picking research doesn't even begin with stocks; we first look at the investing environment (politics, economics, demographics, and so on) and choose which industry will benefit. After we know which industry will prosper accordingly, then we start to analyze and choose individual stock(s). We start with the big picture first and methodically drill down to the company level afterwards.

After we choose a stock, we wait. Patience is more than just a virtue; patience is to investing what time is to a seed that's planted in fertile soil. The legendary Jesse Livermore said that he didn't make his stock market fortunes by trading stocks; his fortunes were made "in the waiting." Why?

When we tell you to have patience and a long-term perspective, it isn't because we want you to wait years or decades for your stock portfolio to bear fruit. It's because you're waiting for a specific condition to occur: for the market to discover what you have! When you have a good stock in a good industry, it may take time for the market to discover it. When a stock has more buyers than sellers, it rises — it's as simple as that. As time passes, more buyers find your stock. As the stock rises, it attracts more attention and therefore more buyers. The more time that passes, the better your stock looks to the investing public.

REMEMBER

When you're choosing growth stocks, you should consider investing in a company only if it makes a cash profit (in other words, profits without accounting voodoo) and if you understand how it makes that profit and from where it generates sales. Part of your research means looking at the industry and sector and economic trends in general. Chapter 5 in Book 2 helps you avoid voodoo numbers!

Look for leaders in megatrends

A strong company in a growing industry is a recipe for success. If you look at the history of stock investing, this point comes up constantly. Investors need to be on the alert for megatrends because they help ensure success.

A megatrend is a major development that has huge implications for much (if not all) of society for a long time to come. Good examples are the advent of social media and the blockchain (including cryptocurrency) on the Internet (new technology) and the aging of Canada (demographics). (Book 6 covers blockchain and cryptocurrency technology.) Both of these trends offer significant challenges and opportunities for the Canadian economy. Take the Internet, for example. Its potential for economic application is still being developed and honed. Millions keep flocking to its new and exciting applications for many reasons. And census data tells us that senior citizens (over 65) will be the fastest-growing segment of the Canadian population during the next 20 years. How does the stock investor take advantage of a megatrend?

Compare company growth to industry growth

You have to measure the growth of a company against something else to figure out whether its stock is a growth stock. Usually, you compare the growth of a company with the growth of other companies in the same industry or with the stock market in general. In practical terms, when you measure the growth of a stock against the stock market, you're actually comparing it against a generally accepted benchmark, such as the S&P/TSX60, the Dow Jones Industrial Average (DJIA), or the Standard & Poor's 500 (S&P 500). For more on stock indexes, see Chapter 4 in Book 3.

TIP

If a company's earnings grow 15 percent per year over three years or more and the industry's average growth rate over the same time frame is 10 percent, then the stock qualifies as a growth stock. You can easily calculate the earnings growth rate by comparing a company's earnings in the current year to the preceding year and computing the difference as a percentage. For example, if a company's earnings (on a per-share basis) were $1 last year and $1.10 this year, then earnings grew by 10 percent. Many analysts also look at a current quarter and compare the earnings to the same quarter from the preceding year to see whether earnings are growing.

REMEMBER

A growth stock is called that not only because the company is growing but also because the company is performing well with some consistency. Having a single year where your earnings do well versus the S&P/TSX60's or the S&P 500's average doesn't cut it. Growth must be consistently accomplished.

Consider a company with a strong niche

TIP

Companies that have established a strong niche are consistently profitable. Look for a company with one or more of the following characteristics:

» **A strong brand:** Companies such as Coca-Cola, Metro, and Shoppers Drug Mart come to mind. Yes, other companies out there can make soda or sell personal hygiene products, but a business needs a lot more than a similar product to topple companies that have established an almost irrevocable identity with the public.

» **High barriers to entry:** United Parcel Service, Shopify, and BlackBerry have set up tremendous distribution and delivery networks that competitors can't easily duplicate. High barriers to entry offer an important edge to companies that are already established. Examples of high barriers include high capital requirements (like needing lots of cash to start, or significant investment in machinery or infrastructure) or special technology or patented intellectual property that's not easily reproduced or acquired.

» **Research and development (R&D):** Companies such as Celestica and Pfizer spend a lot of money researching and developing new technology and pharmaceutical products, respectively. This investment becomes a new product with millions of consumers who become loyal purchasers, so the company's going to grow. You can find out what companies spend on R&D by checking their financial statements and their annual reports (more on this in Chapter 5 of Book 2).

Check out a company's fundamentals

REMEMBER

When you hear the word *fundamentals* in the world of stock investing, it refers to the company's financial condition and related data. When investors (especially value investors) do fundamental analysis, they look at the company's fundamentals — its balance sheet, income statement, cash flow, and other operational data, along with external factors such as the company's market position, industry, and economic prospects. Essentially, the fundamentals indicate the company's financial condition. Chapter 5 in Book 2 goes into greater detail about analyzing a company's financial condition. However, the main numbers you want to look at include the following:

» **Sales:** Are the company's sales this year surpassing last year's? As a decent benchmark, you want to see sales at least 10 percent higher than last year. Although it may differ depending on the industry, 10 percent is a reasonable, general yardstick.

» **Earnings:** Are earnings (especially cash, not just paper earnings or estimates like accrued interest revenue) at least 10 percent higher than last year? Earnings should grow at the same rate as sales (or better, which is what would happen if the company improved its cost control).

» **Debt:** Is the company's total debt equal to or lower than the prior year? The death knell of many a company has been excessive debt.

A company's financial condition has more factors than are mentioned here, but these numbers are the most important. Using the 10 percent figure may seem like an oversimplification, but you don't need to complicate matters unnecessarily. Someone's computerized financial model may come out to 9.675 percent or maybe 11.07 percent, but keep it simple for now.

Evaluate a company's management

The management of a company is crucial to its success. Before you buy stock in a company, you want to know that the company's management is doing a great job. But how do you do that? If you call up a company and ask, it may not even return your phone call. How do you know whether management is running the company properly? The best way is to check the numbers. Financial numbers are the language of business. The following sections tell you the numbers you need to check. If the company's management is running the business well, the ultimate result is a rising stock price.

Return on equity

REMEMBER

Although you can measure how well management is doing in several ways, you can take a quick snapshot of a management team's competence by checking the company's return on equity (ROE). You calculate the ROE simply by dividing earnings by equity. The resulting percentage gives you a good idea whether the company is using its equity (or net assets) efficiently and profitably. Basically, the higher the percentage, the better, but you can consider the ROE solid if the percentage is 10 percent or higher. Keep in mind that not all industries have identical ROEs.

To find out a company's earnings, check out the company's income statement. The income statement is a simple financial statement that expresses this equation: sales (or revenue) minus expenses equals net earnings (or net income or net profit). You can see an example of an income statement in Table 3-1. (Find more details on income statements in Chapter 5 of Book 2.)

TABLE 3-1

Grobaby, Inc., Income Statement

	2019 Income Statement	2020 Income Statement
Sales	$82,000	$90,000
Expenses	–$75,000	–$78,000
Net earnings	$7,000	$12,000

To find out a company's equity, check out that company's balance sheet. (See Chapter 5 in Book 2 for more details on balance sheets.) The balance sheet is actually a simple financial statement that illustrates this equation: Total assets (TA) minus total liabilities (TL) equals net equity. For public stock companies, the net assets are called shareholders' equity or simply equity. Table 3-2 shows a balance sheet for Grobaby, Inc.

Table 3-1 shows that Grobaby's earnings went from $7,000 to $12,000. In Table 3-2, you can see that Grobaby increased the equity from $35,000 to $40,000 in one year. The ROE for the year 2019 is 20 percent ($7,000 in earnings divided by $35,000 in equity), which is a solid number. The following year, the ROE is 30 percent ($12,000 in earnings divided by $40,000 equity), another solid number. A good minimum ROE is 10 percent, but 15 percent or more is preferred.

TABLE 3-2

Grobaby, Inc., Balance Sheet

	Balance Sheet for December 31, 2019	Balance Sheet for December 31, 2020
Total assets (TA)	$55,000	$65,000
Total liabilities (TL)	–$20,000	–$25,000
Equity (TA minus TL)	$35,000	$40,000

Equity and earnings growth

Two additional barometers of success are a company's growth in earnings and growth of equity:

>> Look at the growth in earnings in Table 3-1. The earnings grew from $7,000 (in 2019) to $12,000 (in 2020), a percentage increase of 71 percent ($12,000 minus $7,000 equals $5,000, and $5,000 divided by $7,000 is 71 percent), which is excellent. At a minimum, earnings growth should be equal to or better than the rate of inflation, but because that's not always a reliable number, we like at least 10 percent.

>> In Table 3-2, Grobaby's equity grew by $5,000 (from $35,000 to $40,000), or 14.3 percent ($5,000 divided by $35,000), which is very good — management is doing good things here. Look for equity increasing by 10 percent or more.

Insider buying

TIP

Watching management as it manages the business is important, but another important indicator of how well the company is doing is to see whether management is buying stock in the company as well. If a company is poised for growth, who knows better than management? And if management is buying up the company's stock en masse, that's a great indicator of the stock's potential.

Notice who's buying and/or recommending a company's stock

TIP

You can invest in a great company and still see its stock go nowhere. Why? Because what makes the stock go up is demand — having more buyers than sellers of the stock. If you pick a stock for all the right reasons and the market notices the stock as well, that attention causes the stock price to climb. The things to watch for include the following:

- » **Institutional buying:** Are mutual funds and pension plans buying up the stock you're looking at? If so, this type of buying power can exert tremendous upward pressure on the stock's price. Some resources and publications track institutional buying and how that affects any particular stock. Frequently, when a mutual fund buys a stock, others soon follow. In spite of all the talk about independent research, a herd mentality still exists in Canada and in other markets as well.

- » **Analysts' attention:** Are analysts talking about the stock on the financial shows? As much as you should be skeptical about an analyst's recommendation (given the past two stock market debacles like the Tech Wreck and the Great Recession), it offers some positive reinforcement for your stock. Don't ever buy a stock solely on the basis of an analyst's recommendation. Just know that if you buy a stock based on your own research and analysts subsequently rave about it on BNN Bloomberg (www.bnnbloomberg.ca/), your stock price is likely to go up. A single recommendation by an influential analyst can be enough to send a stock skyward.

- » **Newsletter recommendations:** Independent researchers usually publish newsletters. If influential Canadian newsletters are touting your choice, that praise is also good for your stock. Although some great newsletters are out there and they offer information that's as good as or better than that of some brokerage firms' research departments, definitely don't base your investment decision on a single tip. However, seeing newsletters tout a stock that you've already chosen should make you feel good.

- » **Consumer publications:** No, you won't find investment advice here. This one seems to come out of left field, but it's a source that you should notice. Publications such as *Consumer Reports* regularly look at products and services and rate them for consumer satisfaction. If a company's offerings are well received by consumers, that's a strong positive for the company. This kind of attention ultimately has a positive effect on that company's stock.

Make sure a company continues to do well

A company's financial situation does change, and you, as a diligent investor, need to continue to look at the numbers for as long as the stock is in your portfolio. You may have chosen a great stock from a great company with great numbers a few years ago, but chances are pretty good that the numbers have changed since then.

WARNING

Great stocks don't always stay that way. A great selection that you're drawn to today may become tomorrow's pariah. Information, both good and bad, moves like lightning. Keep an eye on your stock company's numbers! To help minimize the downside risk, see the sidebar "Protecting your downside" for an example. For more information on a company's financial data, check out Chapter 5 in Book 2.

PROTECTING YOUR DOWNSIDE

Trailing stops are stop-losses that you regularly manage with the stock you invest in. Trailing stops can help you, no matter how good or bad the economy is (or how good or bad the stock you're investing in is).

Suppose that you had invested in Research In Motion (now called BlackBerry), a classic example of a phenomenal Canadian growth stock that went bad. Really bad. Around the year 2000, when its stock was still riding high, investors were as happy as chocoholics at a Cadbury factory. Along with many investors who forgot that sound investing takes discipline and research, some Research In Motion investors thought, "Downside risk? What downside risk?"

Here's an example of how a stop-loss order would have worked if you had invested in Research In Motion. Pretend you're back in 2000 and you buy Research In Motion at a price of, let's say, $65 per share and put in a stop-loss order with your broker at $60. (Remember to make it a GTC, or good-till-cancelled order. If you do, the stop-loss order stays on indefinitely.) As a general rule, you can place the stop-loss order at 10 percent below the market value (to reduce the stop-loss purchase cost). As the stock goes up, you keep the stop-loss trailing upward like a tail. (Now you know why it's called a "trailing" stop; it trails the stock's price.) When Research In Motion hits $75, your stop-loss changes to, say, $70, and so on. Now what?

When Research In Motion starts its perilous descent, you get out at $70. The new price of $70 triggers the stop-loss, and the stock is automatically sold — you stopped the loss! Actually, in this case, you could call it a "stop and cash in the gain" order. Because you bought the stock at $65 and sold at $70, you pocket a respectable capital gain of $5 (7.6 percent appreciation), less the cost of the stop-loss. Now you safely step aside and watch the stock continue its plunge.

What if the market is doing well? Are trailing stops a good idea? Because these stops are placed below the stock price, you're not stopping the stock from rising indefinitely. All you're doing is protecting your investment from loss. That's discipline! The stock market of 2004 to 2007 was fairly good to stock investors because the bear market that started in 2000 took a break — at least until 2008 when another one started. That bear market was even worse and the drop in stock prices ushered in the Great Recession. Ouch! During a bear market, trailing-stop strategies are critical because a potential decline in the stock price will become a greater risk.

Heed investing lessons from history

A growth stock isn't a creature like the Loch Ness monster — always talked about but rarely seen. Growth stocks have been part of the financial scene for nearly a century. Examples abound that offer rich information that you can apply to today's stock market environment. Look at past market winners, especially those during the recent bull market, and the bearish markets found between 2000–2010, and ask yourself, "What made them profitable stocks?" These two time frames offer a stark contrast to each other. The current bull market is a booming time for stocks, especially U.S. stocks, whereas the years before were very tough and bearish. In fact, Canadian stock market indexes, although higher than before, still lag U.S. indexes at the time of this writing.

REMEMBER

Being aware and acting logically are as vital to successful stock investing as they are to any other pursuit. Over and over again, history gives you the formula for successful stock investing:

>> Pick a company that has strong fundamentals, including signs such as rising sales and earnings and low debt. (See Chapter 5 in Book 2.)

>> Make sure that the company is in a growing industry.

>> Fully participate in stocks that are benefiting from bullish market developments in the general economy.

>> During a bear market or in bearish trends, switch more of your money out of growth stocks (such as technology) and into defensive stocks (such as utilities).

>> Monitor your stocks. Hold on to stocks that continue to have growth potential, and sell those stocks with declining prospects.

Exploring Small Caps and Speculative Stocks

Everyone wants to get in early on a hot new stock. Why not? You buy Shlobotky, Inc., at $1 per share and hope it zooms to $98 before lunchtime. Who doesn't want to buy a cheapy-deepy stock today that becomes the next Apple or Walmart? This possibility is why investors are attracted to small cap stocks.

Small cap (or small capitalization) is a reference to the company's market size. Small cap stocks are stocks that have a market value (i.e., market capitalization) under $1 billion. Investors may face more risk with small caps, but they also have the chance for greater gains. Canada's stock market is replete with small cap stocks.

Out of all the types of stocks, small cap stocks continue to exhibit the greatest amount of growth. In the same way that a tree planted last year has more opportunity for growth than a mature 100-year-old redwood, small caps have greater growth potential than established large cap stocks. Of course, a small cap doesn't exhibit spectacular growth just because it's small. It grows when it does the right things, such as increasing sales and earnings by producing goods and services that customers want.

REMEMBER

For every small company that becomes a Financial Post FP500 firm, hundreds of companies don't grow at all or go out of business. When you try to guess the next great stock before any evidence of growth, you're not investing — you're speculating. Have you heard that one before? Of course you have, and you'll hear it again. There's nothing wrong with speculating. But it's important to know that you're speculating when you're doing it. If you're going to speculate in small stocks hoping for the next Alphabet (Google), use the guidelines presented in the following sections to increase your chances of success.

Knowing when to avoid IPOs

Initial public offerings (IPOs) are the birthplaces of public stocks, or the proverbial ground floor. The IPO is the first offering to the public of a company's stock. The IPO is also referred to as "going public." Because a company going public is frequently an unproven enterprise, investing in an IPO can be risky. Here are the two types of IPOs:

>> **Start-up IPO:** This is a company that didn't exist before the IPO. In other words, the entrepreneurs get together and create a business plan. To get the financing they need for the company, they decide to go public immediately by approaching an investment banker. If the investment banker thinks that it's a good concept, the banker will seek funding (selling the stock to investors) via the IPO.

>> **A private company that decides to go public:** In many cases, the IPO is done for a company that already exists and is seeking expansion capital. The company may have been around for a long time as a smaller private concern, but now decides to seek funding through an IPO to grow even larger (or to fund a new product, promotional expenses, and so on). Facebook and Groupon are examples of such IPOs.

Which of the two IPOs do you think is less risky? That's right — the private company going public. Why? Because it's already a proven business, which is a safer bet than a brand-new start-up. Some more great examples of successful IPOs in recent years are United Parcel Service and Google (they were established companies before they went public).

Great stocks started as small companies going public. You may be able to recount the stories of Federal Express, Dell, Home Depot, and other great successes. But do you remember an IPO by the company Lipschitz & Farquar? No? That's because it's among the majority of IPOs that don't succeed.

WARNING

IPOs have a dubious track record of success in their first year. Studies periodically done by the brokerage industry have revealed that IPOs actually decline in price 60 percent of the time (more often than not) during the first 12 months. In other words, an IPO has a better-than-even chance of dropping in price. For Canadian stock investors, the lesson is clear: Wait until a track record appears before you invest in a company. If you don't, you're simply rolling the dice (in other words, you're speculating, not investing!). Don't worry about missing that great opportunity; if it's a bona fide opportunity, you'll still do well after the IPO.

Making sure a small cap stock is making money

REMEMBER

We emphasize two points when investing in stocks:

>> **Make sure that a company is established.** Being in business for at least three years is a good minimum.

>> **Make sure that a company is profitable.** It should show net profits of 10 percent or more over two years or longer.

These points are especially important for investors in small stocks. Plenty of start-up ventures lose money but hope to make a fortune down the road. A good example is a company in the biotechnology industry. Biotech is an exciting area, but it's esoteric, and at this early stage, companies are finding it difficult to use the technology in profitable ways. You may say, "But shouldn't I jump in now in anticipation of future profits?" You may get lucky, but when you invest in unproven, small cap stocks, you're speculating.

Analyzing small cap stocks before investing

The only difference between a small cap stock and a large cap stock is a few zeros in their numbers and the fact that you need to do more research with small caps. By sheer dint of size, small caps are riskier than large caps, so you offset the risk by accruing more information on yourself and the stock in question. Plenty of information is available on large cap stocks because they're widely followed. Small cap stocks don't get as much press, and fewer analysts issue reports on them. Here are a few points to keep in mind:

REMEMBER

>> **Understand your investment style.** Small cap stocks may have more potential rewards, but they also carry more risk. No investor should devote a large portion of his capital to small cap stocks. If you're considering retirement money, you're better off investing in large cap stocks, exchange-traded funds (ETFs; see Chapter 4 in Book 3), investment-grade bonds, bank accounts, and/ or mutual funds. For example, retirement money should be in investments that are either very safe or have proven track records of steady growth over an extended period of time (five years or longer).

>> **Check with the SEC and SEDAR.** Get the financial reports that the company must file with the SEC and SEDAR (such as its quarterly reports). These reports offer more complete information on the company's activities and finances. Go to the Securities and Exchange Commission website at www.sec.gov and check its massive database of company filings at EDGAR (Electronic Data Gathering, Analysis, and Retrieval system). Get the financial reports for Canadian public companies through SEDAR (System for Electronic Document Analysis and Retrieval) at www.sedar.com. You can also check to see if any complaints have been filed against the company.

>> **Check other sources.** See whether brokers and independent research services, such as Value Line, follow the stock. If two or more different sources like the stock, it's worth further investigation.

WARNING

Chapter 1 of Book 2 and Chapter 4 of Book 3 touch on the TSX Venture Exchange. This is the Canadian stock exchange where you can find lots of small, and risky, development-stage companies. All trading here is executed electronically. Be careful when you invest in one of the many stocks listed on this exchange. You can lose a lot of money before you hit that one diamond in the rough!

Chapter **4**

Investing for Income

Investing for income means investing in stocks that provide you with regular cash payments (dividends). Income stocks may not be known to offer stellar growth potential, but they're good for a steady infusion of cash. If you have a lower tolerance for risk, or if your investment goal is anything less than long-term, income stocks are a better bet than growth stocks. Long-term, conservative Canadian investors who need income resources can also benefit from income stocks because of their better track record of keeping pace with inflation (versus fixed-income investments, such as bonds) over the long term.

The bottom line is that dividend-paying stocks deserve a spot in a variety of Canadian portfolios. This chapter explains the basics of income stocks, shows you how to analyze income stocks with a few handy formulas, and describes several typical income stocks.

TIP

Getting your stock portfolio to yield more income is easier than you think. Many investors increase income using proven techniques such as covered call writing. Covered call writing is beyond the scope of this book, but you can find out more about it and whether it applies to your situation. Talk to your financial advisor or read up on it — it's covered more fully in *Trading Options For Dummies,* 3rd Edition, by Joe Duarte (Wiley). You can also find great educational material on this option strategy (and many others) at the Chicago Board Options Exchange (www.cboe.com).

Understanding Income Stocks Basics

Dividend-paying stocks are a great consideration for those investors seeking more income in their portfolios, especially stocks with higher-than-average dividends known as income stocks. Income stocks take on a dual role in that they can not only appreciate but also provide regular income.

Getting a grip on dividends

When people talk about gaining income from stocks, they're usually talking about dividends. A dividend is nothing more than money paid out to the owner of stock. You purchase dividend stocks primarily for income — not for spectacular growth potential.

Dividends are sometimes confused with interest. However, dividends are payouts to owners, whereas interest is a payment to a creditor.

>> A stock investor is considered a part owner of the company she invests in and is entitled to dividends when they're issued.

>> A chartered bank, on the other hand, considers you a creditor when you open an account. The bank borrows your money and pays you interest on it.

Unlike interest payments, a company may choose to cease paying common dividends at any time, without being in default. Although investors would be disappointed if dividends were halted, they are nevertheless a discretionary payment by the company.

A dividend is quoted as an annual number but is usually paid on a quarterly basis. For example, if a stock pays a dividend of $4, you're probably paid $1 every quarter. If, in this example, you have 200 shares, you're paid $800 every year (if the dividend doesn't change during that period), or $200 per quarter. Getting that regular dividend cheque every three months (for as long as you hold the stock) can be a nice perk. It's sort of like a short-term mini-pension!

TIP

A good income stock has a higher-than-average dividend (typically 4 per cent or higher).

REMEMBER

Dividend rates aren't guaranteed — they can go up or down, or in some cases when a company is in financial distress, the dividend can be discontinued. Fortunately, most companies that issue dividends continue them indefinitely and actually increase dividend payments from time to time. Historically, dividend increases have equalled (or exceeded) the rate of inflation.

Recognizing who's well-suited for income

Who is best suited to income stocks? They can be appropriate for many investors, but they're especially well-suited for the following individuals:

» **Conservative and novice investors:** Conservative investors like to see a slow-but-steady approach to growing their money while getting regular dividend cheques. Novice investors who start slowly also benefit.

» **Retirees:** Growth investing (see Chapter 3 in Book 2) is best suited for long-term needs, whereas income investing is best suited to current needs. Retirees may want growth in their portfolios, but they're more concerned with regular income that can keep pace with inflation.

» **Dividend reinvestment plan (DRP) investors:** For those investors who like to compound their money with DRPs, income stocks are perfect. DRPs are exactly what they sound like — they are preset administrative plans that reinvest dividends to buy more stock. They represent a very small portion of stock investing, but it's worthwhile for you to know they exist. Check out www.dripprimer.ca/canadiandriplist for a primer on DRPs and a list of Canadian companies offering these plans. Some people call this the "get rich eventually" approach.

Assessing the advantages of income stocks

Income stocks tend to be among the least volatile of all stocks, and many investors view them as defensive stocks. Defensive stocks are stocks of companies that sell goods and services that are generally needed no matter what shape the economy is in. (Don't confuse defensive stocks with defence stocks, which specialize in goods and equipment for the military.) Food, beverage, and utility companies are great examples of defensive stocks. Many of these utilities are in industries where the firm is a monopoly (sole supplier) or oligopoly (one of a few firms) that control supply in the region, with little competition. Even when the economy is experiencing tough times, people still need to eat, drink, and turn on the lights. Companies that offer relatively high dividends also tend to be large firms in established, stable industries.

TIP

Some industries in particular are known for high-dividend stocks. Utilities (such as electric, gas, and water), real estate investment trusts (REITs), and the energy sector (oil and gas royalty trusts) are places where you definitely find income stocks. You'll have no trouble at all finding a large assortment of high-dividend stocks on the Toronto Stock Exchange, because many of the stocks listed on the TSX, and included in its indexes, fall into one of these industry sectors. Yes, you can find high-dividend stocks in other industries and on foreign stock markets, but you find a higher concentration of them in these industries, especially in Canada. For more details, see the sections highlighting these industries later in this chapter.

Digging into the disadvantages of income stocks

Before you say, "Income stocks are great! I'll get my chequebook and buy a batch right now," take a look at the following potential disadvantages (ugh!). Income stocks do come with some fine print.

What goes up . . .

Income stocks can go down as well as up, just as any stock can. The factors that affect stocks in general — politics, industry and sector changes, and so on — affect income stocks, too. Fortunately, income stocks don't get hit as hard as other stocks when the market is declining, because high dividends tend to act as a support to the stock price. Therefore, income stocks' prices usually fall less dramatically than other stocks' prices in a declining market.

Interest-rate sensitivity

Income stocks can be sensitive to rising interest rates. When interest rates go up, other investments (such as corporate bonds, newly issued Canadian Treasury securities, and bank guaranteed investment certificates) are more attractive. When your income stock yields 4 per cent and interest rates go up to 5 per cent, 6 per cent, or higher, you may think, "Hmm. Why settle for a 4 per cent yield when I can get 5 per cent or better elsewhere?" As more and more investors sell their low-yield stocks, the prices for those stocks fall.

Another point to note is that rising interest rates may hurt the company's financial strength. If the company is highly leveraged with debt and has to pay a lot of interest, that may affect the company's earnings, which in turn may affect the company's ability to continue paying dividends.

REMEMBER

Dividend-paying companies that experience consistent falling revenues tend to cut dividends. In this case, consistent means two or more years.

The effect of inflation

Although many companies raise their dividends on a regular basis, some don't. Or if they do raise their dividends, the increases may be small. Some utilities that are monopolies or oligopolies are heavily regulated by government agencies, which may limit their ability to raise revenues and dividends. If income is your primary consideration, you want to be aware of these facts. If you're getting the same dividend year after year and this income is important to you, rising inflation becomes a problem.

Say that you have XYZ stock at $10 per share with an annual dividend of 30 cents (the yield is 30 cents divided by $10, or 3 per cent). If you have a yield of 3 per cent two years in a row, how do you feel when inflation rises 6 per cent one year and 7 per cent the next year? Because inflation means costs are rising, inflation shrinks the value of the dividend income you receive. In other words, your dividend income alone can't keep up with your inflated cost of living. Fortunately, studies show that in general, dividends do better in inflationary environments than bonds and other fixed-rate investments. Usually, the dividends of companies that provide consumer staples (food, energy, and so on) meet or exceed the rate of inflation.

PLAYING IT SAFE WITH INCOME-GENERATING ALTERNATIVES

If you're an investor seeking income but you're nervous about the potential risks associated with income stocks, here are some non-stock alternatives:

- **Treasury securities:** Issued by the federal government and considered the safest investments in the world. Canadian Treasury securities are sold to the public to pay off maturing debt and raise money to operate the government. Three general types of treasury securities are sold in Canada and the U.S. Treasury bills (T-bills) mature in three months, six months, or one year. Treasury notes (Canada notes) are intermediate-term securities and mature in two to ten years. Treasury bonds (Canada bonds) are long-term securities that have maturities ranging from 10 to 30 years. U.S. T-bills have much larger minimum purchase requirements than Canadian T-bills, which require minimums from $5,000 (for terms of 6 to 12 months) up to $25,000 (for 30- to 60-day terms). A U.S.-denominated Canadian Treasury bill (guaranteed by the Canadian government) has a minimum requirement of US$100,000.

- **Bank certificates of deposit (CDs):** These investments are backed up (to a limit of $100,000) by the Canada Deposit Insurance Corporation (CDIC) and are very safe.

- **Guaranteed Investment Certificates (GICs):** Like CDs, GICs are safe and also guaranteed (again, up to a limit of $100,000) by the CDIC.

- **Income-generating exchange traded funds (ETFs) and mutual funds:** Income ETFs are dividend and diversified income funds that in many cases make periodic payouts of cash. The iShares Dow Jones Canada Select Dividend Index Fund (XDV-T) is one of many ETFs that generate income. (See Chapter 4 in Book 3 for more details.) Also, many mutual funds, such as Canadian Treasury–bond mutual funds and corporate bond funds, are designed for income investors. They offer diversification and professional management, and you can usually invest small amounts. Book 3 has the scoop on mutual funds.

Investing for Income

The Canada Revenue Agency's cut

The Canadian government taxes stock dividends on a more favourable basis than, say, income from employment or interest income. Find out from your tax advisor the extent to which this is (or will be) an issue for you.

Analysing Income Stocks

As you find out in the preceding section, even conservative income investors can be confronted with different types of risk. Fortunately, this section helps you carefully choose income stocks so that you can minimize unwanted outcomes.

TIP

Look at income stocks in the same way you do growth stocks when assessing the financial strength of a company. Getting nice dividends comes to a screeching halt if the company can't afford to pay them. If your budget depends on dividend income, then monitoring the company's financial strength is that much more important. You can apply the same techniques listed in Chapters 3 and 5 of Book 2 for assessing the financial strength of growth stocks to your assessment of income stocks.

Pinpointing your needs first

You choose income stocks primarily because you want or need income now. As a secondary point, income stocks have the potential for steady, long-term appreciation. So if you're investing for retirement needs that won't occur for another 20 years, maybe income stocks aren't suitable for you — a better choice may be to invest in growth stocks because they're more likely to grow your money faster over a lengthier investment term. (You discover who's best suited to income stocks earlier in this chapter.)

If you're certain you want income stocks, do a rough calculation to figure out how big a portion of your portfolio you want income stocks to occupy. Suppose that you need $25,000 in investment income to satisfy your current financial needs. If you have bonds that give you $20,000 in interest income and you want the rest to come from dividends from income stocks, you need to choose stocks that pay you $5,000 in annual dividends. If you have $80,000 left to invest, you need a portfolio of income stocks that yields 6.25 per cent ($5,000 divided by $80,000 equals a yield of 6.25 per cent; yield is explained in more detail in the following section).

You may ask, "Why not just buy $80,000 of bonds (for instance) that yield at least 6.25 per cent?" Well, if you're satisfied with that $5,000 and inflation for the foreseeable future is 0 or considerably less than 6.25 per cent, then you have a point.

Inflation and the relatively higher taxation of interest income from bonds will probably be around for a long time. Fortunately, the steady growth that income stocks provide is a benefit to you.

REMEMBER

Every investor is different. If you're not sure about your current or future needs, your best choice is to consult with a financial planner. Flip to Chapter 2 in Book 2 for more information.

Checking out yield

REMEMBER

Because income stocks pay out dividends — income — you need to assess which stocks can give you the highest income. How do you do that? The main thing to look for is yield, which is the percentage rate of return paid on a stock in the form of dividends. Looking at a stock's dividend yield is the quickest way to find have an estimate oft how much money you might earn versus other investments. Table 4-1 illustrates this point. Dividend yield is calculated in the following way:

Dividend yield = ANNUAL Dividend income ÷ current stock price

TABLE 4-1 **Comparing Yields**

Investment	Type	Investment Amount	Annual Investment Income (Dividend)	Yield (Annual Investment Income Investment Amount)
Smith Co.	Common stock	$20 per share	$1.00 per share	5%
Jones Co.	Common stock	$30 per share	$1.50 per share	5%
Wilson Bank	Savings account	$1,000 deposit	$10.00 (interest)	1%

The following sections use the information in Table 4-1 to compare the yields from different investments and to show how evaluating yield helps you choose the stock that earns you the most money.

REMEMBER

Don't stop scrutinizing stocks after you acquire them. You may make a great choice that gives you a great dividend, but that doesn't mean the stock will stay that way indefinitely. Monitor the company's progress for as long as it's in your portfolio by using resources such as www.bloomberg.com and www.stockhouse.com.

Examining changes in yield

Most people have no problem understanding yield when it comes to bank accounts. If a bank Guaranteed Investment Certificate (GIC) from the Bank of Montreal has an annual yield of 2.5 per cent, you can figure out that if $1,000 is deposited in it, a year later it will generate $1,025 (slightly more if you include compounding). The GIC's market value in this example is the same as the deposit amount: $1,000. That makes it easy to calculate.

REMEMBER

How about stocks? When you see a stock listed in the financial pages, the dividend yield is provided, along with the stock's price and annual dividend. The dividend yield in the financial pages is always calculated as if you bought the stock on that given day. Just keep in mind that based on supply and demand, stock prices change every business day (virtually every minute!) that the market's open, so the yield changes daily as well. So keep the following three things in mind when examining yield:

>> **The yield listed in the financial pages may not represent the yield you're receiving.** What if you bought stock in Smith Co. (see Table 4-1) a month ago at $20 per share? With an annual dividend of $1, you know your yield is 5 per cent. But what if today Smith Co. is selling for $40 per share? If you look in the financial pages, the yield quoted is 2.5 per cent. Gasp! Did the dividend get cut in half? No, not really. You're still getting 5 per cent because you bought the stock at $20 rather than the current $40 price; the quoted yield is for investors who purchase Smith Co. *today*. They pay $40 and get the $1 dividend, and they're locked into the current yield of 2.5 per cent. Although Smith Co. may have been a good income investment for you a month ago, it's not such a hot pick today (from a yield lens) because the price of the stock has doubled, cutting the yield in half. Even though the dividend hasn't changed, the yield has changed dramatically because of the stock price change.

>> **Stock price affects how good of an investment the stock may be.** Another way to look at yield is by looking at the investment amount. Using Smith Co. in Table 4-1 as the example, the investor who bought, say, 100 shares of Smith Co. when they were $20 per share only paid $2,000 (100 shares × $20 — leave out commissions to make the example simple). If the same stock is purchased later at $40 per share, the total investment amount is $4,000 (100 shares × $40). In either case, the investor gets a total dividend income of $100 (100 shares × $1 dividend per share). Which investment is yielding more — the $2,000 investment or the $4,000 investment? Of course, it's better to get the income ($100 in this case) with the smaller investment amount of $2,000 (a 5 per cent yield is better than a 2.5 per cent yield).

>> **The dividend amount itself might change, even if the stock price remains the same.**

Comparing yield between different stocks

All things being equal, choosing Smith Co. or Jones Co. is a coin toss. It's looking at your situation and each company's fundamentals and prospects that will sway you. What if Smith Co. is an auto stock (like General Motors) and Jones Co. is a Canadian utility serving the Vancouver metro area? Now what? During any of the past few recessions, the North American automotive industry struggled tremendously, but utilities in both Canada and the U.S. were generally in much better shape. In that scenario, Smith Co.'s dividend is in jeopardy, whereas Jones Co.'s dividend is more secure. Another issue is the payout ratio (see the next section). Therefore, companies whose dividends have the same yield may still have different risks.

Looking at a stock's payout ratio

REMEMBER

You can use the payout ratio to figure out what percentage of a company's earnings is being paid out in the form of dividends (earnings = sales – expenses). Keep in mind that companies pay dividends from their net (i.e., after-tax) earnings. Therefore, the company's earnings should always be higher than the dividends the company pays out. Here's how to figure a payout ratio:

Dividend (per share) ÷ Earnings (per share) = Payout ratio

Say that the company CashFlow Now, Inc. (CFN), has annual earnings (or net income) of $1 million. Total dividends are to be paid out of $500,000, and the company has 1 million outstanding shares. Using those numbers, you know that CFN's earnings per share (EPS) is $1 ($1 million in earnings ÷ 1 million shares) and that it pays an annual dividend of 50 cents per share ($500,000 ÷ 1 million shares). The dividend payout ratio is 50 per cent (the 50-cent dividend is 50 per cent of the $1 EPS). This number is a healthy dividend payout ratio because even if CFN's earnings fall by 10 per cent or 20 per cent, plenty of room still exists to pay dividends.

TIP

If you're concerned about your dividend income's safety, watch the payout ratio. The maximum acceptable payout ratio should be 80 per cent, and a good range is 50 to 70 per cent. A payout ratio of 60 per cent or lower is considered very safe (the lower the percentage, the safer the dividend).

REMEMBER

When a company suffers significant financial difficulties, its ability to pay dividends is compromised. Good examples of stocks that have had their dividends cut in recent years due to financial difficulties are Canadian oil industry companies, although the price of oil has begun to rebound, and the fortunes of oil and other resource extraction companies may soon improve. So if you need dividend income to help you pay your bills, be aware of the dividend payout ratio.

Studying a company's bond rating

Bond rating? Huh? What's that got to do with dividend-paying stocks? Actually, a company's bond rating is very important to income stock investors. The bond rating offers insight into the company's financial strength. Bonds get rated for quality for the same reasons that consumer agencies rate products like cars or toasters. Standard & Poor's (S&P) is the world's major independent rating agency that looks into bond issuers. S&P looks at the bond issuer and asks, "Does this bond issuer have the financial strength to pay back the bond and the interest as stipulated in the bond indenture?" S&P (www.standardandpoors.com) and similar bond rating agencies like the Canadian-rooted DBRS (http://dbrs.com) are there to help.

To understand why this rating is important, consider the following:

>> **A good bond rating means that the company is strong enough to pay its obligations.** These obligations include expenses, payments on debts, and declared dividends. If a bond rating agency gives the company a high rating (or if it raises the rating), that's a great sign for anyone holding the company's debt or receiving dividends.

>> **If a bond rating agency lowers the rating, that means the company's financial strength is deteriorating.** This is a red flag for anyone who owns the company's bonds or stock. A lower bond rating today may mean trouble for the dividend later on.

>> **A poor bond rating means that the company is having difficulty paying its obligations.** If the company can't pay all its obligations, it has to choose which ones to pay. More often, a financially troubled company chooses to cut dividends or (worst-case scenario) not pay dividends at all.

The highest rating issued by S&P is AAA. The grades AAA, AA, and A are considered investment grade, or of high quality. Bs and Cs indicate a poor grade, and anything lower than that is considered very risky (the bonds are referred to as junk bonds).

Just because a bond rating company issues a rating does not mean that the rating is accurate. It is strictly an estimate. Look no further than all of those banks and other public companies that went under during the financial crisis a decade or so ago. Very few had a rating worse than BB! Right.

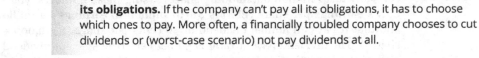

Why do bond rating agencies get it wrong from time to time? Sometimes, it's because the company that an agency evaluates doesn't give the agency complete, relevant, and accurate information from which it can formulate a fair rating. Also, external influences such as the state of the Canadian housing or oil and gas markets weigh heavily on a bond rating but are difficult for the agency to fully assess. In the worst-case scenario, a company may try to unduly influence a bond rating agency in order to get a better rating. Because a company can select and pay a rating agency, you can see how opinion shopping for a favourable rating may become a very real risk.

Diversifying your stocks

REMEMBER

If most of your dividend income is from stock in a single company or single industry, consider reallocating your investment to avoid having all your eggs in one basket. Concerns about diversification apply to income stocks as well as growth stocks. If all your income stocks are in the Canadian electric utility industry, then any problems in that industry are potential problems for your portfolio as well.

Exploring Some Typical Income Stocks

Although virtually every industry has stocks that pay dividends, some industries have more dividend-paying stocks than others. You won't find too many dividend-paying income stocks in the computer or biotech industries, for instance. The reason is that these types of companies need a lot of money to finance expensive research and development (R&D) projects to create new products. Without R&D, the company can't create new products to fuel sales, growth, and future earnings. Computer, biotech, and other innovative industries are better for growth investors. Keep reading for the scoop on stocks that work well for income investors.

Utilities

Utilities generate a large cash flow. (If you don't believe this statement, look at your gas, water, and electric bills!) Cash flow includes money from income (sales of products and/or services) and other items (such as the selling of assets, for example). This cash flow is needed to cover expenses, loan payments, and dividends. Utilities are considered the most common type of income stocks, and many investors have at least one utility company in their portfolio. Investing in your own local utility isn't a bad idea — at least it makes paying the utility bill less painful. Examples of Canadian utility companies are TransAlta (TA) and Fortis (FTS), which both trade on the TSX and pay dividends.

REMEMBER

Before you invest in a public utility, consider the following:

>> **The utility company's financial condition:** Is the company making money, and are its sales and earnings growing from year to year? Make sure the utility's bonds are rated A or higher (bond ratings are covered in the earlier section "Studying a company's bond rating").

>> **The company's dividend payout ratio:** Because utilities tend to have a good cash flow, don't be too concerned if the ratio reaches 70 per cent. From a stability and safety point of view, however, the lower the rate, the better. See the earlier section "Looking at a stock's payout ratio" for more on payout ratios.

>> **The company's geographic location:** If the utility covers an area that's doing well and offers an increasing population base and business expansion, that bodes well for your stock. Good resources for researching population and business data are Statistics Canada (www.statcan.gc.ca) and the U.S. Census Bureau (www.census.gov).

TIP

The utility sector is not alone in having many dividend-paying stocks. Also check out the stocks of large companies participating in sectors such as finance (like banks and insurance companies), pipelines, basic materials (for example, chemicals, aluminum, gold, and steel), services (airlines, media, entertainment, travel, and accommodation), consumer goods (food, automobile, and healthcare products), and industrial goods.

Real estate investment trusts (REITs)

Real estate investment trusts (REITs) are a special breed of stock. A REIT is an investment that has elements of both a stock and a mutual fund (a pool of money received from investors that's managed by an investment company; see Book 3).

>> A REIT resembles a stock in that it's a company whose stock is publicly traded on the major stock exchanges, and it has the usual features that you expect from a stock — it can be bought and sold easily through a Canadian broker, income is given to investors as a dividend distribution, and so on.

>> A REIT resembles an exchange traded fund (ETF) or mutual fund in that it doesn't make its money selling goods and services; it makes its money by buying, selling, and managing an investment portfolio of real estate investments. It generates revenue from rents and property leases, as any landlord does. Also, some REITs own mortgages and gain income from the interest.

TECHNICAL STUFF

A Canadian unitholder of a Canadian REIT typically receives a distribution on a quarterly or monthly basis, depending on the REIT. The Canadian Income Tax Act allows the distribution to represent some combination of income, capital gain, or return of capital.

As a REIT unitholder, you are subject to the appropriate tax on the income and capital gain parts of the distribution, unless you hold the REIT in a tax-exempt vehicle such as a Registered Retirement Savings Plan (RRSP). You will get a T3 slip for Canada Revenue Agency tax filing purposes either from your broker or directly from the REIT. The slip shows how much is income, how much is a capital gain, and so on. You may also be interested to know that the taxable income that flows to unitholders reduces the taxable income of the REIT. In other words, REITs are typically exempt from tax at the trust (company) level as long they distribute at least 90 per cent of their income to their Canadian unitholders. But even REITs that stick to this tax law are still exposed to corporate taxation on retained income.

If you invest in U.S. REITs, you should consult a tax advisor to figure out the exact tax implications of investing in a foreign REIT, because the tax rules and trust rules are different in each country. In general, however, U.S. and Canadian REITs are themselves exempt from corporate taxes as long as they meet certain criteria, such as dispensing almost all of their net income to unitholders. This provision is the reason why REITs generally issue generous dividends or distributions. Beyond this status, REITs are, in a practical sense, like any other publicly traded company. You can find REITs listed on the Toronto Stock Exchange.

The main advantages to investing in REITs include the following:

» Unlike other types of real estate investing, REITs are easy to buy and sell. In other words, they are liquid. You can buy a REIT through your online broker, just as you can to purchase any stock.

» REITs have higher-than-average yields. Because they must distribute a very high percentage of their income to unitholders, their dividends usually yield a return of 4 to 13 per cent.

» REITs involve a lower risk than the direct purchase of real estate because they use a portfolio approach diversified among many properties. Because you're investing in a company that buys the real estate, you don't have to worry about managing the properties — the company's management does that on a full-time basis. Usually, the REIT doesn't just manage one property; it's diversified in a portfolio of different properties.

» Investing in a REIT is affordable for small Canadian investors. REIT shares usually trade in the $10 to $40 range, meaning that you can invest with very little money.

WARNING

REITs do have disadvantages. Although they tend to be diversified with various properties, they're still susceptible to risks tied to the general real estate sector. Real estate investing in the U.S. and Canada has again reached lofty and in many cases record-high levels recently, which means that a downturn may be imminent. In Canada, especially in Vancouver and Toronto, real estate prices are near record highs. Whenever you invest in an asset (like real estate or REITs in recent years) that has already skyrocketed due to artificial stimulants (in the case of real estate, very low interest rates and too much credit and debt, as well as, in some cases, foreign capital inflows), the potential losses can offset any potential (unrealized) income. Also, if interest rates rise, watch for REITs to be pressured downward because real estate companies are often leveraged with debt.

TIP

When looking for a REIT, analyze it the way you'd analyze a property (see Book 7). Look at the location and type of property. If shopping malls are thriving in Edmonton, Toronto, and Winnipeg and your REIT buys and sells shopping malls in those areas, then you'll probably do well. On the other hand, the ongoing rise of online shopping may also threaten these types of REITs. Also, if your REIT invests in office buildings across the country and the office building market is overbuilt and having tough times, you'll have a tough time, too.

TIP

Choosing REITs with a view toward quality and strong fundamentals (location, potential rents, trends, and so forth) is still a good idea.

Royalty trusts

In recent years, the oil and gas sector has generated much interest as the whole sector boomed, then crashed, and is now recovering. Some income investors have capitalized on this price increase by investing in energy stocks called royalty trusts. Royalty trusts are companies that hold assets such as oil-rich and/or natural gas–rich land and generate high fees from companies that seek access to these properties for exploration. The fees paid to the royalty trusts are then disbursed as high dividends to their shareholders. During the early part of this decade, royalty trusts sported yields in the 7 to 12 per cent range. More recently, the yields were much lower. However, with oil prices recovering, this is an equity investment worth, um, exploring.

WARNING

Although energy has been a hot field in recent years and royalty trusts have done well, keep in mind that their payout ratios are very high (often in the 90 to 100 per cent range), so dividends will suffer if their cash flow shrinks. (Payout ratios are discussed in detail earlier in this chapter.)

Chapter **5**

Using Accounting Basics to Choose Winning Stocks

Too often, the only number investors look at when they look at a stock is the stock price quote. Yet what really drives the stock price is the company behind that single number. To make a truly good choice in the world of stocks, you have to consider the company's essential financial information. What does it take to see these important numbers?

This book and a little work on your part are all you need to succeed. This chapter takes the mystery out of the numbers behind the stock. The most tried-and-true method for picking a good stock starts with picking a good company. Picking a company means looking at its products, services, industry, and financial strength. Considering the problems that the market has witnessed in recent years — such as corporate debt problems and derivative meltdowns wreaking havoc on public companies and financial firms around the world — this chapter is more important than ever. Don't underestimate it. Because accounting is the language of business, understanding the basics behind the numbers can save your portfolio.

Recognizing Value When You See It

If you pick a stock based on the value of the underlying company that issues it, you're a value investor — an investor who looks at a company's value to judge whether you can purchase the stock at a good price. Companies have value the same way many things have value, such as eggs or elephant-foot umbrella stands. And there's a fair price to buy them at, too. Take eggs, for example. You can eat them and have a tasty treat while getting nutrition as well. But would you buy an egg for $1,000 (and no, you're not a starving millionaire on a deserted island)? Of course not. But what if you could buy an egg for 5 cents? At that point, it has value and a good price. This kind of deal is a value investor's dream.

Value investors analyze a company's fundamentals (earnings, assets, and so on) to see whether the information justifies purchasing the stock. They see whether the stock price is low relative to these verifiable, quantifiable factors. Therefore, value investors use fundamental analysis, whereas other investors may use technical analysis. Technical analysis looks at stock charts and statistical data, such as trading volume and historical stock prices. Some investors use a combination of both strategies.

History has shown that the most successful long-term investors have typically been value investors using fundamental analysis as their primary investing approach. The most consistently successful long-term investors were — and are — predominately value investors. The following sections describe different kinds of value and explain how to spot a company's value in several places.

Understanding different types of value

Value may seem like a murky or subjective term, but it's the essence of good stockpicking. You can measure value in different ways (as you discover in the following sections), so you need to know the differences and understand the impact that value has on your investment decisions.

Market value

REMEMBER

When you hear someone quoting a stock at $47 per share, that price reflects the stock's market value. The total market valuation of a company's stock is also referred to as its market cap or market capitalization. How do you determine a company's market cap? With the following simple formula:

Market capitalization = Share price × Number of shares outstanding

If Canuck Corp.'s stock is $35 per share and it has 10 million shares outstanding (or shares available for purchase), its market cap is $350 million. Granted,

$350 million may sound like a lot of money, but Canuck Corp. is considered a small market capitalization stock, or "small cap" stock.

Who sets the market value of stock? The market, of course! Millions of investors buying and selling directly and through intermediaries such as mutual funds determine the market value of any particular stock. If the market perceives that the company is desirable, investor demand for the company's stock pushes up the share price.

WARNING

The problem with market valuation is that it's not always a good indicator of a good investment. In recent years, plenty of companies have had astronomical market values, yet they've proven to be very risky investments. For example, think about Valeant Pharmaceuticals of Montreal, which for a brief period was the largest company on the TSX in terms of market capitalization. Shares of Valeant reached a peak of $335 in July 2015. Then things went south. A catastrophic combination of controversial drug price hikes and an alleged multimillion-dollar kickback scheme caused those shares to tumble to as low as $12.75. It has since recovered a bit, but the damage to the company's reputation still places pressure on the stock price today. In fact, the company has since changed its name to Bausch Health Companies to cosmetically distance itself from its troubled past. Because market value is a direct result of the buying and selling of stock investors, it can be a fleeting thing. This precariousness is why investors must understand the company behind the stock price.

Book value and intrinsic value

Book value (also referred to as accounting value) looks at a company from a balance sheet perspective (assets – liabilities = net worth, or stockholders' equity). It's a way of judging a firm by its net worth to see whether the stock's market value is reasonable compared to the company's intrinsic value. *Intrinsic* value is tied to what the market price of a company's assets — both tangible (such as equipment) and intangible (such as patents) — would be if sold.

Generally, market value tends to be higher than book value. However, If market value is substantially higher, the value investor becomes more reluctant to buy that particular stock — it may be overvalued. The closer the stock's market capitalization is to the book value, the safer the investment, if the company is well-run.

WARNING

Be cautious with a stock whose market value is more than twice its book value. If the market value is $1 billion or more and the book value is $500 million or less, that's a good indicator that the business may be overvalued, or valued at a higher price than its book value and ability to generate a profit. Just understand that the farther the market value is from the company's book value, the more you'll pay for the company's real potential value. And the more you pay, the greater the risk that the company's market value (the stock price, that is) can decrease.

Sales value and earnings value

A company's intrinsic value is directly tied to its ability to make money. For this reason, many analysts like to value stocks from the perspective of the company's income statement. Two common and very important barometers of value are expressed in ratios: the price-to-sales ratio (P/S) and the price-to-earnings (P/E) ratio. In both instances, the price is a reference to the company's market value (as reflected in its share price), while sales and earnings are references to the firm's ability to make money. These two ratios are covered more fully in the later section "Tooling around with ratios."

REMEMBER

For investors, the general approach is clear. The closer the market value is to the company's intrinsic value, the better. And, of course, if the market value is lower than the company's intrinsic value, you have a potential bargain worthy of a closer look. Part of looking closer means examining the company's income statement (which is discussed later in this chapter), also called the profit and loss statement, income statement, or simply the P&L. A low price-to-sales ratio is 1 or below (say, for example, 0.7), a medium P/S is between 1 and 2, and a high P/S is 3 or higher.

Putting the pieces together

When you look at a company from a value-oriented perspective, here are some of the most important items to consider (see the later section "Accounting for Value" for more information):

>> **The balance sheet, to figure out the company's net worth:** A value investor doesn't buy a company's stock because it's "cheap," but because it's *undervalued* (the company is worth more than the price its stock reflects — its market value is as close as possible to its book value).

>> **The income statement, to figure out the company's profitability:** A company may be undervalued from a simple comparison of the book value and the market value, but that doesn't mean it's a screaming buy. For example, what if you find out that a company is in trouble and losing money this year? Do you buy its stock then? No, you don't. Why invest in the stock of a losing company? (If you do, you aren't investing — you're gambling or speculating.) The heart of a firm's value, besides its net worth, is its ability to generate profit and cash.

>> **Ratios that let you analyze just how well (or not so well) the company is doing:** Value investors basically look for a bargain. That being the case, they generally don't look at companies that everyone is talking about, because by that point, the stock of those companies ceases to be a bargain. The value

investor searches for a stock that will eventually be discovered by the market and then watches as the stock price goes up. But before you bother digging into the fundamentals to find that bargain stock, first make sure that the company is making money.

The more ways that you can look at a company and see value, the better:

>> **Examine the P/E ratio.** One of the first things to look at is the P/E ratio. Does the company have one? (This question may sound dumb, but if the company's losing money, it may not have one.) Does the P/E ratio look reasonable, or is it in triple-digit, nosebleed territory?

>> **Check out the debt load.** Next, look at the company's debt load (the total amount of liabilities). Is it less than the company's equity? Are sales healthy and increasing from the prior year? Does the firm compare favourably in these categories versus other companies in the same industry? This is a critical piece of information because in today's unforgiving economy, high debt loads can quickly destroy a company.

TIP

>> **Think in terms of tens.** There's beauty in simplicity. You'll notice that the number ten comes up frequently as this chapter measures a company's performance, juxtaposing all the numbers you need to be aware of. If net income is rising by 10 per cent or more, that's fine. If the company is in the top 10 per cent of its industry, that's great. If the industry is growing by 10 per cent or better (sales and so on), that's terrific. If sales are up 10 per cent or more this year, that's wonderful. A great company doesn't have to have all these things going for it, but it should have as many of these things happening as possible to ensure greater potential success.

Does every company/industry have to neatly fit these criteria? No, of course not. But it doesn't hurt you to be as picky as possible. You need to find only a handful of stocks from thousands of choices.

TIP

Value investors can find thousands of companies that have value, but they can probably buy only a handful at a truly good price. The number of stocks that can be bought at a good price is relative to the market. In mature bull markets (ones in a prolonged period of rising prices), a good price is hard to find; most stocks have probably seen significant price increases, but in bear markets (markets in a prolonged period of falling prices), good companies at bargain prices are easier to come by and represent great stock investing opportunities.

Accounting for Value

Profit is to a company what oxygen is to a human. Without profit, a company can't survive, much less thrive. Without profit, it can't provide jobs, pay taxes, or invest in new products, equipment, or innovation. Without profit, it eventually goes bankrupt, and the price of its stock plummets toward zero.

In the heady days leading up to both of the last two bear markets, many investors lost a lot of money simply because they invested in stocks of companies that weren't making a profit. Lots of public companies ended up like bugs that just didn't see the windshield coming their way. Companies such as Nortel and Lehman Brothers entered the graveyard of rather-be-forgotten stocks. Research In Motion, now called BlackBerry, escaped the graveyard but still superficially changed its name in a move designed to escape its mistake-ridden past. Stock investors as a group lost trillions of dollars investing in glitzy or derivative-fuelled companies that sounded good but weren't making money. When their brokers were saying, "buy, buy, buy," their hard-earned money was saying, "bye, bye, bye!" What were they thinking?

Stock investors need to pick up some rudimentary knowledge of accounting to round out their stock-picking prowess and to be sure that they're getting a good value for their investment dollars. As mentioned earlier, accounting is the language of business. If you don't understand basic accounting, you'll have difficulty being a successful investor. Investing without accounting knowledge is like travelling without a map. However, if you can run a household budget, using accounting analysis to evaluate stocks is easier than you think, as you find out in the following sections.

TIP

Finding the relevant financial data on a company isn't difficult in the age of information and 24-hour Internet access. Websites such as www.nasdaq.com and www.sedar.com can give you the most recent balance sheets and income statements of most public companies. You can find out more about public information and company research in Chapter 1 of Book 2.

Breaking down the balance sheet

REMEMBER

A company's balance sheet gives you a financial snapshot of what the company looks like in terms of the following equation:

Assets – liabilities = Net worth (or net equity)

The following sections list questions that a balance sheet can answer and explain how to use it to judge a company's strength over time.

Answering a few balance sheet questions

Analyze the following items that you find on the balance sheet:

>> **Total assets:** Have they increased from the prior year? If not, was it because of the sale of an asset or a write-off (uncollectable accounts receivable, for example)?

>> **Financial assets:** In recent years, many companies (especially U.S. banks and some Canadian resource companies) had questionable financial assets (such as subprime mortgages and heavy debt loads) that went bad, and they had to write them off as unrecoverable losses or sell large assets to meet debt repayment obligations. Does the company you're analyzing have a large exposure to financial assets that are low-quality (and hence, risky) debt?

>> **Inventory:** Is inventory higher or lower than last year? If sales are flat but inventory is growing, that may be a problem, perhaps caused by obsolete inventory.

>> **Debt:** Debt may be the biggest weakness on the corporate balance sheet. Make sure that debt isn't a growing item and that it's under control. In recent years, debt has become a huge problem.

>> **Derivatives:** A *derivative* is a speculative and complex financial instrument that doesn't constitute direct ownership of an asset (such as a stock, bond, or commodity) but, in the case of equity derivatives, is a promise to convey ownership. Some derivatives are quite acceptable because they're used as protective or hedging vehicles. But they're frequently used to generate income and can then carry risks that can increase liabilities. Standard options and futures are examples of equity-oriented derivatives on a regulated exchange, but these types of derivatives are a different animal and in a less regulated part of the financial world. Some economists estimate that the worldwide derivatives market is more than ten times total world gross domestic product. The number or notional value often mentioned is one *quadrillion,* or 1,000 times one trillion dollars. These stratospheric numbers can easily devastate a company, sector, or market (as the credit crisis and Great Recession of over a decade ago showed).

Find out whether the company dabbles in these complicated, dicey, leveraged financial instruments. Find out (from the company's regulatory filings in SEDAR or EDGAR) whether it has derivatives and, if so, the total amount. Having derivatives that are valued higher than the company's net equity may cause tremendous problems. Derivatives problems sank many, ranging from stodgy banks (Barings Bank of England) to affluent counties (Orange County, California) to once-respected hedge funds (LTCM) to corporations (Lehman Brothers).

>> **Equity:** Equity is the company's net worth (what's left in the event that all the assets are used to pay off all the company debts). The stockholders' equity should be increasing steadily by at least 10 per cent per year which, in turn, usually reflects increasing retained earnings (as opposed to new equity issuance). If not, find out why.

Table 5-1 shows you a brief example of a balance sheet.

TABLE 5-1

XYZ Balance Sheet — December 31, 2020

Assets (What the Company Owns)	Amount
1. Cash and inventory	$5,000
2. Equipment and other assets	$7,000
3. TOTAL ASSETS (Item 1 + Item 2)	$12,000
Liabilities (What the Company Owes)	Amount
4. Short-term debt	$1,500
5. Other debt	$2,500
6. TOTAL LIABILITIES (Item 4 + Item 5)	$4,000
7. NET EQUITY (Item 3 – Item 6)	$8,000

By looking at a company's balance sheet, you can address the following questions:

>> **What does the company own (assets)?** The company can own assets, which can be financial, tangible, and/or intangible. An asset is anything that has value or that can be converted to or sold for cash. Financial assets can be cash, investments (such as stocks or bonds of other companies), or accounts receivable. Assets can be tangible items such as inventory, equipment, or buildings. They can also be intangible things such as licences, patents, trademarks, or copyrights. For example, companies like Facebook and Alphabet (which is better known as Google and includes its other subsidiaries) are not just enormous "cash asset" generators — they also have tremendously valuable patent, licence, and other intangible or intellectual property "assets."

>> **What does the company owe (liabilities)?** A liability is anything of value that the company must ultimately pay someone else for. Liabilities can be invoices (accounts payable) or short-term or long-term debt. Watch liabilities carefully when you study financial statements. If they are growing quickly when other parts of the business, such as sales, are not doing well or keeping pace, this may spell trouble.

>> **What is the company's net equity (net worth)?** After you subtract the liabilities from the assets, the remainder is called net worth, net equity, or net stockholders' equity. This number is critical when calculating a company's book value.

Assessing a company's financial strength over time

The logic behind the assets/liabilities relationship of a company is the same as that of your own household. When you look at a snapshot of your own finances (your personal balance sheet), how can you tell whether you're doing well? Odds are that you start by comparing some numbers. If your net worth is $5,000, you may say, "That's great!" But a more appropriate remark is something like, "That's great compared to, say, a year ago."

TIP

Compare a company's balance sheet at a recent point in time to a past time. You should do this comparative analysis with all the key items on the balance sheet, which are listed in the preceding section, to see the company's progress (or lack thereof). Is it growing its assets and/or shrinking its debt? Most important, is the company's net worth growing? Has it grown by at least 10 per cent since a year ago? All too often, Canadian investors stop doing their homework after they make an initial investment. You should continue to look at the firm's numbers regularly so that you can be ahead of the curve. If the business starts having problems, you can get out before the rest of the market starts getting out (which causes the stock price to fall).

REMEMBER

To judge the financial strength of a company, ask the following questions:

>> **Are the company's assets greater in value than they were three months ago, a year ago, or two years ago?** Compare today's asset size to the most recent two years to make sure that the company is growing in size and financial strength.

>> **How do the individual items compare with prior periods?** Some particular assets that you want to take note of are cash, inventory, and accounts receivable.

>> **Are liabilities such as accounts payable and debt about the same, lower, or higher compared to prior periods? Are they growing at a similar, faster, or slower rate than the company's assets?** Debt that rises faster and higher than items on the other side of the balance sheet is a key warning sign of potential financial problems.

>> **Is the company's net worth or equity greater than the preceding year? And is that year's equity greater than the year before?** In a healthy company, the net worth is constantly rising. As a general rule, in good economic times, net worth should be at least 10 per cent higher than the preceding year. In tough economic times (such as a recession), 5 per cent is acceptable. Seeing the net worth grow at a rate of 15 per cent or higher is great. Don't lose sight of this important financial indicator.

TIP

When evaluating a stock, look under the management discussion and analysis (MD&A) section of the annual report for discussion about commitments, contingencies, and pledged assets. Determine roughly how big the potential impact can be if some of these commitments turn into reality.

WARNING

Whenever the economy goes into a period of recession, many Canadian and U.S. companies will suffer losses. This typically qualifies them for tax credits to be received in a future tax period. Many companies will recognize this as a special item (revenue) on the income statement in the current year to boost the bottom line. A tax asset is also booked on the balance sheet. Invariably, after a year or so, window dressers make the tax asset (tax credit receivable) disappear — the company reevaluates the likelihood of actually qualifying for the credit and determines that it stands no chance of collecting from the Canada Revenue Agency (CRA) or Uncle Sam. The tax asset gets written off, a special charge is created (in the year a company would prefer to see a charge), and the investor is left with even more distorted financial statements.

WARNING

Many, if not most, public companies have pension plans for employees, and corresponding obligations to adequately fund those plans. If there's any deficiency in the amount that's contributed to the plan, the company ultimately has to fund the shortfall. Cash infusions dig into the company's cash balances and can potentially impair its ability to do the things it wants to. During any challenging economic period, this becomes an important issue. Many companies will fail to adjust downward the assumptions underpinning their pension plans, such as the returns the plan's investments will generate in upcoming years. Some pension plans are still based on assumptions that their investment funds will grow at 7 per cent or more, when in fact future forecasted returns are expected to be lower.

Looking at the income statement

REMEMBER

Where do you look if you want to find out what a company's profit is? Check out the firm's income statement. It reports, in detail, a simple accounting equation that you probably already know:

Sales – expenses = Net profit (or net earnings, or net income)

Look at the following figures found on the income statement:

>> **Sales:** Are they increasing? If not, why not? By what percentage are sales increasing? Preferably, they should be 10 per cent higher than the year before. Sales are, after all, where the money comes from to pay for all the company's activities (such as expenses) and create subsequent profits.

>> **Expenses:** Do you see any unusual items? Are total expenses reported higher than the prior year, and if so, by how much? If the total is significantly higher, why? A company with large, rising expenses will see profits suffer, which isn't good for the stock price.

>> **Research and development (R&D):** How much is the company spending on R&D? Companies that rely on new product development (such as pharmaceuticals or biotech firms) should spend at least as much as they did the year before (preferably more) because new products mean future earnings and growth.

>> **Earnings:** This figure reflects the bottom line. Are total earnings higher than the year before? How about earnings from operations (leaving out expenses such as taxes and interest)? The earnings section is the heart and soul of the income statement and of the company itself. Out of all the numbers in the financial statements, earnings have the greatest single impact on the company's stock price.

Table 5-2 shows you a brief example of an income statement.

TABLE 5-2

XYZ Income Statement for Year Ending 12/31/2020

Total Sales (or Revenue)	Amount
1. Sales of products	$11,000
2. Sales of services	$3,000
3. TOTAL SALES (Item 1 + Item 2)	$14,000
Expenses	**Amount**
4. Marketing and promotion	$2,000
5. Payroll costs	$9,000
6. Other costs	$1,500
7. TOTAL EXPENSES (Item 4 + Item 5 + Item 6)	$12,500
8. NET INCOME (Item 3 – Item 7) (In this case, it's a net profit)	$1,500

Using Accounting Basics to Choose Winning Stocks

Looking at the income statement, investors can try to answer these questions:

>> **What sales did the company make?** Businesses sell products and services that generate revenue (known as sales or gross sales). Sales also are referred to as the *top line*.

>> **What expenses did the company incur?** In generating sales, companies pay expenses, like payroll, utilities, advertising, and administration.

>> **What is the net profit?** Also called net earnings or net income, net profit is the bottom line. After paying for all expenses, what profit did the company make?

The information you glean should give you a strong idea about a firm's current financial strength and whether it's successfully increasing sales, holding down expenses, and ultimately maintaining profitability. You can find out more about sales, expenses, and profits in the sections that follow.

Sales

Sales refers to the money that a company receives as customers buy its goods or services. It's a simple item on the income statement and a useful number to look at. Analyzing a business by looking at its sales is called top line analysis.

REMEMBER

Investors should take into consideration the following points about sales:

>> **Sales should be increasing.** A healthy, growing company has growing sales. They should grow at least 10 per cent from the prior year, and you should look at the most recent three years. The extent to which sales increase from quarter to quarter greatly influences a stock's price movement, one way or another.

>> **Core sales (sales of those goods or services that the company specializes in) should be increasing.** Frequently, the sales figure has a lot of stuff lumped into it. Maybe the company sells widgets (what the heck is a widget, anyway?), but the core sales shouldn't include other things, such as the sale of a building or other one-time or unusual items. Take a close look. Isolate the firm's primary and regular offerings and ask whether these sales are growing at a reasonable rate (such as 10 per cent).

>> **Does the company have odd items or odd ways of calculating sales?** To this day and in the context of the still-low-interest-rate environment, many companies boost their sales by aggressively offering affordable financing with easy repayment terms. Say you find out that Suspicious Sales Inc. (SSI) had annual sales of $50 million, reflecting a 25 per cent increase from the year before. Looks great! But what if you find out that $20 million of that sales number comes from sales made on credit that the company extended to

non-creditworthy buyers? Some companies that use this approach later have to write off losses as uncollectable debt because the customers ultimately can't pay for the goods.

TIP

If you want to get a good clue as to whether a company is artificially boosting sales, check its accounts receivable (listed in the asset section of its balance sheet). Accounts receivable refers to money that is owed to the company for goods that customers have purchased on credit. If you find out that sales went up by $10 million (great!) but accounts receivable went up by $20 million (uh-oh), something just isn't right. That may be a sign that the financing terms were too easy, and the company may have a problem collecting payment (especially in a recession).

Expenses

How much a company spends has a direct relationship to its profitability. If spending isn't controlled or held at a sustainable level, it may spell trouble for the business.

REMEMBER

When you look at a company's expense items, consider the following:

>> **Compare expense items to the prior period.** Are expenses higher than, lower than, or about the same as those from the prior period? If the difference is significant, you should see commensurate benefits elsewhere. In other words, if overall expenses are 10 per cent higher compared to the prior period, are sales *at least* 10 per cent more during the same period? If advertising expenses are up, did sales rise in a meaningful and predictable way?

>> **Are some expenses too high?** Look at the individual expense items. Are they significantly higher than the year before and as compared to industry peers? If so, why?

>> **Have any unusual items been expensed?** An unusual expense isn't necessarily a negative. Expenses may be higher than usual if a company writes off uncollectable accounts receivable as a bad debt expense. Doing so inflates the total expenses and subsequently results in lower earnings. Pay attention to nonrecurring charges that show up on the income statement, and determine whether they make sense.

Profit

Earnings, or profit, is the single most important item on the income statement. It's also the one that receives the most attention in the financial media. When a company makes a profit, it's usually reported as earnings per share (EPS). So if you hear that XYZ Corporation (yes, the infamous XYZ Corp.!) beat last quarter's earnings by a penny, here's how to translate that news. Suppose that the company made $1 per share this quarter and 99 cents per share last quarter. If that company had 100 million shares of stock outstanding, its profit this quarter is $100 million (the EPS times the number of shares outstanding), which is $1 million more than it made in the prior quarter ($1 million is 1 cent per share times 100 million shares).

TIP

Don't simply look at current earnings as an isolated figure. Always compare current earnings to earnings in past periods (usually a year). For example, if you're looking at a retailer's fourth-quarter results, don't compare them with the retailer's third-quarter outcome. Doing so is like comparing apples to oranges. What if the company usually does well during the December holidays but poorly in the fall? In that case, you don't get a fair comparison.

A strong company should show consistent earnings growth from the period before (the prior year or the same quarter from the prior year), and you should check the period before that, too, so that you can determine whether earnings are consistently rising over time. Earnings growth is an important barometer of the company's potential growth and bodes well for the stock price.

REMEMBER

When you look at earnings, here are some things to consider:

>> **Total earnings:** This item is the most watched. Total earnings should grow year to year by about 10 per cent and more.

>> **Operational earnings:** Break down the total earnings and look at a key subset — that portion of earnings derived from the company's core and regular activity. Is the company continuing to make money from its primary goods and services?

>> **Nonrecurring items:** Are earnings higher (or lower) than usual or than expected, and if so, why? Frequently, the difference results from irregularly occurring and atypical items such as the sale of an asset or a large depreciation write-off.

TIP

Keep percentages as simple as possible. Ten per cent is a good number because it's easy to calculate and it's a good benchmark. However, 5 per cent isn't unacceptable if you're talking about tough times, such as a recession. Obviously, if sales, earnings, and/or net worth are hitting or surpassing 15 per cent, that's great.

WARNING

Some retailers, and especially Internet e-tailers, use coupon promotions to promote higher sales volumes. That's fine. What is not fine is when companies engage in window dressing where they exclude the value (cost) of promotional giveaways when booking revenue. They have found a more dubious approach. Assume for a moment that someone buys a shirt for $30 and uses a $10 coupon to make the purchase. Under generally accepted accounting rules, just $20 of revenue ought to be booked. But some retailers would book $30 in revenue and charge the $10 in promotional costs to marketing expenses. The auditors should catch this, but tell that to Sino-Forest or Lehman Brothers investors who also relied on auditors. Such accounting voodoo may result in artificially higher sales and gross margin, better top-line comments from financial analysts, and inflated share price. Can you spell "distortion"?

WARNING

A company can turn a variety of what should be expenses into assets by depreciating capital assets (resources that last more than one year) more slowly than otherwise required under the principle of reasonableness (in other words, by easing it slowly into expenses). With certain types of costs incurred, management can judgmentally overestimate a period of useful benefit to longer than one year. That would let management justify recording part of it on the balance sheet (as an asset) instead of on the income statement (as an expense). This serves to artificially boost profits.

Tooling around with ratios

A ratio is a helpful numerical tool that you can use to find out the relationship between two or more figures found in a company's financial data. A ratio can add meaning to a number or put it in perspective. Ratios sound complicated, but they're easier to understand than you may think.

Say that you're considering a stock investment and the company you're looking at has earnings of $1 million this year. You may think that's a nice profit, but in order for this amount to be meaningful, you have to compare it to something. What if you find out that the other companies in the industry (of similar size and scope) had earnings of $500 million? Does that change your thinking? Or what if the same company had earnings of $75 million in the prior period? Does that change your mind?

Two key ratios to be aware of are

>> Price-to-earnings (P/E) ratio

>> Price-to-sales (P/S) ratio

TIP

Every investor wants to find stocks that have a 20 per cent average growth rate over the past five years and have a low P/E ratio (sounds like a dream). Use stock screening tools available for free on the Internet to do your research. A stock screening tool lets you plug in numbers, such as sales or earnings, and ratios, such as the P/E ratio or the debt to equity ratio, and then click! — up come stocks that fit your criteria. These tools are a good starting point for serious investors. Most Canadian brokers have them at their websites (such as TD Waterhouse at www.tdwaterhouse.ca and BMO InvestorLine www.bmo.com/investorline/). Some excellent stock screening tools can also be found at TMX (www.tmxmoney.com), Bloomberg (www.bloomberg.com), Nasdaq (www.nasdaq.com), and Market-Watch (www.marketwatch.com).

The P/E ratio

The price-to-earnings (P/E) ratio is very important in analyzing a potential stock investment because it's one of the most widely regarded barometers of a company's value, and it's usually reported along with the company's stock price in the financial page listing. The major significance of the P/E ratio is that it establishes a direct relationship between the bottom line of a company's operations — the earnings (or net profit) — and the stock price.

The P in P/E stands for the stock's current price. The E is for earnings per share (typically the most recent 12 months of earnings). The P/E ratio is also referred to as the earnings multiple or just multiple.

REMEMBER

You calculate the P/E ratio by dividing the price of the stock by the earnings per share. If the price of a single share of stock is $10 and the earnings (on a per-share basis) are $1, then the P/E is 10. If the stock price goes to $35 per share and the earnings are unchanged, then the P/E is 35. Basically, the higher the P/E, the more you pay for the company's earnings.

Why would you buy stock in one company with a relatively high P/E ratio instead of investing in another company with a lower P/E ratio? Investors buy stocks based on expectations. They may bid up the price of the stock (subsequently raising the stock's P/E ratio) because they feel that the company will have increased earnings in the near future. Perhaps they feel that the company has great potential (a pending new invention or lucrative business deal) that will eventually make it more profitable (think Tesla). More profitability in turn has a beneficial impact on the firm's stock price. The danger with a high P/E is that if the company doesn't achieve the hoped-for results, the stock price can fall.

TIP

Look at two P/E ratios to get a balanced picture of the company's value:

>> **Trailing P/E:** This P/E is the most frequently quoted because it deals with existing data. The trailing P/E uses the most recent 12 months of earnings in its calculation.

>> **Forward P/E:** This P/E is based on projections or expectations of earnings in the coming 12-month period. Although this P/E may seem preferable because it looks into the near future, it's still considered an estimate that may or may not prove to be accurate.

The following example illustrates the importance of the P/E ratio. Say that you want to buy a business and we're selling a business. You come to us and say, "What do you have to offer?" We say, "Have we got a deal for you! We operate a retail business downtown that sells spatulas. The business nets a cool $2,000 profit per year." You say, "Uh, okay, what's the asking price for the business?" We reply, "You can have it for only $1 million! What do you say?"

If you're sane, odds are that you politely turn down that offer. Even though the business is profitable (a cool $2,000 a year), you'd be crazy to pay a million bucks for it. In other words, the business is way overvalued (too expensive for what you're getting in return for your investment dollars). The million dollars would generate a better rate of return elsewhere and probably with less risk. As for the business, the P/E ratio of 500 ($1 million divided by $2,000) is outrageous — definitely an overvalued company, and a lousy investment.

What if we offered the business for $12,000? Does that price make more sense? Yes. The P/E ratio is a more reasonable 6 ($12,000 divided by $2,000). In other words, the business pays for itself in about 6 years (versus 500 years in the prior example).

REMEMBER

Looking at the P/E ratio offers a shortcut for investors asking the question, "Is this stock overvalued?" As a general rule, the lower the P/E, the safer (or more conservative) the stock is. The reverse is more noteworthy: The higher the P/E, the greater the risk.

REMEMBER

When someone refers to a P/E as high or low, you have to ask the question, "Compared to what?" A P/E of 30 is considered very high for a large cap electric utility but quite reasonable for a small cap, high-technology firm. Keep in mind that phrases such as large cap and small cap are just a reference to the company's market value or size. Cap is short for capitalization (the total number of shares of stock outstanding × the share price).

The following basic points can help you evaluate P/E ratios:

>> **Compare a company's P/E ratio with its industry.** Electric utility industry stocks, for example, generally have a P/E that hovers in the 9–14 range. So, an electric utility with a P/E of 45 indicates something is wrong with that utility.

>> **Compare a company's P/E with the general market.** If you're looking at a small cap stock on the Nasdaq that has a P/E of 100 but the average P/E for established companies on the Nasdaq is 40, find out why. You should also compare the stock's P/E ratio with the P/E ratio for major indexes such as the Dow Jones Industrial Average (DJIA), the Standard & Poor's 500 (S&P 500), the S&P/TSX Composite, and the Nasdaq Composite. Stock indexes are useful for getting the big picture.

>> **Compare a company's current P/E with recent periods** (such as this year versus last year). If it currently has a P/E ratio of 20 and it previously had a P/E ratio of 30, you know that either the stock price has declined or earnings have risen. In this case, the stock is less likely to fall. That bodes well for the stock.

>> **Low P/E ratios aren't necessarily a sign of a bargain,** but if you're looking at a stock for many other reasons that seem positive (solid sales, strong industry, and so on) and it also has a low P/E, that's a good sign.

>> **High P/E ratios aren't necessarily bad,** but they do mean that you should investigate further. If a company is weak and the industry is shaky, heed the high P/E as a warning sign. Often, a high P/E ratio means that investors have bid up a stock price, anticipating future income.

WARNING

>> **Watch out for a stock that doesn't have a P/E ratio.** In other words, it may have a price (the P), but it doesn't have earnings (the E). No earnings means no P/E, meaning that you're better off avoiding the stock. Can you still make money buying a stock with no earnings? You can, but you aren't investing; you're speculating (think Amazon in its early stages).

The P/S ratio

The price-to-sales (P/S) ratio is a company's stock price divided by its sales. Because the sales number is rarely expressed as a per-share figure, it's easier to divide a company's total market value (explained earlier in this chapter) by its total sales for the last 12 months.

TIP

As a general rule, a stock trading at a P/S ratio of 1 or less is a reasonably priced stock worthy of your attention. For example, say that a company has sales of $1 billion and the stock has a total market value of $950 million. In that case, the P/S is 0.95. In other words, you can buy $1 of the company's sales for only 95 cents. All things being equal, that stock may be a bargain.

Analysts use the P/S ratio as an evaluation tool in these circumstances:

>> In tandem with other ratios to get a more well-rounded picture of the company and the stock.

>> When they want an alternate way to value a business that doesn't have earnings (earnings are negative).

>> When they want a true picture of the company's financial health, because sales are tougher for companies to manipulate than earnings.

>> When they're considering a company offering products (versus services). The P/S ratio is more suitable for companies that sell items that are easily counted (such as products). Firms that make their money through loans, such as banks, aren't usually valued with a P/S ratio because deriving a usable P/S ratio for them is more difficult.

REMEMBER

Compare the company's P/S ratio with other companies in the same industry, with the industry average, to get a better idea of the company's relative value.

3 Investing in Mutual Funds

Contents at a Glance

Chapter **1**

What Is a Mutual Fund?

Unless you've been living in a cave high in the mountains for the past decade, railing against the evils of humankind, you've heard a lot about mutual funds. Chances are you or someone in your family already owns some. Mutual funds seem complicated — even though they are incredibly popular — so lots of people shy away. Many people aren't sure where to start, or they just buy the first fund their banker or financial planner suggests. All too often Canadians end up disappointed with their funds' performance, because they've been sold something that's either unsuitable or just too expensive. It's a shame, because building a portfolio of excellent funds is easy if you follow a few simple rules and use your own common sense. This stuff isn't complicated — a mutual fund is just a money-management service that operates under clear rules. Yes, it involves a lot of marketing mumbo-jumbo and arcane terminology, but the basic idea could be written on a postage stamp: In return for a fee, the people running the fund promise to invest your money wisely and give it back to you on demand.

The fund industry is competitive and sophisticated, which means plenty of good choices are out there. This chapter shows how funds make you money — especially if (only if!) you leave your investment in place for several years. It also touches on the different types available and describes the main places you can go to buy funds.

Beginning with Mutual Fund Basics

REMEMBER

A *mutual fund* is a pool of money that a company gets from investors like you and divides up into equally priced *units.* Each unit is a tiny slice of the fund. When you put money into the fund or take it out again, you either buy or sell units. For example, say a fund has *total assets* — that is, money held in trust for investors — of $10 million and investors have been sold a total of 1 million units. Then each unit is worth $10. If you put money into the fund, you're simply sold units at that day's value. If you take money out, the fund buys units back from you at the same price. (Handling purchase and sale transactions in units makes it far simpler to do the paperwork.) And the system has another huge advantage: As long as you know how many units you own, you can simply check their current price to find out how much your total investment is worth. For example, if you hold 475 units of a fund whose current unit price is $15.20, then you know your holding has a value of 475 times $15.20, or $7,220.

REMEMBER

Owning units of a mutual fund makes you — you guessed it — a *unitholder.* In fact, you and the other unitholders are the legal owners of the fund. But the fund is run by a company that's legally known as the *fund manager* — the firm that handles the investing and also deals with the fund's administration. The terminology gets confusing here because the person (usually an employee of the fund manager) who chooses which stocks, bonds, or other investments the fund should buy is also usually called the fund manager. To make things clear, this book refers to the company that sells and administers the fund as the *management company* or *fund sponsor.* The term *fund manager* is used for the person who picks the stocks and bonds. His or her skill is one of the main benefits you get from a mutual fund. Obviously, the fund manager should be experienced and not too reckless — after all, you're trusting him or her with your money.

Under professional management, the fund invests in stocks and bonds, increasing the pool of money for the investors and boosting the value of the individual units. For example, if you bought units at $10 each and the fund manager managed to pick investments that doubled in value, your units would grow to $20. In return, the management company slices off fees and expenses. (In the world of mutual funds, just like almost everywhere else, you don't get something for nothing.) Fees and expenses usually come to between 0.3 percent and 3 percent of the fund's assets each year, depending on how a fund invests. Some specialized funds charge much more.

Confused? Don't be; it isn't rocket science. This example should help. Suppose that units in a fund were bought from and sold to people like you at $21.83 each at the end of March. So if you invested $1,000 in the fund that day, you owned 45.8 units ($1,000 divided by $21.83). The price you pay for each unit is known as the fund's *net asset value* per unit. The net asset value is the fund's assets minus its liabilities, hence the "net" (which means after costs and debts are taken away), divided by the number of units outstanding.

So a fund company buys and sells the units to the public at their net asset value. This value increases or decreases proportionally as the value of the fund's investments rises or falls. Let's say in March you pay $10 each for 100 units in a fund that invests in oil and gas shares, always a smelly and risky game. Now, say, by July, the value of the shares the fund holds has dropped by one-fifth. Then your units are worth just $8 each. So your original $1,000 investment is now worth only $800. But that August, a bunch of companies in which the fund has invested strike oil in Alberta. That sends the value of their shares soaring and lifts the fund's units to $15 each. The value of your investment has now grown to $1,500.

Where can you go from here? You've made a tidy profit after a bit of a letdown, but what happens next? Well, that depends on you. You can hang in there and see if more oil's in them there hills, or you can cash out. With most funds, you can simply buy or sell units at that day's net asset value. That flexibility is one of the great beauties of mutual funds. Funds that let you come and go as you please in this way are known as *open-end funds,* as though they had a giant door that's never locked. Think of a raucous Viking banquet where guests are free to come and go at will because the wall at one end of the dining hall has been removed.

That means most mutual funds are marvelously flexible and convenient. The managers allow you to put money into the fund on any business day by buying units, and you take money out again at will by selling your units back to the fund. In other words, an investment in a mutual fund is a *liquid asset.* A liquid asset is either cash or it's an investment that can be sold and turned into good old cash at a moment's notice. The idea is that cash and close-to-cash investments, just like water, are adaptable and useful in all sorts of situations. The ability to get your cash back at any time is called *liquidity* in investment jargon, and professionals prize it above all else — more than they prize red Porsches with very loud sound systems or crystal goblets in lovely velvet-lined boxes with their initials engraved in gold.

WARNING

The other type of fund is a *closed-end fund.* Investors in these funds often are sold their units when the fund is launched, but to get their money back they must find another investor to buy the units on the stock market like a share, often at a loss. The fund usually won't buy the units back, or may buy only a portion. You can make money in closed-end funds, but it's very tricky. As craven brokerage analysts sometimes say when they hate a stock but can't pluck up the courage to tell investors to sell it: "Avoid."

The Nitty-Gritty: How a Fund Makes You Money

The following sections define returns when it comes to mutual funds, explain how funds make money for you, and describe what exactly a fund buys.

WARNING

With most companies' funds you're free to come and go as you please, but companies often impose a small levy on investors who sell their units within 90 days of buying them, a so-called "back-end load." That's because constant trading raises expenses for the other unitholders and makes the fund manager's job harder. The charge (which should go to the fund, and usually does) is generally 2 percent of the units sold, but it can be more. Check this out before you invest, especially if you're thinking of moving your cash around shortly after you buy.

Returns: What's in it for you?

REMEMBER

The main reason why people buy mutual funds is to earn a *return*. A return is simply the profit you get in exchange for either investing in a business (by buying its shares) or for lending money to a government or company (by buying its bonds). It's money you get as a reward for letting other people use your cash — and for putting your money at risk. Mutual fund buyers earn the same sorts of profits but they make them indirectly because they're using a fund manager to pick their investments for them. The fund itself earns the profits, which are either paid out to the unitholders or retained within the fund itself, increasing the value of each of its units.

When you invest money, you nearly always hope to get the following:

>> **Trading profits** or *capital gains* (the two mean nearly the same thing) when the value of your holdings goes up. Capital is just the money you've tied up in an investment, and a capital gain is simply an increase in its value. For example, say you buy gold bars at $100 each and their price rises to $150 each. You've earned a capital gain of $50, on paper at least.

>> **Income** in the form of interest on a bond or loan, or dividends from a company. *Interest* is the regular fee you get in return for lending your money, and *dividends* are a portion of a company's profits paid out to its shareowners. For example, say you deposit $1,000 at a bank at an annual interest rate of 5 percent; each year you'll get interest of $50 (or 5 percent of the money you deposited). Dividends are usually paid out by companies on a per-share basis. Say, for example, you own 10,000 shares and the company's directors decide to pay a dividend of 50 cents per share. You'll get a cheque for $5,000.

THE SOMEWHAT SLEAZY DAWN OF THE MUTUAL FUND

The modern mutual fund evolved in the 1920s in the United States. In 1924, one Edward Leffler started the world's first open-end fund, the Massachusetts Investors Trust. It's still going. Mr. Leffler's fund had to be purchased through a broker, who charged a sales commission, adding to an investor's cost. Four years later, Boston investment manager Scudder Stevens & Clark started First Investment Counsel Corp., the first no-load fund (a fund you buy with no sales commission). The fund was called no-load because instead of purchasing it through a commission-charging broker, investors bought it directly from the company.

Nothing was wrong with those early open-end funds. They were run well and they survived the Great Crash of 1929 and the subsequent Depression, in part because the obligation to buy and sell their shares every day at an accurate value tended to keep managers honest and competent. But closed-end funds were the main game in the 1920s. (Closed-end funds don't buy back your units on demand, meaning you're locked into the fund until you find another investor to buy your units from you on the open market.) And a crooked game it was. By 1929, investors were paying ridiculous prices for closed-end shares. Brokers charged piratical sales commissions of 10 percent, annual expenses topped 12.5 percent, and funds kept their holdings secret. Needless to say, most collapsed in the Crash and ensuing Depression.

Following that debacle, mutual funds in Canada and the United States were far more tightly regulated, with laws forcing them to disclose their holdings at least twice a year and report costs and fees to investors. Plenty of badly run funds are still out there, not to mention plenty of greedy managers who don't put their unitholders' interests first, but at least now clear rules that protect investors who keep their eyes open exist.

You also hope to get the money you originally invest back at the end of the day, which doesn't always happen. That's part of the risk you assume with almost any investment. Companies can lose money, sending the value of their shares tumbling. Or inflation can rise, which nearly always makes the value of both shares and bonds drop rapidly. That's because inflation eats away at the value of the money, which makes it less attractive to have the money tied up in such long-term investments where it's vulnerable to steady erosion.

Here's an example to illustrate the difference between earning capital gains and dividend income. Say you buy 100 shares of a company — a Costa Rican crocodile farm, for example — for $115 each and hold them for an entire year. Also, say you get $50 in dividend income during the year because the company has a policy of paying four quarterly dividends of 12.5 cents, or 50 cents per share, annually (that is, 50 cents times the 100 shares you own — $50 right into your pocket).

Now imagine the price of the stock rises in the open market by $12, from $115 to $127. The value of your 100 shares rises from $11,500 to $12,700, for a total capital gain of $1,200.

REMEMBER

Your capital gain is only on paper unless you actually sell your holdings at that price.

Add up your gains and income, and that's your total return — $50 in dividends plus a capital gain of $1,200, for a total of $1,250.

Returns as a percentage

Returns on mutual funds, and nearly all other investments, are usually expressed as a percentage of the capital the investor originally put up. That way you can easily compare returns and work out whether or not you did well.

After all, if you tied up $10 million in an investment to earn only $1,000, you wouldn't be using your cash very smartly. That's why the return on any investment is nearly always stated in percentages by expressing the return as a proportion of the original investment. In the example of the crocodile farm in the preceding section, the return was $50 in dividends plus $1,200 in *capital appreciation,* which is just a fancy term for an increase in the value of your capital, for a total of $1,250. At the beginning of the year you put $11,500 into the shares by buying 100 of them at $115 each. To get your *percentage return* (the amount your money grew expressed as a percentage of your initial investment), divide your total return by the amount you initially invested and then multiply the answer by 100. The return of $1,250 represented 10.9 percent of $11,500, so your percentage return during the year was 10.9 percent.

It's the return produced by an investment over several years, however, that people are usually interested in. Yes, it's often useful to look at the return in each individual year — for example, a loss of 10 percent in Year 1, a gain of 15 percent in Year 2, and so on. But that's a long-winded way of expressing things. It's handy to be able to state the return in just one number that represents the average yearly return over a set period. It makes it much easier, for instance, to compare the performance of two different funds. The math can start getting complex here, but don't worry — just stick to the basic method used by the fund industry.

Fund returns are expressed, in percentages, as an *average annual compound return.* That sounds like a mouthful, but the concept is simple. Say you invested $1,000 in a fund for three years. In the first year, the value of your investment dropped by

10 percent, or one-tenth, leaving you with $900. In Year 2, the fund earned you a return of 20 percent, leaving you with $1,080. And in Year 3, the fund produced a return of 10 percent, leaving you with $1,188. So, over the three years, you earned a total of $188, or 18.8 percent of your initial $1,000 investment. When mutual fund companies convert that return to an "average annual" number, they invariably express the number as a "compound" figure. That simply means the return in Year 2 is added (or compounded) onto the return in Year 1, and the return in Year 3 is then compounded onto the new higher total, and so on. A return of 18.8 percent over three years works out to an average annual compound return of about 5.9 percent. The average annual compound return is also known as the "geometric average" return.

As the example demonstrates, the actual value of the investment fluctuated over the three years, but say it actually grew steadily at 5.9 percent. After one year, the $1,000 would be worth $1,059. After two years, it would be worth $1,121.48. And after three years, it would be worth $1,187.65. The total differs from $1,188 by a few cents because we rounded off the average annual return to one decimal place, instead of fiddling around with hundredths of a percentage point.

REMEMBER

Keep these important points in mind when looking at an average annual compound return:

>> **Average:** That innocuous-looking average usually smoothes out some mighty rough periods. Mutual funds can easily lose money for years on end — it happened, for example, when the world economy was hurt by inflation and recession in the 1970s.

>> **Annual:** Obviously, this means per year. And mutual funds should be thought of as long-term holdings to be owned for several years. The general rule in the industry is that you shouldn't buy an equity fund — one that invests in shares — unless you plan to own it for five years. That's because stocks can drop sharply, often for a year or more, and you'd be silly to risk money you might need in the short term (to buy a house, say) in an investment that might be down from its purchase value when you go to cash it in. With money you'll need in the near future, you're better off to stick to a super-stable, short-term bond or money market fund that will lose little or no money (more about those later).

Of course, mutual fund companies sometimes use the old "long-term investing" mantra as an excuse. If their funds are down, they claim it's a long-term game and that investors should give their miraculous strategy time to work. But if the funds are up, the managers run ads screaming about the short-term returns.

>> **Compound:** This little word, which means "added" or "combined" in this context, is the plutonium trigger at the heart of investing. It's the device that

makes the whole thing go. It simply means that to really build your nest egg, you have to leave your profits or interest in place and working for you so you can start earning income on income. After a while, of course, you start earning income on the income you've earned, until it becomes a very nicely furnished hall of mirrors.

Another example will help. Mr. Simple and Ms. Compound each have $1,000 to invest, and the bank's offering 10 percent a year. Now, let's say Mr. Simple puts his money into the bank, but each year he takes the interest earned and hides it under his mattress. Simple-minded, huh? After ten years, he'll have his original $1,000 plus the ten annual interest payments of $100 each under his futon, for a total of $2,000. But canny Ms. Compound leaves her money in the account, so each year the interest is added to the pile and the next year's interest is calculated on the higher amount. In other words, at the end of the first year, the bank adds her $100 in interest to her $1,000 initial deposit and then calculates the 10-percent interest for the following year on the higher base of $1,100, which earns her $110. Depending on how the interest is calculated and timed, she'll end the ten years with about $2,594, or $594 more than Mr. Simple. That extra $594 is interest earned on interest.

How funds can make you rich

REMEMBER

The real beauty of mutual funds is the way they can grow your money over many years. "Letting your money ride" in a casino — by just leaving it on the odd numbers in roulette, for example — is a dumb strategy. The house will eventually win it from you because the odds are stacked in the casino operator's favour. But letting your money ride in a mutual fund over a decade or more can make you seriously rich. Funds let you make money in the stock and bond markets almost effortlessly.

Here's an example: An investment in Investors Dividend Fund (offered by Investors Group) from its launch in 1961 through the end of June 2008 produced an annual average compound return of about 8 percent. If your granny had been prescient enough to put $10,000 into the fund when it was launched, instead of blowing all her dough on sports cars and wild men, it would have been worth $5.4 *million* by mid-2008.

Of course, no law says you have to buy mutual funds in order to invest. You might make more money investing on your own behalf, and lots of people from all walks of life do. But it's tricky and dangerous. So millions of Canadians too busy or scared to learn the ropes themselves have found that funds are a wonderfully handy and reasonably cheap alternative. Buying funds is like going out to a restaurant compared with buying food, cooking a meal, and cleaning up afterward.

Yes, eating out is expensive, but it sure is nice not to have to face those cold pots in the sink covered in slowly congealing mustard sauce.

What mutual funds buy

REMEMBER

Mutual funds and other investors put their money into just two long-term investments:

>> **Stocks and shares:** Tiny slices of companies that trade in a big, sometimes chaotic but reasonably well-run electronic vortex called, yes, the stock market

>> **Bonds:** Loans made to governments or companies, which are packaged up so that investors can trade them to one another

Folk memories run deep, and after ugly stock market meltdowns in the 1920s and 1970s, mutual funds and stocks in general had unhealthy reputations for many years. For generations, Canadians, like people all over the world, preferred to buy sure things, usually bonds or fixed-term deposits from banks, the beloved guaranteed investment certificate (GIC). But as inflation and interest rates started to come down in the 1990s, it became harder and harder to find a GIC that paid a decent rate of interest — research shows most people are truly happy when they get 8 percent.

The Canadian mutual fund industry really started growing like a magic mushroom on a wet morning in Victoria in the mid-1990s, after rates on five-year GICs dropped well below that magic 8 percent. At that point, Canadians decided they were willing to take a risk on equity funds.

Checking Out Types of Funds

REMEMBER

Mutual funds fall into four main categories:

>> **Equity funds:** By far the most popular type of fund on the market, equity funds hold stocks and shares. Stocks are often called "equity" because every share is supposed to entitle its owner to an equal portion of the company. These funds represent an investment in raw capitalism — ownership of businesses.

>> **Balanced funds:** The next biggest category is balanced funds. They generally hold a mixture of just about everything — from Canadian and foreign stocks

to bonds from all around the world, as well as very short-term bonds that are almost as safe as cash.

>> **Bond funds:** These beauties, also referred to as "fixed-income" funds, essentially lend money to governments and big companies, collecting regular interest each year and (nearly always) getting the cash back in the end.

>> **Money market funds:** They hold the least volatile and most stable of all investments — very short-term bonds issued by governments and large companies that usually provide the lowest returns. These funds are basically savings vehicles for money you can't afford to take any risks with. They can also act as the safe little cushion of cash found in nearly all well-run portfolios.

Discovering Where to Buy Funds

Chapter 3 in Book 3 goes into detail about some of the legal and bureaucratic form–filling involved in buying a fund (don't worry, it's not complicated). In essence, you hand over your money and a few days later you get a transaction slip or confirmation slip stating the number of units you bought and what price you paid. You can buy a mutual fund from thousands of people and places across Canada, in one of four basic ways:

>> **Buying from professional advisers:** The most common method of making a fund purchase in Canada is to go to a stockbroker, financial planner, or other type of adviser who offers watery coffee, wisdom, and suggestions on what you should buy. These people will also open an account for you in which to hold your mutual funds. They are essentially salespeople and they nearly always make their living by collecting sales commissions on the funds they sell you, usually from the fund company itself. Their advice may be excellent and they can justifiably claim to impose needed discipline on their clients by getting them into the healthy habit of saving. But always keep in mind that they have to earn a living: The funds they offer will tend to be the ones that pay them the best commissions.

Examples of fund companies that sell exclusively through salespeople, planners, and stockbrokers are Mackenzie Financial Corp., Fidelity Investments Canada Ltd., CI Financial Corp., AGF Management Ltd., and Franklin Templeton, all based in Toronto. Investors Group Inc. of Winnipeg, Canada's biggest fund company, also sells through salespeople, but the sales force is affiliated with the company.

>> **Bank purchases:** The simplest way to buy funds is to walk into a bank branch. You also can call your bank's toll-free telephone number or buy funds online

at banks' websites. Banks never charge sales commissions to investors who buy their funds. The disadvantage to this approach is limited selection, because most bank branches are set up to sell only their company's funds. And not all bank staff are equipped or trained to give you detailed advice about investing. But the beauty of this approach is that you can have all your money — including your savings and chequing accounts and even your mortgage or car loan — in one place, making it simple to transfer money from one account to another. Buying your mutual funds at your bank can also earn you special rates on loans.

>> **Buying direct from fund companies:** For those who like to do more research on their own, excellent "no-load" companies sell their funds directly to investors. They're called no-load funds because they're sold with no sales commissions. No-load funds can avoid levying sales charges because they don't market their wares through salespeople. Because these funds don't have to make payments to the advisers who sell them, they often come with lower expenses. Examples of no-load companies include Beutel Goodman; Leith Wheeler; Mawer; MFS McLean Budden; Phillips, Hager & North (PH&N); and Saxon. Once again, limited selection of funds is a drawback.

>> **Buying from discount brokers:** Finally, for the real do-it-yourselfers who like to make just about every decision independently, you can find discount brokers that operate on the Internet or over the phone. Mostly but not always owned by the big banks, they sell nearly every fund from nearly every company, usually free of commissions and sales pitches.

Discount brokers are a huge force in the United States and they've gained popularity in Canada. The advantages, and they're significant, are low costs and a wide selection of funds. But don't expect personal help from a discounter.

Chapter **2**

Buying and Selling Mutual Funds

M utual funds were one of the 20th century's great wealth-creating innovations. Funds transformed stock and bond markets by giving people of modest means easy access to investments previously limited to the rich. The fund-investing concept is likely to remain popular for years, letting ordinary and not-so-ordinary people build their money in markets that would otherwise intimidate them. That's because the idea of packaging expert money management in a consumer product, which is then bought and sold in the form of units, is so brilliantly simple. Even journalists can understand it.

This chapter takes another look at funds, assessing their great potential as well as their nasty faults. It wraps up with a chat about the relative merits of no-load and load funds.

A Few Reasons to Buy Funds

Chapter 1 in Book 3 discusses how and why mutual funds work and why they make sense in general. The following sections give you some specific, significant reasons to make them a big part of your financial plan.

Offering safety in numbers: Public scrutiny and accountability

Perhaps the best thing about mutual funds is that their performance is public knowledge. When you own a fund, you're in the same boat as thousands of other unitholders, meaning the fund company is pressured to keep up the performance. If the fund lags its rivals for too long, unitholders will start *redeeming,* or cashing in, their units, which is the sort of thing that makes a manager stare at the ceiling at 4 a.m., sweat rolling down his or her grey face.

Fund companies are obliged to let the sun shine into their operations — and sunlight is the best disinfectant — by sending unitholders clear annual *financial statements* of the fund's operations. These statements are tables of figures showing what the fund owns at the end of the year, what expenses and fees it paid to the management company, and how well it performed. Statements are audited (that is, checked) by big accounting firms. The management company must also at least offer to send you the semi-annual statements, showing how the fund was doing halfway through the year.

TIP

To get the semi-annual statement, you often have to mail back a fiddly little card requesting it. Make sure you do. It costs you nothing, and knowing that investors are interested in what's happening to their money helps to keep fund companies on their toes. If you want to reduce paper burden, make a note of looking for this information on the fund company's website. For more on the financial statements for funds, see Chapter 3 in Book 3.

A lot of the information in the statements is hard to understand and not particularly useful, but always check one thing: Look at the fund's main holdings. If you bought what you thought was a conservative Canadian fund, for example, then you want to see lots of bank stocks and other companies you've at least heard of.

REMEMBER

Don't confuse the *financial statements* — which describe how the fund is doing — with your own individual *account statement.* Your account statements are personal mailings that show how many units you own, how many you've bought and sold, and how much your holdings are worth. Companies usually must send you personal account statements at least twice a year. Some fund sellers, such as banks, send quarterly statements, and discount brokers often mail them monthly. Fund companies also have Internet-based and telephone-based services that let you verify the amount of money in your account every day. See Chapter 3 in Book 3 for more on account statements.

The following sections help you decipher price and performance figures. When you know what to look for, you can accurately track your funds' performance.

Your fund manager should give you the straight story, but getting a second opinion is never a bad plan, especially when it comes to your cash.

Finding and reading price tables

Time was you could check a mutual fund's unit price, or net asset value per share (NAVPS), in most daily newspapers. (Refer to Chapter 1 in Book 3 for a definition of net asset value.) But daily tables are now virtually extinct, and the few that remain are on the endangered species list. You can look up fund prices on individual fund company websites instead.

Most mutual funds calculate and publish a value for their units every day that stock and bond markets are open. Some small or very specialized funds do this only monthly or weekly, and some take a day or two getting the information out, but unit prices for most widely available funds are available the next day on fund information websites and, to a limited extent, in major newspapers. The listing also usually shows the change in unit price from the previous day.

Checking and reading mutual fund performance

Newspapers' monthly fund performance reports have gone the way of the dodo bird. This is unfortunate if you liked to opened up those broad pages full of wide tables and highlight and circle things. Checking fund performance is now strictly an Internet operation. Assuming you are comfortable online, this is a very good thing. Apart from saving countless trees that used to be chopped up into newsprint pulp, you can get more immediate information and easily compare a fund against its peers and other investments.

Because mutual fund investing is primarily a longer-term undertaking, performance statistics should command more of your attention than daily prices do. How often should you check your fund's performance? Unfortunately, this question has no easy answer. But it's a good idea to look every three months or so to see how your manager is doing. Even if you bought your funds through a financial planner or other salesperson — who's supposed to be looking out for your interests — it never hurts to keep an eye on how well the recommendations are turning out.

Funds that buy the same sorts of investments are listed together, by category. Determining how a fund is categorized isn't easy nowadays, because data providers, who are members of the Canadian Investment Funds Standards Committee, use more than 40 asset categories. Your first step, then, is to enter the name of a fund in a website's general fund search tool, and then check its category on the page that appears.

A table typically provides the fund name at far left and, at the far right, its price, or net asset value per share, at the end of the most recent business day. In between are the percentage changes in price over one day, one week, one month, and three months, as well as the change from the beginning of the year. Morningstar (https://www.morningstar.ca/ca/) provides data for all fund categories. Similar information is available at *The Globe and Mail* (www.theglobeandmail.com/investing/markets/funds/).

Making sense of the numbers

TIP

What can you do with this jumble of numbers? The unit price is useful information, because by multiplying the price by the number of units you own you can work out the value of your holdings. You can also make sure the unit price you find online matches the price shown on the statement you get from your broker or fund company, in order to double-check their bookkeeping. Keep the mutual fund reports for June 30 and December 31 in your little sequined satchel until you've done your checking, because you'll be getting reports from your fund company showing the value of your holdings as of those dates.

The unit price is also handy if you're hazy on which fund you actually own. Don't laugh — a lot of smart people aren't always sure. With thousands of funds, versions of funds, and fund-like products available in Canada, it's easy to get confused. Often, several different versions of a particular fund, known as share classes, are on sale, depending on how you buy it (such as a front-end or back-end load) and other factors such as investment guarantees or minimum initial purchase amount. If your account statement shows you own a fund with a unit price of $10.95, for instance, and your research reports the same price, chances are you're talking about the same fund. However, you might have to go so far as to check your statements for the precise name of the fund, including the series or class letter — or even check the fund sales code, which is used by fund salespeople when making transactions.

REMEMBER

The meat of the subject is contained in the performance numbers. These returns are after the fund's fees and expenses have been deducted. Some exceptions to this practice exist in the monthly report — that is, funds that levy extra charges that reduce the performance shown — but the returns for all of the biggest companies are after charges. The companies that deduct fees and expenses *after* the returns shown in such tables are generally fund companies that sell funds as part of a comprehensive financial package. Clients get a customized statement that lists their fees separately, instead of lumping in the charges with the fund's overall return. Always check whether the returns you're being shown are before or after the deduction of all charges and costs.

THE DIFFERENCE BETWEEN THE AVERAGE AND THE MEDIAN

Sometimes figuring out whether a fund has done better than other funds in its group is harder than it looks. When you look at a fund report, you'll come across two terms used to describe the typical fund's performance: The *average* and the *median.* The average and the median are both numbers that attempt to show how funds in a particular category have done. That way, if you're interested in a fund you can compare its performance with that of its rivals. For example, if you're considering buying your bank's U.S. equity fund, it's a good idea to see how it has done compared with other funds in the U.S. equity category. However, sometimes the average can be distorted upward or downward by a few extreme cases, so the median acts as a middle point, giving a good idea of what the typical return for funds was. Here's how it works:

- The **average** is calculated by simply adding up the return figures for all funds for a particular period and then dividing by the number of funds involved.

- The **median** is the halfway mark. Half of the funds were below that point and half were above.

Normally, the two numbers are very similar, but a sprinkling of very high or low returns in the sample can pull them apart. An "average" figure can be a misleading comparative, because it gives equal weight to each and every member of that group — regardless of the significance of each member. To be truly useful, an average must be "weighted" according to, in the case of a fund category, each individual fund's assets.

For an example, take a look at the Canadian small/mid-cap equity category, which includes more volatile funds that focus on stocks of smaller companies. In 2006, the average fund in this category gained 14.0 percent, while the median return was just 10.9 percent. Why such a great difference? Because the average was pumped up by enormous returns — as high as 60.5 percent — from a handful of funds that happened to ride some red-hot little shares. Although 2006 was a good year for this type of fund, about one-third of them made less than 10 percent — nowhere near the stratospheric numbers put in by the category leaders.

Putting your eggs in many baskets

Another good reason to buy mutual funds is the fact that they instantly mitigate your risk by letting you own lots of stocks and bonds, ideally in many different markets. *Diversification,* spreading your dollars around, is the cornerstone of successful investing. Diversifying means you won't be slaughtered by a collapse in the price of one or two shares.

WARNING

Some people learn about diversification the hard way. Investors think they've lucked into the next big thing, hand over their entire fortune, and then lose it all in a cruel market correction. Pinning your hopes on just one stock or handful of stocks is never a wise move, so don't let this happen to you.

Mutual funds let ordinary investors buy into faraway markets and assets. It would be difficult and expensive for most ordinary people to purchase shares in Asia or Europe, or bonds issued by Latin American governments (go easy on those, though), if they couldn't buy them through mutual funds. Although events of global impact such as terrorist activity, natural disasters, and the price of oil have an impact on markets worldwide, some respond positively to developments, and others respond negatively. It's tough to keep track of it all and predict which markets will be affected and by how much. So the question is this: Why even try? History demonstrates that a portfolio with lots of different and varied asset classes will tend to suffer fewer speed bumps.

REMEMBER

Most equity mutual funds own shares in at least 50 companies — fund managers who try to go with more "concentrated" portfolios have been known to get their fingers burned. In fact, academic research suggests that only seven stocks may be enough to provide adequate diversification for an investor, but seeing dozens of names in a portfolio offers a lot more reassurance.

Getting good returns from professional management

One of the most entertaining and informative books ever written on the subject of investing is *A Fool and His Money: The Odyssey of an Average Investor* by John Rothchild. First published in 1988, the book describes Mr. Rothchild's own abject failure in the market and includes his observation that most amateur investors are less than frank about how they've actually done. Even if they've had their heads handed to them, they tend to claim they ended up "about even." The moral of the story: Even if your relatives and pals claim to have made a fortune in the market, treat their boasts with a goodly dose of skepticism.

REMEMBER

Yes, bad funds abound. But chances are you'll do better in a mutual fund than you would investing on your own. At least the people running funds are professionals who readily dump a stock when it turns sour, instead of hanging on like grim death, as amateurs tend to do. The habit of selling quickly and taking the loss while it's still small is said to be one of the main traits that distinguishes the pro from the amateur.

Making investing convenient

Funds are just so darned handy, no wonder hundreds of millions of people around the world buy them. Yes, you could make your own lip balm. You could gather the eucalyptus bark and the deer's eyelid secretions, and boil them up in a big copper pot for days while chanting your head off. But it's easier just to walk into the drugstore and buy a stick. Likewise, it's a snap to sign a cheque or let the fund company deduct cash from your bank account regularly — a lot easier than worrying about the market and finding out the difference between investing in a long-dated strip bond and an exciting, newly listed, Internet solutions startup with scalable technology.

Critics of funds claim, with some justification, that the industry has brainwashed members of the public into thinking they're too stupid to invest for themselves. And it does seem fund companies want you to believe it's necessary to have some 25-year-old pup in a suit do it for you, in return for a fat fee. But the reality is that most people are just too busy, confused, or plain lazy to figure out the investing game. This book will make you an educated fund investor, whether you choose to deal with that young pup or go it alone.

Investing without breaking the bank

The typical Canadian stock fund rakes off about 2.3 percent of your money each year in fees and costs. That's a hefty charge, but the fund company also relieves you of a lot of drudgery and tiresome paperwork in return. Funds offer a lot of convenience. The fund company keeps your money safe and handles the record-keeping for your savings. It all leaves you free and clear to get on with your life.

In fact, mutual funds are a positive bargain if you're just starting to invest. Quite a few companies will let you put as little as $500 into their funds, and you can often open up a regular investment plan — where the money is simply taken out of your bank account — for as little as $50 a month. That's a pretty good deal when you realize that fund companies actually lose money on small accounts. If an investor has, say, $1,000 in an equity fund with a management expense ratio (MER) of 2.3 percent, then the company is collecting only $23 in fees and expenses, barely enough to cover postage and administration costs let alone turn a profit. Even the cheapest "discount" stockbroker in Canada will let you do only one trade for about 25 bucks.

The costs of a mutual fund investment are buried in the MER and the relatively incomprehensible statement of operations, but at least you can work them out with a bit of digging. Try asking traditional full-service stockbrokers for a clear explanation of their commission rates. You'll get a lot of mumbling and long sentences containing the phrase "it depends," but no clear answers.

Watching over your investment

Mutual fund companies are pretty closely watched, not only by overworked provincial securities regulators, but also, believe it or not, by rival companies. Competing companies don't want a rotten peach spoiling the reputation of the whole barrel. The Investment Funds Institute of Canada (IFIC), the industry lobby group, is a mouthpiece for the companies, naturally. But it also generally keeps an eye on things. And Toronto, where most of the industry is based, is a village where everyone knows everyone. You'd be surprised how many industry executives tell reporters about skullduggery *off the record* — always about competing fund sellers, of course.

Yes, greed abounds. Despite some improvements in recent years, fees are still too high, unitholder reports are often difficult to decipher, salespeople are given goodies, and funds are sometimes used as horns of plenty when managers divert their trading, and the resulting flow of commissions, to their brokerage buddies. The good news is most companies are simply making too much money honestly to risk it all by running scams.

REMEMBER

The stocks, bonds, and other securities a fund buys with your money don't even stay in the coffers of the fund company: Under provincial securities laws, the actual assets of the fund must be held by a separate "custodian," usually a big bank or similar institution. Just stick with regular mutual funds, those that come with a document called a "simplified prospectus" and are managed by widely known companies, and you should be okay.

Getting out your money if you need it

If you decide to move your hard-earned cash out of a fund, your fund company will normally get your money to you within three days. Removing money from a fund effortlessly whenever you like may not seem like a big deal — but in the world of investing, being able to do so whenever you want to, with no hassles or questions, is especially good.

WARNING

Don't forget that lots of other investments, including guaranteed investment certificates (GICs), hit you with a penalty if you take your cash out early. Selling a stock invariably costs you a brokerage commission with no guarantee you'll get a decent price for your shares. Sell a bond and you're often at the mercy of your dealer, who can pluck a price out of the air.

The Perils and Pitfalls of Funds

So now that you're convinced funds are the right place to be, this section is going to throw you for a bit of a loop. An informed investor is a wealthy investor, after all, and it's important to realize that funds aren't perfect. None of these disadvantages mean you shouldn't buy mutual funds. But keeping them in mind will help you stay out of overpriced and unsuitable investments.

Excessive costs

When you start amassing serious money in mutual funds, your costs can get outrageous. For example, if you invest $100,000 in a set of typical equity funds with a management expense ratio of 2.3 percent, the fund company is siphoning off $2,300 of your money every year. The math gets truly chilling when you extrapolate the cost of management fees over long periods. Over 20 years, at an MER of 2.3 percent, the fund company will end up with an incredible 50 percent or so of the total accumulated capital. How so? Simply by slicing that little 2.3 percent off the top each year.

In theory, that's what it costs to pay a fund manager to actively invest on your behalf. But if you're content to accept whatever return — good or bad — the overall market can achieve, then you can save a bundle by owning *index funds* or, better still, *exchange-traded funds* (ETFs). Index funds are funds with low expenses that simply track the whole stock or bond market by producing a return in line with a market index, such as the Standard & Poor's/Toronto Stock Exchange composite index of approximately 300 well-known companies. An ETF is similar to an index fund except it trades on a stock exchange. They don't have a portfolio manager as they simply own all of the stocks in an index. A typical index fund, such as RBC Canadian Index Fund, has expenses of 0.71 percent. See Chapter 4 in Book 3 for more on index funds and ETFs.

Style drift: When managers get lost in the jungle

In the past, some managers would *drift* or depart from the type of investments they told you they'd buy when you signed on, usually because they were chasing hot returns or because they were scared. You can keep tabs on the biggest portfolio holdings in your fund by checking the fund company's website, but your only legal entitlement to a full list of all of the portfolio contents is when the company sends you annual and semi-annual financial statements, and these typically do not arrive until three months following the period end.

The most prominent type of drift involves value and growth investing styles (see Chapters 3 and 4 in Book 2). The most glaring example of a value manager holding a growth stock was Nortel Networks in the late 1990s, which value managers held in their portfolios long after its price had multiplied many times. However, style drift has largely been a non-issue in recent years. The issue is this: How long should a value manager hold a stock that no longer provides value because its price is sky high?

REMEMBER

Whether or not such examples represent style drift is highly debatable. It's an example of how you as an investor need to monitor your fund investments. Ultimately, it's your responsibility to make sure you're headed in the right direction.

When bad managers attack

They may be smart and they may be professionals, but fund managers sure can blow it, leaving behind nothing but a lot of little scraps of grey polyester and a bunch of ugly minus signs in front of their returns. Companies, however, usually replace managers of big funds after just a couple years of bad performance.

Having a decent Canadian equity fund, in particular, is a marquee attraction for a company. It's the fund category carrying the most prestige, partly because it wins the most attention from the media. You can be sure that just about every manager running a large equity or balanced fund, Canadian or global, is working his or her silk socks off trying to top the performance league. Every so often, companies get in bidding wars for managers with a great reputation. So everyone running a fund is trying to get public notice for earning hot returns, because it increases his or her market value.

Vague explanations of poor performance

No matter how badly a fund did, the analysis given to investors is frequently a languid description of the stock or bond market and a few of the manager's choice reflections on the future of civilization. All written in a sort of Old Etonian detached and refined tone, as though the person running the fund was really just dabbling, old chap. Don't really have to work at all, don't you know, what with the estate in Scotland and the trust funds. Only really drop by the office for half an hour every two weeks or so, dash it all. Busy with the golf and usually comatose by 5 p.m.

WARNING

What unitholders deserve, but too often are denied, is an honest discussion of whether their fund kept up with the market and its peers. Securities regulators are putting the squeeze on companies to improve their reports, but it'll take time. You shouldn't have to pull on a grubby deerstalker hat and smoke a smelly pipe to discover what went wrong with performance and what the manager plans to do about it.

In the meantime, if your fund lags the market and other funds in the same category, ask for a clear explanation from your broker or financial planner if you got advice when buying funds. If you bought a no-load fund (covered later in this chapter), look for a written set of reasons in the company's regular mailings to unitholders. Because no-load companies deal directly with their investors — instead of going through a salesperson — their reports are often clearer than the information provided by companies that market their funds through advisers.

WARNING

Another big problem in the reporting of performance is that all too often it's not at all clear who is actually running your fund and how long they've been doing it. Fund companies rarely, if ever, print the length of a manager's tenure, and they usually don't warn investors in a timely way if he or she quits or is fired. Yes, a few veteran managers have been running the same fund for years. And some companies such as Fidelity Investments Canada Ltd. make it reasonably plain who's actually calling the shots. But at many companies, managers come and go with such unpredictable frequency that it's difficult if not impossible to keep track of them. Rather than worry about finding a genius to pick your stocks, you're much better off looking at the fund itself. Make your decision about investing with an eye to how the fund has performed and what it currently holds, rather than trying to figure out who is in the top spot.

Prospectuses that don't say enough

It's often hard to tell from a company's website, promotional handouts, and even official reports to unitholders whether the returns from its funds have been any good. That's because most companies, incredibly, still don't show their performance against an appropriate market benchmark, such as the Standard & Poor's/Toronto Stock Exchange composite index (S&P/TSX) for Canadian equity funds or the MSCI World Index for global equity funds. However, things have gotten better since the fund industry began producing *prospectuses* that are fairly easy to understand. A prospectus is the document that must be given to the purchasers of a fund, describing its rules and risks. A prospectus must provide performance numbers that compare a fund to a benchmark, such as the S&P/TSX for Canadian equity funds. Prospectuses also give the fund's returns on a year-by-year calendar basis, which is invaluable for checking whether unitholders have enjoyed steady returns or suffered through insane swings.

However, prospectuses are still of only limited usefulness because they don't say *why* the fund has lagged or outperformed its benchmark. Fortunately, an additional document, the *management report of fund performance,* has taken a big step toward providing useful comparative data and explanations of a fund's recent performance. More on these is in Chapter 3 of Book 3.

Too many funds and too few long-term results

Fund managers love to talk about how investing is a long-term game — especially when they're losing money — but have you noticed how many ads you see touting performance over periods as short as one year? And companies seem unable to resist launching new funds that invest in the hottest new asset class — just in time to lose money for investors when the bubble bursts.

It happened with science and technology funds in the early 2000s. At the beginning of the decade, the number of funds in this category had multiplied to more than 120, but the group then tanked with huge losses in 2001 and 2002. Today, fewer science and technology funds exist, but the group's median compound annual returns are mostly negative over most time spans. Did Canadians really need such a selection of science and technology funds? As the performance numbers attest, they arguably didn't need any of the wretched things.

REMEMBER

It's easy to get dizzy amid the flashing lights and loud music, and jump aboard the fund industry's carousel of new products. But steer clear of the fancy stuff and stick to plain old conservative equity and bond funds with your serious long-term money, and you'll end up ahead.

Load versus No-Load: The Great Divide

You can buy mutual funds in two main ways:

>> **Through a professional seller:** You can get a salesperson such as a broker or financial planner to help. The broker has to earn a living, so you'll almost certainly end up buying load funds — a load is a sales charge or commission that's paid to the broker, either by you or by the fund company.

>> **Going it alone:** You can pick your funds on your own, with perhaps some advice from a bank staffer or mutual fund employee. In that case, you'll often end up buying *no-load* funds, which don't levy a sales commission.

Grey areas abound. You can buy *load* funds on your own and pay no commissions (through a discount broker, which will provide little or no advice). Some brokers will sell you no-load funds or load funds on which they waive commissions. And banks can fall in between the two stools. But those are the two essential methods.

Load funds: The comfort zone

Most mutual funds in Canada are sold to investors by a salesperson who is in turn paid by way of a sales commission. Millions of people love the feeling of having an advocate and adviser who seems to know his or her way through the jungle of investing. And why not hire a professional? After all, you probably don't fix your own plumbing yourself or remove your own appendix (too hard to get the stains out of the kitchen tiles).

Your adviser might work for a stockbroker, a financial planning firm, or an insurance brokerage — or he or she might be self-employed. But the important point is this: If you buy funds through a salesperson, your primary relationship is with them, not with the fund company.

Any fund company should be able to answer your questions about your account. Always make sure you get a regular account statement from the fund company itself (unless you're with one of the big stockbrokers; the big brokers usually handle all of the recordkeeping). But load companies, such as Fidelity Investments Canada, won't even sell you funds directly. You have to open an account with a broker or planner, who will then put the order through for you. The companies' systems and much of their marketing are designed to deal with salespeople, not members of the public, so your buy and sell orders must come from your broker.

Sales commissions on load funds come in a bewildering number of variations and forms. And discount brokers have dreamed up even more ways to make the whole thing even more complicated. But when you buy a load fund from a broker or planner, you have three basic options.

You can negotiate and pay an upfront commission — known as a *sales charge* or *front load* — to the salesperson. Savvy investors usually pay 2 percent or less. That entitles you to sell the fund at any time with no further charges, and it sometimes gets you lower annual expenses.

Alternately, you can buy funds on a "low-load" basis. Some firms refer to this as "no-load," even though you must buy them through an adviser. There's no free lunch, of course, as a low-load fund generally will have higher annual expenses than the front-end version of the same fund.

Finally, you can buy funds with a *back-end load* or *redemption charge.* In that case, the fund company itself pays the commission to the broker — usually 5 percent in the case of an equity fund or a balanced fund and less for a bond fund. However, you, the investor, are on the hook for a "redemption charge" if you sell the fund within a set number of years. The redemption charge is based either on the original purchase cost of the units you're redeeming or their value at the time you sell. The policy varies by company. The first option is slightly better for you because, presumably, the value of your units will have increased by the time you redeem. For example, say you invest $10,000 in a fund on a back-end-load basis and the fund gains 20 percent, leaving you with $12,000. Say you decide to redeem half of your holding, incurring a 4.5-percent back-end load. If the redemption charge is based on your original investment, you pay $225 (which is 4.5 percent of $5,000), but if it's based on the current market value, you pay $270 (4.5 percent of $6,000).

But a difficulty exists for the fund industry with back-end loads. If the adviser doesn't have to wangle a commission out of the client every time he or she buys a fund, more of a temptation exists for brokers and planners to switch customers from fund to fund, collecting commissions from the fund companies along the way. So the fund industry borrowed a technique from the life insurers, who have been dealing with salespeople's naughty tricks for generations, and introduced the *trailer fee*. Trailers are essentially yet another commission — usually between 0.5 percent and 1 percent of the value of the client's holding annually — that's paid by the company to the salesperson each year as long as his or her customer stays in the fund. It's a payment for loyalty. The trailer comes out of the management fee, not out of your account, so you never see it.

Many load companies pay a higher trailer to salespeople when they sell the fund on a front-load basis, getting their sales commission directly from the investor. That's because the company itself hasn't had to pay the charge. So on front-load fund sales, where *the investor* negotiates and pays the commission, a company might pay a trailer of 1 percent of the client's holding of equity funds each year; but on deferred-load sales, where *the company* paid the original sales commission, the trailer might be only 0.5 percent. It all gets pretty confusing — and it gets more complicated as you go further in — but that's the basis of the commission structure in mutual funds.

No-load funds: The direct approach

The other great branch of the fund industry is the no-load sector — funds that sell directly to the public with no sales commissions. Here, life is much simpler. A no-load shop will open an account for you when you contact them; you do this without the involvement of a broker, planner, or any other kind of adviser. You're not charged to buy or sell a fund, although remember that to discourage in-and-out trading you often face a *penalty* of 2 percent or so if you dump a fund within three months of buying.

The banks dominate the no-load fund business through their vast customer bases, discount brokerage arms, and branch networks. Until recently they had difficulty building a strong record, and big market share, in equity funds. However, the Big Five banks in Canada have made gains in this area through improved performance and marketing through their branch networks, which has helped propel them to the top rungs of the fund-asset rankings.

Because no-load funds usually don't pay sales commissions to brokers — although they sometimes pay trailer fees to persuade advisers to sell their funds — their annual expenses and fees should be much lower than those of load funds. Should be, but aren't. Bankers aren't known for cutting fees where they can get away with keeping them high, and most no-load funds in Canada are only slightly cheaper than broker-sold funds. In other words, you can expect to part with about 1 percent of your assets each year when you invest in most equity or balanced funds, no matter where you buy them. Some bank-run equity funds charge less — mostly income-oriented dividend funds, which generally are less complicated to manage than more aggressive stock funds.

The banks and a few other no-load-fund sellers also are the place to find index funds, which have ultra-low expenses — mostly less than 1 percent. An index fund costs very little to manage because its portfolio simply tracks the whole market by mimicking an index. These are known as passively managed funds, with no investment decisions necessary on the part of the managers. Because index funds generate such small management fees, load companies can't afford to sell them and also pay commissions to brokers. See Chapter 4 in Book 3 for more about index funds and even less expensive passive investments known as exchange-traded funds, or ETFs.

No-load fund sellers' main bread and butter, like other fund companies, are actively managed funds — some of which also have relatively low expenses. Actively managed funds, unlike index funds, buy and sell particular stocks in an attempt to beat the market and other managers. However, no-load shops' bargain funds often have relatively high minimum investments in order to keep costs low (servicing tiny accounts isn't profitable, remember). For example, a minimum account size of $25,000 with the company may be required.

HOW AN IRISH CHARMER REVOLUTIONIZED THE MUTUAL FUND

Until the late 1980s, investors had to cough up the sales charge for load mutual funds themselves — it ran as high as 10 percent of the investor's money in some iniquitous cases. But in 1987 a brilliant fund marketer named Jim O'Donnell at Mackenzie Financial had a brainwave: Consumers loathed having to part with cash off the top just to pay a salesperson; they wanted to see all their money going to work for them right away. So why not have the *company* pay the commission to the broker and get the money back through the management fee?

There was at least one problem with the strategy: Investors who hadn't paid a sales charge upfront might be inclined to simply dump the fund whenever they wanted. They hadn't paid a sales load, after all, so they wouldn't feel like they were wasting the commission. So Mackenzie also introduced its redemption charges, which kicked in if you cashed out early. The back-end idea was a smash hit and the company's first back-end-load fund, the Industrial Horizon Fund, attracted hundreds of millions of dollars within months of its launch in 1987. The rest of the load fund industry soon copied it.

IN THIS CHAPTER

» Making a fund purchase

» Figuring out a prospectus in a few seconds

» Getting to know the management report of fund performance

» Seeing what your account statement has to say

» Checking on how your investment is growing through annual reports

Chapter **3**

Paperwork and Your Rights

Ever get work done on your house and notice how contractors talk? They use expressions such as "six of one and half a dozen of another" or "you could do that," and they'll pound 'em out in a barrage that leaves you more confused than before. People in the investment business like to drone on in the same way. They produce documents that explain every angle and aspect, but skip the stuff you really want to know: Is this fund any good and how has it done?

Investors hate getting piles of paper in the mail, but the glossy brochures keep coming. To some extent, the verbiage isn't the companies' fault. Securities law obliges those selling investments to disclose trivia their clients couldn't care less about. Still, it's pretty simple to filter out the noise in the mailings you get from a fund company — and cut straight to the information that really matters. And the documents from fund companies have improved, especially prospectuses, the all-important fact sheets that tell you about the promise and perils of a fund before you buy it. Industry regulators have gone further, requiring fund companies to provide performance update reports, written in plain English, to unitholders twice a year.

In general, the documents and forms you have to deal with are pretty straightforward. Mutual fund forms are set up to be easy to fill out. Some special questions apply for opening a registered retirement savings plan, or you may need to fill in sections of your tax return to report investment income and gains, but they tend to be simple.

This chapter goes over the important paperwork to demystify your account statement (the regular mailing that shows how you're doing) and walk you through a simplified prospectus (the brochure that describes the fund). As always, what to watch out for are the costs loaded on your account — and you find out where to sniff around.

Signing Up

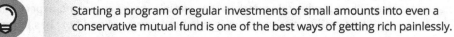

The big thing to decide straightaway is whether you're investing inside a registered retirement savings plan (RRSP) — a special tax-sheltered account in which investment profits pile up tax-free — or in an ordinary, taxable account in which your money is subject to taxes (see Chapter 3 in Book 1 for more on how RRSPs work). You can expect to fill out two main types of forms when you buy mutual funds:

>> An account application form — which may just be called a "retirement savings plan" form if it's for an RRSP.

>> A form allowing the fund company to take fixed amounts out of your bank account for investment in funds, if you've decided to start a regular investing program. People usually have the money taken out monthly, but some fund companies allow you to use different periods, such as every week.

Starting a program of regular investments of small amounts into even a conservative mutual fund is one of the best ways of getting rich painlessly.

TIP

Filling in your account (or RRSP) application form

When you decide to buy a mutual fund, the first thing you'll be asked to fill out is an "account application" form — which tells the company who you are, what you want to buy, and how much you want to spend. An account is like a little shelf on which all your investments are kept at the broker's or the mutual fund company's office.

The account application is the document that tells the fund company the following:

>> Your name

>> Address

>> Level of investment knowledge

>> The amount of money you want to put into each fund

For investors, it's actually one of the most useful and informative documents mutual fund sellers print. That's because it contains hard information the fund company needs itself, so the new account form is free of vagueness and verbosity. For example, in the space where the form asks how much you want to invest in each fund, it nearly always clearly states the minimum investment.

REMEMBER

Before you agree to buy anything, have a good look at the application form. And if you have any questions at all, approach your seller for a clear explanation. The form will also sometimes disclose what extra fees — such as charges for administration — you're expected to cough up. That's not a sudden attack of candour on the company's part — it's simply that the bureaucrats need to know how you'll be paying, directly or by having it taken out of your account.

The form for opening a new account includes some odd-looking questions. The fund company or broker wants to know

>> How experienced you are as an investor

>> Your income

>> Your *net worth* (the value of your personal assets after your debts are taken away)

They're not just being nosy here. One of the pillars of provincial securities law is a requirement that people selling investments should recommend only securities that are suitable for the customer — a principle referred to in the jargon as *Know Your Client* or KYC. In fact, the account application form is often just referred to as the KYC. The idea is this: An elderly investor on a limited income shouldn't have a big chunk of his or her portfolio rammed into a Low-Coupon Speculative High-Yield Unsecured Sub-Saharan Junk Bond Fund.

REMEMBER

The KYC can be a useful protection for you if it turns out later that your adviser put you into funds that were too risky for your circumstances, but it also works to the salesperson's advantage. He or she has an automatic out if you lost money on a volatile fund but you claimed when you opened the account that you knew a fair bit about investing. This is no place to put on a brave face — if you're a complete novice, say so and be proud of it. Pretending to know more than you do could really get you into hot water here if a dispute erupts between you and your broker about an investment that went sour.

WARNING

If you're investing with a bank or other no-load, direct fund seller (see Chapter 2 in Book 3), the application form will be issued by the company and it'll be clear that your deposit's going straight to them. But if you're buying funds through a financial planner or other independent fund salesperson, make sure you fill out an application form issued by the fund company itself. For your own security and convenience, it's important that you're recorded as a customer *on the books of the fund company,* giving you an extra measure of protection if the dealer or financial planner makes an error or even runs into cash-flow or regulatory problems. For example, if you're investing in a Franklin Templeton Investments fund, see that the form you fill out is a Franklin Templeton form.

When money is held on the books of the mutual fund company itself, the account is said to be *in client name.* In other words, the account bears the name of the individual investor at the head office of the fund company. It's a good arrangement for you because that way, if you ever have a dispute with your broker or you want to move your account elsewhere, your units and your name are in the fund company's records, making it much easier to shift your money.

Nearly every big financial planning chain and mutual fund dealer is set up so that mutual fund units are held in client name on the books of the fund company. That means you can expect to get statements at least twice a year from both the dealer and the fund companies you've invested with; always check them against each other. However, with traditional stockbrokers such as RBC Dominion Securities Inc., or with discount brokers such as TD Waterhouse Canada Inc., your money may be held only on the broker's books. In that case, the fund company may have no record of your account. Wherever you invest, it usually pays to keep an eye on the securities listed for your account and the transactions shown.

REMEMBER

Discount brokers and traditional stockbrokers tend to have sophisticated *back offices* or administration systems because their clients usually own stocks and bonds as well as funds. That means mutual funds are held in the same big pot as other securities, so these brokers don't pass their clients names on to the mutual fund company. Unfortunately, that means the fund company may have no record of your investment, and therefore isn't able to send you an annual and semi-annual statement of your personal holdings. That could make it harder to resolve any disputes with your broker over what you bought and how much it's worth. And very early in your investing career, someone is certain to get an order wrong. As in any business, mistakes can happen when dealing with discount brokers, mutual fund companies, and fund dealers. However, the good news is that these are large organizations that have the resources to fix errors. But get everything in writing, retain copies of all of the forms you fill out, and keep brief notes of the orders you issue over the phone or online. Retain transaction confirmation numbers until you see evidence in your account that a purchase or sale has been conducted properly and according to your wishes.

Getting confirmed

REMEMBER

Fund companies are required to send you a *confirmation* or *transaction slip* in the mail a few days after a transaction. This document confirms you've purchased units and for what amount, and whether you bought them with an upfront or "front-end" commission, on a "low-load" basis, or with a *back-end load* or redemption charge (assuming it's a fund that's sold with commissions). A back-end load or redemption charge applies when you sell fund units. Read the confirmation or transaction slip very carefully, and if you spot any errors, immediately contact the salesperson (or fund company, if you purchased directly) to get the mistake fixed.

Also, when writing your cheque to pay for your funds, make it payable to the fund company. Or, if it must be made out to your adviser's firm as opposed to the fund company, write "in trust" on the cheque. That gives you extra protection if the dealer hits financial problems, potentially tying your money up in bankruptcy proceedings.

REMEMBER

The main thing, when you've decided what fund to buy, is keeping a brief note of what you asked for and what you were told. And hang on to copies, photocopies, or scanned images of everything. If a dispute arises, an investor who can calmly produce notes from his or her meetings with the adviser, along with copies of documents, will be taken far more seriously.

Prospectuses: Not Always Your Friend

A mutual fund *prospectus* is the document that must be given to you when you buy a mutual fund. It's the crucial method the fund industry uses to set out the purpose of the fund, describe the fees, costs, and charges, and warn buyers of the risks involved in investing in the fund. Always ask to see the prospectus before you buy a fund (the salesperson should offer it) and then make sure you read at least these two sections:

>> The investment objectives of the fund — that is, the sort of things it invests in.

>> The charges and fees — if they aren't clearly explained, then get your salesperson to help.

Prospectuses traditionally were written using vague language, laden with legalese or with so many technical terms that it was impossible to figure out whether a fund was worth buying. But securities regulators have forced fund companies to produce prospectuses and other documents that are clear and concise. Nowadays, prospectuses (and their new companions, management reports of fund performance) are summaries that allow investors to put their finger on important information quickly.

The prospectus itself actually comes in two parts:

>> Part A is a very broad, catch-all piece that serves to provide the bulk of the information required to inform you and, perhaps more important, satisfy the lawyers that the regulatory requirements are being met. It covers absolutely every minute detail that could possibly be applied to all funds offered by a company. In some cases, such as when a fund company has various "families" or brands of funds, more than one Part A prospectus exists; be sure to obtain the one that applies to your fund.

>> A second document — somewhat predictably labelled Part B — provides information specific to your fund. Most fund companies have a list of Part B prospectuses, grouping related funds into individual documents. However, individual funds each have their own sections within this document. This is the part of the prospectus that contains the all-important historical performance and portfolio holdings information.

The third piece of the disclosure puzzle is the management report of fund performance (MRFP), which mercifully is a self-contained piece. (Find out about the MRFP later in this chapter.)

You've been warned

The mutual fund prospectus is not entirely your friend, or at least it's not a true do-anything-for-you, hoops-of-steel, give-you-her-last-smoke type of friend. The prospectus, the document describing a mutual fund that's given to purchasers, is designed to inform you, but it's also there to protect the fund salesperson and fund company. Because after it's been given to you, the law assumes you've been *adequately warned* about the dangers and disadvantages of the fund. No point whining about the losses on funny foreign currencies when you were told of the danger right there on page 137.

Mutual fund prospectuses — which usually cover all or at least several of the funds in a company's lineup under one cover — have always contained the following information:

>> **The name of the fund and its investment objectives:** For example, providing a steady income while preserving capital for a money market fund, or capital gains for a stock fund. Usually it's a bland statement that tells you little — after all, it would be an odd equity fund that didn't seek capital gains. (Perhaps someday they'll invent a fund that tries to *lose* as much money as possible, and also dream up a way to get investors to buy it!)

>> **The risks of investing in the fund:** A good prospectus will warn of the dangers of losing money in bonds if inflation returns or interest rates turn up. And you can count on seeing a warning that an equity fund will be vulnerable if the stock market tanks. Special warnings about the dangers of foreign funds are almost always included, such as the chance of currency losses if the Canadian dollar climbs relative to overseas currencies — a danger that countless investors who were heavily diversified in foreign funds discovered to be very real in recent years. And small-company fund prospectuses invariably point to the unpleasant volatility and unique dangers of small stocks. But, once again, the risks section usually consists of stating the bleeding obvious, as our Australian friends would say.

>> **The company's idea of an appropriate investor:** Look for clues as to the sort of investor who should buy the fund and the sort who should avoid it. For example, Franklin Templeton Investments — one of the more conservative fund companies — warns prospective investors in its emerging markets fund that they must be "willing to accept high investment risk." After reading that, you have no cause to whine if you get beaten up by volatile markets in Brazil, Russia, or Thailand. Sure enough, although Templeton Emerging Markets has made tons of money for its investors in some years — including returns in excess of 20 percent in 2005 and 2006 — it also has produced some spectacular losses in other years. Most infamously, it crashed 27 percent in 2000 — but the crash came on the heels of a 43 percent gain the year before!

>> **The costs and fees imposed on investors:** By law you'll find the management fees for a fund and the expenses that have recently been charged to investors. You'll also see any sales charges or commissions. Because most load funds can be bought with a front-end or a deferred load, you'll usually find both options explained (see Chapter 2 in Book 3 for more about front-end and deferred-load funds). Along with the charges to investors, the prospectus must also list the commissions, annual fees, and other incentives given to salespeople. In principle, that's a great idea because it tells fund buyers how their advisers may be biased or influenced. Unfortunately, though, disclosure of commissions is often hedged around with "up to" or "may," leaving most investors no wiser than before. The prospectus also includes a table showing the hypothetical total of expenses and fees an investor in the fund could expect to pay over periods ranging from one to ten years. It's a fairly useful indication as to how much mutual fund investing can cost.

PULLING OUT OF THE DEAL

A mutual fund prospectus (the term comes from a Latin word meaning "view") is one of the central pieces of mutual fund regulation. In fact, it's considered so important that in most provinces you have two business days after you get the prospectus to cancel your purchase of a fund *for any reason.* So even if you pull on a clown costume and dance around as you demand your money back, they have to pay up, no matter how silly your explanation.

Interestingly, in many provinces you also have the right to cancel your mutual fund purchase within 48 hours of getting your order confirmation. But don't expect the fund company or broker to welcome your business in the future if you cancel your order without a reasonable justification. The law assumes that until you've had a chance to read the prospectus, you haven't been properly told about the fund. But after you've read it, you're pretty well on your own. Unless you can show that the fund isn't sticking to the promises made in the prospectus, the people selling and running the fund can reasonably argue that all the risks and expenses have been explained to you — and you'll have a tough time cancelling your agreement to buy the fund.

Prospectuses for bank-sold funds will also talk vaguely about "incentives" given to their employees, and nearly all mutual fund companies will reserve the right to "participate" (as one fund seller delicately puts it) in advertising by brokers and in "conferences" for salespeople. In other words, the fund managers hand over money to help brokers pay for these things. However, the good — or bad — old days of flying to Maui for a "seminar" at a fund company's expense are over. The public, media, and regulators just got so tired of the piggery that the fund industry agreed to introduce a sales code, which bans the worst of the excesses.

REMEMBER

Always remember that a fund company often has two sets of customers: its unitholders (the people who actually own the funds), and the brokers and financial planners who sell its wares. If a broker-sold fund company doesn't keep them sweet, it's in trouble.

More charges to look for

Here are some of the other charges the prospectus must disclose:

>> **Fees for administering registered retirement savings plans (RRSPs), registered retirement income funds (RRIFs), and registered educational savings plans (RESPs):** These range from zero to about $75 annually. Ask if you can pay them separately by cheque — especially where it'll save your

precious RRSP dollars — but some companies claim that their systems are set up only to take the money directly out of your account (which is handier for them).

>> **Fees for closing your account and moving the money to another institution:** Expect to pay $40 or $50.

>> **Fees for short-term trading:** If you sell a fund within a short period after buying it, usually one to three months, you'll often face a penalty of 2 percent of the amount you sold. That's because funds are supposed to be a long-term holding, and investors who hop on and off over and over again increase costs for everyone.

Introducing the Management Report of Fund Performance

In 2005, regulators forced the funds industry to produce annual and semi-annual summaries of fund performance and holdings. These reports, called *management reports of fund performance* (MRFP), also include basic information on the fund's investment mandate and its recent risk experience, and, perhaps most useful of all, a discussion of the fund's recent performance.

Although a fund company must provide you with a copy of a fund's prospectus and its periodic MRFPs, the most recent MRFP is the only document you really need to read to gain a clear picture of a fund's mandate and how the fund's been faring. If the fund seller doesn't give you a copy, ask for it or download it from the fund company's website or from SEDAR, the official online depositary of all securities documents filed in Canada. (We discuss SEDAR more later in this chapter.)

Looking at what goes into an MRFP

An MRFP must contain certain information for the specified period and be presented in a prescribed sequence. The format ensures that consistent and up-to-date information will be available for every mutual fund sold in Canada. Here's a summary of the information that must be included in an MRFP:

>> **Investment objectives:** A summary of the fund's fundamental investment objective and strategies.

>> **Risk experience:** How changes to the investment fund over the financial year affected the overall level of risk associated with an investment in the investment fund.

THE MYSTERIOUS ANNUAL INFORMATION FORM

Pick up any mutual fund prospectus and you'll notice that it's referred to as the "simplified" version. As you get further into mutual funds, and hopefully more interested in them, you might get a hankering to look at the "complicated" version. Well, actually, no such thing exists. The prospectus given to investors is called "simplified" because it's only part of the full prospectus document: The rest of it, technically speaking, is the fund's annual and semi-annual statements and a little-known document called the "annual information form." The AIF is available if you ask for it (the prospectus should provide a contact address or phone number), or you can download it from the Internet at www.sedar.com, the central clearinghouse where just about all Canadian public companies and mutual funds must file their reports and other required disclosure documents. The AIF contains things like the names of the trustees for the funds (who are supposed to be looking out for the interest of the investors), more detail on the commissions paid to brokers and other salespeople, and a bit more information about the outside portfolio managers hired to help run the funds.

>> **Results of operations:** This section covers the fund's performance during the period in question, as compared to its benchmark index. It summarizes noteworthy changes in portfolio holdings, the impact of these changes on the fund's stated objectives, and details of any borrowing in which the fund might have engaged. Portfolio holdings are expressed in terms of individual investments as well as industry sectors, geographic regions, bond investment quality, and currency, as applicable.

>> **Recent developments:** This section includes a discussion of market events and how the fund's overall strategies might have been amended (or not) to respond to the situation. It also must disclose any changes in portfolio managers, or in accounting policies.

>> **Related party transactions:** Any transactions involving parties related to the fund must be disclosed.

>> **Financial highlights:** These are tables showing a breakdown of the calculation of the net asset value per share (NAVPS), various ratios including the management expense ratio and portfolio turnover ratio.

>> **Management fees:** A breakdown of the services received by the fund that constitute its management fees.

>> **Past performance:** Tables show the fund's rates of return for the past ten calendar years, plus one-, three-, five-, and ten-year compound annual returns.

When securities regulators first unveiled the MRFP concept, fund company executives, investment advisers, and investors all greeted it with groans because they feared it would be yet one more level of tedious and expensive documentation. But, in practice, MRFPs have turned out to be a source of pretty good information, all presented in a document typically less than a dozen pages long.

Checking out an MRFP

Have a look at an annual MRFP for a large equity income fund, CI Signature Dividend, for the year ended March 31, 2020. Figures 3-1 through 3-3 show some key information about the fund's performance and portfolio holdings:

» **Year-by-year returns:** These are great for letting you know what kind of swings in value you can expect. The bar charts show annual returns for four share classes of the CI Signature Dividend fund (the "Year-by-Year Returns" section actually shows returns for all 10 classes). The mainstream units, class A, had slightly lower returns than the other classes, which have lower annual expenses because they're sold only by advisers who charge a separate management fee directly to their clients. Regardless of the class, the bars clearly denote the fund's good years and bad.

FIGURE 3-1:
Management report of fund performance showing performance information for the CI Signature Dividend fund.

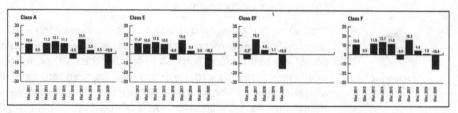

Source: CI Investments

FIGURE 3-2:
Management report of fund performance showing portfolio holdings information for the CI Signature Dividend fund.

SUMMARY OF INVESTMENT PORTFOLIO as at March 31, 2020

Category	% of Net Assets	Category	% of Net Assets	Top 25 Holdings	% of Net Assets
Country allocation		**Sector allocation**			
Canada	54.0	Financials	41.4	Cash & Cash Equivalents	3.7
U.S.A.	22.8	Utilities	9.5	Manulife Financial Corp.	3.0
Cash & Cash Equivalents	3.7	Energy	9.0	Power Corporation of Canada	2.4
Switzerland	3.6	Health Care	8.6	The Bank of Nova Scotia	2.0
France	2.8	Consumer Staples	8.2	Novartis AG, Registered Shares	1.6
U.K.	2.6	Communication Services	4.7	Enbridge Inc.	1.5
Netherlands	2.2	Information Technology	4.6	Merck & Co., Inc.	1.4

Source: CI Investments

FIGURE 3-3:
Management report of fund performance showing annual compound returns for Class A shares of the CI Signature Dividend fund.

	One Year (%)	Three Years (%)	Five Years (%)	Ten Years (%)	Since Inception (%)
Class A	(15.9)	(4.3)	(0.9)	4.0	n/a
Blended Index (new)	(13.9)	(2.4)	0.5	4.4	n/a
Blended Index (old)	(14.1)	(2.6)	0.6	4.5	n/a
MSCI ACWI Global High Dividend Yield Total Return Index	(7.6)	2.0	4.2	8.4	n/a
S&P/TSX Preferred Share Total Return Index (new)	(21.0)	(8.0)	(4.4)	(0.4)	n/a
S&P/TSX Composite Total Return Index	(14.2)	(1.9)	0.9	4.1	n/a
BMO Capital Markets 50 Preferred Total Return Index (old)	(21.7)	(8.6)	(4.1)	0.0	n/a
Class E	(16.2)	(4.7)	(1.3)	n/a	4.3
Blended Index (new)	(13.9)	(2.4)	0.5	n/a	3.8
Blended Index (old)	(14.1)	(2.6)	0.6	n/a	3.9
MSCI ACWI Global High Dividend Yield Total Return Index	(7.6)	2.0	4.2	n/a	8.9
S&P/TSX Preferred Share Total Return Index (new)	(21.0)	(8.0)	(4.4)	n/a	(1.9)
S&P/TSX Composite Total Return Index	(14.2)	(1.9)	0.9	n/a	3.4
BMO Capital Markets 50 Preferred Total Return Index (old)	(21.7)	(8.6)	(4.1)	n/a	(1.6)

Source: CI Investments

TECHNICAL STUFF

>> **Annual compound returns:** This shows the rates of return, compounded annually, over one-, three-, five-, and ten-year periods ended March 31, 2020, for all share classes. It also shows the share class compound annual return since its inception in October 1996, compared with the performance of two benchmark blended indices, the MSCI ACWI Global High Dividend Yield Index, the S&P/TSX Preferred Share Index, the Standard & Poor's/Toronto Stock Exchange composite index, and the BMO Capital Markets 50 Preferred Shares Total Return Index. The S&P/ TSX Composite Index tracks the broad Canadian stock market, and the BMO index is a barometer of the performance of preferred shares. *Preferreds,* as they're called, are the traditional form of dividend-paying stock, but nowadays fewer companies issue them, preferring (no pun intended) to pay dividends to shareholders via common stock.

We'll spare you a lengthy discussion on the reasons why — although the serious lag in performance by preferreds, as shown in this table, might have something to do with it. Suffice it to say that the BMO preferred index is a worthwhile benchmark to use in this case. Blended returns of the two indices also are provided. The A units (which are fee-inclusive and are what most people buy) have underperformed (4 per cent vs. 4.4 per cent) the blended index over the long term (10 years) and also lagged the broader S&P/TSX, although by very little (4 per cent versus 4.1 per cent).

>> **Portfolio breakdown:** This table shows in which sectors the fund invests, as well as other types of investments such as cash and cash equivalents. In CI Signature Dividend's case, more than 40 per cent of the portfolio was in the Financials sector as of March 2020 — not surprising, given the fund's mandate to produce dividend income.

>> **Top-25 holdings:** The big holdings of an equity fund represent the manager's true loves. They're a reliable guide to the personality of the fund. Check 'em out — if they're natural resource producers or small companies you've never heard of, or bonds issued by technology outfits or developing nations, you're

in for interesting times. The top holdings of CI Signature Dividend are all big blue-chip companies (Manulife Financial Corp., Power Corporation of Canada, The Bank of Nova Scotia, Novartis AG, Enbridge Inc., and so on) that normally pay dividends. Their shares aren't likely to shoot up ten times in value, but they're not likely to go bust either.

The financial section (see Figure 3-4) has some lines of tabular data well worth noting, specifically the following:

>> **Net assets:** Asset growth (or shrinkage) is a key indicator of a fund's health. As you can see, this fund's assets have decreased since 2016, likely due to investors' thirst for higher income-producing investments, and a reflection of investor "search for yield" given low global interest rates.

>> **Management expense ratio (MER):** This is useful information when you're looking for low-cost funds (and you are). Seeing the figures for five years shows whether the fund company has been able to reduce its MER, particularly if its assets have decreased. In mutual funds, economies of scale don't seem to apply. However, in this case, the after-tax MER has decreased slightly from 1.89% to 1.88%.

>> **Portfolio turnover rate:** This measures the speed at which the manager changes the fund's holdings — a 100-per cent turnover rate is high, indicating that trading equivalent to the value of the entire fund took place during the year. High turnover in a fund, of course, means higher transaction costs and greater expenses to the fund. This value has been a staple of U.S. fund reporting for years and was adopted as a Canadian requirement during a reporting upgrade. As for this chapter's example, CI Signature Dividend's turnover rate has been in general going down since 2016, no doubt a contributing factor to its slightly decreasing MER.

FIGURE 3-4: Management report of fund performance showing some of the financial information for CI Signature Dividend fund.

	Total net assets [1] $000's	Number of units outstanding [2] 000's	Management expense ratio before taxes [3] %	Harmonized sales tax [4] %	Management expense ratio after taxes [5] %	Effective HST rate for the year [6] %	Trading expense ratio [7] %	Portfolio turnover rate [8] %
Class A								
Commencement of operations October 29, 1996								
Mar. 31, 2020	485,143	43,896	1.70	0.18	1.88	10.85	0.08	43.88
Mar. 31, 2019	384,798	28,255	1.70	0.18	1.88	10.85	0.12	44.29
Mar. 31, 2018	584,221	41,598	1.70	0.19	1.89	10.91	0.11	53.14
Mar. 31, 2017	798,115	54,294	1.70	0.19	1.89	10.98	0.10	51.99
Mar. 31, 2016	790,578	58,905	1.70	0.19	1.89	10.97	0.10	57.28

Source: CI Investments

Paperwork and Your Rights

WHAT IS THE S&P/TSX COMPOSITE INDEX?

The S&P/TSX composite is Canada's main stock market barometer, measuring the value of nearly 300 of our most important publicly traded companies, such as Royal Bank of Canada or Trans-Canada PipeLines Ltd. It's a fine way of checking how good the returns from stocks in general have been. For example, the index climbed above 15,000 for the first time in May 2008, doubling its value in less than five years. High prices for energy and other commodities propelled the TSX's surge.

Every country has benchmarks for measuring returns from its local stock market. The United States has the old-fashioned Dow Jones Industrial Average, a relic of the 1800s that contains 30 giant companies. But the more representative Standard & Poor's index of 500 companies and the technology-heavy Nasdaq Composite Index also exist. The wildest index name you may come across is Finland's: The Hex Index.

The S&P/TSX composite used to contain a fixed 300 companies — when it was known as the TSE 300 — but the Canadian market turned out to be too small to produce 300 companies large enough for big pension funds and mutual funds to invest in. After persistent criticism that the index was full of little stocks that were hard to trade, the exchange brought in Standard & Poor's Corp. of New York to redesign the market benchmark. The revamped edition was launched in 2002. These days, the index has no fixed number of stocks. Find out more about stock investing in Book 2.

Surveying Your Account Statement

Account statements, which show how much your holdings are worth and how much you've bought and sold since the last report from your fund company, are one area where the fund industry still needs to make progress. Investors often have trouble understanding what they actually own and even more difficulty figuring out their rates of return. Every company uses its own system and layout, and jargon such as "book value" isn't much help.

You may get an account statement only twice a year if you invest through a stock-broker or financial planner. The broker or planner and the fund company you've used will often both send you statements for the six months ending June 30 and for the year ending December 31. Usually the people who invest through a sales-person aren't interested in monitoring their investments frequently (that's why they hired someone to advise them), so twice-yearly statements are fine. Some-times, a company will agree to send you statements more frequently — so try asking — but the fund seller's system may not be set up to do this. However, as more brokerages and planning firms make statement downloading available via their websites, monthly frequency is becoming more common.

If you hold your funds directly with a bank or no-load company, then you'll probably get a statement every quarter. That's because investors who go directly to their bank or to a fund company usually enjoy making their own decisions about investing — so they want to check their holdings more frequently. If you invest through a discount broker, your statement will often arrive monthly, especially if you've done some buying or selling in your account during the previous month. Discount brokerage customers tend to be very interested in investing, so they insist on regular updates. All companies still send out account statements, but just about every large fund seller also now lets you check your account and recent transactions over the phone or at their Internet site.

Besides your name, address, account number, and the nature of your account (that is, taxable or tax-deferred), your statement will almost certainly show the following:

» The total value of your investment in each fund you hold, plus a total value for your account.

» The number of fund units you held and their price or net asset value at the end of the reporting period. Be sure to check these against the unit value shown for the fund in an online monthly report for the period — and it's not a bad idea to verify that the number of units matches the number shown in your previous statement, adjusting for any sales or purchases you may have made or for any distributions (in the form of new units) the fund declared.

» Any purchases or redemptions of units, and at what prices.

Beyond that, statements vary, but many big fund companies also provide the following information:

» The change in the value of your account, and ideally of your investment in each fund, since your last statement.

» The book value of your holdings. This technically means the amount you've ever put into the fund, which is useful for calculating whether you're using up your complete foreign content limit in a tax-sheltered plan. That's because the foreign content is calculated as a percentage of the book value, not of the current market value.

TIP

Some more service-oriented forms calculate compound rates of return for client portfolios. Although this should be a standard service in this era of high technology and regulation, it is an extreme exception to the rule. If your adviser provides this information to you, express how much you appreciate it. If on the other hand they don't provide portfolio compounded returns, bug them about doing so.

Annual and Semi-Annual Financial Statements (or Annual Reports)

At least once a year, a glossy brochure turns up in the mail filled with rows of dull-looking figures and dry terms such as "statements of operations" or "net realized gain (loss) on sale of investment (excluding short-term notes)." These are the fund's financial statements, which, like the prospectus discussed earlier in this chapter, usually group several funds into one document. Fund companies produce the statements twice a year. They have to send the report for the fund's financial year-end to all unitholders, but they're generally allowed to send the half-year report only to investors who actually request it. There should be a mail-in card for you to do this.

TIP

Unless this stuff really puts you to sleep, ask to have the six-month report mailed to you. You'll be reminding the fund company that you take your money seriously.

Getting worked up about the financial details in the statements is pointless, but some important items to check include the following:

>> The report must show the complete portfolio for the fund, not just the top holdings. It's worth it, and interesting, to glance down the list to see whether the manager has any funny-looking stuff that may be an attempt to jazz up performance while taking on more risk. The full portfolio listing will also show how much the fund paid for each stock and bond and what it's worth now: It's always fun to see which investment has proved to be a disaster for the fund, although managers often "window dress" by dumping a turkey so it doesn't show up in the report.

TIP

>> The statements often contain a commentary by the manager or fund company on what went right or wrong for the fund. As usual with mutual fund handouts, these tend to be bland and boring descriptions of the market or economic outlook, rather than an honest discussion of the manager's good and bad moves. But look for some important clues. If the portfolio manager has been replaced or if the fund's strategy is being changed in a major way, it may be time to dump it. And keep an eye on the top holdings. If they look riskier than you want, or if they leave out major sectors of the economy, then the fund company may be rolling the dice in order to jack up returns and attract more investors.

DON'T THROW THE BOOK VALUE AT YOUR MANAGER

Be careful when comparing the book value of your investment in a fund with its market value. The book value is the total sum that's been put into the fund, so in that sense it represents your total investment. But it also includes the value of any distributions made by the fund in the form of new units, even though they weren't real investments that came out of your pocket. The reinvested distributions have the effect of increasing the book value, and they can make it grow larger than the market value — making it appear the fund has lost you money when it may have been a winner.

For example, say you originally invest $10,000 in a fund that produces a return of 20 percent, leaving you with a market value of $12,000. But say the manager is an active trader and she pays out $4,000 in capital gains distributions along the way. Then your fund could have a book value of $14,000, or $2,000 more than its market value on your statement, even though the manager has done a good job.

Chapter **4**

Investing in Canadian Exchange-Traded Funds

When it comes to stock investing, there's more than one way to do it. Buying stocks directly is good; sometimes, buying stocks indirectly is equally good (or even better) — especially if you're risk averse. Buying a great stock is every stock investor's dream, but sometimes you face investing environments that make finding a winning stock a hazardous pursuit. Prudent stock investors should consider adding Canadian and U.S. exchange-traded funds (ETFs) to their wealth-building arsenal.

An exchange-traded fund (ETF) is basically a mutual fund that invests in a fixed basket of securities but with a few twists. This chapter shows you how ETFs are similar to (and different from) mutual funds, provides some pointers on picking ETFs, and notes the fundamentals of stock indexes (which are connected to ETFs).

Comparing Exchange-Traded Funds and Mutual Funds

For many folks and for many years, the only choice besides investing directly in stocks was to invest indirectly through mutual funds (the topic of Book 3). After all, why buy a single stock for roughly the same few thousand dollars that you can buy a mutual fund for and get benefits such as professional management and diversification?

For small investors, mutual fund investing isn't a bad way to go. Investors participate by pooling their money with others and get professional money management in an affordable manner. But mutual funds have their downsides too. Many, in fact. Mutual fund fees, which include management fees and sales charges (referred to as *loads*), eat into gains, and investors have no choice about investments in a mutual fund. Whatever the fund manager buys, sells, or holds on to is pretty much what the investors in the fund have to tolerate. Investment choice is limited to either being in the fund . . . or being out.

But now, with ETFs, investors have greater choices than ever, a scenario that sets the stage for the inevitable comparison between mutual funds and ETFs. The following sections go over the differences and similarities between ETFs and mutual funds.

The differences

Simply stated, in a mutual fund, securities such as stocks and bonds are constantly bought, sold, and held; in other words, the fund is actively managed by a third-party portfolio manager. An ETF holds similar securities, but the portfolio typically isn't actively managed. Instead, an ETF usually holds a fixed basket of securities that may reflect an index or a particular industry or sector. (An index is a method of measuring the value of a segment of the general stock market. It's a tool used by money managers and investors to compare the performance of a particular stock to a widely accepted standard; see the later section "Taking Note of Indexes" for more.)

For example, an ETF that tries to reflect the S&P/TSX 60 will attempt to hold a securities portfolio that mirrors the composition of the S&P/TSX 60 Index as closely as possible. Here's another example: A water utilities ETF may hold the top 15 or 20 publicly held water companies. (You get the picture.)

REMEMBER

Where ETFs are markedly different from mutual funds (and where they're really advantageous) is that they can be bought and sold like stocks. In addition, you can do with ETFs what you can generally do with stocks (but can't usually do with mutual funds): You can buy in share allotments, such as 1, 50, or 100 shares more. Mutual funds, on the other hand, are usually bought in dollar amounts, such as 1,000 or 5,000 dollars' worth. The dollar amount you can initially invest is set by the manager of the individual mutual fund.

Here are some other advantages of ETFs: You can put various buy/sell brokerage orders on ETFs, and many ETFs are optionable (meaning you may be able to buy/sell put and call options on them). Mutual funds typically aren't optionable or can't be sold short.

In addition, many ETFs are marginable (meaning that you can borrow against them with some limitations in your brokerage account). Mutual funds usually aren't marginable in Canada or the U.S. (although it is possible if they're within the confines of a stock brokerage account).

REMEMBER

Sometimes an investor can readily see the great potential of a given industry or sector but is hard-pressed to get that single really good stock that can take advantage of the profit possibilities of that particular segment of the market. The great thing about an ETF is that you can make that investment very easily, knowing that if you're unsure about it, you can put in place strategies that protect you from the downside (such as stop-loss orders or trailing stops). That way, you can sleep easier!

The similarities

Even though ETFs and mutual funds have some major differences, they do share a few similarities:

>> First and foremost, ETFs and mutual funds (MFs) are similar in that they aren't direct investments; they're "conduits" of investing or "investment vehicles," which means that they act like a connection between the investor and the investments.

>> Both ETFs and MFs basically pool the money of investors and the pool becomes the "fund," which in turn invests in a portfolio of investments.

>> Both ETFs and MFs offer the great advantage of diversification (although they accomplish it in different ways).

>> Investors don't have any choice about what makes up the portfolio of either the ETF or the MF. The ETF has a fixed basket of securities (the money manager overseeing the portfolio makes those choices), and, of course, investors can't control the choices made in a mutual fund.

REMEMBER

For those investors who want more active assistance in making choices and running a portfolio, the MF may very well be the way to go. For those who are more comfortable making their own choices in terms of the particular index or industry/sector they want to invest in, the ETF is a much better venue.

Choosing an Exchange-Traded Fund

Buying a stock is an investment in a particular company (as you find out in Book 2), but an ETF is an opportunity to invest in a block of stocks. In the same way a few mouse clicks can buy you a stock at a stock brokerage website, those same clicks can buy you virtually an entire industry or sector (or at least the top-tier stocks).

For investors who are comfortable with their own choices and do their due diligence, buying a winning stock is a better (albeit more aggressive) way to go. For those investors who want to make their own choices but aren't that confident about picking winning stocks, getting an ETF is definitely a better way to go.

You had to figure that choosing an ETF wasn't going to be a coin flip. You should be aware of certain considerations, some of which are tied more to your personal outlook and preferences than to the underlying portfolio of the ETF. The following sections give you the info you need on bullish and bearish ETFs.

Main types of ETFs

You may wake up one day and say, "I think the stock market or a special segment of it will do very well going forward from today," and that's just fine if you think so. Maybe your research on the general economy, financial outlook, and political considerations make you feel happier than a starving man on a cruise ship. But you just don't know (or don't care to research) which stocks would best benefit from the good market moves yet to come. No problem! That's because the following sections cover the primary types of ETFs you can choose from. ETFs represent one of the best examples of what is often referred to as *story investing*.

TIP

To find out more about ETFs in general and to get more details on the ETFs mentioned throughout this chapter (Horizons AlphaPro Managed S&P/TSX 60 ETF, SPY, PBJ, and SH), go to websites such as www.etfdb.com. A great way to see whether ETFs exist to fit a theme you have in mind is to simply search for the term in your favorite search engine. For example, if you are intrigued by artificial intelligence, use the search term "ETFs for artificial intelligence."

Major market equity index ETFs

Why not invest in ETFs that mirror a general major market index such as the U.S. S&P 500 or Canadian S&P/TSX 60? This type of index ETF tracks the overall market. Other index ETFs track a specific subset of the overall market, such as small capitalization (small cap) stocks or large capitalization (large cap) stocks. Subset indexes also exist for sectors such as technology, oil and gas, and consumer goods. The slicing and dicing can go further — much further, in fact, as each year passes and the ETF industry continues to grow.

Index ETFs typically include equities. The equities may be from Canada, the U.S., or elsewhere in North America, or they may be global or international in scope. Perhaps the ETF is a combination of all of these. The bottom line is *anything goes*, so don't worry too much about the categories. What's important is *what* the ETF contains by way of underlying securities, and the stories those stocks and other securities tell.

An index-based ETF tries to earn the return of the market or subset of the market that it seeks to mimic, less the fees. American ETFs such as SPY construct their portfolios to track the composition of the S&P 500, known as its "benchmark," as closely as possible. Canadian ETFs such as the Horizons AlphaPro Managed S&P/TSX 60 ETF track component stocks within the S&P/TSX 60 Index. As they say, why try to beat the market when you can match it? It's a great way to go when the market is having a good rally. (See the later section "Taking Note of Indexes" for the basics on indexes.)

When the S&P 500 and the S&P/TSX 60 were battered in late 2008 and early 2009, the respective U.S. and Canadian ETFs, of course, mirrored that performance and hit the bottom in March 2009. But from that moment on and well into the time of the writing of this book, the S&P 500 (and the ETFs that tracked it like the iShares Core S&P 500 ETF) did really well. The ETFs that tracked the S&P/TSX 60 did reasonably well during this same period. It paid to buck the bearish sentiment of early 2009. Of course it did take some contrarian gumption to do so, but at least you had the benefit of the full S&P 500 stock portfolio, which at least had more diversification than a single stock or a single subsection of the market.

ETFs that include dividend-paying stocks

ETFs don't necessarily have to be tied to a specific industry or sector; they can be tied to a specific type or subcategory of stock. All things being equal, what basic categories of stocks do you think would better weather bad times: stocks with no dividends or stocks that pay dividends? (The question answers itself, pretty much like "What tastes better: apple pie or barbed wire?") Although some sectors are known for being good dividend payers, such as utilities (and there are some good ETFs that cover this industry), some ETFs cover stocks that meet a specific criteria.

You can find ETFs that include high-dividend income stocks (typically 4 percent or higher), as well as ETFs that include stocks of companies that don't necessarily pay high dividends but do have a long track record of dividend increases that meet or exceed the rate of inflation.

Given these types of dividend-paying ETFs, it becomes clear what is good for what type of stock investor:

>> If we were stock investors who were currently retired, we'd probably choose the high-dividend stock ETF, along with a bond ETF. Dividend-paying stock ETFs are generally more stable than those stock ETFs that don't pay dividends and, for most Canadians, are important vehicles for generating retirement income.

>> If we were in pre-retirement (some years away from retirement but clearly planning for it), we'd probably choose the ETF with the stocks that had a strong record of growing the dividend payout, along with a bond ETF. That way, those same dividend-paying stocks would grow in the short term and provide better income down the road during retirement.

For more information on dividends, flip to Chapters 1 and 4 in Book 2.

Currency ETFs

Currency ETFs are designed to track the performance of a single currency in the foreign exchange market against a benchmark currency or basket of currencies. The way ETFs do this is quite exotic and beyond the scope of this book. But in short, the ETFs consist of cash deposits, debt instruments denominated in a certain currency, and futures or swap contracts.

Currency markets used to be the playground of experienced traders. However, exchange-traded funds kicked open the doors of foreign exchange to Canadian investors. Through a stock market gateway, currency ETFs are used by Canadians who look for exposure to the foreign exchange market, seek diversification, and prefer to transact outside of the complex and cumbersome futures or foreign exchange market.

Fixed-income ETFs

Fixed-income or *bond* ETFs are still in their infancy. However, they may have a role during times of instability. They are a form of ETF that exclusively invests in fixed-income financial instruments. These holdings can be a portfolio of corporate or government bonds or a combination of the two. They can employ different strategies such as high-yield only, and can hold within the ETF long-term or short-term maturity financial instruments. These are called *maturity-themed ETFs.* Take note that the ETF itself has no maturity, and bond ETFs are passively managed. Fixed-income ETFs trade like stock ETFs on a major exchange.

Alternative ETFs related to a strategy

What are alternative ETFs? In a nutshell, they're anything that doesn't fit nicely into the equity or other types of ETFs covered so far. Some ETFs cover industries such as food and beverages, water, energy, and other things that people will keep buying no matter how good or bad the economy is. Without needing a crystal ball or having an iron-willed contrarian attitude, a stock investor can simply put money into stocks — or in this case, ETFs — tied to human need.

TIP

Keep in mind that dividend-paying stocks, described earlier in this chapter, generally fall within the criteria of "human need" investing because those companies tend to be large and stable, with good cash flows, giving them the ongoing wherewithal to pay good dividends.

Another type of alternative strategy is to focus on a sector such as commodities. Sub-sectors may include oil and gas, agriculture, sugar, coffee, precious metals, livestock — just about anything! This is where stock investor creativity can pay off.

ETFs may also be thematic by focusing, for instance, on stocks of growth companies, or stocks of value companies.

To give you a better sense of the wide array of Canadian ETFs that are out there, check out the following list of ETFs trading on the TSX Canadian stock exchange, as of June 2020, arranged by decreasing order of YTD trading volume (note that this list isn't exhaustive):

- » iShares S&P/TSX 60 Index ETF
- » BetaPro Crude Oil Daily Bull ETF

- » BetaPro Natural Gas 2x Daily Bull ETF

- » BetaPro Crude Oil -1x Daily Bear ETF

- » iShares S&P/TSX Capped Energy Index ETF

- » BetaPro S&P 500 -2x Daily Bear ETF

- » iShares S&P/TSX Capped Financials Index ETF

- » iShares S&P/TSX Global Gold Index ETF

- » BetaPro Canadian Gold Miners -2x Daily Bear ETF

- » BMO Equal Weight Banks Index ETF

Bearish ETFs

Most ETFs are bullish in nature because they invest in a portfolio of securities that they expect to go up in due course. But some ETFs have a bearish focus. Bearish ETFs (also called short ETFs) maintain a portfolio of securities and strategies that are designed to go the opposite way of the underlying or targeted securities. In other words, this type of ETF goes up when the underlying securities go down (and vice versa). Bearish ETFs employ securities such as put options (and similar derivatives) and employ strategies such as going short.

Take the S&P/TSX 60, for example. If you were bullish on that index, you might choose an ETF such as Horizons AlphaPro Managed S&P/TSX 60. If you were bearish, you could invest in the Horizons BetaPro S&P/TSX 60 Inverse ETF, which seeks investment returns that fully correspond to the inverse of the S&P/TSX 60 Index.

If you were bearish on the US S&P 500 index because of Fiscal Cliff and other concerns and wanted to seek gains by betting that it would go down, you could choose an ETF such as the ProShares Short S&P 500 ETF (SH).

You can take two approaches on bearish ETFs:

- » **Hoping for a downfall:** If you're speculating on a pending market crash, a bearish ETF is a good consideration. In this approach, you're actually seeking to make a profit based on your expectations. Those folks who aggressively went into bearish ETFs during early or mid 2008 made some spectacular profits during the tumultuous downfall during late 2008 and early 2009.

>> **Hedging against a downfall:** A more conservative approach is to use bearish ETFs to a more moderate extent, primarily as a form of hedging, whereby the bearish ETF acts like a form of insurance in the unwelcome event of a significant market pullback or crash. We say "unwelcome" because you're not really hoping for a crash; you're just trying to protect yourself with a modest form of diversification. In this context, diversification means that you have a mix of both bullish positions and, to a smaller extent, bearish positions.

Taking Note of Indexes

For stock investors, ETFs that are bullish or bearish are ultimately tied to major market indexes. You should take a quick look at indexes to better understand them (and the ETFs tied to them).

Whenever you hear the CBC or other media commentary, or the scuttlebutt at the local watering hole about "how the market is doing," it typically refers to a market proxy such as an index. You'll usually hear them mention "the Dow" or perhaps the "S&P/TSX 60." There are certainly other major market indexes, and there are many lesser, yet popular, measurements such as the Dow Jones Transportation Average. Indexes and averages tend to be used interchangeably, but they're distinctly different entities of measurement.

Most people use these indexes basically as standards of market performance to see whether they're doing better or worse than a yardstick for comparison purposes. They want to know continually whether their stocks, ETFs, mutual funds, or overall portfolios are performing well.

In Canada, the TSX (https://tsx.com/) is now Canada's main exchange for the trading of equities. The S&P/TSX 60 Index includes 60 large capitalization stocks for Canadian equity markets. The index is market-capitalization weighted (weighted for company stock market value), weight-adjusted for things like share float (shares readily available to the public), and also balanced across ten industry sectors. Table 4-1 shows the current lineup of 60 stocks tracked on the S&P/TSX 60.

Even though the S&P/TSX 60 Index contains the "big guns" as its constituent companies, it's the S&P/TSX Composite Index that's the headline benchmark Canadian index, and the one you hear on the radio about the most. It represents about 70 percent of the total market capitalization on the Toronto Stock Exchange (TSX) with about 250 companies out of the total 1,500 companies that make up the Toronto Stock Exchange. (See Chapter 1 of Book 2 for more about stock exchanges.)

TABLE 4-1   Stocks on the S&P/TSX 60

Company	Symbol
Agnico Eagle Mines Limited	AEM
Algonquin Power & Utilities Corp.	AQN
Alimentation Couche-Tard Inc. Class B Subordinate Voting Shares	ATD.B
BCE Inc.	BCE
Bank of Montreal	BMO
Bank of Nova Scotia (The)	BNS
Barrick Gold Corporation	ABX
Bausch Health Companies Inc.	BHC
Brookfield Asset Management Inc. Class A Limited Voting Shares	BAM.A
Brookfield Infrastructure Partners L.P. Limited Partnership Units	BIP.UN
Brookfield Property Partners L.P. Limited Partnership Units	BPY.UN
CCL Industries Inc. Unlimited Class B Non-Voting Shares	CCL.B
CGI Inc. Class A Subordinate Voting Shares	GIB.A
Cameco Corporation	CCO
Canadian Apartment Properties Real Estate Investment Trust Trust Units	CAR.UN
Canadian Imperial Bank Of Commerce	CM
Canadian National Railway Company	CNR
Canadian Natural Resources Limited	CNQ
Canadian Pacific Railway Limited	CP
Canadian Tire Corporation Limited Class A Non-Voting Shares	CTC.A
Canopy Growth Corporation	WEED
Cenovus Energy Inc.	CVE
Constellation Software Inc.	CSU
Dollarama Inc.	DOL
Emera Incorporated	EMA
Enbridge Inc.	ENB

Company	Symbol
First Quantum Minerals Ltd.	FM
Fortis Inc.	FTS
Franco-Nevada Corporation	FNV
George Weston Limited	WN
Gildan Activewear Inc.	GIL
Imperial Oil Limited	IMO
Inter Pipeline Ltd.	IPL
Kinross Gold Corporation	K
Kirkland Lake Gold Ltd.	KL
Loblaw Companies Limited	L
Magna International Inc.	MG
Manulife Financial Corporation	MFC
Metro Inc.	MRU
National Bank of Canada	NA
Nutrien Ltd.	NTR
Open Text Corporation	OTEX
Pembina Pipeline Corporation	PPL
Power Corporation of Canada Subordinate Voting Shares	POW
Restaurant Brands International Inc.	QSR
Rogers Communications Inc. Class B Non-voting Shares	RCI.B
Royal Bank of Canada	RY
SNC-Lavalin Group Inc.	SNC
Saputo Inc.	SAP
Shaw Communications Inc. Class B Non-voting Shares	SJR.B
Shopify Inc. Class A Subordinate Voting Shares	SHOP
Sun Life Financial Inc.	SLF

(continued)

TABLE 4-1 *(continued)*

Company	Symbol
Suncor Energy Inc.	SU
TC Energy Corporation	TRP
TELUS Corporation Common	T
Teck Resources Limited Class B Subordinate Voting Shares	TECK.B
Thomson Reuters Corporation With New Deposit Receip	TRI
Toronto-Dominion Bank (The)	TD
Waste Connections Inc.	WCN
Wheaton Precious Metals Corp.	WPM

IN THIS CHAPTER

» **Checking out old, reliable, guaranteed investment certificates**

» **Looking at regular bonds and strip bonds**

» **Taking stock of stocks**

» **Sniffing out income trusts**

» **Investigating managed products**

Chapter 5

Beyond Mutual Funds

So you've got your debt under control and your insurance taken care of. Time to start saving money. But what are you going to do with those vast piles of cash? Think of this chapter as an investment primer, a rundown on the drawbacks and attractions of the different types of financial assets you can buy with your savings. If you're certain by now that funds are the way to go for you, then feel free to skip to Chapter 2 in Book 3, which introduces where you can go to buy them. But it's useful to know about the other investment choices you have — including Canada Savings Bonds and guaranteed investment certificates, which can't be bought through mutual funds at all.

Don't worry, though. The decisions you need to make are fairly simple when you come down to it. The investment business is an incredibly conservative industry. For all the dot-com flash and techno-trading systems, your basic investment options are the same as they were in the 1920s or even the 1820s — stocks, bonds, or cash. Here's what's out there: everything from the mundane to the manic. This chapter takes you for a stroll down Risk Road, moving from the very safest choices to the most unpredictable. Along the way, it points out some of the dangers and delights of each investment — so that even if you end up handing your money over to a fund company to manage, you'll at least have an idea of what they're going to do with it.

The Good Old GIC: You Know Where You Sleep

You've no doubt noticed that most banks offer miserable rates of interest — 1 percent if you're lucky — on money dumped in a "savings" account. You may be able to get more if you keep a very high balance in the account, or if you opt for an account with a higher rate but exorbitant transaction fees. And some "e-savings" accounts pay a decent rate with low fees if you abide by certain transaction rules. But without getting bogged down in bank-account research, you can do better if you put the cash in a *guaranteed investment certificate* (GIC) with a bank, insurance company, or trust company for a fixed period.

REMEMBER

A GIC is a deposit that a financial institution accepts on the understanding that the money, plus a guaranteed amount of interest, will be returned after a set number of years. The interest is calculated on an annual basis and each year's interest is usually added or "compounded" onto the total for the purpose of calculating the next year's interest — so you earn interest on interest. A drawback is that you may not be able to get the deposit back before the term is up, or, if you can, you might have to forfeit the interest earned. In other words, these deposits aren't as *liquid* — cashable — as you might think. The great beauty of GICs, though, is that you know exactly where you stand: For example, a five-year deposit of $10,000 at a rate of 3 percent compounded annually will give you $11,592.74 after 60 months — no more and no less.

For years, generations even, the GIC was Canada's favourite investment, and it's still the number-one choice of many Europeans. And why not? Consider this example: In 1990, when interest rates were high and prices for food and shelter were rising fast, you could leave money on deposit at a big, safe bank and come back a year later to collect a lump sum that had magically grown by 12 percent (see bar 8 in Figure 5-1). Well, it wasn't magic, actually. Banks had to offer those kinds of rates to attract any money because inflation was rising.

But as you can see from Figure 5-1, a steady drop in the rate of inflation during the 1990s meant a remorseless decline in GIC rates. And after rates slumped below the 7- to 8-percent mark in the early part of the decade, the stage was set for a flood of hundreds of billions of dollars into mutual funds as Canadians demanded a decent return on their money.

The recession of the early 1980s and fears of a recurrence around 1990 kept interest rates high until 1992, when the economy strengthened and rates began their plummet to historic lows before rising ever so slightly the past few years. So, no bonanza.

FIGURE 5-1:
One-year
average
GIC rates,
1983–2020.

Source: Bank of Canada

Types of GICs

GICs come in a sometimes-bewildering range of shapes and flavours, so always make sure you understand all of the mechanics before you buy one. Get an employee of the financial institution to write down the value of the deposit when it matures (except in the case of index-linked GICs, whose returns are tied to the stock market).

Here are some common variations above and beyond the traditional non-cashable GIC (even more specific types exist):

>> **Cashable GICs:** Traditional GICs tie your money up or at least reduce the interest you get if you cash out early. But cashable GICs let you take all or part of your money out early with no penalty. Expect to get a lower annual rate, though. It can be a full percentage point lower than the return on a normal non-cashable GIC.

>> **Index-linked GICs:** These pay you little or no fixed interest but they promise to return your initial investment and pay a return that's linked to the performance of a stock market index — always a bit watered-down, though, in order to pay for the guaranteed return of capital and leave a profit margin for the bank. In other words, your money is safe from loss but your potential return isn't as good as it would have been investing directly in stocks. For example, a typical GIC linked to the Canadian stock market might pay no guaranteed interest but give the investor a return identical to the change in the Standard & Poor's/ Toronto Stock Exchange 60 index — subject to some limitations.

WARNING

Index GICs are popular when interest rates on ordinary GICs are low. The problem with these products is that their rules and terms are so complicated it can be difficult or impossible to know how well you're doing as you go along. Yes, they offer some stock market action for investors who would otherwise be too nervous to go into equities, but most investors will do better with an index fund and a couple of conservative equity funds, especially if they can ride out downturns in the market over a few years.

Some institutions have rolled out GICs linked to the performance of a specific mutual fund. Royal Bank has one linked to its RBC O'Shaughnessy International Equity Fund. Bank of Montreal links one of its "Progressive GICs" to returns of its BMO Dividend Fund.

>> **Convertible GICs:** RRSP marketing season (for registered retirement savings plans) is the first 60 days of the calendar year, when money put into your RRSP can be used to reduce taxable income for the previous year. For example, if you earned $50,000 during 2019 but managed to put $5,000 into a plan by March 1, 2020, then you'd have to pay tax on income of only $45,000 for 2019. During that two-month period, institutions offer flexible GICs that let you invest your money at the one-year rate, but then allow you to switch to a longer-term deposit or to the company's mutual funds.

>> **Escalating-rate GICs:** These GICs also don't lock you in. You can cash out without penalty after one or two years, but if you stay on, the interest rate gets higher. The design of these GICs varies among institutions, and some offer more than one type. Like index-linked GICs, the returns offered by some of these "escalator" GICs are based on some pretty complex formulas.

Finding the best rates

A quick way to find out the various GIC rates on offer from a wide variety of institutions is to check websites like ratehub.ca (https://www.ratehub.ca/gics) or print newspapers. Both online and print tables list rates at a range of lenders and deposit takers, from the biggest bank to the most obscure trust company.

REMEMBER

You often can get a higher rate by going to a smaller company, but dealing with the little outfit may be more troublesome because it won't have the same branch network and resources. Wherever you go, make sure the institution is a member of the Canada Deposit Insurance Corp. See the next section for more on the deposit insurance protection provided by this government agency.

Checking out the benefits of GICs

REMEMBER

Don't spurn the humble GIC out of hand. They never lose money. Remember bad-news years for the stock market, such as 2001 and 2002, when the median Canadian equity fund lost 8 percent and 14 percent, respectively? Sticking to one-year GICs would have kept you in the black those years, gaining an average 2.7 percent and 1.6 percent, respectively. GICs offer other advantages:

» **Simplicity:** They're simple and quick to buy, with no extra fees or complicated forms to fill out. Just about any bank, insurance company, or stockbroker will sell you one.

» **Income generating:** They're a useful planning tool if you need your portfolio to throw off a regular stream of income. That can be done by "laddering" GICs — putting the money into deposits with separate terms, each maturing on a different date to match your spending needs. Even if you don't need the money for income, having your GICs come due at different times is also handy for reducing "reinvestment risk." That's the problem of getting a pile of money to reinvest from a maturing bond or deposit just as interest rates are low. If the money comes up for reinvestment at different times, you can reinvest it at a variety of interest rates.

» **Safe and secure:** If you buy a GIC from a bank, trust company, or loan company, as long as the GIC's term to maturity doesn't exceed five years, your money is protected by insurance provided by the federal government's Canada Deposit Insurance Corporation. If the financial institution fails, CDIC will cover an individual for up to $100,000 in deposits (including chequing accounts and the like but *not* mutual funds) at that institution. When buying a GIC, always make sure the company you're dealing with has CDIC coverage. Go to www.cdic.ca for more information.

Watching out for inflation

WARNING

Before you abandon all thoughts of buying mutual funds and plunge into GICs instead, note that fixed-rate deposits are a dangerous investment in one important sense. Their rates of return can be so low that they do little to protect you against inflation. As Table 5-1 shows, even quite modest rates of inflation eat away alarmingly quickly at the real value of your savings. The U.S. dollar, still the world's main store of wealth, lost its value at an average of about 5 percent during the 1980s and 1990s — in other words, prices in the United States rose by about 5 percent per year. The inflation rate has been much lower in recent years, dipping to less than 2 percent in Canada, before inching back up thanks to rising commodity prices. Inflation of just 3 percent a year wipes out about one-fifth of the value of your money in five years.

TABLE 5-1 ## How Inflation Destroys Money over Time

Time Elapsed	Approximate Value of $10,000 at 3 Percent Inflation
Initial amount	$10,000
One year	$9,700
Two years	$9,215
Three years	$8,754
Four years	$8,317
Five years	$7,901
Six years	$7,506
Seven years	$7,130
Eight years	$6,774
Nine years	$6,435
Ten years	$6,113

The curse of inflation means that, as an investor, you're constantly clambering up a slippery, moving staircase covered in rotting mackerel and parts of Scotsmen. Stand still or go forward too slowly, and you end up sliding backward.

Bonds and Strip Bonds

Bonds are loans to governments or corporations that have been packaged into certificates that trade on the open market. They usually pay a fixed rate of interest, often twice a year. And they "mature" or come due after a set number of years, when the holder of the bond gets back the value of the original loan, known as the "principal." But don't bother buying individual bonds until you've got $10,000 or so to spend, because the cost of buying a cheap bond index mutual fund is so low. Index funds, which just earn a return in line with an entire bond market or index, are particularly suitable for the bond market because normal human managers find it very difficult to earn much more than their rivals without taking risks.

The median Canadian fixed income fund has annual expenses of about 1.8 percent, but many bond funds can be held for less than 1 percent a year. That's less than $100 out of a $10,000 investment, so you're doing fine.

Considering bond alternatives

If you're comfortable buying and selling on the stock exchange (see Book 2), it's worth thinking about buying a *bond exchange-traded fund* — bond ETFs are units in a simple trust that give you ownership of bonds but trade on the exchange like a share. (Get an introduction to exchange-traded funds — which are perhaps the best deal of all for small investors — in Chapter 4 of Book 3.) The big advantage to buying bonds or a bond ETF is that you save on fees. One domestic bond ETF, iShares Core Canadian Universe Bond Index ETF, charges just 0.10 per cent.

You can also consider bond funds. The annual fund expenses will cut into your yield, yes — but you may just decide the cost is worth it.

WARNING

Don't forget, though, that with a bond fund you are essentially playing the bond market without the backup security of being able to hold a bond to its maturity date, and thus recover your original investment, or principal, in addition to the periodic interest payments. Bond fund managers buy and sell bonds on the market, and thus you are signing on to a pretty aggressive form of investing. No, you won't exactly be a "master of the universe," as in Tom Wolfe's *The Bonfire of the Vanities,* but you will be participating in a fairly active market.

Investing directly in bonds

You can obtain a far better yield than bond funds by investing directly in bonds. However, the bond market is not always the friendliest place for small investors — it can be difficult to get information or do trades. It's just not a popular product, and profit margins for the dealer are thin.

WARNING

The trouble with bonds is that, unlike stocks, they don't trade in a central marketplace where the prices are posted. If you buy stocks, your broker usually just acts as an "agent" who connects you with the seller's broker, collecting a commission for the service. But your broker generally buys and sells bonds as a "principal" — that is, the firm actually owns the bonds it trades, holding them in "inventory" like a store. That means when you're trading bonds, you generally have to ask your broker what the firm's price quote is for a bond you want to buy or sell. And then you more or less have to accept the price that's offered.

Even bigger problems can occur in buying and selling *strip bonds,* which are components of coupon bonds that have been "stripped" or separated to reflect the fact that many long-term buyers who hold bonds until maturity aren't interested in collecting periodic interest payments. In fact, such dribs and drabs of interest are a liability because they must constantly be reinvested. So strip bonds pay no interest until they mature — the interest payments have been "stripped" away. Instead, they're bought at a deep discount to their face value, maturing at full value or "par" like a normal bond.

For example, you might pay your broker 50 cents on the dollar for a strip bond maturing in ten years. That will give you an annual compound yield of about 7.2 percent. In other words, an investment of $5,000 becomes $10,000 after a decade. Because strip bondholders are prepared to wait until they get any of their money back, they're rewarded with a higher yield to maturity. It's often 0.5 to 1 percentage point of extra yield yearly compared with a regular bond with a similar term to maturity.

WARNING

Strip bonds can be difficult to unload. They're volatile, losing their market value quickly when interest rates rise. That's because higher rates offer better interest-earning opportunities in the here and now, so they rapidly devalue money you don't get for a long time. And strip bonds are all about waiting for a faraway payoff. Because strip bonds are often sold as a retail product, your broker may be reluctant to buy one back from you at a decent price if the firm has no demand for strips from other clients. So if you're buying a strip, plan on holding it to maturity.

So if you have at least $10,000 to play with, buy bonds and hold them to maturity by all means. You know exactly what yield you're getting and how much money you'll have when the bonds mature. With a bond mutual fund, which is constantly rolling over its holdings, you won't have nearly that much certainty.

WARNING

If you plan to try trading bonds, note that making money in this market ("going forward," an annoying expression Bay Street types like to use a dozen times before breakfast) will be tougher in the long run. That's because bond prices usually only go up when interest rates and the rate of inflation fall — if inflation stays unchanged, then all you're likely to get from a bond is its yield to maturity at the time of purchase.

Stocks: Thrills, Spills, and Twisted Wreckage

Although you can spot stocks trading at crazy prices and make money buying those individual shares, it's hard. This section is an introduction to stocks; see Book 2 for more information.

Going with index funds

Unless you plan to spend quite a bit of time tracking stocks and reading the financial press, you're probably best off in equity funds. The easiest strategy of all: Just climb aboard the madness by putting a chunk of your money into stock index funds — which track the whole stock market — and you'll be doing what a lot of smart pros do. The indexes themselves go crazy from time to time, as they did in 2005 and 2006 when investors rushed to buy income trusts and then rushed even more quickly to sell them off when the government removed income trusts' tax advantages in late 2006. More recently, skyrocketing crude-oil prices sent the S&P/TSX Composite Index on a wild ride, while U.S. and other markets slumped. Perhaps the most spectacular example of abrupt stock market activity was in 1999 and 2000, when technology and telecommunications stocks dominated the market benchmarks.

It might all seem too much to stomach, but when you look at the long-term record of stock market performance, particularly in North America, it's hard to stay away from the index-investing party. You're only alive three times, after all, and the last two times you come back as something in the sea, so why not have fun now?

Here's just one example from recent history. As Figure 5-2 shows, an investment of $10,000 in Canadian dollars in stocks outside Canada and the United States grew at a compound annual rate of 5.7 percent to about $30,400 between mid-1988 and mid-2008. The same $10,000 put into U.S. stocks grew to about $62,000 — a 9.5-percent, 25-year compound annual return — while Canadian stocks left you with more than $67,100, or a 10-percent growth rate.

If you're intrigued by this brief glimpse into the world of index funds, head over to Chapter 4 in Book 3.

FIGURE 5-2:
$10,000 initial investment, held from mid-1983 to mid-2008.

Source: Morningstar

Buying individual stocks

Think you can beat the market? Go ahead and dive into the shark . . . er, whatever . . . water where loads of sharks are swimming around. Picking good stocks consistently is really, really hard (but Book 2 can help). You also need a broker to put through your trades. Your shares get held in the brokerage's computer system under an account in your name. Always check your statement and transaction confirmation slips carefully, because mistakes happen.

If you want to buy individual stocks, you will need a bit of money to make it worth the trouble and expense — say, at least $10,000 — unless you're just throwing a few thousand at the market for laughs (and it is enjoyable, so try it when you get a chance). Most trades go through in "board lots" of 100 shares at a time, for efficiency. If you're dealing in blue-chip companies, buying 100 shares can add up — it costs $2,500 for 100 shares trading at $25 each. Buying fewer than 100 shares at a time is generally inefficient because it means dealing in an "odd" or "broken" lot of less than 100. If you deal in odd lots, you'll often get a lower price when you sell and have to pay more per share when you buy.

And, as usual in investing, you must make a choice between having a salesperson take care of all the humdrum stuff at a cost, or doing it yourself at less expense. The price of buying stock through a full-service traditional stockbroker is usually shrouded in black curtains and dry ice. Establishing commission rates can be like bargaining in a grim, sweaty bazaar on the edge of a poisoned desert — in other words, full-service brokerage commissions are completely negotiable. A small trade typically might cost 4 percent of a transaction's value. That's quite a haircut to take when you buy and again when you sell, but most frequent traders could haggle for much less. But don't expect a full-service broker to be too thrilled about your business unless you've got at least $50,000 or even $100,000 to throw into the market, because with any less than that you're more of an annoyance than a revenue stream. And it's not unusual for an experienced and acclaimed broker to accept only "high-net-worth accounts" of $1 million or more.

So investors with modest means are left with a discount broker, which may impose no minimum account size at all but also provides little or no advice or help. Their commission rates vary, but discounters' minimum commissions typically run from $5 to $20, depending on whether you use the Internet or a live human to do your trade. (See Chapter 2 in Book 2 for more about brokers.)

Buying and selling stocks profitably and reliably is difficult — perhaps impossible — but evidence indicates that ordinary investors can do well by investing in a few well-run, growing companies and simply holding them for years. Mind you, that's emotionally tough to do. Check out an example from recent history: Bombardier Inc. is a Montreal company that sells planes, trains, and other transportation equipment all over the world. If you'd bought Bombardier shares in the summer of 2003, you'd have roughly doubled your money in five years. But it would have been a tough buy-and-hold experience, with the share price moving from about $4.50 a share at the end of June 2003 to above $7 in the winter of 2004, thanks to strong sales, then tumbling to below $2 at the end of 2004, at which point the company's retired chief executive, Laurent Beaudoin, returned to the executive suite. Investors clearly embraced this move, and the shares soared to the $7 neighbourhood by mid-2007. Industry challenges caused the stock to fall back to nearly $4 by the winter of 2008 before rallying big-time to around $9 by mid-2008, largely on the back of strong business-jet sales.

Have a look at Figure 5-3 to see the rises and falls of Bombardier stock. The area graph along the bottom of the chart shows monthly trading volume, which indicates how much attention a stock is attracting in the market. High volumes often accompany a significant rise or fall in price.

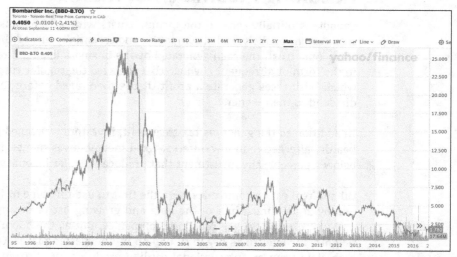

FIGURE 5-3: Bombardier's share price over twenty years.

Source: Yahoo! Finance

Taking a wilder ride with stock alternatives

WARNING

For those who find even stocks too staid, options, warrants, futures, and rights are the wonder drug of investing — volatile ways to play or speculate on a share, market, or commodity. They're structured to offer faster price changes than the underlying asset itself. The general principle is that for a little money you get to "buy risk" from someone who doesn't want it. But the downside is that your wild party has a time limit, because the speculative instrument always expires after a set period. That's a huge drawback: Many a market veteran will testify that picking the right investment is tough enough, without having the clock ticking against you. Buy these things only with money you don't care about.

Income Trusts: No Longer the Taxpayer's Best Friend

Income trusts are businesses that have been turned into a sort of fund that pays out regular — usually monthly — distributions to holders of their units. Say an income trust's *yield*, or yearly payout to investors per dollar invested, is 8 percent. On a $10,000 investment, you could expect $800 in income payments annually.

Income trusts trade on the stock exchange like an ordinary share, so they're simple to buy and sell. Look for them under "trust units" in stock market listings and on stock-quote websites.

Recalling income trust mania

Canadians initially took to the income trusts with wild enthusiasm. Financiers took regular publicly traded companies and essentially turned them inside out. As an income trust, the cash generated by the business is paid directly to investors in the form of a frequent cheque. That replaced the regular corporate system, in which businesses generate a profit that is then taxed before they can pay out a dividend to their owners.

In addition to the generous tax treatment, investors welcomed the prospect of a healthy alternative to low-interest fixed income investments. In an era of rates below 2 percent, any investment that produced regular income was welcome.

Oil and real estate companies were the first to use this type of financing vehicle, and by 2006 almost half of the long and growing list of income trusts were oil and gas, electricity, and pipelines companies. But as the boom approached new heights, income trusts began to pop up in unexpected places. One fund paid out cash flow from an international sardine producer, two frozen-food warehouse funds, a pet food fund, and another fund that paid income from a burger chain.

Income trusts' popularity as a substitute for common shares had become so great that by mid-2006 it was common to see a horde of income trusts mentioned in daily stock market summaries in the news media.

Clamping down on income trusts

However, the wheels fell off the income trust bandwagon in late 2006, when the federal government pulled the plug on the favourable tax treatment this type of investment had enjoyed. As trusts, they had provided a considerable tax-deferral on income paid out. But income trusts were in danger of replacing traditional stocks as the main product traded on the Toronto Stock Exchange (picture it: the Toronto Income Trust Exchange), and Ottawa acted suddenly to level the fiscal playing field. Income trust income is now taxed in the same way as dividend income.

While most existing income trusts survived the loss of their tax advantages, based on their investment fundamentals, the parade of stock-issuing companies heading to the trust conversion machine has slowed to a small line of stragglers.

Considering investing in income trusts

WARNING

Most income trusts generally kept their distributions flowing as promised (oil and gas trusts have had to cut theirs when commodity prices fell, but that was obvious to investors all along). Yields have remained quite generous — up to 13 percent. Those are pretty generous income streams, but income trusts are riskier than a bond — particularly now that they're no longer the taxpayer's best friend. The bottom line? Evaluate an investment in an income trust in exactly the same way as you would a stock. Just as no certainty exists that a company's share price will go up or it will be able to continually pay dividends, no guarantee exists that an income trust's underlying business will indeed be able to keep up the profits or revenue needed for the distributions. The trusts' structures tend to be horrendously tangled, with corporate diagrams that would make your hair stand on end — complexity is always a red flag in investing. And the danger exists that the necessity to pay out cash will in fact bleed some of the businesses dry.

But the small investor who buys a trust has one thing on his or her side: Mutual funds are also investing in them. Anxious to get in on the act, mutual fund companies have started funds that buy the trusts. We're a little skeptical here: When you combine the trusts' management fees with the fees on the new funds (the median Canadian income trust equity mutual fund has an annual management expense ratio of 2.5 percent), you end up paying a lot of money to a lot of people. But at least professional investors are keeping an eye on the folks running the trusts.

The bottom line here is that income trusts are potentially too volatile to go overboard on, but the generous yield means they're a reasonable bet for many investors. As with any investment area, make sure you buy more than one to spread your risk. Better yet, you can invest in an income trust fund.

Managed Products: A Fee Circus

Every year, the investment industry comes up with warehouses full of glittering, new, nougat-flavoured, candy-coloured, "managed" investment products, each holding out the prospect of riches and implying your savings will be exposed to only the barest smidgeon of risk. And pretty well every year, a lot of these exciting innovations fail to deliver the golden eggs. The problem is that when investments are done up in such fancy packages, somebody has to pay for all the frills and gorgeous ribbons — and it's always the retail buyer. The investment may be called a *unit trust*, a *structured* or *hybrid fund*, a *royalty trust*, a *closed-end fund*, a *partnership*, or an *income trust* — whatever the name and no matter how wonderful the sales spiel, never forget that if someone's trying to sell the thing to you, they are collecting a fee somewhere down the line.

WARNING

A number of complex investment vehicles are best left to sophisticated, experienced investors. Although they can be difficult to understand, it should be noted that some are, however, well managed, underpriced, and lucrative to own. But all carry disadvantages:

>> **Limited partnerships:** These things are so complicated you need to have a lawyer look them over for you, and even then you're vulnerable. They usually produce tax breaks for the buyers by investing in risky things such as movies or natural resources, but unless you have money to burn, don't consider these highly speculative investments.

>> **Hedge funds:** These began as privately run funds for the very rich, but are now sold to the small investor, often through hedge "funds of funds." Hedging is the practice of protecting your investments against loss — by selling borrowed shares at the same time as you buy others, for example. And that's what the rich are mostly interested in when it comes to investing: protecting what they have. Hedge funds are no longer all about avoiding losses, though. Some, although not all, use exotic or risky techniques to chase high returns. Hedge funds used to require a minimum investment of $25,000, but they now can be had for as little as $1,000. But absolutely make sure you get professional advice before putting any serious money into this type of product.

>> **"Structured" or "hybrid" funds:** These things don't represent Bay Street's finest hour. Investors plowed hundreds of millions of dollars into the funds in 2001, attracted by their promise of a high yield plus the guaranteed return of capital after ten years. The typical fund sold units at $25 each with the pledge to refund that purchase price at the end of a decade — while also trying to pay a rich yield in the range of 8 to 10 percent annually. The funds planned to pull off the neat trick with financial engineering — it involved a risk-free

strategy of selling options to other investors that gave *them* the right to buy the fund's stock holdings. Didn't work. The market for options turned tail, which forced many of the funds to reduce their hoped-for distributions to unitholders.

WARNING

In your investing career, stick to the things the professionals buy — bonds and stocks and simple mutual funds that invest in bonds and stocks. Buying a fancy, managed product adds a level of cost and complexity that can only reduce your returns. Buying a stock or a royalty or income trust at the issue price when it's first sold to the public is risky, too, even though you traditionally get it commission-free. Grab it later when the price has fallen, which it likely will eventually. The issue price has often been inflated to pay for brokerage commissions and other marketing expenses, not to mention general hype — so let some other poor investor pay for all those shiny new Mercedes and BMW automobiles you see parked in Bay Street garages.

4

Investing in Precious Metals

Contents at a Glance

Chapter **1**

Beginning with the Benefits and Risks of Metals

Investments are generally intangibles; you can't touch or taste them (not that you would want to munch on a stock certificate), but they are more or less abstract things. On the other hand, precious metals — like gold and silver — can be beautiful things that you can actually hold and admire. Fortunately, the beauty can also extend to your wealth-building picture as well. This chapter covers the benefits of precious metals and their related investments. Don't be mesmerized, though; this chapter also goes into the ugly side of metals (risk).

Protecting Your Portfolio Against Inflation

Inflation is one of the greatest dangers to your investing and wealth-building pursuits. Many people make the common error of thinking of inflation in terms of its symptoms instead of seeing inflation for what it really is.

Perhaps you've thought, "Gee whiz . . . how much for that bag of groceries? Here, why not take my whole freakin' wallet! Never mind . . . I'll just put back the breath mints. Harrumph." But high prices aren't the cause of inflation; they are the result or symptom. Inflation means that the government is printing a lot of money (dollars or euros or whatever the currency is of that particular country), and this increasing supply of money is used to buy a limited basket of goods and services. The following sections show you why diversifying your portfolio with precious metals can strengthen your wealth building.

Precious metals against the dollar

REMEMBER

Monetary inflation refers to increasing the money supply ("monetary" is just an official way of referring to "money" such as dollars). Monetary inflation then leads to price inflation, which is what most people are familiar with. The bottom line is that you end up paying more for the stuff you regularly buy. The end result isn't that goods and services cost more — the money you use is worth less. That's the insidious side of inflation; it acts like a hidden tax that destroys your purchasing power.

Keep in mind that whatever investments you have, they are denominated in dollars. If you are a Canadian citizen, then the odds are pretty good that virtually everything you own is measured and valued in Canadian dollars. Therefore, as the dollar goes down in value, that will have an adverse effect on your financial well-being.

If you had $1,000 tucked away in your sock drawer in 2019 and you checked in 2020 and it's still there, you might say that you still have $1,000 (or "Thank God no one checks this drawer!"). From a nominal point of view, your wealth hasn't budged. It's still $1,000 and you feel fine. But before you check your mattress, understand that your wealth actually shrunk. According to Statistics Canada, between January 2019 and January 2020, Consumer Price Index (CPI) inflation was 2.4 per cent. That means you would have needed an additional $24 in your sock drawer just to buy the same "basket of goods" as the original $1,000 from a year ago.

Inflation is not a short-term problem, either. In the preceding example, whether the actual difference is $24 or $60 or $90 is not that big a deal. But it becomes a very big deal over an extended period of time. Currencies can lose (and have lost) value across decades. That's a problem and that's why diversifying into tangible assets such as precious metals makes sense.

Diversification against all currencies

You encounter a purchasing-power risk in any man-made currency that could be produced at will by a government authority (such as a government central bank).

What does this mean for you going forward? A growing (mismanaged?) money supply is at the heart of the problem. Because paper or *fiat* currencies first started being used centuries ago, governments have never resisted the temptation to print up lots of it. This is why the dustbin of history is top heavy in currencies that were over-printed into oblivion. Could that be the case today? Are currencies being created in ever increasing amounts?

Oh yeah. Inflation isn't just a problem for you. It's affecting many people across the globe. Gold and silver are doing well and should continue to do well regardless if we are talking dollars, euros, yen, or salt. It is safe to say that hyper-inflation, a currency crisis, or collapse is destined to hit currencies at some point in the coming years.

What does this have to do with the benefits of precious metals? It's like looking through a window, watching a torrential downpour, and discussing the benefits of umbrellas. Yes . . . inflation will rain on your wealth-building parade and the forecast is for a batch of storms on everyone's radar screens for the foreseeable future.

The most obvious and familiar precious metals are gold and silver, and these two should suffice for most portfolios. However, precious metals also encompass platinum, palladium, uranium, and obscure precious metals such as rhodium.

TIP

Base metals like copper, aluminum, nickel, zinc, lead, and tin deserve a spot in some portfolios. In recent years, some base metals have seen their prices double and triple. Those gains would qualify as "precious" (at least in this book). Even though copper and nickel are readily found in the composition of your pocket change, they are base metals that offer investment opportunities as well.

Seeing Benefits for Investors

You always need a good reason to do something, especially when you're talking about where to put your hard-earned, inflation-ravaged money. Precious metals in their various formats offer many benefits (see the following sections), and the sum total of these benefits makes them a compelling choice as a part of your portfolio.

Safe haven

One point that you will hear on a regular basis from gold aficionados is that gold and silver are real money that are not someone else's liabilities. For newcomers to the world of precious metals that would be an intriguing statement. What does it mean?

A currency such as the U.S. dollar is backed up by the "full faith and credit of the United States." You can surmise that a currency is not money in the truest sense of the word; it is a type of claim or liability backed up by the issuing authority, which is in this example the U.S. federal government.

There was a time when the U.S. dollar was redeemable in gold and silver. That dollar was backed up by something that was universally considered a "unit of exchange" and a "store of value," which is what gold and silver were considered for literally thousands of years. This was the whole point behind the "gold standard."

As long as the U.S. dollar was backed by gold, it had strength and people had confidence in it. Starting in 1913 with the creation of the Federal Reserve (America's "government central bank"), the dollar started to decouple from gold until the connection between gold and silver was totally severed during the Great Depression. At that point, the spigots on producing dollars opened up. The U.S. dollar started a long, slow-motion bear market (in terms of purchasing power) where a dollar in 1913 is only worth a few cents today.

Precious metals such as gold were a different story. It has been said that a single ounce of gold could have bought you a decent suit during the 1800s. If you sold a single ounce of gold on December 24, 2006, you would have gotten $620 USD (not including transaction fees) and that would have been plenty of dollars to buy a nice suit for Christmas.

REMEMBER

In good times and bad, precious metals have retained their value and earned their title as a safe haven.

Privacy

In the world of financial assets, tax reporting is common. With certain types of precious metals vehicles, there is no reporting (for transactions under $10,000 value). This is especially true of gold and silver collectibles such as numismatic coins. Of course this does not relieve you of the obligation of paying taxes in the case of capital gains transactions.

WARNING

Rules can change obviously, so make sure that you discuss your purchases and sales with your tax advisor.

Inflation hedge

In early 2006, Harry Browne died. His claim to fame is that he is a legendary investor who was right on the money during the 1960s and '70s. One of the last books that he wrote was a short book that was a concise, true gem of financial wisdom called *Fail-Safe Investing: Lifelong Financial Security in 30 Minutes*

(St. Martin's Press). In it he detailed a model portfolio that was easily constructed by the average investor and it had performed very well in a variety of economic conditions. It consisted of 25% each of cash, stocks, bonds, and . . . gold. He suggested that you rebalance it each year to keep the 25% allocation.

Mr. Browne was keenly aware of the dangers of inflation, recession, and other systemic problems that occur because of political and governmental mismanagement (such as through inflation, taxes, and regulation). He recognized that gold was not easily produced and manipulated by government. One question that may pop up is "Can't gold be produced as well?" Gold is mined but the average annual addition of gold to the world gold supply is just a few per cent. That physical limitation keeps gold growing at a pace that helps it to retain its value yet plentiful enough to keep pace with population growth.

Dollar hedge

A dollar hedge seems synonymous with an inflation hedge since you're dealing with the same issue. But *dollar hedge* is more related to those who see the Canadian dollar as an entity worth trading against. You can invest or speculate based on the direction of the Canadian dollar as its own investment vehicle.

In the same way you can look at the relationship of a common stock to the company it is attached to, you can look at a currency as it is attached to a country. There are definite similarities. When a country's currency is strong, it is to the rest of the world a representation of how strong or well-managed the country is.

TECHNICAL STUFF

For example: During the 1980s and 1990s, the U.S. dollar was considered a strong currency, but since then, due to factors including a ballooning national debt and a large trade deficit, the dollar started a long decline.

A hedge against the dollar can manifest itself in a variety of ways. For example, some will speculate in the currencies of other countries because if one currency declines in value, then some other currency is probably rising. Of course, the other currencies could also decline as well. The bottom line is that gold and silver are solid choices as dollar hedges.

Confiscation protection

Later in this chapter, you find out about the risks of precious metals, and one segment focuses on political risk. Simply stated: The government can affect your investment. In the 1930s, for example, the Franklin D. Roosevelt administration in the United States authorized government confiscation of gold and essentially banned ownership of gold. But they exempted gold coins, having a recognized special value to collectors of rare and unusual coins.

Even in the extreme case of heavy-handed government intervention, gold can still be a store of value.

Liquidity

Liquidity is an important benefit for investors. All *liquidity* really means is how quickly you convert an asset to cash. Securities such as stocks and bonds are very liquid assets. Assets such as real estate are not. Precious metals and their related investments tend to be very liquid. Mining stocks, like other stocks, can easily be sold in seconds either with a call to the broker or a visit to a website. You can do likewise with options and futures (you get them and get rid of them through your brokerage account).

In terms of physical metals, the most liquid precious metals are gold and silver. If you have gold and/or silver coins, they are very liquid as you can go to virtually any coin dealer store or website and quickly convert bullion or numismatic coins to cash.

WARNING

Numismatic coins (coins that have achieved value due to their rarity) carry a high markup, so if you were to liquidate them, you may get only 70 cents on the dollar (or less). Most people sell their coins to coin dealers, but these dealers will basically offer you wholesale prices since they will end up trying to resell the coins at retail. Consider selling coins to other investors or collectors as they are easier to find now through the Internet.

Portfolio diversification

In the book *Stock Investing For Dummies* (Wiley), I (coauthor Paul) write extensively on portfolio diversification. It's important to have stocks in different sectors so that the overall portfolio can be safer yet still grow without you having to reach for the antacid on those volatile days. Here, I get to tell you what I think is a good part of the diversification. Metals mining stocks (and uranium) have been among the top-performing stocks in this millennium. Yet I am sure that many in the public haven't realized it. You already know about physical metals and their performance along with their advantages. Their "disadvantages" are covered in later in this chapter. How about the stocks?

Take Agnico-Eagle Mines Ltd. (symbol: AEM) for example. AEM is a Canadian gold-mining stock listed on the New York Stock Exchange. You could have purchased it at the turn of the century for around $5 a share. It hit $45 in 2006 for a total long-term gain of 800% (not including dividends). At the time of this writing, it's nearly $66. If that's diversification, don't you want more of it? Other selective mining stocks in gold as well as other metals (and uranium) had similar results.

Your retort after that paragraph might be, "Gee, Paul, I'm sure that if I look hard enough that I will certainly find stocks that did just as well and probably a heck of a lot better in totally different sectors. Why choose stocks in the metals sector if there are also healthcare, biotech, and so on?" I'm glad you asked. Or I'm glad that I wrote down that you asked what I'm glad you asked.

In the realm of investing and speculating, the past is something you learn from so that you can prepare for the future. In that prior example, AEM went up 800% in the same time frame that the asset it mined (primarily gold) went from under $300 to over $650 an ounce (gold more than doubled). I, along with an army of gold experts, saw economic conditions that were very fertile for gold to shoot past $1,000 and much higher in later years. What happens to gold-mining companies that are profitably sitting on millions of ounces of the stuff? Can you say "jackpot"?

It doesn't stop there. Gold is great but there are also silver, uranium, and so much more. Cool profits in hot markets; don't you like the sound of that?

Checking Out Benefits for Traders and Speculators

Traders and speculators want a market that makes profits easier to achieve. The current and pending precious metals market offers an environment for just that. The following sections consider supply and demand as the ultimate factors in your wealth-building pursuits.

Supply and demand

As a trader or a speculator, what do you think of when you hear the phrase "supply and demand"? Say what? Do you think of Mrs. Krapalbee in your university economics course on the first day of class? Let me change that dynamic. Think "profits." When you understand this simple, age-old, foundational economic idea and apply its eternal wisdom to today's fast-moving, modern markets, you can make a profit easier. This idea sits at the heart of your trading/speculating success.

The natural resource (or commodities) sector is wonderfully positioned for gains in the coming years. Breaking it down a step further, natural resources can be neatly separated into two segments: finite natural resources and renewable natural resources.

Renewable natural resources include things such as corn, sugar, coffee, and so on. They have been profitable markets since natural resources have been in a multiyear bull market and it will continue for years to come. But you know what happens with renewable resources. The news reports "the coffee crop in Brazil will be down this season" and the price of coffee goes up on the news and you say "time to percolate some profits!" and you buy coffee futures. Then . . . as you smell the aroma of fresh-brewed money . . . wham! The next report says "Chile expects record coffee harvest" and your coffee futures nose-dive as you say "I knew I shoulda done cocoa instead!" These are great markets with great opportunities but I prefer to speculate with finite natural resources. Yes . . . by a country mile. Why?

Finite natural resources refer to resources that are not readily renewable or replaceable. Good examples are oil, natural gas, base metals, uranium, and precious metals. In other words, whatever people find that is above and below ground . . . that's it! No more. Society ultimately finds substitutes, but only if it really, really, really has to. That's humanity. We go through a painful transition as we move from one resource to the next but we hang on to the original resource until a suitable substitute comes along.

A good example is oil. Modern societies use oil and will keep using it until it's gone, but progress has been too slow into cleaner substitutes such as solar and wind energy. In the meanwhile, think about the following dynamic:

>> The world population keeps growing.

>> The nations of the world keep expanding their money supplies.

>> Finite natural resources are slowly being used up.

Put those three together and you have dynamic opportunities in things such as . . . precious metals. The benefits for traders and speculators then become obvious.

Huge gains potential

I have one client who opened a commodities brokerage account in late 2003 with $40,000. Options on silver futures were purchased. After a roller-coaster ride complete with bone-jarring corrections, the account was worth over $300,000 by May 2006. A 650% return in about two and a half years. Nice! That doesn't include the fact that the original $40,000 was taken out of the account and sent back to her. Nicer! This was of course speculation but it was done with only 10 per cent of her money. Silver in that time frame went from under $5 in 2003 to over $14 in May 2006.

What would happen to an account like that if silver was to go to its old high of $50? Of course, $50 was its old high in 1980. Adjusted for inflation it would be in three figures. That's the type of potential that makes speculators salivate.

Trading versus speculating

I know an associate who likes to speculate and he hates trading. Trading requires a lot of time, attention, and timing (as you find out in Book 5 on day trading). Plus you add in the transactions costs. After you factor it all in, you may make a profit of . . . say a few hundred bucks. Now there are traders out there who make some great profits and even a good living at it. Trading with options and/or futures has a lot of advantages.

Successful trading takes a lot if you are going to make it work. I prefer speculating because I can do all of my homework and make a few transactions such as buying that small stock with great potential or getting a long-dated option on, say, a silver futures contract and then wait for the fireworks. This has worked better for me.

The benefits of speculating

Speculating is akin to financial gambling, but if you do your homework, you can greatly increase the odds in your favour. It is possible to take a small amount of risk capital and parlay it into a much larger sum. Here are some benefits of speculating:

>> **With knowledge, research and discipline it is possible to make great money.** I know real-life examples of clients who turned $5,000 into $20,000 or more in a few months.

>> **You can do it with little money.** I know several clients and students who started with as little as $1,000 in futures options and some who started with as little as $500 in stock speculating and all have made great profits.

>> **You can minimize your risk.** Many think that to turn a small sum into a great sum that you need more leverage. Not really; you can utilize vehicles that have leverage with the risk of leverage (such as options).

Futures is a great area for speculating, but my favourite for speculating is options. Whether it's options on stocks or on futures, my belief and experience tell me that it is a great way to profit without incurring undue risk. The phrase "undue risk" sounds loaded, but it will make sense. Futures carry risk beyond your purchase price. You could get into futures with, say, $5,000 and within days lose the entire sum plus still owe thousands. Yikes . . . who needs that?

This is why it is important that besides knowing the benefits of speculating, you should understand the risks before you begin transacting. For those who want to speculate with unlimited profits while limiting risk and loss, consider options.

Recognizing the Risks of Precious Metals

It goes without saying that the age-old equation in the world of investing is risk versus return. This equation states that if you want a greater return on your investment, then you have to tolerate greater risk. If you don't want greater risk, then you have to tolerate a lower rate of return. The world is full of pitfalls and precious metals are no different, but keep in mind that precious metals can excel when your other investments don't. Precious metals guard or hedge against risks that can hurt conventional stocks, bonds, or other fixed-rate vehicles.

A good example of the value of, say, gold or silver is what happened in Zimbabwe in 2006. At that time, on paper almost everyone was a millionaire but most people were really poor! The country underwent hyper-inflation as the inflation rate hit the nose-bleed level of 914% in March 2006. Basic goods like a roll of toilet paper soared to $145,750 (only 69 cents in U.S. dollars). Gee, that might encourage some of their citizens to . . . uh . . . use Zimbabwe's currency instead. As incredible as that hyper-inflation was, it is actually not an odd example because it also occurred in Argentina and Serbia and numerous times across history. Those folks who had gold, silver, or other hard assets fared much better than those who didn't.

In this section, you not only get the chance to check out what types of risks are associated with precious metals investing, but you also find ways to minimize those risks.

Distinguishing types of risk

Keep in mind that risk is ubiquitous and just a normal part not only in building wealth but also in living life. Heck, just getting out of bed in the morning could pose a problem. Here are the various types of risks (now that you are out of bed).

Physical risk

Now I don't mean that you may hurt your back from picking up precious metals (heavy metal is a different animal altogether). It just means that if you have gold in physical form, then you have to understand that having it has risks as does owning any valuable property. You have to keep it safe. For some that means keeping your physical metal (such as gold, silver, and platinum) possessions in a safe-deposit box at the bank. For others it means in a secure hiding place at home.

You have to decide. Gold as a physical holding means you need to be concerned about the risk of loss or theft. Then there's relative risk; in other words, what if your relative finds out? Removing some risk always means common sense. After all, if gold hits $3,000 an ounce, you shouldn't be boasting about your investing skills at the local bar.

Market risk

REMEMBER

Market risk may be the most prevalent risk associated with gold. *Market risk* refers to the fact that whenever you buy an asset (physical, common stock, and so on) its price is subject to the ups and downs of the marketplace. In gold, as in many investments, the price can fluctuate and it could do so very significantly. What if you buy today but tomorrow there are more sellers than buyers in the gold market? Then obviously the price of gold would go down. The essence of market risk in commodities such as precious metals is supply and demand.

Another element of market risk can occur when you are involved in a *thinly traded market* — in other words, there may not be that many buyers and sellers involved. This is also called *liquidity risk.* This can happen, for example, in futures. Although futures are usually a liquid market (an adequate pool of buyers and sellers), there may be some aspects of it when it might not be that liquid. Say that you want to sell a futures contract that you recently bought that is not an actively traded contract. What if there are no buyers when you want to sell? Your order to sell through the broker may sit there for a long time. The sale price of the contract would drop and you would lose some gain or even end up with a loss. Be sure to communicate with the broker regarding how active that particular market is.

It is probably appropriate to place in this segment the market risk of mining stocks. The stock of mining companies certainly can go up and down like most any other publicly traded stock. Stock investors can sell stock when they see or expect problems with the company. If, for example, you are considering a gold-mining company, the risk to consider is more than just the fact that it is into gold and the commensurate market risks with gold itself. Also consider the company. Is management doing a good job? Is the company profitable? Are sales increasing? How about their earnings? Do they have too much debt . . . and so on.

Exchange risk

What the heck is exchange risk? Well, it's not a reference to currency exchange; *exchange risk* is a reference to the risks that could occur at the exchanges where futures and options are traded. When futures and options are transacted at the exchange such as at the Chicago Board of Trade (CBOT), they are done so under the rules and regulations of the exchange. The exchange can either purposely or accidentally encourage market outcomes by changing the rules and regulations on an ongoing basis.

A real-life example happened in the spring of 2006 with silver futures at the New York Mercantile Exchange (NYMEX). Silver was rallying nicely as speculators were buying into silver futures contracts. There were great expectations for silver due to the then-pending silver exchange-traded fund (ETF). The exchange decided to raise the margin requirements on margin contracts to try to quell over-speculation. When normally you could put down 10% to speculate on a futures contract, the new amount would be raised to, say, 12% or 15% or possibly more. When you require people to put more funds in for the ability to speculate, then of course you will diminish that activity. If the margin requirements are raised too high, that will result in more selling. More selling results in prices dropping.

The exchanges want an orderly market and they may change regulations or adjust requirements to encourage or exact an outcome. Sometimes that outcome may result either purposely or accidentally in a negative way for you. Here are the three events that may happen at an exchange:

>> **Changing margin requirements:** This section gives an example earlier and it is the most common event that an exchange could enact.

>> **Liquidation only:** This is a rare event but it can happen. This means that the exchange may temporarily restrict the buying side and only selling can occur thus forcing the price down. This occurred with silver in 1980 when it hit its then all-time high of $50.

>> **Halt trading:** Another rare event. The exchange may temporarily halt trading in a particular futures contract.

Political risks

Political risk is probably one of the biggest dangers that investors and speculators don't see coming. It is the one that comes out of the blue and blindsides your portfolio. *Political* refers to politicians who in turn run government. As far as we are concerned, political risk and governmental risk can be synonymous. In my seminars I (coauthor Paul) mention that politicians are Dr. Frankenstein while government is Frankenstein's monster. The bottom line is that *political risk* means that government can change laws and regulations in a way that can harm your investment or financial strategy. This can happen in your own country (O Canada!) or by another country.

Consider what happened in the 1930s in the United States. In 1934, President Franklin D. Roosevelt and Congress passed the Gold Reserve Act which made gold ownership illegal. Had you bought gold in prior years to preserve your wealth in the midst of the Great Depression, well . . . you were now out of luck. FDR then issued a presidential order fixing the price of gold at $35 an ounce which stuck for decades to come. FDR didn't want private citizens to have an alternative outside of the official paper currency.

Fast forward to our times. Political risk is alive and well (unfortunately). In many countries such as Bolivia and Venezuela, the government nationalized properties (government taking private property by force) by foreign companies, among them, mining companies. Had you owned stock in these mining companies you would have seen the share prices drop. Sometimes the share prices drop at the mere threat of government action. In 2005, for example, the Venezuelan government mentioned that it may take property owned by the Toronto-based gold-mining company Crystallex International. Its share price fell by a whopping 50% in a single day. Venezuela's dictator Hugo Chavez did increase taxes on many foreign companies while nationalizing some industries (maybe he needed the funds to buy toilet paper from Zimbabwe).

That's the problem with political risk. As an investor or speculator, you could do all your homework and make a great decision with your portfolio backed up by great research and unflinching economic logic and still lose money because of a government action that could have been unforeseen.

WARNING

An ounce of prevention is worth a pound of cure. It is best to stay away from investments (such as mining companies) that are too exposed to risk in a politically unstable or unfriendly nation. There are still plenty of precious metals opportunities in politically friendly environments such as Canada, the United States, Australia, and Mexico (at least until the next election!).

The risk of fraud

The risk of fraud is as real in precious metals as in every other human endeavour. It's tough enough trying to make a buck when the market seems honest. But you must understand that as a market becomes popular or "hot," it becomes a target for scam artists. Fraud can materialize in a variety of ways but it can be safely categorized into three segments: scams, misrepresentations, and market manipulation.

>> **Scams:** Scams are those events that the consumer organizations always warn about. The image is conjured up about those boiler-room operations where a slick con artist calls up a little old lady in Winnipeg and talks to her about riches to be made in gold and silver if she could crack open her piggy bank and send off a nice money order chunk of her savings. This is certainly a real risk and it becomes more apparent when the source of potential fraud is popular. When Internet auctions became a hot consumer area, there were more Internet auction–related scams. When the real estate market became red-hot in 2005, there were more real estate scams. When precious metals become the "bubble du jour" then you will need to be wary of scammers here as well.

>> **Misrepresentations:** This is a separate topic because it can be a different animal. Basically the point is that you may put your money into a venue and you may not be getting what you think you are buying. A good example is what the respected silver analyst Ted Butler once warned about regarding silver certificates. There have been millions of silver certificates issued in recent decades but there is the real possibility that there isn't any real silver backing them up. In other words there are purchasers of silver certificates who believed that they could convert their paper into actual silver in due time but in fact will not be able to. That sounds like misrepresentation.

>> **Market manipulation:** Short selling can send a stock's price plummeting. Some large brokers and their clients have been caught illegally profiting through a manipulative technique called naked short selling. This is an especially egregious activity with the stock of smaller mining companies. In *naked short selling,* the perpetrator can sell massive quantities of stock essentially created out of thin air to force the price of the stock to come crashing down. Imagine if you owned shares of a small mining company and you saw the share price plummet by 40% or 50% or more for no apparent reason.

Minimizing your risk

REMEMBER

Including precious metals (to whatever extent) in your portfolio minimizes risk because precious metals, such as gold and silver, have historically helped investors in times of economic uncertainty and political and financial tensions in the world at large. The long-term picture for precious metals should continue to bear this out. But nothing is without risk. Precious metals do carry risks and you can minimize your risks — just check out the following sections.

Gaining knowledge

I remember getting into options on silver futures some years ago. It was early 2004 and silver was rising very well and my account was performing superbly. I thought to myself "gee what a genius am I!" then along came April 2004. Silver plummeted by nearly 40 per cent. I thought to myself "gee what a moron am I!" In retrospect, it worked out just fine and I made some great profits but I was sweating bullets that spring. Seeing the value of your "investment" drop by 40% can make you freak out. I would have jumped out the window but I'm on the first floor. The point is that I learned that precious metals futures and options can have very wide and scary price swings. That is the nature of the market.

In fact it is not uncommon for precious metals to correct by 20 per cent to 30 per cent or even more at least once a year (I've come to learn that a "correction" seems awfully incorrect at the time).

REMEMBER

The terms *correct* or *correction* means that a market comes back down after going up too far and/or too fast. Don't confuse a market correcting with a market experiencing a bear market. The correction is a temporary pull-back in the price of the asset that is in a long-term bull market or rising market. The term *bear market* means that the asset is in a long-term falling or decreasing market. In other words, the difference between a correction and a bear market is the same difference as fainting and dropping dead. In the former you recover and get back on track.

Being disciplined

When markets go up and down, it can be difficult to stay disciplined. Markets can't be controlled by individual investors, but investors can and should exercise self-control. People can let their emotions overrule their thinking and do the wrong things when they ought to do the opposite. It happens especially in fast-moving markets.

My client (you can call him Bob) had put $2,000 in a commodities brokerage account. Under my guidance he purchased some options on silver futures. Within a few weeks the value shrunk to $900. Imagine that; he was down 55%. Of course he was very concerned (wouldn't you be?), and we discussed the situation. I told him to stay the course because my research told me that the underlying asset (silver) was in a bull market and that this drop in price was a temporary condition. In addition, the options that were purchased had two full years to go before they expired. This is an example of what happens in the marketplace; no matter how solid your research and logic, the market can go against you. If your research and logic were sound then the odds would swing back in your favour in due course. He decided not to panic and stay the course.

For Bob, the discipline paid off. The $2,000 he speculated with became $4,000 a few months later as the silver market rebounded. Those options were finally cashed in for $5,000 about 12 months after the initial purchase for a gain of 150 per cent. To this day, the account is still growing as we stayed disciplined and bought (and cashed in) at points that made sense. Bob could have panicked when it was at $900, cashed out, and leaped out the nearest window, but thankfully he stayed disciplined and reaped some excellent profits.

REMEMBER

When you are in fast-moving markets, have a plan in place regarding how much you will put at risk, when you plan to get in, and under what conditions and price points you will take profits (or losses).

Being patient

Everyone wants to get rich quick. Who wouldn't like to make a fast buck? Well, people who reach for the fast gains end up with fast losses. I can say with confidence (verifiably) that the vast majority of my long-term clients made money and in many cases a lot of money, but the key to their increase has been patience. The year 2006 is a great example.

A new batch of stock-investing clients came on board during the spring of 2006. At this time, the precious metals (and base metals) were having a fantastic rally. In this real-life example I want to highlight those that were in mining stocks. There were investors who came in and immediately saw their accounts go down by mid-summer as a correction took place. Take a different client (a real client with the fictitious name Fred). Fred came on board in February 2006 with $10,000 and closed out his account 16 weeks later with $9,800. He got impatient and ended up losing $200. I feel bad that he lost $200 and I wasted my time coaching him during that brief period of time. The amazing thing is that had he continued his account, he would have been profitable in a few weeks and he would have had over a 30% gain on his positions in only a few months. A little patience could have made Fred a winner soon enough.

REMEMBER

In a nutshell I think that impatience has been the greatest "personal" problem among investors in this decade. I'm not just saying this for long-term investors; the same goes for traders and speculators. Very often, that investment or speculative position you underwent may go down or sideways for what seems like forever. Sooner or later, if you chose wisely, others notice it too and the payoff can then be swift and impressive.

Using diversification

The advice to use diversification is probably the oldest advice in investing (right after "don't loan money to your relatives"). Diversification in precious metals can mean several things. It could mean spacing out your money among different metals (some precious metals and some base metals). It could mean spreading your money among different classes of investment vehicles (a mix of gold- and silver-mining stocks along with a precious metals mutual fund). For speculators it may mean deploying strategies that could benefit in up or down markets (such as using an option combination like the long straddle).

You can even diversify when you are speculating on a single vehicle. One year most of my clients with commodities accounts were overwhelmingly in silver futures options. It is indeed a high-risk approach but it paid off very well. Silver that year ended up 45% and most of the silver futures options were up in triple digit percentages (sweet!). But, where possible, the options strategies involved a diversified mix of strike prices, time frames, and some *hedging,* meaning that you do something in the account that could do well if the market goes against you.

REMEMBER

It's important to understand that this singular area should only be a single slice of your total financial picture. You need to address other areas of your situation such as

- Money in savings

- Reduce and manage liabilities (such as debt, taxes, and so on)

- Money in conventional investments such as stocks and bonds

- Real estate and other tangible assets

- Insurance and other risk-management tools and strategies

- Pension matters and retirement security

It's not a complete list but it's important to point out that whatever you do in precious metals, it doesn't happen in a vacuum. Hopefully you've looked at your entire financial picture (see Chapter 3 in Book 1) and the economic/political landscape, and you've discovered that the best way to protect and grow your wealth in these times is by diversifying into . . . precious metals!

REMEMBER

Diversification can be accomplished in two ways:

- Add precious metals into your portfolio to gain benefits that may not be there with other, more traditional investments.

- Have both physical metal (such as gold and/or silver bullion coins) and paper investments (such as mining stocks and precious metals ETFs), which make you diversified inside the precious metals portion of your portfolio.

Making risk your friend

REMEMBER

The world can be an uncertain place and many potential events and entities out there have no problem with raining some bad news on the economy in general (and your portfolio in particular). When those types of risks become evident, precious metals revert to their historical role as a safe haven. Without risk, how can you grow your money faster? It is a necessary part of your success and in many cases it is the *reason* for your success.

Risk management tools

Risk is not like the weather ("Everyone talks about it but nobody does anything about it!"). It is something that you can manage and profit from. Here are some proven strategies:

- **Buy the dips.** If you bought what you think is a great stock at $10 per share and a correction hit sending it down to $8, don't just crawl under a rock and wait it out; if possible buy some more. Why not? If it is truly a great stock and your research and logic tell you it's still a solid investment, buy some more.

Ultimately time will pass and the odds are good that when that stock goes to $12 or $15 or more you'll end up saying, "Gee whiz! I coulda had it at $8!" No guts . . . no glory.

>> **Keep cash on the sidelines.** This goes in tandem with the previous point. Have some money sitting somewhere safe, liquid, and earning interest waiting for an opportunity. I tell my students that if they're ready to take the plunge with, say, $10,000 don't invest everything in one shot. Invest half now and stagger the rest in over a few weeks or a few months. Opportunities go hand-in-hand with risks, so do the Boy Scout thing and be prepared.

>> **Utilize stop-loss orders.** If you have a brokerage account, and it's with a major firm with a full-featured website, that firm has some excellent risk management tools available for you. The most commonly used tool for keeping your portfolio's value intact is the stop-loss order. If you bought a stock at $10 then put a stop-loss order in at, say $9, or 10% below the purchase price. That way, if the stock goes up there is no limit to the upside but if the stock goes down and hits $9 a sell order is triggered and you get out. You minimize loss. A stop-loss order can be activated for a single trading day or for an extended period of time (referred to as a GTC order or good-'til-cancelled order). Stop-loss orders are a common feature in a stock brokerage account, but they may not be in a commodities brokerage account.

REMEMBER

Risk (or the lack of it) isn't just where you put your money; it's also how you go about doing it. 'Nuff said.

Weighing risk against return

After considering the risks, you may say, "Gee, why have metals at all?" Well, risk is a double-edged sword. Any (and all investments) have risks, and some invest-ments have great value because they protect you from risk, which is, perhaps, the greatest value of precious metals.

TIP

To offset some of the risk potential that is inherent in any place you put your money, use a very simple criterion, which I like to call the 10% rule: The most you should have in any single vehicle is 10% of your money. Easy! Yes . . . you could make it more precise, more customized, and more complicated. Go ahead, but it's good to have a starting point and a simple strategy before you start to tweak and "optimize."

Chapter **2**

Going for the Gold

"**G**oing for the gold" and "good as gold" and many other familiar phrases mentioning gold have been around for what seems like forever but for good reason. Few things conjure up thoughts of wealth and affluence the way gold does. No pirate in a B-movie shouts "Aargh! There's aluminum buried on that island, mateys!" On the other hand — gold . . . now we're talking. Few things have had the endurance of gold both as a metal and as a store of value. It is then the first precious metal to consider for wealth-builders today. It has through the ages become the quintessential precious metal.

Gold is an element that is found on the standard periodic table of the chemical elements. Gold is listed there with the symbol AU and the atomic number 79 (don't worry, the quiz has been cancelled). The most malleable and ductile of the metals, you could actually take a single ounce of gold and essentially stretch it out into 300 square feet (no one knows why you would do it but it sounds impressive). Gold is a good conductor of heat and electricity (and probably thieves as well). Because it is generally resistant to rust and corrosion, gold quickly became an ideal material to fashion into jewelry, coins, and therefore . . . money! The desirability of gold now became ensured.

However, every major society is inflating its currency at record rates. All the major currencies are subsequently losing their value slowly but surely. Because paper currencies are easily inflated, each unit of currency (dollar, euro, yen, and so on) loses value — not so for gold. As a tangible investment, use this chapter to find out how gold stacks up amidst all the investment choices available today.

Gold: The Ancient Metal of Kings

Since the early days of civilization, gold achieved its status as a symbol of wealth, a unit of exchange, and the essence of money. As an object of desire, it had the qualities virtually everyone deemed as necessary to be called "money": It was a rare element that was easily carried and exchanged, and was also a universal form of money that crossed nationalities and cultures. When nations traded goods and services, gold could have easily had the slogan "Don't leave home without it." For centuries gold had a place of honour in society — even after paper currencies came on the scene.

Paper currencies (also called *fiat currencies*) started coming into usage in the days of Mesopotamia when the drachma was used. Paper currencies didn't have any intrinsic value like gold; it was more or less a *claim* to intrinsic value. In other words, a paper currency had value because it had a claim of value from another asset such as grain or precious metals. So, paper currency was really an IOU. Paper currency gained popularity because it was easier to carry and transact with versus carrying bags of coins.

Many ancient societies used paper currencies as an IOU, attaching precious metals held at a bank or secure storage facility as the backing asset. So, the paper currency had value as long as you could redeem the currency in precious metals such as gold. During the course of history, paper currency soon decoupled from gold and became a competitor instead. First kings and then governments saw that paper currencies were a better alternative to gold . . . or so they thought.

They discovered that paper currencies issued by the government had certain advantages over gold — the main advantage was that paper currencies could be printed at will while gold was not easily produced. The supply of gold throughout history only grew at about 2 per cent per year. On the other hand, paper currencies could be produced very easily and very quickly. Although this may have been the advantage of currency, this was also currency's fatal flaw.

REMEMBER

During the past 3,000 years, there have been literally thousands of different paper currencies that came into existence and ultimately ended up vanquished. When governments can create money by printing up endless supplies of paper currencies, then the temptation to inflate becomes too great. If you can create money at will, why not? This would fill up the government's treasury early on, but as more money is created, its value diminishes and it becomes worth less and less until it's . . . well, worthless. Paper currencies end up with the intrinsic value of nothing, but in the long run, gold is still gold. Gold endures. Aargh, mateys!

CAUSING TROUBLE WITH KEYNES

In 1923, the economist John Maynard Keynes said that gold was "a barbarous relic." He was actually referring to the gold standard (having paper currencies backed up by gold), which was abandoned by governments. The abandonment of the gold standard by so many governments back then (and no major country has one today) will probably be the primary reason why gold investors today will ultimately benefit.

As the Great Depression unfolded during the 1930s, most of the major industrialized nations abandoned the gold standard in an attempt to stabilize their economies. This unfortunately opened up a long-term problem as inflating their currencies became a way of life. The subsequent result is something that everyone is paying now . . . much higher prices.

Reviewing Recent Trends in Gold

Gold has a track record dating back thousands of years, but fast-forward to recent times. In the late 1970s, gold experienced a 20-year bear market, and then the bull market started in the 21st century. The late '70s was a time of inflation, energy problems, international conflict, and economic hardship. Hmmm . . . does that sound familiar? The conditions in the '70s definitely have a lot in common with the first decade of the 21st century. From 2000 to mid-2007, though, gold began a bullish, upward slope. Examining gold's history and trends impacts how you decide to invest, so take a close look at the sections that follow to get an idea of gold's history as well as its promising future.

Explaining all the bull

So after a 20-year bear market, gold awakened at the start of the millennium. Gold (along with other natural resources) was in the early stages of a bull market in the early part of the 2000s. Several reasons explain gold's historic bull market:

>> **China and India:** These two countries alone will have an economic impact that will reverberate across the globe. Virtually every major economy and financial market will be affected, directly or indirectly. As they modernize their economies and as their collective 2.5 billion occupants increase their consumer spending, this will require much in the way of natural resources.

More specifically to the topic of gold, both of these countries have a long history of being very gold friendly. India is a huge consumer market for gold. China is loosening its formerly strict regulations and allowing its ample citizenry the ability to own gold and build wealth in a freer economy. All of this adds up to great news for gold aficionados. Whew . . . 2 billion people with money who like gold! Can you say "soaring demand"?

» **The Middle East:** In spite of all the conflict and turmoil, this area has great potential. Although these countries wield economic and political clout that offers great challenges, this area is yet another gold-friendly region. Many in the region are using their oil profits to buy precious metals. This means more demand.

» **Inflation everywhere:** Perhaps the most compelling bullish reason is that every major country in the world is growing its money supply at historically high levels; most of them are growing their money supply at double-digit rates making this an unprecedented inflationary environment. This means more dollars chasing fewer goods.

Telling the tale of the tape: Gold versus other investments

Gold has retained its value through good times and bad, but make no mistake about it: It has an edge over other investments during difficult or uncertain economic times. In the 1930s, gold was resilient during the Great Depression; stock prices plummeted yet gold was strong. Gold did drop in price during the 1930s but not because of market supply-and-demand factors; the U.S. government banned private ownership of gold so people were essentially forced to sell it.

So you're better off comparing gold with other investments starting with the 1970s and moving onward. As of December 1974, gold ownership became legal for private citizens in the United States. Just in time! Table 2-1 is a snapshot of gold compared to other investments and inflation in the first decade of the millennium, when it started its upward swing. *Note:* Prices are in U.S. dollars.

REMEMBER

Gold shines brightest during periods of inflation (especially hyper-inflation). In a period of stagflation, such as in the 1970s, hard assets (precious metals, real estate, natural resources, and so on) tend to do better than paper assets (such as stocks and bonds).

TABLE 2-1 Comparing Gold to Other Investments and Inflation

Asset	Time Frame	Quote 1/2/00	Quote 6/3/07	Initial Investment Amount	Ending Investment Amount	Annualized Rate	Total Return for 6½ Times	Did It Beat Inflation?
Gold	6½ years	282.05	650.50	$10,000	$23,063	12.90%	131.00%	Yes
Inflation*	6½ years	See rates	n/a		$14,755 (amount you need to retain purchasing power from initial investment)	6.00% + (using the real rate of inflation)	45.00%	n/a
Bonds	6½ years	n/a	n/a	$10,000	$13,250	5.00%	38.00%	No
Stocks (based on Dow Jones Industrial Average)	6½ years	n/a	n/a	$10,000	$11,806	2.78%	18.00%	No
Passbook account	6½ years	n/a	n/a	$10,000	$11,023	1.50%	9.75%	No

* Inflation isn't an asset, of course, but it's important to compare.

Table 2-1 is very telling. Certainly, a year here and a month there show that gold performed poorly. But then, you're not investing; you're trading or speculating. The table clearly shows that during the specific period analyzed, some common paper investments just couldn't keep pace with inflation. Notice the column for inflation illustrates that you would need to have at least $14,755 in 2007 just to match the same purchasing power of $10,000 in 2000. Gold resoundingly beat inflation while paper investments fell short.

TECHNICAL STUFF

By the way, Table 2-1 might make you ask about gold-mining stocks and how they fared during this period. A good barometer of the gold mining industry would be an index called the NYSE Arca Gold BUGS Index (HUI). BUGS stands for "Basket of Unhedged Gold Stocks." The HUI is an index representing a batch of stocks that are gold-mining stocks that do little or no hedging. Basically, hedging is the practice of selling next year's production at this year's prices to lock in a profit. This practice is fine if gold's price is flat or declining. But if gold is rising, then the company foregoes the potential profit. Done too excessively in the wrong market conditions could spell bankruptcy for the company. Hedging isn't a good practice in a rising gold bull market.

Anyway, back to the HUI. How did it perform during the time frame as compared to the other investments in the table? At the beginning of the decade, the HUI started at 73.77 (1/3/00), and it ended the day of trading on June 30, 2007, at 329.35 for a total percentage gain of 346 per cent. In other words, a $10,000 investment in a representative portfolio of gold-mining stocks that made up the HUI index at the beginning of the decade would have been worth $44,645. Sweet! Yes . . . gold mining stocks are "paper" investments, but fortunately they derive their value from a desirable underlying asset . . . gold.

Assuring gold's success

REMEMBER

Gold is a tangible investment that has its own intrinsic value. It sounds weird, but this concept is important when you compare it to "paper" investments. All paper investments are basically "derivatives," meaning they derive their value from another entity or from a promise from another party. Think about paper investments, and you see that they're essentially a promise that needs to be fulfilled. Paper investments have major risk associated with them: the risk of default by the other party. This is also referred to as *counterparty risk.* Look at the panorama of paper investments:

>> **The dollar and other currencies:** When you hold a dollar in your hand, what are you holding? The dollar is a piece of paper with official printing on it. It has no intrinsic value; it is a promise of value backed up by the full faith and credit of the government. However, if the government (any government for that

matter) prints up lots and lots of dollars (monetary inflation), the risk is that each dollar becomes diminished in value.

» **Stock:** Stock, common or otherwise, represents a piece of ownership in a public company. If the company is in business and doing well, the stock for that company will have value. But what happens if the company goes bankrupt? In that case, what will be the value of that stock beyond just being a printed piece of paper? Therefore, stock also has the risk of default. (Flip to Book 2 for more about stocks.)

» **Bonds:** A bond is a form of debt (as you find out in Chapter 5 of Book 3). If you have a bond investment, it is a piece of paper that states that another party will pay you interest and ultimately pay you back the sum of money (the principal) that was loaned. In the bond investment, you are the lender and the person obligated to pay you back is the borrower. What happens if the borrower can't (or won't) pay you back? You could lose some or all of your money in a bond. Because bonds are a paper investment, they have the risk of default.

» **Mortgages and loans:** In this century, markets across the globe have been in turmoil because of problems with sub-prime mortgages. A sub-prime mortgage is where money was loaned for the purpose of buying real estate (typically a home) to individuals who have below-average credit. The point is that mortgages and loans, like bonds, are paper investments that have . . . you guessed it . . . the risk of default. All situations of extending credit — whether it is a bond from a corporation, a government agency, or some cash you loaned to your Uncle Stanley — run the risk of default.

Securing a Safe Haven from the Coming Storm

Understanding the value of gold is like understanding an umbrella without discussing rain. People quickly see the value of an umbrella when it rains. They also understand the value of buying an umbrella on a sunny day, especially when rain is forecast for the next day. To understand gold (as the umbrella), you should understand its role in bad economic conditions (the rain).

Comparing monetary and price inflation

As more and more people wise up to inflation, ultimately they will do something about it. Although inflation has been high in recent years and has the potential to go higher, much of the public hasn't caught on. You can't blame them; the responsibility for informing the public rests squarely on the shoulders of the government and the financial media. The reporting of inflation is in fact dreadful. You should understand inflation not only because of how it helps gold go up, but you should also understand it because it is a pernicious and pervasive problem. The following sections should help you sort through and gain an understanding of inflation.

There are two types of inflation. One is a "problem" while the other is a "symptom." The "problem" is monetary inflation. That is just a fancy phrase for the government's central bank practice of printing money (actually, printing currency). The more a government prints, the more the supply of money could grow. After the money is created, it's circulated through member banks. This money makes its way into the economy through actually printed currency (such as the dollar), electronic transfer, or through loans (credit). This is the problem.

The end result of the problem of monetary inflation is the next phenomenon, price inflation. Price inflation is the one everyone talks about. That's when your uncle goes to the store and says to the sales clerk, "You're charging how much for this?!" Price inflation can be a problem for everyone, but in the big picture, price inflation actually is the "symptom."

TIP

You can find out more about inflation in Canada via the Bank of Canada (www.bankofcanada.ca/core-functions/monetary-policy/inflation/) and Statistics Canada (www.statcan.gc.ca/eng/subjects-start/prices_and_price_indexes/consumer_price_indexes).

Watching the dollar

The dollar is the "other side of the coin" so to speak. When people refer to "rising inflation," they're really referring to the falling value of the dollar (or other currency). If, for example, you look at the long-term chart of gold versus the U.S. dollar, you will see the dollar zig-zagging downward and gold zig-zagging upward. It stands to reason that the more and more dollars you add to the system, the less each unit is worth.

TIP

To monitor the price of trading currencies, you can go to major financial websites, such as BNN Bloomberg (www.bnnbloomberg.ca/). Futures markets-related websites also track currencies, so you can check out places such as FXStreet (https://www.fxstreet.com/) and Yahoo! Finance (https://ca.finance.yahoo.com/).

Buying and owning gold

So maybe you have thrown in the towel screaming, "Okay, okay! Stop it, you win! I see the light! I'll buy some gold (and aspirin)! How do I do it?" Thanks for asking.

The following list shows you the many ways that you can get involved with gold:

>> **You can buy physical gold:**

- **Bullion coins:** Gold as coins

- **Bars and ingots:** Another form of physical gold

- **Numismatic coins:** Gold through collectible coins

- **Jewelry and other forms (such as collectibles):** Make sure that your spouse doesn't see this. Where's that aspirin?

>> **You can buy paper gold:**

- Gold certificates

- Gold exchange-traded funds

- Gold mutual funds

- Gold-mining stocks

- Gold futures

- Gold futures options

- Gold indexes

- Gold managed accounts

Checking Out the Gold Market

Gold is a worldwide market and the long-term supply-and-demand fundamentals are very bullish. The following sections give you some insights into the gold market.

Gold market data and information

The more you know about what is happening in the gold market, the better prepared you will be to profit. The following organizations provide extensive research and data on the yellow metal:

>> **GFMS (formally Gold Fields Mineral Services):** GFMS does specialized research on the world's precious metals market, specifically gold, silver, platinum, and palladium. Find out more about GFMS at www.refinitiv.com/en/products/eikon-trading-software/gfms-precious-metals.

>> **CPM Group:** CPM is another leading consulting firm that specializes in commodities and precious metals research. They provide extensive research on the precious metals markets and publish their work in several annual yearbooks: *The Gold Yearbook, The Silver Yearbook,* and *The Platinum Group Metals Yearbook.* The CPM Group was founded in 1986 by Jeffrey Christian, a metals analyst and the author of the book *Commodities Rising.* Its website is www.cpmgroup.com.

>> **Gold Anti-Trust Action Committee (GATA):** The Gold Anti-Trust Action Committee was formed in January 1999 by well-known gold analyst Bill Murphy. GATA advocates and undertakes litigation against illegal collusion between financial institutions (such as central banks and large brokerage firms) that intervene in the gold market. GATA's aim is to foster a freer market for gold since the central banks and brokerage firms have on an ongoing basis managed to control the price and supply of gold and related financial securities. GATA's website is www.gata.org.

>> **World Gold Council (WGC):** The World Gold Council was created by gold mining companies and refiners in 1987. Its mission is the promotion of investment and usage of gold by consumers, investors, industry, and central banks. The WGC's website is www.gold.org.

>> **Mining Association of Canada (MAC):** The MAC is the national voice of the Canadian mining industry in Ottawa. Visit its website at https://mining.ca/.

>> **National Mining Association (NMA):** The NMA is the voice of the American mining industry in Washington, D.C. and the only national trade organization that represents the interests of mining before Congress, the administration, federal agencies, the judiciary, and the media (www.nma.org).

Industrial supply and demand

The major determinants for gold's performance (its price going up or down) boil down to inflation and supply-and-demand factors.

Total demand and supply

Time for the big picture first. In 2010, total annual worldwide demand was about 4,200 tons (according to www.gold.org/goldhub/data/gold-supply-and-demand-statistics), and the total annual worldwide supply was a little over 4,300 tons. In 2019, total annual worldwide demand was between 4,300 and 4,400 tons, and the total annual worldwide supply was about 4,820 tons.

No matter which way you slice it, the big picture in the long term is that supply-and-demand factors for gold are bullish.

Demand

Demand for gold comes from two places: investment and industry. Gold has unique properties which mean more applications of it in technology, healthcare, and other vital industries. Gold is extremely resistant to corrosion and it has high thermal and electrical conductivity. Therefore, it is an excellent component in electrical devices. Gold is also used in medical equipment because it is resistant to bacteria. New uses for gold have been found in pollution control equipment and fuel cells. In addition, gold has promising application in the new area of nano-technology. The practical uses for gold keep growing.

TIP

For current news on the many new ways gold is being used in industry and medicine, check out gold's growing uses at www.gold.org/goldhub/research/relevance-of-gold-as-a-strategic-asset-2020.

Supply

Gold is mined on all the major continents. Specifically, it has been most plentiful in places such as South Africa, Canada, the United States, Russia, and Australia. (There is no mining in Antarctica but then again, why would you want to?)

For thousands of years, gold was (and is) considered money. It has outlived thousands of currencies, and in due course, it will outlive more currencies. Part of the reason for its durability as a desirable form of money is directly tied to its rarity. You can create lots of paper currencies almost instantly, but you can only increase gold by a mere 2 per cent per year. It is easy to inflate man-made currencies and history tells you this has happened very, very often. It is happening today! But . . . it's not easy to inflate gold.

Although new mines do come on board every year, it doesn't have a significant impact on total worldwide supply since old mines do close down after no more gold is found. In addition, it often takes mines 5 to 10 years (sometimes longer) to go from discovery to production. Although increased market prices for gold are indeed an incentive for more gold exploration, it doesn't happen quickly. It does take years to translate higher market prices into new gold mine discovery and production.

When the price of gold does go up significantly, gold "scrap" does find its way into the marketplace. Scrap is basically recycled gold. As the price of gold goes up, it becomes more economical to recover scrap to refine it and reuse it.

Investment demand

Since the beginning of the new millennium and obviously due to gold's bull market, investment demand has grown tremendously. Actually, according to market studies by the CPM Group, a very unusual situation rose during 2006–07. In that time, private investors (as a collective group) owned more gold than the group of central bankers. The first time in world history!

Much of the new investment demand comes from two sources: the popularity of precious metals-related exchange-traded funds (ETFs) and from international investors such as from China, India, and the Middle East. More and more investors are seeing the big picture, and they understand that gold has unique advantages and is a good part of a well-balanced portfolio.

Central banks

Central banks play a pivotal role in the gold market and sometimes that role can be a controversial one. It stems from the "love/hate relationship" that central banks have with gold (maybe they need therapy). On the one hand, central banks are the single largest holders of gold in the world. Most governments have gold as an asset in their official reserves. Yet, on the other hand, gold is a "competitor" to the currency that is issued by the central bank on behalf of its government.

You'll notice that whenever gold is rallying, one or more of the central banks will either announce a large sale of gold or actually sell a large amount of it. And they have a considerable amount of the yellow metal; it is estimated that central banks along with other governmental institutions (such as the International Monetary Fund) held roughly 17 per cent of the world's above-ground stock of gold at the end of 2019 (see www.gold.org/about-gold/gold-supply/gold-mining/how-much-gold). This stockpile is nearly 34,000 tons (that's tons, not ounces) of gold.

Keep in mind that not all central banks work in unison. Some are buying gold while others are selling. Although the central banks have much autonomy about how to manage their individual gold reserves, most of the major central banks have agreed to do their buying and selling according to guidelines stipulated in agreements such as the 2014 Central Bank Gold Agreement (CBGA; see www.gold.org/what-we-do/official-institutions/central-bank-gold-agreements). Some interesting developments have occurred in recent years.

Central banks in "the West" such as the U.S. Federal Reserve and central banks in Western European governments (such as the United Kingdom, France, Spain, and others) have been net sellers of gold. Meanwhile, central banks in the East (both middle and far) have been net buyers of gold. This tends to generally reflect attitudes about gold in both spheres. Folks in Asia and peripheral regions as groups embrace gold far more than those in North America and Europe. As a total group, it has been a net seller which was a contributing factor to some of those steep corrections that have been experienced by precious metals investors in recent years.

Central banks don't have to just buy and sell their gold to influence the market. They are also involved in activities such as gold derivatives and in leasing gold. For a discussion, see `https://www.gold.org/goldhub/research/gold-investor/central-banks-return-to-gold`.

TIP

Central banks report their gold position and activities to the International Monetary Fund (IMF) and you can view some of this information at the website at `www.imf.org`.

Meeting a Few Gold Bugs

The term "gold bugs" has sometimes been used as a pejorative but many veteran gold analysts and well-known commentators have come to wear the name like a badge of honour. The following is really like a "hall of fame" for the world of gold since some of these stalwarts (actually most of them) were successful and active back in the late 1970s.

What these folks have in common goes beyond an affinity for gold investing. Through the years they have offered research and insights that benefited the gold-investing community for decades. Some of their forecasts became legendary. Yes, they have had their misses, but in the investment world, when you have far more hits than misses and keep doing it for years and even decades, this is something you can't ignore.

To me (coauthor Paul), another reason for checking them out is that I like to know that you just don't talk the talk; you need to also walk the walk. If I know that the person involved made a lot of money on his or her own advice, that goes much further than people who tell you to invest in X and then you find out that they made most of their money by selling reports and newsletters about "How to invest in X." In other words, these folks are primarily self-made in their financial independence due to the adherence and application of their own knowledge.

TIP

Drum roll please! Here is a pantheon of gold bugs worthy of the name:

>> Jay Taylor (www.miningstocks.com)

>> Doug Casey (www.caseyresearch.com/)

>> James Sinclair (www.jsmineset.com)

>> James Dines (www.dinesletter.com)

>> James Turk (www.goldmoney.com)

>> Mary Anne and Pamela Aden (www.adenforecast.com)

>> Harry Schultz (www.hsletter.com)

>> Adam Hamilton (www.zealllc.com)

Digging into Other Gold Investing Resources

The gold market can be a fascinating one and if your money is riding on it then it better be a well-researched one as well. Here are some solid websites for gold investors:

>> Le Metro Pole Café (www.lemetropolecafe.com)

>> Gold Sheet Mining Directory (www.goldsheetlinks.com)

>> Gold Eagle (www.gold-eagle.com)

>> 3 2 1 Gold (www.321gold.com)

Staying informed about the gold price and getting the latest news:

>> Kitco (www.kitco.com)

>> Fastmarkets (www.fastmarkets.com/commodities/precious-metals/gold-prices-and-charts)

>> INO.com (www.ino.com)

IN THIS CHAPTER

» Understanding a unique metal with dual benefits

» Finding silver market information

» Owning physical and paper silver

» Exploring a future with a silver lining

» Meeting legends in the world of silver

Chapter **3**

Discovering the Secret of Silver

Silver is hands-down my favourite precious metal (this is coauthor Paul). Maybe it's because it's more affordable than gold. Maybe it's because I like the color better. Oh wait . . . now I remember: When I buy my wife silver jewelry instead of gold, I still have some cash left to buy something for my boys! Well, really . . . I like silver most because of the great profit potential that I think it will generate. It has served me well in recent years and there is no reason why that shouldn't continue (and get better!) in the coming years. I think devoting a whole chapter to the poor man's gold is a good idea. Silver's future profit potential is truly its silver lining (you were expecting that line . . . right?).

Understanding the Hybrid Potentials of Silver

Silver is a fascinating metal and it has the unique, dual quality of being both a monetary metal (used as money) and an industrial metal. This lies at the heart of its potential. There are countries that are reconsidering the use of silver again in their currencies. Meanwhile, more uses for silver in technology and healthcare mean more opportunities for silver investors and speculators.

Silver is unique in that no other metal combines strength with a softness that allows it to be formed and stretched. You would be hard-pressed to find a metal that conducts electricity as well or is as pliable, corrosion, or fatigue resistant. Nothing else has such high-tensile strength, is wear resistant, has such a long functional life, or is as light sensitive. Silver endures extreme temperatures, conducts heat, reflects light, provides catalytic action, and has a great reputation for its bactericidal qualities. It alloys (easily combines with other metals) and helps to reduce friction. Due to its exceptional properties and reasonable price, there is no substitute for silver.

Monetary uses for silver

For centuries gold and silver were used as money. Silver was probably more widely used since gold was too expensive for day-to-day use. Silver was not as valuable as gold as a monetary unit so it served nicely for the smaller transactions. Silver was used in ancient times, and the first coin minted in Canada by the Royal Mint's Ottawa branch was a silver 50-cent piece in 1908.

The Royal Canadian Mint issued the silver dollar in 1935, but after 1968, the silver dollar was made out of nickel instead. Commemorative silver dollars for collectors still contain silver.

Canada's government issues the Silver Maple Leaf every year, with a face value of five dollars. It's a silver bullion coin produced by the Royal Canadian Mint.

Industrial uses for silver

TECHNICAL STUFF

In the past, the primary engine of industrial usage for silver was photography. As traditional photography started slowly going the way of the buggy and the corset, the true strength and versatility of silver started to come forward. David Morgan of www.silver-investor.com makes a fascinating point about silver: There are more new patents with silver than with all other metals combined. There are thousands of industrial applications for silver. As a matter of fact, out of all the commodities in use in the economy, only petroleum is used in more different ways.

The largest use of silver comes from industrial demand, jewelry/silverware, and photography, in that order. Although photography has gotten all the attention in recent years, of the three major categories, it is the smallest. Industrial demand for silver makes up most of the total demand, and this area is also the fastest *growing* area of silver demand. It is important to understand that in almost all instances, the amount of silver used in a cellphone, laptop computer, or microwave oven is so small that it cannot be recovered. For all practical purposes, the silver used in these applications is lost and unrecoverable.

SORTING THROUGH SILVER'S MANY USES

The multiple uses for silver started growing almost exponentially as industry figured out that silver's unique properties made it an ideal component in a broad array of products. Here is a partial list:

- Bactericide
- Batteries
- Bearings
- Brazing and soldering
- Catalysts
- Clothing (lining to kill bacteria)
- Coins
- Computer components
- Electrical
- Electronics
- Electroplating
- Jewelry and silverware
- Medical applications
- Mirrors and coatings
- Nanotechnology
- Photography
- Plasma screens
- Solar energy
- Super conductivity
- Surgical instruments
- Washing machines
- Water purification

Yes . . . it is a partial list and it keeps growing.

This type of demand is called *price-inelastic* by economists. The small amount of silver that is used makes it an insignificant factor in the price of the product. The amount of silver used in the manufacture of a battery, an automobile, a computer, or cellphone is insignificant when compared to the price of labour and other materials. A doubling in the price of silver would not affect, for example, what Honda uses in making an automobile. Since the price of silver has such a small relationship to the cost of the finished product, there is really no substitute. If the price of silver went to over $100 per ounce, for example, the only possible substitute for silver would be palladium or platinum, both costing much more than $100 per ounce.

Researching Silver

Making fantastic profits in anything is not easy, and silver is no different. Even when you think a speculation is a slam dunk, it can backfire in the short term. You need to be armed with market intelligence. You need the facts, and if you're seeking options, then get informed opinions from long-established sources.

Sources of data

Sometimes opinions are no more valuable than fiat currency (normally a solid laugh line at precious metals conferences). In other words, get the facts. Silver investors and speculators fortunately live in the best of times when it comes to gaining access to reliable information. With some time and effort at a good business library and the Internet, of course, you can find the information necessary to render an informed decision. The following sections list the top sources.

The Silver Institute

Established in 1971, the Washington, D.C.–based Silver Institute is a nonprofit international association with members that span across the silver industry. They regularly track the sources and uses of silver and they publish their research in their World Silver Survey. Their recent research was made available in reports covering topics such as the Chinese Silver market and a study of stockpiles of silver around the world. More information can be found at www.silverinstitute.org.

The CPM Group

The CPM Group is a research and consulting firm that specializes in the metals industry. They produced annual studies in the individual precious metals (called yearbooks) and the most relevant one is the *CPM Silver Yearbook*. Their research includes data on production, consumption, and silver output. More details are at www.cpmgroup.com.

CME Group

For those seeking market data on silver futures and options, go to the source: www.cmegroup.com/trading/metals/. Silver is just one commodity traded at the CME Group (which runs several exchanges), but you can find relevant information on silver and this fast-moving market.

Sources of informed opinion

As silver and precious metals in general become more popular and visible, more and more newsletters and advisory services start to come out of the woodwork. When a new batch of "experts" and "gurus" emerge, that might tell you that it's a popular market, but it becomes a dart-throwing exercise when it comes to choosing the ones that have helpful guidance and information. Who do you turn to?

TIP

It's good to turn to those sources that have had a consistent track record and have followed the silver market for years in both up and down markets. One that specializes in silver is the Morgan Report at silver analyst David Morgan's www.silver-investor.com. Ted Butler's essays and features are provided at www.investmentrarities.com. Doug Casey also does a great job covering silver stocks at www.caseyresearch.com/.

Owning Silver

To maximize your profit opportunities and provide some safety and a measure of diversification, get involved in both physical ownership as well as paper investments of silver. Owning physical silver is a solid, long-term, buy-'n'-hold strategy that should work well. For those seeking more growth (along with more risk) then consider paper investments such as mining stocks. The following sections give you some pointers for both.

Physical silver

TIP

The easiest way to get into silver is through bullion silver coins produced by the Royal Canadian Mint (www.mint.ca/store/template/home.jsp), and they're readily available either directly or through coin shops and dealers.

The benefit of buying bullion is that the price you pay primarily covers the silver content. A silver bullion coin, as you shop around, could be bought for whatever is the spot price of silver plus a premium of 5% to 12% to cover production and marketing costs. Therefore, if the spot price of silver is $10, you could find the cost for a silver coin to vary from $10.50 to $11.20. Be careful as there are dealers that have higher premiums, so do shop around.

There are silver commemoratives, medallions, ingots, and other collectibles available, but you'll find that the price of what you are buying will cost far more than the silver content. You may not even get as much silver as you think. The standard is .999 fine silver so find out as quality can vary.

Keep in mind that another benefit of buying bullion coins is that you can easily sell them as it's a large and liquid market. Collectibles and numismatic coins require more diligence, effort, and expertise in both buying and selling them.

Paper silver

You can invest in silver without actually holding or storing the physical silver. Many people buy silver through things such as silver certificates or through brokers and dealers that store it for you and provide proof of ownership such as through a warehouse receipt.

WARNING

There are some pitfalls so you would need to choose reputable dealers that document the existence of the silver it holds on your behalf. It was a common problem where people bought silver (or so they thought) only to find out that they paid good money for a piece of paper that was not backed up by actual physical silver allegedly held by the vendor.

Another way to invest in silver is through buying common stock of silver-mining companies. There are a few large silver-mining companies and several dozen smaller companies. To invest in them it requires not only some due diligence in understanding the silver market but also about public companies in general. You need to know how they make money and what their financials tell you. In addition you need to know what the pitfalls are. There are companies that can be good choices for either conservative or aggressive investors.

TIP

A safer way to invest in mining stocks (especially for beginning or novice investors) is through mutual funds and exchange-traded funds (ETFs), and Book 3 gives you more guidance. You will find very few (if any) mutual funds that are purely into silver-mining stocks, but there are many precious metals funds that have silver mining stocks as part of their portfolio.

Lastly, the most aggressive and/or speculative way to be in paper silver vehicles is futures and options. This requires much more due diligence and a greater tolerance to risk. Between the two, my personal preference for speculating is options since I can still get "the bang for my buck" similar to futures but I can limit my risk.

Focusing on Silver's Compelling Future

There was a time when silver was plentiful. At one time, for example, the U.S. government had over two billion ounces of silver stockpiled during the 20th century, but as of 2003 it has no more. As people consume more silver than they produce, a major drawdown of supplies begins to occur. You begin to see how rare silver is when you compare it to gold. Virtually all the gold that has been mined is still around in some form. You can find large supplies held by central banks, and gold ownership (through coins and jewelry) is at an all-time high. Silver, though, is a different story.

One of the most incredible things regarding silver is that demand for it has outstripped supply for years. Annual silver supply deficits have run as high as 200 million ounces in boom years, and as low as 70 million ounces in years of recession. It is important to realize that even in years of decreased silver demand, the mining supply on an annual basis did not meet demand. There is nothing more bullish for a commodity than such a deficit condition, a condition where demand is greater than available supply.

Because the vast majority of silver is mined as a byproduct of mining lead, zinc, copper, and gold, the price of silver can be sensitive to the amount produced as a byproduct. This, however, is a condition that has a flipside. When the total amount of silver produced by mining falls short of total demand and the price of silver starts to climb, there is little incentive for base metal miners to rev up their production because the silver produced is not instrumental to their business. The ongoing commodity boom will continue, and base metal production will increase in the future, but it is highly doubtful that the increase will keep pace with the increasing demand for silver for many years.

In today's global economy, the United States is no longer the 800-pound gorilla. While America is slowing down, the rest of the world is speeding up. Precious metals (and commodities in general) could easily have a long-term bull market with just two reasons: China and India (and the rest of Asia).

Asia will be a tremendous factor for two reasons:

>> Asia's growth and accelerating industrialization mean it will need more natural resources. Remember that precious metals are finite natural resources.

>> China and India have always embraced gold and silver in their cultural and social circles. There is natural demand that will only increase as their respective nations become more affluent.

Looking at the Legends of Silver

Every market has those trailblazers that stay on the cutting edge of market movements. The stock market had Benjamin Graham and Warren Buffett. The mutual fund industry had Peter Lynch and John Bogle. If you had followed their research, you would have very done well in those markets. The precious metals market is no different. The following sections profile the trailblazers in silver.

Jerome Smith

One of the first legendary "silver bulls" was Jerome Smith. In 1972 his book *Silver Profits in the Seventies* accurately detailed the bull market for silver during the high-flying '70s. At the time, he was also very accurate about the rise in gold and other precious metals. His writings influenced the Hunt brothers in their infamous attempt at cornering the silver market.

TECHNICAL STUFF

Smith expected silver to explode during the 1980s but was way off the mark. The reasons he cited are probably more appropriate now, decades later, since he did not foresee how much silver would enter the marketplace from government sources that depressed the price. He also didn't foresee the extent that large financial firms in the silver market would be active in forcing the price of silver down (referred to as *shorting* the market). Fortunately, his work influenced others to continue tracking the silver market and its great potential today.

Ted Butler

In recent years, landmark studies and research into the silver market was undertaken by silver analyst Ted Butler (`www.butlerresearch.com`). He has been one of the very few analysts to track and research the silver market on a full-time basis. Although he usually doesn't issue specific forecasts and recommendations, he was correct on a consistent basis on warnings about problems with silver and other metals. He warned about practices such as forward selling, naked short selling, and metals leasing.

Butler is on record that silver has the long-term realistic potential of going into three figures ($100 or more). He also embraces Jerome Smith's forecasts that silver has an outside chance of becoming more valuable than gold when the world marketplace realizes that silver is actually rarer than gold. He cites the following points as the fundamental reasons to be bullish on silver long term:

» **The huge supply and demand imbalance:** As new industrial applications need silver and as the rest of the world continues modernizing and growing (again, places like China and India), demand will outpace (and is already outpacing) new silver being mined. Long-term, a very bullish condition.

» **The huge short position in silver:** In the futures market, you can go long in silver (buying a contract) or you can go short (selling a contract) as a market strategy. Shorting futures contracts means you become a counterparty to trader X's contract to buy silver at a specific price in the future. If prices go down, you make a mark-to-market gain and can exit the position by entering into a long offsetting position with trader Y. Then, trader Y's short position replaces your short position versus trader X.

The bottom line is that Butler warns that there is a huge short position in silver that exceeds the known inventory of silver available — a very unusual situation that could prove to be explosive for the price of silver in due course. In other words, there's not enough silver to cover potential purchases of silver. When a forced purchase in a shorting situation occurs, this is called a *short squeeze*. Long term, this is a very bullish condition.

» **Unbacked silver bank certificates:** Over a period of decades, approximately one billion silver bank certificates were sold with the provision that they can be converted to physical silver. However, there aren't a billion ounces available to back up these certificates. In due course, as some certificates begin to be converted, what happens when the point is reached and no silver is readily available? The signal to the marketplace is that there is a silver shortage and . . . yes . . . this would be yet another reason that silver would increase in price.

The preceding major points come from Ted Butler's research and from publicly available data. Butler makes additional points about the bullish case for silver, but you get the picture.

David Morgan

For years David Morgan of www.silver-investor.com tracked the silver market and offered cutting-edge research on silver and especially silver mining companies. His book *Get the Skinny on Silver* (www.gettheskinnyonsilver.com) quickly became a key reference source especially for beginners. Although Morgan made a number of accurate short-term forecasts for silver, his research indicates that long-term silver is heading for an all-time high price since the supply-and-demand fundamentals are so strong. After surveying the industry, Morgan noted that silver supplies are at historically low levels to the point that if any large investor or industrial firm wanted a significant supply of silver, it could trigger a buying panic causing the price of silver to spike (move upward very quickly).

5
Day Trading

Contents at a Glance

IN THIS CHAPTER

» Figuring out just what day traders do anyway

» Being committed to a trading business

» Concentrating on a few assets, a few dollars at a time

» Knowing what it takes to be a successful trader

» Dispelling some of the myths of trading

Chapter **1**

Waking Up to Day Trading

Make money from the comfort of your home! Be your own boss! Beat the market with your own smarts! Build real wealth! Tempting, isn't it? Day trading can be a great way to make money all on your own. It's also a great way to lose a ton of money, all on your own. Are you cut out to take the risk?

Day trading is a crazy business. Traders work in front of their computer screens, reacting to blips, each of which represent real dollars. They make quick decisions, because their ability to make money depends on successfully executing a large number of trades that generate small profits. Because they close out their positions in the stocks, options, and futures contracts they own at the end of the day, some of the risks are limited. Each day is a new day, and nothing can happen overnight to disturb an existing profit position.

But those limits on risk can limit profits. After all, a lot can happen in a year, increasing the likelihood that your trade idea will work out. But in a day? You have to be patient and work fast. Some days nothing seems good to buy. Other days it feels like every trade loses money. Do you have the fortitude to face the market every morning?

This chapter gives you an overview of day trading. It covers what exactly day traders do all day, goes through the advantages and disadvantages of day trading, describes some of the personality traits of successful day traders, and gives you some information on your likelihood of success.

REMEMBER

You may find that day trading is a great career option that takes advantage of your street smarts and clear thinking — or that the risk outweighs the potential benefits. That's okay: The more you know before you make the decision to trade, the greater the chance of being successful. If it turns out that day trading isn't right for you, you can apply strategies and techniques that day traders use to improve the performance of your investment portfolio.

It's All in a Day's Work

The definition of day trading is that day traders hold their securities for only one day. They close out their positions at the end of every day and then start all over again the next day. By contrast, *swing traders* hold securities for days and sometimes even months, whereas *investors* sometimes hold for years.

The short-term nature of day trading reduces some risks, because no chance exists of something happening overnight to cause big losses. Meanwhile, many investors have gone to bed thinking their position is in great shape, then woken up to find that the company has announced terrible earnings or that its CEO is being indicted on fraud charges.

But there's a flip side (there's always a flip side, isn't there?): The day trader's choice of securities and positions has to work out in a day, or it's gone. There's no tomorrow for any specific position. Meanwhile, the swing trader or the investor has the luxury of time, as it sometimes takes a while for a position to work out the way your research shows it should. In the long run, markets are efficient, and prices reflect all information about a security. Unfortunately, it can take a few days of short runs for this efficiency to kick in.

Day traders are speculators working in zero-sum markets one day at a time. That makes the dynamics different from other types of financial activities you may have been involved in.

REMEMBER

When you take up day trading, the rules that may have helped you pick good stocks (see Book 2) or find great mutual funds (see Book 3) over the years will no longer apply. This is a different game with different rules.

Speculating, not hedging

Professional traders fall into two categories: speculators and hedgers. Speculators look to make a profit from price changes. Hedgers are looking to protect against a price change. They're making their buy and sell choices as insurance, not as a way to make a profit, so they choose positions that offset their exposure in another market.

For example, a food-processing company might look to hedge against the risks of the prices of key ingredients — like corn, cooking oil, or meat — going up by *buying futures* contracts on those ingredients. That way, if prices do go up, the company's profits on the contracts help fund the higher prices that it has to pay to make its products. If the prices stay the same or go down, it loses only the price of the contract, which may be a fair trade-off to the company.

The farmer raising corn, soybeans, or cattle, on the other hand, would benefit if prices went up and would suffer if they went down. To protect against a price decline, the farmer would *sell futures* on those commodities. Then, his futures position would make money if the price went down, offsetting the decline on his products. And if the prices went up, he'd lose money on the contracts, but that would be offset by his gain on his harvest.

REMEMBER

The commodity markets were intended to help agricultural producers manage risk and find buyers for their products. The stock and bond markets were intended to create an incentive for investors to finance companies. Speculation emerged in all of these markets almost immediately, but it was not their primary purpose.

Markets have both hedgers and speculators in them. Day traders are all speculators. They look to make money from the market as they see it now. They manage their risks by carefully allocating their money, using stop and limit orders (which close out positions as soon as predetermined price levels are reached) and closing out at the end of the night. Day traders don't manage risk with offsetting positions the way a hedger does. They use other techniques to limit losses, like careful money management and stop and limit orders (all of which you can read about in Chapter 2 of Book 5).

Knowing that different participants have different profit and loss expectations can help a day trader navigate the turmoil of each day's trading. And that's important, because in a zero-sum market you only make money if someone else loses.

Understanding zero-sum markets

A zero-sum game has exactly as many winners as losers. No net gain exists, which makes it really hard to eke out a profit. And here's the thing: Options and futures markets, which are popular with day traders, are zero-sum markets. If the person who holds an option makes a profit, then the person who *wrote* (which is option-speak for *sold*) that option loses the same amount. No net gain or net loss exists in the market as a whole.

Now, some of those buying and selling in zero-sum markets are hedgers who are content to take small losses in order to prevent big ones. Speculators may have the profit advantage in certain market conditions. But they can't count on having that advantage all the time.

REMEMBER

So who wins and loses in a zero-sum market? Some days, it all depends on luck, but over the long run, the winners are the people who are the most disciplined. They have a trading plan, set limits and stick to them, and can trade based on the data on the screen — not based on emotions like hope, fear, and greed.

Unlike the options and futures markets, the stock market is not a zero-sum game. As long as the economy grows, company profits will grow, and that will lead to growing share prices. There really are more winners than losers over the long run. That doesn't mean there will be more winners than losers today, however. In the short run, the stock market should be treated like a zero-sum market.

If you understand how profits are divided in the markets that you choose to trade, you'll have a better understanding of the risks that you face as well as the risks that are being taken by the other participants. People do make money in zero-sum markets, but you don't want those winners to be making a profit off of you.

REMEMBER

Some traders make money — lots of money — doing what they like. Trading is all about risk and reward. Those traders who are rewarded risked the 80 percent washout rate. Knowing that, do you want to take the plunge? If so, read on. And if not, read on anyway, as you might get some ideas that can help you manage your other investments.

Keeping the discipline: Closing out each night

Day traders start each day fresh and finish each day with a clean slate. That reduces some of the risk, and it forces discipline. You can't keep your losers longer than a day, and you have to take your profits at the end of the day before those winning positions turn into losers.

And that discipline is important. When you're day trading, you face a market that doesn't know or care who you are, what you're doing, or what your personal or financial goals are. No kindly boss who might cut you a little slack today, no friendly coworker to help through a jam, no great client dropping you a little hint about her spending plans for the next fiscal year. Unless you have rules in place to guide your trading decisions, you will fall prey to hope, fear, doubt, and greed — the Four Horsemen of trading ruin.

So how do you start? First, you develop a business plan and a trading plan that reflect your goals and your personality. Then, you set your working days and hours and you accept that you will close out every night. Both of these steps are covered in Chapter 2 of Book 5. As you think about the securities that you will trade (Chapter 3 in Book 5) and how you might trade them, you'll also want to test your trading system to see how it might work in actual trading.

REMEMBER

In other words, you do some preparation and have a plan. That's a basic strategy for any endeavour, whether it's running a marathon, building a new garage, or taking up day trading.

Committing to Trading as a Business

For many people, the attraction of day trading is that traders can very much control their own hours. Many markets, like foreign exchange, trade around the clock. And with easy Internet access, day trading seems like a way to make money while the baby is napping, on your lunch hour, or working just a few mornings a week in between golf games and woodworking.

REMEMBER

That myth of day trading as an easy activity that can be done on the side makes a lot of traders very rich, because they make money when traders who are not fully committed lose their money.

Day trading is a business, and the best traders approach it as such. They have business plans for what they will trade (see Chapter 2 in Book 5), how they will invest in their business, and how they will protect their trading profits. If you catch a late-night infomercial about trading, the story will be about the ease and the excitement. But if you want that excitement to last, you have to make the commitment to doing trading as a business to which you dedicate your time and your energy.

Trading part-time: An okay idea if done right

Can you make money trading part-time? You can, and some people do. To do this, they approach trading as a part-time job, not as a little game to play when they have nothing else to going on. A part-time trader may commit to trading three days a week, or to closing out at noon instead of at the close of the market. A successful part-time trader still has a business plan, still sets limits, and still acts like any professional trader would, just for a smaller part of the day.

Part-time trading works best when the trader can set and maintain fixed business hours. Your brain knows when it needs to go to work and concentrate on the market, because the habit is ingrained.

The successful part-timer operates as a professional with fixed hours. Consider this example: a kindergarten teacher only works half days. She shows up when she's scheduled and, when she's there, she's doing as much work as any of the other educators. She commits her attention to her job when she's in the classroom; when she's not there, she's teaching spin classes and is as focused on getting people into shape as she is getting children to learn. She doesn't pop into school to teach an extra lesson during a break from her spin class gig, nor does she sneak around setting up meetings with parents while she's helping people exercise. If she worked on one job while she was at the other, her work would suffer. And what parent wants their children to be taught by someone who won't dedicate themselves to the kids, even if it's just for a few hours a day?

TIP

If you want to be a part-time day trader, approach it the same way that a part-time teacher, part-time lawyer, or part-time accountant would approach work. Find hours that fit your schedule and commit to trading during them. Have a dedicated office space with high-speed Internet access and a computer that you use just for trading. If you have children at home, you may need to have child care during your trading hours. And if you have another job, set your trading hours away from your work time. Trading via cellphone during your morning commute is a really good way to lose a lot of money (not to mention your life if you try it while driving).

Trading as a hobby: A bad idea

Because of the excitement of day trading and the supposed ease of doing it, you may be thinking that it would make a great hobby. If it's a boring Saturday afternoon, you could just spend a few hours day trading in the forex market (foreign exchange), and that way you'd make more money than if you spent those few hours playing video games! Right?

Uh, no.

WARNING

Trading without a plan and without committing the time and energy to do it right is a route to losses. Professional traders are betting that there will be plenty of suckers out there, because they create the *situations* that allow the pros to take profits in a zero-sum market.

WARNING

The biggest mistake an amateur trader can make is to make a lot of money the first time trading. That first success was almost definitely due to luck, and that luck can turn against a trader on a dime. If you make money your first time out, take a step back and see if you can figure out why. Then test your strategy to see if it's a good one that you can use often.

Successful day traders commit to their business. Even then, most day traders fail in their first year. Brokerage firms, training services, and other traders have a vested interest in making trading seem like an easy activity that you can work into your life. But it's a job — a job that some people love, but a job nonetheless.

TIP

If you really love the excitement of the markets, there are ways to invest on a hobbyist's schedule. First, you can spend your time doing fundamental research to find long-term investments. You can look into alternative investments to help diversify your portfolio; Chapter 3 in Book 5 can get you started on that. You can also trade with play money, either in demo accounts or in trading contests, to try out trading without committing real money.

Working with a Small Number of Assets

Most day traders pick one or two markets and concentrate on those to the exclusion of all others. That way, they can learn how the markets trade, how news affects prices, and how the other participants react to new information. Also, concentrating on just one or two markets helps a trader maintain focus.

And what do day traders trade? Chapter 3 in Book 5 has information on all of the different markets and how they work, but here's a quick summary:

>> **Derivatives:** Futures, options, and CFDs (contracts for difference) allow traders to profit from price changes in such market indexes as the TSX/S&P Composite Index in Canada, or the Dow Jones Industrial Average in the United States. They give traders exposure to the prices at a much lower cost than buying all of the stocks in the index individually. Of course, they tend to be more volatile than the indexes they track, because they are based on expectations.

>> **Forex:** *Forex,* short for *foreign exchange,* involves trading in currencies all over the world to profit from changes in exchange rates. Forex is the largest and most liquid market, and it's open for trading all day, every day except Sunday. Traders like the huge number of opportunities. Because most price changes are small, they have to use *leverage* (borrowed money) to make a profit. The borrowings have to be repaid no matter what happens to the trade, which adds to the risk of forex. (Leverage isn't unique to forex — investors can borrow money to trade derivatives and stocks too.)

>> **Common stock:** The entire business of day trading began in the stock market, and the stock market continues to be popular with day traders. They look for news on company performance and investor perception that affects stock prices, and they look to make money from those price changes. Day traders are a big factor in some industries, such as technology. The big drawback? Stock traders can get killed at tax time if they are not careful.

Managing your positions

A key to successful trading is knowing how much you're going to trade and when you're going to get out of your position. Sure, day traders are always going to close out at the end of the day — or they wouldn't be day traders — but they also need to cut their losses and take their profits as they occur during the day.

Traders rarely place all their money on one trade. That's a good way to lose it! Instead, they trade just some of it, keeping the rest to make other trades as new opportunities in the market present themselves. If any single trade fails, the trader still has money to place new trades. Some traders divide their money into fixed proportions, and others determine how much money to trade based on the expected risk and expected return of the security that they are trading. Careful money management helps a trader stay in the game longer, and the longer a trader stays in, the better the chance of making good money. Chapter 2 in Book 5 has more information on this.

To protect their funds, traders use *stop and limit orders.* These are placed with the brokerage firm and kick in whenever the security reaches a predetermined price level. If the security starts to fall in price more than the trader would like, *bam!* It's sold, and no more losses will occur on that trade. The trader doesn't agonize over the decision or second-guess herself. Instead, she just moves on to the next trade, putting her money to work on a trade that's likely to be better.

REMEMBER

Day traders make a lot of trades, and a lot of those trades are going to be losers. The key is to have more winners than losers. By limiting the amount of losses, the trader makes it easier for the gains to be big enough to generate more than enough money to make up for them.

Focusing your attention

Day traders are often undone by stress and emotion. It's hard, looking at screens all day, working alone, to keep a steady eye on what's happening in the market. But traders have to do that. They have to concentrate on the market and stick to their trading system, staying as calm and rational as possible.

Those who do well have support systems in place. They are able to close their positions and spend the rest of the day on other activities. They do something to get rid of their excess energy and clear their minds, such as running or yoga or meditation. They understand that their ability to maintain a clear mind when the market is open is crucial.

Traders sometimes think of the market itself, or everyone else who is trading, as the enemy. The real enemies are emotions: doubt, fear, greed, and hope. Those four feelings keep traders from concentrating on the market and sticking to their systems.

REMEMBER

One of the frustrations of trading is that some days, there will be more opportunities to trade than you have time or money to trade. Good trades are getting away from you. You simply don't have the resources to take advantage of every opportunity you see. That's why it's important to have a plan and to concentrate on what works for you.

A Few Personality Traits of Successful Day Traders

Traders are a special breed. They can be blunt and crude, because they act fast against a market that has absolutely no consideration for them. For all their rough exterior, they maintain strict discipline about how they approach their trading day and what they do during market hours.

The discipline begins with a plan for how to start the day, including reviews of news events and trading patterns. It includes keeping track of trades made during the day, to help the trader figure out what works and why. And it depends on cutting losses as they occur, reaping all profits that appear, and refining a set of trading rules so that tomorrow will be even better. No, it's not as much fun as just jumping in and placing orders, but it's more likely to lead to success.

Not everyone can be a day trader, nor should everyone try it. This section covers some of the traits that make up the best of them.

Independence

For the most part, day traders work by themselves. Although some cities have offices for traders, known as *trading arcades,* the number of these places has been declining over the years because the cost of setting up at home has gone down dramatically. Computers and monitors are relatively inexpensive, high-speed Internet connectivity is easier to get, and many brokerage firms cater to the needs of traders who are working by themselves.

So that leaves the day trader at home, alone, stuck in a room with nothing but the computer screen for company. It can be boring, and it can make it hard to concentrate. Some people can't handle it.

But other traders thrive on being alone all day, because it brings out their best qualities. They know that their trading depends on them alone, not on anyone else. The trader has sole responsibility when something goes wrong, but he also gets to keep all the spoils. He can make his own decisions about what works and what doesn't, with no pesky boss or annoying corporate drone telling him what he needs to do today.

If the idea of being in charge of your own business and your own trading account is exciting, then day trading might be a good career option for you.

TIP

And what if you want to trade but don't want to be working by yourself? Consider going to work for a brokerage firm, a hedge fund, a mutual fund, or a commodities company. These businesses need traders to manage their own money, and they usually have large numbers of people working together on their trading desks to share ideas, cheer each other on, and give each other support when things go wrong.

REMEMBER

No matter how independent you are, your trading will benefit if you have friends and family to offer you support and encouragement. That network will help you better manage the emotional aspects of trading. Besides, it's more fun to celebrate your success with someone else!

Quick-wittedness

Day trading is a game of minutes. An hour may as well be a decade when the markets are moving fast. And that means a day trader can't be deliberative or panicky. When it's time to buy or sell, it's time to buy or sell, and that's all there is to it.

Many investors prefer to spend hours doing a careful study of a security and markets before committing money. Some of these people are enormously successful. Warren Buffett, the CEO of Berkshire Hathaway, amassed $37 billion from his careful investing style, money that he is giving to charity. But Buffett and people like him are not traders.

Traders have to have enough trust in their system and enough experience in the markets that they can act quickly when they see a buy or sell opportunity. Many brokerage firms offer their clients demonstration accounts or backtesting services that allow traders to work with their system before committing actual dollars, helping them learn to recognize market patterns that signal potential profits.

A trader with a great system who isn't quick on the mouse button has another option: automating trades. Many brokerage firms offer software that will execute trades automatically whenever certain market conditions occur. For many traders, it's a perfect way to take the emotion out of a trading strategy. Others dislike automatic trading, because it takes some of the fun out of it. And let's face it, successful traders find the whole process to be a good time.

Decisiveness

Day traders have to move quickly, so they also have to be able to make decisions quickly. There's no waiting until tomorrow to see how the charts play out before committing capital. If the trader sees an opportunity, she has to go with it. Now.

But what if it's a bad decision? Well, of course some decisions are going to be bad. That's the risk of making any kind of an investment — and no risk, no return. Anyone playing around in the markets has to accept that.

But two good day trading practices help limit the effects of making a bad decision. The first is the use of stop and limit orders, which automatically close out losing positions. The second is closing out all positions at the end of every day, which lets traders start fresh the next day.

REMEMBER

If you have some downside protection in place, then it's psychologically easier to go ahead and make the decisions you need to make in order to make a profit. And if you're one of those people who has a hard time making a decision, day trading probably isn't right for you.

What Day Trading Is Not

Much mythology exists about day trading: Day traders lose money. Day traders make money. Day traders are insane. Day traders are cold and rational. Day trading is easy. Day trading is a direct path to alcoholism and ruin.

This section is going to bust a few day trading myths. Someone has to do it, right? This section brings both good news and bad news, so read it through to get some perspective on what, exactly, the day trader can expect from this new endeavour.

It's not investing . . .

Day traders never hold a position for more than a day. Swing traders hold positions for a few days, maybe even a few weeks, but rarely longer than that. Investors hold their stakes for the long term, with some looking to hang on to their securities for decades and maybe even hand them down to their children.

REMEMBER

Day trading is most definitely not investing. It's an important function to the capital markets because it forces the price changes that bring the supply and demand of the market into balance, but it doesn't create new sources of funding for companies and governments. It doesn't generate long-term growth.

Many day traders withdraw their trading capital on a regular basis to put into investments, helping them build a long-term portfolio for their retirement or for other ventures they might want to take on. A good chance exists the trader will have someone else manage this money, because investing and trading have different mindsets.

But it's not gambling . . .

One of the biggest knocks on day trading is that it's just another form of gambling. And as everyone knows, or should know: In gambling, the odds always favour the house.

In day trading, the odds are even in many markets. The options and futures markets, for example, are zero-sum markets with as many winners as losers, but those markets also include people looking to hedge risk and who thus have lower profit expectations than do day traders.

The stock market has the potential for more winning trades than losing trades, especially over the long run, so it's not a zero-sum market. The odds are ever-so-slightly in the trader's favour.

And in all markets, the prepared and disciplined trader can do better than the frantic, naïve trader. That's not the case when gambling, because no matter how prepared the gambler is, the casino has the upper hand.

WARNING

People with gambling problems sometimes turn to day trading as a socially acceptable way to feed their addiction. If you know you have a gambling problem or suspect you are at risk, it's probably not a good idea to take up day trading. Day traders who are closet gamblers tend to make bad trades and have trouble setting limits and closing out at the end of the day. They turn the odds against them. Chapter 4 in Book 5 has some information on the line between day trading and gambling.

It's hardly guaranteed . . .

Given the participation of day traders in securities markets, researchers are always trying to figure out whether they make money. And the answers aren't good. This section reviews some of the literature to show you the state of day trading success rates. Note that they are low. Few people who take this up succeed, in part because few people who take this up are prepared. And even many of the prepared traders fail.

Much of the research covers performance in the late 1990s, when day trading became wildly popular. It grew along with the commercial Internet, and it fell out of favour when the Internet bubble burst.

REMEMBER

Day trading is difficult, but it is not impossible. You can improve your chances of success by taking the time to prepare and by having enough money to fund your initial trading account. During the first year, you'll want to handle trading losses and still be able to pay your rent and buy your groceries. Knowing that the basics of your life are taken care of will give you more confidence, and that will help your performance.

"Do Individual Day Traders Make Money? Evidence from Taiwan"

This paper, written in 2004 by Brad Barber, Yi-Tsung Lee, Yu-Jane Liu, and Terrance Odean (and available at `http://faculty.haas.berkeley.edu/odean/papers/Day%20Traders/Day%20Trade%20040330.pdf`) found that only 20 percent of day traders in Taiwan tracked between 1995 and 1999 made money in any six-month period, after considering transaction costs. Median profits, net of costs, were US$4,200 for any six-month period, although the best traders showed semi-annual profits of US$33,000. The study also found that those who placed the most trades made the most money, possibly because they are the most experienced traders in the group.

"Report of the Day Trading Project Group"

In 1999, the North American Securities Administrators Association, which represents state and provincial securities regulators in the United States, Canada, and Mexico, researched day trading so that its members could provide appropriate oversight. The report, which you can see at `www.nasaa.org/wp-content/uploads/2011/08/NASAA_Day_Trading_Report.pdf`, did not include performance data. However, it cited several cases where brokerage firms were sanctioned by regulators for misrepresenting their clients' performance numbers, including one firm that had no clients with profits.

"Trading Profits of SOES Bandits"

Paul Schultz and Jeffrey Harris looked into the profits made by the so-called SOES bandits, day traders who took advantage of loopholes that existed in NASDAQ's Small Order Entry System in the 1990s. These people were the first day traders. Did they make money? The authors looked at a few weeks of trade data from two different firms. What they found was that about a third of all round-trip trades (buying and then later selling the same security) lost money before commissions. Only a quarter of the round-trip trades had a profit of $250 or more before commissions. The 69 traders in the study made anywhere from one to 312 round-trip trades per week. They had an average weekly profit after commission of $1,690; however, almost half of the traders, 34 of them, lost money in an average week.

You can see the abstract at http://papers.ssrn.com/sol3/papers.cfm?abstract_id=137949. The full article is available through many libraries.

But it's not exactly dangerous . . .

Yes, a lot of day traders lose money, and some lose everything that they start out with. Many others don't lose all of their trading capital; they just decide that there are better uses of their time and better ways to make money.

A responsible trader works with *risk capital*, which is money that she can afford to lose. She uses stop and limit orders to minimize her losses, and she always closes out at the end of the day. She understands the risks and rewards of trading, and that keeps her sane.

REMEMBER

Many day trading strategies rely on *leverage*, which is the use of borrowed money to increase potential returns. That carries the risk of the trader losing more money than is in his account. However, the brokerage firm doesn't want that to happen, so it will probably close a leveraged account that's in danger of going under. That's good, because it limits your potential loss.

It's not easy . . .

WARNING

Along with the relatively low rate of success, day trading is really stressful. It takes a lot of energy to concentrate on the markets, knowing that real money is at stake. The profit amounts on any one trade are likely to be small, which means the trader has to be persistent and keep placing trades until the end of the day.

Some traders can't handle the stress. Some get bored. Some get frustrated. And some can't believe that they can make a living doing something that they love.

But then again, neither are a lot of other worthwhile activities

Day trading is tough, but many day traders can't imagine doing anything else. The simple fact is that a lot of occupations are difficult ways to make a living, and yet they are right for some people. Every career has its advantages and disadvantages, and day trading is no different.

When you finish this book, you should have a good sense of whether or not day trading is right for you. If you realize that it's the career you have been searching for, we hope it leaves you with good ideas for how to get set up and learn more so that you are successful.

And if you find that maybe day trading isn't right for you, we hope you get some ideas that can help you manage your long-term investments better. After all, the attention to price movements, timing, and risk that is critical to a day trader's success can help any investor improve their returns. What's not to like about that?

Putting day trading success in perspective

A very successful trader once said two things. First, he was suspicious of all the books and training programs on day trading, because he didn't think that they really helped people learn to trade. Despite that, he liked that they existed, because trading had proven to be a great way for him to make a good living and support his family, and he thought it would be great if those people who are cut out for trading discovered the business.

REMEMBER

Yes, most day traders fail — about 80 percent in the first year, as noted earlier. But so do a large percentage of people who start new businesses or enter other occupations. If you understand the risks and keep them in perspective, you'll be better able to handle the slings and arrows of misfortune on the way to your goal.

IN THIS CHAPTER

» **Organizing your business**

» **Planning trades to start your day**

» **Making short-term and long-term choices**

» **Raining clichés like cats and dogs**

» **Taking a peek into the life of a day trader**

Chapter **2**

Making a Day Trade of It

D ay trading is sometimes presented as a profitable hobby. Anyone who buys a day trading course via infomercial can make money easily in just a few hours a week, right? Well, no. Day trading is a job. It can be a full-time job or a part-time job, but it requires the same commitment to working regular hours and the same dedication to learning a craft and honing skills as any other job.

The best traders have plans for their business and for their trades. They know in advance how they want to trade and what they expect to do when they face the market. They may find themselves deviating from their plans at times, due to luck or circumstance or changing markets, but in those cases at least they understand why they are trying something else.

REMEMBER

Failing to plan is planning to fail. And if you can't remember that right now, don't worry. It's repeated several times in this book.

Here's another reason for planning: Trading comes in many flavours, and many of those who call themselves day traders are actually doing other things with their money. If you know in advance what you want to do, you'll be less likely to panic or follow fads. You'll be in a better position to take advantage of opportunities in a way that suits your personality, trading skills, and goals. And that's why this entire chapter is devoted to planning.

Planning Your Trading Business

The day trader is an entrepreneur who has started a small business that trades in securities in hopes of making a return. You'll get your business off to a good start if you have a plan for what you want to do and how you're going to do it. That way, you know what your goals are and what you need to do to achieve them.

You can find a lot of sample business plans in books and on the Internet, but most of them are not appropriate for a trader. A typical business plan is designed not only to guide the business, but also to attract outside financing. Unless you're going to take in partners or borrow money from an outside source, your day trading business plan is for you only. No executive summary and no pages of projections needed.

So what do you need instead? How about a list of your goals and a plan for what you will trade, what your hours will be, what equipment you'll need, and how much to invest in the business?

Setting your goals

The first thing you need in your plan is a list of your goals, both short term and long term. Here is a sample list to get you started:

>> Where do you want to be in the next three months, six months, nine months, a year, three years, five years, and ten years?

>> How many days a year do you want to trade?

>> What do you need to know to trade better?

>> How much do you want to make?

>> What will you do with your profits?

>> How will you reward yourself when you hit your goals?

Be as specific as possible when you think about what you want to do with your trading business, and don't worry if your business goals overlap with your personal goals. When you're in business for yourself, the two often mix.

WARNING

You might be tempted to say, "I want to make as much money as I possibly can," and forget the rest, but that's not a goal that's quantifiable. If you don't know that you've reached your goal, how can you go on to set new ones? And if you don't meet your goal, how will you know how to make changes?

Picking the markets

There are so many different securities and derivatives that you can day trade! Sure, you want to trade anything that makes money for you, but what on earth is that? Each market has its own nuances, so if you flit from futures to forex (foreign exchange), you might be courting disaster. That's another reason why you need a plan. If you know what markets you want to trade, you'll have a better sense of what research services you'll need, what ongoing training you might want to consider, and how to evaluate your performance.

Chapter 3 in Book 5 covers different asset classes and how day traders might use them in great detail. For now, Table 2-1 gives a little cheat sheet that covers those that are most popular with day traders. Think about your chosen markets in the same way: What do you want to trade, where will you trade it, what is the risk and return, and what are some of the characteristics that make this market attractive to you?

TABLE 2-1 **Popular Things for Day Traders to Trade**

Item	Main Exchange	Risk/Reward	Characteristics
Stock index futures	MX, CME	Zero sum/leverage	Benefits from movements of broad markets
Treasury bond futures	CBOT	Zero sum/leverage	Best way for day traders to play the bond market
Foreign exchange	OTC	Zero sum/leverage	Markets open all day, every day, except Sunday
Commodities	CBOT, CME	Zero sum/leverage	An agricultural market liquid enough for day traders
Large-cap stocks	TSX, NYSE	Upward bias	Good stocks for day trading, large and volatile

Key: TSX = Toronto Stock Exchange, MX = Montreal Exchange, CME = Chicago Mercantile Exchange, CBOT = Chicago Board of Trade, OTC = Over the counter, NYSE = New York Stock Exchange

And what do zero sum, leverage, and upward bias mean?

>> Well, *zero sum* means that for every winner, there is a loser. No net gain exists in the market.

>> *Leverage* is the use of borrowed money, which increases potential return and also increases risk.

>> *Upward bias* means that in the long run, the market is expected to increase in price, but that doesn't mean it will go up on any given day that you are trading.

The characteristics of the different markets and assets will affect both your business plan and your trading plan. The business plan should include information on what you will trade and why, as well as on what you hope to learn to trade in the future. The trading plan looks at what you want to trade each day and why, so that you can channel your efforts.

TIP

Many day traders work in a few different markets, depending on their temperament and trading conditions, but successful traders have narrowed down the few markets where they want to concentrate their efforts. Start slowly, working just one or two different securities, but consider adding new markets as your experience and trading capital grows.

Fixing hours, vacation, and sick leave

The markets are open more or less continuously. Although many exchanges have set trading hours, there are traders working after hours who are willing to sell if you want to buy. Some markets, such as foreign exchange, take only the briefest of breaks over the course of a week. This gives day traders incredible flexibility — no matter what hours and what days are best for you to trade, you can find something that works for you. If you are sharpest in the evenings, you might be better off trading Asian currencies, because those markets are active when you are. Of course, this can be a disadvantage, because no one is setting limits for you. Few markets are great places to trade every hour of every day.

If you want to, you can trade almost all the time. But you probably don't want to. To keep your sanity, maintain your perspective, and have a life outside of your trading, you should set regular hours and stick to them. In your business plan, determine when you're going to trade, how often you're going to take a vacation, how many sick days you'll give yourself, and how you'll know to take a day off. One of the joys of self-employment is that you can take time off when you need to, so give yourself that little perk in your business plan.

REMEMBER

Trading is a stressful business. You need to take time off to clear your head, and you'll probably find that working while sick is a sure-fire route to losses. Build in some sick and vacation time.

Getting yourself set up

Part of your business plan should cover where you work and what equipment you need. What can you afford now, and what is on your wish list? Do you have enough computing equipment, the right Internet connection, and a working filing system? This is part of your plan for getting your business underway, so put some thought into your infrastructure.

And yes, this is important. You don't want to lose a day of trading because your computer has crashed, nor do you want to be stuck with an open position because your Internet service provider has a temporary outage. And you certainly don't want to lose your concentration because you're trying to work in the family room while other members of your household are playing video games.

Investing in your business

You won't have the time and money to do everything you want to do in your trading business, so part of your business plan should include a list of things that you want to add over time. A key part of that is continuous improvement: No matter how good a trader you are now, you can always be better. Furthermore, the markets are always changing. New products come to market, new trading regulations are passed, and new technologies appear. You will always need to absorb new things, and part of your business plan should consider that.

Ask yourself the following questions:

>> What percentage of your time and trade gains will go into expanding your knowledge of trading?

>> Do you want to do that by taking seminars or by allocating the time to simulation testing?

>> What upgrades will you make to your trading equipment?

>> How are you going to set yourself up to stay in trading for the long haul?

REMEMBER

It takes money to make money — another cliché. It doesn't mean that you should spend money willy-nilly on any nifty gadget or fancy video seminar that comes your way. Instead, it means that an ongoing, thoughtful investment in your trading business will pay off in a greater likelihood of long-run success.

Evaluating and revising your plan

One component of your business plan should be a plan for revising it. Things are going to change. You may be more or less successful than you hope, market conditions may change on you, and you may simply find out more about how you trade best. That's why you should set a plan for updating your business plan to reflect where you are and where you want to be as you go along. At least once a year, and more often if you feel the need for a change, go through your business plan and revise it to reflect where you are now. What are your new goals? What are your new investment plans? What are you doing right, and what needs to change?

REMEMBER

Business plans are living documents. Use your plan to run your trading business; as your business runs, use the results to update your plan. You can keep the old ones around to show you how much progress you have made, if you're so inclined.

A SAMPLE BUSINESS PLAN

Not sure what should be in a business plan? Here's a sample to get you thinking about how to plan your trading business.

Where I Am Now

I am about to start a career as a day trader. I have $50,000 in capital that I can risk without affecting my livelihood. I will rely on my spouse's job to cover our family spending needs and our health insurance. This trading account will be used to meet our long-term goals: paying off the mortgage, sending the children to university, paying for our retirement, and ultimately buying a vacation house in the mountains.

This business plan covers what I need to get started.

My Business Goals

In three months, I will have spent $5,000 of my capital on a functional office and will have a tested trading strategy that works well in simulation.

In six months, I will be trading daily. I will have lost no more than $5,000 of my trading capital.

In nine months, I will be trading daily, and I will have more winning trades than losing trades.

In a year, I will have gained 10 percent on my account. I will withdraw $1,000 to pay toward our mortgage and another $1,000 toward an ergonomic chair and other office equipment upgrades. I will have mastered my first trading system and will be testing a second one in order to expand my trading opportunities.

In three years, my trading account will have $150,000 in it from my trading successes, after making investments in my business and paying an additional $10,000 in principal on the mortgage. I will be trading three different systems with satisfactory success.

In five years, I will have $300,000 in my trading account. I will have made enough money to have paid off our mortgage, after making regular payments on principal and interest every month, paying $10,000 in year three, and paying off the rest with the profits that I expect to earn between years three and five. I will be known as a successful trader.

In ten years, I will have a second house, and I will continue my record of trading success. I will take $100,000 out of my trading account to cover university tuition.

Markets Traded

My primary trading strategy will involve momentum trades on the S&P/TSX Composite Index Mini Futures, E-Mini NASDAQ, and E-Mini Russell 2000 futures contracts traded on the Chicago Mercantile Exchange. I will put no more than 10 percent of my capital into any one trade and I will close out positions each night.

I am interested in news-driven *swing trading* (holding for short periods of time but longer than a day) in large technology companies, so I will research and test strategies with those. I am also interested in trading Asian currencies, so I will make the time to learn more about those markets and determine whether I can trade them effectively during my preferred trading hours.

Trading Hours and Days

Because my primary strategy is equity driven, I will trade only while the equity markets are open, from 9:30 a.m. until 4:00 p.m. Monday through Friday. I will spend an hour before the markets open researching current trends and news events so that I know what people will be looking for that day. I will spend an hour after the market closes doing paperwork and reviewing the day's trades.

I will take off three full weeks for vacation: the week of my children's spring break, a week in August for a family vacation, and the last week of December. I will also take off any day that I am ill so that I can maintain my health and my concentration.

My Business Setup

I work from a home office. I use my startup funds to purchase two monitors working off of one computer, with a second clone computer on hand in case something goes wrong. I have cable Internet access as well as a DSL backup through my phone line. I have a wireless router, so that I can check my email and instant messages through a third computer, a laptop, instead of through my trading computer. I also have a smartphone so I can read the news, check e-mail, and stay on top of relevant current events when I'm not at a computer during the day.

I have an account with a full-service online brokerage firm that can offer me the necessary research services. I also subscribe to *The Globe and Mail,* the *National Post,* and *The Wall Street Journal,* which I read each morning to help me gauge sentiment.

I track my trades on a paper form that I collect in ring binders. I collect my other paperwork in ring binders that I keep on the shelf in my office.

(continued)

(continued)

Investing in My Business

To stay successful in the long run, I need to keep my skills sharp. To do this, I will read one book on trading psychology or a successful trader's memoir each month. I will also work on simulation trading for swing trading in technology stocks, as I plan to add that to my trading system.

As my trade profits grow, I will invest some of them in trying new trading techniques, knowing that I may have short-term losses until I understand a market better. I will spend one day at the end of each quarter on backtesting and simulation of new strategies.

My wish list includes a more comfortable chair for my office.

Evaluating My Business Plan

Before each vacation, I will read over this business plan. I will use the time away from the markets to think about what changes I need to make and will revise the plan upon my return.

Planning Your Trades

A good trader has a plan. She knows what she wants to trade and how to trade it. She knows what her limits are before she places the order. She's not afraid to take a loss now in order to prevent a bigger loss in the future, and she's willing to sit out the market if nothing is happening that day. Her plan gives her the discipline to protect her capital so that she has money in her account to profit when the opportunities present themselves.

This section covers the components of trade planning. When you start trading, you'll probably write notes to set up a trading plan for each day that covers what you expect for the day, what trades you hope to make, and what your profit goals and loss limit are. As you develop experience, trade planning may become innate. You develop the discipline to trade according to plan, without needing to write it all down — although you might find it useful to tape a list of the day's expected announcements to your monitor.

REMEMBER

Like a business plan, a trading plan is flexible. The markets don't know what you've planned, and you'll probably end up deviating on more than one occasion. The key thing is knowing *why* you deviated: Was it because of the information that you saw when you were looking at your screen, or was it because you became panicky?

What do you want to trade?

The first step in your trading plan should also be addressed in your business plan: What is it that you want to trade? Many traders work in more than one market, and each market is a little different. Some trade different products simultaneously, whereas others choose one for the day and work only on that. (See the earlier section "Picking the markets.")

You need to figure out which markets give you the best chance of getting a profit that day. It's going to be different. Some days, no trades will be good for you in one market. If you're too antsy for that, then find another market to keep you busy so that you don't trade just to stay awake. (Of course, many traders report that the big money opportunities are in the slower, less glamorous markets.)

REMEMBER

As a day trader, you are self-employed. You don't answer to a boss and don't have to trade today if you don't want to. So if you have a headache, or if no good trades are available to you, or if recent losses have gotten you down, take the day off and do something fun.

How do you want to trade it?

Figuring out how to trade an asset involves a lot of considerations: What is your mood today? What will other traders be reacting to today? How much risk do you want to take? How much money do you want to commit? This is the nitty-gritty stage of trade planning that can help you manage your market day better.

Starting the day with a morning review

Before you start trading, take some time to determine where your head is relative to the market. Is today a day that you can concentrate? Are there things happening in your life that might distract you, are you coming down with the flu, or were you out too late last night? Or are you raring to go, ready to take on whatever the day brings? Your mindset should influence how aggressively you want to trade and how much risk you want to take. You have to pay attention to do well in the markets, but you also have to know when to hang back during the day's activities. For example, many traders find that their strategies work best at certain times of the day, such as at the open or before major news announcements.

Think about what people will be reacting to. Go through the newspapers and check the online newswires to gather information. Then figure out the answers to these questions:

>> Are there big news announcements scheduled for today? At what time? Do you want to trade ahead of the news or want to wait and see what the market does?

>> Did something happen overnight? Will that affect trading on the open, or is it already in the markets? Do you want to trade on the open or wait?

>> What are the other people who trade the same future, commodity, stock, or currency that you do worried about today? How are they likely to respond? Do you want to go with the market or strike a contrary position?

TIP

For a handy list of expected news announcements on any given trading day, check out www.tradethenews.com/. For Canadian company news, visit Cision at www.newswire.ca and review the day's press releases.

Drawing up a sample order

After you have a sense of how you're going to tackle the day, you want to determine how much you're going to trade. The key considerations are the following:

>> Do you want to be long or short? That is, do you want to bet that the asset you're trading is going up in price or down?

>> Do you want to borrow money? If so, how much? Borrowing — also known as *margin* or *leverage* — increases your potential return as well as your risk.

REMEMBER

Some contracts, such as futures, have built-in leverage. As soon as you decide to trade them, you are borrowing money.

>> How much money do you want to trade — in dollars, and as a percentage of your total account size?

After you have those items detailed, you're in good shape to get started for the day.

Figuring out when to buy and when to sell

After you get insight into what the day might be like and how much money you want to allocate to the markets, your next step is to figure out when you will buy and when you will sell. Ah, but if that were easy, do you think we'd be writing a book on day trading? No.

The very best traders aren't selling trading advice; they're already retired. Everyone else is figuring it out as they go along, with varying degrees of success.

Many traders rely on *technical analysis*, which involves looking at patterns in charts of the price and volume changes. Other traders look at news and price information as the market changes, rather than looking at price patterns. Still others care only about very short-term price discrepancies. But *the most important thing, no matter what approach you prefer, is that you backtest and simulate your trading before you commit real dollars.* That way, you have a better sense of how you'll react in real market conditions.

Setting profit goals

When you trade, you want to have a realistic idea how much money you can make. What's a fair profit? Do you want to ride a winning position until the end of the day, or do you want to get out quickly when you've made enough money to compensate for your risk? No one answer to this question exists, because so much depends on market conditions and your trading style. In this section you get some guidelines that can help you determine what's best for you, and you find definitions for all the different terms for profits you might come across.

The language of money

Profits are discussed differently in different markets, and you may as well have the right lingo when you write your plan:

>> **Pennies:** Stocks trade in decimal form, so each price movement is worth at least a penny — one cent. It's an obvious way to measure a profit.

>> **Pips:** A *pip* is the smallest unit of currency that can be traded. In foreign exchange markets (forex), a pip is generally equal to one one-hundredth of a cent. If the value of the euro moves from $1.2934 to $1.2935, it has moved a pip.

WARNING

Do not confuse a pip in the forex market with an investment scheme known as *PIP*, sometimes called People in Profit or Pure Investor. (The fraud also operates as *HYIP*, for High Yield Investment Program.) PIP has been promoted as a trading system with a guaranteed daily return, but it's really a pyramid scheme that takes money from participants and returns little or nothing. You can get more information from the U.S. Securities and Exchange Commission's website, www.sec.gov/divisions/enforce/primebank.shtml.

>> **Points:** A *point* is a single percentage. A penny is a point, as is a 1 percent change in a bond price. A related number, a *basis point,* is a percent of a percent, or .0001.

>> **Teenies:** Many securities, especially bonds and derivatives on them, trade in increments of ⅛ of a dollar. Half of an eighth is a sixteenth, also known as a *teeny.*

>> **Ticks:** A *tick* is the smallest trading increment in a futures contract. It varies from product to product. How much it works out to be depends on the contract structure. For the S&P/TSX Composite Index Mini Futures (SCF), one tick value equals five index points, and each index point represents $5. That means the tick value is equal to $25. The value of an SCF futures contract is

calculated by multiplying the current level of the contract by the tick value. On the Chicago Mercantile Exchange's E-Mini S&P 500 contract, a tick is equal to US$12.50, calculated as a 0.25 change in the underlying S&P 500 index multiplied by a US$50 multiplier. A tick on a Chicago Board of Trade E-Mini soybean contract is US$1.25, calculated as ⅛ cent on a bushel of soybeans in a contract covering 1,000 bushels. You can get information on the tick size of contracts that interest you on the website of the offering exchange (they're listed in Chapter 3 of Book 5).

TIP

No one ever lost money taking a profit, as the cliché goes. (The trading business is rife with clichés, if you haven't noticed.) The newer you are to day trading, the more sense it makes to be conservative. Close your positions and end your day when you reach a target profit — and then make note of what happens afterward. Can you afford to hold on to your positions longer in order to make a greater profit?

Thinking about profits

Your profit goals can be sliced and diced a few different ways:

>> The first is the *gain per trade,* on both a percentage basis and an absolute basis.

>> The second is the *gain per day,* also on both a percentage basis and an absolute basis.

What do you have to do to reach these goals? How many successful trades will you have to make? Do you have the capital to do that? And what is right for the trade you're making right now, regardless of what your longer-term goals are?

Setting limits on your trades

It's a good idea to set a *loss limit* along with a profit goal.

TIP

For example, many futures traders have a rule to risk two ticks in pursuit of three ticks. That means they'll sell a position as soon as it loses two ticks in value, and they'll also sell a position as soon as it gains three ticks in value. And for anything in between? Well, they close out their positions at the end of the day, so whatever happens happens.

Even traders who do not have a rule like that often set a limit on how much they will lose per trade. Other traders use computer programs to guide their buys and their sells, so they need to sell their positions automatically. Brokers make this easy by giving customers the choice of a stop order or a limit order to protect their positions.

REMEMBER

You want to limit your loss per trade *as well as* your loss per day. If today is not a good one, close up shop, take a break, and come back fresh tomorrow.

Stop orders

A *stop order*, also known as a *stop loss order*, is an order to sell a security at the market price as soon as it hits a predetermined level. If you want to make sure you sell a block of stock when it falls below $30 per share, for example, you could enter a stop order at $30 (telling your broker "Sell Stop 30"). As soon as the stock hits $30 the broker sells it, even if the price goes to $29 or $31 before all the stock is sold.

Limit orders

A *limit order* is an order to buy or sell a security at a specific price or better: lower than the current price for the buy order, higher than the specific price for a sell order. If you want to make sure you sell a block of stock when it reaches $30 per share, for example, you could enter a limit order at $30 (telling your broker "Sell Limit 30"). As soon as the stock hits $30, the broker sells it, as long as the price stays at $30 or higher. If the price goes even a penny below $30, the limit is no longer enforced. After all, no buyers are going to want to pay an above-market price just so you can get your order filled all the way!

Stop limit orders

A *stop limit* order is a combination of a stop order and a limit order. It tells the broker to buy or sell at a specific price or better, but only after the price reaches a given stop price. If you want to make sure you sell a block of stock when it falls below $30 per share, but you do not want to sell it if it starts to go back up, for example, you could enter a stop order at $29 — the price is usually set lower than your stop price — with a limit of $31 (telling your broker "Sell 29 Limit 31"). As soon as the stock hits $29, the broker sells it as long as the price stays under $31. If the price goes above $31, the order is no longer enforced. The price range where this order will be executed is very small. Stop limit orders aren't typically used as a trading strategy, but it can come in handy if there's a sudden drop in the market like we saw with the "flash crash" on May 6, 2010. On that day the market fell, for reasons not fully understood, by 600 points and then minutes later shot back up. A stop limit order would have prevented your stocks from selling.

Are you confused? Well, the differences may be confusing, but understanding them is important to helping you manage your risks. That's why Table 2-2 and Table 2-3 are a handy breakout of the different types of orders.

TABLE 2-2   # Different Types of Orders for Buying

Buy Orders	Stop Order	Limit Order	Stop Limit Order
Order instructions	Buy Stop 30	Buy Limit 30	Buy Stop 30 Limit 31
Market Price ($)	**Action after the stock hits $30**		
28.50	Buy	Buy	Buy
29.00	Buy	Buy	Buy
29.50	Buy	Buy	Buy
30.00	Buy	Buy	Buy
30.50	Buy	Nothing	Buy
31.00	Buy	Nothing	Nothing
31.50	Buy	Nothing	Nothing

TABLE 2-3   # Different Types of Orders for Selling

Sell Orders	Stop Order	Limit Order	Stop Limit Order
Order Instructions	Sell Stop 30	Sell Limit 30	Sell Stop 30 Limit 29
Market Price ($)	**Action after the stock hits $30**		
28.50	Sell	Nothing	Nothing
29.00	Sell	Nothing	Sell
29.50	Sell	Nothing	Sell
30.00	Sell	Sell	Sell
30.50	Sell	Sell	Sell
31.00	Sell	Sell	Sell
31.50	Sell	Sell	Sell

A SAMPLE TRADING PLAN

A trading plan may be good for only a short time, but having an idea of what to expect in the market and how you will react goes a long way toward keeping trading discipline, which improves your likelihood of long-run profits. What does such a plan look like? Well, here's a sample to get you started.

What I'm Trading Today

Today, I'll be trading the S&P/TSX Composite Index Mini Futures. They closed down yesterday, but I'm expecting an uptick in the market today as companies report good earnings, so I'm going to trade on the long side. My plan is to start the day buying two contracts with stop orders to sell if they decline more than three ticks each. These contracts will remain open until the end of the day unless the stop is reached. I will add a third contract if the market shows momentum in the morning and a fourth contract if it shows momentum in the afternoon. These two additional contracts can be long or short, depending on the market direction, although it's unlikely that the purchasing manager or home sales surveys will have a large effect on the market's direction. (Naturally, I will not take out a short contract during the day if my two initial long contracts are still open.) I will close all positions at the end of the day, if not sooner.

Because the margin on each contract is $3,500, my maximum exposure today will be approximately 28 percent of my total account, with no contract accounting for more than 7 percent of my account.

Today's Expected News Announcements

Before the open: earnings announcements from RIM (expect $0.62), PG (expect $0.74)

10:00 a.m. Ivey Purchasing Managers Index — survey of purchasing managers — market expects 51.0

10:00 a.m. Pending Home Sales — market expects up 0.2 percent

After the close: earnings announcements from AC.B (expect $0.20), AGU (expect $1.29)

5:00 p.m. Auto Sales — market expects up 10%

5:00 p.m. Merchandise exports — market expects down 2 percent

(continued)

(continued)

My Profit and Loss Goals for the Day

My profit goal is five ticks or $125 per contract traded, for a target of $500 if I acquire my planned maximum of four contracts, but I plan to ride my profits until the end of the day. If all four contracts decline in value, I will close when they fall three ticks apiece, for a maximum loss of $75 per contract or $300 for the day.

What if the trade goes wrong?

No matter how in tune you feel with the market, no matter how good your track record, and no matter how disciplined you are with setting stops, stuff is going to happen. Just as you can make more money than you plan to, you can also *lose* a lot more. If you're going to day trade, you have to accept that you'll have some really bad days.

So what do you do? You suck it up, take the loss, and get on with your life.

Yes, the market may have blown past your stops. That happens sometimes, and it's hard to watch real dollars disappear into someone else's account, someone you will never know. Still, close your position and just remember that tomorrow is another day with another chance to do better.

Don't hold in hopes of making up a loss. The market doesn't know what you own, and it won't reward your loyalty and best hopes.

WARNING

After you take the loss and clear your head, see if you can learn something for next time. Sometimes a loss can teach you valuable lessons that make you a smarter, more disciplined trader in the long run.

TIP

Closing Out Your Position

By definition, day traders hold their investment positions only for a single day. This is important for a few reasons:

REMEMBER

>> Closing out daily reduces your risk of something happening overnight.

>> Margin rates — the interest rates paid on money borrowed for trading — are low and in some cases zero for day traders, but the rates go up on overnight balances.

>> It's good trade discipline that can keep you from making expensive mistakes.

But like all rules, the single-day rule can be broken and probably should be broken sometimes. This section covers a few longer-term trading strategies you may want to add to your trading business on occasion.

Swing trading: Holding for days

Swing trading involves holding a position for several days. Some swing traders hold overnight, whereas others hold for days or even months. The longer time period gives more time for a position to work out, which is especially important if it is based on news events or if it requires taking a position contrary to the current market sentiment. Although swing trading gives traders more options for making a profit, it carries some risks because the position could turn against you while you're away from the markets.

REMEMBER

A trade-off always exists between risk and return. When you take more risk, you do so in the hopes of getting a greater return. But when you look for a way to increase return, remember that you will have to take on more risk to do it.

Swing trading requires paying attention to some basic fundamentals and news flow. It's also a good choice for people who have the discipline to go to bed at night instead of waiting up and watching their position in hopes that nothing goes wrong.

Position trading: Holding for weeks

A *position trader* holds a stake in a stock or a commodity for several weeks and possibly even for months. This person is attracted to the short-term price opportunities, but he also believes that he can make more money holding the stake for a long enough period of time to see business fundamentals play out. This increases the risk and the potential return, because a lot more can happen over months than minutes.

Investing: Holding for months or years

An *investor* is not a trader. Investors do careful research and buy a stake in an asset in the hopes of building a profit over the long term. It's not unusual for investors to hold assets for decades, although good ones sell quickly if they realize that they have made a mistake. (They want to cut their losses early, just as any good trader should.)

Investors are concerned about the prospects of the underlying business. Will it make money? Will it pay off its debts? Will it hold its value? They view short-term price fluctuations as noise rather than as profit opportunities.

Many traders pull out some of their profits to invest for the long term (or to give to someone else, such as a mutual fund manager or hedge fund, to invest). It's a way of building financial security in the pursuit of longer goals. This money is usually kept separate from the trading account. (Flip to Book 2 for more about stock investing and Book 3 for more about mutual fund investing.)

Maxims and Clichés That Guide and Mislead Traders

This section covers a few of the many maxims traders use to think about their trading, such as

>> The stock doesn't know you own it.

>> Failing to plan is planning to fail.

>> Your first loss is your best loss.

A lot more are out there.

Clichés are useful shorthand for important *rules* that can help you plan your trading. But they can also mislead you because some are really obvious — too obvious to act on effectively. (Yes, everyone knows that you make money by buying low and selling high, but how do you tell what low is and high is?) Here's a runthrough of some you'll come across in your trading career, along with our take on what they mean.

Pigs get fat, hogs get slaughtered

Trading is pure capitalism, and people do it for one primary reason: to make money. Sure, a ton of economic benefits come from having well-functioning capital markets, such as better price prediction, risk management, and capital formation. But a day trader just wants to make money.

However, get too greedy and you're likely to get stupid. You start taking too much risk, deviating too much from your strategy, and getting careless about dealing with your losses. Good traders know when it's time to take a profit and move on to the next trade.

This is also a good example of an obvious but tough-to-follow maxim. When are you crossing from being a happy little piggy to a big fat greedy hog that's about to be turned into a pork belly? Just know that if you're deviating from your trading plan because things are going so great, you might be headed for some trouble.

In a bear market, the money returns to its rightful owners

A *bull* market is one that charges ahead; a *bear* market is one that does poorly. Many people think they're trading geniuses because they make money when the entire market is going up. It was easy to make money day trading just about any stock in 2009, when the market recovered from near economic collapse, but it wasn't so easy the year before when the frighteningly out-of-control financial crisis began. It's when the markets turn negative that those people who really understand trading and who know how to manage risk will be able to stay in until things get better, possibly even making nice profits along the way.

The corollary cliché for this is *"Don't confuse brains with a bull market."* When things are going well, watch out for overconfidence. It might be time to update your business and trading plans, but it's not to time to cast them aside.

The trend is your friend

When you day trade, you need to make money fast. You don't have the luxury of waiting for your unique, contrary theory to play out. An investor may be buying a stock in the hopes of holding it for decades, but a trader needs things to work now.

Given the short-term nature of the market, the short-term sentiment is going to trump long-term fundamentals. People trading today may be wrong about the direction of foreign exchange, interest rates, or share prices, but if you're closing out your positions tonight, you need to work with the information in the market *today.*

REMEMBER

In the short run, traders who fight the market lose money.

Two problems exist with *The trend is your friend.* The first is that by the time you identify a trend, it may be over. Second, there are times when it makes sense to go against the herd, because you can collect when everyone else realizes their mistakes. This is where the psychology of trading comes into play. Are you a good enough judge of human behaviour to know when the trend is right and when it's not?

Buy the rumour, sell the news

Markets react to information. That's ultimately what drives supply and demand. Although the market tends to react quickly to information, it can overreact, too. Lots of gossip gets traded in the markets as everyone looks to get the information they need in order to gain an advantage in the markets. And despite such things as confidentiality agreements and insider-trading laws, many rumours turn out to be true.

These rumours are often attached to such news events as corporate earnings. For whatever reason — good news, analyst research, a popular product — traders might believe that the company will report good quarterly earnings per share. That's the rumour. If you buy on the rumour, you can take advantage of the price appreciation as the story gets more play.

When the earnings are actually announced, one of two things will happen:

>> They will be as good as or better than rumoured, and the price will go up. The trader can sell into that and make a profit.

>> They will be worse than rumoured, everyone will sell on the bad news, and the trader will want to sell to get out of the loss.

Of course, if the rumour is *bad*, you want to do the opposite: sell on the rumour, and buy on the news.

The problem with *Buy the rumour, sell the news* is that rumours are often wrong, and there may be more opportunities to buy on bad news when other traders are panicking, thus driving prices down for a few minutes before sanity sets in. But it's one of those rules that everyone talks about, whether or not they actually follow it.

Cut your losses and ride your winners

A reminder: You need to cut your losses before they drag you down. No matter how much it hurts and no matter how much you believe you're right, you need to close out a losing position and move on.

But the opposite is not necessarily true. Although good traders tend to be disciplined about selling winning positions, they don't use stops and limits as rigorously on the upside as they might on the downside. They're likely to stick with a profit and see how high it goes before closing out a position.

REMEMBER

Note that this conflicts a little with *Pigs get fat, hogs get slaughtered.* (Trading maxims can be so contradictory!) To prevent overconfidence and sloppiness from greed, ride your winners *within reason.* If your general discipline is to risk three ticks on a futures contract in order to make five, and a contract goes up six ticks before you can close it out, you might want to stick with it. But if you also close out at the end of every day, don't give in to the temptation of keeping that position open just because it's still going up. Keep to your overall discipline.

You're only as good as your last trade

The markets churn on every day with little regard for why everyone trading right now is there. Prices go up and down to match the supply and the demand at any given moment, which may have nothing to do with the actual long-term worth of an item being traded. And it certainly has nothing to do with how much you really, really want the trade to work out.

One of the biggest enemies of good traders is overconfidence. Especially after a nice run of winning trades, a trader can get caught up in the euphoria and believe that he finally has the secret to successful trading under control. While he's checking the real estate listings for that beachfront estate in Maui, *bam!* The next trade is a disaster.

Does that mean that the trader is a disaster, too? No, it just means that the markets won this time around.

REMEMBER

Most day traders are working in zero-sum markets, which means that for every winner there is a loser. Hence, not everyone can make money every day. The challenge is to maintain an even keel so as not to be distracted by confidence when the trading is going well or by fear when the trading is going poorly. The next trade is a new trade.

IN THIS CHAPTER

» Finding good assets for day trading

» Seeking securities to trade

» Counting cash and currency

» Making money from mundane commodities

» Deriving profits from derivatives

Chapter **3**

Signing Up for Asset Classes

t's one thing to day trade, but *what* are you going to trade? Stocks, pork bellies, or hockey cards? You have myriad choices, but you have to choose so that you can learn the market, know what changes to expect, and make your trades accordingly.

Although it may be tempting, you can't trade everything. There are only so many hours in a day and only so many ideas you can hold in your head at any one time. Furthermore, some trading strategies lend themselves better to certain types of assets than others. By learning more about all the various investment assets available to a day trader, you can make better decisions about what you want to trade and how you want to trade it.

What Makes a Good Day Trading Asset?

In academic terms, the universe of investable assets includes just about anything you can buy at one price and sell at another, potentially higher price. That means artwork and collectibles, real estate, and private companies would all be considered to be investable assets.

Day traders have a much smaller group of assets to work with. It's not realistic to expect a quick one-day profit on price changes in real estate. Online auctions for collectible items take place over days, not minutes. If you're going to day trade, you want to find assets that trade easily, several times a day, in recognized markets. In other words, you want *liquidity*. As an individual trading your own account, you want assets that can be purchased with relatively low capital commitments. And finally, you may want to use *leverage* — borrowed money — to improve your return, so you want to look for assets that can be purchased using other people's money.

Liquidity

Liquidity is the ability to buy or sell an asset in large quantity without affecting the price levels. Day traders look for *liquid assets* so they can move in and out of the market quickly without disrupting price levels. Otherwise, they may not be able to buy at a good price or sell when they want.

At the most basic level, financial markets are driven by supply and demand. The more of an asset supplied in the market, the lower the price; the more of an asset that people demand, the higher the price. In a perfect market, the amount of supply and demand is matched so that prices don't change. This happens if a high volume of people are trading, so that their supply and demand is constantly matched, or if a very low frequency of trades are happening, so that the price never changes.

REMEMBER

You may be thinking, *Wait, don't I want big price changes so that I can make money quickly?* Yes, you want price changes in the market, but you don't want to be the one causing them. The less liquid a market is, the more likely your buying and selling is going to affect market prices, and the smaller your profit will be.

Volume

Volume is the total amount of a security that trades in a given time period. The greater the volume, the more buyers and sellers are interested in the security, and the easier it is to get in there and buy and sell without affecting the price.

Day traders also look at the relationship between volume and price. This is an important technical indicator. The simple version is this:

>> High volume with no change in price levels means an equal match between buyers and sellers.

>> High volume with rising prices means more buyers than sellers, so the price will continue going up.

>> High volume with falling prices means more sellers than buyers, so the price will keep going down.

Frequency

Another measure of liquidity is *frequency*, or how often a security trades. Some assets, like stock market futures, trade constantly, from the moment the market opens until the very last trade of the day, and then continue into overnight trading. Others, like agricultural commodities, trade only during market hours or only during certain times of the year. Other securities, like stocks, trade frequently, but the volume rises and falls at regular intervals related to such things as *options expiration* (the date at which options on the stock expire).

TIP

The more frequently a security trades, the more opportunities you'll have to identify the short-term profit opportunities that make day trading possible.

Volatility, standard deviation, and variance

The *volatility* of a security is how much the price varies over a period of time. It tells you how much prices fluctuate and thus how likely you are to be able to take advantage of that. For example, if a security has an average price of $5 but trades anywhere between $1 and $14, it will be more volatile than one with an average price of $5 that trades between $4 and $6.

One standard measure of volatility and risk is *standard deviation*, which is how much any given price quote varies from a security's average price. You can calculate it with most spreadsheet programs and many trading platforms.

For each of the prices, you calculate the difference between it and the average value. So if the average price is $5, and the closing price today is $8, the difference would be $3. (More likely, the research service that you use would calculate the difference for you.)

After you have all the differences between the prices and the average, you find the square of these differences. If the difference for one day's price is $8, then the square would be $64. You add up all the squared differences over the period of time that you're looking at and then find the average of them. That number is called the *variance*. Finally, calculate the square root of the variance, and you have the standard deviation.

REMEMBER

The higher the standard deviation, the higher the volatility; the higher the volatility, the more a security's price is going to fluctuate, and the more profit — and loss — opportunities exist for a day trader.

TECHNICAL
STUFF

Standard deviation is also a measure of risk that can be used to evaluate your trading performance.

Capital requirements

You don't necessarily need a lot of money to begin day trading, but you do need a lot of money to buy certain securities. Stocks generally trade in *round lots,* which are orders of at least 100 shares. For example: If you want to buy a stock worth $40 per share, you need $4,000 in your account. Your broker will probably let you borrow half of that money, but you still need to come up with the other $2,000.

Options and futures trade by contract, and one contract represents some unit of the underlying security. For example, in the options market, one contract is good for 100 shares of the stock. These contracts also trade in round lots of 100 contracts per order.

WARNING

No one will stop you from buying a smaller amount than the usual round lot in any given security, but you'll probably pay a high commission and get worse execution for your order. Because the returns on each trade tend to be small anyway, don't take up day trading until you have enough money to trade your target asset effectively. Otherwise, you'll pay too much to your broker without getting much for yourself.

Bonds do not trade in fractional amounts; they trade on a per-bond basis, and each bond has a face value of $1,000. Some trade for more or less than that, depending on how the bond's interest rate differs from the market rate of interest, but the $1,000 is a good number to keep in mind when thinking about capital requirements. Many dealers have a minimum order of 10 bonds, though, so a minimum order would be $10,000.

Marginability

Most day traders make money through a large volume of small profits. One way to increase the profit per trade is to use borrowed money in order to buy more shares, more contracts, or more bonds. *Margin* is money in your account that you borrow against, and almost all brokers will be happy to arrange a margin loan for you, especially if you're going to use the money to make more trades and generate more commissions for the brokerage firm.

Generally, a stock or bond account must hold 50 percent of the purchase price of securities when you borrow the money. So if you want to buy $100 worth of something on margin, you need to have $50 in your account. The price of those securities can go down, but if they go down so much that the account now holds only 30 percent of the value of the loan, you'll get a margin call.

In Canada, margin requirements for each security are set by the Canadian regulators, though brokerage firms sometimes set their own, higher amounts. There are no rules that limit the maximum amount of money you can borrow, but the brokerage firms will lose a lot of money if you don't pay them back. That's why they may set a limit on the loan. Each firm has its own rules, so check with your broker on how they set their margin requirements.

TECHNICAL STUFF

You probably think that the 1929 crash was responsible for the Great Depression of the 1930s, right? Think again. Most economic historians believe that the crash was a distraction. Instead, the real problem was that interest rates fell so rapidly that banks refused to lend money, while prices fell so low that companies had no incentive to produce. It's a situation known as *deflation*, and it's relatively rare, but it is devastating when it occurs.

Most stocks and bonds are marginable (able to be purchased on margin), and the Investment Industry Regulatory Organization of Canada (IIROC) allows traders to borrow up to 70 percent — you have to put at least 30 percent down — of their value. But not all securities are marginable. Stocks priced below $5 per share, those traded on the OTC Bulletin Board (discussed later in this chapter), and those in newly public companies often cannot be borrowed against or purchased on margin. Your brokerage firm should have a list of securities that are not eligible for margin.

REMEMBER

If leverage is going to be part of your day trading strategy, be sure the assets you plan to trade are marginable.

Securities and How They Trade

In the financial markets people buy and sell securities every day, but just what are they buying or selling? *Securities* are financial instruments. In the olden days, they were pieces of paper, but now they are electronic entries that represent a legal claim on some type of underlying asset. This asset may be a business, if the security is a stock, or it may be a loan to a government or a corporation, if the security is a bond. This section covers different types of securities that day traders are likely to run across and tells you what you need to jump into the fray.

REMEMBER

In practice, *asset* and *security* are synonyms, and *derivative* is considered to be a type of asset or security. But to be precise, these three are not the same:

>> An asset is a physical item. Examples include a company, a house, gold bullion, or a loan.

>> A security is a contract that gives someone either the right of ownership of an asset, such as a share of stock, or a promissory note that is in turn backed by an asset, such as a bond.

>> A derivative is a contract that draws its value from the price of a security.

DAY TRADING IN CANADA VERSUS THE REST OF THE WORLD

Nary a day goes by that you don't hear something about the Toronto Stock Exchange. It's up, it's down, BlackBerry's quarterly report sent investors scrambling out of the tech sector — if you watched just the Canadian news you'd think the TSX was the only market on the planet.

In reality, most day traders stay away from Canadian markets. There are really only three places to trade in this country — the TSX, the TSX Venture Exchange, and the Montreal Exchange. That doesn't leave a lot of choice. The markets are also much smaller compared to their U.S. counterparts. Two industries — commodities and financials — make up most of the index, so again choice is limited. Because the markets are small they're less liquid than the New York Stock Exchange (NYSE) or Nasdaq, making it difficult for traders to make any money.

Fortunately, Canadians have access to a whole swath of markets and products that are based in other countries. A trader can buy an Australian dollar, a stock on the NYSE, or an option on the Chicago Board Options Exchange (CBOE). And most people do choose to forgo Canadian stocks for American ones, even when trading a Canadian company. Because the U.S. market is more liquid, a trader may want to buy and sell RIM (BlackBerry's stock symbol) on the NYSE instead of the TSX. This chapter lists Canadian and American options; pick what you think is the best place to trade for your style and expertise.

Stocks

A *stock*, also called an *equity*, is a security that represents a fractional interest in the ownership of a company (see Book 2 for the full scoop). Buy one share of Microsoft, and you're an owner of the company, just as Bill Gates is. He may own a much larger share of the total business, but you both have a stake in it. Shareholders elect a board of directors to represent their interests in how the company is managed. Each share is a vote.

A share of stock has *limited liability*. That means you can lose all your investment, but no more than that. If the company files for bankruptcy, the creditors cannot come after the shareholders for the money they are owed.

Some companies pay their shareholders a dividend, which is a small cash payment made out of firm profits. Because day traders hold stock for really short periods of time, they don't normally collect dividends.

How stocks trade

Stocks are priced based on a single share, and most brokerage firms charge commissions on a per-share basis. Despite this per-share pricing, stocks are almost always traded in round lots of 100 shares. The supply and demand for a given stock is driven by the company's expected performance.

A stock's price is quoted with a *bid* and an *ask:*

>> The bid is the price that other buyers will buy the stock from you if you're selling.

>> The ask is the price that other sellers will sell you if you're the one buying.

Bid-ask prices on Canadian exchanges are a centralized quote — they represent the best bid and ask prices from all participants on the market. In the U.S. it's the broker who sets the bid ask price — and often profits off the spread — but in Canada quotes are posted for everyone to see regardless of broker.

Here's an example of a price quote:

```
MSFT $27.70 $27.71
```

That's a quote for Microsoft (ticker symbol: MSFT on the Nasdaq). The bid is listed first: $27.70; the ask is $27.71. That's the smallest spread you'll ever see! The spread here is so small because Microsoft is a liquid stock, and no big news events at the moment might change the balance of buyers and sellers.

TIP

If your American trading buddy is talking about how his broker takes a cut of the spread, don't panic and wonder why you haven't noticed those same fees. In Canada brokers make money off commission — it's unlikely they're taking a percentage of the spread.

TECHNICAL STUFF

People tend to use the words *broker* and *dealer* interchangeably, but a difference does exist. A broker simply matches buyers and sellers of securities, whereas a dealer buys and sells securities out of its own account. Almost all brokerage firms are both brokers and dealers.

Where stocks trade

Stocks trade mostly on organized *exchanges* such as the Toronto Stock Exchange (TSX) and the New York Stock Exchange (NYSE), but more and more they trade on electronic communications networks, also called alternative trading systems, some of which are operated by the exchanges themselves. Brokerage firms either belong to the exchanges themselves or work with a correspondent firm that handles the trading for them, turning over the order in exchange for a cut of the commission.

When you place an order with your brokerage firm, the broker's trading staff executes that order wherever it can get the best deal. But is that the best deal for you? You'll be happy to know, that yes it is. Canadian dealers have an obligation to get the best execution for their client — it's written right in the rules set out by the regulators.

REMEMBER

The financial markets are in a state of flux, with a lot of mergers and acquisitions among the exchanges. The information here might be obsolete when you read it, which really is fascinating. It wasn't so long ago that these exchanges were staid organizations run like private clubs.

TORONTO STOCK EXCHANGE (TSX)

The TSX is *the* Canadian exchange. If a Canadian company wants the public's cash, it's going to list on the TSX — and almost all major corporations in the Great White North do. However, not all companies can trade on the exchange — you definitely won't see the corner store take out an IPO, and even larger businesses can't automatically list. More than 1,570 companies are listed on the exchange, with a total market cap — the total dollar market value of a company's outstanding shares — of more than $3.1 trillion.

All the companies listed on the exchange paid a fee to be there. Depending on the size of the company, businesses have to pay between $10,000 and $200,000 to list. In most cases companies are assigned a three-letter ticker symbol — BlackBerry (originally called Research In Motion) uses RIM, for example — but not always. Gold company Kinross's symbol is, appropriately, K, and Toronto Dominion Bank can be found under TD. Some companies, like Toronto-based media company Torstar, have a ".B" after their symbol (TS.B), which means investors can purchase only non-voting class B shares.

TECHNICAL STUFF

Companies have to meet a number of requirements to list, and the requirements vary depending on the industry. You can find out all about the wonderful world of listing at www.tmx.com, but here are the basics: Company execs have to show they're successful, or, if it's a new venture, that the management has a record of experience. Companies must also have a certain amount of assets, though it varies per sector.

TSX VENTURE EXCHANGE (TSXV)

The Calgary-based TSX Venture Exchange operates like the TSX, but it's for junior companies or new businesses looking for startup capital. More than 1,600 companies are listed on the exchange, with a total market cap of $45 billion. The mining industry makes most use of the TSXV — 56 percent of the companies are from that sector — and technology companies come in a distant second. Some of these companies will eventually move to the TSX, and others will close shop and delist. Because it's mostly for smaller operations it's a slightly more volatile place to invest.

BRINGING THE TSX INTO THE 21ST CENTURY

In 1861, 24 men got together at Toronto's Masonic Hall and started the TSX. Membership cost $5, there were only 18 listed securities, and trading was limited to one 30-minute session a day. In 1997, TSX closed its trading floor and went virtual — becoming, at that time, the largest floorless exchange in North America.

In 1999, Canada's trading landscape underwent a major change. At the time there were stock exchanges in most big Canadian cities, but that year it was decided the TSX would become the sole place to trade senior equities. The Montreal Exchange stuck to derivatives, and the rest of the exchanges formed the Canadian Venture Exchange (CDNX). Two years later the TSX Group (the company that owns and operates the TSX) bought the CDNX, and in 2002 renamed it the TSX Venture Exchange (TSXV). Since then the TSX Group has become a public company itself, attracted international listings, merged with the Montreal Exchange, and changed its name to the TMX Group.

TIP

The TSXV is a good place for traders to play resource-based companies, because that's what makes up most of the index.

ALTERNATIVE TRADING SYSTEMS (ATS) AND ELECTRONIC COMMUNICATION NETWORKS (ECN)

Once upon a time the TSX was the only exchange in town. That monopoly meant it could charge brokers high fees for trades. And, if something went wrong with the TSX's software — like it did in December 2008, when a technical glitch cancelled an entire day of trading — investors would be out of luck. Alternative trading systems, also called electronic communication networks, have been around since the turn of the century, but only in the last decade have they begun to be a viable alternative to the standard exchanges.

Canada has a number of alternative trading systems — Chi-X Canada and Omega ATS, to name a couple — and all list the exact same securities as the TSX, but at different prices. Share prices don't vary too much, though; RIM's open price could be $46.15 and Omega ATS lists it at $46.50. Luckily, traders don't have to worry about the different exchanges because the broker will automatically sort through every exchange and buy the stock at the best price. A good chance exists you won't even know that you purchased a stock on Chi-X instead of the TSX.

TIP

Some traders swear like sailors as they rapidly buy and sell, but one F-word is worse than anything you'd hear a few minutes to close: *fees*. Brokers have to pay them every time they trade, and those costs are often passed down to the trader. When the TSX had a monopoly it could charge whatever it wanted; alternative trading systems were created in part to bring those fees down. Fortunately, fees have fallen, and as alternative trading systems gain more ground they could drop more. That's good news for traders who will hopefully see commission costs tumble as brokers pass on their savings to their customers.

THE NEW YORK STOCK EXCHANGE (NYSE)

Why is an American exchange listed in a Canadian day traders book? Because most day traders spend money on U.S. exchanges. It's important to know just as much about them — if not more — than the TSX. The New York Stock Exchange is the Big Kahuna of stock exchanges. Most of the largest U.S. corporations trade on it, and, like the TSX, they pay a fee for that privilege. The more than 2,000 companies listed on the exchange also have ticker symbols with three or fewer letters; many old companies have one-letter symbols, like F for Ford and T for AT&T.

To be listed on the New York Stock Exchange, a company generally needs to have at least 2,200 shareholders, trade at least 100,000 shares a month, carry a *market capitalization* (number of shares outstanding multiplied by price per share) of at least $100 million, and post annual revenues of at least $75 million.

The New York Stock Exchange is more than 200 years old, and has been going through some big corporate changes in order to stay relevant. Unlike its Canadian counterpart, it's a *floor-based exchange.* The trading area is a big open space in the building, known as the *floor.* The floor broker, who works for the member firm, receives the order electronically and then takes it over to the trading post, which is the area on the floor where the stock in question trades. At the trading post, the floor broker executes the order at the best available price.

NYSE AMERICAN

NYSE American, once known as the American Stock Exchange (AMEX), is a floor-based exchange also headquartered in New York City. Like the New York Stock Exchange, floor brokers receive orders and take them to trading posts to be filled. NYSE American specializes in growing companies, but some other types of businesses are also listed on it. Listed companies have two- or three-letter ticker symbols and generally are profitable, have a market capitalization (number of shares outstanding multiplied by price per share) of at least $75 million, and have a price per share of at least $2. These companies tend to be smaller and more speculative than New York Stock Exchange companies.

NASDAQ

Nasdaq used to stand for the National Association of Securities Dealers Automated Quotation System, but now it's just a name, not an acronym, pronounced just like it's spelled. When Nasdaq was founded, it was an electronic communication network (more on those earlier in this chapter) that handled — like the TSXV — companies that were too small or too speculative to meet New York Stock Exchange listing requirements. What happened was that brokers liked using the Nasdaq network, while technology companies (like Microsoft, Intel, Oracle, and Apple) that were once small and speculative became international behemoths. But the management teams of these companies saw no reason to change how they were listed.

Nasdaq companies have four-letter ticker symbols. When a customer places an order, the brokerage firm looks to see whether a matching order is on the network. Sometimes, it can be executed electronically; in other cases, the brokerage firm's trader needs to call other traders at other firms to see whether the price is still good. A key feature of Nasdaq is its *market makers*, who are employees of member brokerage firms who agree to buy and sell minimum levels of specific stocks in order to ensure some basic level of trading is taking place.

Nasdaq divides its listed companies into three categories:

>> **The Nasdaq Global Select Market** includes the 1,400 largest companies on the exchange and has high governance and liquidity standards for participating firms.

>> **The Nasdaq Global Market** includes companies that are too small for the Global Select Market, but that in general have a market capitalization of at least $75 million, at least 1.1 million shares outstanding, at least 400 shareholders, and a minimum price per share of $5.

>> **The Nasdaq Capital Market** is for companies that do not qualify for the Nasdaq Global Market. To qualify here, companies need a market capitalization of at least $50 million, at least one million shares outstanding, about 300 shareholders, and a minimum price per share of $4.

TIP

Day traders will find that Nasdaq Global Select Market companies are the most liquid. They may also notice changes in trading patterns when a company is close to being moved between categories. An upgrade is a sign of good news to come and increased market interest. A downgrade means that the company most likely isn't doing well and will be of less interest to investors.

OVER-THE-COUNTER BULLETIN BOARD (OTC BB)

The Over-the-Counter Bulletin Board is the market for companies that are reporting their financials to the provincial securities commissions (and, in the States, the U.S. Securities and Exchange Commission) but that do not qualify for listing on the TSXV or Nasdaq. Canada's OTC market is tiny; you can buy these types of companies on the TMX Group-run NEX. The exchange is for companies that have low levels of business activity or aren't active anymore. In other words, they're too small to trade on other exchanges.

TIP

In many cases, a Bulletin Board listing is often a last hurrah before oblivion.

Bonds

A *bond* is a loan. The bond buyer gives the bond issuer money. The bond issuer promises to pay interest on a regular basis. The regular coupon payments are why bonds are often called *fixed income investments.* Bond issuers repay the money borrowed — the principal — on a predetermined date, known as the *maturity.* Bonds generally have a maturity of more than ten years; shorter-term bonds are usually referred to as *notes,* and bonds that will mature within a year of issuance are usually referred to as *bills.* Most bonds in North America are issued by corporations (corporate bonds) or by the federal governments (called government bonds in Canada and Treasury bonds in the States). Some local governments in the U.S. also issue municipal bonds, but that's much less common in Canada.

The interest payments on a bond are called *coupons.* You've probably seen "car for sale" or "apartment for rent" signs with little slips of paper carrying a phone number or e-mail address cut into the bottom. If you're interested in the car or the apartment, you can rip off the slip and contact the advertiser later. Bonds used to look the same. The bond buyer would receive one large certificate good for the principal, with a lot of smaller certificates, called coupons, attached. When a payment was due, the owner would cut off the matching coupon and deposit it in the bank. (Some old novels refer to rich people as "coupon clippers," meaning that their sole labour in life was to cut out their bond coupons and cash them in. Nowadays, bond payments are handled electronically, so the modern coupon clipper is a bargain hunter looking for an extra 50 cents off a jar of peanut butter.)

Over the years, enterprising financiers realized that some investors needed regular payments, but others wanted to receive a single sum at a future date. So they separated the coupons from the principal. The principal payment, known as a *zero-coupon bond,* is sold to one investor, while the coupons, called *strips,* are sold to another investor. The borrower makes the payments just like with a regular bond. (Regular bonds, by the way, are sometimes called *plain vanilla.*)

The borrower who wants to make a series of payments with no lump-sum principal repayment would issue an *amortizing* bond to return principal and interest on a regular basis. If you think about a typical mortgage, the borrower makes a regular payment of both principal and interest. This way, the amount owed gets smaller over time so that the borrower does not have to come up with a large principal repayment at maturity.

Other borrowers would prefer to make a single payment at maturity, so they issue *discount bonds.* The purchase price is the principal reduced by the amount of interest that otherwise would be paid.

REMEMBER

If a company goes bankrupt, the bondholders get paid before the shareholders. In some bankruptcies, the bondholders take over the business, leaving the current shareholders with nothing. See Chapter 5 in Book 3 for more about bonds.

How bonds trade

Bonds often trade as single bonds, with a face value of $1,000, although some brokers will only take on minimum orders of ten bonds. They don't trade as frequently as stocks do because most bond investors are looking for steady income, so they hold their bonds until maturity. Bonds have less risk than stocks, so they show less price volatility. The value of a bond is mostly determined by the level of interest rates in the economy. As rates go up, bond prices go down; when rates go down, bond prices go up. Bond prices are also affected by how likely the loan is to be repaid. If traders don't think that the bond issuer will pay up (that is, perceive default risk), then the bond price will fall.

REMEMBER

Generally speaking, only corporate (and municipal in the U.S.) bonds have repayment risk. It's possible that the U.S. government could default, but that's unlikely as long as it can print money. Most international government bonds have similarly low default risk, but some countries *have* defaulted, especially when they borrow in foreign currencies. The most notable was Russia, which refused to print money to repay its debts in the summer of 1998. This caused huge turmoil in the world's financial markets, including the collapse of a major hedge fund, Long-Term Capital Management.

The global financial crisis also put many countries at risk, especially in Europe. In 2010 fears spread that Greece would default on its loans after Standard & Poor's — a U.S.-based company that rates borrowers — downgraded the country's debt rating to junk bond status. That sent stock markets plunging and spread fear that other financially strapped European countries, like Spain and Portugal, would default too. So, as you can see, just because a bond is issued by a government doesn't mean your investment is guaranteed.

In the past, investment banks and governments would sell new bonds directly to institutional investors, like pension plans or mutual funds. Now, anyone can buy bonds — but because they are usually purchased in large quantities, it's rare that a retail investor would buy a few bonds to complement her stocks. Traders, though, have more access to the bond market thanks to their broker. The broker will buy hundreds of thousands of dollars in bonds (or much more) and then sell them piecemeal to traders. Most bonds trade over-the-counter, meaning dealers trade them among themselves rather than on an organized exchange.

A bond price quote looks like this:

```
3 3/4 Mar 21 n 99:28 99:29
```

This is a U.S. Treasury note maturing in March 2021 carrying an interest rate of 3.75 percent. Similar to stocks, the numbers right after the "n" (for *note*) list the bid and ask.

>> The first number is the bid, and it's the price at which the dealer will buy the bond from you if you're selling.

>> The second number is the ask, and it's the price the dealer will charge you if you're buying. The difference is the spread, and that's the dealer's profit.

But wait, there's more: Corporate bonds trade in eighths of a percentage point, and government bonds trade in 32nds. The bid of 99:28 means that the bond's bid price is $99\frac{28}{32}$ percent of the face value of $1,000, or $998.75.

TECHNICAL STUFF

Why on earth do bonds trade in eighths or fractions of eighths? Do traders just like to show off their math skills? No, it goes back to before the American Revolution. The dominant currency in most of the Americas then was the Spanish doubloon, a large gold coin that could be cut into fractions to make trade easier. Like a pie, it would be cut into eight equal pieces, so prices throughout the colonies were often set in eighths. (In Robert Louis Stevenson's book *Treasure Island,* the parrot keeps squawking "Pieces of eight! Pieces of eight!" This is why.)

The fractional pricing convention carried over to North American securities markets, and has persisted because it guarantees dealers a bigger spread than pricing in decimals. After all, $\frac{1}{32}$ of a dollar is more than $\frac{1}{100}$. U.S. and Canadian stocks were priced in sixteenths until 2001. You'll notice a difference between the U.S. and Canadian bond markets, though. If you're purchasing an American bond it will be priced using the old convention, but buy a Canadian bond and you'll be dealing in decimals.

WARNING

Most bonds are not suitable for day traders. Only government bonds have enough consistent trading volume to attract a day trader. Because of the capital required to trade and the relatively low liquidity of many types of bonds, many traders prefer to use *futures* to bet on interest rates. Futures are discussed in detail later in this chapter.

Where bonds trade

Are you one of those day traders who wants to buy or sell bonds anyway? Or do you just want to know more about the market? Then read on:

>> **Listed bonds:** Some larger corporate bonds are traded on the TSX, the New York Stock Exchange, and NYSE American. When you want to buy or sell them, you place an order through your brokerage firm, which sends an order to the floor broker. The process is almost identical to the trading of listed stocks.

>> **Over-the-counter trading:** Most corporate and municipal bonds trade over-the-counter, meaning no organized exchange exists. Instead, brokerage firms use electronic price services to find out where the buyers and sellers are for different issues. Over-the-counter bonds don't trade much. Buyers often give their quality, interest rate, and maturity requirements to their broker, and the broker waits until a suitable bond comes to market.

>> **Treasury dealers:** Unlike the corporate and municipal bond market, the Treasury market is one of the most liquid in the world. The best way to buy a new Treasury bond is directly from the government, because no commission is involved. You can get more information from the government of Canada's website, https://www.canada.ca/en/department-finance/programs/financial-sector-policy/securities/debt-program.html, or the U.S. Treasury Department's website, www.savingsbonds.gov. Both have information on different government bonds for various purchasers.

TIP

Note that you can no longer buy bonds from the Canadian government, which stopped selling them in 2017, but the website has information on what to do if you already own them.

After the bonds are issued, they trade on a secondary market of Treasury dealers. These are large brokerage firms registered with the government that agree to buy and sell bonds and maintain a stable market for the bonds. If your brokerage firm is not a Treasury dealer, it has a relationship with one that it can send your order to.

Treasury dealers do quite a bit of day trading in Treasury bonds for the firm's own account. After all, the market is liquid enough that day trading is possible. Few individual day traders work the Treasury market, though, because it requires a great deal of capital and leverage to make a high return.

Exchange traded funds (ETFs)

Exchange traded funds (ETFs) are a cross between mutual funds and stocks, and they offer a great way for day traders to get exposure to market segments that might otherwise be difficult to trade. A money management firm buys a group of assets — stocks, bonds, or others — and then lists shares that trade on the market. (One of the largest organizers of exchange traded funds is Blackrock's iShares at www.ishares.com.) In most cases, the purchased assets are designed to mimic the performance of an index, and investors know what those assets are before they purchase shares in the fund.

Exchange traded funds are available on the big market indexes, like the S&P/TSX Composite Index, the S&P/TSX 60, the S&P 500, and the Dow Jones Industrial Average. They are available in a variety of domestic bond indexes, international stock indexes, foreign currencies, and commodities. (Flip to Chapter 4 in Book 3 for more information on ETFs.)

For day traders, the advantage of exchange traded funds is that they can be bought and sold just like stocks, discussed earlier in this chapter. Customers place orders, usually in round lots, through their brokerage firms. The price quotes come in decimals and include a spread for the dealer.

The firm that sets up the exchange traded fund gets to choose the market where it will trade, as long as the fund meets the exchange's requirements for size, liquidity, and financial reporting. Exchange traded funds trade on the TSX, NYSE, NYSE American, and Nasdaq.

Cash and Currency

Cash is king, as they say. It's money that's readily available in your day trading account to buy more securities. For the most part, the interest rate on cash is very low, but if you're closing out your positions every night, you'll always have a cash balance in your brokerage account. The firm will probably pay you a little interest on it, so it will contribute to your total return.

Money market accounts are boring. For day trading excitement, cash can be traded as foreign currency. Every day, trillions (yes, that's trillions with a t) of dollars are exchanged, creating opportunities to make money as the exchange rates change. Currency is a bigger, more liquid market than the U.S. stock and bond markets combined. It's often referred to as the *forex* market, short for *foreign exchange*.

How currency trades

The exchange rate is the price of money. It tells you how many dollars it takes to buy yen, pounds, or euros. The price that people are willing to pay for a currency depends on the investment opportunities, business opportunities, and perceived safety in each nation. If American businesses see great opportunities in Thailand, for example, they'll have to trade their dollars for baht in order to pay rent, buy supplies, and hire workers there. This will increase the demand for baht relative to the dollar, and it will cause the baht to go up in price relative to the dollar.

Exchange rates are quoted on a bid–ask basis, just as are bonds and stocks. A quote might look like this:

```
USDJPY=X 118.47 118.50
```

This is the exchange rate for converting the U.S. dollar into Japanese yen. The bid price of 118.47 is the amount of yen that a dealer would give you if you wanted to sell a dollar and buy yen. The ask price of 118.50 is the amount of yen the dealer would charge you if you wanted to buy a dollar and sell yen. The difference is the dealer's profit, and naturally, you'll be charged a commission, too.

Note that with currency, you're a buyer and a seller at the same time. This can increase the profit opportunities, but it can also increase your risk.

Day traders can trade currencies directly at current exchange rates, which is known as *trading in the spot market.* They can also use currency exchange traded funds (discussed earlier in this chapter) or currency futures (discussed later in this chapter) to profit from the changing prices of money.

Where currency trades

Spot currency — the real-time value of money — does not trade on an organized exchange. Instead, banks, brokerage firms, hedge funds, and currency dealers buy and sell among themselves all day, every day.

Day traders can open dedicated forex accounts through their broker or a currency dealer (one is `https://forex.ca/`) and then trade as they see opportunities during the day.

How the Canadian dollar is traded

The most common currency transaction is the euro against the U.S. dollar, mainly because Europe is one of the largest trading blocs in the world and a lot of business is done between those two countries. But Canadians often trade the loonie against the greenback for two reasons: America's our biggest trading partner, and it's just what we know. You can, of course, trade the Canadian dollar against any other currency too.

Beginners may want to stick to the Canada–U.S. relationship, simply because most news outlets in the Great White North report on currency fluctuations relative to the American buck. Understanding how to trade the loonie against the yen takes a bit more work.

Commodities and How They Trade

Commodities are basic, interchangeable goods sold in bulk and used to make other goods. Examples include oil, gold, wheat, and lumber. Commodities are popular with investors as a hedge against inflation and uncertainty. Stock prices can go to zero, but people still need to eat! Although commodity prices usually tend to increase at the same rate as in the overall economy, so they maintain their real (inflation-adjusted) value, they can also be susceptible to short-term changes in supply and demand. A cold winter increases demand for oil, a dry summer reduces production of wheat, and a civil war could disrupt access to platinum mines.

TIP

Day traders aren't going to buy commodities outright — if you really want to haul bushels of grain around all day, you can do that without taking on the risks of day trading. You'd get more exercise, too. Instead, day traders who want to play with commodities can look to other investments. The most popular way is to buy *futures* contracts, which change in price with the underlying commodity (discussed later in this chapter). Increasingly, many trade commodities through exchange traded funds (covered earlier in this chapter) that are based on the value of an underlying basket of commodities.

Derivatives and How They Trade

Derivatives are financial contracts that draw their value from the value of an underlying asset, security, or index. For example, an S&P/TSX 60 futures contract would give the buyer a cash payment based on the price of the S&P/TSX 60 index on the day that the contract expires. The contract's value thus depends on where the index is trading. You're trading not the index itself, but rather a contract with a value derived from the price of the index. The index value changes all the time, so day traders have lots of opportunities to buy and sell.

Types of derivatives

Day traders are likely to come across three types of derivatives. Options and futures trade on dedicated derivatives exchanges, whereas warrants trade on stock exchanges.

Options

An *option* is a contract that gives the holder the right, but not the obligation, to buy or sell the underlying asset at an agreed-upon price at an agreed-upon date in the future. An option that gives you the right to buy is a *call,* and one that gives you the right to sell is a *put.* A call is most valuable if the stock price is going up, whereas a put has more value if the stock price is going down.

TIP

Here's one way to remember the difference: you *call up* your friend to *put down* your enemy.

For example, a MSFT 2021 Mar 22.50 call gives you the right to buy Microsoft at $22.50 per share at the expiration date on the third Friday in March 2021. (Did you know that traders refer to Microsoft as "Mr. Softy"? Clever, huh?) If Microsoft is trading above $22.50, you can exercise the option and make a quick profit. If it's selling below $22.50 you could buy the stock cheaper in the open market, so the option would be worthless.

TIP

You can find great information on options, including online tutorials, on the Montreal Exchange's website, www.m-x.ca. For an American perspective, visit the Chicago Board Options Exchange's website, www.cboe.com.

Futures

A *futures* contract gives one the obligation to buy a set quantity of the underlying asset at a set price and a set future date. These started in the agricultural industry because they allowed farmers and food processors to lock in their prices early in the growing season, reducing the amount of uncertainty in their businesses. Futures have now been applied to many different assets, ranging from pork bellies (which really do trade — they are used to make bacon) to currency values. A simple example is a locked-in home mortgage rate; the borrower knows the rate that will be applied before the sale is closed and the loan is finalized. Day traders use futures to trade commodities without having to handle the actual assets.

Most futures contracts are closed out with cash before the settlement date. Financial contracts — futures on currencies, interest rates, or market index values — can only be closed out with cash. Commodity contracts may be settled with the physical items, but almost all are settled with cash. No one hauls a side of beef onto the floor of the Chicago Board of Trade!

Warrants

A *warrant* is similar to an option, but it's issued by the company rather than sold on an organized exchange. (After they are issued, warrants trade similarly to stocks.) A warrant gives the holder the right to buy more shares in the company at an agreed-upon price in the future.

A cousin of the warrant is the *convertible bond,* which is debt issued by the company. The company pays interest on the bond, and the bondholder has the right to exchange it for stock, depending on where interest rates and the stock price are. Convertibles trade on the stock exchanges.

Contract for difference (CFD)

A *contract for difference* allows traders to get exposure to an underlying asset, such as a share, index, currency, or commodity, without actually owning the asset itself. Because you don't own the asset commissions are often less — CMC Markets, one of the main CFD brokers, charges $5 for buying a contract on a stock;

if you bought the actual stock through a discount broker you'd pay anywhere between $7 and $20.

CFDs are similar to futures contracts, but they have no fixed expiry date or contract size. A trader makes money depending on what the difference is between the initial contract price and the time the CFD is sold.

Buying and selling derivatives

Derivatives trade a little differently than other types of securities because they are based on promises. When someone buys an option on a stock, they aren't trading the stock with someone right now, they're buying the right to buy or sell it in the future. That means that the option buyer needs to know that the person on the other side is going to pay up. So, the derivatives exchanges have systems in place to make sure that those who buy and sell the contracts will be able to perform when they have to. Requirements for trading derivatives are different than in other markets.

How derivatives trade

Remember the earlier section on marginability? Well, the word *margin* is used differently when discussing derivatives, but that's in part because derivatives are already leveraged — you aren't buying the asset, just exposure to the price change, so you can get a lot of bang for your buck.

Margin in the derivatives market is the money you have to put up to ensure that you'll perform on the contract when it comes time to execute it. In the stock market, margin is collateral against a loan from the brokerage firm. In the derivatives markets, margin is collateral against the amount you might have to pay up on the contract. The more likely it is that you will have to pay the party who bought or sold the contract, the more margin money you will have to put up. Some exchanges use the term *performance bond* instead.

To buy a derivative, you put up the margin with the exchange's clearing house. That way, the exchange knows you have the money to make good on your side of the deal — if, say, a call option that you sell is executed, or you lose money on a currency forward that you buy. Your brokerage firm will arrange for the deposit.

At the end of each day, derivatives contracts are *marked-to-market,* meaning that they are revalued. Profits are credited to the trader's margin account, and losses are deducted. If the margin falls below the necessary amount, the trader will get a call and have to deposit more money.

By definition, day traders close out at the end of every day, so their options are not marked-to-market. The contracts will be someone else's problem, and the profits or losses on the trade go straight to the margin account, ready for the next day's trading.

Where derivatives trade

Traditionally, derivative trading involves *open-outcry* on physical exchanges. Traders on the floor get orders and execute them among themselves, shouting and using hand signals to indicate what they want to do. No central trading post or market maker controls the activities or guarantees a market. Most traders are employees of large commodities brokerage firms, but some are independent. No matter who employs them, traders may be executing someone else's orders for a fee, or they may be working for proprietary accounts.

Open-outcry has fewer economies of scale than the electronic trading systems that dominate activity in other assets. That's why there are more derivatives exchanges in the United States than active stock exchanges. Still, all the exchanges offer some electronic trading services, and that has become more and more popular. It's also causing much restructuring and consolidation among the exchanges. In July 2007, the Chicago Board of Trade merged with the Chicago Mercantile Exchange because floor traders at both exchanges were losing market share to electronic trading.

WARNING

Sometimes, the people in the pits start messing around with each other, and that can cause unusual volatility in the trading of the securities. Day traders who deal in commodities will often notice short periods of irrational trading for those derivatives that trade primarily in pits. The more human involvement, the less efficient a market will be.

Here are a few places where derivatives trade:

>> **Montreal Exchange (MX):** Most day traders will access American exchanges to trade derivatives, but some instruments can be bought and sold right here in Canada, on the TMX Group's Montreal Exchange.

TECHNICAL STUFF

The MX is Canada's oldest exchange, starting up in 1832. In the early 1900s Montreal was Canada's financial centre; it used to execute many more trades than its Toronto counterpart. The ME was, at one time, so integral to Canada's financial markets that the terrorist group Front de libération du Québec bombed it in 1969. Over time the exchange began trading options and futures.

In 1999 the TSX became the recognized place to sell stocks, and the MX became Canada's main derivatives exchange. Nine years later the MX merged with the TSX Group to form the TMX Group. These days, the MX's business is primarily in equity, exchange traded funds, and currency options, and index, interest rate, and energy derivatives.

» **Chicago Board of Trade (CBOT):** At the top of the Chicago Board of Trade's building is a statue of Ceres, the Greek goddess of grain. That's because this is the centre of futures trading in corn, wheat, rice, oats, and soybeans. The Board of Trade has branched out over the years and now offers futures contracts on financial commodities like Treasury bonds and the Dow Jones Industrial Average. Recently, it added trading in ethanol futures, an expansion from its history with corn. When a brokerage firm gets a customer order for a future traded on the Board of Trade it can send it to floor brokers to fill in the trading pits, or it can use the exchange's electronic trading system.

» **Chicago Mercantile Exchange (CME):** Futures in non-grain agricultural products, such as milk, butter, cattle, pork bellies, and fertilizer, trade at the Chicago Mercantile Exchange, known more colloquially as "the Merc." Other key futures traded here include foreign exchange, interest rates, and the Standard & Poor's and Nasdaq indexes. The Merc has also added some alternative products such as futures in weather and real estate. When brokerage firms receive orders for the Merc's futures they send them to floor brokers, who can fill them in the trading pits, or they can use the Merc's electronic trading system.

» **New York Mercantile Exchange (NYMEX):** Fuels and metals trade at the New York Mercantile Exchange, which is the largest physical commodities exchange in the United States. Most trading takes place in open-outcry pits, but an electronic system is available for overnight trading.

» **New York Board of Trade (NYBOT):** The New York Board of Trade was founded in 1998, when the Coffee, Sugar, and Cocoa Exchange merged with the New York Cotton Exchange. Here, traders can buy and sell futures and options on those commodities as well as on orange juice, the New York Stock Exchange, the U.S. dollar, and the euro. Orders are filled in the trading pits or through an electronic trading system.

» **Chicago Board Options Exchange (CBOE):** The Chicago Board Options Exchange, often known by the acronym CBOE (pronounced *see-bow*), is the largest options market in the United States. This is where orders for stock options are traded. Brokerage firms use floor brokers in the trading pits or the CBOE's electronic trading system to handle customer orders.

GETTING TO KNOW THE CME GROUP

The CME Group (www.cmegroup.com/) is the largest futures exchange in the world. It was formed in July 2007, after the Chicago Board of Trade merged with the Chicago Mercantile Exchange; in 2008 it acquired the fuels and metals–focused New York Mercantile Exchange (NYME) and the Commodity Exchange (COMEX). Even though these exchanges are owned by one company, they still have separate locations and traders access the individual exchanges.

IN THIS CHAPTER

» Taking on risk and getting a return

» Investing for the long haul

» Trading for the day

» Gambling it all away

» Managing the risks you take

Chapter **4**

Investing, Trading, and Gambling

Day trading isn't investing, nor is it gambling — at least not if done right. But the lines among the three can be thin, and if you know where they are you'll be in a better position to follow your trading strategy and make more money. And if you can avoid the trap of gambling, you'll be better able to preserve your trading capital.

The difference between investing and gambling is the *risk and return tradeoff.* In investing, the odds are generally in your favour, but that doesn't mean you're going to make money. Some day traders end up gambling, and then the odds are moving against them. And unlike in the finer establishments in Las Vegas, no one is going to bring the failed day trader free drinks to help ease the pain. A lot comes down to personality; if you are on a casino's "do not admit" list, you probably aren't a great candidate for day trading.

This chapter starts off with a lot of gory details about risk and return. It helps you understand how the securities markets price risk and reward those who are willing to take it. Then it explains the differences in risk and reward for investors, traders, and gamblers to give you better information to help you plan your day trading.

Understanding Risk and Return

Investors, traders, and gamblers have this in common: They are putting some of their money at risk and they expect to get a return. Ideally, that return comes in the form of cold, hard cash — but at a casino, you might get your return in the form of tickets to a Celine Dion concert after you lose a lot of money at the tables.

Trading is a business: The more you know about the potential risks and the sources of your potential return, the better off you'll be. Your risk is that you won't get the return you expect, and your reward is that you get fair compensation for the risk you take.

What is risk, anyway?

REMEMBER

Risk is the measurable likelihood of loss. The riskier something is, the more frequently a loss will occur, and the larger that loss is likely to be. Playing in traffic is riskier than driving in traffic, and skydiving is riskier than gardening. This doesn't mean that you can't have losses in a low-risk activity or big gains in a high-risk one. It just means that with the low-risk game, losses are less likely to happen, and those that do are likely to be small.

TECHNICAL STUFF

What's the difference between risk and uncertainty? Risk involves the *known likelihood* of something good or bad happening so that it can be priced. What's the likelihood of your living to be 100? Or of getting into a car accident tonight? Your insurance company knows, and it figures your rates accordingly. What's the likelihood of aliens from outer space arriving and taking over the Earth? Who knows! It could happen, but that event is uncertain, not risky — at least until it happens.

The ability to measure risk made modern business possible. Until mathematicians were able to use statistics to quantify human activities, people assumed that bad things were simply the result of bad luck or, worse, the wrath of the gods. But when they could understand probability, it could be applied and used. If a sailor agreed to join a voyage of exploration, what was the probability that he would return home alive? And what would be fair compensation to him for that risk? What was the probability of a silo of grain going up in flames? And how much should the farmer charge the grain buyers for the risk that he was taking, and how much should someone else charge to insure the farmer against that fire?

Considering the probability of a loss

Whenever you take risk, you take on the probability of loss. If you know what that probability is, you can determine whether the terms you are being offered are fair and you have a reasonable expectation for the size of the loss.

Imagine that you are presented with this opportunity: You put up $10. You have an 80 percent chance of getting back $11 and a 20 percent chance of losing everything. Should you take it? To find out, you multiply the expected return by the likelihood and add them together: (80% × $11) + (20% × $0) = $8.80. Your expected return of $8.80 is less than the $10 cost of this contract, so you should pass on it.

Now, suppose you are offered this opportunity: You put up $10. You have a 90 percent chance of getting back $11 and a 10 percent chance of getting back $6. Your expected return is (90% × $11) + (10% × $6) = $10.50. This contract would be in your favour, so you should take it.

Now here's a third proposition: You put up $10. You have a 90 percent chance of getting back $13.89 and a 10 percent chance of losing $20 — even more than you put up. Your expected return is (90% × $13.89) + (10% × −$20) = $10.50. It's the same expected return as the previous proposition, but do you like it as much?

REMEMBER

When thinking about loss, most people tend to put too much weight on the absolute dollar amount that *they* can lose, rather than thinking about the likelihood. The problem is that the markets don't trade on your personal preferences. This is one of the psychological hurdles of trading that those who are successful can overcome. Can you?

Securities markets rely on the concept of *limited liability*. That is, you cannot lose any more money than you invested in the first place. If you buy a stock, it can go down to zero, but it can't go any lower. If the company goes bankrupt, no one can come to you and ask you to cover the bills. On the other hand, the most the stock can go up in price is infinity, so the possible return for your risk is huge.

WARNING

Most day trading strategies have the same limited liability: You can lose what you trade, and no more. Some strategies have unlimited liability, however, such as selling short or using leverage. If you sell a stock short (borrow shares and then sell them in hopes that the stock goes down in price, allowing you to repay the loan with cheaper shares), and if the stock goes up to infinity, you have to repay the loan with those infinitely valued shares! Most likely, you're going to close out your position before that happens, but keep in mind that even if you close out your positions every night like a good day trader should, some strategies have the potential to cost you more money than you have in your trading account.

REMEMBER

To protect themselves and to protect you against losing more money than you have, brokerage firms and options exchanges will require you to keep enough funds in your account to cover shortfalls (known as *margin,* discussed in Chapter 3 of Book 5). You will have to be approved before you can trade in certain securities. For example, anyone trading options has to fill out an agreement that the brokerage firm must first approve and then keep on file.

Many day trading strategies are *zero-sum games,* meaning that for every winner on a trade, there is a loser. This is especially true in options markets. Now, the person on the other side of the trade might not mind being a loser; she may have entered into a trade to *hedge* (protect against a decline in) another investment and is happy to have a small loss instead of a much larger one.

WARNING

The problem for you as a day trader is that little wiggle room exists in a zero-sum game. Every trade you make is going to win or lose, and your losses may exactly offset your winners. If your strategy takes place in a market that is a zero-sum game, such as the options market, make sure that you've tested your strategy thoroughly so that you know whether your odds are better than even.

Finding the probability of not getting the return you expect

In addition to absolute measures of risk and liability, consider another factor: *volatility.* That's how much a security's price might go up or down in a given time period.

The math for measuring volatility is based on standard deviation (discussed in Chapter 3 of Book 5). A standard deviation calculation starts with the average return over a given time period. This is the *expected* return — the return that, on average, you'll get if you stick with your trading strategy. But any given week, month, or year, the return might be very different from what you expect. The more likely you are to get what you expect, the less risk you take in the form of volatility.

TIP

Standard deviation shows up many times in trading. The key thing to know is this: The higher the standard deviation of the underlying securities, the more risk you take with your trade. However, the same volatility creates trading opportunities for day traders to exploit. A security with a low standard deviation isn't going to offer you many chances to make money over the course of a day.

Standard deviation is used to calculate another statistic: beta. *Beta* tells you how risky a security is relative to the risk of the market itself. If you buy a stock with a beta of more than 1, then that stock is expected to go up in price by a larger percentage than the market when the market is up, and it's expected to go down by a larger percentage than the market when the market is down.

REMEMBER

High-beta stocks, and options on high-beta stocks, are riskier than low-beta stocks, but they offer a greater potential for return.

TECHNICAL STUFF

The word *beta* comes from the Capital Asset Pricing Model (CAPM), an academic theory that says that the return on an investment is a function of the risk-free rate of return (discussed in the next section), the extra risk of investing in the market as a whole, and then the volatility — beta — of the security relative to the market. Under the CAPM, no other sources of risk and return exist. Any other sources would be called *alpha*, but in theory, alpha doesn't exist. Not everyone agrees with that, but the terms *alpha* and *beta* have stuck.

Getting rewarded for the risk you take

When you take risk, you expect to get a return. That's fair enough, right? That return comes in a few different forms related to the risk taken. Although you might not really care how you get your return as long as you get it, thinking about the breakdown of returns can help you think about your trading strategy and how it works for you.

Opportunity cost

The *opportunity cost* of your money is the return you could get doing something else. Is your choice day trading or staying at your current job? Your opportunity cost is your current salary and benefits. You'd give up that money if you quit to day trade. Is the opportunity cost low enough that it's worth your while? It may be. Just because taking advantage of an opportunity carries a cost doesn't mean that the opportunity isn't worth it.

REMEMBER

When you trade, you want to cover your opportunity cost. Your cost will be different than someone else's, but if you know what it is up front, you'll have a better idea of whether your return is worth your risk.

You can think about opportunity cost in another way, too. When you make one trade, you give up the opportunity to use that money for another trade. That means you want to trade only when you know the trade is going to work out, more likely than not. That's why you need to plan your trades (see Chapter 2 in Book 5) and backtest (run a simulation using your strategy and historical securities prices) and evaluate your performance so that you know you're trading for the right reasons, and not just out of boredom.

Risk-free rate of return and the time value of money

The value of money changes over time. In most cases, this is because of *inflation*, which is the general increase in price levels in an economy. But it's also because you give up the use of money for some period of time. That's why any investment or trading opportunity should include compensation for the *time value of your money.*

In day trading, your return from time value is small, because you hold positions for only a short period of time and close them out overnight. Still, some time component is relevant to the money you make. That smallest return is known as the *risk-free rate of return.* That's what you demand for giving up the use of your money, even if you know with certainty that you'll get your money back. In practice, investors think of the risk-free rate of return as the rate on Canadian or U.S. government Treasury bills, which are bonds that mature in less than one year. This rate is widely quoted in newspapers and electronic price quote systems.

REMEMBER

If you cannot generate a return that's at least equal to the risk-free rate of return, you shouldn't be trading.

Risk–return tradeoff

Economists say there's no such thing as a free lunch. Whatever return you get, you get because you took some risk and gave up another opportunity for your time and money. In that sense, making money is all about work and risk.

This is known as the *risk–reward tradeoff.* The greater the potential reward, the greater the amount of risk you're expected to take, and thus the greater potential you have for loss. But if you understand the risks you're taking up front, you may well find that they are worth taking. That's why you have to think about the risks and rewards up front.

The magic of market efficiency

The reason why a balance between risk and reward exists is that markets are reasonably efficient. This efficiency means that prices reflect all known information about the companies and the economy, and it means that all participants understand the relative tradeoffs available to them. Otherwise, you'd have opportunities to make a riskless profit, and that just won't do according to the average economist. "You can't pluck nickels out of thin air," they like to say. In an efficient market, if an opportunity exists to make money without risk, someone would have taken advantage of that already.

It works like this: You have information that says Company A is going to announce good earnings tomorrow, so you buy the stock. Your increased demand causes the price to go up, and pretty soon, the stock price is where it should be given that the company is doing well. The information advantage is rapidly eliminated. And in most cases, everyone gets the news — or hears the rumour — of the good earnings at the same time, so the price adjustment happens quickly.

WARNING

Wouldn't it be great if you could get the news of a good earnings report before everyone else, to make a quick trading profit? Yep. At least until the RCMP show up and haul you off to prison — talk about your opportunity costs! It's illegal to trade on *material inside information* (which would be information that is not generally known that would affect the price of the security). Canada's provincial securities commissions, the Investment Industry Regulatory Organization of Canada (IIROC), and the individual brokers monitor trading for patterns that suggest illegal trading based on inside information. They want all investors and traders to feel confident that the investment business is fair. Be very wary of tips that seem too good to be true.

Now, you'll notice in the example that it was the activity of traders that caused the price of Company A's stock to go up to reflect the expected good earnings report. The markets may be more or less efficient, but that doesn't mean they work by magic. Price changes happen because people act on news, and those who act the fastest are day traders.

In economic terms, *arbitrage* is a riskless profit. A hard-core believer in academic theory would say that arbitrage opportunities don't exist. In practice, though, they do. Here's how it works: Although Company A is expected to have a good earnings announcement tomorrow, you notice that the stock price has gone up faster than the price of a call option on Company A, even though premium should reflect the stock price. So, you sell Company A (borrowing shares and selling it short if you have to), and then use the proceeds to buy the option. When the option price goes up to reflect the stock price, you can sell it and lock in a riskless profit — at least, before your trading costs are considered.

THE OLDEST ECONOMICS JOKE EVER TOLD

When you're wise to the ways of risk and return, this joke should make sense to you: Two economists are walking down the street. One sees a $20 bill on the sidewalk and stops to pick it up. "Don't bother," says the other. "If it were real, someone would have taken it already."

"Don't be so sure," says the first economist. He picks it up, sees that it is real, then turns to his friend and says, "How about if I buy you a free lunch?"

Defining Investing

Investing is the process of putting money at risk in order to get a return. It's the raw material of capitalism. It's the way that businesses get started, roads get built, and explorations get financed. It's how the economy matches people who have too much money, at least during part of their lives, with people who need it in order to grow society's capabilities.

Investing is heady stuff. And it's very much focused on the long term. Good investors do a lot of research before committing their money, because they know that it will take a long time to see a payoff. That's okay with them. Investors often invest in things that are out of favour, because they know that with time others will recognize the value and respond in kind.

TIP

One of the best investors of all time is Warren Buffett, Chief Executive Office of Berkshire Hathaway. His annual letters to shareholders offer great insight. You can read them at `www.berkshirehathaway.com/letters/letters.html`.

What's the difference between investing and saving? When you save, you take no risk. Your compensation is low — it's just enough to cover the time value of money. Generally, the return on savings equals inflation and no more. In fact, a lot of banks pay a lot less than the inflation rate on a federally insured savings account, meaning that you're paying the bank to use your money.

In contrast to investing, day trading moves fast. Day traders react only to what's on the screen: no time to do research, and the market is always right when you are day trading. You don't have two months or two years to wait for the fundamentals to work out and the rest of Wall Street to see how smart you were. You have today. And if you can't live with that, you shouldn't be day trading.

Talking about Trading

Trading is the act of buying and selling securities. All investors trade, because they need to buy and sell their investments. But to investors, trading is a rare transaction, and they get more value from finding a good opportunity, buying it cheap, and selling it at a much higher price sometime in the future. But traders are not investors.

Traders look to take advantage of short-term price discrepancies in the market. In general, they don't take a lot of risk on each trade, so they don't get a lot of return on each trade, either. Traders act quickly. They look at what the market is telling them and then respond. They know that many of their trades will not work out, but as long as more than half work, they'll be okay. They don't do a lot of in-depth research on the securities they trade, but they know the normal price and volume patterns well enough that they can recognize potential profit opportunities.

Trading keeps markets efficient, because it creates the short-term supply and demand that eliminates small price discrepancies. It also creates a lot of stress for traders, who must react in the here and now. Traders give up the luxury of time in exchange for a quick profit.

TECHNICAL STUFF

Speculation is related to trading, in that it often involves short-term transactions. Speculators take risks assuming a much greater return than might be expected, and a lot of what-ifs may have to be satisfied for the transaction to pay off. Many speculators hedge their risks with other securities, such as options or futures.

Getting a Grip on Gambling

A *gambler* puts up money in the hopes of a payoff if a random event occurs. *The odds are always against the gambler and in favour of the house,* but people like to gamble because they like to hope that if they hit it lucky, their return will be as large as their loss is likely.

Some gamblers believe that the odds can be beaten, but they are wrong. (Certain card games are more games of skill than gambling, assuming you can find a casino that will play under standard rules. Yeah, you can count cards when playing blackjack with your friends, but it's a lot harder in a professionally run casino.) They get excited about the potential for a big win and get caught up in the glamour of the casino, and soon the odds go to work and drain away their stakes.

TIP

A *fair lottery* takes place when the expected payoff is higher than the odds of playing. You won't find it at most casinos, although sometimes the odds in a sports book or horse race favour the bettor, at least in the short term. A more common example takes place in lotteries when the jackpots roll over to astronomical amounts. Canadian lotteries don't get high enough to fit this description, but if you're travelling through the States you may want to pick up a multi-state Mega Millions ticket. In March 2007, for example, the lottery had a jackpot of $390 million, but the odds of winning were 1 in 175 million. This means that a $1.00 ticket had an expected value of $2.28, making it a fair proposition.

WARNING

Trading is not gambling, but traders who are not paying attention to their strategy and its performance can cross over into gambling. They can view the blips on their computer screen as a game. They can start making trades without any regard for the risk and return characteristics. They can start believing that how they do things affects the trade. And pretty soon, they are using the securities market as a giant casino, using trading techniques that have odds as bad as any slot machine.

Managing the Risks of Day Trading

After you know more about the risks, returns, and related activities of day trading, you can think more about how you're going to run your day trading business. Before you flip through the book to find out how to get started, consider two more kinds of risk you need to be aware of:

>> Business risk

>> Personal risk

Business risk is the uncertainty of the timing of your cash flow. Not every month of trading is going to be great, but your bills will come due no matter what. You'll have to pay for subscriptions while keeping the lights turned on and the computer connected to the Internet. Taxes come due four times a year, and keyboards hold a mysterious attraction for carbonated beverages, causing them to short out at the most inopportune times.

TIP

Regardless of what happens to your trading account, you need cash on hand to pay your bills or you'll be out of business. The best way to protect yourself is to start out with a cash cushion just for covering your operating expenses. Keep it separate from your trading funds. Replenish it during good months.

The *personal risk* of trading is that it becomes an obsession that crowds out everything else in your life. Trading is a stressful business, and the difference between those who succeed and those who fail is psychological.

REMEMBER

The key to successful day trading is controlling your emotions. After all, the stock doesn't know that you own it, as equity traders like to say, so it isn't going to perform well just because you want it to. This can be infuriating, especially when you're going through a draw-down of your capital. Those losses look mighty personal. You have to figure out a way to manage your reactions to the market, or you shouldn't be a day trader. Day traders talk about their enemies being fear and greed. If you panic, you'll no longer be trading to win, but trading not to lose. The distinction is important: If your goal is not to lose, you won't take appropriate risk, and you won't be able to respond quickly to what the market is telling you.

IN THIS CHAPTER

» Looking at a history of day trading and regulations

» Wondering who all these regulators are, anyway

» Considering some basic brokerage requirements

» Handling hot tips

» Trading with other people

Chapter **5**

Understanding Regulations

The financial markets are wild and woolly playgrounds for capitalism at its best. Every moment of the trading day, buyers and sellers get together to figure out what the price of a stock, commodity, or currency should be at that moment given the supply, the demand, and the information out there. It's beautiful.

One reason why the markets work so well is that they are regulated. That may seem like an oxymoron: Isn't capitalism all about free trade, unfettered by any rules from nannying bureaucrats? Ah, but for capitalism to work, people on both sides of a trade need to know that the terms will be enforced. They need to know that the money is in their account and safe from theft. And they need to know that no one has an unfair advantage. *Regulation* creates the trust that makes markets function.

Day traders may not be managing money for other investors, and they may not answer to an employer, but that doesn't mean they don't have rules to follow. They have to comply with applicable securities laws and exchange regulations, some of which specifically address those who make lots of short-term trades. Likewise, brokers and advisers who deal with day traders have regulations that they need to follow, and understanding them can help day traders make better decisions about whom to deal with. In this chapter, you find out who does the regulating, what they look at, and how it all affects you.

How Regulations Created Day Trading

Canada's regulatory system is very different from that in the U.S., though it all stems from the same place. The American system came first, and so we borrowed many rules from our southern neighbours. Things have developed significantly since then, and although many similarities exist you'll also find a lot of differences. But first, a quick course in American history is in order so you can see how regulation in fact helped create trading.

With the advent of the telegraph, traders could receive daily price quotes. Many cities had *bucket shops,* which were storefront businesses where traders could bet on changes in stock and commodity prices. They weren't buying the security itself, even for a few minutes, but were instead placing bets against others. These schemes were highly prone to manipulation and fraud, and they were wiped out after the stock market crash of 1929.

After the 1929 crash, small investors could trade off the ticker tape, which was a printout of price changes sent by telegraph, or wire. In most cases, they would do this by going down to their brokerage firm's office, sitting in a conference room, and placing orders based on the changes they saw come across the tape. Really serious traders could get a wire installed in their own office, but the costs were prohibitive for most individual investors. In any event, traders still had to place their orders through a broker rather than having direct access to the market, so they could not count on timely execution.

Another reason why so little day trading happened back then is that until 1975, all American brokerage firms charged the same commissions. That year, the U.S. Securities and Exchange Commission (SEC) ruled that this amounted to price fixing, so brokers could then compete on their commissions. Some brokerage firms, such as Charles Schwab, began to allow customers to trade stock at discount commission rates, which made active trading more profitable.

TIP

Today, Canadian fees are all over the map and getting cheaper, so compare commission prices before you settle on a broker.

The system of trading off the ticker tape more or less persisted until the stock market crash of 1987. Brokerage firms and market makers were flooded with orders, so they took care of their biggest customers first and pushed the smallest trades to the bottom of the pile. After the crash, the exchanges and the SEC called for several changes that would reduce the chances of another crash and improve execution if one were to happen. One of those changes was the Small Order Entry System, often known as SOES, which gave orders of 1,000 shares or fewer priority over larger orders.

Similar regulation was developed in Canada at about the same time. The Order Exposure Rule was created to make sure smaller orders were given the same priority as larger ones. Here, 50 standard trading units or fewer (about 5,000 shares) have to be immediately entered on a market place. Brokers can't fill their larger orders first.

In the 1990s, when Internet access became widely available, this became less of a problem because traders could place orders in real time. But the rule still applies. Brokers could, theoretically, wait to execute Internet orders so they could deal with their 100,000-share trades first. Of course, that would be terrible for business — and with so much competition, fast execution is a selling point. Still, this rule, plus the speed of the Internet, put traders on the same footing as brokers and made day trading look like a pretty good way to make a living.

Who Regulates What?

In Canada, financial markets get regulatory oversight from various bodies, but most of the rules come from the provincial security commissions (such as the Ontario Securities Commission, or OSC) and the Investment Industry Regulatory Organization of Canada (IIROC). Both have similar goals: to ensure that investors and traders have adequate information to make decisions, and to prevent fraud and abuse.

Unlike in the United States, which has the Securities and Exchange Commission, Canada has no *national* regulator. IIROC governs dealers (the institutions whose trading software you're using) across the country, and the securities commissions enforce the provincial Securities Act and Commodity Futures Act. The commissions' mandate, says the OSC's website, is to protect investors from "unfair, improper or fraudulent practices and to foster fair and efficient capital markets and confidence in capital markets."

Both IIROC and Canada's other self-regulatory organization, the Mutual Fund Dealers Association (MFDA), which oversees dealers who sell only mutual funds, police their own members, but the former self-regulatory organization (SRO) does a lot more. IIROC regulates the Toronto Stock Exchange (TSX), the Canadian

Securities Exchange (formerly the Canadian National Stock Exchange), and various alternative trading systems such as Bloomberg Tradebook and Omega ATS.

When it comes to equity exchanges, IIROC's main job is to make sure nothing fishy is happening. The organization monitors trading activity and can place halts or delays if market integrity is compromised. It also enforces Universal Market Integrity Rules — the rules in Canada that govern trading.

IIROC also monitors how securities are traded in order to look for patterns that might point to market manipulation or insider trading. It works with brokerage firms to make sure they know who their customers are and that they have systems in place to make certain these customers play by the rules.

Because the stock and corporate bond markets are the most popular markets and have a relatively large number of relatively small issuers, regulators are active and visible. Not just one government is issuing currency — a whole bunch of companies issue shares of stock. When it turns out that one of these companies has fraudulent numbers the headlines erupt, and suddenly everyone cares about what the regulators are up to. That's just the first layer in regulating this market.

TIP

Serious talk has happened in the hallowed halls of the Legislature about creating a single national securities regulator in Canada, much like the SEC in the United States. Governments have been debating the question of whether Canada needs one for decades, so the chances of it happening soon are slim. However, if you're reading this book a few years after its publication date, be aware that some of what is written here may be obsolete.

Provincial securities commissions

Each province has its own agency to ensure the markets work efficiently. Although rules may vary, they all share a common goal: to keep capital markets safe from fraud. Each commission governs its own jurisdiction, but they do work together. The commissions also work with the SEC or other governing bodies when fraud crosses country borders.

The provincial securities commissions have various functions, including the following:

>> Regulating provincial capital markets by enforcing the provincial Securities Act and, depending on where, the Commodity Futures Act. The commissions ensure that any companies that have securities listed on exchanges in their jurisdiction report their financial information accurately and on time, so that investors can determine whether investing in the company makes sense for them.

>> Working with various stakeholders — retail investors, pensions funds, dealers, advisers, stock exchanges, alternative trading systems, SROs, and more — in ensuring compliance, investor protection, and keeping fair and efficient markets.

>> Prosecuting firms and individuals who violate securities law. Although the commissions spend a lot of time investigating allegations of misconduct, they hold hearings over takeover bids and other regulatory issues, too.

Investment Industry Regulatory Organization of Canada (IIROC)

IIROC (www.iiroc.ca) was created in 2008 when the Investment Dealers Association and Market Regulation Services merged. The IDA was an SRO that oversaw Canadian dealers, and MRS provided regulation services for Canadian markets. The union has brought better oversight to the industry, making it more difficult for nefarious crooks to take advantage of investors.

The combined SRO oversees investment dealers in Canada that trade stocks, bonds, mutual funds, options, forex, and other securities. It also looks after trading activity on debt and equity markets. It has hundreds of member firms, with thousands of people who are registered to sell securities. IIROC administers background checks and licensing exams, regulates securities trading and monitors how firms comply, and provides information for investors so that they are better informed about the investing process.

IIROC also requires advisers to know as much as they can about their clients, via Know Your Client (KYC) forms. This includes determining whether an investment strategy is suitable for them. Find out more about suitability in the later section "Are you suitable for day trading?" — for now, just know that it's an IIROC function.

TIP

The first thing a day trader should do is check IIROC and MFDA's media release pages and the security commissions' registration sites. Every time a disciplinary hearing against a firm or adviser takes place, the progress of the proceedings is posted on the site. Find out whether the firm you want to trade with has violated any regulations. The security commissions' registrations sites allow you to type in the name of a person or firm and see whether they are in fact registered, what category they're registered in, and if any conditions were attached to that registration. These tools help ensure you're not dealing with a criminal.

Mutual Fund Dealers Association of Canada (MFDA)

Unlike IIROC, which oversees dealers who trade stocks and bonds, the MFDA (www.mfda.ca) represents members who work only with mutual funds. Despite operating under its own set of rules, it shares many of the same goals as IIROC. It regulates operations, standards, and business conduct of its members and tries to improve investor protection. It can fine members for violating rules, and works with authorities when criminal charges are laid.

The MFDA represents nearly 100 firms, or over 78,000 mutual fund sales persons, with about $550 billion in assets under administration. It's highly unlikely the brokerage firm you use will be an MFDA member. Because you're trading more than just mutual funds, you'll be working in an IIROC environment.

The exchanges

It wasn't long ago that each major city had its own exchange. But through mergers and an agreement that Toronto would host a central stock exchange, the TSX became the main exchange in the country. However, depending on what you trade, the TSX is not the only game in town — you'll also find the TSX Venture Exchange (TSXV), the Montreal Exchange (MX), and other exchanges and alternative trading systems.

Canada's main exchanges are owned by the TMX Group (www.tmx.com/). It oversees the TSX, the TSXV, the MX, and a few others. The group has outsourced its regulation duties of the TSX and TSXV to IIROC, and the others regulate trading activity in-house.

Brokerage Basics for Firm and Customer

No matter how they are regulated, brokers and futures commission merchants have to know who their customers are and what they are up to. That leads to some basic regulations about suitability and money laundering — and extra paperwork for you. Don't be too annoyed by all the paperwork you have to fill out to open an account, though — your brokerage firm has even more.

Are you suitable for day trading?

Brokerage firms have to make sure the activity surrounding their customers is appropriate. The firms need to know their customers and be sure that any recommendations are suitable. When it comes to day trading, firms want to be sure their customers are dealing with *risk capital* — money they can afford to lose. They also want to be sure that their customers understand the risks they are taking. Depending on the firm, and what you're trying to do, you might have to submit financial statements, sign a stack of disclosures, and verify that you have had previous trading experience.

REMEMBER

It's no one's business but your own, of course, except that the regulators want to make sure that firm employees aren't talking customers into taking on risks they should not be taking. Sure, you can lie about it. You can tell the broker you don't *need* the $25,000 you're putting in your account, even if that's the money paying for your kidney dialysis. But when it's gone, you can't say you didn't know about the risks involved.

Staying out of the money laundromat

Money laundering is a way to receive money acquired from illegal activities. Your average drug dealer, Mafia hit man, or corrupt politician doesn't accept credit cards, but he really doesn't want to keep lots of cash in his house. How can he collect interest on his money if it's locked in a safe in his closet? And besides, his friends are an unsavory sort. Can he trust them to stay away from his cache? If this criminal fellow takes all that cash to the bank, those pesky bankers will start asking a lot of questions, because they know that most people pursuing legitimate business activities get paid through cheques or electronic direct deposit.

Hence, the felon with funds will look for a way to make it appear that the money is legitimate. It happens in all sorts of ways, ranging from making lots of small cash deposits to engaging in complicated series of financial trades and money transfers, especially between countries, that become difficult for investigators to trace. Sometimes these transactions look a lot like day trading, and that means that legitimate brokerage firms opening day trade accounts should be paying attention to who their customers are.

Fighting money laundering took on urgency after the September 11, 2001 attacks, because it was clear that someone somewhere had given some bad people a lot of cash to fund the preparation and execution of their deadly mission. Several nations increased their oversight of financial activities during the aftermath of the strikes on the World Trade Center and Pentagon. That's why one piece of paperwork from your broker will be the anti–money laundering disclosure. The Financial Transactions and Reports Analysis Centre of Canada (FINTRAC) is the government body that looks after money laundering activities, but brokers track this as well. If they suspect a trader is laundering money they'll report it to FINTRAC, which will then investigate.

MONEY LAUNDERING: AL CAPONE OR WATERGATE?

Although some believe that the term *money laundry* dates back to Al Capone's attempts to evade taxes by owning laundries — businesses that had a large number of small cash transactions — the U.S. Federal Reserve Board says the term didn't come into use until the Watergate scandal, when Richard Nixon's campaign staff had to hide the money used to pay the people who broke into his opponent's psychiatrist's office.

REMEMBER

In order for your brokerage firm to verify that it knows who its customers are and where their money came from, you'll probably have to provide the following when you open a brokerage account:

>> Your name

>> Date of birth

>> Street address

>> Place of business

>> Social Insurance Number

>> Driver's licence and passport

>> Copies of financial statements

Rules for day traders

Here's the problem for regulators: Many day traders lose money, and those losses can be magnified by the use of *leverage strategies* (trading with borrowed money, meaning that you can lose more money than you have in the quest for large profits). If the customer who lost the money can't pay up, then the broker is on the hook. If too many customers lose money beyond what the broker can absorb, then the losses ripple through the financial system, and that's not good.

IIROC has a long list of rules that its member firms have to meet in order to stay in business. The organization sets margin requirements and, depending on the type of account, the requirements are stricter to reflect the greater risk. You can get more information on industry compliance at www.iiroc.ca/industry/industrycompliance/Pages/default.aspx.

REMEMBER

The rules set by IIROC are minimum requirements. Brokerage firms are free to set higher limits for account size and borrowing in order to manage their own risks better.

Tax reporting

If you're a long-term investor receiving dividends, your online broker will send you a slip at the end of the year detailing how much income you've made. Traders will also receive tax forms if they received dividends or interest income — this mostly applies to people who hold overnight positions. Brokers may also send out a summary of trades to help track capital gains and losses.

Hot Tips and Insider Trading

The regulations are very clear for things about suitability and money laundering. You get a bunch of forms, you read them, you sign them, you present documentation, and everyone is happy. The rules that keep the markets functioning are clear and easy to follow.

Another set of rules also keeps markets functioning — namely, that no one has an unfair information advantage. If you knew about big merger announcements, interest rate decisions by the Bank of Canada, or a new sugar substitute that would eliminate demand for corn syrup, you could make a lot of money in the stock market, trading options on interest rate futures, or playing in the grain futures market.

Insider trading is a broad term. Any non-public information that a reasonable person would consider when deciding whether to buy or sell a security could apply, and that's a pretty vague standard — especially because the whole purpose of research is to combine bits of immaterial information together to make investment decisions.

WARNING

Day traders can be susceptible to hot tips, because they are buying and selling so quickly. If these hot tips are actually inside information, though, the trader can become liable. If you get great information from someone who is in a position to know — an officer, a director, a lawyer, an investment banker — you may be looking at stiff penalties. According to the Canada Business Corporations Act, courts can assess civil penalties of "any measure of damages it considers relevant in the circumstances." A criminal conviction can land someone in jail for up to ten years.

TECHNICAL
STUFF

Insider trading is difficult to prove, so federal regulators use other tools to punish those it suspects of making improper profits. In the United States, Martha Stewart wasn't sent to prison on insider trading charges; she was charged with obstructing justice by lying to investigators about what happened.

Whenever a big announcement is made, such as a merger, the exchanges go back and review trading for several days before to see whether any unusual activities occurred in relevant securities and derivatives. Then they start tracing them back to the traders involved through the brokerage firms to see whether it was coincidence or part of a pattern.

REMEMBER

The bottom line is this: You may never come across inside information. But if a tip seems too good to be true, it probably is — so be careful.

Taking on Partners

After your day trading proves to be wildly successful, you might want to take on partners to give you more trading capital and a slightly more regular income from the management fees. You can do it, but it's a lot of work.

If you start trading as a business a good chance exists you'll have to register with your provincial securities commission as a dealer, an investment fund manager, or perhaps something else depending on what you're doing. What triggers registration is complicated. If you're thinking about bringing people on board, it's best to call your securities commission or a lawyer and ask them what you need to do. You may also want to read part 25.1 of the Ontario Securities Act (www.ontario.ca/laws/statute/90s05) to find out which category you'd fall under.

WARNING

Registration is not a do-it-yourself project. An error or omission may have tremendous repercussions down the line, from fines to jail time. If you want to take on partners for your trading business, spend the money for qualified legal advice. It will protect you and show prospective customers that you're serious about your business.

6

Cryptocurrency Investing

Contents at a Glance

Chapter **1**

What Is a Cryptocurrency?

So you've looked at the title of Book 6, and your first question is probably this: "What the heck is a cryptocurrency, anyway?" Simply stated, a *cryptocurrency* is a new form of digital money. You can transfer your traditional, non-cryptocurrency money like the Canadian dollar digitally, but that's not quite the same as how cryptocurrencies work. When cryptocurrencies become mainstream, you may be able to use them to pay for stuff electronically, just like you do with traditional currencies.

However, what sets cryptocurrencies apart is the technology behind them. You may say, "Who cares about the technology behind my money? I only care about how much of it there is in my wallet!" The issue is that the world's current money systems have a bunch of problems. Here are some examples:

» They require a "trusted" third party to verify transactions.

» Payment systems such as credit cards and wire transfers are outdated.

» In most cases, a bunch of middlemen like banks and brokers take a cut in the process, making transactions expensive and slow.

» Financial inequality is growing around the globe.

» Around 3 billion unbanked or underbanked people can't access financial services. That's approximately half the population on the planet!

Cryptocurrencies aim to solve some of these problems, if not more. This chapter introduces you to crypto fundamentals.

TIP

The Canadian government has information on cryptocurrencies at www.canada. ca/en/revenue-agency/programs/about-canada-revenue-agency-cra/ compliance/digital-currency.html.

Beginning with the Basics of Cryptocurrencies

You know how your everyday, government-based currency is reserved in banks? And that you need an ATM or a connection to a bank to get more of it or transfer it to other people? Well, with cryptocurrencies, you may be able to get rid of banks and other centralized middlemen altogether. That's because cryptocurrencies rely on a technology called *blockchain*, which is *decentralized* (meaning no single entity is in charge of it). Instead, a network of computers is in charge of verifying transactions.

The following sections go over the basics of cryptocurrencies: their background, benefits, and more.

The definition of money

Before getting into the nitty-gritty of cryptocurrencies, you need to understand the definition of money itself. The philosophy behind money is a bit like the whole "which came first: the chicken or the egg?" thing. In order for money to be valuable, it must have a number of characteristics, such as the following:

>> Enough people must have it.

>> Merchants must accept it as a form of payment.

>> Society must trust that it's valuable and that it will remain valuable in the future.

Of course, in the old days, when you traded your chicken for shoes, the values of the exchanged materials were inherent to their nature. But when coins, cash, and credit cards came into play, the definition of money and, more importantly, the trust model of money changed.

Another key change in money has been its ease of transaction. The hassle of carrying a ton of gold bars from one country to another was one of the main reasons cash was invented. Then, when people got even lazier, credit cards were invented. But credit cards carry the money that your government controls. As the world becomes more interconnected and more concerned about authorities who may or may not have people's best interests in mind, cryptocurrencies may offer a valuable alternative.

Here's a fun fact: Your normal, government-backed currency, such as the Canadian dollar, must go by its fancy name, *fiat currency,* now that cryptocurrencies are around. Fiat is described as a legal tender like coins and banknotes that have value only because the government says so.

Some cryptocurrency history

The first ever cryptocurrency was (drumroll please) Bitcoin! You probably have heard of Bitcoin more than any other thing in the crypto industry. Bitcoin was the first product of the first blockchain developed by some anonymous entity who went by the name Satoshi Nakamoto. Satoshi released the idea of Bitcoin in 2008 paper and described it as a "purely peer-to-peer version" of electronic money.

**TECHNICAL
STUFF**

Bitcoin was the first established cryptocurrency, but many attempts at creating digital currencies occurred years before Bitcoin was formally introduced.

Cryptocurrencies like Bitcoin are created through a process called *mining.* Very different than mining ore (but certainly named after it), mining cryptocurrencies involves powerful computers solving complicated mathematical problems. Flip to Chapter 4 in Book 6 for more on mining.

Bitcoin remained the only cryptocurrency until 2011. Then Bitcoin enthusiasts started noticing flaws in it, so they decided to create alternative coins, also known as *altcoins,* to improve Bitcoin's design for things like speed, security, anonymity, and more. Among the first altcoins was Litecoin, which aimed to become the silver to Bitcoin's gold.

Key crypto benefits

Following are a number of solutions that cryptocurrencies may be able to provide through their decentralized nature:

>> **Reducing corruption:** With great power comes great responsibility. But when you give a ton of power to only one person or entity, the chances of their abusing that power increase. The 19th-century British politician Lord Acton

said it best: "Power tends to corrupt, and absolute power corrupts absolutely." Cryptocurrencies aim to resolve the issue of absolute power by distributing power among many people or, better yet, among all the members of the network. That's the key idea behind blockchain technology anyway.

>> **Eliminating extreme money printing:** Governments have central banks, and central banks have the ability to simply print money when they're faced with a serious economic problem. By printing more money, a government may be able to bail out debt or devalue its currency. However, this approach is like putting a bandage on a broken leg. Not only does it rarely solve the problem, but the negative side effects also can sometimes surpass the original issue.

For example, when a country like Iran or Venezuela prints too much money, the value of its currency drops so much that inflation skyrockets and people can't even afford to buy everyday goods and services. Their cash becomes barely as valuable as rolls of toilet paper. Most cryptocurrencies have a limited, set amount of coins available. When all those coins are in circulation, a central entity or the company behind the blockchain has no easy way to simply create more coins or add on to its supply.

>> **Giving people charge of their own money:** With traditional cash, you're basically giving away all your control to central banks and the government. With cryptocurrencies, you and only you can access your funds. (Unless someone steals them from you, that is.)

>> **Cutting out the middleman:** With traditional money, every time you make a transfer, a middleman like your bank or a digital payment service takes a cut. With cryptocurrencies, all the network members in the blockchain are that middleman; their compensation is formulated differently from that of fiat money middlemen's and therefore is minimal in comparison. Flip to Chapter 4 in Book 6 for more on how cryptocurrencies work.

>> **Serving the unbanked:** A vast portion of the world's citizens has no access or limited access to payment systems like banks. Cryptocurrencies aim to resolve this issue by spreading digital commerce around the globe so that anyone with a mobile phone can start making payments. And yes, more people have access to mobile phones than to banks. In fact, more people have mobile phones than have toilets, but at this point the blockchain technology may not be able to resolve the latter issue. (Flip to Chapter 2 in Book 6 for more on the social good that can come from cryptocurrencies and blockchain technology.)

Common crypto and blockchain myths

During the 2017 Bitcoin hype, a lot of misconceptions about the whole industry started to circulate. These myths may have played a role in the cryptocurrency crash that followed the surge. The important thing to remember is that both the blockchain technology and its by-product, the cryptocurrency market, are still in their infancy, and things are rapidly changing. Time to get some of the most common misunderstandings out of the way:

>> **Cryptocurrencies are good only for criminals.** Some cryptocurrencies boast anonymity as one of their key features. That means your identity isn't revealed when you're making transactions. Other cryptocurrencies are based on a decentralized blockchain, meaning a central government isn't the sole power behind them. These features do make such cryptocurrencies attractive for criminals; however, law-abiding citizens in corrupt countries can also benefit from them. For example, if you don't trust your local bank or country because of corruption and political instability, the best way to store your money may be through the blockchain and cryptocurrency assets.

>> **You can make anonymous transactions using all cryptocurrencies.** For some reason, many people equate Bitcoin with anonymity. But Bitcoin, along with many other cryptocurrencies, doesn't incorporate anonymity at all. All transactions made using such cryptocurrencies are made on public blockchain. Some cryptocurrencies, such as Monero, do prioritize privacy, meaning no outsider can find the source, amount, or destination of transactions. However, most other cryptocurrencies, including Bitcoin, don't operate that way.

>> **The only application of blockchain is Bitcoin.** This idea couldn't be further from the truth. Bitcoin and other cryptocurrencies are a tiny by-product of the blockchain revolution. Many believe Satoshi created Bitcoin simply to provide an example of how the blockchain technology can work. Almost every industry and business in the world can use the blockchain technology in its specific field.

>> **All blockchain activity is private.** Many people falsely believe that the blockchain technology isn't open to the public and is accessible only to its network of common users. Although some companies create their own private blockchains to be used only among employees and business partners, the majority of the blockchains behind famous cryptocurrencies such as Bitcoin are accessible by the public. Literally anyone with a computer can access the transactions in real time. For example, you can view the real-time Bitcoin transactions at www.blockchain.com.

Risks

Just like anything else in life, cryptocurrencies come with their own baggage of risk. Whether you trade cryptos, invest in them, or simply hold on to them for the future, you must assess and understand the risks beforehand. Some of the most talked-about cryptocurrency risks include their volatility and lack of regulation. Volatility got especially out of hand in 2017, when the price of most major cryptocurrencies, including Bitcoin, skyrocketed above 1,000 percent and then came crashing down. However, as the cryptocurrency hype has calmed down, the price fluctuations have become more predictable and followed similar patterns of stocks and other financial assets.

Regulations are another major topic in the industry. The funny thing is that both lack of regulation and exposure to regulations can turn into risk events for cryptocurrency investors. Chapter 3 in Book 6 explores these and other types of risks, as well as methods of managing them.

Gearing Up to Make Transactions

Cryptocurrencies are here to make transactions easier and faster. But before you take advantage of these benefits, you must gear up with crypto gadgets, discover where you can get your hands on different cryptocurrencies, and get to know the cryptocurrency community. Some of the essentials include cryptocurrency wallets and exchanges.

Wallets

Some *cryptocurrency wallets,* which hold your purchased cryptos, are similar to digital payment services like Apple Pay and PayPal. But generally, they're different from traditional wallets and come in different formats and levels of security.

REMEMBER

You can't get involved in the cryptocurrency market without a crypto wallet. Be sure to get the most secure type of wallet, such as hardware or paper wallets, instead of using the convenient online ones.

Exchanges

After you get yourself a crypto wallet (see the preceding section), you're ready to go crypto shopping, and one of the best destinations is a cryptocurrency exchange. These online web services are where you can transfer your traditional money to buy cryptocurrencies, exchange different types of cryptocurrencies, or even store your cryptocurrencies.

WARNING

Storing your cryptocurrencies on an exchange is considered high risk because many such exchanges have been exposed to hacking attacks and scams in the past. When you're done with your transactions, your best bet is to move your new digital assets to your personal, secure wallet.

Exchanges come in different shapes and forms. Some are like traditional stock exchanges and act as a middleman — something crypto enthusiasts believe is a slap in the face of the cryptocurrency market, which is trying to remove a centralized middleman. Others are decentralized and provide a service where buyers and sellers come together and transact in a peer-to-peer manner, but they come with their own sets of problems, like the risk of locking yourself out. A third type of crypto exchange is called *hybrid*, and it merges the benefits of the other two types to create a better, more secure experience for users.

TIP

For an introductory list of cryptocurrency exchanges in Canada, see `https://cryptohead.io/canada/best-exchanges/`.

Communities

TIP

Getting to know the crypto community can be the next step as you're finding your way in the market. The web has plenty of chat rooms and support groups to give you a sense of the market and what people are talking about. Here are some ways to get involved:

>> **Crypto-specific Telegram groups.** Many cryptocurrencies have their very own channels on the Telegram app. To join them, you first need to download the Telegram messenger app on your smartphone or computer; it's available for iOS and Android.

>> **Crypto chat rooms on Reddit or BitcoinTalk:** BitcoinTalk (`https://bitcointalk.org/`) and Reddit (`www.reddit.com/`) have some of the oldest crypto chat rooms around. You can view some topics without signing up, but if you want to get involved, you need to log in. (Of course, Reddit isn't exclusive to cryptos, but you can search for a variety of cryptocurrency topics.)

>> **TradingView chat room:** One of the best trading platforms out there, TradingView (`www.tradingview.com/`) also has a social service where traders and investors of all sorts come together and share their thoughts, questions, and ideas.

>> **Invest Diva's Premium Investing Group:** If you're looking for a less crowded and more investment/trading-focused place to get support, you can join our investment group (and chat directly with me, coauthor Kiana, as a perk too) at `https://learn.investdiva.com/join-group`.

REMEMBER

On the flip side, many scammers also target these kinds of platforms to advertise and lure members into trouble. Keep your wits about you.

Making a Plan Before You Jump In

You may just want to buy some cryptocurrencies and save them for their potential growth in the future. Or you may want to become more of an active investor and buy or sell cryptocurrencies more regularly to maximize profit and revenue. Regardless, you must have a plan and a strategy. Even if your transaction is a one-time thing and you don't want to hear anything about your crypto assets for the next ten years, you still must gain the knowledge necessary to determine things like the following:

>> What to buy

>> When to buy

>> How much to buy

>> When to sell

The following sections give you a quick overview of the steps you must take before buying your first cryptocurrency.

If you're not fully ready to buy cryptocurrencies, no worries: You can try some alternatives, like mining, stocks, and more.

Select your cryptos

Over 1,600 cryptocurrencies are out there at the time of writing, and the number is growing. Some of these cryptos may vanish in five years. Others may explode over 1,000 percent and may even replace traditional cash. The most famous cryptocurrencies right now include Ethereum, Ripple, Litecoin, Bitcoin Cash, and Stellar Lumens.

You can select cryptocurrencies based on things like category, popularity, ideology, the management behind the blockchain, and its economic model.

Because the crypto industry is pretty new, it's still very hard to identify the best-performing cryptos for long-term investments. That's why you may benefit from diversifying among various types and categories of cryptocurrencies in order to manage your risk. By diversifying across 15 or more cryptos, you can stack up the odds of having winners in your portfolio. On the flip side, overdiversification can become problematic as well, so you need to take calculated measures.

Analyze, invest, and profit

When you've narrowed down the cryptocurrencies you like, you must then identify the best time to buy them. For example, in 2017 many people started to believe in the idea of Bitcoin and wanted to get involved. Unfortunately, many of those people mismanaged the timing and bought when the price had peaked. Therefore, they not only were able to buy fewer bits of Bitcoin (pun intended), but they also had to sit on their losses and wait for the next price surge.

By analyzing the price action and conducting proper risk management, you may be able to stack the odds in your favour and make a ton of profit in the future.

Chapter **2**

Why Invest in Cryptocurrencies?

Whether you're a seasoned investor who has been exposed only to investment assets other than cryptos or you're just starting to invest (in anything!) for the first time, you're probably wondering why you should consider including cryptocurrencies in your portfolio. You've probably heard about Bitcoin here and there. Heck, you may have even heard of other cryptocurrencies such as Ethereum and Litecoin. But what's the big deal about all these funny-sounding coins anyway? Is Litecoin just a very light coin that won't take much space in your physical wallet? Is a Bitcoin made of bits and pieces of other valuable coins? Why on earth should you invest in bits of coins?

Cryptocurrency investing may make sense for many investors, for a growing number of reasons — from things as simple as diversification to more exciting stuff like joining the revolutionary movement toward the future of how we perceive money. This chapter shows you some exciting features of this new investment kid on the block and gives you a general overview of the market as a whole. That way, you can decide whether the cryptocurrency industry is the right route for you to grow your wealth.

TIP

Although you can read this book in any order, consider reading Chapter 3 in Book 6 right after this one. That chapter explains the other side of the coin, which involves the risks surrounding cryptocurrencies.

Diversifying from Traditional Investments

Diversification is the good ol' "don't put all your eggs in one basket" thing. You can apply this advice to literally anything in life. If you're travelling, don't put all your underwear in your checked-in luggage. Put an emergency pair in your carry-on in case your luggage gets lost. If you're grocery shopping, don't buy only apples. Even though they say "an apple a day keeps the doctor away," you still need the nutrition in other kinds of vegetables and fruit.

You can go about investment diversification in so many ways. You can diversify with different financial assets, like stocks, bonds, foreign exchange (forex), and so on. You can diversify based on industry, like technology, healthcare, and entertainment. You can allocate your investment by having multiple investment time frames, both short-term and long-term. Adding cryptocurrencies to your investment portfolio is essentially one way of balancing that portfolio. Especially because the cryptocurrency industry is vastly different from traditional ones, this diversification may increase the potential of maximizing your portfolio's growth. One of the main reasons for this higher potential is that the cryptocurrency market may react differently to various global and financial events.

The following sections explain more by briefly looking into some of the traditional markets and exploring their differences from the cryptocurrency market.

Stocks

The stock market gives you the opportunity to take a bite of the profits a company makes (as you find out in Book 2). By buying stocks of that company, you become a part-owner of that firm. The more stocks you buy, the bigger your slice of the cake. And of course, the higher the risk you face if the whole cake is thrown out in the garbage.

The stock market is perhaps one of the most appealing investment assets. Novice investors may pick up a stock or two just because they like the company. For most investors, the charm of stock investing is the possibility that the prices will increase over time and generate significant capital gains. Some stocks even provide you with a periodic income stream through something called *dividends*. (Chapter 3 in Book 6 explains more about capital gains and dividend income.) Regardless, for most stocks, the dividends paid within a year are nothing compared to the increase of the stock's value, especially when the economic environment is upbeat.

REMEMBER

This is precisely what stocks and cryptocurrencies have in common: When their respective markets are strong, you can generally expect to benefit from price appreciation.

Make no mistake, though, both markets have their bad days and sometimes even bad years. The stock market has a longer history that can guide investors through navigating the future. For example, even though it may not always seem like it, bad days happen less often than good ones. Figure 2-1 shows that for the 70 years between 1947 and 2017, the Dow, one of the main stock market indexes in the United States, ended the year at a lower price only 28.6 percent of the time (20 years). The other 71.4 percent (50 years), it went up.

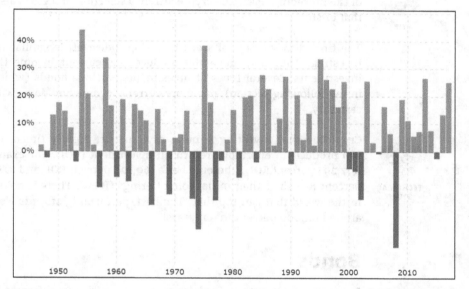

FIGURE 2-1:
Dow Jones 70-year historical chart by year.

Source: Macrotrends.net

However, stock investing naturally has some disadvantages. For example,

>> **Stocks face different types of risks.** Even the most awesome stocks have risks that you can't easily eliminate, such as the following (see Chapter 3 in Book 6 for details):

- Business and financial risk

- Purchasing power risk

- Market risk

- Event risk

- Government control and regulations
- Foreign competition
- The general state of the economy

>> **The stock selection process can be a pain in the neck.** You have literally thousands of stocks to choose from. Predicting how the company will perform tomorrow can also be very difficult. After all, the price today only reflects the current state of the company or what the market participants perceive it to be.

TIP

By investing in the cryptocurrency market, you may be able to average out some of the preceding risks. The cryptocurrency selection process is also different from that of stocks.

The final disadvantage of stock investing, however, is similar to that of crypto investing. They both generally produce less current income than some other investments. Several types of investments, such as bonds (which are discussed in the following section), pay more current income and do so with much greater certainty.

TECHNICAL
STUFF

Cryptocurrency investing is quite asymmetric. Rightly timed, crypto investing can produce an enormous return on investment (ROI). For example, NXT has a 697,295 percent ROI, Ethereum has a 160,100 percent ROI, and IOTA has a 282,300 percent ROI since their initial coin offerings (ICOs). There is no other investment in the world that can top that. The best-performing stock is Netflix, and that's around 64,000 percent in ten years!

Bonds

Bonds are also known as *fixed-income securities.* They're different from cryptocurrencies and stocks in that you loan money to an entity for a period of time, and you receive a fixed amount of interest on a periodic basis. Hence its categorization as "fixed income."

Just like with cryptocurrencies and stocks (see the preceding section), you can also expect capital gains from bonds. But these capital gains work a bit differently. Because the companies issuing bonds promise to repay a fixed amount when the bonds mature, bond prices don't typically rise in correlation with the firm's profits. The bond prices rise and fall as market interest rates change.

Another similarity among bonds, cryptocurrencies, and stocks is that they're all issued by a wide range of companies. Additionally, many governmental bodies issue bonds. So if you're looking to diversify only within the bonds market, you still can choose from a range of relatively safe ones to highly speculative ones.

Compared to cryptocurrencies and stocks, bonds are generally less risky and provide higher current income. But they still are subject to a variety of risks. Some of the risks involved with bonds investing are similar to those of cryptocurrencies and stocks — namely, purchasing power risk, business and financial risk, and liquidity risk. Bonds have an additional type of risk known as the *call risk* or *prepayment risk.* Call risk is the risk that a bond will be *called,* or retired, long before its maturity date. If the bond issuer calls its bonds, you'll have to find another place for your funds.

REMEMBER

The potential for very high returns on bonds is much lower compared to cryptocurrencies and stocks, respectively. But the risk involved with bonds is also comparatively lower. You can find more about cryptocurrency risks in Chapter 3 of Book 6.

Forex

Here's an alternative investment that may be even riskier than cryptocurrencies. *Forex* is the geek term for the foreign exchange market. It's the first thing I (coauthor Kiana) ever invested in. I've written books about it (*Invest Diva's Guide to Making Money in Forex* [McGraw-Hill Education] and *Ichimoku Secrets* [CreateSpace Independent Publishing Platform]). In fact, my company's original name was Forex Diva! We then switched to Invest Diva, literally in order to emphasize the importance of diversification.

By participating in the forex market, you buy and sell currencies. Not cryptocurrencies, but fiat currencies such as the Canadian dollar, the U.S. dollar, the euro, the British pound, the Australian dollar, or any other currency any government issues. A *fiat currency* is a country's legal tender that's issued by the government.

Before Bitcoin became the celebrity of financial assets in 2017, most people associated cryptocurrencies such as Bitcoin with the traditional forex market because "cryptocurrency" includes the word "currency," and crypto owners hoped to use their assets to make payments. However, as mentioned earlier in this chapter, cryptocurrencies also have a lot in common with stocks.

When you participate in the forex market, you don't necessarily invest for long-term capital gains. Even the most popular currencies such as the U.S. dollar are subject to a ton of volatility throughout the year. A good U.S. economy doesn't always translate into a stronger U.S. dollar.

TECHNICAL STUFF

Heck, sometimes some countries, such as Japan, prefer to have a weaker currency because they rely heavily on exports. If their currencies are stronger than the currency of the country they're trying to sell stuff to, they get a lower rate to sell the same product abroad than domestically.

Participating in the forex market as an investor mainly consists of short-to-medium-term trading activity between different currency pairs. You can buy the euro versus the U.S. dollar (the EUR/USD pair), for example. If the euro's value appreciates relative to the U.S. dollar's, you make money. However, if the U.S. dollar's value goes higher than the euro's, you lose money.

Analyzing the forex market needs a very different approach when compared to stock and cryptocurrency analysis. When looking at the forex markets, you need to focus on the issuing country's economic state, its upcoming economic figures such as its *gross domestic product* (GDP, or the value of the goods produced inside the country), unemployment rate, inflation, interest rate, and so on, as well as its political environment.

However, just like the cryptocurrency market, you need to trade forex in pairs. In my online forex education course, the *Forex Coffee Break,* I compare these pairs to dancing couples — international couples who push each other back and forth. Traders can make money by speculating which direction the couple will move next. You can see this metaphor in Figure 2-2, where the Australian dollar (AUD, or Mr. Aussie) is dancing against the U.S. dollar (USD, or Ms. USA).

FIGURE 2-2:
Forex metaphor: Australian dollar dancing against U.S. dollar.

Source: InvestDiva.com

You can apply a similar concept to the cryptocurrency market. For example, you can pair up Bitcoin (BTC) and Ethereum (ETH) against each other. You can even pair up a cryptocurrency such as Bitcoin against a fiat currency such as the Canadian dollar and speculate their value against each other. However, in these cases you need to analyze each currency, crypto or fiat, separately. Then you need to measure their relative value against each other and predict which currency will win the couple's battle in the future.

TIP

You can also consider cryptocurrencies as a cross between stocks and forex. Though many investors invest in cryptocurrencies for capital gain purposes, you can also trade different cryptocurrencies against each other, the way you can in the forex market.

Precious metals

Time to compare one of the most recent man-made means to buy stuff (cryptocurrencies) to one of the most ancient ones! No, not *bartering,* where people exchanged their goods and services to fulfill their needs. The following sections talk about the stuff with a bling. Before the advent of paper money, precious metals such as gold and silver were long used to make coins and to buy stuff.

REMEMBER

The precious metals comparison is actually the best argument when someone tells you cryptocurrencies are worthless because they don't have any intrinsic value. Flip to Book 4 for more about precious metals.

Getting a little background

Back in the days of bartering, people would exchange stuff that provided real value to their human needs: chickens, clothes, or farming services. Supposedly, people in the ancient civilization of Lydia were among the first to use coins made of gold and silver in exchange for goods and services. Imagine the first shopper who tried to convince the seller to accept a gold coin instead of three chickens that could feed a family for a week. This change was followed by leather money, paper money, credit cards, and now cryptocurrencies.

Some may argue that precious metals like gold do too have intrinsic value. They're durable. They conduct both heat and electricity and therefore have some industrial application. But to be honest, most people don't invest in precious metals because they're trying to conduct electricity. They primarily buy them to use as jewelry or currency. Today, market sentiment mainly determines the value of gold and silver.

TECHNICAL STUFF

Silver has more use as an industrial metal than gold does. Silver is used in batteries, electrical appliances, medical products, and other industrial items. However, despite the additional demand, silver is valued lower than gold.

Even though precious metals don't have an arguable intrinsic value, they have long been a favourite investment tool among market participants. One of the main reasons is their historical association with wealth. Often, when investments such as bonds, real estate, and the stock market go down or the political environment is uncertain, people flock to precious metals. People prefer to own precious metals at these times because they can actually physically touch metals and keep them in their homes right next to their beds.

Comparing precious metals to cryptocurrencies

Besides the fact that you need to mine in order to get your hands on precious metals and some cryptocurrencies, one key similarity between precious metals and cryptocurrencies is that both categories have unregulated characteristics. Gold has been an unregulated currency at various times and in various places. Unregulated currencies become more valuable when investors don't trust the official currency, and cryptocurrencies just seem to be another example of this trend.

REMEMBER

Investing in precious metals comes with a number of risk factors you need to keep in mind. For example, if you're buying physical precious metals as an investment, you must consider their portability risk. Transferring precious metals can be expensive given their weight, high import taxes, and the need for a high level of security. In contrast, you don't need to make a physical transfer with cryptocurrencies, besides hardware crypto wallets. But moving cryptocurrencies is much faster and less expensive, even with a hardware wallet, than transferring precious metals.

On the other hand, cryptocurrency prices have been more volatile in the short time they've been available on the markets than all precious metals combined have. The 2017 volatility in particular was due to the hype in the market, as Chapter 3 in Book 6 explains. As cryptocurrency investing becomes more mainstream and more people use it for everyday transactions, crypto prices may become more predictable.

Gaining Capital Appreciation

Capital appreciation refers to the increase in the price or value of cryptocurrencies. And it's one of the reasons many investors (and noninvestors, for that matter) look to jump on the cryptocurrency train. Initial Bitcoin owners sure waited years before they saw any sort of capital appreciation.

The following sections look at the history of capital appreciation for cryptocurrencies and discuss their growth potential — a big reason to consider investing in them.

REMEMBER

With great expectations of capital appreciation and huge growth potential come great expectations of capital losses. That's why you should read Chapter 3 in Book 6 before starting your trading activity in the cryptocurrency market.

Historical returns

Most of the gains in the cryptocurrency market up to 2017 were a result of market hype. In 2013, for example, many people bought Bitcoin as its price approached $1,000 (in U.S. dollars) for the first time. As you can see in Figure 2-3, shortly after, its price crashed to around $300, where it stayed for the following two years.

FIGURE 2-3:
Bitcoin price between 2013 and January 2017.

Source: tradingview.com

The next big wave of growth came in January 2017, when Bitcoin's price broke above the $1,000 level.

If you had bought one Bitcoin at $300 at the end of 2015, by January 2017 you would've had $700 worth of capital appreciation (when the price hit $1,000). But of course, the gains didn't stop there. As you can see in Figure 2-4, after the break above $1,000, Bitcoin's price managed to go all the way up to close to $20,000 by the end of 2017, when it came crashing down to a range around $6,000.

For people who had bought (or mined) Bitcoin when it was valued at around $300 and held on to it throughout the volatility, the crash to $6,000 wasn't that big of a deal. For every Bitcoin they'd bought at $300, they had around $5,700 worth of capital appreciation even if they didn't cash their Bitcoins in when the value reached above $19,000.

FIGURE 2-4:
Bitcoin price
between 2016
and July 2018.

Source: tradingview.com

People who bought Bitcoin at around $1,000 and cashed it out at $19,000 at its 2017 peak would've made $18,000 for every Bitcoin they owned. Of course, those who bought Bitcoin at $19,000 had to sit on their hands and eat their losses after the crash.

Many market participants compare Bitcoin and other cryptocurrencies' appreciation to the dot-com bubble from the mid-1990s and early 2000s. According to *Fortune* magazine, since its creation in 2009 until March 2018, Bitcoin saw four bear (falling) waves, where prices dropped 45 to 50 percent, typically rebounding an average of 47 percent afterward. During the dot-com bubble, the Nasdaq composite index had five of those waves, averaging 44 percent declines followed by 40 percent rebounds. Trading volume patterns are also eerily similar.

Nasdaq has clearly rallied nicely from its low in 2002. Though history and past performance aren't indicative of future behaviour, crypto enthusiasts have reasons to believe that growth potential for cryptocurrencies may be similar to the Nasdaq rebound, if not better.

Huge growth potential

Bitcoin and cryptocurrencies were the biggest investment story of 2017. Stories appeared daily on CNBC, and in the *Wall Street Journal* and *New York Times*, about people becoming millionaires practically overnight.

However, after January 2018, the price of Bitcoin fell 63 percent. The media followed suit appropriately, saying the opportunity had passed — that the cryptocurrency bull market was over and the bubble had burst.

This tune was interesting, especially because many billionaires became crypto investors at this point. For example, J.P. Morgan CEO Jamie Dimon (who had called Bitcoin a fraud and said any J.P. Morgan traders caught trading Bitcoin would be fired) became one of the most active buyers of a fund that tracks the price of Bitcoin. The price of Bitcoin fell as much as 24 percent in the few days that followed Dimon's statement, and sure enough, right in that period, J.P. Morgan and Morgan Stanley started buying for their clients at low prices.

This story isn't alone in the crypto market. For example, after slamming Bitcoin at the World Economic Forum in Davos, Switzerland, in January 2018, calling it a "bubble," hedge fund titan George Soros gave the green light to his $26 billion family office to begin buying cryptocurrencies just eight weeks later.

TECHNICAL STUFF

Interestingly, Soros attributes part of his success to his understanding of what he calls "reflexivity." In simple terms, this theory states that investors base their decisions not on reality but on their perception of reality. Soros once said, "The degree of distortion may vary from time to time. Sometimes it's quite insignificant, at other times it is quite pronounced. Every bubble has two components: an underlying trend that prevails in reality and a misconception relating to that trend."

The problem is that most people have no clue what's really going on in the cryptocurrency market. And most have no idea where the price is about to go next. The majority of those interested in the market are taking their cues from market noise, making it way easier for the prices to fall when the big movers downplay for their own benefit.

"Going against the crowd" is one of the key pillars in my *Invest Diva Diamond Analysis (IDDA)*, as well as in the *Make Your Money Work for You PowerCourse* at https://learn.investdiva.com/free-webinar-3-secrets-to-making-your-money-work-for-you. When the majority of the market panics about the drops in the value of an asset, it is often the best time to stack up on it. You can say the same about the cryptocurrency market. For the cryptocurrencies with strong blockchain technology behind them, once the price bottoms out, there is nowhere for its value to go but up.

Increasing Income Potential

Although gaining capital appreciation is one of the most attractive features of cryptocurrency investing (as explained earlier in this chapter), you can also take advantage of some cryptocurrencies that pay something similar to dividends in the stock market.

A bit about traditional dividends

By definition, a *dividend* is a sum of money public companies pay their share-holders on a regular basis. Corporations pay billions of dollars' worth of dividends every year. Yet in spite of these numbers, many investors (especially young ones) don't pay much attention to dividends. They prefer capital gains because the rewards can be quicker and can way exceed any amount of dividend payment.

TECHNICAL STUFF

In the traditional stock market, companies typically pay dividends on a quarterly basis. A firm's board of directors decides how much to pay shareholders in dividends or whether to pay dividends at all. Sometimes, the directors decide to pay dividends because the stock value isn't doing so well. So they select a higher dividend rate to keep investors interested in buying the stocks.

REMEMBER

Investors with lower risk tolerance may prefer dividend payments to capital gains because dividend payments don't fluctuate as much as the value of stocks do. Furthermore, if the markets crash like they did in 2008, dividends can provide nice protection. The best way to accumulate dividends is to hold onto your assets long-term.

The basics on crypto dividends

During the crypto mania of 2017, many cryptocurrency platforms were quick to realize the importance of regular payments to keep investors happy. But these payments can be a bit different than traditional stock dividends. You can generate regular, passive income in the crypto market in several ways. Here are the two most popular ones:

>> **HODLing:** No, this term is not a typo for "holding," although it has a similar meaning. It stands for "Hold On for Dear Life." It is the closest payment to traditional dividends. Some cryptocurrencies pay out the HODLers, who simply purchase and carry the digital coins in their wallets.

>> **Proof-of-stake (PoS):** This is a lighter version of proof-of-work in cryptocurrency mining (see Chapter 4 in Book 6). When you "stake" a coin, it means you put it aside so it can't be used in the blockchain network. If you have a ton of stakes, you have a higher chance of getting paid at a random selection by the network. Annual returns for staking vary between 1 percent and 5 percent, depending on the coin.

Some popular dividend-paying cryptos are NEO, ARK, and exchange cryptocurrencies like Binance and KuCoin.

REMEMBER

While receiving cash (or digital coins) just for holding onto your assets is pretty cool, sometimes it makes more sense to cash out and reinvest your holdings to get a better return.

Fueling Ideological Empowerment

Just as oil is the lubricant that allows a machine to operate, blockchain technology is the lubricant that enables the cryptocurrency market. *Blockchain* is the underlying technology for cryptocurrencies, not to mention one of those breakthrough developments that has the potential to revolutionize nearly every industry in the world completely.

Blockchain can offer so much more as it's aiming to resolve many economic and financial problems in the world today, from dealing with the flaws of the sharing economy to banking the unbanked and underbanked. Here are some of the kinds of social good that come through cryptocurrencies and the blockchain technology.

The economy of the future

We live in an era where the *sharing economy* is exploding. The sharing economy allows people to rent out their own property for use by others. Internet giants such as Google, Facebook, and Twitter rely on the contributions of users as a means to generate value within their own platforms. If you've ever taken an Uber or Lyft rather than a taxi or rented a room on Airbnb instead of a hotel, you're a part of the sharing economy crowd.

However, the traditional sharing economy has its issues, such as the following:

>> **Requiring high fees for using the platforms.**

>> **Hurting individual users but benefitting the underlying corporation:** In most cases, the value produced by the crowd isn't equally redistributed among all who have contributed to the value production. All the profits are captured by the large intermediaries who operate the platforms.

>> **Playing fast and loose with consumer info:** Some companies have abused their power by getting access to private data without customers knowing.

As the sharing economy expands in the future, its problems will likely become more complicated.

In order to combat these issues, several companies are developing blockchain-based sharing economy platforms. These platforms are much more affordable to use and provide much-needed transparency. They limit, and sometimes completely cut out, the need for a centralized middleman. This shift allows true peer-to-peer interactions, eliminating the 20-to-30-percent transaction fees that come with centralized platforms. Because all transactions are logged on blockchains, all users can audit the network's operations.

This approach is possible because of the decentralized nature of blockchain technology, which is ultimately a means for individuals to coordinate common activities, to interact directly with one another, and to govern themselves in a more trustworthy and decentralized manner.

WARNING

Some cryptocurrency transactions aren't entirely free. In many cases, every time there is a transaction on a blockchain, you have to pay the "network fees," which are funds payable to the blockchain network members who are mining your coins/transactions. If you take into consideration the time "wasted" waiting for a transaction to clear (for example, it takes 78 minutes for a Bitcoin transaction to reach consensus), then in reality you may not save anything in fees by going to some blockchain applications.

Blockchain remains the fuel behind the economy of the future, and cryptocurrencies are a by-product to pave the way by distributing the global economy.

Freedom from government control of currency

The rise of Bitcoin and other cryptocurrencies as a trillion-dollar asset class in 2017 was spurred without the oversight of a central bank or monetary authority guaranteeing trust or market conduct. Unlike fiat currencies such as the Canadian dollar and the euro, most cryptocurrencies will never be subject to money printing (officially called *quantitative easing*) by central banks. Most cryptocurrencies operate under controlled supply, which means no printing of money. In fact, networks limit the supply of tokens even in cases where the demand is high. For example, Bitcoin's supply will decrease in time and will reach its final number somewhere around the year 2140. All cryptocurrencies control the supply of the tokens by a schedule written in the code. Translation: The money supply of a cryptocurrency in every given moment in the future can roughly be calculated today.

The lack of government control over cryptocurrencies can also help with lower inflation risk. History has shown over and over again that when a particular government applies bad policies, becomes corrupt, or is faced by crisis, the country's individual currency suffers. This fluctuation in the currency value can lead to the printing of more money. Inflation is the reason why your parents paid less than a dollar for a gallon of milk while you have to pay at least three dollars. How awesome would it be if cryptocurrencies can get rid of government-controlled inflation so that your grandchildren don't have to pay more for stuff than you do?

Help for the unbanked and underbanked

One of the most noble problems cryptocurrencies can solve is banking the *unbanked*. According to Cointelegraph, "2 billion people in the world still don't have a bank account. Most of them live in low- and middle-income emerging markets, but even in high-income countries, large numbers of people are unable to use banks to meet their day-to-day financial needs. This means they don't have access to the convenience, security, and interest that banks provide."

Moreover, many people are *underbanked*; they have access to a bank account but don't have adequate access to the financial services that banks can provide. For example, research indicates that 6 percent of Canadians are unbanked and 28 percent of Canadians are underbanked (see www.greedyrates.ca/blog/unbanked-canadians-turning-away-traditional-financial-institutions/). Without access to savings and credit, these people can't participate in the cycle of economic growth.

TIP

Cryptocurrencies, with the help of blockchain technology, have the potential to help the unbanked and underbanked by letting them create their own financial alternatives efficiently and transparently. All someone needs to start using cryptocurrencies such as Bitcoin and send and receive money is a smartphone or laptop and Internet connection.

IN THIS CHAPTER

» Understanding the concept of return in crypto investing

» Getting to know cryptos' risks

» Seeing an example of cryptocurrency return versus risk

» Exploring different types of cryptocurrency risks

» Applying your risk tolerance to your investment strategy

Chapter **3**

Recognizing the Risks of Cryptocurrencies

So you're excited to jump on the crypto wagon, perhaps because you expect a gigantic *return* (profit) on your investment. That's basically the reward for investing. However, you can't consider return without also looking at risk. *Risk* is the uncertainty surrounding the actual return you generate. What may represent high risk for others may not be as risky for you due to everyone's unique lifestyles and financial circumstances.

Cryptocurrencies have shown their fair share of volatility, which has made some investors millions of dollars while wiping out some others' initial investment. This chapter looks at cryptocurrencies' price volatility, defines cryptocurrency rewards and risk, describes different types of risk, and gives you pointers on managing risk.

Reviewing Cryptocurrency Returns

Different assets generate different types of returns. For example, one source of return is the change in the investment's value. Also, when you invest in the stock market or the forex (foreign exchange) market, you may generate an income in the form of dividends or interest. Investors call these two sources of return *capital gains* (or *capital losses*) and *current income,* respectively.

REMEMBER

Although most people invest in the cryptocurrency market for capital gains, some cryptocurrencies actually offer current income opportunities. You get an introduction to cryptocurrency returns in Chapter 2 of Book 6.

Capital gains (or losses)

The most popular reason for crypto investing is to see gains in the coins' value. Some people associate the coins with precious metals such as gold. Doing so makes sense because, just like gold, a limited amount is available for most cryptocurrencies, and one way to extract many of them is to "mine." (Of course, you don't need to gear up with a pickax and headlamp when mining cryptocurrencies; head to Chapter 4 in Book 6 for an introduction to cryptocurrency mining.)

With that, many investors consider cryptocurrencies to be assets even though the Canada Revenue Agency (CRA) considers cryptos as commodities. People buy these currencies in hopes of selling them when the prices rise more. If the value of your cryptocurrency token goes higher from the time you purchase, you get capital gains when you sell the token. Congrats! If the prices go lower, you end up with capital losses.

Income

Income is a lesser-known type of return in the cryptocurrency market. Income is generated from something called *crypto dividends.*

Traditionally, dividends occur when public companies distribute a portion of their earnings to their shareholders. Traditional types of dividends include cash payments, shares of stock, or other property.

Earning dividends in the crypto market can get a bit more complicated. Different currencies have different operating systems and their own rules and regulations. However, the concept still remains the same. Crypto dividend payments are becoming increasingly popular among altcoins, which are the alternative cryptocurrencies besides Bitcoin. When choosing a cryptocurrency for your portfolio, you can consider looking into crypto dividends as well as the potential of capital gains (discussed in the preceding section).

Some of the most popular ways to earn crypto dividends are

>> **Staking:** Holding a proof-of-stake coin in a special wallet (see Chapter 4 in Book 6)

>> **Holding:** Buying and holding a crypto in any wallet

TIP

At the time of writing, some dividend-paying cryptocurrencies include NEO, KuCoin, BridgeCoin, Neblio, and Komodo. In addition, besides staking and holding, you can earn regular interest payments by participating in crypto lending. For example, you can earn up to 5 percent interest on your cryptos by allowing companies like Celsius Network to give out loans to the general public against cryptos.

Risk: Flipping the Other Side of the Coin

Investment returns are exciting, but you can't consider return without also looking at risk. The sad truth about any type of investment is that the greater the expected return, the greater the risk. Because cryptocurrencies are considered riskier than some other assets, they may also provide higher returns. The relationship between risk and return is called the *risk-return trade-off*.

REMEMBER

Cryptocurrency investing isn't a get-rich-quick scheme. You shouldn't invest in cryptocurrencies by using your life savings or taking out a loan. You must consider your risk tolerance, understand the different sources of cryptocurrency risks, and then develop an investment strategy that's suitable for you — just you, not anyone else — because you're unique, and so is your financial situation.

Also keep in mind that early Bitcoin investors waited years to see any returns. If you don't have the patience required to see meaningful returns on your investment, you may need to forget about investing altogether.

That being said, a healthy amount of risk appetite is essential not only when investing but also in life. Don't get so paranoid about risk that you just never leave the house for fear of getting into an accident!

Glimpsing Cryptocurrencies' Reward versus Risk

One of the main reasons cryptocurrency investing became such a hot topic in 2017 was the crazy surge in the value of major cryptocurrencies such as Bitcoin.

Although you may have heard of Bitcoin the most, it wasn't even among the ten best-performing crypto assets of 2017. Bitcoin's value grew by more than 1,000 percent, but other, lesser-known cryptocurrencies such as Ripple and NEM were among the biggest winners, with a whopping 36,018 percent and 29,842 percent growth, respectively.

Where did Bitcoin stand on the performance list? Fourteenth!

These returns made investors and noninvestors alike super excited about the cryptocurrency market. By the beginning of 2018, almost everyone you knew — your doctor, your rideshare driver, perhaps even your grandmother — was probably talking about Bitcoin, whether or not the person had any experience in any sort of investing.

However, as is true of any type of investment, what goes up must come down, including the cryptocurrency market. Because the cryptocurrency prices had gone up so much, so quickly, the crash was as hard and as speedy. For example, by February 2018, Bitcoin had dropped to the three-month lows of $6,000 from highs of nearly $20,000 (in U.S. dollars).

The cryptocurrency then started to consolidate above the $6,000 support level, forming lowering highs as you can see in Figure 3-1. In this context, *support level* is a price that the market has had difficulty going lower than in the past. In this case, the price had difficulty breaking below $6,000 back in November 2017. *Lower highs* are those mountain-like peaks on the chart. Every peak (high) is lower than the previous one, which indicated a decrease of popularity among market participants.

Many analysts considered the great appreciation of major cryptocurrencies' value to be a bubble. This fluctuation is a heck of a roller-coaster ride in such a short period of time! The returns were great for those who invested early and took profit at the highs. But just imagine investing in the market when the prices were up and watching the value of your investment going lower and lower. That's one of the major risk factors in any type of investing.

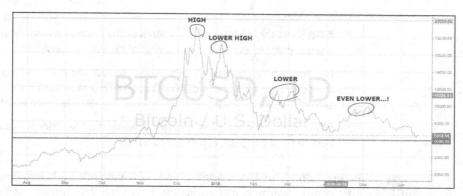

FIGURE 3-1:
Bitcoin's price action versus the U.S. dollar from 2017 to 2018.

Source: *tradingview.com*

Digging into Different Kinds of Risk

Getting educated about risk puts you right on top of your game. Knowing your risk tolerance, you can create a strategy that protects you and your wealth. The risks associated with cryptocurrencies come from many different sources. Here are the various types of crypto risks.

Crypto hype risk

Though getting hyped up in the thought of buying your dream car is a good thing, the hype surrounding cryptocurrencies isn't always as exciting. The main reason cryptos have a lot of hype is that most people don't know about what they're investing in; they just end up listening to the crowd. The crypto hype back in 2017 was one the many drivers of the fast-and-furious market surge. After people started to figure out what they'd invested in, the prices crashed. This type of behaviour became so popular that crypto geeks created their very own lingo around it. Here are a few terms:

>> **FOMO:** This crypto-geek term stands for "Fear of missing out." This happens when you see a massive surge in a crypto you don't own and you hurry in to get your hands on it as the price goes up. Hint: Don't do it! What goes up must come down, so you may be better off waiting for the hype to calm down and buy at lower prices.

>> **FUD:** This is short for "Fear, uncertainty, and doubt." You can use this in a Reddit post when you hear one of those Doctor Doomsdays talking down the market. JPMorgan Chase's CEO, Jamie Dimon, spread one of the biggest FUDs in September 2017 by calling Bitcoin a fraud. In January 2018, he said he regretted saying that.

- **ATH:** Short for "All-time high." Whenever the price of an asset reaches the highest point in its history, you can say, "It's reached an ATH."

- **Bag holder:** You don't want this to be your nickname! Bag holders are those investors who bought out of FOMO at an ATH and missed the chance of selling. Therefore, they are left with a bag (wallet) filled with worthless coins.

- **BTFD:** This one stands for "Buy the f@#&ing dip!" In order for you not to become a bag holder, you've got to BTFD.

REMEMBER

Before falling for the market noise, arm yourself with knowledge on the specific cryptos you're considering. You have plenty of opportunities to make lots of money in the crypto market. Be patient and acquire the right knowledge instead of betting on the current hype. An investor who trades on the hype probably doesn't even have an investment strategy — unless you call gambling a strategy!

Security risk

Scams. Hacking. Theft. These issues have been a common theme in the cryptocurrency market since Bitcoin's inception in 2009. And with each scandal, the cryptocurrencies' values are compromised as well, although temporarily. Your cryptocurrency can be compromised in three main ways, which are outlined in the following sections. You should definitely follow safety precautions in every step of your cryptocurrency investing strategy.

Safety check #1: The cryptocurrency itself

Hundreds of cryptocurrencies are already available for investments, with thousands of new ICOs (initial coin offerings) on the way. When choosing the cryptocurrency to invest in, you must educate yourself on the blockchain's protocol and make sure no bugs (or rumours of bugs) may compromise your investment. The protocol is the common set of rules that the blockchain network has agreed upon. You may be able to find out about the nature of the cryptocurrency's protocol on its white paper on its website. The white paper is an official document that the crypto founders put together before their ICO, laying out everything there is to know about the cryptocurrency. But companies are unlikely to share their shortcomings in their white papers. That's why reading reviews on savvy websites like Reddit and InvestDiva.com can often be your best bet.

These types of bugs appear even in the major cryptocurrencies. For example, a lot of negative press surrounded EOS's release of the first version of its open source software before June 2, 2018. A Chinese security firm had found a bug in the EOS code that could theoretically have been used to create tokens out of thin air. However, EOS was able to fix the bugs. To further turn the bad press into positive,

Block.one, the developer of EOS, invited people to hunt for undiscovered bugs in return for monetary rewards (a process known as a *bug bounty*).

WARNING

Reliable cryptocurrency issuers should take matters into their own hands immediately when a bug is found. But until they do, you're wise to keep your hands off their coins!

Safety check #2: The exchange

Exchanges are where you trade the cryptocurrency tokens. You need to make sure that your trading host is trustworthy and credible. Countless numbers of security incidents and data breaches have occurred in the crypto community because of the exchanges.

One of the famous initial hacks was that of Japan-based Mt. Gox, the largest Bitcoin exchange, in 2013. At the time, Mt. Gox was handling 70 percent of the world's Bitcoin exchanges. However, it had many issues, such as lack of a testing policy, lack of a version control software, and lack of a proper management. As all these problems piled up, in February 2014 the exchange became the victim of a massive hack, where about 850,000 Bitcoins were lost. Although 200,000 Bitcoins were eventually recovered, the remaining 650,000 have never been recovered.

Many exchanges have learned a lesson from this incident and are keeping up with the latest safety measures. However, exchange hacks still happen almost on a monthly basis.

WARNING

In centralized exchanges, which are like traditional stock exchanges, the buyers and sellers come together, and the exchange plays the role of a middleman. These exchanges typically charge a commission to facilitate the transactions made between the buyers and the sellers. In the cryptoworld, *centralize* means "to trust somebody else to handle your money." One of the main issues with centralized cryptocurrency exchanges is their vulnerability to hacks. In some past hacking scandals, however, the exchange has paid the customers back out-of-pocket. That's why choosing a centralized exchange wisely, knowing it has the financial ability to combat hackers and pay you in case it gets hacked, is important. Of course, with the popularity of cryptocurrencies, more centralized cryptocurrency exchanges are bound to pop up in the market. Some will succeed, and some may fail. Therefore, you need to pick your crypto shop wisely.

TIP

As time goes by, the market learns from previous mistakes and works on a better and safer future. However, you still need to take matters into your own hands as much as possible. Before choosing an exchange, take a look at its security section on its website. Check on whether it participates in any bug bounty programs to encourage safety. And, of course, ask the right people about the exchange. In

Invest Diva's Premium Investing Group, we keep an eye on the latest developments in the market and keep our members informed about any shady activities. So feel free to stop by `https://learn.investdiva.com/join-group`!

Safety check #3: Your wallet

The final round of security check is all in your own hands because what kind of crypto wallet you use is entirely up to you. Though you don't physically carry your crypto coins, you can store them in a secure physical wallet. You actually store the public and private keys, which you can use for making transactions with your altcoins, in these wallets as well. You can take your wallet's security to a higher level by using a backup.

Volatility risk

Volatility risk is essentially the risk in unexpected market movements. Though volatility can be a good thing, it can also catch you off guard sometimes. Just like any other market, the cryptocurrency market can suddenly move in the opposite direction from what you expected. If you aren't prepared for the market volatility, you can lose the money you invested in the market.

The volatility in the cryptocurrency market has resulted from many factors. For one, it's a brand-new technology. The inception of revolutionary technologies — such as the Internet — can create initial periods of volatility. The blockchain technology and its underpinning cryptocurrencies take a lot of getting used to before they become mainstream.

REMEMBER

The best way to combat the cryptocurrency volatility risk is looking at the big picture. Volatility matters a lot if you have a short-term investing horizon because it's an indicator of how much money you may make or lose over a short period. But if you have a long-term horizon, volatility can turn into an opportunity.

TIP

You can also offset volatility risk by using automated trading algorithms on various exchanges. For example, you can set up an order like "sell 65 percent of coin 1," "100 percent of coin 2," and so on if the price drops by 3 percent. (This is essentially a stop-loss order but for the case of cryptos where one can trade fractional amounts.) This strategy can minimize the risk of volatility and allow you to sleep well at night.

Liquidity risk

By definition, *liquidity risk* is the risk of not being able to sell (or *liquidate*) an investment quickly at a reasonable price. Liquidity is important for any tradable asset. The forex market is considered the most liquid market in the world. But even in the forex market, the lack of liquidity may be a problem. If you trade currencies with very low volume, you may not even be able to close your trade because the prices just won't move!

Cryptocurrencies can also see episodes of illiquidity. Heck, the liquidity problem was one of the factors that led to the high volatility in Bitcoin and other altcoins described earlier in this chapter. When the liquidity is low, the risk of price manipulation also comes into play. One big player can easily move the market to his or her favour by placing a massive order.

TIP

The crypto community refers to these types of big players as *whales*. In the cryptocurrency market, whales often move small altcoins by using their huge capital.

On the bright side, as cryptocurrency investing becomes more available and acceptable, the market may become more liquid. The increase in the number of trusted crypto exchanges will provide opportunity for more people to trade. Crypto ATMs and payment cards are popping up, helping raise the awareness and acceptance of cryptocurrencies in everyday transactions.

Another key factor in cryptocurrency liquidity is the stance of countries on cryptocurrency regulations. If the authorities are able to define issues such as consumer protection and crypto taxes, more people will be comfortable using and trading cryptocurrencies, which will affect their liquidity.

REMEMBER

When choosing a cryptocurrency to trade, you must consider its liquidity by analyzing its acceptance, popularity, and the number of exchanges it's been traded on. Lesser-known cryptocurrencies may have a lot of upside potential, but they may put you in trouble because of lack of liquidity.

Vanishing risk

Hundreds of different cryptocurrencies are currently out there. More and more cryptocurrencies are being introduced every day. In ten years' time, many of these altcoins may vanish while others flourish.

A familiar example of vanishing risk is the dot-com bubble. In the late 1990s, many people around the world dreamed up businesses that capitalized on the popularity of the Internet. Some, such as Amazon and eBay, succeeded in conquering the world. Many more crashed and burned. Following the path of history, many of the booming cryptocurrencies popping up left and right are destined to bust.

REMEMBER

To minimize the vanishing risk, you need to analyze the fundamentals of the cryptocurrencies you choose to invest in. Do their goals make sense to you? Are they solving a problem that will continue in the years to come? Who are their partners? You can't vanish the vanishing risk entirely (pun intended), but you can eliminate your exposure to a sudden bust.

Regulation risk

One of the initial attractions of cryptocurrencies was their lack of regulation. In the good old days in cryptoland, crypto enthusiasts didn't have to worry about governments chasing them down. All they had was a white paper and a promise. However, as the demand for cryptocurrencies grows, global regulators are scratching their heads on how to keep up — and to not lose their shirts to the new economic reality.

REMEMBER

To date, most digital currencies aren't backed by any central government, meaning each country has different standards.

You can divide the cryptocurrency regulation risk into two components: the regulation event risk and regulation's nature itself.

>> The *regulation event risk* doesn't necessarily mean that the cryptocurrency market is doing poorly. It just means the market participants reacted to an unexpected announcement. In recent years, every seemingly small regulation announcement drove the price of many major cryptocurrencies and created a ton of volatility.

>> At the time of writing, there are no global cryptocurrency regulators, so existing regulations are all over the board. In some countries, cryptocurrency exchanges are legal as long as they're registered with the financial authorities. Other countries have been stricter on the cryptocurrencies but more lenient on the blockchain industry itself.

TIP

>> To stay updated on Canada's cryptocurrency rules, visit www.canada.ca/en/financial-consumer-agency/services/payment/digital-currency.html.

The future of cryptocurrency regulations seems to be bright at this writing, but it may impact the markets in the future. As the market grows stronger, though, these impacts may turn into isolated events.

Tax risk

When cryptocurrency investing first got popular, hardly anyone was paying taxes on the gains. A lot of underreporting was going on. However, as the market gets more regulated, the authorities may become stricter on taxation.

Different countries have different rules. In the United States, for example, tax risk involves the chance that the authorities may make unfavourable changes in tax laws, such as limitation of deductions, increase in tax rates, and elimination of tax exemptions. In other countries, tax risk can get more complicated. For example, at the time of writing, the Philippines hasn't clearly established whether the Bureau of Internal Revenue will treat cryptocurrencies as equities, property, or capital gains tax.

TIP

According to the Canadian government, "Tax rules apply to digital currency transactions, including those made with cryptocurrencies. Using digital currency does not exempt consumers from Canadian tax obligations. This means digital currencies are subject to the Income Tax Act." Stay informed by visiting `canada.ca/en/financial-consumer-agency/services/payment/digital-currency.html`. The tax treatment of cryptocurrencies is covered at `canada.ca/en/revenue-agency/programs/about-canada-revenue-agency-cra/compliance/digital-currency/cryptocurrency-guide.html`.

REMEMBER

Although virtually all investments are vulnerable to increases in tax rates, cryptocurrency taxation is a fuzzy area. Most regulators can't even agree on the basic concept of what a token represents!

Exploring Risk Management Methods

The only way you can achieve your investment goals is to invest at a risk level consistent with your risk tolerance assessment. You can measure your risk tolerance by considering objective measures like your investment goals, your time horizon for each goal, your need for liquidity, and so on. You can increase your risk tolerance by setting longer-term goals, adding to your savings by using methods other than online investing, and lowering your need for current liquidity.

These things are certainly easier said than done, especially considering you never know when you're gonna get hit financially. The following sections provide guidance on how to manage risk by building an emergency fund, being patient with your investments, and diversifying.

TIP

Check out this master class on my website where I (coauthor Kiana) explain how you can calculate your personal risk tolerance and give you all the analysis tools and questionnaires in order to make your money work for you: `https://learn. investdiva.com/free-webinar-3-secrets-to-making-your-money-work-for-you`. See the nearby sidebar "Measuring your own risk tolerance" for more information, too.

MEASURING YOUR OWN RISK TOLERANCE

Risk tolerance has two main components:

- Your willingness to risk
- Your ability to withstand risk

A financial planner is likely to have you fill out a risk tolerance questionnaire that measures your willingness to risk. This questionnaire evaluates your willingness to take on risk by asking about risk issues. It can help you determine whether you are risk averse or risk tolerant. A *risk averse* investor requires significantly more return in order to consider investing in a higher-risk investment. A *risk tolerant* investor is more willing to accept risk for a small increase in return.

However, to really get an understanding about the amount you can invest in the markets, you must also find out your ability to withstand risk based on your unique financial situation and living circumstances. To calculate your risk tolerance, you must prepare your financial statements and analyze some ratios such as

- **Your emergency fund ratio:** You can calculate this by dividing your accessible cash by your monthly necessary spending. The result must be greater than 6.
- **Your housing ratio:** Divide your housing costs by your gross pay.
- **Your debt ratio:** This one calculates your total debt divided by your total assets. The benchmark varies depending on your age and financial goals.
- **Your net worth ratio:** You can calculate this by dividing your net worth (which is all your assets minus your debt) by your total assets.

Using these ratios and comparing them to benchmark numbers, you can then fill out a simple questionnaire to figure out your risk tolerance.

Build your emergency fund first

My husband and I were recently exposed to an unpredicted financial burden. After a year of financial success for both of us, we went ahead and upgraded our budget, bought a new house in an awesome neighbourhood, and added some luxury expenses we normally wouldn't go after. It was good times!

Then the unexpected tax law change in the United States put us in a higher tax bracket than usual and took away some of our previously sought tax exemptions and deductions. Right after that, our daughter, Jasmine, was born, and our plans to have our parents take care of her for the first six months fell through because of sudden health issues on both sides of the family. As the saying goes, when it rains, it pours — figuratively and literally. Our area got hit by a few storms, which flooded our basement, damaged our trees, and dropped a few branches on our house. We now needed an additional budget for the damages.

I tell this story simply to point out the importance of having an emergency fund, no matter what you're investing in or what your strategy is. Thanks to our emergency fund, we were able to overcome this financially challenging time and turn our focus back on raising our little bundle of joy. Of course, now we had to rebuild the fund from scratch.

TIP

You can calculate your emergency fund by dividing the value of your total immediately accessible cash by your necessary monthly expenses. That will give you the number of months you can survive with no additional cash flow. The result *must* be greater than six months. But the more the merrier. For more on risk tolerance calculation, visit `https://learn.investdiva.com/free-webinar-3-secrets-to-making-your-money-work-for-you`. Also, check out Chapter 3 in Book 1 for more on establishing an emergency reserve.

REMEMBER

You must have an emergency fund before creating an investment portfolio, let alone adding cryptocurrencies to it.

Be patient

The risks involved with cryptocurrencies are slightly different from those of other, more established markets such as equities and precious metals. However, you can use similar methods for managing your portfolio risk regardless of your investments.

The most common reason many traders lose money online is the fantasy of getting rich quick. I can say with confidence (verifiably) that the vast majority of my long-term students made money, and in many cases a lot of money. The key has been patience.

"Patience is a profitable virtue" is the mantra of our investment group. The majority of our portfolio holding had been equities and forex, but the same has been true to Bitcoin holders. It took years (nine years, to be exact) for early Bitcoin enthusiasts to make any return on their holdings. And although a bit of a bubble occurred in 2017, nothing is stopping the markets from reaching and surpassing the all-time-high levels in the coming years.

The patience mantra doesn't help only long-term investors. It also goes for traders and speculators. Very often, that investment or speculative position you took may go down or sideways for what seems like forever. Sooner or later, the market will take note of the sentiment and either erase losses or create new buy opportunities.

In Figure 3-2, you can see the role patience can play in an investor's returns. Of course, you'd love for the markets to just march up to your profit target (that is, exit) price level straightaway. But more often than not, it just doesn't work that way.

>> The chart on the left shows a fantasy most traders have when they buy an asset. They hope the price will march up toward their profit target within their trading time frame, whether short-term or long-term, and make them money.

>> The chart on the right shows the reality. Traders and investors alike often see a lot of dips in the price before the market reaches their profit target. Some investors panic on the dips and call it quits. But in the end, those who were patient and held their position through the rough times win. This can be true to both short-term and long-term investors, so the chart's time frame doesn't really matter.

REMEMBER

Success follows a bumpy road. Your portfolio may even turn into negative territory at times. However, if you've done your due diligence of analyzing your investment, you must make time your friend in order to see long-term profit.

A great example of this idea is the crash of 2008. Almost all markets around the world dropped like a hot rock because of economic issues such as the mortgage crisis. Most people panicked and started to get out of their investments with massive losses. Had they given it some (well, a lot of) patience, they would've seen their portfolios in positive territory in around five years.

FIGURE 3-2:
Demonstrating why patience is a profitable virtue.

Source: *InvestDiva.com*

Diversify outside and inside your cryptocurrency portfolio

As Chapter 2 in Book 6 notes, diversification is the "don't put all your eggs in one basket" rule, and this age-old investing advice remains true to the revolutionary cryptocurrency market. Besides diversifying your portfolio by adding different assets such as stocks, bonds, or exchange-traded funds (ETFs), diversification within your cryptocurrency portfolio is also important.

For example, Bitcoin is perhaps the celebrity of all cryptocurrencies, so everyone wants to get hold of it. But Bitcoin is also the oldest cryptocurrency, so it has some unresolvable problems. Every day, younger and better-performing cryptocurrencies make their way into the market and offer exciting opportunities.

Besides age, you can group cryptocurrencies in several different ways for diversification purposes. Here are some examples:

>> **Major cryptocurrencies by market cap:** This category includes the ones in the top ten. At the time of writing, these options include Bitcoin, Ethereum, Ripple, and Litecoin.

- » **Transactional cryptocurrencies:** This group is the original category for cryptocurrencies. Transactional cryptocurrencies are designed to be used as money and exchanged for goods and services. Bitcoin and Litecoin are examples of well-known cryptos on this list.

- » **Platform cryptocurrencies:** These cryptocurrencies are designed to get rid of middlemen, create markets, and even launch other cryptocurrencies. Ethereum is one of the biggest cryptos in this category. It provides a backbone for future applications. NEO is another prime example. Such cryptocurrencies are generally considered good long-term investments because they rise in value as more applications are created on their blockchain.

- » **Privacy cryptocurrencies:** These options are similar to transactional cryptocurrencies, but they're heavily focused toward transaction security and anonymity. Examples include Monero, Zcash, and Dash.

- » **Application-specific cryptocurrencies:** One of the trendiest types of cryptos, application-specific cryptocurrencies serve specific functions and solve some of the world's biggest problems. Some examples of such cryptos are VeChain (used for supply chain applications), IOTA (Internet of Things applications), and Cardano (cryptocurrency scalability, privacy optimizations, and so on). Some get super specific, such as Mobius, also known as Stripe for the blockchain industry, which was seeking to resolve the payment issues in the agriculture industry in 2018. Depending on the specifics of each project, a number of these cryptos may prove highly successful. You can pick the ones that are solving issues closer to your heart; just be sure to analyze their usability, application performance, and project team properly.

REMEMBER

One key problem the cryptocurrency market faces when it comes to diversification is that the whole market appears to be extremely correlated. The majority of cryptocurrencies go up when the market sentiment turns bullish (upward), and vice versa. Despite this tendency, you can diversify away risk in a crypto-only portfolio by adding more crypto assets to your portfolio. By investing in multiple crypto assets, you can spread out the amount of risk you're exposed to instead of having all the volatility of the portfolio come from one or a few assets.

Chapter 4

How Cryptocurrencies Work

C ryptocurrencies, and more specifically Bitcoin, have been one of the first use cases for blockchain technology. That's why most people may have heard about Bitcoin more than they have about the underlying blockchain technology.

This chapter gets into more detail about how cryptocurrencies use blockchain technology, how they operate, and how they're generated, as well as some crypto geek terms you can impress your date with.

Explaining Basic Terms in the Cryptocurrency Process

Cryptocurrencies are also known as digital coins, but they're quite different from the coins in your piggy bank. For one thing, they aren't attached to a central bank, a country, or a regulatory body.

Here's an example. Say you want to buy the latest version of *Cryptocurrency Investing For Dummies* from your local bookstore. Using your normal debit card, this is what happens:

1. You give your card details to the cashier or the store's point-of-sale system.
2. The store runs the info through, essentially asking your bank whether you have enough money in your bank account to buy the book.
3. The bank checks its records to confirm whether you do.
4. If you do have enough, the bank gives a thumbs-up to the bookstore.
5. The bank then updates its records to show the movement of the money from your account to the bookstore's account.
6. The bank gets a little cut for the trouble of being the middleman.

Now if you wanted to remove the bank from this entire process, who else would you trust to keep all these records without altering them or cheating in any way? Your best friend? Your dog walker? In fact, you may not trust any single person. But how about trusting *everyone* in the network?

REMEMBER

Blockchain technology works to remove the middleman. When applied to cryptocurrencies, blockchain eliminates a central record of transactions. Instead, you distribute many copies of your transaction ledger around the world. Each owner of each copy records your transaction of buying the book.

Here's what happens if you want to buy this book using a cryptocurrency:

1. You give your crypto details to the cashier.
2. The shop asks everyone in the network to see whether you have enough coins to buy the book.
3. All the record holders in the network check their records to see whether you do. (These record holders are called nodes; their function is explained in more detail later in this chapter.)
4. If you do have enough, each node gives the thumbs-up to the cashier.
5. The nodes all update their records to show the transfer.
6. At random, a node gets a reward for the work.

That means no organization is keeping track of where your coins are or investigating fraud. In fact, cryptocurrencies such as Bitcoin wouldn't exist without a whole network of bookkeepers (nodes) and a little thing known as *cryptography*.

The following sections explain that and some other important terms related to the workings of cryptocurrencies.

Cryptography

Shhh. Don't tell anyone. That's the *crypto* in *cryptography* and *cryptocurrency*. It means "secret." In the cryptocurrency world, it mainly refers to being "anonymous."

Historically, cryptography is an ancient art for sending hidden messages. (The term comes from the Greek word *krypto logos*, which means *secret writing*.) The sender *encrypts* the message by using some sort of key. The receiver then has to *decrypt* it. For example, 19th-century scholars decrypted ancient Egyptian hieroglyphics when Napoleon's soldiers found the Rosetta Stone in 1799 near Rosetta, Egypt. In the 21st-century era of information networks, the sender can digitally encrypt messages, and the receiver can use cryptographic services and algorithms to decrypt them.

What does Napoleon have to do with cryptocurrencies? Cryptocurrencies use cryptography to maintain security and anonymity. That's how digital coins, even though they're not monetized by any central authority or regulatory body, can help with security and protection from double-spending, which is the risk of your digital cash being used more than once.

**TECHNICAL
STUFF**

Cryptography uses three main encryption methods:

>> **Hashing:** Hashing is something like a fingerprint or signature. A *hash function* first takes your input data (which can be of any size). The function then performs an operation on the original data and returns an output that represents the original data but has a fixed (and generally smaller) size. In cryptocurrencies such as Bitcoin, it's used to guess the combination of the lock of a block. Hashing maintains the structure of blockchain data, encodes people's account addresses, and makes block mining possible. You can find more on mining later in this chapter.

>> **Symmetric encryption cryptography:** *Symmetric encryption* is the simplest method used in cryptography. It involves only one secret key for both the sender and the receiver. The main disadvantage of symmetric encryption is that all parties involved have to exchange the key used to encrypt the data before they can decrypt it.

>> **Asymmetric encryption cryptography:** *Asymmetric encryption* uses two keys: a public key and a private key. You can encrypt a message by using the receiver's *public* key, but the receiver can decrypt it only with his or her *private* key.

Nodes

A *node* is an electronic device doing the bookkeeping job in the blockchain network, making the whole decentralized thing possible. The device can be a computer, a cellphone, or even a printer, as long as it's connected to the Internet and has access to the blockchain network.

Mining

As the owners of nodes (see the preceding section) willingly contribute their computing resources to store and validate transactions, they have the chance to collect the transaction fees and earn a reward in the underlying cryptocurrency for doing so. This process is known as *mining,* and the owners who do it are *miners.*

REMEMBER

To be clear: Not all cryptocurrencies can be mined. Bitcoin and some other famous ones can. Some others, such as Ripple (XRP), avoid mining altogether because they want a platform that doesn't consume a huge amount of electricity in the process of mining; power usage is one of the issues with blockchain, actually. Regardless, for the most part, mining remains a huge part of many cryptocurrencies to date.

Here's how mining works: Cryptocurrency miners solve cryptographic puzzles (via software) to add transactions to the ledger (the blockchain) in the hope of getting coins as a reward. It's called mining because of the fact that this process helps extract new cryptocurrencies from the system. Anyone, including you, can join this group. Your computer needs to "guess" a random number that solves an equation that the blockchain system generates. In fact, your computer has to calculate many 64-character strings or 256-bit hashes and check with the challenge equation to see whether the answer is right. That's why it's so important that you have a powerful computer. The more powerful your computer is, the more guesses it can make in a second, increasing your chances of winning this game. If you manage to guess right, you earn Bitcoins and get to write the "next page" (or "block") of Bitcoin transactions on the blockchain.

Because mining is based on a form of guessing, for each block a different miner guesses the number and is granted the right to update the blockchain. Whoever has the biggest computing power combined, controlling 51 percent of the votes, controls the chain and wins every time. Thanks to the law of statistical probability, the same miner is unlikely to succeed every time. On the other hand, this game can sometimes be unfair because the biggest computer power will be the first to solve the challenge equation and "win" more often.

Proof-of-work

If you're a miner and want to actually enter your block and transactions into the blockchain, you have to provide an answer (proof) to a specific challenge. This proof is difficult to produce (hence all the gigantic computers, time, and money needed for it), but others can very easily verify it. This process is known as *proof-of-work*, or PoW.

For example, guessing a combination to a lock is a proof to a challenge. Going through all the different possible combinations to come up with the right answer may be pretty hard, but after you get it, it's easy to validate — just enter the combination and see whether the lock opens! The first miner who solves the problem for each block on the blockchain gets a reward. The reward is basically the incentive to keep on mining and gets the miners competing to be the first one to find a solution for mathematical problems. Bitcoin and some other minable cryptocurrencies mainly use the PoW concept to make sure that the network isn't easily manipulated.

REMEMBER

This whole proof-of-work thing has some downsides for blockchain technology. One of the main challenges is that it wastes a lot of computing power and electricity just for the sake of producing random guesses. That's why new cryptocurrencies have jumped on an alternative wagon called proof-of-stake (PoS), covered in the next section.

Proof-of-stake

Unlike PoW, a *proof-of-stake* (PoS) system requires you to show ownership of a certain amount of money (or *stake*). That means the more crypto you own, the more mining power you have. This approach eliminates the need for the expensive mining extravaganza. And because the calculations are pretty simple to prove, you own a certain percentage of the total amount of the cryptos available.

Another difference is that the PoS system offers no block rewards, so the miners get transaction fees. That's how PoS cryptos can be several thousand times more cost-effective than PoW ones. (Don't let the PoS abbreviation give you the wrong idea.)

REMEMBER

But of course, PoS also can have its own problems. For starters, you can argue that PoS rewards coin hoarders. Under the proof-of-stake model, nodes can mine only a percentage of transactions that corresponds to their stake in a cryptocurrency. For example, a proof-of-stake miner who owns 10 percent of a cryptocurrency would be able to mine 10 percent of blocks on the network. The limitation with this consensus model is that it gives nodes on the network a reason to save their coins instead of spending them. It also produces a scenario in which the rich get richer because large coin holders are able to mine a larger percentage of blocks on the network.

Proof-of-importance

Proof-of-importance (PoI) was first introduced by a blockchain platform called NEM to support its XEM cryptocurrency. In some ways PoI is similar to PoS because participants (nodes) are marked as "eligible" if they have a certain amount of crypto "vested." Then the network gives a "score" to the eligible nodes, and they can create a block that is roughly the same proportion to that "score." But the difference is that the nodes won't get a higher score only by holding onto more cryptocurrencies. Other variables are considered in the score, too, in order to resolve the primary problem with PoS, which is hoarding. The NEM community in particular uses a method called "harvesting" to solve the PoS "hoarding" problem.

Here's how Investopedia defines harvesting: "Instead of each miner contributing its mining power in a cumulative manner to a computing node, a harvesting participant simply links his account to an existing supernode and uses that account's computing power to complete blocks on his behalf." (Find out more about harvesting later in this chapter.)

Transactions: Putting it all together

REMEMBER

Here's a summary of how cryptocurrencies work (check out the preceding sections for details on some of the terminology):

1. When you want to use cryptos to purchase something, first your crypto network and your crypto wallet automatically check your previous transactions to make sure you have enough cryptocurrencies to make that transaction. For this, you need your private and public keys.

2. The transaction is then encrypted, broadcast to the cryptocurrency's network, and queued up to be added to the public ledger.

3. Transactions are then recorded on the public ledger through mining. The sending and receiving addresses are wallet IDs or hash values that aren't tied to the user identification so they are anonymous.

4. For PoW cryptos, the miners have to solve a math puzzle to verify the transaction. PoS cryptos attribute the mining power to the proportion of the coins held by the miners, instead of utilizing energy to solve math problems, in order to resolve the "wasted energy" problem of PoW. The PoI cryptos add a number of variables when attributing the mining power to nodes in order to resolve the "hoarding" problem that's associated with PoS.

Cruising through Other Important Crypto Concepts

Earlier in this chapter, you find out about basics of cryptocurrencies and how they're related to blockchain technology. This section gets a few more concepts out of the way, just in case someone starts talking to you about them. Other factors make cryptocurrencies so special and different from your government-backed legal tender, also known as *fiat currency*, such as the Canadian dollar.

Adaptive scaling

Adaptive scaling is one of the advantages of investing in cryptocurrencies. It means that it gets harder to mine a specific cryptocurrency over time. It allows cryptocurrencies to work well on both small and large scales. That's why cryptocurrencies take measures such as limiting the supply over time (to create scarcity) and reducing the reward for mining as more total coins are mined. Thanks to adaptive scaling, mining difficulty goes up and down depending on the popularity of the coin and the blockchain. This can give cryptocurrencies a real longevity within the market.

Decentralization

The whole idea behind blockchain technology is that it's *decentralized*. This concept means no single entity can affect the cryptocurrencies.

TECHNICAL STUFF

Some people claim cryptocurrencies such as Ripple aren't truly decentralized because they don't follow Bitcoin's mining protocol exactly. Ripple has no miners. Instead, transactions are powered through a "centralized" blockchain to make it more reliable and faster. Ripple in particular has gone this route because it wants to work with big banks and therefore wants to combine the best elements of fiat money and blockchain cryptocurrency. Whether non-minable currencies such as Ripple can be considered true cryptocurrencies is up for discussion, but that fact doesn't mean you can't invest in them, which is the whole purpose of this book anyway!

Harvesting

Harvesting is an alternative to the traditional mining used to maintain the integrity of a blockchain network. It was designed by a blockchain platform called NEM to generate its own currency called XEM. According to finder.com, this is how harvesting works: "Every time someone carries out a transaction, the first computer to see and verify the transaction will notify nearby users of that transaction, creating a cascade of information. This process is called 'generating a block.' Whenever someone with more than 10,000 vested XEM generates a block in NEM, they receive the transaction fees on that block as payment." Also, as explained earlier in this chapter, harvesting uses a PoI system rather than PoS and PoW.

Open source

Cryptocurrencies are typically *open source.* That means that miners, nodes, and harvesters alike can join and use the network without paying a fee.

Public ledger

A ledger is the age-old record-keeping system for recording information and data. Cryptocurrencies use a *public ledger* to record all transactional data. Everyone in the world can access public blockchains and see entire transactions happening with cryptocurrencies.

Note that not all blockchains use a public ledger. Some businesses and financial institutions use private ledgers so that the transactions aren't visible to the world. However, by doing so, they may contradict the original idea behind blockchain technology.

Smart contracts

Smart contracts are also called *self-executing contracts, blockchain contracts,* or *digital contracts.* They're just like traditional contracts except that they're completely digital. Smart contracts remove the middleman between the buyer and the seller so you can implement things like automatic payments and investment products without the need of a central authority like a bank.

A smart contract is actually a tiny computer program that's stored and runs on a blockchain platform. Because of that, all the transactions are completely distributed, and no centralized authority is in control of the money. Also, because it's stored on a blockchain, a smart contract is *immutable.* Being immutable means that after a smart contract is created, it can never be changed again; it can't be tampered with, which is an inherited feature from blockchain technology.

WARNING

However, being immutable comes with its own disadvantages. Because you can't change anything in the smart contract, that means that if the code has any bugs, you can't fix them either. This makes smart contract security more difficult. Some companies aim to combat this problem by auditing their smart contracts, which can be very costly.

As time goes by, we can expect better coding practices and development life cycles to combat smart contract security problems. After all, smart contracts are still a pretty young practice with their whole life of trial and error ahead of them.

Stick a Fork in It: Digging into Cryptocurrency Forks

What you get from a cryptocurrency fork won't fill your tummy, but it may fill your crypto wallet with some money! Many popular cryptocurrencies were born as a result of a split (fork) in another cryptocurrency like Bitcoin. The following sections explain the basics of these cryptocurrency splits and how you may be able to profit from them.

What is a fork, and why do forks happen?

Sometimes when a group of developers disagrees with the direction a specific cryptocurrency is going, the members decide to go their own way and initiate a *fork*. Imagine an actual physical fork. It has one long handle, and then it divides into a bunch of branches. That's exactly what happens in a cryptocurrency fork.

As explained earlier in this chapter, some cryptocurrencies are implemented within open source software. Each of these cryptocurrencies has its own protocol that everyone in the network should follow. Examples of such rule topics include the following:

>> Block size

>> Rewards that miners, harvesters, or other network participants get

>> How fees are calculated

REMEMBER

But because cryptocurrencies are essentially software projects, their development will never be fully finished. There's always room for improvement. Crypto developers regularly push out updates to fix issues or to increase performance. Some of these improvements are small, but others fundamentally change the way the original cryptocurrency (which the developers fell in love with) works. Just as in any type of relationship, you either grow together or grow apart. When the disagreements among a group of developers or network participants intensify, they can choose to break up, create their own version of the protocol, and cause a potential heartbreak that requires years of therapy to get over. Okay, the last part doesn't really happen.

Hard forks and soft forks

Two types of forks can happen in a cryptocurrency: a hard fork and a soft fork.

Most cryptocurrencies consist of two big pieces: the protocol (set of rules) and the blockchain (which stores all the transactions that have ever happened). If a segment of the crypto community decides to create its own new rules, it starts by copying the original protocol code and then goes about making changes to it (assuming the cryptocurrency is completely open source). After the developers have implemented their desired changes, they define a point at which their fork will become active. More specifically, they choose a block number to start the forking. For example, as you can see in Figure 4-1, the community can say that the new protocol will go live when block 999 is published to the cryptocurrency blockchain.

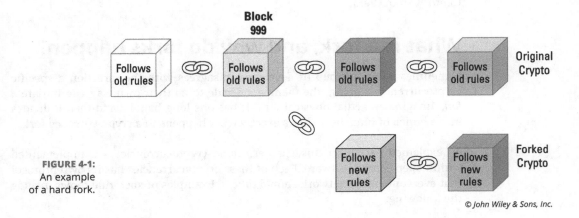

© John Wiley & Sons, Inc.

FIGURE 4-1:
An example
of a hard fork.

When the currency reaches that block number, the community splits in two. Some people decide to support the original set of rules, while others support the new fork. Each group then starts adding new blocks to the fork it supports. At this point, both blockchains are incompatible with each other, and a *hard fork* has occurred. In a hard fork, the nodes essentially go through a contentious divorce and don't ever interact with each other again. They don't even acknowledge the nodes or transactions on the old blockchain.

On the other hand, a soft fork is the type of breakup where you remain friends with your ex. If the developers decide to fork the cryptocurrency and make the changes compatible with the old one, then the situation is called a *soft fork*. You can see the subtle difference in the example shown in Figure 4-2.

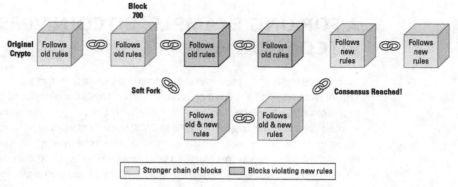

Block 700

Original Crypto | Follows old rules | Follows old rules | Follows old rules | Follows old rules | Follows new rules | Follows new rules

Soft Fork

Follows old & new rules | Follows old & new rules

Consensus Reached!

Stronger chain of blocks | Blocks violating new rules

FIGURE 4-2:
An example of a soft fork.

© John Wiley & Sons, Inc.

Say the soft fork is set to happen at block 700. The majority of the community may support the stronger chain of blocks following both the new and old rules. If the two sides reach a consensus after a while, the new rules are upgraded across the network. Any non-upgraded nodes (that is, stubborn geeks) who are still mining are essentially wasting their time. The community comes back together softly, and everyone lives happily ever after — until the next major argument, of course.

Free money on forks

Because a new fork is based on the original blockchain, all transactions that previously happened on the blockchain also happen on the fork. The developers of the new chain take a "snapshot" of the ledger at a specific block number the fork happened (like 999 in Figure 4-1) and therefore create a duplicate copy of the chain. That means if you had a certain amount of cryptocurrencies before the fork, you also get the same amount of the new coin.

REMEMBER

To get free coins from a fork, you need to have the cryptocurrency on a platform that supports the fork before the block number at which the fork occurs. You can call this free money. But how valuable the coins are all depends how well the new fork performs and how popular it gets within the community.

A FORKING EXAMPLE: BITCOIN VERSUS BITCOIN CASH

Even the celebrity of cryptocurrencies, Bitcoin (BTC), has seen forks. One of the well-known Bitcoin forks happened on August 1, 2017. That's the birthday of Bitcoin Cash. In this case, the developers couldn't agree on what the size for a block should be. Some wanted the block size to go from 1MB to 2MB, but others wanted to increase it even more, to 32MB. Some people in the community loved the new big idea, while others thought the other group was crazy. So both groups decided to go their own ways. Bitcoin Cash adapted a brand-new symbol (BCH), too. People who already had BTC got the same amount of BCH added to their crypto wallets.

As of June 2020, BCH is valued at around $250 (in U.S. dollars), while BTC is around $9,625. Only time will tell whether BCH ever surpasses the original protocol's value. But hey, at least the forkers got some value out of it!

7

Investing in Real Estate

Contents at a Glance

Chapter **1**

Thinking about Real Estate

O wning land has been a status symbol for generations. It once gave people a right to vote and a degree of independence from the demands of the world. Today, it promises financial independence, which amounts to the same thing for most people. Land is tangible; you can stand on it and live on it, things you can't do with investments bought and sold online, and represented by numbers on a page. Whether you have a handful of homes you rent to university students, renovate a run-down character house to be sold at a profit, or buy the local strip mall and make it a gathering point for the neighbourhood, you've got opportunities for making money as well as making a contribution to your community.

Real estate is everywhere: the apartment or house you call home, the mall where you go shopping for groceries and clothes, and the office where you work. Even the park where you take your kids and walk your dog is property with potential investment value. But like any other investment, real estate has its risks, too. Remember the old saying "land rich, cash poor"? There's real wealth in land but some equally real financial dangers, too, if you don't have a strategy for making the most of it. What kind of real estate interests you most? Have you considered the skills — and weaknesses — you bring to your role as an investor? Successful investment in real estate means becoming land rich in order to become cash rich, too. You want to do it right!

This chapter discusses the various opportunities awaiting you as an investor and some of the risks associated with real estate. It looks at the considerations worth bearing in mind as you're sizing up the different investment tools available. Finally, this chapter investigates how real estate can fit into a long-term financial plan and the implications that it can have for your retirement and your estate.

Investigating Real Estate Investing

So what's the real deal about real estate? What makes it such a hot topic and critical investment for everyone from the government honchos who manage the Canada Pension Plan down to the tech nerd from school who's making oodles of money as a programmer? This section checks out the advantages of real estate and compares property relative to other kinds of investments you may consider as part of your portfolio.

Discovering the opportunities

Statistics from the Canadian Real Estate Association (CREA) indicate that residential real estate has increased in value by an average of more than 5 percent a year over the past 30 years. Even though there have been some significant dips during that period, and not every property will make the same gains in every year or from city to city, the trend is unmistakable: The long-term potential for your real estate investment to appreciate is significant. Several reasons support the argument that an investment in real estate makes sense.

Leverage opportunities

REMEMBER

Leverage is all about using a small amount of your own money and letting someone else's cash do the rest of the work. Because real estate provides the loan's *security* — a guarantee of repayment if you're unable to pay off the loan — the risk is low. If you run into financial trouble and your *creditors*, the people who've loaned you cash, demand immediate repayment and call your loan, your property could be subject to proceedings that lead to its sale. Providing that the property sells for more than the amount owing, you stand to emerge relatively unscathed. The nature of a forced sale of your property depends on the province and the mortgage documents you have signed. For example, in Ontario, the power-of-sale process doesn't require court approval, whereas in some other provinces, the foreclosure and sale process requires the court to be involved throughout.

Some of the basics of setting your limits as an investor so you can avoid the sale of your properties due to default of payment are discussed in the later section "Figuring Out Whether You're Right for Real Estate Investing." Chapter 4 in Book 7 discusses financing at greater length.

Equity opportunities

By paying down a mortgage, you're paying the purchase value of the property and making its value your own over several years. Real estate is therefore unlike many other investments because it gives you a chance to build *equity* — your share of the property's net worth at the time of sale — over the course of the investment rather than invest everything up front and hope for the best. Because the value of a property will change while you're paying down the original value, you have two ways to build wealth, not just one.

WARNING

Beware of negative equity! Although real estate is a convenient way to build equity (and that's a good thing), a drop in the market can bring destruction and result in *negative equity*, a situation in which the market value of a property is less than the mortgage it secures. This typically happens when an investment is financed with too much debt, a condition known as being overleveraged. This was a common scenario in the United States during the subprime mortgage crisis of 2006 when interest rates on some high-risk mortgages saddled buyers with payments they couldn't afford. The financial crisis of 2008 brought further trouble, when some lenders called loans on borrowers suddenly considered to be poor risks.

To some investors, negative cash flow is a bigger concern than negative equity because negative cash flow leaves them short of cash to cover immediate expenses. However, negative equity is *an unrealized loss* that could turn into positive equity when the market improves. The key to successful investing in both cases is avoiding *overleveraging*, which means having more debt than you can handle. It implies excessive risk-taking, which most investors consider an imprudent investment strategy.

Return opportunities

When investors talk about returns, they're talking about the money they'll see — not the option to return their property for a refund! You're quite right to ask for your money back when you invest in real estate, but the smart investor will get to keep the property, too. In fact, our calculations estimate that it's not impossible to enjoy a net return of more than 75 percent annually on your investment. How do we figure that? Here's the math.

If you buy a $300,000 property with a $30,000 down payment and the property increases in value by half over five years, the increase in equity is $150,000. That amounts to approximately $112,500 after the government taxes the appreciation in the property's value, or *capital gain.* This would represent a return of 375 percent over five years, or at least 75 percent annually on your original investment of $30,000. Assuming the debt you incurred to buy the property decreased over the course of the five years, and the property generated rental income, you would enjoy an even greater return on your investment.

Tax opportunities

Real estate offers several tax advantages for you as an investor, especially if you've developed an investment strategy that accounts for taxes. Taxes erode the return you'll see on investments yielding a fixed return, such as bank accounts, bonds, and guaranteed investment certificates (GICs), but not Tax-Free Savings Accounts (TFSAs). Stocks and other equities put your principal at risk. Real estate investments, however, frequently enjoy a reduced tax rate. Between tax-free capital gains on your principal residence to savings of up to 50 percent on taxes levied on capital gains from investment properties, there are many tax advantages to investing in real estate. You're also able to deduct investment expenses and *write off any depreciation* in property values on your real estate purchases.

Hedge opportunities

No, don't hide from your creditors in a bush! The kind of hedging discussed here means taking shelter from the effects of inflation, which works to erode your buying power. The rate of inflation varies from month to month, year to year, and even country to country. But real estate typically appreciates at a rate 3 to 5 percentage points *above* the inflation rate. So if inflation is running at 3 percent, look for your investment in real estate to appreciate at 6 to 8 percent. If you choose wisely, your investment stands a good chance of increasing at a rate greater than that of inflation, as Figure 1-1 shows.

REMEMBER

You're paying off your mortgage in dollars that reflect inflation, also known as *real dollars.* So, although the value of your mortgage will diminish over time, you'll typically enjoy a higher income thanks to salary increases or rental revenue increases that will help make your mortgage more affordable to carry over the long term.

Flexibility opportunities

Real estate offers a variety of investment options that give you flexibility in terms of how much attention they demand and the amount of risk you'll bear. By investing in just one property rather than several, or in partnership with family or friends, you can limit (or increase) your involvement to the level that suits you.

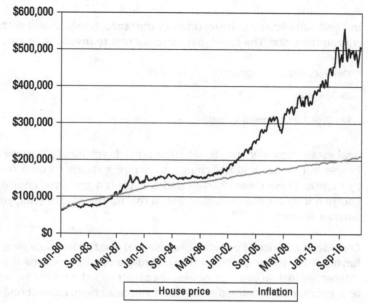

FIGURE 1-1:
Average home prices haven't always increased at the same rate as inflation, but long-term gains have steadily outpaced the inflation rate.

Source: Canadian Real Estate Association

Learning opportunities

Most investments entail some sort of learning process. Real estate is no different. Prior involvement in buying property, such as a home, may make it easier, but don't underestimate the need to find out about the particular dynamics of investing in real property. Real estate investment also offers opportunities to discover community issues and economic trends at work in neighbourhoods. And, if you're game for the role of landlord, you'll also have a chance to improve your people-management skills.

Considering alternatives

But wait! Do you really want to buy a patch of dirt or a stack of bricks? Why not let someone else worry about the paperwork associated with ownership and the hassles of managing an investment property? You have better things to do and better places to put your money, right?

True enough — and if these are your nagging doubts, you'll do well to consider other types of investments. Fear not, though: Some investments even let you enjoy indirect benefits from the fortunes of the real estate business without direct exposure to the risks! The three main alternatives to investing in real estate include

>> Fixed-term investments

>> Equities

>> Direct investment in businesses

Real estate typically stands out from other investments because of its stable and long-term nature and the chance to derive a steady income from assets month by month. These three characteristics make it a preferred choice for many, but if you're not up for the risks inherent in real estate investments, you might be safer with an alternative.

REMEMBER

Consider a balanced portfolio. Because real estate carries its own measure of risk, having a diversified portfolio that includes a mix of investment vehicles is in your interest — just so your entire nest-egg isn't wiped out by, say, fire, flood, locusts, or a swarm of determined termites. If you need help, consult one of the many reference works available, such as the latest edition of *Personal Finance for Canadians For Dummies* by Eric Tyson, MBA, and Tony Martin, B.Comm (Wiley).

Fixed-term investments

Guaranteed investment certificates (GICs) and bonds are stable investments with minimal risk and a guaranteed return. Fixed-term investments are great if you don't have a lot of cash to play with or need readily accessible funds, but if you're holding a lot of them, consider real estate a step up to a more sophisticated form of investing.

The difference in return can be significant, with the appreciation in real estate values often outpacing inflation. And unlike real estate earnings, interest received on term deposits and bonds is fully taxable as income and also subject to inflation. A GIC may offer a 4 percent return on your cash, but if inflation is 3 percent, you're seeing an effective return of just 1 percent on those dollars. Even if you're in the lowest tax bracket, you're probably just breaking even.

Equities

Not to be confused with the equity you build by paying down your mortgage, *equities* such as stocks trade on the open market and expose investors to fluctuations in value on a per-share or per-unit basis. The return is never guaranteed, though depending on your portfolio you may do better at some points than others. The stock market can offer good returns to dedicated, savvy investors; it's also subject to downturns that can wipe out the value of your investment. Although the past 10 years have seen the longest bull market in history, boosting the fortunes of many, it followed the financial crisis of autumn 2008 when equity markets staged a significant correction and many stocks lost at least a fifth of their value.

Mutual funds, though not strictly speaking equities, also fluctuate in value in response to market conditions but tend to be more diversified, reducing exposure to market volatility and in turn minimizing risk.

REMEMBER

Stocks, income trusts, and mutual funds may carry greater risk than real estate. The value of equities will fluctuate with daily market forces, but a good real estate investment typically delivers a steady cash flow as a result of consistent demand from a mix of short- and long-term tenants, or stable leasing relationships. Find the basics of stocks in Book 2 and mutual funds in Book 3.

Direct investment in businesses

Supporting a business venture you believe in by providing it with a start-up loan may be one of the most rewarding investments you make, but it also comes with the uncertainties associated with the company's business. Though the return isn't guaranteed, if the business succeeds, you can be paid back handsomely depending on the terms of the financing arrangement (which should be in your favour, because you get to have a hand in writing them).

Figuring Out Whether You're Right for Real Estate Investing

If you're serious about real estate investing (and if you're reading Book 7, you probably are), the first thing you need to do is determine whether you and real estate are a good investment match. This determination is key to your financial future. This section helps you figure that out.

Real estate, like other investment options, demands that you have a plan for building your portfolio. Just as you're careful not to contribute too much in a given month or year to your Registered Retirement Savings Plan (RRSP), you don't want to sink too much of your available cash resources into a real estate investment you may not be able to sell for several years. Why own a palace if you can't live like royalty?

Knowing your financial limits is just one aspect of determining your capacity for investing in real estate. Assessing your appetite for risk is equally important.

Risks are both real and perceived. For example, buying a property when the market is at its peak entails a real risk that the property could fall in value, leaving you open to a loss. Or you may be tempted to buy a property on the grounds that City Hall will let you renovate it. You might have reasonable grounds for believe this, but your success will depend on how well you or your representatives make the case to the local planning department. Other variables in the success of your investment include whether you're able to work within local zoning bylaws or can obtain a variance from the bylaws to achieve your goals. The potential is there, but you'll need to ensure that you can make the desired alterations to a property as part of your due diligence before the purchase.

WARNING

Equally important to successful investing is knowing yourself and how much confidence you have as an investor. Avoid situations that could undermine your confidence and cloud your decision-making abilities, such as buying or renovating properties for nostalgic or emotional reasons without first drafting a solid business plan.

Determining how much you can invest

Getting a handle on your personal finances is an important part of financing your real estate investment (something discussed at greater length in Chapter 4 of Book 7). Financing the actual purchase is just one part of the picture. Costs that crop up every day — from necessities such as shoes for the kids to luxuries like your gym membership or a night out on the town — determine how much cash you have available for investment purposes. Don't forget to take into account unexpected expenses such as an interruption in employment income. These factors each affect the amount you can invest, and the amount of risk you're willing to take on.

REMEMBER

Conventional wisdom suggests you should put aside three months' worth of living expenses to draw on in case of emergency, and the same holds true for your real estate investments. In case of emergency, you'll not only have to service the mortgage, you'll have to service the property itself — that is, cover ongoing maintenance of your building or property.

Assessing your risk tolerance

The risks associated with real estate stem from its disadvantages. Chances are you're attracted to real estate and the stability it offers; after all, land isn't about to get up and walk away, and they're not making a whole lot more of it. But land also has its own limitations that can affect how you can use it and its value to investors. Some common risks include

>> **Changes to surrounding properties and the local neighbourhood:** More than likely, you know houses where the grass has grown long and shaggy, the curtains are faded, and newspapers sit yellowing on the front step. Now, imagine that house is right next door to your investment property. Or perhaps a few of them stand in the neighbourhood where you're thinking of buying. Chances are you won't find the neighbourhood as appealing. Changes in the condition of other properties can seriously affect the value of your own real estate, and may prompt you to try selling a property earlier than you had intended.

On the other hand, positive changes to nearby properties can boost the value of your property and even prompt you to make improvements that will keep up not only with the Joneses but also with the broader market.

>> **Changes in the political climate and government policies:** Regardless of who forms the government, real estate investments may be subject to policy changes. A city council may need extra funding and pass a bylaw requiring owners of apartment buildings to pay significantly more for city services than homeowners. Some cities have introduced speculation and vacancy taxes, unheard of a decade ago. Or perhaps city staff are about to rezone the lot down the street for commercial development; depending on whether they allow a tea boutique or a bar with exotic dancers, your property is likely to see a change in value. Whether you can make the most of such changes will determine the success of your investment.

>> **Changes in the local economy:** You've probably heard of ghost towns. When companies pack up and takes the jobs with them, property values are sure to follow. A sudden change in the local economy can mean boom or bust for your portfolio. Are you able to anticipate the changes or find ways to meet them head-on when they occur?

REMEMBER

The amount of risk you can accept and manage will determine the kind of property you purchase but also whether you purchase at all. Take a close look at your background and the skills you bring to the challenges of being an investor. Are you familiar with the risks you face, or will they be new challenges for you? They might help you to discover and develop new skills, but you don't want to jeopardize your investment in the process. Becoming familiar with the risks you face — and recognizing when you need assistance, or even when you should reject an opportunity — is key to a successful investment.

Are you ready for the long haul?

Real estate isn't usually a form of investment that yields a quick profit, though some investors have been known to *flip* properties (selling them at a gain shortly after buying them). Instead, most investors hold real estate for at least one cycle of the real estate market. A *market cycle* is the period in which a market goes from high to low, from a buyer's market to a seller's market (this concept is discussed at length in Chapter 3 of Book 7). A standard cycle in the real estate market typically lasts as few as 5 and as many as 12 years. Some observers believe market cycles are actually lengthening, which means longer holding periods before you'll be able to realize a return.

Determining your readiness for a long-term investment and establishing realistic financial goals will help you select the kind of property that will suit your needs.

Are you ready for a soft market?

A *soft market* occurs when demand is slack for a product or service. Think of it as kind of like a soft-boiled egg: If you don't know what you're dealing with before you crack into it, you'll find yourself with a mess on your hands. As an investor, a soft market is an opportunity to pick up properties at a lower price than you might otherwise. If you've already got property, you may find yourself unable to sell at the price you expected. The situation will force you to make some hard choices: Are you comfortable holding the property a bit longer, or are you willing to accept a slightly lower return in exchange for a quick sale? This is worth thinking about, in case your financial circumstances change and you need to access the equity that's accumulated in your property since you bought it.

TIP

Soft markets are also periods during which you can invest in property with a view to preparing it for sale when markets improve.

Getting into Real Estate Investing

After you examine the alternatives and determine your limits, if you still think real estate investing is for you, you'll need to decide what sort of investment you want and where to invest. Your motivation for investing will influence where you search, so be sure to prioritize the criteria you want in an investment property so you can focus your search and have a better view to what you're seeking. Your interests will also influence the goals you set in the financial plan supporting your investment strategy.

Knowing your needs

Before you start looking at prospective locations, figure out what your investment intentions are. For example:

>> You want a property close to your current home so that you can address tenants' needs (and admire your purchase on a daily basis).

>> You want a vacation getaway you can rent out when you're not there or a home for your retirement.

>> You want a property you can renovate and resell, a strategy that could take you into older communities or run-down neighbourhoods poised for revival.

TIP

After you determine whether you're seeking a straightforward investment property or one you can also use and a general price range, you'll be able to narrow your search to a few prospective investment areas. Identify at least three locales; if your first choice falls through, you'll have an alternative ready to go. Chapter 2 of Book 7 reviews the different types of investments that are out there, and Chapter 3 of Book 7 helps you figure out what you want from a property.

Keeping your goals in mind

Any interest you have in using the property should mesh with your long-term goals. Don't move to a city just because you enjoyed a visit you once had. A recreational property may seem an attractive investment today but lose its appeal after the novelty of the locale wears off and your preferences change. In this case, even if the market where you've bought offers the best prospects for resale in the world, the property won't have lived up to at least one of your original expectations.

Say, for example, you live in Calgary but have dreams of retiring in 10 to 15 years. Vancouver Island, the Okanagan Valley, or the outskirts of Calgary are three areas that appeal to you as potential retirement locales. Although Vancouver Island and the Okanagan would require a significant amount of travel time to visit over the next 15 years, you're not that keen on staying in Calgary. Maybe you found a great deal on a property on Vancouver Island and your research indicates strong potential for an appreciation in its value. But wait — you've found an equally promising property in the Okanagan, and strong local demand for housing means you can rent the house to a local family until you're ready to take occupancy. Weighing the merits of each, you eventually decide on the Okanagan: You've set your heart on eventually leaving Calgary, the Okanagan is closer than Vancouver Island, and you're certain cash flow from the Okanagan property will be steady. Chapter 3 in Book 7 talks more about meshing your investment strategy with your goals.

Understanding your limitations

Your ability to afford a property, both the basic purchase price and the carrying cost of the mortgage, factor into where you scout opportunities. If you're financing your purchase by selling off a parcel of land in rural Saskatchewan, chances are that purchasing the same-sized parcel in an industrial park on the outskirts of Edmonton won't be in the cards (unless you can obtain additional financing). But if you sell a summer home in the Laurentians with dreams of buying a seaside cottage in Nova Scotia, your potential investment options will probably be greater. Chapter 4 in Book 7 helps you take a cold, hard look at your resources and how they'll affect your investing strategy.

And don't forget, time is money, so you'll probably want to factor in travel time for visiting and administering your prospective purchase. An investment shouldn't be a burden, so be sure you can effectively manage it without the task consuming too much of your time.

TIP

A standard rule for determining where to invest rules out properties located more than four hours' driving distance of where you live. This ensures you can easily reach the property in a timely fashion if required.

Looking for locations

If you're new to real estate investing, you might have a hard time figuring out where you should invest. The following questions should help you put your finger on it:

>> What are demographic trends for the area you're looking at? Are people moving in or out, and why?

>> What are the economic indicators for the region? Are the prospects for employment growth and residential development strong?

>> What have land values been doing in the areas where you're looking?

>> Is the kind of property you're buying in short supply in the area? Why or why not?

>> What are observers, both inside and outside the real estate industry, saying about the prospects for the various areas where you're considering making an investment?

The fortunes of the region can affect your fortunes as an investor. A region that seems unfavourable in the near term may offer investors some good opportunities as the economy improves or your imagination (and research) find ways to adapt your investment to meet local needs. Such opportunities will be less obvious if you don't understand the local dynamic. And they could be more difficult to sell when the time comes for you to move on, because you'll have to attract the attention of a buyer and educate them on the property's merits and potential. Chapter 5 in Book 7 discusses the search for a property at greater length.

CROSS-BORDER INVESTING

U.S. real estate investing isn't a focus of this book, but you can't ignore the fact that about 90 percent of Canada's population lives within 160 kilometres of the U.S. border and more than a million Canadian nationals live in the United States. These factors, among others, make U.S. real estate a tempting investment option. Yet despite the fact that Canada and the United States share the world's longest undefended border, you can't count on being welcomed with open arms. Canadian citizens investing in U.S. real estate should bear in mind a few facts:

- The U.S. Department of Homeland Security continues to tighten its monitoring and control of cross-border traffic. Though regular visitors to the United States may enjoy faster passage across the line, take time to consider how much inconvenience you're prepared to handle in managing an investment in another country.

- Private property rights tend to be more vigorously defended in the United States than in Canada. Becoming a property owner in the United States will also subject you to U.S. tax laws at the municipal level, if not the state and federal levels. You'll also have to comply with U.S. legislation affecting your property as well as any policies or measures that may determine how you use and dispose of real estate.

- The U.S. Internal Revenue Service withholds 30 percent of rental income and 10 to 15 percent of the proceeds from the sale of foreign-owned properties, unless certain elections are made and the appropriate paperwork is completed. This is an important consideration, potentially limiting the cash flow you're able to enjoy and impacting any reinvestment on the close of any sale.

Canada taxes its residents' worldwide income, meaning that personal income you derive from investment properties outside Canada is subject to taxes in this country. But holding the property through a corporate entity in the United States will subject it to U.S. tax laws, which could significantly complicate matters.

Mexico is another country that enjoys significant interest from property investors, especially in the wake of the 1994 North American Free Trade Agreement and reforms to Mexico's property ownership and land tenure legislation. Make absolutely certain to review any Mexican property investments you're considering with a lawyer and other advisers who can coach you on the unique complexities of Mexican real estate.

Be sure to take a look at what other authors have written on the topic. Researching the tax policies of the jurisdiction where you hope to invest — be it the United States or anywhere else — is also imperative. In addition to books such as the latest edition of *The Canadian Snowbird Guide: Everything You Need to Know about Living Part-time in the USA and Mexico* by Douglas Gray, LLB (Wiley), seek professional advice from lawyers and accountants familiar with the implications of cross-border and overseas investing.

Fitting Real Estate into a Financial Plan

Before you charge ahead with real estate investing, make a plan, because the day will likely come when you want to retire, relaxing with a cool beverage on a beach instead of talking to your real estate agent. A financial plan is about how you'll *get* to that beach with a drink in your hand. Financial planning includes five basic steps:

1. **Select your professional advisers (see Chapter 3 in Book 7).**

2. **Assess your current and future financial situation (see Chapter 4 in Book 7).**

3. **Establish your goals and priorities.**

4. **Develop a financial plan.**

5. **Evaluate your progress toward your goals.**

An objective plan, prepared with the assistance of professional advisers, will equip you to develop a portfolio of real estate that will ultimately see you sipping umbrella drinks in the sand (see Chapter 3 in Book 7 for all you need to know about assembling your crack team of advisers). The plan should address the following:

>> Personal insurance coverage

>> Your entire investment portfolio

>> Debts

>> Tax considerations of your particular situation

>> Your retirement strategy

>> Estate plans

The following sections focus on the latter two aspects, which have a direct impact on how you manage your real estate investments.

Considering when to sell

An investment not only helps you to make more of your resources in the present, it promises to help you do more in the future. Many people invest with a view to funding their retirement, so drafting a strategy for the sale of your portfolio that helps achieve your financial goals should be integral to the financial plan you develop.

Major reasons for disposing of assets include rebalancing your portfolio in favour of more liquid or higher yielding investments, or securing funds for retirement or in accordance with your estate plan.

Regular renewal of your portfolio, either through maintenance of the existing assets or trading up to new or higher yielding properties, is a standard strategy. Consider the strategy of pyramiding. Not to be confused with pyramid schemes, *pyramiding* involves the purchase of one or two select assets on a regular basis, and the sale of others, ensuring that your portfolio constantly renews itself and doesn't become stale.

TIP

Pyramiding also provides an opportunity to review your investments and assess how your financial plan is helping you achieve the goals you've established.

Planning for retirement

With an average life expectancy of just over 82 years, Canadians are living longer and enjoying healthier retirements than ever before. Planning for increased life expectancy will affect how quickly you divest your real estate portfolio. Fortunately, real estate isn't like your Registered Retirement Savings Plan (RRSP), which must be converted to a Registered Retirement Income Fund (RRIF) by the time you turn 71. Other means exist to ensure real estate provides the stable retirement income that will make your golden years golden in fact as well as in name.

Common options include the following:

>> Reverse mortgage

>> Line of credit

>> Sale and lease-back arrangement

>> Living trust

Wills and (real) estate planning

Don't kid yourself — you're not immortal. You will need a will, if only to preserve the good memories people have of you. Not having a will invites frustration for the administrators of your estate, and could result in your paying a lot more tax, essentially defeating your best efforts to be a successful real estate investor. A will ensures that your investments are efficiently and promptly distributed as you wish, not by a government formula.

REMEMBER

A will isn't the only tool available to manage your estate. Powers of attorney also help facilitate the orderly management and transfer of your investments prior to your death.

IN THIS CHAPTER

» Investing in residential properties

» Buying commercial and industrial properties

» Understanding condo and recreational properties

» Acquiring raw land

» Exploring syndicates and similar creatures

» Trusting your fortunes to income trusts

Chapter **2**

Exploring Real Estate Investments

I f you're new to the world of real estate investing, you're in the right place. This chapter introduces you to the various kinds of real estate on the market — residential, commercial and industrial, condos, recreational, and raw land — as well as alternatives such as old-style syndicates, newfangled crowdfunding initiatives, and tried-and-true real estate investment trusts (REITs).

If you're a more seasoned investor, fear not. You'll find something of value here too: good, solid information that shows how one investment stacks up against another and may spark fresh ideas for developing a diversified portfolio, taking into consideration risk versus reward. You'll be inspired to consider how less-common options like industrial real estate or retail units in a condo development can work for you.

Homing In on Residential Properties

Buying a principal residence — in other words, your home — is typically the first major real estate purchase you'll make. But if you've never considered your home as the starting point for an investment portfolio, why not? Even tycoons need somewhere to lay their heads, and finding a home for yourself is a convenient way to explore and hone the skills you'll need to tackle more complex deals as an investor.

Home-buying is a chance to practise the basic acquisition skills you'll need to select and secure properties. If you decide to rent out a suite in your house, you'll be able to test your management and people skills, as well as other joys of being a landlord. And, of course, home ownership brings regular opportunities to familiarize yourself with the hands-on maintenance that makes up the practical side of managing a real estate investment.

The following sections discuss your home or even a secondary residence, such as a cottage, as an investment property. They focus on many of the basic principles you can literally study at home and then apply to pure investment properties, from renovation to leasing.

Investing begins at home

For many, the family home is worth more than its weight in gold. Many people have a deep-seated attachment to it and don't consider it a money-making venture. Yet more than one homeowner has been delighted to find the family nest is in fact a sizeable nest egg, thanks to a steady appreciation in value. For families who have occupied the same house for several decades, the original investment can deliver a return in both happy memories and hard cash, often just in time for retirement.

Go into any bookstore or library and you'll find several guides to advise you on the purchase of your first home. You can also look online for many resources. Many of the steps you'll go through and features you're looking for in your own home are equally important when you're buying a house as an investment property.

Buying a home with the added motive of seeing it double as an investment property will intensify the importance of many of these issues. You'll be scouting features your family will want as the primary occupants but could appeal to potential tenants, too. You'll also be conscious of points that could help the house fetch a higher resale value when it comes time to sell.

Renting a suite, paying a mortgage

Tenants aren't called "mortgage-helpers" for nothing. Homeowners looking to build equity in their property can do so far faster with the help of rental income. Most lenders will also factor rental income when calculating the amount of a mortgage you can obtain to purchase the home. (Calculations will differ among lenders, so be sure to shop around.)

Tenants can help you pay off a mortgage faster, whether it's for your primary residence or a full-fledged rental property. Figure 2-1 shows why tenants can give you something to rave about — at least from a financial perspective.

FIGURE 2-1:
A mortgage-helper can shorten the standard life of a $160,000 mortgage significantly.

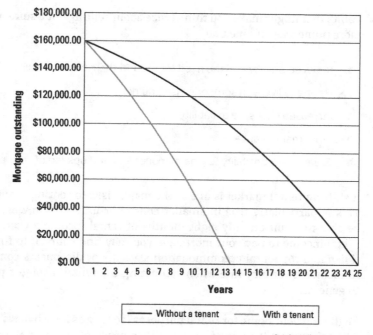

© John Wiley & Sons, Inc.

Take the example of a $200,000 bungalow with a finished basement (separate entrance, of course) in Charlottetown. Renting the basement to a student at University of Prince Edward Island for $800 a month would give you enough to add an extra $200 a week to your mortgage payments. Assuming a 20 percent down payment and an average interest rate of 5 percent over a standard 25-year term, with payments made biweekly, the extra cash could reduce the length of your mortgage by nearly 12 years and save you more than $60,000 in interest.

Being a landlord isn't for everyone, however. Renting a suite in your home to a tenant, even temporarily, not only gives you some extra cash to put toward the mortgage, but also gives you a good idea of whether you want to become a full-time landlord on a larger property or multiple properties.

On the plus side, being a landlord gives you

>> Rental income

>> Opportunities for tax deductions related to business expenses

>> Opportunities to indulge your penchant for home improvements

Points that might make you think twice about renting out a suite in your house are more numerous and include

>> Reduced privacy and the need for around-the-clock availability

>> Having to live with someone else's quirks

>> Increased exposure to liability

>> More maintenance

>> Greater responsibility for the management and upkeep of your property

WARNING

A shifting rental market is one of the major risks to renting a suite in your home. This is particularly true in smaller college or university towns, where you may be able to count on only eight months of rental income a year. If you count on rental income to pay your mortgage, you may find yourself in financial difficulty if demand for rental accommodation slackens or disappears completely. Be sure to include a vacancy rate when estimating the rental income a property is likely to generate.

TIP

Modifying your home for rental purposes (so long as local bylaws allow, of course) will affect your insurance coverage. For peace of mind, make sure your policy protects you with additional coverage. You can't require tenants obtain apartment insurance, but you can encourage them to do so and ask them to provide proof of coverage. You need to be sure you're covered in case a fire starts in the rental suite and your own property is consumed.

CAUTIONARY TALES FROM THE BASEMENT

Ask anyone who's been a tenant why someone may want to think twice before renting out a basement suite, and you're guaranteed to get an earful.

Many tenants have horror stories about hearing the landlord and his wife energetically making love upstairs or being awoken by the sound of the landlord's newborn daughter crying. You can easily address these problems with some good soundproofing. But if you don't have soundproofing, know that your tenant will hear even the most intimate moments of your daily life.

Landlords with basement suites have their own tales of woe. You want to make sure you have your privacy and aren't going to be aware of the details of the carousing of the first-year students to whom you've rented your basement. Nor do you want to be the victim of a fire caused by the space heater a tenant has brought in to keep warm.

And don't get those landlords started on the smokers and pet owners who, even if you prohibit them, may try to find a way around your house rules. The smoker, for example, may respect your desire that she not smoke in her suite, but she may leave a crop of crushed butts littering the ground around her doorway. Guess who's most likely to have to clean those up?

Proper screening will go a long way to protecting you from the worst of tenants, but be aware that personal habits can still create unexpected hassles and even conflicts within a property.

Managing tenants

Even the best tenants and properties require attention. From maintenance you might otherwise ignore to keeping track of and collecting rent, you have to keep on top of issues that you wouldn't have to watch if you were just counting on your property to rise in value rather than generate revenue. Knowing some of the scenarios that could arise will help you prepare and be a more confident landlord — and a more successful investor! Right now it's worth emphasizing the importance of having a rental agreement, especially if you're renting a suite in your primary residence.

TIP

To cut off potential problems at the pass, ask prospective tenants to complete a tenancy application form soliciting information such as rental history and names of previous landlords and other references and giving you permission to do a credit check.

Some people rent a part of their home on an informal basis, but doing so could cause problems. If you need to terminate a tenancy, for example, you'll have less legal recourse if things go sour than if you have a formal lease agreement. Some provinces such as B.C. provide a standard form of lease, available at https:// www2.gov.bc.ca/gov/content/housing-tenancy/residential-tenancies/ forms, or you can consult a real estate lawyer who will prepare and approve a lease agreement for your tenants. Doing so will help ensure that in the case of a dispute, the contract is (more or less) bulletproof.

REMEMBER

Rental contracts should include the following:

>> The number of permanent residents allowed in the unit

>> The term of the lease — whether month-to-month, renewable after a year, or reverting to month-to-month after an initial term (usually a year)

>> Whether or not pets and smoking are allowed

>> The damage deposit and grounds for its return or forfeiture

Managing property

Your ability to attract tenants and charge a higher rent will increase with the quality of the suite you offer. Be prepared to make modest, ongoing investments in the suite that will allow you to maximize the rent you can reasonably expect a tenant to pay. Painting the suite may enable you to charge a higher rent that will more than pay for the paint job over the course of the tenancy. Getting in the habit of investing in regular maintenance and upgrades in your own home will prepare you for the economics of managing a stand-alone residential investment.

Renovating for fun and profit

Making over a home can be a lot of fun and pay off in a property worth more than straight *appreciation*, or increase in market value, would allow. Renovating also allows you to build a home that you'll enjoy living in, at least until you sell it. Though this can be fun and satisfying, the major drawback is that it requires a lot of hard work.

For those willing to make the effort, homes suitable for renovation generally come for a better price than homes with the latest features and finishes. Buying a fixer-upper that you've carefully inspected with the help of a contractor can get you into an up-and-coming market earlier than other buyers. The fixing up you do allows you to offer a modernized home to buyers who probably wouldn't have looked twice at the place before you worked your magic.

WARNING

Another option for minor makeovers is giving the tenant an allowance for work such as painting or providing a temporary discount in rent in lieu of paying for improvements or repairs. However, be sure to confirm the details of the arrangement with the tenant in writing to avoid misunderstandings of what the deal entails, including the scope of the work to be done, the amount of the allowance or other discount or incentive and — if trades are required — the need for licensed workers.

Owning second homes and cottages

Nearly one in six Canadians have a second residence, with a condo or cottage being among the most popular choices. As well as being another place to hang your hat, a second home is also a simple means of developing a successful real estate portfolio.

WARNING

Some municipalities now regulate property owners who use short-term rental sites such as Airbnb. British Columbia has introduced vacancy taxes to make sure local homes house local residents rather than sit vacant more than six months each year. While owning a second home may sound attractive, make sure you're compliant with local government regulations targeting second-home owners.

Second residences

A second house, a condo for the kids while they go to university, or even your own future retirement home can each be a practical answer to your personal needs and desires as well as work as an investment. Consider how a second (or third, or fourth) home can serve your current needs *and* those of your investment strategy.

For example, if you're shopping for a condo for the kids to use while they're attending university, you'll probably be scouting neighbourhoods that will allow you to rent to other students when your kids graduate. Research the market and see if you can serve a need for student housing in a desirable locale that's currently undersupplied. Perhaps you want to be in a certain area when you retire; finding someone to rent the house or apartment you buy until you're ready to move in will help reduce your retirement costs.

Cottages

Chances are you can't spend every day in cottage country, however appealing that sounds. But if local bylaws allow it, you may be able to derive a small amount of income from leasing your cottage to others for a few days or weeks at a time. It's a sensible way of making sure your property is occupied and allows you to recover some of the purchase cost.

You may need to substantially upgrade the property, however, to make it appealing to renters. You've probably heard the stories of rustic cottages in such poor repair that the vacation became a nightmare — you don't want to be *that* landlord. As with other rental properties, make sure what you're offering is in good repair. Also, confirm that the renovations you have in mind are allowed. Limitations exist in many areas regarding the type of upgrades permitted, especially for waterfront properties.

Another common concern is that absentee landlords could lead to a hollowing out of the local community. The last thing many year-round residents of any neighbourhood want is for a significant portion of homes to be vacant most of the year. If you intend to rent out the cottage you're buying, check what local and provincial regulations allow.

WARNING

Some communities with large numbers of cottages limit the use of properties by anyone other than the owners. Short-term rentals to vacationers through sites such as Airbnb may sound like a good idea, but they may also invite the wrath of locals. Common concerns include the potential for short-term residents to disrespect community standards, overburden local resources such as groundwater, or change a community's character by introducing a more transient population.

Securing Commercial and Industrial Properties

Commercial and industrial properties aren't the most glamorous investments, but if they pass muster with the Canada Pension Plan and other institutional investors, why not with you? Buying an office building or warehouse is more complex than buying the average home, but with leases typically running for years at a time, you stand a good chance of enjoying a more stable cash flow than you would from residential properties. The trick is finding the opportunities, especially if you're just starting out. Although anyone can relate to residential housing, investing in commercial and industrial properties requires preparation and the help of experienced advisers.

However high the standards you have for residential real estate, houses are relatively simple propositions when it comes to market influences. By contrast, commercial and industrial properties are subject to diverse factors and influences rooted in economic trends. People shop in only so many places, and only so much office space is required in each community. And warehouses? They're not quite as numerous as coffee shops.

Still, opportunities exist to do well by commercial and industrial properties, which are home to the businesses that can be the lifeblood of communities. However, this is generally not a viable option for investors with less than $50,000 to invest.

TIP

What the Multiple Listing Service (www.realtor.ca) is for residential real estate, ICX (www.icx.ca) is for nonresidential properties. It's one of several services that can help you locate commercial and industrial properties. The larger commercial brokerage firms also publish their listings, not all of which are necessarily linked to the MLS system. Don't forget to check out the various media that publish real estate listings, whether targeted specifically to real estate investors, such as Western Investor (www.westerninvestor.com), or trade publications for specific industries. A wide range of print and electronic resources exist can help you uncover opportunities.

Assessing classes

Several classes of commercial and industrial real estate exist, with the most recognizable being retail, office, and industrial, which are discussed in the following sections. Each has a different level of liquidity, based on the performance of the local economy and the shifting measure known as investor confidence. With several large players involved in these types of real estate, however, you stand a good chance of eventually being able to sell.

Retail

The humble shop front is a mainstay of main streets everywhere. But not every merchant owns the shop, let alone the building where the shop is located. Often, a private landlord owns the building, which may or may not have some residential units above. Indeed, a mixed-use building in a smaller town can provide your portfolio with a measure of diversity by giving you a stake in two asset classes at once. Many large urban centres feature retail units within condo developments. The retail units are sold off like the apartments above and at comparable prices. Providing you can find a tenant who will meet the needs of the surrounding neighbourhood — this often requires some skill, rooted in a knowledge of the neighbourhood and an ability to devise a lease package that will attract the right tenants — you'll be able to reap the benefits of their success.

Small community-oriented plazas with just a few shops can also provide a steady income and, in the right location, appreciation in value if resold for redevelopment.

TIP

Retail units also work well if you need premises for your own business. Just as you buy a home rather than rent an apartment so you can build equity in your own property rather than someone else's, buying commercial space can be a good long-term investment. Car dealerships are typical examples; some auto dealers make more money off the lots from which they sell cars than from car sales. Depending on your business, the property where it operates may earn you more money than your business ever will.

Office

Whether it's for the local accountant or an ambitious entrepreneur, office space is a type of real estate few businesses can do without. Similar to residential, it's available in both stand-alone buildings and larger developments ranging from condo developments to business parks.

Despite exposure to shifts in the economy, office properties generally allow you to implement longer-term leases than are typically possible on other forms of real estate. Businesses value long-term arrangements to ensure the stability of their own operations, and you can use that fact to stabilize your investment portfolio.

Although it's worth noting that vacancies are often higher than for residential real estate, keep in mind that you'll also be able to charge a higher rent and contract for increases over the life of a lease.

Industrial

The workhorses of the real estate sector, industrial properties are probably the least glamorous assets you'll encounter. Bare-bones construction makes them functional rather than fashionable, designed as they are to serve the needs of manufacturers, distributors, or any grab-bag of blue-collar uses. But the basic service they provide also makes them stable investments with a good potential for return.

WARNING

Conducting proper due diligence means that before your purchase and industrial property, you investigate to know what types of businesses are operating on the premises. For example, the activities of some industrial tenants raise the risk of soil contamination, which could leave you on the hook for the cleanup costs and negate the income you get from the property. It could also lead to legal trouble. The leaching of petrochemicals is a common scenario, and many landowners have found themselves on the hook for cleanup costs associated with past activities. If the chemicals have flowed onto an adjacent property, the owner could face a bill for remediating all affected properties. Due diligence can help you avoid being caught out by past problems. It can also help you focus on attracting specific kinds of users who, because of the property's historical uses or location, will be a good fit and pose little risk to its future condition. This also holds true if you're think-ing about building new space. Researching the market will indicate sectors in par-ticular need of industrial space, and some may eventually purchase the property when it comes time for you to sell.

TIP

Prior to Canada legalizing recreational cannabis in October 2018, black market pot was often grown in unlicensed facilities known as grow-ops. Some jurisdictions required the registration of properties that hosted grow-ops and the disclosure to future purchasers due to the risk of moisture damage, moulds, and other issues with the properties. The information helped buyers to know what they were get-ting into. Now that cannabis is legal, with homeowners allowed to grow at least four plants for personal use, a lingering skunky smell may be the biggest risk. Groups such as the Ontario Real Estate Association continue to have concerns and want buyers to know a property's history. However, the reality in most of Canada is that busted grow-ups are unregistered, so buyers need to thoroughly review and inspect properties for damage prior to purchase as part of their due diligence.

Assessing liquidity

A property's *liquidity* — its ability to be sold — is more important in assessing the long-term potential of nonresidential assets than homes and apartments. But it's also more complex to determine, depending on your familiarity with the several factors at play. Most residential buyers, for example, don't examine trends in a specific industry to determine where to buy a home. But you'll want to study the demand for retail space in a community if you're buying a strip mall, or examine commodity price trends if you've been offered a warehouse previously used by the forest sector. Are you up for the challenge?

An asset's liquidity is a function of its attractiveness and appeal to investors, per-haps even more than market cycles (a full cycle consists of a buyer's market, a seller's market, and a balanced market; see Chapter 3 in Book 7). An asset in Mon-treal, for example, may tend to have greater liquidity than a property in Corner Brook — not because Corner Brook is a bad place to invest, but because Montreal is a larger centre with a more diverse economy and, in short, more opportunities for the use of the property. Properties that can deliver a greater return than more expensive assets will also enjoy healthy liquidity, regardless of how the broader market is faring. On the other hand, key assets in a market such as Vancouver are *illiquid* — difficult to sell — because so few alternatives exist that owners simply aren't willing to sell what they have.

REMEMBER

The greater the future demand for a property, the better your chance of seeing a return when the time comes to sell — whether that's next year or five years away. Factors to take into account include

>> The property's proximity to properties used by similar or complementary businesses

>> Prospects for the growth of the sector the property serves

>> The economic strength of the community in which the property is located

>> The property's proximity to transportation networks that may enhance its appeal to users in a sector other than that of the current user

For example, a port is a good location for a warehouse, but an office building located nowhere near other offices or other commercial properties might be a hard sell to potential tenants and therefore future buyers.

COMPETITORS OR POTENTIAL PURCHASERS?

Because some forms of real estate are in stronger demand than others, you're bound to run into competition at some point. Competition isn't necessarily bad, however. The relationships you build with other investors may lead to opportunities in the future. It pays to respect your competitors.

Respect for your competitors is a particularly important attribute in the close-knit world of commercial real estate investment. Relationships you develop now may help you sell a property in the future. Rather than see yourself in competition with other purchasers, consider them future business partners. The people you trump today may be interested in buying the asset in the future.

Many large investors looking to develop their holdings won't enter a new market unless they can find a sizable portfolio that makes entry worth their while. You may have two or three properties, but if you can form partnerships with other small owners, you increase the chance of attracting the interest of a larger buyer. This is true whether you're a group of homeowners selling to a developer or commercial landlords trying to attract a major investor.

Weighing Condos as an Investment

Condos, also known as *strata-titled units* in British Columbia and *co-proprietorships* in Quebec, are more than just apartments. Residential condos (both apartments and townhomes) are the best-known form of this type of real estate, but this type also encompasses commercial, industrial, and hotel properties. Yet when people talk of condos, they almost always mean residential.

WARNING

Because condo units are generally subject to the building council's regulations, condos carry some of the perils of joint ownership. Condo bylaws occasionally limit activities allowed in suites, including the ability to rent units. You need to check the bylaws before you make any commitment. There could be some provinces that permit condo rentals as a right. As provincial legislation can change at any time, you need to do your due diligence research in advance. Read the provincial legislation online, and check with a condo lawyer. Condo fees have the potential to vary, with special levies possible for maintenance and repairs. Just because a problem didn't affect your suite, the mere fact that it happened in the building at all may subject you to these levies and diminish the value of your unit.

A MORE DETAILED LOOK AT CONDOMINIUMS

Condos are organized very differently from other types of property. Residential condominiums include apartments as well as single-detached, semi-detached, and row homes; stack townhomes; and duplexes. Building sites, subdivisions, and mobile home parks also fall into the condo class. Primary elements of the condo are the residential unit and the common elements. Common elements generally include walkways, driveways, lawns and gardens, lobbies, elevators, parking areas, recreational facilities, storage areas, laundry rooms, stairways, plumbing, electrical systems and portions of walls, ceilings, floors, and other items.

Ownership of the common elements is typically distributed among the unit owners according to the size of their units. The exact description of the common elements, and what you own as part of your unit, may differ from development to development, but the documents you receive when you buy your unit will state these clearly. Some unit owners may have exclusive rights to some of the common elements. Typical examples of so-called limited common elements include parking spaces, storage lockers, roof gardens, balconies, patios, and front and back yards.

(continued)

Exploring Real Estate Investments

(continued)

Residential condominiums occur in both urban and suburban settings. Urban condos typically take the following forms:

- A high-rise apartment building
- A three- to five-storey new midrise building
- An older building converted from rental apartments
- A building where unit owners own the street-level floor, which is leased to retailers to help offset the common maintenance fees of the residential condominiums in the rest of the building

Suburban condominiums maximize their use of the available land while affording attractive views, private driveways, and common recreational facilities such as swimming pools, tennis courts, saunas, and even playgrounds. Some of the most common formats include

- Cluster housing consisting of multi-unit structures of two or four units apiece, each with its own private entranceway
- Townhome-type single-family homes distributed in rows
- Garden apartments consisting of a group of apartment buildings surrounding a common green, frequently with each of the floors held by separate condo owners
- Duplexes, triplexes, or fourplexes
- A series of detached single-family homes in a subdivision format, all using the same land and parking areas

Investing in residential condos

Residential condos are popular investments. Vancouver, which boasts one of Canada's most active condo markets, has seen as many as half the units in some new buildings sold to investors. That's an important statistic, but not great news if you're planning to rent a unit in that kind of situation. Investors who purchase a unit with the intention of renting it out want to know they have a reasonable hope of finding tenants, something that's more difficult to do when several landlords are competing for the same limited number of prospects.

On the other hand, condos can be an attractive alternative to standard rental accommodation. And this raises the potential for them to command a higher rent than other forms of residential rentals. Barring a glut of similar product and providing your unit is in an appropriate neighbourhood, condos can be an affordable means for you to claim a slice of the rental market.

TIP

Because condos are run by a council, know what the rules allow before you buy. Some buildings limit the number or percentage of suites available for rental, while others limit the kinds of improvements that can be made and whether pets are allowed. Other issues to consider include management fees and the potential for upcoming expenses, which are usually shared among the owners. Ask to see the minutes of the council meetings and view other records associated with the building's operation and management.

Investing in commercial condos

Retail, office, and industrial condos used to be rare, but they've now become accepted parts of the real estate market in Canada's major cities. Guidelines for investing in these properties are similar to those for other forms of commercial property (covered earlier in this chapter) but with the added precautions regarding condo investments.

Owner-occupiers reap the most advantages of owning a commercial condo, however. Some of the benefits include

>> **Fixed business costs:** Because you own the commercial space, you aren't subject to rising rents. Although operating costs may fluctuate based on condo fees, as a member of the building council, you have some input into what those fees will be.

>> **Tax advantages:** The standard business-related advantages of occupying property you own hold true for condo units, including opportunities to deduct depreciation and business expenses associated with the unit.

>> **Appreciation in value:** Like any other investment, you also reap the benefit from any appreciation in property value — the reason you became an investor in the first place!

Investing in hotel condos

Hotels developed on the condominium model have had a mixed history and are less common today than in the boom leading up to the financial crisis of 2008. Units are typically sold to buyers who in turn contract with a management company to oversee the operation of the hotel. Proceeds from hotel operations then flow back to the suite owners. Disappointment may await investors who expect a certain return on their units.

Exploring Real Estate Investments

WARNING

Real estate is not without risk, and this goes double for hotel investments. Being subject to the vagaries of the tourist trade, a hotel condo suite may actually cost you money. Poor cash flow at the property and paltry returns will diminish your chances of selling your unit, so buy wisely. Select a property that has demonstrated its success in the market. You can find useful tips in the book *101 Streetsmart Condo Buying Tips for Canadians,* by Douglas Gray (Wiley).

WARNING

Some hotel condo managers promise to return a specific amount to you as an investor. Beware of these properties because the variable nature operating costs and hotel occupancies make this a difficult promise to keep and could lead to costly and stressful litigation.

Dreaming of Recreational Properties

Recreational properties are more than a cottage at the lake for investors. From fractional ownership to islands with development potential, the opportunities available are wide-ranging and far-flung.

Recreational properties offer the promise of an enhanced quality of life. They're a retreat where a property owner can enjoy the lifestyle as well as entertain friends and extended and blended families. Many buyers see recreational properties as the homes as a future primary residence, one to which they'll eventually retire.

A purchaser of recreational property can use equity from a principal residence to buy a recreational property and take out high-ratio financing through Canada Mortgage and Housing Corporation (CMHC). This move makes buying a recreational property an affordable proposition. It also reflects the fact that many people will eventually sell their primary residence and put the proceeds towards the recreational properties they're moving into. Unlike in the past, many buyers are seeing recreational properties as an opportunity to trade up or downsize, not as a discretionary purchase.

TIP

Should you have the chance to sell either your principal residence or recreational property, you have the option of *naming* one of the two properties as your principal residence. Generally, this is the one with the largest capital gain; as your principal residence it wouldn't be subject to capital gains tax. The other property would be subject to capital gains tax. Talk to your accountant.

WARNING

CMHC will back high-ratio mortgages on recreational properties only if the properties are suitable — and accessible — for year-round occupancy by the borrower or a relative of the borrower on a rent-free basis.

Cottages and cabins

Cottages and cabins are a simple form of recreational property with the same potential to appreciate in value as any other residential asset. Renovations and the possible renting out of cottages provides the opportunity to boost value and provide cash flow on an ongoing basis. When compared to other forms of recreational real estate, this is probably the one most familiar to people and easily understood.

Many cottages come with an acreage that provides recreational opportunities. The acreage itself may be a good investment if you have the foresight (and good fortune) to buy in the path of urban development. Calgary is a good example of a city that has swallowed up many smaller communities in the course of its growth, turning countless former retreats from city life into part of the city itself — and handing the former owners of the properties a windfall to boot.

Fractional ownership

Fractional ownership, as the name implies, gives you an equity share in a property — usually a resort-style development — with rights to access it in proportion to your share. For example, if you own 10 to 25 percent of a property, you have rights to use it 10 to 25 percent of the time.

Unlike a timeshare, in which you purchase only rights to use the property in proportion to your interest, a fractional ownership purchase puts your name on the title deed, along with those of the other owners. The owners generally have an agreement outlining the procedure for selling interest in the property. To avoid any misunderstandings or conflict, make sure you have a proper legal structure and appropriate documentation of the arrangement.

TIP

One of the draws of fractional ownership is that your unit is often in a rental pool when you're not using it. Even if that option isn't offered, you may be able to rent it yourself. You need to have your real estate lawyer read the unit contract before any commitment. Either way, you'll get to enjoy some income in addition to having a getaway for your own use.

Most fractional ownerships of residential properties where the owner is registered on the land title as a fractional owner tend to be from ¼ to $\frac{1}{10}$. It could have a higher fraction, but that is not the norm. In most cases, based on the per unit cost of the fraction, the actual aggregate purchase value of the "investment" could be valued many times more than the actual market value.

Resorts by the suite

Many resort properties offer investment opportunities similar to the ones discussed in the earlier section "Investing in hotel condos." Like fractional ownership arrangements, these types of property allow owners to acquire stake in a property that's more affordable than if they had full ownership.

Developers have pursued these types of developments because they reduce the risk of proceeding with construction. You benefit from access to the suite for set periods of time each year, as well as proceeds from the net profits of the suite's operation.

WARNING

Some overseas resort projects undertaken by or marketed to Canadians may seem like attractive opportunities, but be sure to thoroughly investigate the risks. Chapter 1 in Book 7 briefly discusses cross-border investing, but resort properties are worth special scrutiny — most people want a vacation property that's a slice of heaven rather than a taste of, er, the other place. Moreover, local factors may complicate development of a project you're considering solely based on the plans. Be sure you understand what safeguards exist for investors, and know your exit strategy.

TIP

For further information and more tips on recreational property, consult the book *The Complete Guide to Buying and Owning Recreational Property in Canada,* by Douglas Gray (Wiley).

Developing a Taste for Raw Land

Just because a property is vacant doesn't mean it's worthless. Sometimes the value has yet to be realized. As a *land banker,* someone who buys up properties for the value of the land alone, you can be there at ground zero — literally! — and be the first to profit from property that has a great future ahead of it. The next purchaser may be another investor, an individual who wants to build a home, or even a developer with visions of a subdivision. The land you bank doesn't have to be in the city, either; it can just as easily be in a rural community with a growing residential population.

REMEMBER

Raw land is good if you're an investor with a long-term plan. The downside of land banking is the chance you'll find yourself waiting a long time before the value of the land increases enough to make it worth selling. Regardless of what you do with land, it's what underpins all real estate and they're not making any more of it! It's a starting point worth considering.

Staking your claim

You may feel like an old-time prospector when you first buy a piece of raw land. It might not pan out for you, regardless of your gut feeling. But for the low price at which you can buy undeveloped land in many parts of Canada, raw land is frequently a gamble worth taking. Whether you're in the city or the countryside, several alternatives can help you make good on your investment.

Choosing a locale, as with every other real estate purchase, requires research into the area's current conditions and future prospects. Because the return you're looking for probably requires the development of the property into something new, your attitude should be similar to that of a renovator: Look for a site with the potential to be popular, and one that is showing signs of a turnaround. For a rural community, the clues might lie in proximity to an urban centre, and demographic trends such as an influx of retirees or younger couples.

TIP

Try to find the best fit between the land you purchase and what your research tells you is fuelling the long-term potential of the surrounding community. You want to be where the action is, so that you can benefit from the potential future interest in your site. Civic planning departments and local public transit authorities post their development plans publicly, allowing you to see where residential and commercial building is likely to occur.

REMEMBER

Raw land comes with just as many responsibilities as any other property. You have to make sure your property conforms to any local bylaws, especially with regards to appearance and cleanliness. You don't want it to become a liability, and you will be liable if hazards exist on it that could bring others to harm. You also want to ensure it meets environmental conditions, so that you don't find yourself with a nasty surprise when the time comes to sell.

Goin' country or swingin' in the city

Development often follows a relentless pace. The patch of grass where you played as a kid has become a block of town houses. As a real estate investor you may not want to lose what was, but you can't help thinking of what's to come.

This country wouldn't have any cities had someone not first put up a house and begun developing undeveloped land. Because the cost of urban property is often quite high, opportunities to secure vacant lots are sometimes most frequent in rural communities. British Columbia and Ontario considered the trend so significant that legislation in these two provinces limits the use of farmland.

Vacant lots in urban settings are subject to far more variables, including the use of surrounding properties, local zoning, and carrying costs (especially property taxes). You must often be prepared to hold land for a long time before you see a return. Often, the payoff comes from having a property someone else needs to pursue a development. Through strategic buying, a small investment can deliver a decent return relative to the time spent managing it.

This is true in small towns as well as cities. A small town won't always be small, especially if it is adjacent to a growing city. Calgary is a good example of a city that's grown, absorbing smaller communities in its path. Had you owned a parcel of land in some of those communities when they were outside the city, you might be enjoying a wealthy retirement today.

Banking on land

Rather than holding a single lot, you may have the opportunity to acquire a large tract of land. As a land banker you may add to this tract or wait patiently to sell it either in whole or in part to a developer. Although land bankers typically deal with residential land, some bank land for other uses.

REMEMBER

The main risk to banking land is that you're *not receiving any income* from it but still have to pay the taxes and other costs of ownership. Some cities offer owners a tax break for creating parks and community gardens on vacant land; rural proper-ties can be leased to farmers for a small amount of income (or in British Columbia, a tax break). Quebec and British Columbia both have home-to-land-matching programs that link landowners with farmers in need of property. Knowing how long you can afford to carry a property, or knowing what you intend to do with it until you sell, is key to being a successful land banker.

Deciding to build

Because you won't see a significant return on your investment in raw land until it's developed, it's important to have a vision for the property. What kind of devel-opment promises the greatest payoff? Are you willing to do it yourself? If not, are you willing to *joint venture,* or partner, with a fellow investor or developer? Per-haps, in rare cases, you will be able to see a return by merely holding the land and selling it at a profit.

Becoming a developer

You're not likely to become a developer with your first piece of property, unless you're undertaking renovations. But if you have the cash to fund development, why not add value to part or all of the land you've been acquiring? This can include everything from a single building on a rural acreage to an urban in-fill project that takes a sliver of land to a higher and better use.

Partnering with others

Sometimes it can pay to enter into an arrangement with a partner that allows you to reap a return from the development of your land. Perhaps you supply the land alone or you commit to arranging the servicing; perhaps you do more, such as undertake the rezoning process that primes it for development. Whatever arrangement you choose can allow you to see a better return than you would by selling off the raw land to an eager developer.

A partnership could also speed the sale of the land if your hopes for the area where you bought haven't quite come true. One developer had a tract of land subdivided for sale as development lots for single-family homes. But the lots weren't selling. So the developer approached a home builder who designed custom homes on the lots. The partnership added value to the land, allowing the developer to sell the lots for much more than the market value of the bare land, and the home builder was able to make a few sales, too.

Holding out for gain

Occasionally, the land you've assembled and patiently held will yield a return without any improvement at all. This can happen when development happens on surrounding properties and the prospects for your property become brighter by association. Or perhaps the land itself is suitable for a particular use, such as growing grapes rather than apples, and the price of vineyard land is rising. You'll be able to take advantage of the shift.

REMEMBER

Needless to say, if you're planning to hold land, you should have a long-term plan that supports that objective.

Howdy, Partners: Buying into Syndicates

Syndicates, in which money from investors supports a property's acquisition for investment purposes, have a checkered past (see the nearby sidebar "Acknowledging history"). Reforms to the regulations governing them have boosted their favour among investors who have an appetite for real estate but no desire to actually own or manage property themselves. Buying into a syndicate requires that the investor get an independent legal opinion, however, and a clear understanding of the risks involved.

Syndicated properties offer several benefits, including potentially a lower degree of risk because the syndicator rigorously scrutinizes properties before investors join the syndicate. Syndicated properties also typically offer a higher return to investors than comparable properties investors manage themselves. This may be because the investment is genuinely expected to deliver a better return; alternatively, it may reflect a higher degree of risk, depending on whether the investors directly participate in the purchase or are simply providing the funds to a mortgage investment corporation. (Higher returns often signal a higher level of risk.)

Syndication generally occurs through investment firms charged with selling the investment to clients. The investment managers at such firms should be alert to trends in the investment world and determined to manage assets for the best return possible. A wise investor must know the syndicate's track record and read the prospectus carefully.

ACKNOWLEDGING HISTORY

During the 1970s and 1980s, developers in Canada could take advantage of the federal multi-unit residential building (MURB) program to solicit investment in their multi-family rental projects. Such investments were effectively *tax shelters*, places where investors could put money to defer or reduce tax payments. During the late 1980s, many of the old MURBs were converted to condos, nixing the cash flow on which investors depended. A lack of adequate federal oversight didn't protect some investors from receiving the short end of the stick in the course of some conversions, and ultimately gave the investments a bad name.

Similarly, several mortgage investment corporations failed investors in the 1990s. Like syndicates, the mortgage investment corporation (MIC) would invest in real estate, but on the mortgage side. Investors would take a share of the interest paid on the mortgages. Though investors believed the MICs were reliable investment vehicles with limited risks, many turned out to be quite the opposite.

Today, syndicates and their kin are subject to strict regulations established by the province in which they operate. They typically identify properties and solicit funds for the purchase of the asset from established investment firms. The investment firms in turn offer shares in the properties to their clients, who receive both dividends from the ongoing operation of the property and a share in the proceeds from the property when it's eventually sold. Shares can be priced from $5,000.

Gaining strength in numbers

The benefit of syndicates is that you're not alone. The acquisition of the property is through a partnership, meaning your share is one of several.

The syndicator typically takes a cut of the proceeds on the property's sale, and the profits are shared with other investors. Among the benefits you enjoy are capital appreciation and even deferred taxes. As with any service for which you pay, however, shop around and find an investment and management team with which you feel comfortable.

Turning to the crowd

Crowdfunding is a new twist on the syndicate. Similar to crowdfunding campaigns for charitable causes (think GoFundMe), crowdfunding for real estate takes place via a public platform online and investors plunk down $500 or $1,000 for a stake in the next big development. It's a way for small investors to gain exposure to real estate. Although relatively untested, the model has sourced funds for a variety of redevelopment projects in the United States and has been tested on a small scale in Canada by the likes of NexusCrowd Inc.

The platforms typically serve as intermediaries that connect investors with opportunities or developers with capital (depending on your perspective). Because the platforms themselves aren't selling securities, they're largely unregulated. It pays to research the terms of each site thoroughly and ensure your interests are protected.

Knowing the risks

Syndicates aren't risk-free. You run the risk that the money you're investing in a syndicate will be lost. It's up to you to know the risks. Don't be taken in by a sales pitch. Ask your lawyer to analyze the syndicate in terms of what investments drive its business and the nature of your exposure.

REMEMBER

Before anteing up your hard-earned cash for either a syndicated investment opportunity or a crowdfunded development, speak with your tax accountant, financial planner, and lawyer for their opinions on the investment and the relevant safeguards. (Chapter 3 in Book 7 discusses finding and adding these professionals to your team.)

Researching Real Estate Investment Trusts

Real estate investment trusts (REITs) are a popular investment option because they pay regular dividends from the ongoing operations of their assets — that is, real estate. Like syndicates, they offer an efficient means of investing in real estate while avoiding direct ownership of property. The relatively low degree of risk (beyond fluctuations in market value) makes them a good choice for conservative investors who want a stake in the real estate market.

The following sections help you understand what income trusts are, how they operate, and how to understand the value they're delivering to you as an investor.

Trusted alternatives

Just like public companies, *income trusts* trade on the public markets. Shares in the company are known as *units*, which can fluctuate in value but which entitle their holders to a share in the taxable earnings resulting from the business of the trust. For REITs, the business is the operation of the various buildings in its portfolio. These can include apartment buildings, seniors' care facilities, shopping centres, office buildings, hotels, or any other class of real estate in which the REIT chooses to invest. The trust's managers are accountable to unit holders for distributions that aren't made.

TECHNICAL STUFF

Trust units trade on the public markets like stocks but are different. Although stocks represent an ownership stake in the company that issues them, trust units entitle holders to *distributions* from the business or businesses that deliver their profits to the trust.

The range of REITs in Canada offers investors opportunities to invest in most classes of real estate.

TIP

Searching for the perfect trust begins with plugging the terms *investment trust*, *REIT*, and even *income fund* and *income trust* into your favourite search engine. You can then identify the trusts that interest you most and dig into their financial statements on SEDAR (www.sedar.com) if they're Canadian or consult your investment broker.

Regardless of the trust structure, the assets managed by the operating business of the trust are subject to the same forces that apply to every other building in their class. Multi-family residential properties tend to have stable incomes, for example. Hotels operate in a more volatile environment and will tend to see greater fluctuations in the returns they can deliver. Shopping centres also offer a measure of stability, but they'll provide a return that reflects the strength of the retail sector.

WARNING

Don't take the word *trust* literally! The trust's assets remain subject to the trends influencing the sector in which they operate. These trends will have an impact on their operations, profitability, and, in turn, the amount of the distributions you receive. In extreme cases, if the operating business of the trust performs poorly, a distribution may not land in your lap at all. On the other hand, as witnessed when stock markets took a dive in late 2008, an otherwise solid REIT may be discounted by the market regardless of how well its real estate is performing because the units of the REIT are seen as just one more equity.

Reading financial statements

To get a better grasp of what the trust in which you're considering investing is all about, one of the most important things you can do is crack open its books. Thanks to SEDAR (www.sedar.com), an electronic database handling the filings of all public companies in Canada, this is relatively easy to do. SEDAR, which stands for System for Electronic Document Analysis and Retrieval, logs quarterly financial statements, annual reports, and annual information forms and all other public documents issued by the various real estate investment trusts that operate in Canada.

TIP

Studying the statements SEDAR collects gives you some insight into the performance of a trust, any issues it may have faced, and how its executives handled them. Don't neglect the notes to the financial statements, which can harbour extra information not expressly stated in the formal part of the quarterly and annual reports. Before you even glance at a trust's financial statements, look at the annual information form. It provides an overview of the trust's business, its development, and observations on the risks to the operating business from which it receives the profits.

Understanding the operation of a given trust can be invaluable in helping you decide whether to buy units in the trust, or to opt for one involved in an asset class more to your taste.

Exploring Real Estate
Investments

Chapter **3**

Establishing Your Investment Strategy

P eople can talk as much as they like about making money in real estate, but the proof is in the doing. And to do it right, you need a strategy. This chapter discusses the importance of understanding market cycles, setting investment goals, and identifying the properties that can help you achieve them. It also covers the need for a group of trusted advisers to guide and direct you as you make the choices that will help you reach (hopefully) your investment goals.

REMEMBER

Take time to research and develop your investment strategy, independently and in consultation with your advisers. (Don't have advisers yet? Don't worry — you get help with that in this chapter, too.) The topics in this chapter help you build your strategy, but the outcomes will reflect your own unique circumstances and goals.

Studying Market Cycles

Some people think the markets are on a perpetual wash cycle: Somehow, they always end up taken to the cleaners and wind up a sock short of a full pair. The pros know that market cycles are more like a life cycle, rising and falling with economic cycles and investor sentiment. The typical cycle will see both supply and demand grow, mature, and eventually die. All markets are cyclical to some degree, thanks to the forces of supply and demand, seasonal trends, or the latest fashion. The property market is no different. Certain types of real estate regularly pass in and out of favour, home sales typically slump in winter and rebound in spring, and the balance between buyer and seller is constantly shifting.

Understanding market cycles is important to your success as an investor, whether you're a buyer or a seller. Purchasing a property for a good price when demand is weak improves your chances of selling at a gain, if you're able to gauge the direction in which the market is heading! As a seller, a market with many buyers allows you to command a higher price, especially if the property is unique or one that commands plenty of interest.

The following sections help you understand market cycles, the variables influencing them, and how you can navigate the challenges and opportunities they present.

The real estate cycle

The typical length of a cycle in the real estate market is five years, though it can last as long as 12 years. Some observers argue that market cycles are lengthening under the influence of global investment trends and interest in real estate as an investment. The basic cycle itself hasn't changed, however.

The market goes through three stages in the course of a full cycle. These include the buyer's market, the seller's market, and the balanced market. A balanced market is the most fleeting of the three, but the following sections give each of them equal time.

Buyer's market

The *buyer's market* typically comes at the bottom of a cycle, when properties are plentiful in relation to the number of potential buyers. Properties take longer to sell, prompting vendors to offer incentives such as lower prices and the opportunity to negotiate concessions. You also have an opportunity to shop around for better properties or lower prices on comparable assets, and to leverage existing assets to make purchases with a better chance of appreciation than those already in your portfolio.

Seller's market

A *seller's market* is the opposite of a buyer's market. Many buyers mean good demand, shorter sales times, and fewer properties to go around. Sale prices typically rise, and in extreme cases competition between potential buyers can lead to rapid appreciation in market value. Less room for bargaining means that as a buyer you have to know what you want, be prepared to pay for it, and expect conditional offers to come under closer scrutiny as vendors try to secure the best deal for themselves.

Balanced market

Don't expect to find an exact balance in the market, which usually tends more to one side of the spectrum than the other. When it happens, however, a balanced market provides a stable environment for both buyers and sellers. Properties tend to sell in a reasonable length of time that allows for relaxed negotiation, adequate due diligence, and reasonable offers. The various parties to the deal have the best chance under these conditions of reaching a mutually satisfying conclusion.

MESHING WITH MARKETS

Jon and Joan had planned to buy a home for many years. They saved their money religiously, planning to use Jon's money for expenses and Joan's money towards a down payment on a house that would be close to where they worked. They were each planning on using some of their Registered Retirement Savings Plans (RRSPs) for a first-home purchase. They didn't like debt, so they aimed to save at least 50 percent of the house price before they would buy.

At the time, interest rates were 5 percent. However, over the five years they were saving, home prices in their area of choice went up 10 percent a year, from $200,000 to $300,000 — 50 percent more than what they had budgeted. The shift in values meant what they'd saved for a down payment now amounted to a mere 10 percent of the purchase price. Moreover, new lending rules meant their combined income was too low to qualify for the 90 percent mortgage. Even though interest rates had dropped, they had to qualify at a rate two percentage points higher to demonstrate that they could carry the loan in the future.

Jon and Joan decided that the only place they could afford was two hours from town. It had a nice rural ambience, but the long drive and high gas prices made them think hard about the arrangement. However, it was too good to pass up, so after they bought the property, they decided to launch a home-based business that allowed them to work remotely. Thanks to technology, they could run their business from home without having to commute to town every day. The moral of the story? A *clear sense of the reality* of the real estate marketplace, supply and demand, interest rates, and affordability, and a realistic game plan is critical to choosing the right property.

Factors affecting market conditions

Supply and demand, capital available for investment, and confidence in the market may help define market conditions, but they're not the only elements at play. Several factors affect the market directly and indirectly, influencing when you decide to buy and sell.

Don't expect all of these factors to produce the same results every time they mix. Knowing the role they each play in the market, however, gives you an understanding that enables you to make the right choice for your portfolio.

Supply and demand

REMEMBER

The two main components of the cycle are supply and demand. It's basic economics — supply relieves demand, whereas demand works to limit supply. Too much supply reduces value, whereas strong demand inflates prices.

Within general market areas, variations in supply and demand might occur at the regional and neighbourhood levels that aren't necessarily consistent with the broader trend. For example, Manitoba might be seeing a lacklustre market generally while Winnipeg might be strong; within Winnipeg, some areas may be doing better than others, depending on what kind of properties are on offer.

BEARING WITH THE MARKETS

Goldilocks used to break into abandoned houses in seedy neighbourhoods to find places to sleep. She decided that was not the quality of lifestyle that met her emotional and aesthetic needs. So, she decided to get her own place. In true fairy-tale form, she was fortunate enough, through the assistance of her unbearable family, to borrow enough money to buy a little house in a buyer's market. She worked hard renovating and decorating it over several years, in an area of "cute" starter homes on big lots.

The real estate market started to heat up and eventually became very hot. Goldilocks sold her home at the top end of a seller's market because her neighbourhood was now trendy and in high demand. She kept the money in the bank and looked around for a home near the woods. By the time she found her dream home, the real estate market was no longer in a frenzy, and normalcy reigned supreme — the market was now balanced. Goldilocks was able to buy her dream home mortgage-free with the large amount of money she had saved from her first home sale, invest the rest of her cash through a financial planner, and live happily ever after. The End.

Availability of financing and credit

The availability of financing, in the form of cash, credit, or through loans and mortgages (though of course financing is often credit) help deals to get done. Real estate investors need cash to do deals, and the willingness of partners, banks, and other lenders to make funds available helps investors purchase properties.

When financing and credit are readily available, developers will buy land and build, while investors will move in. When mortgage rates rise or capital flows tighten, activity cools. Confidence in the market reflects the prevailing sense of which way those involved believe the market is going to turn. That call is a judgment based on the amount of cash flowing through the market as well as the supply of and demand for available real estate.

Confidence

Confidence is the willingness of investors and other participants in the market to engage in deals and to favour long-term opportunities over various types of risk. When confidence is high, deals get done; when it's absent, there may be people willing to sell and get out of the market but it's hard to get financing. Keeping on top of the mood requires knowing what drives the flow of capital and the market itself.

Drivers of capital and confidence

The supply of capital and confidence in the market are two elements that help drive the real estate market through its regular cycle. But the supply of capital and confidence is influenced by the following:

>> **Interest rates:** Because interest rates have a direct effect on the financing of both development and investment properties, real estate professionals keep a close eye on where rates are heading. Typically, high rates help cool the market by prompting price reductions. Lower rates spur the market by making more cash available to investors and developers. Low interest rates may also stimulate demand and result in heightened competition for assets.

>> **Tax rates:** Property taxes vary by community and type of property. A high tax rate typically discourages purchasers and may push investors into municipalities where rates are lower. Taxes levied by higher levels of government, such as federal capital gains tax and provincial property transfer taxes, may also have an influence over investors' decisions. The introduction of taxes aimed at limiting speculation and encouraging rentals in British Columbia and Ontario are new phenomena investors need to heed.

>> **Occupancy rates:** Tenants play a role in real estate markets by indicating demand for certain types of assets. High vacancy levels mean assets return less income to owners, narrowing margins and potentially lowering investor expectations for real estate in the neighbourhood and ultimately property prices. This could create opportunities for purchasers. High occupancies typically boost the perceived value of an asset.

>> **Perceived value:** Public perception of any particular piece of real estate plays a key role in determining what buyers are willing to pay. Good neighbourhoods, or those whose potential for growth is strong, enjoy stronger pricing than those with less favourable characteristics.

REMEMBER

What the public perceives as good value isn't necessarily rooted in scientific research, however. Marketing, fashion, and simple word-of-mouth may all contribute to some areas becoming hot whereas others fall into decline. Keep your ears open to find out what people are saying about particular areas on the street and online, and put the buzz to the test by trying to find supporting facts (as the saying goes, the plural of "anecdote" isn't "data"). Become a student of local fortunes to know which areas deserve attention and which don't.

The impact of other markets

Because real estate deals are part of the larger economy, they're subject not just to the forces rippling through the property market, but also to those of the national, provincial, and local economies. The four are interrelated, so pay attention not just to what's selling (or not), but why. A boom, for example, may lead to a surge in the housing market, new retail openings, and demand for commercial properties to serve the bustling sectors of the economy. A recession, by contrast, will see depressed prices for real estate and force you to take a closer look at the sectors showing the greatest long-term promise.

TIP

Recessions are typically the time to prepare for the next boom. You may be able to scoop up underperforming assets and transform them into the gems of your portfolio. Have a look at reports on the local market from your local real estate brokerages, as well as growth forecasts that the Bank of Canada and other major financial institutions release on a regular basis.

The economic fortunes of a particular community are also important. One-industry towns do well so long as their industry prospers, but economic diversity is better for a community's long-term prospects. Diversity offers some protection against national and regional fortunes, as well as trends affecting specific industries. That's not to say single-job towns can't transform themselves, but the risk of a prolonged downturn is greater. An investor typically won't want to wait that long to see a return.

WARNING

Communities, especially smaller ones, are also more subject to demographic changes and other shifts in local character that can affect the prospects for real estate. These changes are sometimes sparked by events in the local economy (a plant closure, for example, or the creation of new jobs), whereas others reflect the age of the incoming (or outgoing) owners.

Many of Canada's small towns, especially resource-dependent ones, have seen their stars rise and fall on the back of changing circumstances and trends. The British Columbia ski resort of Whistler, for example, is a small village turned international four-season resort as investors developed properties and amenities that attracted skiers, hikers, and convention-goers.

In Thunder Bay, Ontario, the growth of Lakehead University has stabilized the city's economic core and provided ancillary economic activity. A similar transformation is underway in the resource town of Prince George, British Columbia, where the University of Northern B.C. has drawn in a younger population.

Buying real estate in St. John's, Newfoundland, and Labrador might not have been a wise choice when the fishing business was going down the tubes, but oil and natural gas have replaced fish and the boom has helped reinvigorate real estate markets.

Growth

When governments — federal, provincial, or municipal — commit resources to building new highways, bridges, and airports, opportunity will follow. On a smaller scale, new zoning in a town or city opens the door to opportunity. Often, a level of speculative investment may precede the actual funding announcements because the projects will have been discussed well in advance of any government commitments.

Savvy investors will stay updated on major infrastructure and community planning discussions and watch for opportunities to make their own investments. Many investors with a long-term investment horizon buy in the path of development, allowing them to buy relatively affordable properties that will one day be prime redevelopment opportunities.

Knowing the Market, Knowing Yourself

Real estate investing probably isn't an exercise in self-discovery for you. But even if you think you know yourself, the experience of buying and selling property may shed light on skills and traits you didn't know you had. Those revelations may be empowering or they could be chilling — particularly if they're pushing you into negative-return territory. That's why knowing what you bring to the table is as important as knowing the kind of market you're operating in, and having a sound strategy that helps you reach your goals.

REMEMBER

Don't forget to include details about your financial standing and potential needs when you take stock of your own attributes. Although you're hoping real estate makes you money, you need at least some to start with, so it makes sense to consider all your assets — real and personal — when developing your investment strategy.

Taking stock of your real assets is easier than figuring out your personal skills and attributes. For real assets, you can review your most recent income tax return, tally personal net worth (assets less liabilities), and draw up a brief budget reflecting projected income and expenses for yourself. Together, these give you an idea of where you stand and of the kinds of investments you can consider. For a more detailed treatment of this topic, consult Chapter 3 in Book 1 as well as the latest edition of *Personal Finance For Canadians For Dummies* by Eric Tyson, MBA, and Tony Martin, B.Comm (Wiley).

This chapter talks about selecting an advisory team, and this section discusses the person without whom that team wouldn't exist — you! You need to focus on two areas as you consider your approach to real estate investing: your skills and how your personal financial goals mesh with the long-term economic outlook.

Taking stock of your skills

Being a successful investor depends in large measure on the skills, personal experiences, and research you've accumulated. Research and education can train you in ways of thinking about real estate, but real estate investing is a business and requires business acumen. It won't make up for a disinclination toward certain types of properties or a total lack of interest in real estate. Fortunately, because everyone needs a place to live, you've likely had some dealings with real estate in the past and have a basic sense of the skills you bring to buying, selling, and renting property.

First, however, some sobering news: There's no simple way to assess your skills. You won't find a special Myers-Briggs test or Rorschach blot for determining your aptitude for investing in real estate. Taking an inventory of acquired skills and stacking them up against those needed to acquire and manage property is probably a better way to lay the groundwork for your investing career.

Some advocate an assessment of strengths, weaknesses, opportunities, and threats (SWOT). As cliché as it sounds, it's good advice. A SWOT assessment requires you to take a close look at your abilities and shortcomings, and to consider the advantages and challenges facing the particular business in which you're involved. It gives you an idea of the opportunities you're best suited to pursue and the kinds of threats to which you're particularly vulnerable.

REMEMBER

We can't guess your skills and vulnerabilities, but we can offer the following list of attributes we believe are important to real estate investors. This list isn't exhaustive or exclusive, but we hope it provides food for thought:

>> **Initiative:** Being a self-starter who knows how to hustle is an important skill for a real estate investor. After all, your first deal isn't likely to come to you: You have to find it.

>> **Self-confidence:** A strong sense of self-confidence complementing your ability to take control will bolster your chances of success. And remember, self-confidence means being able to admit when you've made a mistake and adjusting your plans accordingly.

>> **People skills:** These skills help you relate to others and even win them over to your cause, whether they be partners, brokers, bank managers, or bureaucrats. Being a shy introvert won't necessarily work against you (especially if you exude confidence), but you may not make as many connections in the course of your investments. Then again, that could allow you to possess a mystique that awes — and inspires — those around you. (At least that's what we introverted writer types keep telling ourselves.)

>> **Sales and communications skills:** These skills help you make your pitch to those with property to sell, buyers, and tenants; they can also help you convince planners that a development you'd like to undertake on a property will benefit all concerned. Being able to sell your project, whether for money or goodwill, is becoming more and more important as the demands and issues facing landowners and developers increase.

>> **Research and analysis skills:** These are important for gathering and understanding the various threads of information that relate to your market, and knowing which information to ignore. The more efficiently you can absorb market information and the faster you can respond, the more dynamic an investor you'll be.

>> **Decision-making skills:** When you have completed your research and analysis, you must make a decision about how to proceed. Fortunately, as this chapter discusses, you have a supportive team of advisers around you as a guide.

Establishing Your Investment Strategy

You can also ask yourself a few key questions that give you some insight into your personal investing style:

» **Do I like risk, or do I prefer stability?** Real estate has a reputation as a stable investment choice with a proven record of returns over the long term, but some assets are more stable than others.

» **Do I have the time needed to realize a return on my investment?** If personal circumstances limit your investment time frame, consider investments with a greater degree of liquidity.

» **Do I have a sense of place that will evoke gut feelings about a particular market?** Although a personal connection can get in the way of sound investing, familiarity with the community, local history, and people with whom you're dealing can enhance your ability as an investor.

Gauging the market's future — and yours

Market cycles — discussed earlier in this chapter — play a key role in determining your investment strategy. You can't predict the future, but knowing general trends helps you plot out a strategy to keep you on track regardless of market movements.

For example, with real estate cycles running 5 to 12 years on average, you can bet that a 30-year investment career will take you through about three major cycles. The frequency may be greater in local markets, based on economic factors, but the big picture is what you want to keep in mind at the moment. It means that if the market is declining right now, odds are good that in a year or two you might be able to pick up some bargains, and in another 5 to 10 years sell them for a profit.

REMEMBER

Cycles are never exact, so timing your deals requires keeping an eye on circumstances as they evolve and create opportunities. In the meantime, you can estimate the time you have to hold, develop, and enjoy properties. Regularly review the time frames you establish for each property to develop a portfolio positioned to take advantage of cyclical trends, regardless of what the future brings.

Determining your own personal investment future based on who you are now and what you want to do in the future requires some introspection and, of course, planning. Ask a few basic questions:

» What are your long-term investment goals?

» Do you have plans to start a business?

» Do you plan on having children?

» When do you want to retire?

TIP

Though your goals may change from year to year, at least one stable element remains: You're not getting any younger! Knowing when you want to have kids, when your kids are likely to leave home, when you want to retire, and other key transitions in your life will help you develop an investment schedule.

For example, you may be 26 and single, with a career just kicking into gear. You have a bit of money and can afford a down payment on a simple condo that gets you into the market. Perhaps in six years you'll marry and be able to trade on the value of that condo for a larger place, and then use the condo to generate income. Or perhaps you'll decide to sell and trade up.

On the other hand, you may be 40 years old with kids bound for college in a few years and plans to retire in 15 years. Your investment strategy reflects those plans. After you check your strategy against the current market cycle, you may consider an income-producing property for a medium-term hold, and something with potential for longer-term appreciation that you can sell when retirement approaches. Of course, if the market peaks in 12 years or is in a slump at 15, you'll want to choose a property that lets you respond to shifting circumstances without jeopardizing your own plans.

WARNING

No one can read the future, so don't invest what you can't afford to lose. Although you can understand the market and make sound judgment calls, a measure of risk always exists.

Selecting an Investment Type

Finding your kind of property isn't quite as easy as taking out a personals ad ("Single real estate investor seeks hot property for fun and profit"). Locating a property that advances your investment goals comes down to a lot of homework, an educated guess, and a gut feeling about what kind of property is going to serve you best (so maybe finding your kind of property is more like scouting a highly compatible match on OkCupid and finding out *they really are*).

Whether you invest in residential, commercial, or industrial properties, or any of the myriad types of real estate investments in Chapter 2 of Book 7, your success depends on matching them with your need to use them for personal use as well as investment purposes; the desire for relatively liquid assets or long-term investments; and the overall resilience of the assets to market cycles.

Establishing Your
Investment Strategy

Investing with intent

Do you want a property you can use for your own purposes or one strictly for investment? Knowing what you want from a property will help you determine the type of properties you'll consider buying:

>> **Personal use:** Some forms of real estate are better suited to personal use than others. Investing in a property that will double as your home or place of business will have practical benefits for you as well as delivering a return.

>> **Alternative uses:** Savvy property investment requires that you balance your personal needs against the characteristics of the properties you're considering as investments. If and when you don't need the property for your purposes, who will? Will there be a market for it, or are your needs unique? Perhaps you've seen fashion shops become cafés and industrial properties transformed into housing in growing urban areas. Perhaps you've also seen a fancy new restaurant in a small town sit empty for years after the initial owner went bankrupt. Smart investing requires knowing what comes next, not only for you, but for your investments.

>> **Straight investment:** A property bought strictly for investment purposes may be just what you're looking for, because you have no interest in using it. For example, you may buy an apartment building with the sole purpose of being a landlord. Although the neighbourhood the building is in and the maintenance of the building appeals to you (not to mention the regular cash flow), you are quite happy not to live there.

Lapping up liquidity

Some properties have greater *liquidity* (its ability to be sold) than others (find out more about liquidity in Chapter 2 of Book 7). Depending on the amount of time you have to hold an investment, you may want to buy a property to sell after a few years of generating income or one to hold for years in anticipation of long-term appreciation in value. Gauging the liquidity of a property and making it work in your favour is a good aim. The possibilities are as follows:

>> **High liquidity:** Residential properties are generally the most liquid real estate investment. If your strategy is to buy and sell in the near term, residential properties are your best bet.

>> **Medium liquidity:** Suites in resorts and other forms of recreational properties are subject to trends in the sectors they serve, potentially reducing their liquidity. This makes them a good medium-term hold in a diversified portfolio.

>> **Low liquidity:** Properties with a low level of liquidity come from a range of sectors and asset classes. No one type of property has a monopoly on low liquidity. The least liquid properties in a given market are those in least demand. Buying a property of this sort is typically a decision made with a long-term horizon and a strategy to match.

REMEMBER

Balance a property's liquidity with your needs, something discussed in the previous section. Between the two, you have the information you need to gauge a time frame for your investment.

Staying strong in soft times

Whether you're looking for a stable cash flow or are just plain conservative, a stable property is a good thing to have. The two main gauges of stability when it comes to investing are the following:

>> **Stability in value:** You want a property that's not going to lose its value — in other words, one that will appreciate over time. A good means of ensuring this happens is to buy a property in a growing neighbourhood where land values are likely to increase. An established community is generally a good place to buy, whereas a home in a single-employer town carries more risk. But don't forget to look ahead and to buy in the path of development; a property can increase significantly in value if it finds itself engulfed by an expanding city (as landowners around Calgary have discovered in recent years).

>> **Stability in cash flow:** Cash flow also depends on neighbourhood fundamentals. Because income-producing properties are often subject to cyclical factors, you may want to consider them for short- to medium-term investment. But less volatility means greater stability, so if you have an apartment block in an established residential area, chances are you're going to see both long-term cash flow and an appreciation in land values.

Doing your research

No matter what investment type you're leaning towards, you need to do your homework. If you're going to find properties with the potential to meet your needs and expectations, you need to not only know where to look, but also understand the specific trends affecting the *asset classes* (groupings of specific categories of assets, such as office properties, according to relative value) and properties that interest you.

TIP

A wealth of data-driven blogs have taken over from traditional media to keep investors in the loop on local trends. Many are written by professionals, either those in the real estate industry or urban planners. Still others are written by fellow investors. Try to find one you like and that wins your trust (and has the trust of others), and then use it for a daily dose of insight. The monthly and quarterly reports from real estate brokerages and their brokers, as well as most major financial institutions, can provide a deeper diver into the trends. The reports are usually available online or from the companies themselves, free of charge. Provincial, regional, and local associations for building owners, developers, and landlords are also useful sources of information, whether through newsletters or regular meetings.

Selecting Advisers

Even if you're relatively certain you don't want any partners in your real estate venture, you shouldn't go it completely alone. You need a team of independent advisers who will offer support — and challenge your assumptions — to make sure you stay on the right track as you pursue your investment goals.

You'll want several people with different sets of expertise on board, each with a particular contribution to make. At various times during your real estate investing career, you might consult a real estate agent, a lawyer, an appraiser, an accountant, and a financial planner. This section explains why you're only as good as the people who surround you and offers some tips on selecting them, including some leads on organizations that can help you find the professional who's right for you.

TIP

These advisers can offer specific professional advice and expertise. Many of them are also potential mentors, people able to coach and guide, and sounding boards as you develop your portfolio. Many people find having a dedicated mentor accelerates their professional growth, and provides an outside perspective independent of the advice they're paying others to provide. Depending on the ownership structure you choose for your portfolio, a mentor can also be a useful advisory board member guiding the development of your company. If your advisers can't suggest some mentors, consider cultivating relationships with candidates by participating in local networking and professional organizations.

Before you begin: The criteria

Knowing what to look for when you're sizing up potential members of your advisory team is important — and we're not just talking about qualifications and experience. Just because a real estate agent is right for one person doesn't mean the same agent is right for you. Although references from family and friends can help, criteria for choosing your team of trusted advisers go beyond qualifications and experience to include personality, professional competence, and fees.

You're going to have to depend on your interviewing skills because, let's face it, you won't get along with everybody and some good questions may help you figure out who's right — and who's wrong — for you. Draft some questions that will provide a basis for interviewing your potential advisers. Don't be afraid to ask tough questions — the answers you get might prompt you to think twice about the candidate and steer you away from trouble before it finds you. You don't need something as formal (or as harsh) as the Spanish Inquisition — just a thorough but relaxed interview that makes candidates feel comfortable. You want them to open up and tell you how they can help you.

TIP

References and word-of-mouth referrals are particularly important when selecting any adviser offering a holistic perspective on your financial affairs. Ask for professional references and then contact those professionals to discover about their sense of the adviser's strengths and weaknesses. Also, ask how long the individuals have been dealing with each other. Don't ask for or expect an adviser to provide you with a list of clients, because doing so would breach confidentiality.

REMEMBER

A short list of three candidates can help you compare the relative merits of each as well as provide alternatives in case your top choice falls through.

Evaluating qualifications and experience

Some of the advisers you're scouting, such as lawyers, have professional qualifications; others have specialized training, such as Realtors. Be sure to ask whether the people you're interviewing have the appropriate training and certification, and request the documentation to back up their claims. Find out how much experience they've had since receiving their training. Has the lawyer or appraiser cultivated any special experience that can help you? For example, an accounting firm that has a sizable clientele of small to medium-sized businesses will have in-depth expertise regarding small businesses, but if the firm also has several clients engaged in real estate, you'll be better served.

Determining personal compatibility

You may have a business relationship with your advisers, but don't discount the fact you'll have to deal with them on a personal level, too. The best candidate for the job should also be someone who doesn't tick you off. Attitude, approach, candour, and communication skills are all factors to take into account.

For example, expect your adviser to respond to your requests promptly. If your adviser is too busy for you or is slack in returning your calls, emails, or texts, you'll soon be grumbling about the situation. That doesn't make for a good relationship! Take charge and make sure your needs are a priority.

Ask yourself these questions when selecting advisers:

>> Do you feel good chemistry (that is, do you like them and sense they like you)?

>> Do you feel they understand your wants and needs clearly?

>> Do they communicate clearly orally and in writing?

>> Do you trust their motivation and judgment?

>> Do you have confidence in their objectivity and expertise?

>> Do they respond to your questions quickly and effectively?

>> Do you feel they respect you and your opinion?

>> Do you feel they will meet your needs in a timely way?

REMEMBER

A solid rapport with your advisers will give you more confidence in their ability to assist you. Being uncomfortable with them could make you more prone to dissatisfaction, which cloud your judgment when presented with a perfectly good deal.

Fees

Fees should be affordable, but also on a par with what others in the adviser's field are charging and — above all — a reflection of the adviser's training and experience. Accountants' fees, for example, typically reflect the work being done, so you may have to pay a bit more to receive the advice you need. But make sure you're comfortable with the rate, and that it's within your budget; otherwise, in an attempt to reduce expenses, you may not use the adviser as effectively as you might. Remember, not seeking professional advice when you need it is poor management! Table 3-1 provides a look at the cost of a range of advisers.

TABLE 3-1   ## Adviser Costs

Adviser	Cost
Buyer's real estate agent	No cost on standard residential properties because the agent obtains the commission or part of the commission from the vendor; both parties owe commissions to their respective agents in the case of commercial properties.
Mortgage broker	Usually no cost to arrange financing, unless you're having difficulty obtaining financing; here, more time and skill are involved, so the cost could be a percentage of the loan's value. The lender frequently waives survey and appraisal costs in the case of residential real estate, unless location, market conditions, or lender criteria dictate otherwise. However, for commercial real estate, due diligence and risk management criteria are much higher, and fees are the norm as well as surveys and appraisals.
Property inspector	The fee depends on the nature, age, and size of property. It could range from $300 to $1,000+ for a residential property. However, if you're investing in commercial property, you'd normally have expenses for many other types of inspections and reports, such as an engineer's report and environmental assessment. The costs vary by report.
Real estate lawyer	Depends on the cost of the property being purchased and amount of the mortgage, plus related disbursements such as search fees and filing costs; can range from $500 to thousands of dollars (taxes are extra).
Accountant	Can vary based on the time, skill, qualifications, and the complexity and nature of the advice and services. Typically begins at $500 (fees only).

The real estate agent

Real estate agents are important because they're the ones licensed to act on your behalf when you buy or sell a property. For the purchaser, the agent can identify properties and provide valuable background and analysis that may interest you. An agent will also represent your interests to the listing broker. This arm's-length position can have its advantages when the time comes to negotiate a deal. Equally important, the agent may know mortgage brokers willing to arrange financing for your purchase. You benefit from the agent's listing services and ability to represent your interests and advocate for you in the marketplace. Agents may also have market knowledge that expedites the sale of your property, ensuring that you see a return faster than if you handled the sale yourself.

Real estate agents each have a different level of skill and sometimes a unique area of expertise. To match your own needs with the talents of an agent, consult family, friends, and colleagues regarding particular agents. Real estate firms that handle the kind of property that interests you and work regularly with investors may also have recommendations. You can do some preliminary research by talking to people at open houses or checking out the agent's website.

Provincial real estate associations and your local real estate board can provide further information on Realtors that may be experienced in the kinds of properties that interest you. This would include providing relevant statistical data, as well as Buyer Agency Agreements, and so on.

TECHNICAL STUFF

Coined in the United States in 1916, the word *Realtor* legally applies in Canada only to members of the Canadian Real Estate Association (CREA). The code of conduct to which Realtors adhere is available at www.crea.ca.

The lawyer

The number of potential risks accompanying real estate transactions make legal advice indispensable when you're buying or selling a property, and especially so when it's intended as an investment.

A lawyer will provide advice and guidance that helps protect your legal interests with respect to residential real estate. Having a lawyer is also crucial for commercial real estate because the potential legal risks are even greater. All the real estate and mortgage documents you sign and the property you purchase have legal implications and obligations you're required to meet. Having the counsel of an experienced real estate lawyer can mitigate those risks.

A lawyer who specializes in real estate law is critical because you want an expert who is savvy and experienced in the area you're making your investments. The specialization will enhance the lawyer's ability to meet your needs with respect to due diligence and risk management. For example, have your lawyer review your prospective offer and contract documents before you make an offer. Alternatively, the offer may have a condition that stipulates your lawyer's review within a certain time frame before the deal goes firm. Your lawyer can also review any condo *bylaws* to ensure there are no restrictions. Your lawyer will also do a *property search* to review any financial or legal encumbrances against the property or restrictions on the nature of use. The payoff can be significant: In one recent case, the purchase price for a 16-unit rental building fell 20 percent when the lawyer examining the purchase contract found that four units in the building were illegal.

References for lawyers are available from family, friends, or colleagues, or via a referral service operated by provincial law societies across Canada. You can easily locate law firms with expertise in particular areas of real estate law via the law societies or using your favourite Internet search engine.

TIP

You may be able to save a bit of cash by having the lawyer handling your mortgage documents also handle the documents related to your property transaction. You must be careful that no conflict of interest exists, but doing so may not be easy if you live in a smaller community with a limited number of lawyers.

The bar association for your province or territory should be able to provide further information on lawyers who may be of service to you.

A WORD ABOUT NOTARIES

Though lawyers are almost always notaries public, not all notaries public are lawyers. This distinction is important for you to remember, because a lawyer is trained and qualified to provide a legal opinion, whereas notaries public may not be. But in Quebec, notaries (not advocates) are the people you want handling your property deal — they're what the rest of Canada knows as lawyers.

The appraiser

Traditionally, appraisers were trained in the valuation of real property. That makes them an important resource when you're trying to determine the value of your portfolio or what kind of financing you might be able to secure. They aren't always integral to a transaction but their knowledge may assist you in securing a better deal on a mortgage or taking a more strategic view of your investment.

Many appraisal firms have also branched into consulting work. This can assist you when you're scouting properties to purchase, by helping you understand not just the financial worth of the property, but opportunities for increasing its value. Appraisers will often provide assistance when you opt to appeal your property tax assessment.

TIP

The local chapter of the Appraisal Institute of Canada (www.aicanada.ca) maintains a list of appraisers for your area.

The accountant

In addition to always being the life of the party, accountants are integral to the financial health of your investments. Even if you keep close tabs on the day-to-day operating costs of your properties, an accountant can ensure you claim the appropriate deductions on your income tax and make prudent decisions toward achieving your long-term financial goals.

Unfortunately, anyone in Canada can call herself an accountant. However, the professional designation Chartered Professional Accountant (CPA), introduced in 2012, identifies that the person you want to employ as an accountant has credible and recognized professional training and credentials.

That didn't happen for a guy named Don, unfortunately. Don wanted some money-saving tax strategies. Don decided that staff at the tax preparation shop in his local mall were up-to-date on the latest tax rules. But the advice Don received was inappropriate for the type of investment he was considering. The Canada Revenue Agency audited Don on receipt of his first tax return because of the strategy he employed on the basis of the tax shop's advice. The outcome of the audit cost him a pretty penny. If Don had used the services of a professionally qualified tax adviser, the outcome would have been very different.

Your lawyer may be able to recommend a suitable choice. Some provincial chapters of Chartered Professional Accountants Canada (www.cpacanada.ca) also have searchable databases of their members. A call to any one of the provincial chapters can help narrow your search for an accountant specializing in real estate issues.

The financial planner

A financial planner complements the services your accountant offers by helping you set long-term goals for your *investments*. A planner can help determine whether a specific property serves your long-term investment goals and perhaps suggest alternative means of achieving those.

Because financial planners aren't required to undergo any specific professional training, and only Quebec places legal requirements upon those who offer financial planning services, be cautious about the person you engage as your planner. You want to make sure that the financial planner has at least a CFP (Certified Financial Planner) designation and preferably is a "fee only" financial planner (not providing services based on commission). You pay the planner a fee for his advisory services, of which real estate investment would be part of your portfolio. Be cautious, because a commission-based financial planner is interested in making commissions off investments (that is, generating sales volume), so any real estate investments would dilute your investment capital.

References are essential, as are background checks. Family, friends, and accountants may be able to supply references, and a number of industry associations can also provide recommendations for your area. An interview can test whether you have the rapport necessary to work effectively together, which is especially important because your relationship will include frank discussions about your attitudes toward life, death, family, and business. Speak to a minimum of three financial planners so you have a benchmark comparative research reference point. Don't make any final investment decisions without speaking with your professional accountant about the tax strategic planning and with your legal adviser on the estate planning and will preparation aspects. You want an integrated portfolio and professional feedback to manage your risk and meet your overall objectives.

Organizations able to assist you in your search for a financial planner include the Financial Planning Standards Board (www.fpsb.org) and the Financial Advisors Association of Canada (www.advocis.ca).

ROUNDING UP ADVISERS

You can consult several types of advisers regarding your real estate investments. Keep in mind that prices for their services vary considerably depending on your requirements. Furthermore, be sure to comparison-shop a minimum of three people in each area before you make your decision. You need that background as a benchmark, and also to make sure that the advice, recommendations, and price quotes you're given are consistent. And if they aren't, find out why!

Put your questions in writing in advance of any meeting or telephone discussion so that you don't forget. Prioritize your questions in case you run out of time — a possibility, especially when you're paying by the hour. Make notes of all discussions with your advisers.

Other professional advice

A number of professionals may not have a high profile in your efforts to buy and sell property, but they can make important contributions during the due diligence period and other phases. These include building inspectors, structural engineers, and architects.

The building inspector

Building inspectors are responsible for ensuring newly built buildings conform to local building codes. Making sure any building you buy conforms to local standards and best practices for its particular kind of construction is in your interest.

Home inspectors are similar to building inspectors insofar as they examine a property to ensure it is structurally sound prior to your purchase. The regulations governing their activities vary from province to province; in some cases, no formal set of regulations governs their activities. B.C. and Alberta license home inspectors, for example, though certification is also available through trade associations.

TIP

For more information on the organization operating in your area, contact the Canadian Association of Home and Property Inspectors (www.cahpi.ca).

The structural engineer

Planning a renovation? Check with a structural engineer to see whether your plans impact the basic structure of the building. This includes walls, beams, and other elements that if removed or otherwise altered during renovations could destabilize the building. You may change your mind regarding your purchase if your plans do not meet with the approval of a structural engineer.

Structural engineers, like civil, electrical, and mechanical engineers, are registered professionals. Be sure to check their qualifications with the provincial registering body.

The architect

Architects are known as the coordinating consultants on building projects and play a key role in managing the major renovation of a property. They're also important in providing design services that can make the renovation you plan even better.

Though only registered architects are allowed to call themselves architects, intern architects and foreign architects living in Canada can provide basic design services for home renovation projects. You can obtain references to architects and designers willing to assist in your project from the local registering office and through local home builders' associations.

Chapter **4**

Pulling Together the Cash: Assessing Your Resources

R emember when you were a kid and saw something you really liked? If you didn't have enough money, your parents probably told you to save up or maybe shovel the neighbour's driveway for some extra cash.

Being a real estate investor is kind of like that. But because most of the things you want to buy are a whole lot more expensive than what you can afford with a single paycheque, it helps to have a strategy that helps you accumulate the cash you want faster than by doing odd jobs around the neighbourhood (lucky you). This chapter discusses some of the ways you can optimize your saving strategies and scrape together as much of your own cash as possible before approaching banks, private lenders, and other sources of capital.

This chapter also covers finding, and cultivating, workable partnerships. Because many of the sources discussed here are friends and family, you also get some tips on making sure you stay on good terms with them. Just because they're family doesn't mean you can be any less professional with them. Nor should they expect anything other than professional behaviour from you.

Assessing Your Financial Situation

It sounds obvious, but if you're going to sink money into something, whether it's a hole in the ground, a new car, a bank account, or a piece of real estate, you need money. And if you're going to fill the hole, save a particular amount of money, or buy a property worth a specific amount, you're going to want to know how much you'll need to do the job — and do it right.

Knowing your resources and whom to ask for the extra capital you need to do a deal are key elements of successful real estate investing. Resources include not only you — your own finances, present and future — but the people with whom you partner, or who can put you in touch with prospective partners. These partners ideally include people who can match your investment with their own deep pockets to buy a property that can make you both rich (and maybe even famous).

Before you turn to others for help, look at your own financial situation. Take stock of your *assets*, the funds you have at your disposal, and *liabilities*, such as outstanding debts and other claims that reduce the amount you have to invest. You won't be able to secure a great rate on a mortgage if you're carrying hefty debts, as this will determine your net worth — an important factor that lenders look at in determining your eligibility for a loan.

Financial resources to tally may include the following:

>> Cash and savings, including Tax-Free Savings Accounts (TFSAs), Registered Retirement Savings Plans (RRSPs; see Chapter 3 in Book 1), and Registered Education Savings Plans (RESPs)

>> Investments, such as term deposits, mutual funds, equities, and properties

REMEMBER

When you've tallied up your financial resources, subtract the amount of debt you're carrying. Calculating your net personal worth based on the difference between your assets and liabilities helps you determine how much money you have to invest.

Tallying your assets will give you a sense of your net worth, which in turn helps lenders determine the size of loan you'll receive. However, if you want to use registered investments such as RRSPs, there may be tax implications. The later section "Identifying Resources" discusses these.

TIP

Running a credit check on yourself could reveal important information about your eligibility for a loan. Even when all else indicates you could be a good risk, a bad credit rating will weigh against your ability to secure the best possible financing deal. The major agency providing credit reports in Canada is Equifax (www.equifax.ca), which will provide you with information about your own credit rating free of charge. TransUnion Canada (www.transunion.ca) also provides credit reports.

The most recent edition of *Personal Finance For Canadians For Dummies*, by Eric Tyson, MBA, and Tony Martin, B.Comm (Wiley), can provide you with further tips on laying a firm financial foundation for your first foray into the world of real estate investing.

Identifying Resources

So, how much cash do you have to play with, anyway? And how are you going to use it to fund your real estate purchase? Tapping a mix of resources is just as important as investing in a diverse range of assets. Reducing your reliance on a single source of funds limits the chance you will be caught short if that source of financing dries up. Cultivating other sources may also create opportunities for funding future investments as you grow your portfolio.

Resources fall into three categories:

>> *Liquid,* such as savings in your piggy bank or bank account, which you can access and pour into alternative investments relatively easily

>> *Illiquid,* which aren't easily converted to cash you can use to fund other types of investment and typically include bonds and other long-term, locked-in investments or investments whose risk inhibits conversion

>> *Vaporous* (okay, *vaporous* isn't a legitimate financial term but it fits!), which are difficult to pin down until they take the form of liquid resources; they usually come from other sources on request

Typically, you want to supplement any liquid resources you're ready to invest with illiquid resources converted for the purposes of the investment you're about to make. Shortfalls in your own resources can be made up by collecting funds from others who are game to support your investment: friends, family, or even strangers.

REMEMBER

Social capital is just as important as financial capital. Some cultures avoid financial institutions in favour of cooperating among themselves, and some of these groups have enjoyed huge success in the real estate market. Don't underestimate the value of your social connections when assessing your own investment abilities. This is why this chapter spends time discussing the importance of approaching friends and acquaintances for financing. You may even wish to establish a formal partnership with your supporters, an option discussed later in this chapter.

Liquid: Savings

Savings and other liquid resources typically account for no more than one-third of a balanced investment portfolio. Whether you're working with an old-fashioned bank account, TFSA, or a low-risk, income-oriented mutual fund (see Book 3), you've got cash on hand.

The advantage of liquid resources is that they're available in the event of unexpected circumstances such as job loss, emergency travel, or medical expenses. But compared to other investments (discussed in Chapter 1 of Book 7), they're probably not advancing your personal wealth to any extent. Most low-risk investments don't offer high returns and tend to grow slowly. Some low-risk investments lose value over the long term in exchange for a greater degree of liquidity. Fortunately, they're available when an investment opportunity comes around.

Depending on your investment strategy, however, you may not have a lot of liquid resources sitting around waiting for an investment opportunity. You may have been paying off student debts with a view to increasing your ability to secure new loans. Perhaps you're debt-free and have put your savings into aggressive investments aimed at building the little you have into something greater. It might be time to shift some of those funds into a high-interest savings account earmarked for your first real estate purchase.

TIP

The amount of cash you keep in liquid investments should be the equivalent of three months' worth of expenses, plus what you need for ongoing monthly expenses. This frees up more cash for investment in higher-yielding options that may offer better returns, building the amount you're able to invest in less time.

TIP

Savings include more than just the money you set aside for a rainy day or a major purchase, however. Putting aside a specific amount each month is a good plan, but don't forget to review your spending habits and look for savings in your day-to-day expenses. You probably have heard (and maybe even taken) the advice to cut down on expenses such as that daily hit of java, but don't forget that unused gym membership, public transit or car-share membership rather than owning a car (if possible), and service charges. The same advice holds if you already own property and are saving up for an additional purchase.

Illiquid: Long-term investments

Planning is critical if you hope to use long-term investments to finance a real estate purchase. Whether you're waiting for market conditions to improve before you cash out, or simply waiting for a bond or guaranteed investment certificate (GIC) to mature, planning can help ensure your illiquid investments melt together to provide you with the cash you need when you need it for other purposes.

The challenge you face highlights the need for a diverse investment portfolio. We're not talking just diversity of investment types but diversity of liquidity. Although the latest darling of the stock market (such as TSLA) may have spectacular growth potential, you want to be sure you have the freedom to cash out when you want, rather than when the market dictates. A stable stock may offer a lower return but ensure you get to see a reasonable gain over the course of your ownership. With the advice of a financial planner or broker, consider a mix of stock types and set goals for the ongoing sale of shares that will allow you to secure the greatest gains possible for your ultimate goal of real estate investment. (Book 2 introduces you to stocks.)

Similarly, if you favour bonds and other fixed-term investments, make sure they mature on a regular basis rather than all at once. Known as *laddering,* spacing maturity dates limits your exposure to changes in interest rates. You also have an opportunity to top up your investments or shift them into either higher-yielding vehicles or more liquid forms for investing in property. (Chapter 5 in Book 3 discusses bonds.)

RRSPs and RESPs are illiquid so far as they've been designed as tax shelters with a long-term investment timeline. While first-time homebuyers can tap them for a home purchase — a home that may also have a rental suite — a property investor can't withdraw the funds without incurring a *penalty.* Withdrawals will be considered part of your annual income, and will potentially boost your personal rate of income tax. That would be a bad thing if, say, it boosted you into the highest tax bracket. However, you may be able to remove a judicious portion to complement the other assets you're allocating to a real estate investment. Just beware of the tax implications, and consult with your advisers.

WARNING

Something you want to minimize — and if at all possible completely avoid — are penalties and fees for early redemption or transfers. In addition, review management fees with a view to avoid paying too much for the oversight of your investments. Tax implications may also accompany the redemption of shares, so consult your accountant for advice on how to minimize taxes as you line up your resources to invest in real estate.

TIP

TFSAs are a convenient alternative to RRSPs when building — and tapping — funds for property investment. Although cash placed in an RRSP is sheltered from taxes until withdrawal, funds you place in a TFSA are taxed in the year they were earned. The growth of TFSA funds is tax-free, however. Depending on the options your financial institution offers, you may be able to grow your TFSA deposits faster — and more cheaply — than if they were in a standard fixed-term investment or RRSP because the gain is tax-free.

TALLYING CASH

Determining the amount of cash you have available at any given time for real estate investment depends largely on your having a clear financial plan in place and sticking to it. No formula exists, as the amount you have depends on your appetite for risk or debt, your goals and priorities, your borrowing leverage from a lender or mortgage broker, the possibility that the seller could carry you in terms of a mortgage (vendor-back financing), your family connections and borrowing abilities through them, and your creativity and initiative. However, here are some tips on elements of your spending and saving habits you may want to monitor, assess, and update on an ongoing basis:

- The amount of cash you need and want for a down payment

- Your disposable income, net after tax

- The maximum personal line of credit that you can get from your lender

- Additional sources of income that might be available to you, such as working a second job, working overtime, or starting a part-time home-based business on the side

- Money your family or relatives may be prepared to lend you, or possibly invest with you in real estate, and the amount, their expectations for the investment, and any restrictions

- How much RRSP borrowing room exists for a first-time home buyer, if that is applicable for you and your partner

- Your credit rating (set out a plan to improve it if required)

- A pre-approved mortgage for the maximum amount possible and to be held for the maximum length of time possible (say, 90 to 120 days)

- The amount of rental revenue you could obtain from a property through a basement suite as well as the rest of the house to maximum revenue for mortgage eligibility purposes, if that's the investment scenario you're interested in

- The members of your investment group and why they would be assets (if you are thinking of group investing); also look at developing such a group of people with a clear investment plan in writing so that you can exploit purchase opportunities

REMEMBER A financial planner can advise you on balancing your short-term and long-term needs and identifying the resources you should keep in liquid, short-term investments and less liquid, higher-yielding long-term investments. Financial planners are important people to have on your advisory team (see Chapter 3 in Book 7).

Vaporous: Friends and acquaintances

Other people's money may be as important to the success of your investment as your own. Don't forget the people you see every day. You may not have told people you're thinking about investing in real estate, but they may not have told you *they're* thinking about it, either!

A shortfall in your own resources and a desire to not involve an institutional lender, for whatever reason, may make a friend or other acquaintance an important source of funding. That's especially true if they're also looking for investment opportunities. A casual conversation may be an effective way of broaching your need for capital and gauging a friend's interest, but having a plan ready to discuss won't hurt. To reflect a professional approach, be able to tell potential investors the following:

>> What you need and for how long

>> Why you need it

>> The way you hope their participation will benefit them

A realistic and confident attitude about the amount you need and willingness to offer a competitive return (either through interest payments, a share of the cash flow if it's an income-producing property, or a stake in the property itself that will deliver a return when you decide to sell the property — see also the later section "Working with Professional Financial Partners") bolsters your ability to secure the support you need. Setting a realistic time frame for the investment will also give your potential financier the information required to decide whether to buy in.

WARNING Because you're approaching someone you know, be sure to limit the potential for personal conflict by having a legal agreement in place that safeguards interests on all sides. Be sure anyone prepared to loan you money receives independent legal advice before doing so. Don't let the convenience of tapping a friend for the cash you need become a source of bad feeling. You want the deal to be a winning prospect for all concerned. By the same token, don't promise something you can't deliver.

Banking on family

Rising real estate values have focused attention on the so-called "Bank of Mom and Dad" in markets across Canada in recent years. Older property owners hold clear title to billions of dollars of real estate while the younger generation has found it tough to gain a foothold in the market. Many have turned to their parents to help them buy their first home, so why not a first investment property, too?

Approaching family to invest in your next real estate venture is no longer an option of last resort (and frankly it never was). In several situations it's more than just a convenient idea, it's good business sense, too:

>> When a family member has the cash you need to close a deal

>> When a family member has not only cash but also expertise that can help you develop your investment portfolio as well as your investing skills

>> When a family member is willing to become a full partner and meets the criteria you would set for any other business partner

FAMILY MATTERS

Jordan recently moved to Halifax and was enthusiastic about buying a property in a part of the city that was beginning to see a lot of redevelopment. The upside was good, and he wanted to get in early. He found a property with a two-bedroom suite in the basement and planned to renovate and find tenants for the upstairs. He would live in the basement with Kim, his partner. Jordan's parents agreed to provide a $50,000 loan toward the purchase and renovation of the house, but they didn't insist on a written agreement outlining the terms. After all, Jordan had always been a responsible person and this was a way of helping him out.

But after a year of renovations and a few months of renting the upstairs portion, Kim and Jordan broke up. She went to a lawyer and brought a claim forward arguing that because she had helped make monthly payments and contributed to renovations and maintenance of the property, she was entitled to half the equity in the house.

Because there was nothing in writing proving that the money from Jordan's parents was a loan, and there was no mortgage securing the funds, the cash was accounted as a gift. After much legal haggling, Jordan and Kim reached an out-of-court settlement for $25,000 (not to mention legal fees). Proper documentation could have avoided the mess that resulted, and ensured that all parties benefitted, at least financially, from the breakup.

There's an upside for everyone: Existing property owners have a chance to reinvest accumulated equity whereas younger buyers have a chance to jump-start their real estate careers.

WARNING

Don't let the ties that bind blind you to professional practice. Some people make a habit of treating their family differently than they treat their friends — and that often means worse rather than better. However, you should treat everyone with whom you do business in a professional manner, which is especially true of family, because there's not just money involved but expectations of kinship and trust that can become highly charged when money's involved. Make sure you have a formal contract outlining the terms of the loans and their repayment as well as any other support that family members provide. Clearly state the benefit to them of the arrangement and your obligations to them. Don't take the support of family for granted, unless you wish to invite resentment. Honour your agreement as you would that with any other lender.

Providing cash

Many tycoons got their start with a bit of seed money from a parent, an uncle, or some other family member. Whether as start-up capital or last-minute financing needed to close a deal, family money can play an important role in your career as a real estate investor.

Having financial support from family is an advantage insofar as your family knows your needs and you know the source of the cash. The ties that bind should guarantee that each side respects the other's interests, making for a durable long-term partnership. You may even enjoy easier terms from family than any institutional lender would offer. In some ways, family can play the role of so-called "angel investors."

TIP

To reassure any family members from whom you secure financing, provide some form of security, either through a mortgage agreement or a security agreement. Doing so will ensure that they're ranked as secured creditors should you be unable to meet your obligations and declare bankruptcy. The security will guarantee that they have a chance of seeing something when your assets undergo liquidation, whereas unsecured creditors enjoy no such guarantee.

REMEMBER

If you buy a home with a brother or sister (say, during university), make sure you have an agreement outlining your respective rights and responsibilities associated with the property and the particulars of your ownership stakes.

Passing on skills

Family members are sometimes logical sources of financing because you can also learn more about investment from them. Giving them a stake in the success of your investment may encourage them to share advice based on their own experiences as investors.

Having an older, wiser, better-heeled family member serve as both an investor and mentor has its advantages if you're a younger investor. The experience can teach you how to handle a purchase through negotiation to close, and how to manage the property. In exchange, on top of simple repayment of the loan, you could offer an equity stake in the property.

REMEMBER

Clearly define the involvement of the relative with whom you're working. This ensures your relative knows the limits of her participation in the venture and also limits her exposure to potential legal claims in the event the investment goes sour. If the family member is older, a clear agreement can also mitigate issues that may arise during settlement of the member's estate in the event of his untimely demise.

Defining roles and responsibilities is particularly important where family is involved because emotional sensitivities may heighten the tension or any feelings of betrayal when things don't work out as expected. Safeguards in the shape of formal agreements help ensure you don't act solely on emotions.

Partnering up

Finding out that a family member wants to go into business with you may be the last thing you expect when you approach him for financing. But it's not necessarily a bad idea. You have a right to consider your options, however, and subject your potential partner to the standard gamut of trials you would put any other business partner through. Chapter 3 in Book 7 discusses some of these factors.

Family members deserve both greater and less scrutiny. Less, because you have a long-standing connection with them that gives you special insights into their character and some expectation of how they'll behave. Greater scrutiny of their role in your venture is necessary, however, because even if you've known each other since birth, your objectives won't necessarily be the same. Make sure you're on the same page, and have a common understanding of your respective motivations, long-term goals, and the skills you will each be bringing to the investment.

REMEMBER

Family includes spouses! Although a business relationship with a blood relative can be sensitive enough, you probably don't have to go home with him at the end of the day. Not so with a spouse! Before you enter an investment or business relationship with your spouse, make sure you're prepared for the venture — or the relationship — going sour. Discuss what would happen, for instance, if other creditors called their loans or the bank started to foreclose on your primary residence. Could the relationship handle it? And if you and your spouse decide to separate, are there clear terms that will allow both of you to recoup your respective share of equity from the investment without a costly legal battle?

KEEPING THE PEACE

Peace of mind is difficult enough to maintain in your business when family aren't involved. Their involvement can open up whole new possibilities for frustration and anxiety. Many disagreements are avoidable if you follow a few simple principles:

- **Be careful about requesting personal guarantees from family members or friends.** Asking a spouse, family member, or friend to guarantee or co-sign a loan may sound innocuous enough, but it invites bad feelings if the lender requests immediate payment (a step colloquially known as *calling the loan*). The relationship may not survive the financial loss, depending on the amount and the related circumstances. It's always best, where possible, to bear the responsibility yourself. If doing so isn't possible, you need to be very aware and wary of the relationship impacts if your investment doesn't work out as planned. You need to discuss the risks and expectations and rewards if you're planning on giving a financial benefit or incentive, openly with family members or friends. Better still, have the deal put in writing by your lawyer so there are no misunderstandings. Many relationships have disintegrated and resulted in lawsuits because an investor wanted to tap into the convenience and leverage of a credit benefit of a friend/family, and things didn't work out.

- **Collateral mortgages on your primary residence.** Secured lines of credit on a home are a major source of investment capital, which also adds tax deductibility to your mortgage payment costs. However, each investment situation and investor tolerance and comfort level is different. Some people deal with debt and potential liability risk well. Others don't and worry about it. If you're in the latter situation, you need to adopt an investment strategy that works for your relationship. If you're concerned about failing as a real estate investor, or creditors could place a claim against your home, be cautious. You need a roof over your head, and losing your home would rob you not only of that but possibly of your marriage as well.

- **Don't assign life insurance proceeds.** Among the assets you shouldn't calculate among your available financial resources when you're gearing up to do a deal is your life insurance policy. If you assign the proceeds of the policy to your creditors and you die unexpectedly, your creditor could receive the money without your family ever seeing a cent. A far better option is securing mortgage insurance, which assures concerned creditors that any loans you've taken will be satisfied on your death.

- **Don't ask family or friends to serve as directors of your investment company.** Directorships carry a lot of responsibility, not to mention liability for claims made against the company. This can leave directors open to personal lawsuits from creditors, threatening their own assets rather than just those of the investment company.

WARNING

Most jurisdictions in Canada treat the gain in an individual's assets after marriage as so-called *matrimonial property,* meaning it accrues to the family rather than the individual. This means a couple may come to a marriage, civil partnership, or common-law relationship with separate levels of savings, but any *increase* in those savings becomes subject to division (typically 50-50) if the relationship breaks down. This includes any increase in equity associated with a real estate investment. To avoid adding to the complication of a potential divorce, especially in cases where spouses don't contribute equally to a property investment, the couple should have an agreement defining their contributions to the purchase and a mechanism for the withdrawal of either partner, as in any other business relationship.

Working with Professional Financial Partners

Given all the cautions issued earlier about working with family, maybe you would prefer to turn to professional or institutional financiers, the folks for whom real estate financing is as natural as breathing. Even if you've enlisted the help of family and friends, you may need a little extra cash to round out your financial backing. The options are many, from financial institutions such as a bank or credit union to independent-minded career investors looking for opportunities to invest their loose cash.

Regardless of whether you seek institutional or independent financiers, shop around. Services and rates vary among financial institutions, and even among branches of the same institution. You want to be sure you're getting not just the best deal, but also the best service for your purposes.

Private lenders, who may be friends of friends or contacts you'll discover in the process of networking, require particular caution to ensure that the deal is fair and equitable for all concerned. Even if they're hoping the purposes to which you're putting their cash brings them a return, you want to make sure interest is reasonable for the purposes and that you're being treated fairly.

This section can help you assess the opportunities and be aware of the risks that accompany outside financial partners.

Squaring accounts

Getting the best deal from a financial partner, and ensuring the best treatment possible, demands attention to the three Rs: rates, results, and references.

Rates

Of course, if you need additional cash to close a deal, you want to receive it for the lowest possible price. The benchmark interest rate is known as the prime rate, which banks give to their best customers. You can find both current and historical rates on the Bank of Canada website (`https://www.bankofcanada.ca/rates/banking-and-financial-statistics/posted-interest-rates-offered-by-chartered-banks/`). Comparing interest rates and the terms of mortgages is vital. Some bargaining room exists if you're looking for a better rate or terms, so muster whatever persuasive skills and goodwill you can in an effort to reach an arrangement that works for you.

Other lenders typically charge a higher interest rate than the major financial institutions, but the persuasion can also help you secure a better deal from them.

Results

After you've identified lenders offering the best rates on the financing you need, have a look at the results they've been able to secure for others. You can tell a lender by the company it keeps, and institutional lenders are generally happy to tell you who they've done business with and the deals they've made happen. It's to their credit if they've played a role in a landmark transaction, and it works in your favour if they know the kind of deal you want to do, whether it's a simple house purchase or a land transaction.

References

References are invaluable whenever you're investigating a partnership. That's especially so when it comes to lenders because their integrity is vital to the success of your venture.

Check with others who've done business with the lender you're considering. What was their experience, especially in terms of service? Was the lender responsive and easy to work with? Knowing the experience of others may bring to light issues that didn't appear in either your preliminary investigation or the documentation they provided.

TIP

Run a credit check of your potential financial partner. You probably don't have to worry about a major financial institution or credit union, but if you're considering receiving financing from an individual or small business, you should check their credentials. A search of provincial court records, for example, may turn up information that steers you to safer partners. Most provincial courts have searchable databases of judgments (or decisions) available online.

Recognizing danger

It usually happens in only the most desperate of cases, but lenders may want to charge interest at levels approaching the maximum rate allowed by law (60 percent in many jurisdictions). That's hardly competitive with prime! Though 60 percent and under isn't legally considered *usury* (the practice of charging an exorbitant rate of interest), in these days of cheap financing it's close (small wonder the Italian poet Dante reserved a special place in Hell for usurers).

More common dangers include inflexible agreements and the lack of adequate leeway for yourself, especially if you run into cash flow difficulties or other circumstances that temporarily prevent you from meeting obligations. References from other investors who have worked with the lender should clear up any concerns in this area.

For a beginning investor, a prudent investment strategy is important. A more sophisticated and experienced investor might feel comfortable with paying a high rate of interest if they look at the overall investment potential and return on investment. For example, an experienced investor might be less concerned about the rate of interest than if the loan can be paid back at any time without penalty. In this scenario, a savvy investor might feel comfortable paying 20 percent interest if there is a realistic prospect of obtaining a 200 percent return on investment within a relatively short period of time, for example.

WARNING

Real estate fraud is for a danger often associated with unscrupulous lenders. It's something that could cost you your investment, your property, and, if identity theft is involved, your ability to invest in the future.

Optimizing Saving Strategies and Leverage

Building your resources to a point where you can actually do something with them is one of the greatest challenges you face as an investor. When you have a stake in the market, however, things gradually become easier because you're able to use your existing assets to back future deals and grow your portfolio.

This section looks at how you can gather together the resources you need to invest, and also takes a look at *leveraging,* which at the most basic level simply means borrowing money to make a purchase. Borrowing money requires security, however, and after you've closed a deal or two, you may have the option of using an existing property to leverage your next buy.

Assembling a war chest

Your real estate empire may be about as tiny and aggressive as Lichtenstein next to some of the bigger dealers in the business, but you still need a war chest, or funds to finance your real estate conquests. Regardless of the kind of assets you include, you've got to make the numbers work before you head out on the acquisitions trail. To get started, you need to stock your chest with enough capital to finance the assets you want.

Developing a comprehensive strategy is key and involves four steps:

1. **Set investment goals.**

2. **Develop a budget that helps you achieve your goals.**

3. **Establish an investment strategy that makes the most of your investments, through laddering and other techniques.**

4. **Plan an exit strategy, or a timeline for when you want to begin pouring your non–real estate investments into property.**

Setting investment goals

Knowing how much you want or need to raise to begin investing is important. In some parts of Canada, you may need just a few thousand dollars to buy a property; in others, the cost of entry will be a lot more. Setting an investment range will help determine your purchase strategy as well as give you a sense of the investment timeline you're looking at.

For example, if you need just $10,000 to make a down payment on a cottage or piece of land, you may have that in the bank. But if you need $50,000, you'll likely have to save up and cash in some investments to become a buyer. Achieving those goals could take one to three years, or more, and requires you to meet ongoing expenses while saving up.

TIP

A wise strategy is to examine your savings, gauge what you expect to be able to save over a specific time frame, and then identify a price range for your investment property based on the down payment you're willing to make and the amount of mortgage you can handle. For example, if you have $20,000 and expect to save

$10,000 a year over the next two years, you can look at properties ranging from $200,000 (based on a 20 percent down payment of $40,000) to $400,000 (if the bank is willing to finance 90 percent of the purchase price). Ideally, you might consider something in the $275,000 to $300,000 range to cushion against market fluctuations or unforeseen financial issues you might encounter.

Developing a budget

A budget keeps you on track as you put together the cash to fund your real estate purchase. The budgeting process forces you to assess your income sources and your expenses, perhaps encouraging you to become a more responsible manager of your cash. You may even find yourself inspired to seek higher-paying employment!

REMEMBER

A disciplined approach to saving for a major investment will also get you in the habit of setting aside funds for ongoing investment in the management and operation of the asset you acquire.

Having set a budget for yourself, calculate the resources you will likely be able to invest in the future. This requires drafting a simple budget, and perhaps setting some realistic goals for savings. Budgets may not be your thing, but they play an integral role in maintaining the discipline you need to invest in real estate. Your budget should identify how much you can afford to devote to real estate investments. This amount is important for two reasons:

>> If you're preparing to invest in real estate, it focuses your saving efforts toward a specific goal, such as a down payment, and signals when you are able to make your move into the market.

>> If you already own a home or investment property, this amount tells you how much you have to pay down existing properties and channel toward new investments.

Finally, because you've likely made some initial contact with lenders (see the earlier section "Working with Professional Financial Partners"), try to identify how much cash you can expect to secure through mortgages, personal loans, and other means. The answer could help determine your investment choices.

Establishing an investment strategy

Money in the bank is great, of course, but it's not going to do a whole lot if it's just sitting there. That's where a solid investment strategy comes into play, helping you reach your goals more effectively — and, we hope, quickly. A mentor can assist you in thinking towards the decisions you'll make as you formulate your investing strategy, and the choices you make to develop or disperse your portfolio. Often, the years of experience and particular expertise a mentor or business coach provides will be instrumental in cultivating your own confidence as an investor.

In addition, a financial adviser can assist you in structuring your portfolio to help you retain the gains you make. Though fluctuations in market value will occur, you need to avoid losses and translate gains into further gains in order to meet your goals faster.

TIP

Many financial planners provide assistance only after your portfolio reaches a certain size, but it doesn't hurt to make contact early. Cultivating a relationship with an adviser familiar with your long-range plan ensures someone has an established understanding of your goals and objectives as your portfolio expands. You reap the reward in advice tailored to your specific needs. See the discussion of financial planners in Chapter 3 of Book 7.

Planning an exit

What do you do when you've reached your investment goals? An exit strategy gives the answer, defining the process by which you can convert part or all of your investments into more liquid (that is, accessible) forms for financing a real estate purchase. It should include a start date, timeline, and what you'll do with the funds (in your war chest) in preparation for acquiring a property. You may opt to convert them into low-yielding liquid investments or scout properties in anticipation of using the funds at a particular date as a way to make the most of them and prevent them from sitting idle.

TIP

Depending on the deal you strike to acquire a property and the kinds of assets you have, full liquidation may not be necessary. You may be able to close a deal by committing to paying your investments to the vendor as they become available, effectively resulting in a graduated purchase. This could shorten the timeline required for your exit strategy. Offering investments in lieu of cash may have tax implications, however. Again, talk to your accountant and financial planner regarding the best way to structure such an arrangement.

Weighing the opportunities and risks of leveraging

Leveraging is the practice of using a small amount of your own resources and borrowing the rest to buy a property. Your resources may be the down payment that allows you to secure a mortgage. Sometimes another property will secure financing for a property or project that will boost the value of your portfolio. The Greek philosopher Archimedes famously boasted, "Give me a place to stand and I will move the earth," a poetic expression of the fact that a fixed point can support a bar capable of shifting great weights. Similarly, real estate investors can use a single property to leverage subsequent purchases several times the value of the original property.

The opportunities leverage offers real estate investors is an advantage of this form of investment, something Chapter 1 in Book 7 discusses. But a deal that's *overleveraged* can also create trouble, and sometimes even cost you a property.

Gaining ground

When successful, leveraging allows you to build a portfolio more rapidly than if you were just paying cash. If property values are increasing and you can trade up, leveraging is a low-risk endeavour that can *rapidly* build your wealth. The risk to the lender is low or nonexistent because the expensive property into which you've leveraged yourself can be sold should you not meet your obligations; the proceeds will cover your outstanding debt.

Risking losses

History is full of investors who purchased properties they couldn't afford to buy, then found themselves forced to sell because the payments were more than they could bear. But a wise investor won't let leveraging opportunities outrun an investment's potential. Building a portfolio by leveraging deals should still respect fundamental principles of good financial management.

Higher-than-desired leveraging can happen if you buy at the top of the market and conditions begin to weaken. A decline in the value of the property puts the lender at risk. The conditions could also jeopardize your ability to see steady cash flow from the property, putting you at risk of defaulting on those hefty payments.

TIP

Staying within your means isn't always easy to do, but guidelines exist. One good rule considers it unwise to leverage a property unless it has seen sufficient appreciation to purchase a property twice the size of the original property. You may not acquire a property worth twice as much as your current holding, but you can at least buy one that's of equal value relatively worry-free.

TIP

Another rule recommends making down payments of no less than 25 percent of an asset's value, regardless of how cheap financing is. However cautious that sounds, it will prevent you (in most circumstances, anyway) from ever being too highly leveraged. It may also establish enough of an equity stake to make you eligible for more favourable financing terms.

IN THIS CHAPTER

» Identifying the best time to buy

» Finding the home or rental property for you

» Choosing a location to invest in

» Understanding the types of land ownership

» Knowing when a property's just right

» Getting help from property resources

Chapter **5**

Scouting Properties: Where to Look and What to Look For

Finding the right property takes skill, maybe some luck, and a whole lot of intuition. But the hard work of scouting properties will give you the gut feelings you need to make the hard decisions successful real estate investors make. This chapter is something of a scout's handbook, and we can't help but advise, "Be prepared!"

This chapter discusses everything about finding properties, from the big picture down to the specific property. Some of the basic issues are tackled in Chapter 1 of Book 7, but this chapter gets into the nitty-gritty of sizing up the conditions in specific markets, neighbourhoods, and even the property you're looking at investing in. We can't know the specifics of every situation you have to choose from, of course, but we hope we can provide some useful examples and guidelines.

Assessing Current Market Cycles

The past two decades have been kind to Canadian real estate. Global threats have attracted international buyers to a country generally seen as stable and safe. The global financial crisis of 2008 came and, in many parts of the country, left until 2015 when the picture became more complicated. Knowing how to read the shifting landscape has been key to staying on top of local markets across the country.

Chapter 3 in Book 7 offers a general overview of market cycles, along with concepts important to understanding the market. These basic elements help you to decide when to buy and sell properties, but putting the concepts to work requires research, keen observation, and a measure of intuition.

This section walks you through an analysis of market cycles as they apply to the process of purchasing a property. Three main steps go into assessing the current market cycle: conducting research, analyzing the facts you've found, and making a decision.

Research: Doing your homework

The first step is to figure out what type of market you're in (Chapter 3 in Book 7 describes the three market types). Is it a *buyer's market*, with plenty of product to choose from? Or a *seller's market*, with rising prices and limited supply? Or are conditions stable, reflecting a relatively *balanced market*?

To help you figure out where the market stands, this section looks at the key factors identified in Chapter 3 of Book 7 as affecting market conditions.

Knowing where to find basic information — and when to dig for more — is an important skill for researching market cycles. This section gives you the pointers you need to be an effective market analyst. More sources of information appear later in this chapter.

Tracking interest rates

Higher interest rates aren't something borrowers appreciate, but the lenders financing real estate investments certainly do! The lower the interest rate charged on a mortgage, the greater the incentive for you to borrow when buying a property. During the early 2000s and then again following the financial turmoil of 2008, rates dropped. Today, they've come off their historic lows, but they remain relatively low compared to the long-term average. When rates rise, borrowing becomes more expensive, but an investor who does her homework will ensure that the property will have positive cash flow even in a high-interest-rate environment.

LOCKING INTO RATES

The Bank of Canada is cautious and conservative in determining when to raise or lower interest rates. Normally, any change — and the reasons for the change — is the focus of economists' speculation for days beforehand and much discussion in financial and other circles. The Bank of Canada looks at various factors when making a decision to change the policy rate. For example, the rate might be increased to dampen inflationary trends by increasing the cost of borrowing, or decreased to encourage borrowing to stimulate the economy. Another reason for the Bank of Canada to change the policy rate is to make the Canadian dollar more attractive for international institutional investors. The bank takes into account a lot of factors prior to making its decision.

The relevance of interest-rate fluctuations to investors is the degree of financing risk. That's why a lot of investors will take out a long-term fixed-rate mortgage — say, for 5, 7, or even 10 years. When interest rates appear to set to rise, some will work with a lender to lock in financing at a lower rate. This way, investors can budget with certainty regardless of what happens to interest rates.

On the other hand, some investors prefer a variable-rate mortgage that fluctuates based on the Bank of Canada rate. However, the interest rate difference can be 1 to 2 percent less than a fixed-rate mortgage. Money can be saved, but the risk is the uncertainty as to when interest rates might go up. It could be that over time the variable interest rate could be higher than if you had locked in your fixed-term mortgage six months earlier. Most investors prefer the stability of a long-term, guaranteed-rate mortgage.

TIP

The Bank of Canada (www.bankofcanada.ca) is the primary source of information on interest rates in Canada. Based in Ottawa, it's the central bank that sets the pace for rates at lending institutions across Canada. The bank provides regular updates on its policy rate, the target for the overnight rate, and reasons for changes. It also offers charts with historical interest-rate data that allows you to see where rates have been and draw conclusions about where they might be heading.

Canada's major chartered banks and other lending institutions regularly issue newsletters with their own commentary on interest rates and the Bank of Canada's policies. These updates and newsletters from their chief economists are important resources to consult when trying to figure out where rates are heading and how real estate markets will respond.

Though you shouldn't try to second-guess interest rates, closely looking at past rates, current trends, and what the various banks are saying should indicate whether rates are set to rise, plateau, or fall. By gauging interest rate trends against other factors including the health of the economy, you can make your own call as to whether financing will be more or less expensive in the future and whether or not you should select a variable or fixed-rate mortgage. Interest-rate trends also indicate whether you should buy now, wait a few months when financing might be cheaper, or sell while low rates are creating opportunities for buyers to hop into the market.

TIP

Rising rates may make financing more expensive, but they can sometimes create opportunities for buyers by putting pressure on owners who have overleveraged their portfolio. Selling when buyers are active can provide financing you can use to purchase properties when debt-burdened owners have to unload assets.

Determining property taxes

Property taxes may seem like fixed costs, but they are important considerations for investors. A booming market with rising sale values pushes up assessors' *valuations* of properties. A slack market, by contrast, could see property values fall. This has a direct impact on the annual tax assessment, not only in the coming year, but often in the three years following the change in value. Taxes levied on a property will affect the return you see as an investor, and possibly your financing costs.

Different investors have different expectations and projections for their profit margins. Most investors want a *double return* — that is, a positive cash flow for a rental revenue stream, and a capital gain over the original purchase price. Traditionally, real estate has gone up an average of about 5 percent a year for the past 30 years. However, that figure can be higher or lower depending on the real estate cycle, location, type of property, and other factors. Most investors would like to see equity in their properties increasing at least 5 percent a year.

This will affect municipal property taxes, which are the primary revenue source for cities. Residential property taxes are often just a small percent of annual assessed value, but those few percentage points will eat into your cash flow. Knowing which way property taxes are likely to head in a particular market will help you determine the kind of cash flow you'll need to get from the property to cover costs, as well as the long-term drag on your return.

REMEMBER

Property tax assessment records are available through the provincial assessment authorities, municipal offices, and online tools maintained by these organizations. You can also find explanations of trends in each municipality's annual financial reports. Often, local media cover trends in property taxation, providing you with insights into overall municipal approaches to setting tax rates (in some provinces, the provincial government sets the rates).

TIP

Be sure to discuss the impact of property taxation policies on your investment with an appraiser, who is often able to coordinate appeals on any assessments you consider out of line with the reality of your holding. Given the range of factors that affect the value of a property and its performance in any given market, you should understand how property taxes will influence your own cash flow as well as the property's appeal to future investors. Assessments that indicate opportunities for investment can easily rise after investors move in, improve the properties, and improve the tone of the surrounding neighbourhood.

Considering capital gains

Capital gains are another consideration. If your property gains an average of 10 percent a year in value over ten years, the property will double in value. If you buy it for $100,000, and sell it for $200,000, you have a $100,000 gain in your original capital investment. You are taxed by the Canada Revenue Agency on 50 percent of your gain. In this example, that means you could keep $50,000 tax-free, and pay tax on the remaining $50,000. At the top marginal tax rate of approximately 50 percent, you would pay approximately $25,000 tax. At the end of the day, you could keep $75,000 of your original $100,000 gain, after tax.

If your original purchase price was $100,000, that would mean a 75 percent return over ten years, or an average of 7.5 percent a year non-compounded. But you'll also have to factor in positive cash flow from rental income to determine your actual return.

On the other hand, maybe you just put down 10 percent and borrowed the other 90 percent on a mortgage. Therefore, you actually received a 75 percent return on your original personal resource down payment of $10,000 over ten years. The reason is that your original $10,000-down "investment" resulted in a $75,000 net gain, or an average of $7,500 a year on your original $10,000, or a 75 percent return per year. Better than obtaining, say, a 3 percent return on a term deposit that is taxed as investment income in your hands in that taxation year. Depending on your tax bracket, you could pay 30 percent or more on that interest income, meaning that net after tax you actually received only about two-thirds of your interest, or 2 percent in the example given.

Reviewing leasing conditions

Fully leased properties with long-term tenants make for great investments from a revenue perspective, but a close look at the tenant mix may reveal nothing more than a good tease. The last thing you want to do is enter a market on the basis of an apparently healthy lease market, only to find that leasing activity is actually heading south and taking property prices with it.

TIP

Fortunately, several sources can help you investigate the current and long-term history and prospects for local leasing markets. If you're looking at residential rental properties, have a gander at the annual rental housing market survey that the Canada Mortgage and Housing Corporation (www.cmhc.ca) produces. Commercial brokerages such as Colliers International (www.colliers.com), CBRE (www.cbre.ca), and Avison Young (www.avisonyoung.ca) prepare similar reports on a quarterly basis for commercial and industrial markets. Retail leasing reports are also available from the big brokerages, but high rates of turnover make these more difficult to produce.

Knowing where vacancies stand in your market, and the rents tenants are paying for their spaces, will indicate investment opportunities and reflect landlords' capital requirements. High vacancies may indicate buying opportunities as existing owners may want to sell out because of cash flow pressures; alternatively, low vacancies may make assets attractive to purchasers, resulting in a seller's market as buyers compete for assets.

REMEMBER

A good leasing market doesn't necessarily mean a good investment market. The balance between supply and demand might be just right, and the long-term potential for appreciation in values is low. Conversely, landlords might hold on to properties despite high vacancies because they're willing to wait till the market turns back in their favour. Still, knowing rental conditions can help you build an argument for investing in particular locales and devising a negotiating strategy that will win over vendors.

Gauging buyer confidence

Buyers' confidence in markets is as changeable as the markets themselves. The two, after all, have an intimate relationship. Confident investors contribute to a strong market, while conservative investors limit the volume of activity taking place in the market.

But short of doing psychological assessments of a random sampling of active investors, how can you gauge the level of confidence in the market? Let others skilled in the art research it for you, of course!

TIP

The Conference Board of Canada (www.conferenceboard.ca) is one of several organizations that issue business and consumer confidence surveys. For a fee, the Board provides detailed analyses for specific regions. The information gleaned from these sources, like interest-rate projections, can help you gauge whether markets are in for a boom or a downturn.

Rising consumer confidence may indicate an increased willingness to invest in real estate. As an investor, you may consider preparing your residential property for sale to potential buyers, or perhaps you'll opt to buy before the market heats up. On the other hand, falling confidence in the market may signal purchase opportunities as people retrench in anticipation of harder times.

WARNING

Consumer confidence is less definite than monetary policy and interest rates, and it relies on a good grasp of the current economic climate. Unforeseen events can put the kibosh on existing predictions, so although you should consult assessments of the market's mood, know that the mood is just that — a mood. It won't necessarily obey scientific laws.

Considering local planning

Urban planning activities have a peripheral influence on market cycles but may play a role in spurring demand in local areas. Including a glance at urban planning initiatives in the areas where you're considering investing is therefore a good plan.

Here's how planning has an influence: An area that has languished at the bottom of the local market cycle may find itself at the top of a council's priority list because of public concern over its status or the potential for improvement if it is rezoned for certain purposes. A community planning process may identify certain goals and uses for the area. Perhaps planners will propose development incentives. A combination of these factors may spark a rush into the area.

Knowing the pressures facing specific neighbourhoods and where these areas rank in the city's planning priorities will give you clues to the future direction of the market in these areas. This gives you an advantage over other investors, potentially allowing you to get in when the market is low and sell when the market is high. Conversely, if an area is set for rezoning, you want to be aware that the market for properties with uses allowed under the previous zoning is about to collapse.

Analysis without paralysis: Tallying the variables

Making sense of the information you glean through your research into market conditions and perceptions of the market may seem like voodoo. And to be fair, seeing the big picture takes a good deal of intuition.

To make your job of determining market conditions a bit easier, Table 5-1 assembles various variables and suggests an appropriate action based on the variables most prevalent in your corner of the market. Of course, determining a market's character is hardly an exact science, but this table should help you put circumstances into perspective. Find the set of criteria that come closest to what you've discovered about the market, and gauge how you'll respond.

Scouting Properties: Where to Look and What to Look For

TABLE 5-1 Sizing Up the Cycle

	A	B	C	D	E
Values	Depressed	Increasing	Increasing	Declining	Depressed
Rents	Low	Increasing	Increasing	Declining	Low
Vacancy level	High	Beginning to decrease	Low	Increasing	High
Occupancy level	Low	Increasing	High	Decreasing	Low
New construction	Very little	Increasing	Booming	Slowing	Very little
Profit margins	Low	Improving	Widest	Decline	Low
Investor confidence	Low	Negative to neutral	Positive	Slightly negative	Low
Media coverage	Negative and pessimistic	Positive and encouraging	Positive and optimistic	Negative and pessimistic	Negative and pessimistic
Action	Buy	Second best time to buy	Sell	Be cautious	Buy

The decision: Trust your gut

Whether you're buying or selling, don't make your decision lightly. Consult your long-term investment plan and take stock of what your advisers are saying. Knowing when you're ready to sell is as important as knowing when you're ready to invest. Though you may consider selling a handful of properties in your portfolio, the range of properties you can buy is typically larger. Knowing whether the market is at the right point for a purchase, however, is just one aspect of your investment decision.

REMEMBER

Few markets are uniform, after all. Even an unfavourable market can harbour good investments. Finding the good deals in difficult circumstances is part of the challenge — and joy — of investing in real estate.

X Marks the Spot: Identifying a Target Market

Throwing a dart at a list or map showing the areas where market conditions are favourable is one way of identifying a target market for investing, but you should put a bit more effort than that into your decision. A number of factors may sway you in favour of (or against) a particular locale. The landscape can change rapidly, and although stable, long-term areas may not see much change in their appeal (or lack thereof), shifts in the market often create new opportunities for investors in marginal or transitional areas. Alternatively, sudden shifts in government or popular opinion may send once-robust areas into prolonged doldrums.

The following sections explore some of the considerations you'll want to take into account when you're narrowing down your list of potential neighbourhoods for investment. Keep the fundamentals of the local market in mind, looking past the fads to the actual investment potential of the area. Of course, your perception and affinity for a particular neighbourhood may count more than the hard financial stats. To ensure your investment balances financial wisdom with personal feeling, find out what conditions on the ground are really like.

Separating the fads from the fundamentals

Successful real estate investment requires that you know what you're buying and trust that it's going to deliver a return. Remember the old joke about diplomacy being the skill of telling someone to go to hell in a way that they actually look forward to the trip? Real estate marketing can be a lot like that; a marketer will sell you a piece of hell and you'll enjoy the heat and other amenities!

Although the marketing of new developments tends to focus on lifestyle and neighbourhood options, you may look at other aspects of the property and wonder whether that development is really so great. The hottest new neighbourhood under development or redevelopment may not fit your investment strategy, no matter what advantages the marketers tout.

REMEMBER

Points to consider when comparing a property in a hot neighbourhood to one in a locale generally considered less favourable include not only their price, but also their potential for appreciation, maintenance costs, and cash flow:

>> **Price** is an important factor when stacking up properties, and especially when gauging the relative merits of two properties whose neighbourhoods differ in quality. Check whether the list price of each property is within area norms, and whether either of the two is undervalued. A market correction may create opportunities to buy undervalued properties simply because the original owners have become skittish and want out. An undervalued asset in a good neighbourhood is a wise bet, but steer clear of an overpriced home in an undervalued neighbourhood because you'll have less room for long-term appreciation while the rest of the neighbourhood catches up with your property's value (or the property's value may actually fall in line with the rest of the neighbourhood).

» **Potential for appreciation** will indicate the return you can expect on your investment. The greater the potential for appreciation, the better the investment. Consult an appraiser for a prognosis on the kind of return you can expect on the various properties you're considering.

» **Potential maintenance costs** could cut into your margins, especially in a less-favourable neighbourhood. We're not talking only about deferred maintenance that's contributed to the lower asking price of the property and greater potential for appreciation; we're talking about the ongoing maintenance associated with graffiti, litter, vandalism, and the like. You may be able to make something of the property, but will you be able to *keep* that something?

» **Potential for cash flow** could moderate your enthusiasm for that high-end asset if you find tenants hard to come by. Depending on your investment strategy, it may be better for you to invest in a more modest property with solid cash flow potential than a trophy few can afford to rent from you. On the other hand, if you have a chance to pick up two residential properties, and can swing the financing, you may opt to live in one and rent the other — effectively having *two* slices of cake and eating them too. (Just be sure you know which piece is sweeter.)

Getting to know markets and neighbourhoods

Bearing in mind the fundamentals of sound investing, part of your job as a diligent investor is to familiarize yourself with the neighbourhoods you're targeting for investment. There are several ways to do this, from research to walkabouts, and a number of factors to consider.

TIP

Based on your research into market conditions, identify three neighbourhoods that could yield investment opportunities. Doing so allows you to see how each compares with the others, tally up the relative advantages and disadvantages of each, and generally get a feel for which neighbourhood you're most comfortable with.

Basic factors to consider before you even visit a neighbourhood relate to its age, its character, and its unique mix of properties and infrastructure.

Sizing up age

Older neighbourhoods either are well-to-do and established, or show their age. The good news is that a neighbourhood with an aging stock of properties with rock-bottom values can offer great value. You may be able to renovate the property and make it into something people want, either as tenants or owners. On the other hand, an established neighbourhood with good-quality homes may offer few opportunities for you to enter the market.

A new neighbourhood may be the hottest place for some investors, but it also has the potential for surprises. Where an established neighbourhood has a reputation, a new neighbourhood has yet to prove itself. The quality of the homes may be good and the infrastructure may be there, but what will it become?

Sizing up character

The kind of neighbourhood character we're talking about isn't necessarily the vibe you'll pick up during a stroll down the street. Rather, it's the mix of people actually in the neighbourhood, the age and income levels, and education and employment indicators. These factors are worth considering because they contribute to the kind of tenant you attract, and also how the locale maintains itself.

For example, an upper-income neighbourhood in a suburb with a growing working-class population may have a prime piece of real estate to offer. Buying the upper-end property hoping to lease suites to workers or students may not be the best idea because the rents you'll have to charge to make ends meet on the property probably won't match what the workers and students are able to pay. Chances are the better opportunity will lie in an asset that can provide affordable housing to the growing population of workers.

TIP

Statistics Canada (www.statcan.gc.ca) collates data from each census into profiles for communities across Canada as well as specific tracts within communities. These *community profiles* provide detailed information on the age of residents, the housing stock, as well as income levels and other demographic and socioeconomic information.

REMEMBER

We don't recommend a snobby attitude in selecting properties, but as an investor you should consider what serves the market. Paying attention to the demographics and overall character of a neighbourhood helps you find an asset that's the right fit, not only with your own goals but also with those of the people to whom you hope to lease.

Sizing up the mix

The right mix of properties in a neighbourhood ensures a match made in heaven between the kind of property you want to own and the needs of any tenants you hope to secure.

Perhaps you've got a penchant for a small industrial building. The three mid-size bays inside are perfect for light industrial users. But a glance at the uses of surrounding properties indicates that it's nowhere near any amenities, and neighbouring properties don't really complement the kind of users you hope to secure. However good a deal it is, and whatever the future growth potential of the area where it's situated, chances are the small industrial users you're looking for may not want to lease the premises. If it doesn't suit their needs, the investment won't live up to your expectations.

TIP

Community amenities are key to the users you hope to attract to a revenue-producing property. Several online resources allow you to gauge the potential of a neighbourhood before you even see it. These include Google Street View, of course, but many real estate listings include video tours of listed properties and the surrounding neighbourhood. Many municipalities have mapping tools that can give you a sense of adjacent land uses, rights of way, and other key information. These tools help give a sense of the area's layout as well as what the local amenities are.

Honing your vision

You wouldn't buy a car without kicking the tires, so it makes sense to take a walk-about in each area where you're considering investing. (Don't kick the properties, though. You might break something!) Testing your response to these neighbour-hoods gives you a sense of how others are likely to respond to them.

TIP

To become familiar with a potential neighbourhood, pay it a few visits at various times of day and night. Give yourself a chance to experience it as a driver, a pedes-trian, and a transit user. Are traffic patterns unusual? Is it walkable? Are transit connections frequent, smooth, or a hassle? Your experience of these aspects of the community may give you an understanding of why a neighbourhood is hot or not, and may point you to areas within the neighbourhood that are more convenient places to be than others.

A walkabout is a more intensive way for you to gauge several of the factors discussed in this section. Keep your eyes open for the following:

>> **The fabric of the neighbourhood:** This includes the condition of the properties and landscaping. The better the condition of the neighbourhood, the more attractive it will be to potential tenants and the less risk to the condition and value of your own property. Priming yourself with neighbour-hood history tells you whether the condition of properties is improving or declining.

>> **Local businesses and amenities:** These are important indicators of your fortunes in the neighbourhood. A handful of local businesses serving up staples and a few pleasures is a good sign. Communities that lack a decent grocery store and other basic shops stand to be less favoured by potential tenants and future buyers.

>> **Street vibe:** This is a significant factor in making a neighbourhood a place people want to be. Good traffic flows, people who chat with one another, maybe even street-side decorations are all signs of a vibrant neighbourhood. On the other hand, desolate streets where the windows of the homes have bars may not send the right message to people you're trying to interest in your property.

>> **Noise and environmental factors:** These affect different people in different ways. Unless you're investing in commercial or industrial property, chances are you won't want to buy something on the flight path to the local airport. Similarly, properties that are downwind from a pulp and paper plant or wastewater treatment facility may not be the most attractive assets.

REMEMBER

Be sure to consider the full range of factors at play in the neighbourhoods you're considering. A personal visit may help you make sense of issues local newspapers have raised about the area, or may temper the impressions you've received from others who claim to know what's going on.

KEEPING WATCH

Having an extra pair of eyes scouting properties is a great help when you're looking for a good investment. And who better to ask than a real estate agent, especially one with access to databases such as the Multiple Listing Service (www.mls.ca) for residential properties or ICX (www.icx.ca) for commercial properties?

Take Dan, for example. An experienced real estate investor, Dan regularly buys properties that need some tender loving care. He fixes them up, puts them back on the market, and reaps a profit. To do that, Dan has a long-standing professional relationship with his agent, Pam. Dan sets out the type of property he's interested in buying, the location he wants to buy in, and the price he's prepared to pay. Pam monitors new listings as soon as they're listed, getting the low-down on them even before they've officially hit the MLS site. When a property comes up that meets Dan's requirements, she gets in touch with Dan. Dan quickly checks the properties, and before the market is fully aware of the listing, he puts in his offer.

Knowing what you want and developing a relationship with a listing agent who's able to connect you with properties that meet those criteria can give you an edge over other buyers. The properties Dan scouts need lots of work and typically list for the value of the lot, so he faces a limited number of competitors. Still, without his relationship with Pam, he wouldn't have been as successful as he has been in finding the best deals possible.

Consulting the locals

One of the best things you can do as a potential investor in a neighbourhood is to get to know the locals. This gives you a feel for the area, as well as local concerns and attitudes, and furthers your understanding of the community. You may even discover information about the property you're looking at that may encourage you — or prompt you to think twice about the investment you were hoping to make.

Opportunities for meeting locals abound. Browse the local stores. Visit the local coffee shop (if there is one) and listen to the chatter; maybe strike up a conversation with the people at the neighbouring table. You may not be good at small talk, but even chatting about the weather can create an opportunity to hear what people are saying about the market.

Dimitri took a more direct approach. He wanted to buy a waterfront home for his young family. He found a home for sale in southern New Brunswick, but decided he would do his research homework and check with its neighbours before he made an offer. It was a wise move. He discovered that rats were a serious problem in the area, and that successive attempts to eradicate them had been unsuccessful. The area was also prone to flooding in spring; though none of the people Dimitri spoke with had ever had water in their own homes, they said it wasn't unusual to find it lapping at their basement doors. Dimitri moved on and eventually opted for a house in a new subdivision overlooking a lake.

TIP

Building relationships with locals is something you can never begin too early. This is especially true if you plan a major development of a property or are considering a rezoning. Cultivating an open relationship with members of the community will help bring them onside with your plans. The goodwill you foster by participating in the community as either a homeowner or business operator is invaluable.

Selecting a Property

The property you're seeking in the locale you've chosen may not be simple to find. You have to look for it, or have your broker do so. Chapters 1 and 2 in Book 7 discuss strategies for locating potential investment properties. After you've selected a neighbourhood in which to invest, scan the Multiple Listing Service (www.realtor.ca) listings for your asset class or from brokerages specializing in your area of interest, and keep your eyes open.

Facets of the property to consider include its location, the availability of amenities and services, and the property's potential for appreciation. The criteria are largely refinements of the principles that have allowed you to narrow your search to a handful of properties. By now you should know what you want.

Home sweet home

A house draws out a lot of emotion, regardless of whether you're the owner-occupant or simply a tenant with the option of moving out if it gets on your nerves. You have a lot more conditions you want to satisfy when you're looking for a chunk of residential real estate than, say, a retail unit. Your standards are especially high if you're also planning on living in the house. Any tenants you welcome into the building are there because they've chosen to rent from you and can move on if the place isn't what they expect, but you're going to be stuck with the place as the primary occupant and user. So be selfish and put your own interests first!

REMEMBER

First off, consider where you want to live. Price, affordability, and availability each play a role in determining where you buy, but your own idea of what makes a livable neighbourhood also factors into your decision. Being practical won't hurt; what appeals to you may appeal to tenants or future buyers. Being able to tout a feature of your neighbourhood that has been of particular value to you will help the sales pitch you'll make to the next purchaser.

You have many factors to consider when selecting a home, whether for your own use or as an investment. Here are a few questions to ask yourself:

>> **What is the neighbourhood like?** A thriving neighbourhood promises to be a great place to live, whereas one where not much is going on could make for dull evenings and weekends. Or the run-down nature of some of the buildings could mean more excitement happens than you really care to know about. These factors won't just affect your quality of life as a resident, either; they could be indicative of long-term trends that will either make it easier or more difficult for you to sell your property in the future.

>> **What are traffic flows like?** The local highway may be a great feature if you do a lot of commuting, but you don't necessarily want to be living next door to it. Consider, too, the potential health impacts from living next door to a major traffic artery. These factors could limit the resale value of your property, but convenient access to transportation networks could be an asset for some buyers. Research the traffic patterns and impact on property values in any area in which you're considering buying.

>> **What community amenities are within a 10-kilometre radius?** Nearby schools, places of worship, parks and recreation facilities, transit, and shopping can be points in the favour of residential real estate. The closer your property is to amenities, the more you're able to offer others. The higher value of a location can pay itself back if you approach the purchase as an investment rather than simply your own home.

>> **What does municipal zoning allow for the property?** Favourable zoning can open the door to enhancements that can affect the value of your property. Depending on your neighbourhood, changes may be in the works that will either increase the value of your property or diminish it. Researching what the city plans for a particular residential neighbourhood is an important part of analyzing a property.

>> **What are property tax rates like?** Taxes are one of the few certain things in life, so make sure you study which direction residential property taxes are heading before you buy. Rates typically differ from city to city, so you may be able to find a property comparable to one you like in a municipality that levies a higher tax rate on homeowners, and thus end up paying less tax.

>> **What are the prospects for an increase in property value?** Regardless of where you buy, try to make sure your home has potential to appreciate in value. Some of the basic market research you'll undertake to determine a location (see the earlier section "Separating the fads from the fundamentals") can help you make this call.

>> **What are condo fees and building regulations like?** Don't forget to take condo fees and bylaws passed by the building council into account when you're looking at condominiums. Be sure to review building council minutes prior to buying to become aware of any ongoing issues. (Chapter 2 in Book 7 discusses condos.)

TIP

Having chosen a neighbourhood in which to buy, scout potential homes using the Internet. Here are a few sites to check out:

>> The Canadian Real Estate Association maintains the Multiple Listing Service (MLS) site, which boasts the majority of residential listings across Canada (www.mls.ca). This will give you an idea of the homes available for purchase in a given area, after which you can approach a Realtor to assist your search. You can identify several potential Realtors through listings on the MLS site.

>> Independent agents also exist who can offer insights and connections regarding the area where you hope to buy. You need to find someone with the experience and skills to serve your needs and with whom you can work — so look around.

>> A number of services give owner-vendors a venue for pitching their properties, such as ForSalebyOwner.com and PropertyGuys.com. Approximately a quarter of homes in Canada trade this way. Although we encourage you to use a real estate agent in your various transactions, it's worth remembering that not all people will. You may find a deal on one of these sites that, given some skillful negotiating, will hand you a bargain.

In addition, you can find listings of court-ordered sales, either at the local court-house or through services that collect such data and distribute it for a fee. Web-sites such as www.foreclosuresearch.ca exist, but as often as not vendors facing foreclosure are actively trying to avoid the circumstance and working with brokers who will be able to tip you off to potential opportunities in your locale.

Accommodating tenants

A home isn't a good investment if you can't achieve a return on it. Although appreciation over time is one means of achieving this goal, sharing your home with a tenant provides an ongoing cash flow. To ensure your experience with a tenant has the best chance of success, you want to make sure the home you buy has certain features.

Ideally, if the previous owner of the house has had tenants, you won't need to imagine the modifications needed to make the residence double as a rental prop-erty. Though you may need to make adjustments to the layout, the structure itself should be flexible enough and include some key features:

>> Dividing walls, to ensure a more complete separation of your living area from the tenant's living space

>> Potential for sharing laundry facilities and other amenities, which could eliminate your need to set up a separate laundry area for tenants

>> Wiring and circuitry necessary for the installation of a fridge, stove, and other appliances

These features make the space less hassle for you to adapt for rental use, and cre-ate a more desirable space for potential renters.

TIP

Dividing walls are just one element that help ensure a happy co-existence between your family and your tenants. A separate entrance is often a requirement for both practical and regulatory reasons. On the one hand, it gives the tenants a feeling of privacy and decreases the chance their comings and goings will disturb you. It also establishes the unit as its own dwelling for legal and tax purposes. But if you're buying a two- or three-bedroom condo and want to rent a room to a tenant who will help pay the mortgage, you'll want to put a higher priority on having an extra washroom as well as adequate sound-proofing.

Buying a home located close to a major public transit route will enhance your chance of securing a tenant. A parking spot is another attractive feature.

WARNING

Not all municipalities allow secondary suites, so be sure to check the legality of having tenants before you buy. Some jurisdictions will turn a blind eye to tenants, but you invite a range of hassles by not complying with the letter of the law. For example, the arrangement may compromise your insurance coverage or mail delivery may be denied. Lenders may also refuse to lend if the suite isn't legal, reducing your borrowing power. For peace of mind check what local bylaws have to say, and speak to your lawyer.

Attracting purchasers

Gauging future demand for housing in your neighbourhood is difficult, but you can take steps that will position your home to be attractive to potential purchasers in 5, 10, or even 20 years. Some of these will be reasons that you're attracted to the home yourself, such as proximity to schools, parks, shopping areas, transportation, and other amenities. But looking at the locale is also worthwhile:

>> Is it close to major institutional employers with ongoing employment needs, such as a hospital or university?

>> What is the potential of the home to be adapted for other uses, say rental to tenants, home office use, or the like?

>> Does it have the potential to appeal to buyers completely different from yourself?

>> Does the local zoning allow expansion or redevelopment of the home? You may not be interested in doing this, but the possibility might attract a future owner.

Location, location, location

Okay, "location, location, location" is a time-worn phrase, but it makes sense. And what would a book on real estate be without it? A property's location isn't something to take lightly, given the potential impact on appeal to tenants, your cash flow, and potential resale value.

Appealing to tenants

Many of us, at one time or another, have had a landlord who's baffled us. The rent was good, but property conditions were such that we didn't have to wonder why we were the ones living in the suite rather than the owner!

When you're a landlord, why do the same thing to your tenants? As discussed in the previous section, choosing a property that's in a location where you would want to live yourself makes sense even if you *don't* live there. That's because lots of other people probably would look forward to finding the place you've found.

A decent neighbourhood makes for happy tenants, which makes for stable cash flow and, ultimately, a better return on your investment. (The value that amenities can add to a property's location is covered in the later section "Amenities and services.")

TIP

A property that's attractive to tenants is better than a utilitarian rental property with no cachet at all. Chances are you'll also be able to charge higher rents, potentially securing yourself a long-term advantage that beats buying a larger property in a less attractive neighbourhood commanding lower rents.

Cashing in

The quality of the neighbourhood will affect not only how long tenants stay and the rents they're willing to pay, but also the cash flow the property generates. You'll be able to charge tenants higher rents for suites in well-located properties, and you'll likely face lower operating expenses.

Though you may pay closer attention to the overall appearance of a property that's surrounded by attractive neighbours, the quality of the tenant that a better-groomed property attracts helps your investment property deliver a return. You'll find it easier to secure better-quality tenants — that is, tenants who respect your property — who reduce your maintenance costs. This ensures better margins on the rents you're able to charge.

Trading up

Future buyers will have an interest in the property you've bought if it is in a better-quality location. The chances for appreciation increase if the fortunes of the surrounding area are also on the upswing.

Even if the locale seems to be facing a downturn, a better-quality asset will tend to lose less of its value than one in a poor location in a poor neighbourhood.

Amenities and services

The kinds of amenities and services you hope to have near your investment property vary. Users of residential properties want something different from tenants of commercial and industrial properties. When identifying amenities available to users of the property you're considering buying, you're generally safe to look in a 10-kilometre radius around the property.

TIP

Many property listings now tout scores from www.walkscore.com to highlight the ease of walking, commuting and cycling to local destinations. (You can use the site to check the score of any address you like, of course.)

Residential

Standard residential amenities include schools, places of worship, parks and recreation facilities, transit links, and shopping areas. The closer a property is to a greater selection of amenities, the more you'll be able to command in rent.

Amenities are also increasingly important to resort properties, with those who want to get away from it all not wanting to leave their urban comforts behind. Ensure that the resort property into which you're buying is well-served with amenities suited to the recreational user.

Commercial

Commercial properties, such as office and retail buildings, have their own unique set of needs. Depending on the size and kind of workforce, selling points can include proximity to recreational amenities and shopping facilities as well as food service. Postal outlets and business supply and service centres are also important.

Infrastructure such as parking areas, proximity to main commuting routes, and transit services can also enhance the value of the assets in which you're looking to invest.

Industrial

Connections to transportation infrastructure are among the most important amenities you can provide industrial users. Because these properties are typically where items are made, stored, and distributed, it's important that users have ready access to roads, and even rail and port connections. In many areas of Canada, quick access to the U.S. border is also a consideration.

Like commercial users, industrial tenants appreciate proximity to food service and retail outlets.

Looking to the future

Here's a startling revelation: No one can predict the future. But based on the amount of research you've put into finding a property, you should be able to take an educated guess at what the future holds for the ones you're considering buying. Because the main success of your investment will be in its appreciation, you want to make sure the property itself stands to gain in value. You should also have some confidence that the prospects for the surrounding neighbourhood are good.

Looking in

The future prospects for your investment in and of itself depend on the quality of the building and overall market conditions.

It's worth pointing out here that your property should be structurally sound. A building with potential for adaptation will also have stronger potential to appreciate in value in future years, as residential and other requirements change. The greater the number of uses to which a future owner can put a property, the greater the chances that it will retain its value, and even become a more valuable asset.

The overall market conditions are something over which you have little control. A glance at the history of the property's value should indicate whether or not it has seen a steady appreciation, or whether it has suffered depreciation in the past. Researching the causes for past fluctuations in value may not reveal the potential for appreciation or depreciation, but such research will indicate whether any unusual circumstances were behind the fluctuations.

Looking out

The surrounding neighbourhood can sometimes work to lower or raise the value of your property. Although your property is a passive player in the phenomenon, any increase or decrease in the quality of the community could have an impact.

REMEMBER

As an investor, aim to find a property in a stable neighbourhood with potential for appreciation. Recognizing the warning signs that could indicate the start of a downward trend in value is a skill that should prompt you to sell the property — or stay away from it if you thought it might be a good purchase.

Identifying the Types of Land Ownership

Just as there are different kinds of properties, there are different kinds of ground on which properties stand — and we're not talking about sandy or rocky soil. Rather, two kinds of ownership will define your ownership of land: freehold and leasehold.

TECHNICAL STUFF

Both freehold and leasehold properties can be left in your will as an asset of your estate, or specifically bequeathed.

Holding freely

The most common form of property ownership, especially for investors, is freehold, or *fee simple ownership*. Owning a property freehold allows you to use the property for an indefinite period, and to do as you please with it free of any encumbrances such as lease conditions. Owners of leasehold properties deal directly with the government and are responsible for compliance with the laws and contractual obligations regarding the land as well as any charges that encumber the title of the property, including mortgages, liens, and judgments.

Having freehold ownership is advantageous as an investor because you face virtually no constraints on what you may do with the property, save what liens and laws may require. This allows you to alter, develop, or otherwise maximize its potential as you please so long as what you're doing falls within local planning, zoning, and other guidelines (and of course your own investment strategy).

Holding with limits

Sometimes a landowner will lease rights to the property to a developer who will in turn create *improvements* on the land and sell his interest in the land (complete with lease obligations) and improvements. The improvements are typically buildings or units of buildings developed on the property. A leasehold property allows those holding an interest in land to use it only for fixed periods of time. An agreement between the landlord, who owns the property, and the owner of the leasehold interest, or tenant, sets out the terms and conditions of the relationship. The leaseholder can sell the right to use the land only for the time remaining in the lease — subject, of course, to the conditions of the lease.

Various forms of risk mean this is not the favoured type of property for an investor. A leasehold property may be subject to rent increases if the lease hasn't been prepaid by the developer; alternatively, the tenant may want to hold the property longer than the lease allows. In addition, the lease may place limits on what the tenant can do with a property (sometimes no improvements are allowed, even if the improvements would enhance the property's value).

On the other hand, leasehold properties often have a lower price because of the limitations owners face. This may make them a more accessible starting point for novice investors, especially if they're buying apartments to lease. Toward the end of the lease, however, or in the event lease rates increase significantly, a greater risk of a discount on the price arises because the ownership costs will be significantly higher relative to comparable freehold properties.

Government-owned properties are often available on a leasehold basis. Development is allowed with the goal of generating income for the owner. Many leases for development properties stipulate a 99-year term, although 999-year terms are not unheard of for public amenities. Queen's Park, home of the Ontario legislature, sits on land the University of Toronto leased to the province for a 999-year term expiring in 2858.

Knowing That a Property's Right for You

Just as with falling in love, you know you've found the right investment property when it happens to you. But here are a handful of tips and warnings for you to keep in mind.

TIP

Make sure the property in which you're interested shows potential to serve your investment goals. Check it against the objectives you've set for yourself, and verify your opinion with those of your advisers. You might be missing something that's obvious to them. Consulting them will ensure you're making the best possible decision under the circumstances.

Your actions in the market aren't the only reason to know about market cycles. The information you glean may help you negotiate a better deal, perhaps even a few concessions from the vendor. Building up your knowledge of the local market and the factors affecting it will make you a better negotiator.

WARNING

A property valued at above the current market average could narrow your margins, or potentially become a burden to you if the market slips. This is particularly true in run-down neighbourhoods, where you haven't only general market conditions to worry about but also the conditions of the market in the immediate vicinity of the property.

Run-down neighbourhoods aren't always going to have good long-term potential. Knowing the history of an area will help bring to light any long-term negative perceptions that area faces, and the potential for a turnaround. Although many neglected areas in Canada's major cities have undergone *gentrification* — simply put, the process of being made more attractive, more expensive places to live in — and improvement in recent years, many others have experienced periods of prolonged decline. Your investment may be a glimmer of hope among those who wish for a turnaround, but it's not likely to solve the problem by itself.

Many areas in Canada have older neighbourhoods that boast character buildings and local landmarks. A wave of redevelopment — gentrification, if they've been down-at-the-heel — can give them a new lease on life. Property values could easily double or triple in response to buyer demand as they become the hot new places to live, work, and play. The Cabbagetown and Yorkville areas in Toronto and Yaletown and Gastown neighbourhoods of Vancouver are a just a few examples. Redevelopment of the former Woodward's department store in Vancouver kicked off a wave of redevelopment handed many long-time owners a windfall they never expected to see as the surrounding area — long known as Canada's poorest postal code — spiraled into disarray. On the other hand, persistent social issues and community opposition to redevelopment underscores the importance of a long-term commitment and vision for your investment.

Checking Out Even More Resources for Property Information

All the chapters in Book 7 mention various professionals and professional organizations that offer the skills, expertise, and information that can help you build a successful real estate investment portfolio.

Knowing that help is available is one thing — knowing when to call for help and what the best source of information to help you understand any given situation is another. Sometimes, a combination of sources can be more helpful than the most logical or obvious choice.

This sections highlights some of the resources available, the problems they can help you solve, and the ways you can make use of the expertise they offer to develop a profitable portfolio.

Government agencies

The federal government oversees several ministries and agencies that collect and provide information to help you navigate the real estate market. Some agencies also provide advice, guidance, and even financing to help property investors.

The key federal organizations that can assist property investors include

>> **Canada Mortgage and Housing Corporation:** Commonly known as the CMHC (www.cmhc.ca), this federal organization focuses on residential housing, but it's about a lot more than mortgages and housing. It provides various forms of research and support, including financing to the residential real estate sector that are worth investigating. With respect to property information, it collects and regularly reports data regarding everything from housing starts to rental trends. Snapshots of specific markets and neighbourhoods are available through its housing information portal (find the link at www.cmhc-schl.gc.ca/en/data-and-research). Special interim reports focus on specific issues and opportunities. CMHC produces a variety of guides and reports to help you plan upgrades, full-scale renovations, or even new construction that will improve your property's value as an investment. Many of these are eligible for CMHC financing.

>> **Farm Credit Canada:** Canada's federally backed agricultural lender, FCC (www.fcc-fac.ca) produces an annual report on the value of farmland across Canada among other information related to rural and agricultural properties. It's a good source of information if you're investing in farmland or are involved in an agricultural venture. Some purchase and projects may be eligible for funding if they're directly related to agriculture or supporting activities in the farm sector.

>> **Statistics Canada:** Property information and statistics related to investment in the housing, construction, and real estate sectors generally are available through Statscan (www.statcan.gc.ca/eng/start). Many of its housing statistics are shared through CMHC, but it also has its own regular release schedule for information related to investment intentions, building permits, and other measures of business activity that can help you size up a particular market.

Real estate brokerages and boards

Residential and commercial brokerages and their staff are good sources of information for two reasons:

>> The brokers and agents who work for them have firsthand knowledge about local market conditions and can steer you to areas and properties you might want to consider.

>> Most also issue quarterly and annual reports demonstrating that knowledge. These reports examine sales and sales trends in particular areas, asset classes, and market segments.

TIP

Get to know the firms dealing in the kind of property that interests you; regardless of the firm's size, it will likely produce a report that fills you in on what the firm and its agents are seeing. Most of these reports are available for the asking because they're a good way for the brokerage to keep its name in front of potential clients; you'll often be able to access them online through the brokerage's website.

Some of the firms to contact for reports for residential properties include

>> Century 21 Canada (www.century21.ca)

>> Coldwell Banker Canada (www.coldwellbanker.ca)

>> Re/Max Canada (www.remax.ca)

>> Royal LePage (www.royallepage.ca)

For commercial properties, contact

>> Avison Young (www.avisonyoung.com)

>> CBRE (www.cbre.com/)

>> Colliers International (www.colliers.com)

>> Cushman & Wakefield (www.cushmanwakefield.com/)

Some local firms specialize in project marketing. Although not brokerages in their own right, many also track market conditions, particularly with respect to new homes. If you're considering condominium apartments, investigate the options in your area.

Provincial real estate boards and the regional and local boards they represent also produce monthly reports, typically based on their members' activities. (The local boards represent Realtors and the real estate industry in a given municipality or region.) A portion of this information is aggregated nationally and distributed by the Canadian Real Estate Association (www.crea.ca), the umbrella group that represents the industry nationally. You can sign up to receive these reports to gain a basic sense of local conditions, where the hot areas are, and the number of listings available for a given month. This information can help you determine where a particular market is in a cycle and areas where you might consider investing.

Financial institutions

Banks, credit unions, and other financial institutions that provide mortgages have a vested interest in the state of the real estate market, particularly from an investment standpoint. This means they'll often produce reports examining both general and sector-specific trends. The research typically takes a look at both national and provincial trends, and sometimes includes sections focusing on larger metropolitan areas. The reports sometimes have a direct connection to the investment trends; other times they highlight consumer issues such as housing affordability that may indicate where opportunities lie for investors. To access the reports, simply go to the publications section of the bank's website and see what's available.

The organizations representing and overseeing lenders also produce reports that may be of interest. For example, the Canadian Bankers Association regularly produces a report on mortgages in arrears (https://cba.ca/mortgages-in-arrears), which provides a proxy for court-ordered sale activity in each province. Mortgage Professionals Canada (www.mortgageproscan.ca) produces an annual report on the mortgage market in Canada that provides insight into the market, and how people are investing in real estate.

Policy statements from the Bank of Canada (www.bankofcanada.ca) as well as occasional reports from the Office of the Superintendent of Financial Institutions (www.osfi-bsif.gc.ca), which sets lending guidelines, may also help you gauge the future of the market.

Real estate consultants

A wealth of market reports is available for free, but focused information has a value. For a tailored report that addresses your specific interests or circumstances, you may require the services of a consultant — and can expect to face a bill commensurate with the degree of information you're seeking.

Several options are available in major cities across Canada to help you understand conditions in the local market. Nationally, however, the data solutions team at Altus Group (www.altusgroup.com) issues regular reports, while its team of consultants can provide guidance in applying the data to your specific challenges and questions.

Within specific markets, Urban Toronto (www.urbantoronto.ca) maintains a database of current development projects that provides insights into the state of the condo market and the latest projects to hit the market. Urban Analytics Inc. (www.urbananalytics.ca) maintains its own database for Metro Vancouver, while also producing custom reports for local industry organizations and companies.

Professional appraisers, accredited through the Appraisal Institute of Canada (www.aicanada.ca), have also become more than people who tell you what your property's worth. An increasing number is branching out to provide services ranging from selecting sites for investors to studying the potential for developing specific properties in order to deliver the best return on an investor's dollar. Appraisers can also work in concert with financial planners to ensure your portfolio is acquiring the right kinds of property to produce the maximum value in a given situation or that properties are fulfilling their highest and best use.

TIP

Appraisers know property values, so they're ideal allies when appealing property taxes. They can build a case that may help you avoid a higher levy than you'd pay if you just sized up a property by itself. Similarly, they can also challenge the assessment of a property by a banker or insurer to ensure you're getting the best value for the property.

Owners' associations

Not surprisingly, given the large number of property investors in Canada and the range of issues they face, organizations exist that can help property owners with just about anything they might face. Owner organizations allow property investors to speak with a common voice on important issues ranging from property taxes to major development projects having an impact on a region. Some major organizations in Canada include the following:

>> **Apartment owners' associations:** Most operate on a provincial basis with local divisions. Membership may be most appealing to large property owners, but smaller investors with just a handful of properties are not barred from joining. In fact, if you've got plans to build your portfolio, hooking up with an association like this may allow you to develop relationships that make further investments possible.

>> **Building Owners and Managers Association of Canada:** This national organization (www.bomacanada.ca) represents commercial property owners. Consider joining if you own several commercial properties and would like to meet others responsible for their management.

>> **NAIOP:** This organization (www.naiop.org) represents industrial and office property owners in Canada's major cities. Membership typically includes larger investors and suppliers to the industrial and office sector.

TIP

The cost of an annual membership in any one organization may outweigh the benefits of membership. Many of the events the organizations host are open to non-members for a slightly higher fee than members pay. Even if you aren't a member, you can benefit from the organization's services and events.

Builders' associations

Renovating your property may boost its value as an investment, but make sure you get the proper advice! Several organizations that may not at first glance seem to have a connection to investment property may have the tips to help you make the most of your investment.

Swapping stories with friends who've done projects similar to yours may be a great way to gain tips, but approaching the right organizations can put you in touch with workers who have unique skills, granting agencies willing to support your project, and resource people with guides that can bring you up to speed on current best practices for your type of building.

These organizations include the following:

>> **Canadian Home Builders' Association** (www.chba.ca) and local counter-parts can refer you to companies that have the skills, experience, and credibility that will make sure your job gets done properly.

>> **Canada Mortgage and Housing Corporation** (www.cmhc.ca) whose interest in fostering energy-efficient housing makes it an ideal resource for

background information, tips, and forms of financing that can facilitate your renovation project.

>> **Sustainable building organizations** are able to offer tips on retrofitting your property and direct you to professionals with the expertise to realize your goals. For example, the long-established Canada Green Building Council (www.cagbc.org) set standards for certification of new construction and retrofits and also works to educate industry and the public about green building practices in tandem with provincial and local advocacy groups.

>> **Local heritage organizations** provide not only resources that can help you complete a renovation that reflects a home's history and architecture, but also provide access to funds from various levels of government. Allowing an older property to express its age may make it a more valuable asset to potential purchasers. Moreover, knowing its history may allow you to tap grants for part or all of the renovation.

Provincial land registries

Title to each property in Canada is registered in the province where it lies at the provincial land titles office, or land registry. The title will record (and reveal!) the registered owner, the exact dimensions of the property, and any charges, liens, or encumbrances on the title. For example, a lien may be registered in the event of unpaid construction bills or other charges associated with the property. Rights of way that affect what can be built and where will be noted.

Some of this information may be worth knowing before you purchase, because it may affect how you use the property in future. Other segments of the information may give you insights into why the current owner has offered the property for sale. Regardless, making sure you have the information prior to purchasing a property will be part of your due diligence.

TIP

The information held by the land titles registry in each province is public information, but typically comes at a nominal cost. The cost could be minimal, however, compared to the hit you take if you purchase the property and discover a problem with the title or a condition that limits your use and enjoyment of the real estate.

Property assessment offices

Property assessments are more than numbers. They're a source of valuable information regarding the estimated market value of a given property, the surrounding properties, and the year-to-year shifts in value. Knowing this information for a specific property, or group of properties, can give you a better sense of the property's potential, the state of the market, and the opportunity it presents.

TIP

Many provinces now offer a limited amount of assessment data online, which can help you undertake some rudimentary research on properties so you can make some initial judgment calls and have an informed discussion with your advisory team (see Chapter 3 in Book 7).

City hall

Municipal records and databases offer a surprising amount of property information. Some of this information is mapped, allowing you to quickly compare a specific property with its immediate neighbours and those in the surrounding area.

Some common forms of civic info are zoning and development permit information. Some properties may have come before the local council in the past, and council minutes will provide a record of that history. Most civic sites are searchable, but Google is also a fine option for pulling up the information. A good strategy is to enter both the municipal website URL and your property address in quotations marks so the search is focused; for example, searching the two terms "podunk.ca" "2356 William" would yield any references to 2356 William Street (or avenue) in the town of Podunk.

Major cities are also making a large volume of data available through open data initiatives, revealing everything from crime statistics to dead animals. If you want to avoid buying in a place with high rates of property crime or dead birds, this information could come in handy.

Court records

Clues to why a property has hit the market may turn up by doing a search of provincial courts records for either the owner or the property address. You may discover documents related to the financial woes of the owner or the launch of a court-ordered sale process.

Court records can provide helpful information that lets you understand what went wrong with a property in the past and how you can avoid repeating them. We assume your financial management will be better than the owner who lost it to a lender, but if the property was accused of releasing contaminants, then you might want to take a closer look at what you're buying.

Court records typically fall into higher and lower court proceeds — that is, provincial supreme court and courts of appeal (primarily civil claims and petitions) and provincial court (primarily criminal proceedings). Most of the information of interest to you as an investor and property owner will be found in Supreme Court filings.

Index

I

O

Odean, Terrance, 291

O'Donnel, Jim, 186

Office of the Superintendent of Financial Institutions, 524

office properties, 442

Omega ATS, 325

101 Streetsmart Condo Buying Tips for Canadians (Gray), 448

online resources

  annual information forms, 174

  balance sheets and income statements, 144

  bond ratings, 134

  business and consumer confidence surveys, 504

  CDIC coverage, 221

  cheat sheet (companion to book), 2

  collectibles, 18

  credit reports, 483

  cryptocurrencies, 362, 365, 367, 381, 394, 396–397

  currency prices, 260

  currency trading, 333

  day trading, 291–292, 304, 356

  dividends, 87

  equities exchanges, 213

  exchange-traded funds, 209, 331

  financial news, 79, 90

  financial planners, 478

  financial statements, 457

  futures, 338

  GIC rates, 220

  gold bugs, 265–266

  gold market, 261–266

  income stocks, 125, 131

  inflation, 260

  interest rates, 493, 501

  mutual fund performance, 174

  options, 335

  PIP scheme, 305

  population and business data, 136

  real estate, 438, 522–523

    accountants, 478

    agencies, 523

    appraisers, 477

    boards, 524

    builders' associations, 526–527

    community amenities, 517

    community profiles, 509

    consultants, 525

    financing, 524

    leasing markets, 503–504

    listings, 441, 511–512, 514–515

    owners' associations, 526

    property/building inspectors, 479

  regulation, 353–354

  risk tolerance calculation, 399

  silver market, 268, 270–271, 274–275

  small cap stocks, 124

  stocks

    analysts and pickers, 101, 119

    broker ratings and services, 97–98

    broker registration, 93

    exchanges, 74, 324

    full-service brokers, 94

    screening tools, 153

    tables, 82, 87

  tax laws, 81

  Treasury bonds, 331

  unbanked and underbanked, 385

  university/college funding, 65

  Warren Buffett's letters to shareholders, 346

online wealth managers. *See* robo-advisors

Ontario Real Estate Association, 443

Ontario Securities Act, 358

open source, 410

open-end funds, 161

options, 15–16, 227, 242

Order Exposure Rule, 350–351

overleveraging, 419

over-priced investments, 26

volatility *(continued)*
  beta, 342–343
  cryptocurrencies, 394
  day trading, 342–343
  defined, 319
  standard deviation, 319, 342
  variance, 319
volatility risk, 394

W

Walk Score, 517
Wall Street Journal, The, 79, 87
wallets
  overview, 366
  security risks with, 394
warrants, 227
Watergate, 355
Western Investor, 441
whales, 395
white papers, 392

wills and estate planning, 431
World Gold Council (WGC), 262
World Silver Survey, 270

X

XEM cryptocurrency, 408
XRP (Ripple cryptocurrency), 368, 390, 405

Y

Yahoo! Finance, 260
yield, 86, 131–133
  calculating, 131
  changes in, 132
  comparing, 133
  defined, 32–33
  money market mutual funds, 14

Z

Zcash cryptocurrency, 402

About the Authors

Andrew Bell was an investment reporter and editor with *The Globe and Mail* for 12 years. He joined Business News Network as a reporter in 2001. Bell, an import from Dublin, Ireland, was for 10 years the main compiler of Stars & Dogs in Saturday's *Globe*. He is the coauthor of *Mutual Fund Investing for Canadians For Dummies*.

Bryan Borzykowski has been writing about personal finance and investing for a number of years, and has held editorial positions at several Canadian business magazines and websites. He has written regular features for *Canadian Business* magazine, *PROFIT*, *MoneySense*, the *Toronto Star*, *Moneyville.ca*, and *Advisor.ca*, and he has contributed to *Maclean's, Chatelaine, Yahoo! Finance,* and the *National Post,* among other publications. He has been nominated for several national magazine awards, including one for an article on day trading. He is the coauthor of *Day Trading for Canadians For Dummies*.

Andrew Dagys, CPA, CMA, is a best-selling author who has written and co-authored more than a dozen books, mostly about investing, personal finance, and technology. Andrew has contributed columns to major Canadian publications. He is also a frequently quoted author in many of Canada's daily news publications, including *The Globe and Mail, National Post,* and *Toronto Star*. He has appeared on several national news broadcasts to offer his insights on the Canadian and global investment landscapes. He is the coauthor of *Stock Investing for Canadians For Dummies*.

Kiana Danial is an award-winning, internationally recognized personal investing and wealth management expert. She's a highly sought-after professional speaker, author, and executive coach who delivers workshops and seminars to corporations, universities, and investment groups. She frequently appears as an expert on many TV and radio stations and has reported on the financial markets directly from the floor of the New York Stock Exchange and Nasdaq. Kiana has been featured in the *Wall Street Journal, TIME* magazine, *Forbes, TheStreet.com,* and many other publications as well as on CNN. She has won numerous awards, including Best Financial Education Provider at Shanghai Forex Expo in 2014, New York Business Women of Influence Honoree in 2016, and the Personal Investment Expert of the Year award from Wealth & Finance International in 2018. She is the author of *Cryptocurrency Investing For Dummies*.

Matthew Elder is a writer and communications consultant based in Toronto. Previously he was vice president, content and editorial, of Morningstar Canada. A Montreal native, he was a columnist and editor specializing in personal finance with *The Gazette* for 10 years before moving to the *Financial Post* in 1995, where he was mutual funds editor and columnist until joining Morningstar in 2000. He is the coauthor of *Mutual Fund Investing for Canadians For Dummies*.

Douglas Gray, LLB, is one of the foremost experts on real estate in Canada. He's written more than 25 books on real estate and personal finance, all of them best-sellers. They include ten books on real estate, such as *Making Money in Real Estate, 101 Streetsmart Condo Buying Tips for Canadians, Mortgages Made Easy,* and *The Canadian Landlord's Guide.* He has 35 years of experience investing in residential properties, as well as many years as a lawyer representing buyers, sellers, lenders, borrowers, and developers. Doug is a consultant and columnist, and he regularly gives seminars on real estate across Canada for both professional Realtors and the public. His website is www.homebuyer.ca. He is the coauthor of *Real Estate Investing for Canadians For Dummies.*

Ann C. Logue, MBA, has written for *Barron's, The New York Times, Newsweek Japan, Wealth Manager,* and the International Monetary Fund. She is a lecturer at the Liautaud Graduate School of Business at the University of Illinois at Chicago. Her current career follows 12 years of experience as an investment analyst. She has a BA from Northwestern University and an MBA from the University of Chicago, and she holds the Chartered Financial Analyst (CFA) designation. She is the coauthor of *Day Trading for Canadians For Dummies.*

Tony Martin's widely read column "Me and My Money" appeared in the *Globe and Mail*'s weekend personal finance section. His work has been featured in many leading publications, including *ROB Magazine, Reader's Digest,* and *Canadian Business.* Tony is a frequent commentator and speaker on personal finance and investing and regularly appears on television and radio, including CBC Radio, CBC Television, BCC, and TVOntario. He has led courses across the country on finance and accounting, as well as speaking and presenting, business writing, writing for the web, public speaking and presenting, negotiating, and conflict resolution for national management training leaders, as well as many major companies and organizations, including Shoppers Drug Mart, Siemens, the Ontario Government, and Ontario Power Corp. He is the coauthor of *Investing for Canadians For Dummies.*

Peter Mitham has written about Canadian real estate for publications in Canada and abroad for more than 20 years. He currently contributes a weekly column of real estate news to *Business in Vancouver* (www.biv.com) and covers rural property issues as associate editor of *Country Life in BC* (www.countrylifeinbc.com). Growing up in Quebec, he was fascinated with the catalogues of property listings and mortgage applications in the home office of his father, an appraiser. He has also collaborated with Douglas Gray on *The Canadian Landlord's Guide: Expert Advice for the Profitable Real Estate Investor* (John Wiley & Sons, Inc.). He is the coauthor of *Real Estate Investing for Canadians For Dummies.*

Paul Mladjenovic, CFP, is a certified financial planner practitioner, writer, and public speaker. His business, PM Financial Services, has helped people with financial and business concerns since 1981. In 1985, he achieved his CFP designation. Since 1983, Paul has taught thousands of budding investors through popular national seminars such as "The $50 Wealthbuilder" and "Stock Investing Like a Pro." Paul has been quoted or referenced by many media outlets, including Bloomberg, MarketWatch, Comcast, CNBC, and a variety of financial and business publications and websites. As an author, he has written the books *The Unofficial Guide to Picking Stocks* (Wiley, 2000) and *Zero-Cost Marketing* (Todd Publications, 1995). In recent years, Paul accurately forecast many economic events, such as the rise of gold, the decline of the U.S. dollar, and the housing crisis. He is the coauthor of *Stock Investing for Canadians For Dummies* and the author of *Precious Metals Investing For Dummies.*

Eric Tyson is an internationally acclaimed and best-selling personal finance book author, syndicated columnist, and speaker. He has worked with and taught people from all financial situations, so he knows the financial concerns and questions of real folks just like you. An accomplished personal finance writer, his "Investor's Guide" syndicated column, distributed by King Features, is read by millions nationally, and he is an award-winning columnist. Eric's work has been featured and quoted in hundreds of local and national publications, including *Newsweek, The Wall Street Journal,* the *Los Angeles Times,* the *Chicago Tribune, Forbes, Kiplinger's Personal Finance* magazine, *Parenting, Money, Family Money,* and *Bottom Line/ Personal;* on NBC's *Today Show,* ABC, CNBC, FOX News, PBS *Nightly Business Report,* CNN, and on CBS national radio, NPR's *Sound Money,* Bloomberg Business Radio, and Business Radio Network. Eric's website is www.erictyson.com. He is the coauthor of *Investing for Canadians For Dummies.*

Publisher's Acknowledgments

Senior Acquisitions Editor: Tracy Boggier

Senior Managing Editor: Kristie Pyles

Compilation Editor: Georgette Beatty

Editorial Project Manager: Christina N. Guthrie

Technical Editor: Jesus Antolin Sierra Jimenez

Proofreader: Debbye Butler

Production Editor: Mohammed Zafar Ali

Cover Images: Flag of Canada, round diagram icon © Mikhail Mishchenko/Getty Images, Canadian flag © alexsl/Getty Images

Take dummies with you everywhere you go!

Whether you are excited about e-books, want more from the web, must have your mobile apps, or are swept up in social media, dummies makes everything easier.

Find us online!

dummies.com

dummies
A Wiley Brand

Leverage the power

Dummies is the global leader in the reference category and one of the most trusted and highly regarded brands in the world. No longer just focused on books, customers now have access to the dummies content they need in the format they want. Together we'll craft a solution that engages your customers, stands out from the competition, and helps you meet your goals.

Advertising & Sponsorships

Connect with an engaged audience on a powerful multimedia site, and position your message alongside expert how-to content. Dummies.com is a one-stop shop for free, online information and know-how curated by a team of experts.

- Targeted ads
- Video
- Email Marketing
- Microsites
- Sweepstakes sponsorship

20 MILLION PAGE VIEWS EVERY SINGLE MONTH

15 MILLION UNIQUE VISITORS PER MONTH

43% OF ALL VISITORS ACCESS THE SITE VIA THEIR MOBILE DEVICES

700,000 NEWSLETTER SUBSCRIPTIONS TO THE INBOXES OF *300,000* UNIQUE INDIVIDUALS EVERY WEEK

# of dummies

Custom Publishing

Reach a global audience in any language by creating a solution that will differentiate you from competitors, amplify your message, and encourage customers to make a buying decision.

- Apps
- Books
- eBooks
- Video
- Audio
- Webinars

Brand Licensing & Content

Leverage the strength of the world's most popular reference brand to reach new audiences and channels of distribution.

For more information, visit dummies.com/biz

PERSONAL ENRICHMENT

 **Staying Sharp**
9781119187790
USA $26.00
CAN $31.99
UK £19.99

 **Facebook**
9781119179030
USA $21.99
CAN $25.99
UK £16.99

 **Guitar**
9781119293354
USA $24.99
CAN $29.99
UK £17.99

 Investing
9781119293347
USA $22.99
CAN $27.99
UK £16.99

 **Beekeeping**
9781119310068
USA $22.99
CAN $27.99
UK £16.99

 **Digital Photography**
9781119235606
USA $24.99
CAN $29.99
UK £17.99

 **Meditation**
9781119251163
USA $24.99
CAN $29.99
UK £17.99

 **Pregnancy**
9781119235491
USA $26.99
CAN $31.99
UK £19.99

 **Samsung Galaxy S7**
9781119279952
USA $24.99
CAN $29.99
UK £17.99

 **iPhone**
9781119283133
USA $24.99
CAN $29.99
UK £17.99

 **Crocheting**
9781119287117
USA $24.99
CAN $29.99
UK £16.99

 **Nutrition**
9781119130246
USA $22.99
CAN $27.99
UK £16.99

PROFESSIONAL DEVELOPMENT

 **Windows 10**
9781119311041
USA $24.99
CAN $29.99
UK £17.99

 **AutoCAD**
9781119255796
USA $39.99
CAN $47.99
UK £27.99

 **Excel 2016**
9781119293439
USA $26.99
CAN $31.99
UK £19.99

 **QuickBooks 2017**
9781119281467
USA $26.99
CAN $31.99
UK £19.99

 **macOS Sierra**
9781119280651
USA $29.99
CAN $35.99
UK £21.99

 **LinkedIn**
9781119251132
USA $24.99
CAN $29.99
UK £17.99

 **Windows 10 All-in-One**
9781119310563
USA $34.00
CAN $41.99
UK £24.99

 SharePoint 2016
9781119181705
USA $29.99
CAN $35.99
UK £21.99

 **Fundamental Analysis**
9781119263593
USA $26.99
CAN $31.99
UK £19.99

 **Networking**
9781119257769
USA $29.99
CAN $35.99
UK £21.99

 Office 2016
9781119293477
USA $26.99
CAN $31.99
UK £19.99

 Office 365
9781119265313
USA $24.99
CAN $29.99
UK £17.99

 Salesforce.com
9781119239314
USA $29.99
CAN $35.99
UK £21.99

 **Coding**
9781119293323
USA $29.99
CAN $35.99
UK £21.99

dummies.com

dummies®
A Wiley Brand

Learning Made Easy

ACADEMIC

9781119293576
USA $19.99
CAN $23.99
UK £15.99

9781119293637
USA $19.99
CAN $23.99
UK £15.99

9781119293491
USA $19.99
CAN $23.99
UK £15.99

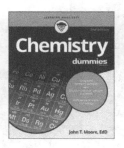

9781119293460
USA $19.99
CAN $23.99
UK £15.99

9781119293590
USA $19.99
CAN $23.99
UK £15.99

9781119215844
USA $26.99
CAN $31.99
UK £19.99

9781119293378
USA $22.99
CAN $27.99
UK £16.99

9781119293521
USA $19.99
CAN $23.99
UK £15.99

9781119239178
USA $18.99
CAN $22.99
UK £14.99

9781119263883
USA $26.99
CAN $31.99
UK £19.99

Available Everywhere Books Are Sold

dummies.com

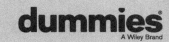

PRINCE ALBERT PUBLIC LIBRARY
31234900123280
Investing for Canadians all-in-one for d

Small books for big imaginations

9781119177173
USA $9.99
CAN $9.99
UK £8.99

9781119177272
USA $9.99
CAN $9.99
UK £8.99

9781119177241
USA $9.99
CAN $9.99
UK £8.99

9781119177210
USA $9.99
CAN $9.99
UK £8.99

9781119262657
USA $9.99
CAN $9.99
UK £6.99

9781119291336
USA $9.99
CAN $9.99
UK £6.99

9781119233527
USA $9.99
CAN $9.99
UK £6.99

9781119291220
USA $9.99
CAN $9.99
UK £6.99

9781119177302
USA $9.99
CAN $9.99
UK £8.99

Unleash Their Creativity

dummies.com

dummies
A Wiley Brand